Fault-Tolerant Systems

Fault-Tolerant Systems

Second Edition

Israel Koren
C. Mani Krishna

MORGAN KAUFMANN PUBLISHERS

ELSEVIER AN IMPRINT OF ELSEVIER

Morgan Kaufmann is an imprint of Elsevier
50 Hampshire Street, 5th Floor, Cambridge, MA 02139, United States

Library of Congress Cataloging-in-Publication Data
A catalog record for this book is available from the Library of Congress

British Library Cataloguing-in-Publication Data
A catalogue record for this book is available from the British Library

ISBN: 978-0-12-818105-8

For information on all Morgan Kaufmann publications
visit our website at https://www.elsevier.com/books-and-journals

Publisher: Katey Birtcher
Acquisitions Editor: Steve Merken
Editorial Project Manager: Andrae Akeh
Publishing Services Manager: Shereen Jameel
Production Project Manager: Kamatchi Madhavan
Designer: Patrick Ferguson
Cover illustration: Yaron Koren

Typeset by VTeX

Printed in the United States of America

Last digit is the print number: 9 8 7 6 5 4 3 2 1

Contents

Preface to the Second Edition

In this second edition of *Fault-tolerant systems,* we have retained the original structure of the book and added material to most chapters. References have been updated to reflect recent advances in the field.

Our principal additions are as follows:

- Chapter 2: A discussion of the principal physical causes of hardware failure.
- Chapter 3: Coverage of low-density parity coding, hierarchical RAID, as well as a discussion of RAID with solid-state devices.
- Chapter 4: Fat-tree topologies, networks-on-a-chip, and wireless sensor networks.
- Chapter 5: We now cover the rejuvenation of hypervisor-based systems and introduce the Ostrand–Weyuker–Bell software fault model.
- Chapter 6: Material on checkpointing with cloud computing utilities and on checkpointing in petascale and exascale computing has been added.
- Chapter 7: This is a new chapter on the increasingly prominent field of cyber-physical systems.
- Chapter 8: Among the additions are sections on aerospace systems, IBM's POWER8 multicore, Intel's Xeon, Oracle and NEC servers and cloud computing.
- Chapter 9: The splitting approach to simulation has been added.

Acknowledgments

Zahava Koren read through the text and made several valuable suggestions. We would also like to thank the staff at Morgan Kaufman for their efforts on behalf of this project. We also thank the funding agencies that have supported our work over the years; in particular, the material in Chapter 7 is partially based on work supported by the National Science Foundation under CNS-1717262.

PRELIMINARIES

The past 50 years have seen computers move from being expensive computational engines used by government and big corporations to becoming an everyday commodity, deeply embedded in practically every aspect of our lives. Not only are computers visible everywhere, in desktops, laptops, and smartphones; it is also a commonplace that they are *invisible* everywhere, as vital components of cars, home appliances, medical equipment, aircraft, industrial plants, and power generation and distribution systems. Computer systems underpin most of the world's financial systems: current transaction volumes, trading in the stock, bond, and currency markets would be unthinkable without them. Our increasing willingness, as a society, to place computers in life-critical and wealth-critical applications is largely driven by the increasing possibilities that computers offer. And yet, as we depend more and more on computers to carry out all of these vital actions, we are—implicitly or explicitly—gambling our lives and property on computers doing their job properly.

Computers (hardware plus software) are quite likely the most complex systems ever created by human beings. The complexity of computer hardware is still increasing as designers attempt to exploit the higher transistor density that new generations of technology make available to them. Computer software is far more complex still, and with that complexity comes an increased propensity to failure. It is probably fair to say that there is not a single large piece of software or hardware today that is free of bugs. Even the space shuttle, with software that was developed and tested using some of the best and most advanced techniques known to engineering at the time, is now known to have flown with potentially serious bugs.

Computer scientists and engineers have responded to the challenge of designing complex systems with a variety of tools and techniques to reduce the number of faults in the systems they build. However, that is not enough: we need to build systems that will acknowledge the existence of faults as a fact of life, and incorporate techniques to tolerate these faults while still delivering an acceptable level of service. The resulting field of *fault-tolerant computing* is the subject of this book.

1.1 FAULT CLASSIFICATION

In everyday language, the terms *fault*, *failure*, and *error* are used interchangeably. In fault-tolerant computing parlance, however, they have distinctive meanings. A *fault* (or *failure*) can be either a hardware defect or a software/programming mistake (bug). In contrast, an *error* is a manifestation of the fault/failure/bug.

As an example, consider an adder circuit, with one output line stuck at 1; it always carries the value 1 independently of the values of the input operands. This is a fault, but not (yet) an error. This fault causes an error when the adder is used, and the result on that line is supposed to have been a 0, rather

Fault-Tolerant Systems. https://doi.org/10.1016/B978-0-12-818105-8.00011-5

than a 1. A similar distinction exists between programming mistakes and execution errors. Consider, for example, a subroutine that is supposed to compute $\sin(x)$, but owing to a programming mistake calculates the absolute value of $\sin(x)$ instead. This mistake will result in an execution error only if that particular subroutine is used and the correct result is negative.

Both faults and errors can spread through the system. For example, if a chip shorts out power to ground, it may cause nearby chips to fail as well. Errors can spread when the output of one unit is used as input by other units. To return to our previous examples, the erroneous results of either the faulty adder or the $\sin(x)$ subroutine can be fed into further calculations, thus propagating the error.

To limit such contagion, designers incorporate *containment zones* into systems. These are barriers that reduce the chance that a fault or error in one zone will propagate to another. For example, a fault-containment zone can be created by ensuring that the maximum possible voltage swings in one zone are insulated from the other zones, and by providing an independent power supply to each zone. In other words, the designer tries to electrically isolate one zone from another. An error-containment zone can be created, as we will see in some detail later on, by using redundant units/programs and voting on their output.

Faults can be classified along multiple dimensions. Some important dimensions are: their duration, when they were introduced, whether or not there was conscious intent behind their introduction, and whether they occurred in hardware or in software. Let us look at each of these dimensions in turn.

Duration: Duration is an important classification dimension for hardware faults. These can be classified into *permanent, transient,* or *intermittent.* A *permanent fault* is just that: it reflects a component going out of commission permanently. As an example of a permanent fault, think of a burned-out lightbulb. A *transient fault* is one that causes a component to malfunction for some time; it goes away after that time, and the functionality of the component is fully restored. As an example, think of a random noise interference during a telephone conversation. Another example is a memory cell with contents that are changed spuriously due to some electromagnetic interference. The cell itself is undamaged: it is just that its contents are wrong for the time being, and overwriting the memory cell will make the fault go away. An *intermittent fault* never quite goes away entirely; it oscillates between being quiescent and active. When the fault is quiescent, the component functions normally; when the fault is active, the component malfunctions. An example for an intermittent fault is a loose electrical connection.

When they were introduced: Faults can be introduced in various phases of the system's lifetime. Faulty design decisions cause faults to be introduced in the design phase. They can be born during system implementation (e.g., software development). They can occur during system operation due to hardware degradation, faulty software updates, or harsh environments (e.g., due to high levels of radiation or excessive temperatures).

Intent: Faults may be intentional or unintentional. Most software bugs are unintentional faults. For example, consider the Fortran instruction `doi=1.35` when the programmer meant to type `do i=1,35`. The programmer was trying to set up a loop; what the system saw was an instruction to assign the value of 1.35 to the variable `doi`.

They may be intentional: consciously undertaken design decisions may lead to faults in the system design. Such faults can be further subclassified into *nonmalicious* and *malicious* categories. Nonmalicious design faults are introduced with the best of intentions; often because of side-effects (often in the way that various modules of the system interact) that were not foreseen at design time, or because the operating environment was imperfectly understood. Malicious faults are introduced with malicious intent: for instance, a programmer may deliberately insert a weak point in software that permits unauthorized access to some data structure. We also include in this subcategory faults, which may not be deliberately introduced, but which behave as if they were the product of nefarious intent. For example, a component may fail in such a way that it "acts as if malicious" and sends differently valued outputs to different receivers. Think of an altitude sensor in an airplane that reports a 1000-foot altitude to one unit, while reporting an 8000-foot altitude to another unit. Malicious faults are also known as Byzantine faults.

1.2 TYPES OF REDUNDANCY

All of fault tolerance is an exercise in exploiting and managing *redundancy*. Redundancy is the property of having more of a resource than is minimally necessary to do the job at hand. As failures happen, redundancy is exploited to mask or otherwise work around these failures, thus maintaining the desired level of functionality.

There are four forms of redundancy that we will study: hardware, software, information, and time. Hardware faults are usually dealt with by using hardware, information, or time redundancy, whereas software faults (bugs) are mostly protected against by software redundancy.

Hardware redundancy is provided by incorporating extra hardware into the design to either detect or override the effects of a failed component. For example, instead of having a single processor, we can use two or three processors, each performing the same function. By having two processors and comparing their results, we can detect the failure of a single processor; by having three, we can use the majority output to override the wrong output of a single faulty processor. This is an example of *static hardware redundancy*, the main objective of which is the immediate masking of a failure. A different form of hardware redundancy is *dynamic redundancy,* where spare components are activated upon the failure of a currently active component. A combination of static and dynamic redundancy techniques is also possible, leading to *hybrid hardware redundancy.*

Hardware redundancy can thus range from a simple duplication to complicated structures that switch in spare units when active ones become faulty. These forms of hardware redundancy incur high overheads, and their use is therefore normally reserved for critical systems, where such overheads can be justified. In particular, substantial amounts of redundancy are required to protect against malicious faults.

The best-known form of information redundancy is error detection and correction coding. Here, extra bits (called check bits) are added to the original data bits so that an error in the data bits can be detected or even corrected. The resulting error-detecting and error-correcting codes are widely used today in memory units and various storage devices to protect against benign failures. Note that these error codes (like any other form of information redundancy) may require extra hardware to process the redundant data (the check bits).

Error-detecting and error-correcting codes are also used to protect data communicated over noisy channels, which are channels that are subject to many transient failures. These channels can be the communication links among either widely separated processors (e.g., the Internet) or processors that form a local network. If the code used for data communication is capable of only detecting the faults that have occurred (but not correcting them), we can retransmit as necessary, thus employing time redundancy.

In addition to transient data communication failures due to noise, local and wide-area networks may experience permanent link failures. These failures may disconnect one or more existing communication paths, resulting in a longer communication delay between certain nodes in the network, a lower data bandwidth between certain node pairs, or even a complete disconnection of certain nodes from the rest of the network. Redundant communication links (i.e., hardware redundancy) can alleviate these problems.

Computing nodes can also exploit time redundancy through reexecution of the same program on the same hardware. As before, time redundancy is effective against *transient* faults. Because the majority of hardware faults are transient, it is unlikely that the separate executions (if spaced sufficiently apart) will experience the same fault. Time redundancy can thus be used to detect transient faults in situations, where such faults may otherwise go undetected. Time redundancy can also be used when other means for detecting errors are in place, and the system is capable of recovering from the effects of the fault and repeating the computation. Compared with the other forms of redundancy, time redundancy has much lower hardware and software overhead, but incurs a high-performance penalty.

Software redundancy is used mainly against software failures. It is a reasonable guess that *every* large piece of software that has ever been produced has contained faults (bugs). Dealing with such faults can be expensive: one way is to independently produce two or more versions of that software (preferably by disjoint teams of programmers) in the hope that the different versions will not fail on the same input. The secondary version(s) can be based on simpler and less accurate algorithms (and, consequently, less likely to have faults) to be used only upon the failure of the primary software to produce acceptable results. Just as for hardware redundancy, the multiple versions of the program can be executed either concurrently (requiring redundant hardware as well) or sequentially (requiring extra time, i.e., time redundancy) upon a failure detection.

1.3 BASIC MEASURES OF FAULT TOLERANCE

Since fault tolerance is about making machines more dependable, it is important to have proper measures (yardsticks) by which to gauge such dependability. In this section, we will examine some of these yardsticks and their application.

A measure is a mathematical abstraction, that expresses some relevant facet of the performance of its object. By its very nature, a measure only captures some subset of the properties of its object. The trick in defining a suitable measure is to keep this subset large enough so that behaviors of interest to the user are captured, and yet not so large that the measure loses focus.

1.3.1 TRADITIONAL MEASURES

We first describe the traditional measures of dependability of a single computer. These metrics have been around for a long time, and measure very basic attributes of the system. Two of these measures are *reliability* and *availability*.

The conventional definition of reliability, denoted by $R(t)$, is the probability (as a function of the time t) that the system has been up continuously in the time interval $[0, t]$, conditioned on the event that it was up at time 0. This measure is suitable for applications, in which even a momentary disruption can prove costly. One example is computers that control physical processes such as an aircraft, for which system-wide computer failure could result in catastrophe.

Closely related to reliability are the *mean time to failure,* denoted by MTTF, and the *mean time between failures,* MTBF. The first is the average time the system operates until a failure occurs, whereas the second is the average time between two consecutive failures. The difference between the two is due to the time needed to repair the system following the first failure. Denoting the *mean time to repair* by MTTR, we obtain

$$MTBF = MTTF + MTTR.$$

Availability, denoted by $A(t)$, is the average fraction of time over the interval $[0, t]$ that the system is up. This measure is appropriate for applications, in which continuous fault-free operation is not vital, but where it would be expensive to have the system down for a significant amount of time. An airline reservation system needs to be highly available, because downtime can put off customers and lose sales; however, an occasional (very) short-duration failure can be tolerated.

The long-term availability, denoted by A, is defined as

$$A = \lim_{t \to \infty} A(t).$$

A can be interpreted as the probability that the system will be up at some random point in time, and is meaningful only in systems that include repair of faulty components. The long-term availability can be calculated from MTTF, MTBF, and MTTR as follows:

$$A = \frac{MTTF}{MTBF} = \frac{MTTF}{MTTF + MTTR}.$$

A related measure, *point availability*, denoted by $A_p(t)$, is the probability that the system is up at the particular time instant t.

It is possible for a low-reliability system to have high availability: consider a system that fails every hour on the average, but comes back up after only a second. Such a system has an MTBF of just 1 hour and, consequently, a low reliability; however, its availability is high: $A = 3599/3600 = 0.99972$.

These definitions assume, of course, that we have a state, in which the system can be said to be "up", and another in which it is not. For simple components, this is a good assumption. For example, a lightbulb is either good or burned out. A wire is either connected or has a break in it. However, for even simple systems, such an assumption can be very limiting. For example, consider a processor that has one of its several hundreds of millions of gates stuck at logic value 0. In other words, the output of this logic gate is always 0, regardless of the input. Suppose the rest of the processor is functional, and that this failed logic gate only affects the output of the processor about once in every 25,000 hours of use. For example, a particular gate in the divide unit when faulty may result in a wrong quotient if the divisor is within a certain subset of values. Clearly, the processor is not fault-free, but would one define it as "down"?

The same remarks apply with even greater force to systems that degrade gracefully. By this, we mean systems with various levels of functionality. Initially, with all of its components operational, the system is at its highest level of functionality. As these components fail, the system degrades from one level of functionality to the next. Beyond a certain point, the system is unable to produce anything of use and fails completely. As with the previous example, the system has multiple "up" states. Is it said to fail when it degrades from full to partial functionality? Or when it fails to produce any useful output at all? Or when its functionality falls below a certain threshold? If the last, what is this threshold, and how is it determined?

We can therefore see that traditional reliability and availability are very limited in what they can express. There are obvious extensions to these measures. For example, we may consider the average computational capacity of a system with n processors. Let c_i denote the computational capacity of a system with i operational processors. This can be a simple linear function of the number of processors, $c_i = ic_1$, or a more complex function of i, depending on the ability of the application to utilize i processors. The average computational capacity of the system at time t can then be defined as $\sum_{i=1}^{n} c_i P_i(t)$, where $P_i(t)$ is the probability that exactly i processors are operational at time t. In contrast, the point availability of the system at time t will be

$$A_p(t) = \sum_{i=m}^{n} P_i(t),$$

where m is the minimum number of processors necessary for proper operation of the system.

1.3.2 NETWORK MEASURES

In addition to the general system measures previously discussed, there are also more specialized measures, focusing on the network that connects the processors together. The simplest of these are classical node and line *connectivity*, which are defined as the minimum number of nodes and lines, respectively, that have to fail before the network becomes disconnected. This gives a rough indication of how vulnerable a network is to disconnection. For example, a network that can be disconnected by the failure of just one (critically positioned) node is potentially more vulnerable than another that requires at least four nodes to fail before it becomes disconnected.

Classical connectivity is a very basic measure of network reliability. Like reliability, it distinguishes between only two network states: connected and disconnected. It says nothing about how the network degrades as nodes fail before, or after, becoming disconnected. Consider the two networks shown in Fig. 1.1. Both networks have the same classical node connectivity of 1. However, in a real sense, network N1 is much more "connected" than N2. The probability that N2 splinters into small pieces is greater than that for N1.

To express this type of "connectivity robustness," we can use additional measures. Two such measures are the average node-pair distance, and the network diameter (the maximum node-pair distance), both calculated given the probability of node and/or link failure. Such network measures, together with the traditional measures listed above, allow us to gauge the dependability of various networked systems that consist of computing nodes connected through a network of communication links.

1.4 OUTLINE OF THIS BOOK

The next chapter is devoted to hardware fault tolerance. This is the most established topic within fault-tolerant computing, and many of the basic principles and techniques that have been developed

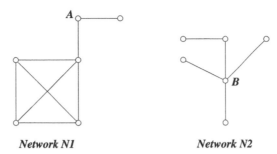

Network N1   *Network N2*

FIGURE 1.1

Inadequacy of classical connectivity.

for it have been extended to other forms of fault tolerance. Prominent hardware failure mechanisms are discussed, as well as canonical fault-tolerant redundant structures. The notion of Byzantine, or malicious, failure is introduced. Techniques to evaluate the reliability and availability of fault-tolerant systems are introduced here, including the use of Markov models.

Next, several variations of information redundancy are covered, starting with the most widely used error-detecting and error-correcting codes. Then, other forms of information redundancy are discussed, including storage redundancy (RAID systems), data replication in distributed systems, and the algorithm-based fault-tolerance technique that tolerates data errors in array computations using some error-detecting and error-correcting codes.

Many computing systems nowadays consist of multiple networked processors that are subject to interconnection link failures, in addition to the already-discussed single node/processor failures. We therefore present in this book suitable fault tolerance techniques for these networks and analysis methods to determine which network topologies are more robust. With the number of transistors on a chip increasing in every hardware generation, networks-on-chip are becoming commonplace. Another recent development is the proliferation of sensor networks. We discuss fault-tolerance techniques for both of these.

Software mistakes/bugs are, in practice, unavoidable, and consequently, some level of software fault tolerance is often necessary. This can be as simple as acceptance tests to check the reasonableness of the results before using them, or as complex as running two or more versions of the software (sequentially or in parallel). Programs also tend to have their state deteriorate after running for long periods of time and eventually crash. This situation can be avoided by periodically restarting the program, a process called rejuvenation. Hypervisor-based systems, where a hardware platform supports multiple virtual machines, each running its own operating system, have gained popularity; we discuss fault-tolerance issues associated with these. Finally, there is the issue of modeling software reliability. Unlike hardware faults, software bugs are very hard to model. Still, a few such models have been developed and several of them are described.

Hardware fault-tolerance techniques can be quite costly to implement. In applications, in which a complete and immediate masking of the effect of hardware faults (especially of a transient nature) is not necessary, checkpointing is an inexpensive alternative. For programs that run for a long time and for which reexecution upon a failure might be too costly, the program state can be saved (once or periodically) during the execution. Upon a failure occurrence, the system can roll back the program to the most recent checkpoint and resume its execution from that point. Checkpointing is especially important in exascale computing, where the computing base may consist of thousands of processors jointly executing programs that take hours, days, or even weeks to execute. Various checkpointing techniques are presented and analyzed in this book, for both general-purpose computing and real-time systems.

Cyber-physical systems, which consist of physical *plants* controlled by computer, have taken off in recent years. Examples include fly-by-wire aircraft, automobiles, spacecraft, power grids, chemical reactors, and intelligent highway systems. Such applications are often life-critical and must therefore be highly reliable. They consist of sensors to assess the state of the plant and the operating environment, computers to run the control software, and actuators to impose their control outputs on the plant. Fault-tolerance issues associated with each are discussed in this book.

Next is a chapter consisting of a few case studies, which serve to illustrate the use of many of the fault-tolerance techniques described previously.

An important part of the design and evaluation process of a fault-tolerant system is to demonstrate that the system does indeed function at the advertised level of reliability. Often, the designed system is too complex to develop analytical expressions of its reliability. If a prototype of the system has already been constructed, then fault-injection experiments can be performed and certain dependability attributes measured. If, however, as is very common, a prototype does not yet exist, statistical simulation may be the only option. Simulation programs for complex systems must be carefully designed to produce accurate results without requiring excessive amounts of computation time. We discuss the principles that should be followed when preparing a simulation program, and show how simulation results can be analyzed to infer system reliability.

We end the book with two specialized fault-tolerance topics: defect tolerant VLSI (very large-scale integration) design and fault tolerance in cryptographic devices. The increasing complexity of VLSI chip design has resulted in a situation, in which manufacturing defects are unavoidable. If nothing is done to remedy this situation, the expected *yield* (the fraction of manufactured chips, which are operational) will be very low. Thus techniques to reduce the sensitivity of VLSI chips to defects have been developed, some of which are very similar to the hardware redundancy schemes.

For cryptographic devices, the need for fault tolerance is twofold. Not only is it crucial that such devices (e.g., smart cards) operate in a fault-free manner in whatever environment they are used, but more importantly, they must stay secure. Fault-injection-based attacks on cryptographic devices have become the simplest and fastest way to extract the secret key from the device. Thus the incorporation of fault tolerance can help to keep cryptographic devices secure.

1.5 FURTHER READING

Several textbooks and reference books on the topic of fault tolerance are available. See, for example, [5–7,10,14,18–20]. Fault tolerance from a software perspective is treated in [3,12,15]. Excellent classifications of the various approaches taken can be found in [2,17]. The major conference in the field is the *Conference on Dependable Systems and Networks* (DSN) [4]; this is a successor to the *Fault-Tolerant Computing Symposium* (FTCS).

Fault tolerance in specific applications are treated in a number of works; for instance embedded/cyber-physical systems in [1,8], cloud computing [9], and high-performance computing [13].

The concept of computing being invisible everywhere appeared in [22], in the context of *pervasive computing*, i.e., computing which pervades everyday living, without being obtrusive.

The definitions of the basic terms and measures appear in most of the textbooks mentioned above and in several probability and statistics books. For example, see [21]. Our definitions of fault and error are slightly different from those used in some of the references. One definition of an error is that it is that part of the system state that leads to system failure. Strictly interpreted, this only applies to a system with state, i.e., with memory. We use the more encompassing definition of anything that can be construed as a manifestation of a fault. This wider interpretation allows purely combinational circuits, which are stateless, to generate errors.

One measure of dependability that we did not describe in the text is to consider everything from the perspective of the application. This approach was taken to define the measure known as *performability*. The application is used to define "accomplishment levels" $L_1, L_2, \cdots, L_n$. Each of these represents a level of quality of service delivered by the application. Now, the performance of the computer affects this quality (if it did not, by definition, it would have nothing to do with the application!). The approach taken by performability is to link the performance of the computer to the accomplishment level that this enables. Performability is then a vector, $(P(L_1), P(L_2), \cdots, P(L_n))$, where $P(L_i)$ is the probability that the computer functions well enough to permit the application to reach up to accomplishment level L_i. For more on performability, see [11,16].

REFERENCES

[1] I. Alvarez, A. Ballesteros, M. Barranco, D. Gessner, S. Djerasevic, J. Proenza, Fault tolerance in highly reliable ethernet-based industrial systems, Proceedings of the IEEE 107 (6) (June 2019) 977–1010.

[2] A. Avizienis, J.C. Laprie, B. Randell, C. Landwehr, Basic concepts and taxonomy of dependable and secure computing, IEEE Transactions on Dependable and Secure Computing 1 (1) (October 2004) 11–33.

[3] B. Baudry, M. Monperrus, The multiple facets of software diversity: recent developments in the year 2000 and beyond, ACM Computing Surveys 48 (1) (September 2015) 16.

[4] Dependable Systems and Networks (DSN) Conference, http://www.dsn.org.

[5] E. Dubrova, Fault-Tolerant Design, Springer, 2013.

[6] W.R. Dunn, Practical Design of Safety-Critical Computer Systems, Reliability Press, 2002.

[7] C.E. Ebeling, An Introduction to Reliability and Maintainability Engineering, McGraw-Hill, 1997.

[8] C. Edwards, T. Lombaerts, H. Smaili, Fault-Tolerant Flight Control, Springer, 2009.

[9] B. Fuhrt, A. Escalante, Handbook of Cloud Computing, Springer, 2010.

[10] J-C. Geffroy, G. Motet, Design of Dependable Computing Systems, Kluwer Academic Publishers, 2002.

[11] R. Ghosh, K.S. Trivedi, V.K. Naik, D.S. Kim, End-to-end performability analysis for infrastructure-as-a-service cloud: an interacting stochastic models approach, in: Pacific Rim International Symposium on Dependable Computing, 2010, pp. 125–132.

[12] R.S. Hammer, Patterns for Fault-Tolerant Software, John Wiley, 2013.

[13] T. Herault, Y. Robert, Fault-Tolerance Techniques for High-Performance Computing, Springer, 2015.

[14] P. Jalote, Fault Tolerance in Distributed Systems, PTR Prentice Hall, 1994.

[15] J. Knight, Fundamentals of Dependable Computing for Software Engineers, Chapman and Hall, 2012.

[16] J.F. Meyer, On evaluating the performability of degradable computing systems, IEEE Transactions on Computers 29 (August 1980) 720–731.

[17] G. Psychou, D. Rodopoulos, M.M. Sabry, D. Atienza, T.G. Noll, F. Catthoor, Classification of resilience techniques against functional errors at higher abstraction layers of digital systems, ACM Computing Surveys 50 (4) (2017) 50.

[18] L.L. Pullum, Software Fault Tolerance Techniques and Implementation, Artech House, 2001.

[19] D.P. Siewiorek, R.S. Swarz, Reliable Computer Systems: Design and Evaluation, A. K. Peters, 1998.

[20] M.L. Shooman, Reliability of Computer Systems and Networks: Fault Tolerance, Analysis, and Design, Wiley-Interscience, 2001.

[21] K.S. Trivedi, Probability and Statistics With Reliability, Queuing, and Computer Science Applications, John Wiley, 2002.

[22] M. Weiser, The computer for the twenty-first century, Scientific American 265 (3) (September 1991) 94–105.

HARDWARE FAULT TOLERANCE

2

Hardware fault tolerance is the most mature area in fault-tolerant computing. Many hardware fault-tolerance techniques have been developed and used in practice in critical applications, ranging from telephone exchanges to space missions. In the past, the main obstacle to a wide use of hardware fault tolerance was the cost of the extra hardware required. With the continued reduction in the cost of hardware, this is no longer a significant drawback, and the use of hardware fault-tolerance techniques is expected to increase. However, other constraints, notably on power consumption, may continue to restrict the use of massive redundancy in many applications.

The hardware can broadly be divided into a hierarchy of three levels. (One can obviously have a more detailed division into sublevels, but three levels will do for our purposes.) At the top is the system level. This is the "face" that the entity presents to the operating environment. An example is the computer hardware that controls a modern aircraft. At the second level, the system is composed of multiple modules or components. Examples include individual processor cores, memory modules, and the I/O subsystem. Obviously, each of these modules will themselves be composed of submodules. At the bottom of the hierarchy are individual nanometer-sized devices.

This chapter first discusses hardware failure at a high level. Then, we dive to the device level to explain some major hardware failure mechanisms. After this, we return to the system level to consider more complex systems consisting of multiple components, describe various resilient structures (which have been proposed and implemented), and evaluate their reliability and/or availability. Next, we describe hardware fault-tolerance techniques that have been developed specifically for general-purpose processors. Finally, we discuss *malicious* faults, and investigate the amount of redundancy needed for protecting against these.

2.1 THE RATE OF HARDWARE FAILURE

The failure rate of a hardware component depends on its current age, any voltage or physical shocks that it has suffered, the ambient temperature, and the technology. The dependence on age is usually captured by what is known as the *bathtub curve* (see Fig. 2.1). When components are very young, their tendency to fail is high. This is due to the chance that some components with manufacturing defects slipped through manufacturing quality control and were released. As time goes on, these components are weeded out, and the component spends the bulk of its life showing a fairly constant failure rate (a precise definition of failure rate is presented a little later, but for now an intuitive understanding is sufficient). As it becomes very old, aging effects start to take over, and the failure rate rises again.

Fault-Tolerant Systems. https://doi.org/10.1016/B978-0-12-818105-8.00012-7

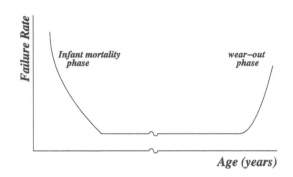

FIGURE 2.1

Bathtub curve.

The impact of the other factors can be expressed through the following empirical failure rate formula for the region where the failure rate is roughly constant:

$$\lambda_{emp} = \pi_L \pi_Q (C_1 \pi_T \pi_V + C_2 \pi_E), \tag{2.1}$$

where the notations represent the following:

λ_{emp} Failure rate of component.

π_L Learning factor, associated with how mature the technology is.

π_Q Quality factor, representing manufacturing process quality control (ranging from 0.25 to 20.00).

π_T Temperature factor, with values ranging from 0.1 to 1000. It is proportional to $e^{-E_a/kT}$, where E_a is the activation energy in electron-volts (eV) associated with the technology, k is the Boltzmann constant (0.8625×10^{-4} eV/K), and T is the temperature in Kelvin (K).

π_V Voltage stress factor for CMOS devices; can range from 1 to 10, depending on the supply voltage and the temperature; does not apply to other technologies (where it is set to 1).

π_E Environment shock factor; ranges from very low (about 0.4) when the component is in an air-conditioned office environment, to very high (13.0) when it is in a harsh environment.

C_1, C_2 Complexity factors; functions of the number of gates on the chip and the number of pins in the package.

Further details can be found in *MIL-HDBK-217E*, which is a handbook produced by the U.S. Department of Defense.

Devices operating in space, which is replete with charged particles and can subject devices to severe temperature swings, can thus be expected to fail much more often than their counterparts in air-conditioned offices; so too can computers in automobiles (which suffer high temperatures and vibration) and industrial applications.

2.2 FAILURE RATE, RELIABILITY, AND MEAN TIME TO FAILURE

In this section, we consider a single component of a more complex system, and show how reliability and mean time to failure (MTTF) can be derived from the basic notion of failure rate. Consider a component that is operational at time $t = 0$ and remains operational until it is hit by a failure. Suppose for the moment that all failures are permanent and irreparable. Let T denote the lifetime of the component (the time until it fails), and let $f(t)$ and $F(t)$ denote the probability density function of T and the cumulative distribution function of T, respectively. These functions are defined for $t \geq 0$ only (because the lifetime cannot be negative) and are related through

$$f(t) = \frac{dF(t)}{dt} \; ; \quad F(t) = \int_0^t f(\tau)d\tau; \tag{2.2}$$

$f(t)$ represents (but is not equal to) the momentary probability of failure at time t. To be exact, for a very small Δt, $f(t)\Delta t \approx \text{Prob}\{t \leq T \leq t + \Delta t\}$. Being a density function, $f(t)$ must satisfy

$$f(t) \geq 0 \text{ for } t \geq 0 \quad \text{and} \quad \int_0^\infty f(t)dt = 1.$$

$F(t)$ is the probability that the component will fail at or before time t,

$$F(t) = \text{Prob}\{T \leq t\};$$

$R(t)$, the reliability of a component (the probability that it will survive at least until time t), is given by

$$R(t) = \text{Prob}\{T > t)\} = 1 - F(t). \tag{2.3}$$

An important quantity is the probability that a good component of current age t will fail in the next short duration of length dt. This is a *conditional* probability, since we know that the component survived at least until time t. This conditional probability is represented by the *failure rate* (also called the *hazard rate*) of a component at time t, denoted by the time-dependent function, $\lambda(t)$, which can be calculated as follows:

$$\lambda(t) = \frac{f(t)}{1 - F(t)}. \tag{2.4}$$

Since $\frac{dR(t)}{dt} = -f(t)$, we obtain

$$\lambda(t) = -\frac{1}{R(t)}\frac{dR(t)}{dt}. \tag{2.5}$$

If a component suffers no meaningful level of aging and has a failure rate that is constant over time: $\lambda(t) = \lambda$. In this case,

$$\frac{dR(t)}{dt} = -\lambda R(t),$$

and the solution of this differential equation (with $R(0) = 1$) is

$$R(t) = e^{-\lambda t}. \tag{2.6}$$

Therefore a constant failure rate implies that the lifetime T of the component has an exponential distribution, with a parameter that is equal to the constant failure rate λ,

$$f(t) = \lambda e^{-\lambda t} ; \qquad F(t) = 1 - e^{-\lambda t} ; \qquad R(t) = e^{-\lambda t} \quad \text{for } t \geq 0.$$

For an irreparable component, the MTTF is equal to its expected lifetime, $E[T]$ (where $E[\ ]$ denotes the expectation or mean of a random variable),

$$MTTF = E[T] = \int_0^\infty t f(t) dt. \tag{2.7}$$

Substituting $\frac{dR(t)}{dt} = -f(t)$ yields

$$MTTF = -\int_0^\infty t \frac{dR(t)}{dt} dt = -tR(t)|_0^\infty + \int_0^\infty R(t) dt = \int_0^\infty R(t) dt \tag{2.8}$$

(the term $-tR(t)$ is equal to zero when $t = 0$ and when $t = \infty$, since $R(\infty) = 0$).

For the case of a constant failure rate for which $R(t) = e^{-\lambda t}$,

$$MTTF = \int_0^\infty e^{-\lambda t} dt = \frac{1}{\lambda}. \tag{2.9}$$

Although a constant failure rate is used in most calculations of reliability (mainly owing to the simplified derivations), there are cases for which this simplifying assumption is inappropriate, especially during the "infant mortality" and "wear-out" phases of a component's life (Fig. 2.1). In such cases, the Weibull distribution is often used. This distribution has two parameters, λ and β, and has the following density function of the lifetime T of a component:

$$f(t) = \lambda \beta t^{\beta-1} \cdot e^{-\lambda t^\beta}. \tag{2.10}$$

The corresponding failure rate is

$$\lambda(t) = \lambda \beta t^{\beta-1}. \tag{2.11}$$

This failure rate is an increasing function of time for $\beta > 1$, is constant for $\beta = 1$, and is a decreasing function of time for $\beta < 1$. This makes it very flexible, and especially appropriate for the wear-out and infant mortality phases. The component reliability for a Weibull distribution is

$$R(t) = e^{-\lambda t^\beta}, \tag{2.12}$$

and the MTTF of the component is

$$MTTF = \frac{\Gamma(\beta^{-1})}{\beta \lambda^{\beta^{-1}}}, \tag{2.13}$$

where $\Gamma(x) = \int_0^\infty y^{x-1} e^{-y} dy$ is the Gamma function. The Gamma function is a generalization of the factorial function to real numbers, and satisfies

- $\Gamma(x) = (x-1)\Gamma(x-1)$ for $x > 1$
- $\Gamma(1) = 1$
- $\Gamma(n) = (n-1)!$ for an integer n, $n = 1, 2, \ldots$

Note that the Weibull distribution includes as a special case ($\beta = 1$), the exponential distribution with a constant failure rate λ.

2.3 HARDWARE FAILURE MECHANISMS

The previous sections introduced us to some factors which affect hardware reliability. In this section, we describe some of the physical failure mechanisms that are at the base of component failure. These failure mechanisms will illustrate the dependence of the failure rate (recall Eq. (2.1)) on the temperature, supply voltage, and the circuit age.

Note that the failure of a device does not automatically result in the failure of the circuit in which the device serves: that depends on the circuit design and usage, which together determine the criticality of the device to component functionality. Different devices within the same circuit see different levels of stress; for instance, their duty cycle (fraction of time for which the device is on) can vary, as can their temperature. It is therefore very hard to map the lifetime of individual devices to the lifetime of the overall circuit.

One cannot therefore create an unbroken chain of reasoning that starts with the individual failure model for each of the billions of transistors in a system and, step by detailed step, go up the hierarchy to accurately model the overall system reliability. Such a model would take too long to evaluate. We have to use approximate models based on experimental tests and on simulation, at the chip or system level.

Rather, device failure models are probably best used to understand how changes in operating parameters (e.g., current, applied voltage, and operating temperature) can change the failure rate. We can then use this knowledge to try to tune the operating parameters to stave off circuit failures to the extent possible. We can also use these models to carry out accelerated failure tests. For example, if we know that failure rates rise exponentially with temperature, we can carry out high-temperature tests of devices, and then use the time-to-failure data to estimate their time-to-failure under normal operating temperatures. If we know that devices can partially recover from stress, we can schedule rest periods to allow them to do so. Knowing that devices slow down as they age, we can clock them more slowly to provide slack time to make up for such slowdown (up to a point). At the design stage, knowing that the aging process will be different for different parts of the circuit (since not all parts are equally stressed), we can size devices differently to provide greater resilience against aging for the more highly stressed portions. And so on.

The failure mechanisms we consider here are those which afflict conventional CMOS devices; such devices are, by far, the most commonly encountered in computing today. The reader should, however, always keep in mind that as device feature sizes continue to drop (e.g., 5 nm devices are being developed at the time of writing), and as new technologies are introduced, new failure mechanisms can become prominent, and failure models can change.

2.3.1 ELECTROMIGRATION

When current flows down a wire, there is momentum transfer between the flowing electrons and the metal atoms that constitute the wire. There is another effect, in the other direction, due to the applied electric field, which is usually insufficient to fully counteract the momentum transfer. As a result, atoms in the metal interconnect can migrate away from their original position, resulting in a thinning of the interconnect or outright separation.

The traditional expression for the median time to failure due to electromigration, denoted by $MedTTF_{EM}$, was derived in the 1960s and is known as Black's formula:

$$MedTTF_{EM} = A_{EM} \cdot J^{-m} \cdot \exp\left(\frac{E_a^{(EM)}}{kT}\right), \tag{2.14}$$

where A_{EM} is a constant of proportionality; J the current density; m an exponent, whose value is typically between 1 and 2; $E_a^{(EM)}$ is the *activation energy* associated with the material of which the interconnect is made; k is Boltzmann's constant; T the absolute temperature, and $\exp(x) = e^x$. The activation energy $E_a^{(EM)}$ is 0.6 eV for aluminium and 0.9 eV for gold. Adding a small quantity of copper (less than 4%) to aluminium is sufficient to significantly increase its activation energy.

Black's formula applies to wires above a certain thickness and length. A metal interconnect can generally be regarded as a polycrystalline film consisting of grains. As the wire width drops below the grain size, the grain boundaries become increasingly perpendicular to the longitudinal direction of the interconnect, and the wire becomes highly resistant to electromigration.

Electromigration tends also to be counteracted by mechanical stress in short wires: below a certain length, called the Blech length, electromigration effects are not significant. The Blech length decreases in proportion to the current density: the product of the Blech length and the applied current density is roughly a constant, depending on the material used.

2.3.2 STRESS MIGRATION

Metal interconnects are deposited on a silicon substrate; the two materials expand at different rates when heated. This causes mechanical stress to the interconnects, which triggers migration among the metal atoms. The mean time to failure caused by stress migration of metal interconnect is often modeled by the following expression:

$$MTTF_{SM} = A_{SM} \cdot \sigma^{-m} \cdot \exp\left(\frac{E_a^{(SM)}}{kT}\right), \tag{2.15}$$

where A_{SM} is a constant of proportionality, σ is the mechanical strain, $E_a^{(SM)}$ is the activation energy for stress migration (often taken as between 0.6 to 1.0 eV), k the Boltzmann constant, and T the absolute temperature. The exponent, m, is usually taken as between 2 and 4 for soft metals like Al and Cu; it rises to between 6 and 9 for strong, hardened materials.

2.3.3 NEGATIVE BIAS TEMPERATURE INSTABILITY

Negative bias temperature instability (NBTI) is an increasingly important failure mechanism in transistors. NBTI can be caused by negative gate voltages and elevated temperatures; it affects pMOS transistors. Its counterpart in nMOS transistors is positive bias temperature instability; we will focus here on NBTI.

When an electric field is applied across the gate oxide of a transistor, charge tends to get trapped below the transistor gate. The amount of trapped charge grows with the time for which the field is applied. The transistor threshold voltage then changes (the threshold voltage is the level beyond which a channel forms between source and drain to allow the transistor to turn on and current to flow); consequently, the current flow across an ON transistor drops, and the gate delay increases. Beyond a certain point, the device can no longer function to specifications. The problem gets worse with increased miniaturization.

Once the gate voltage is removed, this charge can dissipate over time. Such dissipation can be very slow, however: it can take thousands of seconds. Furthermore, complete recovery of the device to its original state tends not to happen; there is always some degradation that carries over from one stress cycle to another. (Recovery is what makes modeling the time to failure of this process so challenging.) Beyond a certain point, timing failures occur, and the circuit composed of such devices fails.

Experimental work has shown that the threshold voltage change increases with temperature, the supply voltage, and the duty cycle. This change grows as a function of the time, t, for which the gate is stressed: the threshold voltage change is proportional to t^m, where m is usually modeled as between $1/4$ and $1/6$.

To reduce the rate of NBTI-induced failure, mitigation by means of using supply voltage scaling and duty cycle reduction can be attempted. Rest periods, where parts of the chip are turned off by power gating, can be regularly scheduled to provide devices the opportunity to partially reverse the voltage threshold shift caused by NBTI. Body biasing, where a voltage is applied to the body of the chip (i.e., the substrate), can be used to compensate for changes in threshold voltage. The supply voltage can be increased to speed up the device to make up for NBTI-induced slowdown; however, this has the unfortunate effect of exacerbating NBTI, and also dramatically increasing the power consumption. In addition, the increase in circuit delay from long-term NBTI-caused degradation can be monitored, and the clock frequency reduced when necessary to prevent timing faults.

2.3.4 HOT CARRIER INJECTION

Charge carriers (electrons for n-channel and holes for p-channel devices) get accelerated by the high fields in the channel of a device. A certain fraction of these carriers gain sufficient energy to be injected into the gate oxide and get trapped there. This can change the current-voltage characteristics of the transistor. After some time, transistors subjected to such defects can become too slow.

The mean time to failure expression depends on whether it is an n-channel or p-channel device; the reason is that electrons and holes have different mobility characteristics. Commonly suggested expressions for the MTTF for n- and p-channel devices are as follows:

$$\text{MTTF}_{n-\text{HCI}} \ = \ A_n I_{sub}^{-m} \cdot w^m \cdot \exp\left(\frac{E_a^{(\text{HCI})}}{kT}\right), \tag{2.16}$$

$$MTTF_{p-HCI} = A_p I_{gate}^{-m} \cdot w^m \cdot \exp\left(\frac{E_a^{(HCI)}}{kT}\right), \tag{2.17}$$

where A_n, A_p are constants of proportionality; I_{sub}, I_{gate} are the substrate and gate currents, respectively; w is the transistor width; $E_a^{(HCI)}$ is the activation energy associated with the HCI process; m an exponent in the range $[2, 4]$; k the Boltzmann constant, and T the absolute temperature. Note that the gate and substrate currents will vary with time, based on the device usage. Using their peak values will provide a lower bound to the MTTF. Also, this expression is useful in providing an indication of how changes in operating conditions will accelerate HCI-based failure.

2.3.5 TIME-DEPENDENT DIELECTRIC BREAKDOWN

When voltage is applied across the gate oxide, electrical defects—called traps—are induced within it. These traps increase leakage current through the gate oxide. As time goes on, these traps can move around and cause variation in leakage current and gate delay. This is the wearout phase, involving *soft breakdown*.

After some time, the traps may overlap, and a conducting path through the oxide results. Once this happens, the leakage current through the gate jumps. This heats up the device; such heating can contribute to the formation of additional traps. These traps may widen the conduction path through the oxide, and the leakage current goes up further. This leads to an increase in temperature, and a highly damaging positive feedback loop is created. The dielectric film suffers *hard breakdown* causing the transistor to fail. The breakdown of the gate dielectric over time is called time-dependent dielectric breakdown (TDDB).

There is no consensus on a model for calculating MTTF for this failure mechanism; there are multiple competing expressions for it. A commonly used expression for the mean time to time-dependent dielectric breakdown is the following:

$$MTTF_{DB} = A_{DB} V^{-(a-bT)} \cdot \exp\left(\frac{X + Y/T + ZT}{kT}\right), \tag{2.18}$$

where A_{DB} is a constant of proportionality, V is the voltage applied across the gate oxide, T is the absolute temperature in Kelvin (K), and k is Boltzmann's constant. Typical values for the other parameters are: $a = 78$, $b = -0.0081$, $X = 0.759$ eV, $Y = -66.8$ eV·K, $Z = -0.37 \times 10^{-4}$ eV/K.

2.3.6 PUTTING IT ALL TOGETHER

Given the many failure mechanisms that exist, how may we put them all together? One approach is to treat each failure mechanism as independent of the others. Assuming a constant failure rate of a given failure mechanism FM, then its rate, denoted by λ_{FM}, will equal the inverse of the mean time to failure (see Eq. (2.9)), i.e., $\lambda_{FM} = MTTF_{FM}^{-1}$. As will be described in greater detail later in this chapter, the *sum of failure rates* model for independent failure mechanisms is followed. Accordingly, the aggregate rate of independent failure mechanisms is the sum of the rates of the individual failure mechanisms, i.e., $\lambda_{total} = \sum_{FM} \lambda_{FM}$. The overall mean time to failure of the device is then estimated as $MTTF_{device} \approx \lambda_{total}^{-1}$. We can then approximate the reliability of the device over some time t as $R_{device}(t) \approx \exp(-\lambda_{total} \cdot t)$.

There are three points that must be made with respect to this approach. First, the failure mechanisms are not necessarily independent; treating them as such and adding up their individual rates may result in estimates of dubious accuracy. For this reason, some have suggested calculating the MTTF of each failure mechanism separately, and taking the minimum of them. Also, when one failure mechanism is dominant, we can simply ignore the others.

Second, these expressions implicitly assume a constant environment. For instance, the temperature dependence in the various formulas above assume a constant temperature. We can use them in a varying environment by means of the following approximation: divide the time axis into small segments, treat the operating conditions as constant over each individual segment, apply the reliability formula over that segment, and then stitch the results together.

Example: Suppose we have an expression for the reliability as a function of temperature. That is, suppose we have the failure rate of a device defined as $\lambda_{device}(T)$, where T is the absolute temperature; this rate has been calculated from a physical model, which assumes a constant temperature. We are given the temperature profile as a function of time: $T(t)$, and are asked to estimate the device reliability over the interval $[0, t]$.

Divide the time axis into short intervals of duration Δ each; interval $I_j = [j\Delta, (j+1)\Delta], j = 0, 1, \cdots$. Assume that the temperature over I_j is constant at T_j. The probability that the device does not fail anytime over I_j, given that it was functional at the beginning of that interval, is given by $\pi(j) = \exp(-\lambda_{device} T_j \Delta)$. Hence, the probability that it does not fail up to the end of I_j is $\prod_{k=0}^{j} \pi(k)$. Note that this is an approximation; it assumes that the failure process in each segment is stochastically independent.

Thirdly, it is very difficult to obtain precise estimates for the variables in the reliability formulas. How, for instance, is one to obtain good estimates for the temperature or duty cycle? We end up having to obtain very approximate estimates based, for example, on circuit simulation.

2.4 COMMON-MODE FAILURES

Redundancy to detect or to mask failure works only so long as the redundant units do not produce incorrect outputs that are all identical. Unfortunately, common-mode failures, where such events occur, are sometimes encountered and greatly reduce the reliability of systems. We will cover common-mode software faults in Chapter 5; here, we focus on hardware.

Common-mode faults occur either at the design/implementation, or at the operational, stage. If the same mistake is made during design or the same vulnerability introduced, multiple circuits can fail identically on the same inputs. At the operational stage, because multiple circuits operate in the same environment, the same environmental disturbance (such as a massive dose of radiation or electromagnetic interference) might introduce identical erroneous outputs. If circuits are powered from a common supply, then surges or other abnormalities in the supply might trigger a similar response from all of them.

Design diversity is used to combat common-mode faults at the design stage. For example, there are different ways of implementing adder circuits (e.g., carry lookahead, carry-select, etc.). One can force one circuit to be implemented using NAND gates, while the corresponding circuit in its redundant partner is implemented using NOR gates. We may place different constraints on gate fan-in, or other circuit parameters in the various circuits, and expect some diversity to emerge from the designs then produced by computer-aided design software tools.

Reducing common-mode faults generated while in operation requires isolation. For example, different circuits may be powered by independent power supplies, or they may be in different zones heavily shielded from radiation or electromagnetic interference.

A metric has been introduced to quantify diversity between two circuits. Let $d_{i,j}$ be the probability that faults f_i, f_j in circuits 1 and 2, respectively, do not cause identically wrong outputs. If $P(f_i, f_j)$ is the probability of the occurrence of such faults, the diversity between these circuits is quantified as $D = \sum_{f_i, f_j} P(f_i, f_j) d_{i,j}$. Unfortunately, this metric is not easy to calculate in practice. For more on this, see the Further Reading section.

2.5 CANONICAL AND RESILIENT STRUCTURES

Having briefly considered some significant physical hardware failure mechanisms, we return now to a higher level. We consider some canonical structures, out of which more complex structures can be constructed. We start with the basic series and parallel structures, continue with nonseries/parallel ones, and then describe some of the many resilient structures that incorporate redundant components (next referred to as modules).

2.5.1 SERIES AND PARALLEL SYSTEMS

The most basic structures are the series and parallel systems depicted in Fig. 2.2. A *series system* is defined as a set of N modules connected together, so that the failure of any one module causes the entire system to fail. Note that the diagram in Fig. 2.2A is a reliability diagram and not always an electrical one; the output of the first module is not necessarily physically connected to the input of the second module. The four modules in this diagram can, for example, represent the instruction decode unit, execution unit, data cache, and instruction cache in a microprocessor. All four units must be fault-free

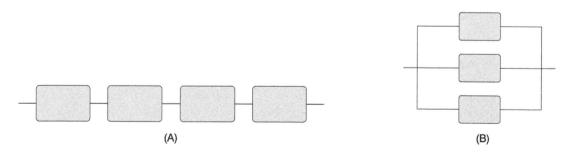

(A)   (B)

FIGURE 2.2

Series and parallel systems. (A) Series system. (B) Parallel system.

for the microprocessor to function, although the way they are connected does not resemble a series system.

Assuming that the modules in Fig. 2.2A fail independently of each other, the reliability of the entire series system is the product of the reliabilities of its N modules. Denoting by $R_i(t)$ the reliability of module i and by $R_s(t)$ the reliability of the whole series system,

$$R_s(t) = \prod_{i=1}^{N} R_i(t), \tag{2.19}$$

if module i has a constant failure rate, denoted by λ_i, then, according to Eq. (2.6), $R_i(t) = e^{-\lambda_i t}$, and consequently,

$$R_s(t) = e^{-\lambda_s t}, \tag{2.20}$$

where $\lambda_s = \sum_{i=1}^{N} \lambda_i$. From Eq. (2.20) we see that the series system has a constant failure rate equal to λ_s (the sum of the individual failure rates), and its MTTF is therefore $MTTF_s = \frac{1}{\lambda_s}$.

A *parallel system* is defined as a set of N modules connected together so that it requires the failure of all the modules for the system to fail. This leads to the following expression for the reliability of a parallel system, denoted by $R_p(t)$:

$$R_p(t) = 1 - \prod_{i=1}^{N} (1 - R_i(t)). \tag{2.21}$$

If module i has a constant failure rate λ_i, then

$$R_p(t) = 1 - \prod_{i=1}^{N} \left(1 - e^{-\lambda_i t}\right). \tag{2.22}$$

As an example, the reliability of a parallel system consisting of two modules with constant failure rates λ_1 and λ_2 is given by

$$R_p(t) = e^{-\lambda_1 t} + e^{-\lambda_2 t} - e^{-(\lambda_1 + \lambda_2)t}.$$

Note that a parallel system does not have a constant failure rate; its failure rate changes with each failure of a module. It can be shown that the MTTF of a parallel system, with all its modules having the same failure rate λ, is $MTTF_p = \sum_{k=1}^{N} \frac{1}{k\lambda}$.

2.5.2 NONSERIES/PARALLEL SYSTEMS

Not all systems have a reliability diagram with a series/parallel structure. Fig. 2.3 depicts a non-series/parallel system, whose reliability cannot be calculated using either Eq. (2.19) or (2.21). Each path in Fig. 2.3 represents a configuration that allows the system to operate successfully. For example, the path ADF means that the system operates successfully if all three modules A, D, and F are fault-free. A path in such reliability diagrams is valid only if all modules and edges are traversed from left to

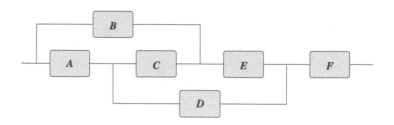

FIGURE 2.3

A nonseries/parallel system.

right. The path BCDF in Fig. 2.3 is thus invalid. No graph transformations that may result in violations of this rule are allowed.

In the following analysis, the dependence of the reliability on the time t is omitted for simplicity of notation, although it is implied that all reliabilities are functions of t.

We calculate the reliability of the nonseries/parallel system in Fig. 2.3 by expanding about a single module i. That is, we condition on whether or not module i is functional, and use the total probability formula,

$$R_{system} = R_i \cdot Prob\{System\ works \mid i\ is\ fault\text{-}free\} + (1 - R_i) \cdot Prob\{System\ works \mid i\ is\ faulty\},$$

$$(2.23)$$

where, as before, R_i denotes the reliability of module i ($i = A, B, C, D, E, F$). We can now draw two new diagrams. In the first, module i will be assumed to be working, and in the second, module i will be assumed faulty. Module i is selected so that the two new diagrams are as close as possible to simple series/parallel structures, for which we can then use Eqs. (2.19) and (2.21). Selecting module C in Fig. 2.3 results in the two diagrams in Fig. 2.4. The process of expanding is then repeated until

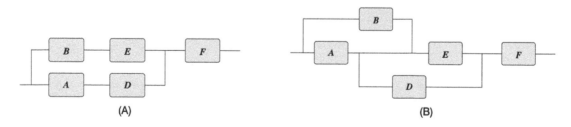

(A)   (B)

FIGURE 2.4

Expanding the diagram in Fig. 2.3 about module C. (A) C not working. (B) C working.

the resulting diagrams are of the series/parallel type. Fig. 2.4A is already of the series/parallel type, whereas Fig. 2.4B needs further expansion about E. Note that Fig. 2.4B should not be viewed as a parallel connection of A and B, connected serially to D and E in parallel; such a diagram will have the path BCDF, which is not a valid path in Fig. 2.3. Based on Fig. 2.4, we can write, using Eq. (2.23),

$$R_{system} = R_C \cdot \text{Prob}\{\text{System works} \mid C \text{ is fault-free}\} + (1 - R_C) \cdot R_F[1 - (1 - R_A R_D)(1 - R_B R_E)]. \tag{2.24}$$

Expanding the diagram in Fig. 2.4B about E yields

$$\text{Prob}\{\text{System works} \mid C \text{ is fault-free}\} = R_E R_F[1 - (1 - R_A)(1 - R_B)] + (1 - R_E)R_A R_D R_F.$$

Substituting this last expression in Eq. (2.24) results in

$$
\begin{aligned}
R_{system} \;=\; & R_C[R_E R_F(R_A + R_B - R_A R_B) + (1 - R_E)R_A R_D R_F] \\
+ \;& (1 - R_C)[R_F(R_A R_D + R_B R_E - R_A R_D R_B R_E)]
\end{aligned}
\tag{2.25}
$$

If $R_A = R_B = R_C = R_D = R_E = R_F = R$, then

$$R_{system} = R^3 \left(R^3 - 3R^2 + R + 2\right). \tag{2.26}$$

If the diagram of the nonseries/parallel structure is too complicated, upper and lower bounds on R_{system} can be calculated instead of using the above procedure.

An upper bound is given by

$$R_{system} \leq 1 - \prod\left(1 - R_{\text{path } i}\right), \tag{2.27}$$

where $R_{\text{path } i}$ is the reliability of the series connection of the modules along path i. The bound in Eq. (2.27) assumes that all the paths are in parallel, and that they are independent. In reality, two of these paths may have a module in common, and the failure of this module will result in both paths becoming faulty. That is why Eq. (2.27) provides only an upper bound, rather than an exact value. As an example, let us calculate the upper bound for Fig. 2.3. The paths are ADF, BEF, and ACEF, resulting in

$$R_{system} \leq 1 - (1 - R_A R_D R_F)(1 - R_B R_E R_F)(1 - R_A R_C R_E R_F). \tag{2.28}$$

If $R_A = R_B = R_C = R_D = R_E = R_F = R$, then $R_{system} \leq R^3(R^7 - 2R^4 - R^3 + R + 2)$, which is less accurate than the exact result in Eq. (2.26).

The upper bound can be used to derive the exact reliability, by performing the multiplication in Eq. (2.28) (or Eq. (2.27) in the general case) and replacing every occurrence of R_i^k by R_i. Since each module is used only once, its reliability should not be raised to any power greater than 1. The reader is invited to verify that applying this rule to the upper bound, Eq. (2.28) yields the same exact reliability as in Eq. (2.25).

A lower bound can be calculated based on minimal cut sets of the system diagram, where a minimal cut set is a minimal list of modules such that the removal (due to faults) of all modules from the set will cause a working system to fail. The lower bound is obtained by

$$R_{system} \geq \prod\left(1 - Q_{\text{cut } i}\right), \tag{2.29}$$

where $Q_{\text{cut } i}$ is the probability that minimal cut i is faulty. In Fig. 2.3, the minimal cut sets are F, AB, AE, DE, and BCD. Consequently,

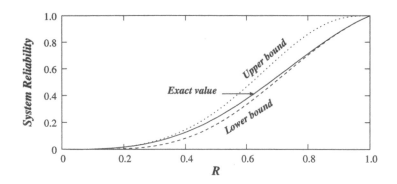

FIGURE 2.5

Comparing the exact reliability of the nonseries/parallel system in Fig. 2.3 to its upper and lower bounds.

$$R_{system} \geq R_F [1 - (1 - R_A)(1 - R_B)] [1 - (1 - R_A)(1 - R_E)] [1 - (1 - R_D)(1 - R_E)]$$
$$\cdot [1 - (1 - R_B)(1 - R_C)(1 - R_D)]. \tag{2.30}$$

If $R_A = R_B = R_C = R_D = R_E = R_F = R$, then $R_{system} \geq R^5 (24 - 60R + 62R^2 - 33R^3 + 9R^4 - R^5)$. Fig. 2.5 compares the upper and lower bounds to the exact system reliability for the case in which all six modules have the same reliability R. Note that in this case, for the more likely high values of R, the lower bound provides a very good estimate for the system reliability.

2.5.3 M-OF-N SYSTEMS

An M-of-N system is a system that consists of N modules and needs at least M of them for proper operation. Thus the system fails when fewer than M modules are functional. The best-known example of this type of systems is the triplex, which consists of three identical modules, whose outputs are voted on. This is a 2-of-3 system: so long as a majority (2 or 3) of the modules produce correct results, the system will be functional.

Let us now compute the reliability of an M-of-N system. We assume, as before, that the failures of the different modules are statistically independent, and that there is no repair of failing modules. If $R(t)$ is the reliability of an individual module (the probability that the module is still operational at time t), the reliability of an M-of-N system is the probability that M or more modules are functional at time t. The system reliability is therefore given by

$$R_{M\_of\_N}(t) = \sum_{i=M}^{N} \binom{N}{i} R^i(t) [1 - R(t)]^{N-i}, \tag{2.31}$$

where $\binom{N}{i} = \frac{N!}{(N-i)!i!}$. The assumption that failures are independent is key to the high reliability of M-of-N systems. Even a slight extent of positively correlated (i.e., common-mode) failures can greatly diminish their reliability. For example, suppose q_{cor} is the probability that the entire system suffers a common failure. The reliability of the system now becomes

$$R^{cor}_{M\_of\_N}(t) = (1 - q_{cor}) \sum_{i=M}^{N} \binom{N}{i} R^i(t)(1 - R(t))^{N-i}. \tag{2.32}$$

If the system is not designed carefully, the correlated failure factor can dominate the overall failure probability.

In practice, correlated failure rates can be extremely difficult to estimate. In Eq. (2.32), we assumed that there was a failure mode, in which the entire cluster of N modules suffers a common failure. However, there are other modes as well, in which subsets of the N modules could undergo a correlated failure. There being $2^N - N - 1$ subsets containing two or more modules, it quickly becomes infeasible to obtain by experiment, or otherwise, the correlated failure probabilities associated with each of the subsets, even for moderate values of N.

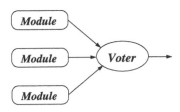

FIGURE 2.6

A triple modular redundant (TMR) structure.

The most important M-of-N system is the *triplex*, or the triple modular redundant (TMR) cluster shown in Fig. 2.6. In such a system, $M = 2$ and $N = 3$, each module carries out the same computation, and a voter selects the majority output. If a single voter is used, that voter becomes a critical point of failure, and the reliability of the cluster is

$$
\begin{aligned}
R_{TMR}(t) &= R_{voter}(t) \sum_{i=2}^{3} \binom{3}{i} R^i(t)(1 - R(t))^{3-i} \\
&= R_{voter}(t) \left(3R^2(t)[1 - R(t)] + R^3(t)\right) \\
&= R_{voter}(t) \left(3R^2(t) - 2R^3(t)\right), \tag{2.33}
\end{aligned}
$$

where $R_{voter}(t)$ is the reliability of the voter.

The general case of TMR is called N-modular redundancy (NMR), and is an M-of-N cluster with N odd, and $M = \lceil N/2 \rceil$.

In Fig. 2.7, we plot the reliability of a simplex (a single module), a triplex (TMR), and an NMR cluster with $N = 5$. For high values of $R(t)$, the greater the redundancy, the higher the system reliability. As $R(t)$ decreases, the advantages of redundancy become less marked; until for $R(t) < 0.5$, redundancy actually becomes a disadvantage, with the simplex being more reliable than either of the redundant

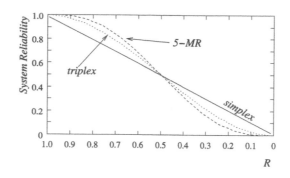

FIGURE 2.7

Comparing NMR reliability (for $N = 3$ and 5) to that of a single module as a function of the single module reliability R (voter failure rate is considered negligible).

arrangements. This is also reflected in the value of MTTF_{TMR}, which (for $R_{voter}(t) = 1$ and $R(t) = e^{-\lambda t}$) can be calculated based on Eq. (2.8) as

$$\text{MTTF}_{TMR} = \int_0^\infty (3R^2(t) - 2R^3(t))dt = \int_0^\infty (3e^{-2\lambda t} - 2e^{-3\lambda t})dt = \frac{5}{6\lambda}$$
$$< \frac{1}{\lambda} = \text{MTTF}_{Simplex}.$$

In most applications, however, $R(t) \gg 0.5$ for realistic t, and the system is repaired or replaced long before $R(t) < 0.5$, so a triplex arrangement does offer significant reliability gains.

Eq. (2.33) was derived under the conservative assumption that every failure of the voter will lead to erroneous system output, and that any failure of two modules is fatal. This is not necessarily the case. If, for example, one module has a permanent logical 1 on one of its outputs, and a second module has a permanent logical 0 on its corresponding output, the TMR (or NMR) will still function properly. Clearly, a similar situation may arise regarding certain faults within the voter circuit. These are examples of compensating faults. Another case of faults that may be harmless are nonoverlapping faults. For example, one module may have a faulty adder, and another module a faulty multiplier. If the adder and multiplier circuits are disjoint, the two faulty modules are unlikely to generate wrong outputs simultaneously. If all compensating and nonoverlapping faults are taken into account, the resulting reliability will be higher than that predicted by Eq. (2.33).

2.5.4 VOTERS

A voter receives inputs $x_1, x_2, \cdots, x_N$ from an M-of-N cluster and generates a representative output. The simplest voter is one that does a bit-by-bit comparison of the outputs, and checks if a majority of the N inputs are identical. If so, it outputs the majority. This approach only works when we can guarantee that every functional module will generate an output that matches the output of every other functional module, bit by bit. This will be the case if the modules are identical processors, use identical inputs and identical software, and have mutually synchronized clocks.

If, however, the modules are different processors, or are running different software for the same problem, it is possible for two correct outputs to diverge slightly, in the lower significant bits. Hence, we can declare two outputs x and y as practically identical if $|x - y| < \delta$ for some specified δ. (Note that "practically identical" is not transitive; if A is practically identical to B, and B is practically identical to C, this does not necessarily mean that A is practically identical to C.)

For such approximate agreement, we can do *plurality* voting. A k-*plurality voter* looks for a set of at least k practically identical outputs (this is a set, in which each member is practically identical to all other members) and picks any of them (or the median) as the representative. For example, if we set $\delta = 0.1$, and the five outputs were $1.10, 1.11, 1.32, 1.49, 3.00$, then the subset $\{1.10, 1.11\}$ would be selected by a 2-plurality voter.

In our discussion so far, we have implicitly assumed that each output has an equal chance of being faulty. In some cases that may not be true; the hardware (or software) producing one output may have a different failure probability than does the hardware (or software) producing another output. In this case, each output is assigned a weight that is related to its probability of being correct. The voter then does weighted voting and produces an output that is associated with over half the sum of all weights.

2.5.5 VARIATIONS ON N-MODULAR REDUNDANCY

Unit-level modular redundancy

In addition to applying replication and voting at the level of the entire system, the same idea can be applied at the subsystem level as well. Fig. 2.8 shows how triple-modular replication can be applied at the individual unit level for a system consisting of four units. In such a scheme, the voters are no longer as critical as in NMR. A single faulty voter will cause no more harm than a single faulty unit, and the effect of either one will not propagate beyond the next level of units. Clearly, the level at which

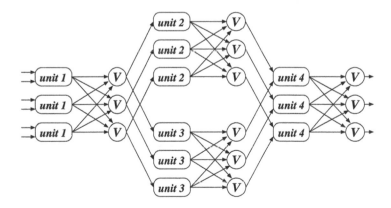

FIGURE 2.8

Subsystem-level TMR.

replication and voting are applied can be further lowered at the expense of additional voters, increasing the overall size and delay of the system.

Of particular interest is the triplicated processor/memory system shown in Fig. 2.9. Here, all communications (in either direction) between the triplicated processors and triplicated memories go through majority voting. This organization is more reliable than a single majority voting of a triplicated processor/memory structure.

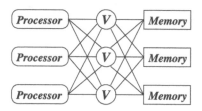

FIGURE 2.9

Triplicated voters in a processor/memory TMR.

Dynamic redundancy

The above variations of NMR employ considerable amounts of hardware to instantaneously mask errors that may occur during the operation of the system. However, in many applications, temporary erroneous results are acceptable as long as the system is capable of detecting such errors and reconfiguring itself by replacing the faulty module with a fault-free spare module. An example of such a dynamic (or active) redundancy scheme is depicted in Fig. 2.10, in which the system consists of one active module, N spare modules, and a *fault detection and reconfiguration* unit that is assumed to be capable of detecting any erroneous output produced by the active module, disconnecting the faulty active module, and connecting instead a fault-free spare (if one exists).

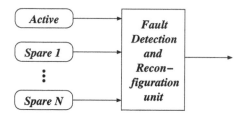

FIGURE 2.10

Dynamic redundancy.

Note that if all the spare modules are active (powered), we expect them to have the same failure rate as the single active module. This dynamic redundancy structure is therefore similar to the basic parallel system in Fig. 2.2, and its reliability is given by

$$R_{dynamic}(t) = R_{dru}(t)\left(1 - (1 - R(t))^{N+1}\right), \tag{2.34}$$

where $R(t)$ is the reliability of each module, and $R_{dru}(t)$ is the reliability of the detection and reconfiguration unit. If, however, the spare modules are not powered (to conserve energy), they may have a negligible failure rate when not in operation. Denoting by c the *coverage factor*, defined as the probability that the faulty active module will be correctly diagnosed and disconnected, and a good spare will be successfully connected, we can derive the system reliability for very large N by arguing as follows:

Failures to the active module occur at rate λ. The probability that such a failure cannot be recovered from is $1 - c$. Hence, the rate at which unrecoverable failures occur is $(1 - c)\lambda$. The probability that no unrecoverable failure occurs to the active processor over a duration t is therefore given by $e^{-(1-c)\lambda t}$; the reliability of the reconfiguration unit is given by $R_{dru}(t)$. We therefore have

$$R_{dynamic}(t) = R_{dru}(t)e^{-(1-c)\lambda t}. \tag{2.35}$$

Hybrid redundancy

An NMR system is capable of masking permanent and intermittent failures, but as we have seen, its reliability drops below that of a single module for very long mission times if no repair or replacement are taking place. The objective of hybrid redundancy is to overcome this by adding spare modules that will be used to replace active modules once they become faulty. Fig. 2.11 depicts a hybrid system consisting of a core of N processors constituting an NMR, and a set of K spares. The outputs of the active primary modules are compared (by the *Compare* unit) to the output of the voter to identify a faulty primary (if any). The *Compare* unit then generates the corresponding disagreement signal, which will cause the *Reconfiguration unit* to disconnect the faulty primary, and connect a spare module instead.

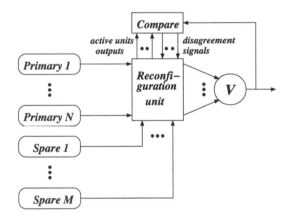

FIGURE 2.11

Hybrid redundancy.

The reliability of a hybrid system with a TMR core and K spares is

$$R_{hybrid}(t) = R_{voter}(t)R_{rec}(t)\left(1 - mR(t)[1 - R(t)]^{m-1} - [1 - R(t)]^m\right), \tag{2.36}$$

where $m = K + 3$ is the total number of modules, and $R_{voter}(t)$ and $R_{rec}(t)$ are the reliability of the voter and the comparison and reconfiguration circuitry, respectively. Eq. (2.36) assumes that any fault in either the voter or the comparison and reconfiguration circuit will cause a system failure. In practice, not all faults in these circuits are fatal, and the reliability of the hybrid system will be higher than what is predicted by Eq. (2.36). A more accurate value of $R_{hybrid}(t)$ can be obtained through a detailed analysis of the voter and the comparison and reconfiguration circuits, and the different ways in which they can fail.

Sift-out modular redundancy

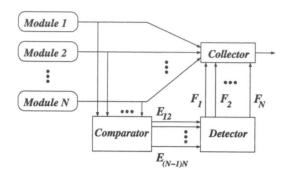

FIGURE 2.12

Sift-out structure.

As in NMR, all N modules in the *Sift-out Modular Redundancy* scheme (see Fig. 2.12) are active, and the system is operational as long as there are at least two fault-free modules. Unlike NMR, this system uses comparator, detector, and collector circuits instead of a majority voter. The comparator compares the outputs of all pairs of modules, so that $E_{ij} = 1$ if the outputs of modules i and j do not match. Based on these signals, the detector determines which modules are faulty and generates the logical outputs $F_1, F_2, \cdots, F_N$, where $F_i = 1$ if module i has been determined to be faulty, and 0 otherwise. Finally, the collector unit produces the system output, which is the OR of the outputs of all fault-free modules. This way, a module, whose output disagrees with the outputs of the other modules, is switched out and no longer contributes to the system output. The implementation of this scheme is simpler than that of hybrid redundancy.

Care must be taken, however, not to be too aggressive in the purging (sifting-out) process. The vast majority of failures tend to be transient and disappear on their own after some time. It is preferable therefore to only purge a module if it produces incorrect outputs over a sustained interval of time.

2.5.6 DUPLEX SYSTEMS

A duplex system is the simplest example of module redundancy. Fig. 2.13 shows an example of a duplex system consisting of two processors and a comparator. Both processors execute the same task, and if the comparator finds that their outputs are in agreement, the result is assumed to be correct. The implicit assumption here is that it is highly unlikely for both processors to suffer identical hardware failures that result in their both producing identical wrong results. If, on the other hand, the results are different, there is a fault, and higher-level software has to decide how it is to be handled.

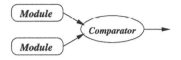

FIGURE 2.13

Duplex system.

The fact that the two processors disagree does not, by itself, allow us to identify the failed processor. This can be done using one of several methods, some of which we will consider below. To derive the reliability of the duplex system, we denote, as before, by c the *coverage factor*, which is the probability that a faulty processor will be correctly diagnosed, identified, and disconnected.

Assuming that the two processors are identical, each with a reliability R(t), the reliability of the duplex system is

$$R_{duplex}(t) = R_{comp}(t)\left(R^2(t) + 2cR(t)(1 - R(t))\right),\tag{2.37}$$

where R_{comp} is the reliability of the comparator. Assuming a fixed failure rate of λ for each processor and an ideal comparator ($R_{comp}(t) = 1$), the MTTF of the duplex system is

$$MTTF_{duplex} = \frac{1}{2\lambda} + \frac{c}{\lambda}.$$

The main difference between a duplex and a TMR system is that in a duplex, the faulty processor must be identified. We discuss next the various ways in which this can be done.

In our discussion above, we have assumed that the duplicated elements are full-fledged processors. This need not be the case; duplication can be carried out at any level. For example, the *Razor* flip-flop (described later in greater detail) includes a shadow latch, which is negative edge-triggered on the clock, as opposed to the main flip-flop, which is positive edge-triggered. Both are fed from the same data source. The shadow therefore samples at a delay equal to the duration of the positive phase of the clock, i.e., the input data is allowed this much extra settling time at the shadow. If the data stored in the main and in the shadow elements differ, then an error is flagged; the data did not settle by the positive clock edge (as it was meant to).

Acceptance tests

The first method for identifying the faulty processor is to carry out a check of each processor's output, known as an *acceptance test*. One example of an acceptance test is a *range test*, which checks if the output is in the expected range. This is a basic and simple test, which usually works very well. For example, if the output of a processor is supposed to indicate the predicted pressure in a container (for gases or liquids), we would know the range of pressures that the container can hold. Any output outside those values results in the output being flagged as faulty. We are therefore using semantic information of the task to predict which values of output indicate an error.

The question is now how to determine the range of acceptable values. The narrower this range, the greater the probability that an incorrect output will be identified as such, but so is the probability that a correct output will be misidentified as erroneous. We define the *sensitivity* of a test as the conditional probability that the test detects an error, given that the output is actually erroneous, and the *false alarm probability* of a test as the conditional probability that the acceptance test declares an error, given that the output is actually good. A narrow range acceptance test will have high sensitivity, but also a high false alarm rate, which means that the test is very likely not to miss an erroneous output, but at the same time, it is likely to get many false-positive results (correct results that the test declares faulty).

The reverse happens when we make this range very wide: then we have low false alarm rates, but also low sensitivity. We will consider this problem again when we discuss recovery block approaches to software fault tolerance in Chapter 5.

Range tests are the simplest, but by no means the only, acceptance test mechanism. Any other test that can discriminate reasonably accurately between a correct and an incorrect output can be used. For instance, suppose we want to check the correctness of a square-root operation; since $(\sqrt{x})^2 = x$, we can square the output, and check if it is the same as the input (or sufficiently close, depending on the level of precision used).

Hardware testing

The second method of identifying the failed processor is to subject both processors to some hardware/logic test routines. Such diagnostic tests are regularly used to verify that the processor circuitry is functioning properly, but running them can identify the processor that produced the erroneous output only if a permanent fault is present in that processor. Since most hardware faults are transient, hardware testing has a low probability of identifying the processor that failed to produce the correct output.

Even if the hardware fault is permanent, running hardware tests does not guarantee that the fault will be detected. In practice, hardware tests are never perfect, and there is a nonzero probability that the test passes as good a processor, which is actually faulty. The test sensitivity, or the probability of the test identifying a faulty processor as such, is in the case of hardware tests often called the *test coverage*.

Forward recovery

A third method for identifying the faulty processor in a duplex is to use a third processor to repeat the computations carried out by the duplex. If only one of the three processors (the duplex plus this new processor) is faulty, then whichever processor the third disagrees with is the faulty one.

It is also possible to use a combination of these methods. The acceptance test is the quickest to run, but is often the least sensitive. The result of the acceptance test can be used as a provisional indication of which processor is faulty, and this can be confirmed by using either of the other two approaches.

Pair-and-spare system

Several more complicated resilient structures have been proposed that use the duplex as their building block. The first such system that we describe is the pair-and-spare system (see Fig. 2.14), in which modules are grouped in pairs, and each pair has a comparator that checks if the two outputs are equal (or sufficiently close). If the outputs of the two primary modules do not match, this indicates an error in at least one of them, but does not indicate which one is in error. Running diagnostic tests, as described in the previous section, will result in a disruption in service. To avoid such a disruption, the entire pair is disconnected and the computation is transferred to a spare pair. The two members of the switched-out pair can now be tested offline to determine whether the error was due to a transient or permanent fault. In the case of a transient fault, the pair can eventually be marked as a good spare.

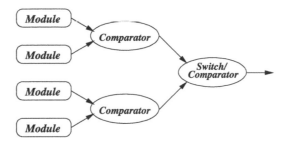

FIGURE 2.14

A pair-and-spare structure consisting of two duplexes.

Triplex-duplex system

Another duplex-based structure is the triplex-duplex system. Here, processors are tied together to form duplexes, and then, a triplex is formed out of these duplexes. When the processors in a duplex disagree, both of them are switched out of the system. The triplex-duplex arrangement allows for the error masking of voting combined with a simpler identification of faulty processors. Furthermore, the triplex can continue to function even if only one duplex is left functional, because the duplex arrangement allows the detection of faults. Deriving the reliability of a triplex-duplex system is reasonably simple and is left for the reader as an exercise.

2.6 OTHER RELIABILITY EVALUATION TECHNIQUES

Most of the structures that we have described so far have been simple enough to allow reliability derivations using straightforward, and relatively simple, combinatorial arguments. Analysis of more complex resilient structures requires more advanced reliability evaluation techniques, some of which are described next.

2.6.1 POISSON PROCESSES

Consider nondeterministic events of some sort, occurring over time with the following probabilistic behavior:

For a time interval of very short length Δt,

1. The probability of one event occurring during the interval Δt is, for some constant λ, $\lambda \Delta t$ plus terms of order Δt^2.
2. The probability of more than one event occurring during Δt is negligible (of the order of Δt^2).
3. Events happening in disjoint intervals are independent. For example, the number of events in the interval $[0, t)$ has no bearing on their number in $[t, t + \Delta]$ for any $\Delta > 0$.

Let $N(t)$ denote the number of events occurring in an interval of length t, and let $P_k(t) = \text{Prob}\{N(t) = k\}$ be the probability of exactly k events occurring during an interval of length t ($k = 0, 1, 2, ...$). Based on (1–3), we have

$$P_k(t + \Delta t) \approx P_{k-1}(t)\lambda\Delta t \; + \; P_k(t)(1 - \lambda\Delta t) \quad (\text{for } k = 1, 2, \ldots),$$

and

$$P_0(t + \Delta t) \approx P_0(t)(1 - \lambda\Delta t).$$

These approximations become more accurate as $\Delta t \to 0$, and lead to the differential equations

$$\frac{dP_k(t)}{dt} \; = \; \lambda P_{k-1}(t) - \lambda P_k(t) \quad (\text{for } k = 1, 2, \ldots)$$

and

$$\frac{dP_0(t)}{dt} \; = \; -\lambda P_0(t).$$

Using the initial condition $P_0(0) = 1$, the solution to this set of differential equations is

$$P_k(t) \; = \; \text{Prob}\{N(t) = k\} \; = \; e^{-\lambda t}\frac{(\lambda t)^k}{k!} \quad (\text{for } k = 0, 1, 2, \ldots).$$

A process $N(t)$ with this probability distribution is called a Poisson process with rate λ. A Poisson process with rate λ has the following properties:

1. The expected number of events occurring in an interval of length t is λt.
2. The length of time between consecutive events is an exponentially distributed random variable with parameter λ and mean value $1/\lambda$.
3. The numbers of events occurring in disjoint intervals of time are independent of one another.
4. The sum of two independent Poisson processes with rates λ_1 and λ_2 is itself a Poisson process with rate $\lambda_1 + \lambda_2$.

As an example for the use of the Poisson process, we consider a duplex system, consisting of two active identical processors with an unlimited number of spares. The two active processors are subject to failures occurring at a constant rate of λ per processor. The spares, however, are assumed to always be functional (they have a negligible failure rate so long as they are not active).

When a failure occurs in an active processor, it must be detected and a new processor inducted into the duplex to replace the one that just failed. As before, we define the coverage factor c as the probability of successful detection and induction. We, however, assume (for simplicity) that the comparator failure rate is negligible, and that the induction process of a new processor is instantaneous.

Let us now calculate the reliability of this duplex system over the time interval $[0, t]$. We first concentrate on the failure process in one of the two processors. When a processor fails (due to a permanent fault), it is diagnosed and replaced instantaneously. Due to the constant failure rate λ, the time between two consecutive failures of the same processor is exponentially distributed with parameter λ. This implies that $N(t)$, the number of failures that occur in this one processor during the time interval $[0, t]$, is a Poisson process with the rate λ.

Since the duplex has two active processors, the number of failures that occur in the duplex is the sum of the numbers of failures of the two processors. The duplex's failure process is therefore also a

Poisson process (denoted by $M(t)$) with rate 2λ. The probability that k failures occur in the duplex over an interval of duration t is thus

$$\text{Prob}\{k \text{ failures in duplex}\} = \text{Prob}\{M(t) = k\} = e^{-2\lambda t} \frac{(2\lambda t)^k}{k!}. \qquad (2.38)$$

For the duplex system not to fail, each of these failures must be detected and the processor successfully replaced. The probability of one such success is the coverage factor c, and the probability that the system will survive k failures is c^k. The reliability of the duplex over the interval $[0, t]$ is therefore

$$
\begin{aligned}
R_{\text{duplex}}(t) &= \sum_{k=0}^{\infty} \text{Prob}\{k \text{ failures in duplex}\} \cdot c^k = \sum_{k=0}^{\infty} e^{-2\lambda t} \frac{(2\lambda t)^k c^k}{k!} \\
&= e^{-2\lambda t} \sum_{k=0}^{\infty} \frac{(2\lambda tc)^k}{k!} = e^{-2\lambda t} e^{2\lambda tc} \\
&= e^{-2\lambda(1-c)t}. \qquad (2.39)
\end{aligned}
$$

In our derivation, we have used the fact that

$$e^x = 1 + x + \frac{x^2}{2!} + \cdots = \sum_{k=0}^{\infty} \frac{x^k}{k!}.$$

We could have obtained the expression in Eq. (2.39) more directly using the type of reasoning we employed in the analysis of hybrid redundancy. To reiterate, the steps are as follows:

1. Individual processors fail at a rate λ, and so processor failures occur in the duplex at the rate 2λ.
2. Each processor failure has a probability c of being successfully dealt with, and a probability $1 - c$ of causing failure to the duplex.
3. As a result, failures that crash the duplex occur with rate $2\lambda(1 - c)$.
4. The reliability of the system is thus $e^{-2\lambda(1-c)t}$.

Similar derivations can be made for M-of-N systems, in which failing processors are identified and replaced from an infinite pool of spares. This is left for the reader as an exercise. The extension to the case with only a finite set of spares is simple: the summation in the reliability expression is capped at that number of spares, rather than going to infinity.

2.6.2 MARKOV MODELS

In complex systems, in which constant failure rates are assumed, but combinatorial arguments are insufficient for analyzing the reliability of the system, we can use *Markov models* for deriving expressions for the system reliability. In addition, Markov models provide a structured approach for the derivation of reliabilities of systems that may include coverage factors and a repair process.

A *Markov chain* is a special type of a stochastic process. In general, a stochastic process $X(t)$ is an infinite number of random variables, indexed by time t. Consider now a stochastic process $X(t)$ that must take values from a set (called the *state space*) of discrete quantities, say the integers $0, 1, 2, \ldots$.

The process $X(t)$ is called a *Markov chain* if

$$\text{Prob}\{X(t_n) = j \mid X(t_0) = i_0, X(t_1) = i_1, \cdots, X(t_{n-1}) = i_{n-1}\}$$
$$= \text{Prob}\{X(t_n) = j \mid X(t_{n-1}) = i_{n-1}\} \quad \text{for every } t_0 < t_1 < \cdots < t_{n-1} < t_n.$$

If $X(t) = i$ for some t and i, we say that the chain is in state i, at time t. We will deal only with continuous time, discrete state Markov chains, for which the time t is continuous ($0 \le t < \infty$), but the state $X(t)$ is discrete and integer valued. For convenience, we will use as states the integers $0, 1, 2, ...$ The Markov property implies that to predict the future trajectory of a Markov chain, it is sufficient to know its present state. This freedom from the need to store the entire history of the process is of great practical importance: it makes the problem of analyzing Markovian stochastic processes tractable in many cases.

The probabilistic behavior of a Markov chain can be described as follows: Once it moves into some state i, it stays there for a length of time that has an exponential distribution with parameter λ_i. This implies a constant *rate* λ_i of leaving state i. The probability that, when leaving state i, the chain will move to state j (with $j \ne i$) is denoted by p_{ij} ($\sum_{j \ne i} p_{ij} = 1$). The rate of transition from state i to state j is thus $\lambda_{ij} = p_{ij} \lambda_i$ ($\sum_{j \ne i} \lambda_{ij} = \lambda_i$).

We denote by $P_i(t)$ the probability that the process will be in state i at time t, given it started at some initial state i_0 at time 0. Based on the above notations, we can derive a set of differential equations for $P_i(t)$ ($i = 0, 1, 2, ...$).

For a given time instant t, a given state i, and a very small interval of time Δt, the chain can be in state i at time $t + \Delta t$ in one of the following cases:

1. It was in state i at time t, and has not moved during the time interval Δt. This event has a probability of $P_i(t)(1 - \lambda_i \Delta t)$, plus terms of order Δt^2.
2. It was at some other state j at time t ($j \ne i$), and moved from j to i during the interval Δt. This event has a probability of $P_j(t)\lambda_{ji}\Delta t$, plus terms of order Δt^2.

The probability of more than one transition during Δt is negligible (of order Δt^2) if Δt is small enough. Therefore for small Δt,

$$P_i(t + \Delta t) \approx P_i(t)(1 - \lambda_i \Delta t) + \sum_{j \ne i} P_j(t)\lambda_{ji}\Delta t.$$

Again, this approximation becomes more accurate as $\Delta t \to 0$, and results in

$$\frac{dP_i(t)}{dt} = -\lambda_i P_i(t) + \sum_{j \ne i} \lambda_{ji} P_j(t),$$

and since $\lambda_i = \sum_{j \ne i} \lambda_{ij}$,

$$\frac{dP_i(t)}{dt} = -\sum_{j \ne i} \lambda_{ij} P_i(t) + \sum_{j \ne i} \lambda_{ji} P_j(t).$$

This set of differential equations (for $i = 0, 1, 2, ...$) can now be solved, using the initial conditions $P_{i_0}(0) = 1$ and $P_j(0) = 0$ for $j \ne i_0$ (since i_0 is the initial state).

Consider, for example, a duplex system that has a single active processor, and a single standby spare that is connected only when a fault has been detected in the active unit. Let λ be the fixed failure rate of each of the processors (when active), and let c be the coverage factor. The corresponding Markov chain is shown in Fig. 2.15. Note that, because the integers assigned to the different states are arbitrary,

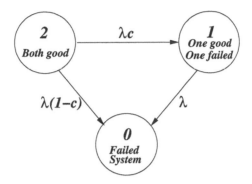

FIGURE 2.15

The Markov model for the duplex system with an inactive spare (state i has i good processors).

we can assign them in such a way that they are meaningful, and thus easier to remember. In this example, the state represents the number of good processors (0, 1, or 2, with the initial state being 2 good processors). The differential equations describing this Markov chain are:

$$\frac{dP_2(t)}{dt} = -\lambda P_2(t),$$
$$\frac{dP_1(t)}{dt} = \lambda c P_2(t) - \lambda P_1(t),$$
$$\frac{dP_0(t)}{dt} = \lambda(1-c)P_2(t) + \lambda P_1(t). \tag{2.40}$$

Solving Eq. (2.40) with the initial conditions $P_2(0) = 1$, $P_1(0) = P_0(0) = 0$ yields

$$P_2(t) = e^{-\lambda t}; \qquad P_1(t) = c\lambda t e^{-\lambda t}; \qquad P_0(t) = 1 - P_1(t) - P_2(t),$$

and as a result,

$$R_{system}(t) = 1 - P_0(t) = P_2(t) + P_1(t) = e^{-\lambda t} + c\lambda t e^{-\lambda t}. \tag{2.41}$$

This expression can also be derived based on combinatorial arguments. The derivation is left to the reader as an exercise.

Our next example of a duplex system that can be analyzed using a Markov model is a system with two active processors, each with a constant failure rate of λ, and a constant repair rate of μ. That is, failures occur as a Poisson process with rate λ; repair time is exponentially distributed with parameter μ (i.e., with mean $1/\mu$). The Markov model for this system is depicted in Fig. 2.16. As in the previous

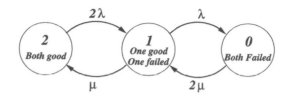

FIGURE 2.16

The Markov model for a duplex system with repair. State variable is the number of functional processors.

example, the state is the number of good processors. The differential equations describing this Markov chain are:

$$\frac{dP_2(t)}{dt} = -2\lambda P_2(t) + \mu P_1(t),$$

$$\frac{dP_1(t)}{dt} = 2\lambda P_2(t) + 2\mu P_0(t) - (\lambda + \mu)P_1(t),$$

$$\frac{dP_0(t)}{dt} = \lambda P_1(t) - 2\mu P_0(t). \tag{2.42}$$

Solving (2.42) with the initial conditions $P_2(0) = 1$, $P_1(0) = P_0(0) = 0$ yields

$$P_2(t) = \frac{\mu^2}{(\lambda + \mu)^2} + \frac{2\lambda\mu}{(\lambda + \mu)^2} e^{-(\lambda + \mu)t} + \frac{\lambda^2}{(\lambda + \mu)^2} e^{-2(\lambda + \mu)t},$$

$$P_1(t) = \frac{2\lambda\mu}{(\lambda + \mu)^2} + \frac{2\lambda(\lambda - \mu)}{(\lambda + \mu)^2} e^{-(\lambda + \mu)t} - \frac{2\lambda^2}{(\lambda + \mu)^2} e^{-2(\lambda + \mu)t},$$

$$P_0(t) = 1 - P_1(t) - P_2(t). \tag{2.43}$$

Note that we solve only for $P_1(t)$ and $P_2(t)$; using the boundary condition that the probabilities must sum up to 1 (for every t) gives us $P_0(t)$ and reduces by one the number of differential equations to be solved.

Note also that this system does not fail completely; it is not operational while at state 0, but is then repaired and goes back into operation. For a system with repair, calculating the availability is more meaningful than calculating the reliability. The (point) availability, or the probability that the system is operational at time t, is

$$A(t) = P_1(t) + P_2(t).$$

The reliability $R(t)$, on the other hand, is the probability that the system never enters state 0 at any time during $[0, t]$, and cannot be obtained out of the above expressions. To obtain this probability, we must modify the Markov chain slightly by removing the transition out of state 0, so that state 0 becomes an *absorbing* state. This way, the probability of ever entering the state in the interval $[0, t]$ is reduced to the probability of being in state 0 at time t. This probability can be found by writing out the differential equations for this new Markov chain, solving them, and calculating the reliability as $R(t) = 1 - P_0(t)$.

Since in most applications processors are repaired when they become faulty, the long-run availability of the system A is a more relevant measure than the reliability. To this end, we need to calculate the long-run probabilities, $P_2(\infty)$, $P_1(\infty)$, and $P_0(\infty)$. These can be obtained either from Eq. (2.43) by letting t approach ∞, or from Eq. (2.42) by setting all the derivatives $\frac{dP_i(t)}{dt}$ ($i = 0, 1, 2$) to 0 and using the relationship $P_2(\infty) + P_1(\infty) + P_0(\infty) = 1$. The availability in the long-run A is then

$$A = P_2(\infty) + P_1(\infty) = \frac{\mu^2}{(\lambda + \mu)^2} + \frac{2\lambda\mu}{(\lambda + \mu)^2} = \frac{\mu(\mu + 2\lambda)}{(\lambda + \mu)^2} = 1 - \left(\frac{\lambda}{\lambda + \mu}\right)^2.$$

2.7 FAULT-TOLERANCE PROCESSOR-LEVEL TECHNIQUES

All the resilient structures described so far can be applied to a wide range of modules, from very simple combinatorial logic modules to the most complex microprocessors, or even complete processor boards. Still, duplicating complete processors that are not used for critical applications introduces a prohibitively large overhead, and is not justified. For such cases, simpler techniques with much smaller overheads have been developed. These techniques rely on the fact that processors execute stored programs and, upon an error, the program (or part of it) can be re-executed as long as the following two conditions are satisfied: the error is detected, and the cause of the error is a short-lived transient fault that will most likely disappear before the program is reexecuted.

The simplest technique of this type mandates executing every program twice, and using the results only if the outcomes of the two executions match. This *time redundancy* approach will clearly reduce the performance of the computer by as much as 50%.

The above technique does not require any means for error detection. If a mechanism (and suitable circuitry) is provided to detect errors during the execution of an instruction, then that instruction can be reexecuted, preferably after a certain delay to allow the transient fault to disappear. Such an *instruction retry* has a considerably lower performance overhead than the brute-force reexecution of the entire program.

A different technique for low-cost concurrent error detection without relying on time redundancy is through the use of a small and simple processor that will monitor the behavior of the main processor. Such a monitoring processor is called a *watchdog processor*, described next.

2.7.1 WATCHDOG PROCESSOR

A watchdog processor (see Fig. 2.17) performs concurrent system-level error detection by monitoring the system buses connecting the processor and the memory. This monitoring primarily targets control-flow checking, verifying that the main processor is executing the correct blocks of code and in the right order. Such monitoring can detect hardware faults and software faults (mistakes/bugs) that cause either an erroneous instruction(s) to be executed or a wrong program path to be taken.

To perform the monitoring of the control flow, the watchdog processor must be provided with information regarding the program(s) that are to be checked. This information is used to verify the correctness of the program(s) execution by the main processor in real-time. The information that is provided to the watchdog processor is derived from the control flow graph (CFG), which represents the control flow of the program to be executed by the main processor (see an example of a five-node CFG

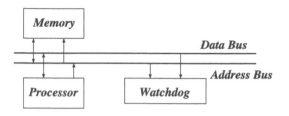

FIGURE 2.17

Error detection using a watchdog processor.

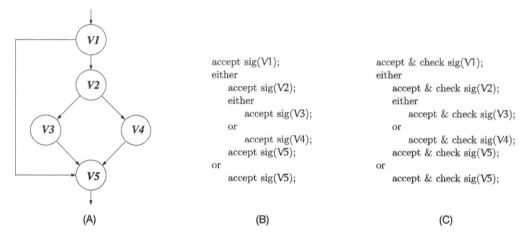

(A)   (B)   (C)

FIGURE 2.18

A control-flow graph and the corresponding watchdog check programs for assigned signatures (B), and for calculated signatures (C). (A) A control flow graph (CFG). (B) Checking control flow. (C) Checking nodes and control flow.

in Fig. 2.18A). A node in this graph represents a block of branch-free instructions; no branches are allowed from and into the block. An edge represents a permissible flow of control, often corresponding to a branch instruction. Labels (called *signatures*) are assigned to the nodes of the CFG and are stored in the watchdog processor. During the execution of the program, run-time signatures of the executed blocks are generated and compared with the reference ones stored in the watchdog processor. If a discrepancy is detected, an error signal is generated.

The signatures of the nodes in the CFG can be either assigned or calculated. Assigned signatures can simply be successive integers that are stored in the watchdog processor along with the CFG. During execution, the signatures of the currently executed nodes are forwarded to the watchdog processor by the main processor. The watchdog processor can then verify that the path taken by the program corresponds to a valid path of the given CFG. The program that the watchdog processor will execute for the CFG in Fig. 2.18A is shown in Fig. 2.18B, where sig(Vi) is the signature assigned to node Vi.

This check program will detect an invalid program path, such as {V1, V4}. Note, however, that an error in one or more instructions within a node will not be detected by this scheme.

To increase the error detection capabilities of the watchdog processor and allow it to detect errors in individual instructions, calculated signatures can be used instead of assigned ones. For a given node, a signature can be calculated from the instructions included in the node by adding (modulo 2) all the instructions in the node, or using a checksum (see Chapter 3) or another similar approach. As before, these signatures are stored in the watchdog processor, and then compared with the run-time signatures calculated by the watchdog processor while monitoring the instructions executed by the main processor. The program that the watchdog processor will execute for the CFG in Fig. 2.18A with calculated signatures is shown in Fig. 2.18C.

Note that most data errors will not be detected by the watchdog processor, since the majority of such errors will not cause the program to change its execution path. The functionality of the watchdog processor can, in principle, be extended to cover a larger portion of data errors by including *assertions* in the program executed by the watchdog processor. Assertions are reasonableness checks that verify expected relationships among the variables of the program. These assertions must be prepared by the application programmer and could be made part of the application software rather than delegated to the watchdog processor. The performance benefits of having the watchdog processor rather than the main processor check the assertions may be offset by the need to frequently forward the values of the relevant application variables from the main processor to the watchdog processor. In addition, the design of the watchdog processor becomes more complicated, since it needs now to be capable of executing arithmetic and logical operations that would otherwise not be required. If assertions are not used, then the watchdog processor must be supplemented by other error-detection techniques (e.g., parity codes described in Chapter 3) to cover data errors.

One of the quoted advantages of using a watchdog processor for error detection is that the checking circuitry is independent of the checked circuitry, thus providing protection against common or correlated errors. Such a protection can also be achieved in duplex structures through the use of design diversity; for example, implementing one of the processors in complementary logic, or simply using processors from different manufacturers. Separation between the watchdog processor and the main processor is becoming harder to achieve in current high-end microprocessors, in which simple monitoring of the processor-memory bus is insufficient to determine which instructions will eventually be executed, and which have been fetched speculatively and will be aborted. Furthermore, the current trend to support simultaneous multithreading greatly increases the complexity of designing a watchdog processor. A different technique for concurrent error checking for a processor supporting simultaneous multithreading is described next.

2.7.2 SIMULTANEOUS MULTITHREADING FOR FAULT TOLERANCE

We start this section with a brief overview of simultaneous multithreading. For a more detailed description, the reader is invited to consult any good book on computer architecture.

High-end processors today improve speed by exploiting both pipelining and parallelism. Parallelism is facilitated by having multiple functional units, with the attempt to overlap the execution of as many instructions as possible. However, because of data and control dependencies, most programs have severe limits on how much parallelism can actually be uncovered within each thread of execution. Indeed, a study of some benchmarks found that on average, only about 1.5 instructions can be overlapped. Therefore most of the time the majority of the functional units will be idle. It is to remedy this problem that the approach of simultaneous multithreading (SMT) was born.

The key idea behind SMT is the following: If data and control dependencies limit the amount of parallelism that can be extracted out of individual threads, allow the processor to execute multiple threads *simultaneously*. Note that we are not talking about rapid context switches to swap processes in and out: instructions from *multiple* threads are being executed at the same time (in the same clock cycle). To support such increased functionality, the architecture must be augmented suitably. A program counter register is needed for each of the threads that the system is simultaneously executing. If the instruction set specifies a k-register architecture, and we want to execute n threads simultaneously, at least nk physical registers are needed (so that there is one k-register set for each of the n threads). These are just the externally visible registers: most high-end architectures have a large number of internal registers that are not "visible" to the instruction set to facilitate register renaming, and thereby improve performance. Unlike the architectural registers, the internal renaming registers are shared by all simultaneously executing threads, which also share a common issue queue. A suitable policy must be implemented for fetching and issuing instructions, and for assigning internal registers and other resources so that no thread is starved.

How is this different from just running the workload on a multiprocessor consisting of n traditional processors? The answer lies in the way the resources can be assigned. In the traditional multiprocessor, each processor will be running an individual thread, which will have access to just the functional units and rename registers associated with that processor. In the SMT, we have a set of threads that have access to a pool of functional units and rename registers. The usage of these entities will depend on the available parallelism within each thread at the moment; it can change with time, as the resource requirements and inherent parallelism levels change in each simultaneously executing thread.

To take advantage of the multithreading capability for fault-detection purposes, *two* independent threads are created for every thread that the application wants to run. These threads execute identical code, and care is taken to ensure that they receive exactly the same inputs. If all is well, they must both produce the same output: a divergence in output signals a fault, and appropriate steps must be taken for recovery. The idea is to provide almost the same amount of protection against transient faults as can be obtained from a traditional approach that runs a total of two copies of the program independently.

To reduce the performance penalty of reexecution, the second execution of the program always trails the first. Call these two executions the leading and the trailing copies of the program, respectively. The advantage of doing this is that information can be passed from the leading to the trailing copy to make the trailing copy run faster, and consume less computational resources. For example, the leading copy can tell the trailing copy the outcome of conditional branches, so that the trailer never makes an incorrect branch guess, or the leading copy can make loading faster for the trailer.

To support the two independent but identical threads, two different sets of several hardware components must be assigned to these threads. For example, two sets of the architectural registers must be used so that a fault in a register being used by one thread will have no impact on the execution of the other thread. With recent developments in computer architecture, such resources are increasingly becoming available. For example, there are general purpose graphics processing units (GPGPUs), which consist of multiple compute units (also known as streaming multiprocessors) on a chip, each of which consists of a large number of processor cores (typically 64 to 128).

This leads to the concept of the *sphere of replication*. Items that are replicated for the two threads are said to be within this sphere; items that are not replicated are outside. Data flows across the sur-

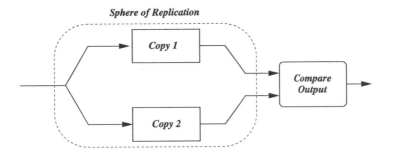

FIGURE 2.19

Sphere of replication.

face of this sphere (see Fig. 2.19). Items that are replicated use such redundancy as a means for fault tolerance and are within the sphere of replication; items that are not must use some other means (such as error-correcting codes discussed in Chapter 3) to protect against the impact of faults. We can decide what items fall within the sphere of replication based on the cost or overhead that they entail, and the effectiveness with which other fault-tolerance techniques can protect them should they be kept outside it. For example, providing two copies of the instruction and data caches may be too expensive, and so, one can rely instead on error-correcting codes to protect their contents.

Note that since redundant results must be compared when leaving the sphere of replication, there is the need for synchronization between the redundant threads at these points. This can cause a loss of performance, since a leading thread will have to wait for the laggard one.

2.8 TIMING FAULT TOLERANCE

As technology has advanced and semiconductor devices become ever smaller and more densely packed, timing variability has increased. The actual delays in a circuit can vary considerably from their nominal values; they can vary considerably both between devices on the same die, as well as between dies (intradie and interdie variability). There are three principal causes for this:

- Process variation increasingly asserts itself at very low feature sizes. That is, there is physical variability in the various parts that go to make up each transistor. Such variability can be considerable even among transistors on the same die. The physical characteristics of a device obviously influence the timing delays of a signal passing through it.
- Circuit delays are a strong function of the supply voltage; they tend to increase as the supply voltage drops. Sometimes, the supply voltage is deliberately changed to adjust the power consumption (which increases exponentially with voltage) at the cost of processing speed. Other times, even with a constant nominal supply voltage, there can be voltage droops that occur when there are large current transients.
- Temperature also affects circuit delay. Devices consume energy; this energy is dissipated as heat. As devices get packed increasingly tightly together (more devices per unit area than formerly),

temperature variation can occur; furthermore, temperatures can vary considerably from one part of a processor core to the next. For example, the integer register file is usually among the hottest parts of a core, whereas a cache is usually quite cool. Furthermore, since power consumption is dynamically varying, so is the temperature. There is also a destabilizing positive feedback effect: increased temperature tends to increase leakage current, which in turn increases temperature. Circuit delays tend to go up with the temperature.

- Device wearout increases delays. The various device aging mechanisms, such as electromigration, time-dependent dielectric breakdown, hot carrier injection, and negative/positive bias temperature instability, all contribute to increased delays. Different devices in a chip age at potentially different rates, increasing spatial timing variability across the chip.

Example: A recent simulation study examined the variation of delay of an inverter. SPICE simulations were run for an inverter cell implemented in 65 nm technology. The fastest inverter in their simulation (at 1 volt supply and $-40°C$) caused a delay of 22.2 ps; the slowest inverter (at 0.9 volt and $-40°C$) imposed a 42.8 ps delay.

Timing faults can occur in clocked systems when the clock interval is too short for signals to propagate through their designated paths. This can result in flip-flops gating in outdated values. An obvious solution to this problem is to lengthen the clock period, i.e., slow down the clock to such an extent that even a significant upward variation in circuit time latency does not cause a signal to arrive too late to "catch" the next clock transition. This is easy to implement; however, it is also very expensive in that it can drastically impair performance.

Timing faults are somewhat different from the other fault types we have encountered. It is not as if wrong results are generated; it is just that the correct results take longer to arrive than expected. Preventing them without slowing down the clock requires a boost of the circuit speed; this can, for example, be done by boosting the supply voltage (up to some tolerable maximum value). This, however, can significantly increase power consumption.

Tolerating errors caused by timing faults consists of two steps: (a) detecting when an error has been generated by longer-than-expected delays, and (b) correcting for it by waiting long enough for the correct value to arrive (i.e., for the result to settle on the wire).

Detecting when an error has been generated can be accomplished by taking two samples of the signal: one at the regular clock transition, and the second after some delay. If the two agree, then the signal has had time to settle before the regular clock transition, and there is no timing error. If the two disagree, then the delayed signal should be used (assuming, of course, that the delay is sufficient to allow even a delayed output to settle).

This is the principle behind the *Razor* latch, which consists of the main flip-flop clocked by the nominal clock and a shadow latch clocked by a delayed clock (see Fig. 2.20). If the shadow latch and the main flip-flop results disagree, after both have received their contents, we have a timing error indication.

Correcting for this can be done in several ways; we describe one approach here in the context of a processor pipeline.[1] This approach is called *counterflow pipelining*. Consider a very simple linear

[1] To understand this discussion, you should be familiar with the basics of pipelining. If you are not, simply skip the rest of this discussion.

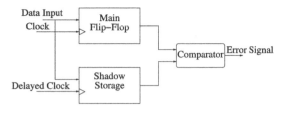

FIGURE 2.20

Detecting a timing error.

pipeline consisting of n stages. A pipeline stage consists of combinational logic ending in storage flip-flops. Such storage is made sensitive to timing errors by having shadow latches in addition to the main flip-flops, used in the manner described above. The main flip-flops are used to deliver inputs to the subsequent stage.

Suppose a timing error is detected in stage k. This means that the wrong inputs were supplied to the combinational logic of stage $k+1$. The output of stage k should therefore be nullified: this is done by inserting a bubble into stage $k+1$ for the current clock cycle. The correct value will be then supplied to stage $k+1$ by the shadow latch of stage k, allowing stage $k+1$ to resume its work after a one-cycle delay. At the same time, a signal is sent from stage k to the earlier stages (i.e., stages $k-1, k-2, \cdots$) telling them to flush their contents. This flushes the pipeline all the way behind stage k to the beginning, Instruction Fetch, stage. Once this flush is complete, Instruction Fetch can resume, fetching (again) the instruction logically following the one which caused the timing problem.

2.9 TOLERANCE OF BYZANTINE FAILURES

We have so far classified failures according to their temporal behavior: are they permanent or do they go away after some time? We will now introduce another important classification, based on how the failed unit behaves.

It is usually assumed that when a unit fails, it goes dead. The picture many people typically have in their minds is that of a lightbulb, which fails by burning out. If all devices behaved that way when they failed, dealing with failures would be relatively simple. However, devices in general, and processors in particular, can suffer *malicious* failures, in which they produce arbitrary outputs. Such failures are known as *Byzantine* failures, and are described below. These failures cause no problem in an M-of-N system with voting, since the voter acts as a centralizing entity, masking out the erroneous outputs. However, when processors are used in a truly distributed way without such a centralizing entity, Byzantine failures can cause subtle problems.

To see this, consider the following example. A sensor is providing temperature information to two processors through point-to-point links between them (see Fig. 2.21). The sensor has suffered a Byzantine failure and tells processor P_1 that the temperature is 25°, while telling P_2 that it is 45°. Now, is there any way in which P_1 and P_2 can figure out that the sensor is faulty? The best they can do is to exchange the messages they have received from the sensor: P_1 tells P_2 that it got 25°, and P_2 tells P_1 that it got 45°. At this point, both processors know that something is wrong in the system, but

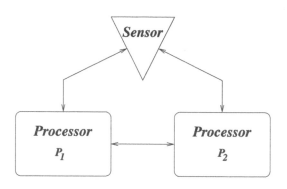

FIGURE 2.21

Network for Byzantine example.

neither can figure out which unit is malfunctioning. As far as P_1 is concerned, the input it received from the sensor contradicts the input from P_2; however, it has no way of knowing whether it is the sensor or P_2 that is faulty. P_2 has a similar problem. No number of additional communications between P_1 and P_2 can solve this problem.

This is known as the *Byzantine generals* problem, since an early paper in this field used as a model a general communicating his attack plans to his lieutenants by messengers. A traitorous commander could send contradictory messages to his lieutenants, or one or more of the lieutenants could be disloyal and misrepresent the commander's orders, and get some divisions to attack and others to retreat. The objective is to get all the loyal lieutenants to agree on the commander's order. If the commanding general is loyal, the order the loyal lieutenants agree on must be the order that the commander sent. Traitorous officers can lie about the order they received.

The solution to this problem is the Byzantine generals algorithm (also known as the interactive consistency algorithm). The model is that of a single entity (such as a sensor or processor) disseminating the value of some variable to a set of receivers. The receivers can communicate among themselves to exchange information about the value they received from the original source. If a unit is functional, it will be truthful in all its messages; a faulty unit may behave arbitrarily. This arbitrary behavior includes the possibility of sending out contradictory messages. All communications are time-bounded, i.e., the absence of a message can be detected by a time-out mechanism. The goal of the algorithm is to satisfy the following *interactive consistency* conditions:

IC1: All functional (nonfaulty) units must arrive at an agreement of the value that was transmitted by the original source.

IC2: If the original source is functional, the value they agree on must be the value that was sent out by the original source.

There are many algorithms for solving the Byzantine generals problem. We will present here the original algorithm, because it is the simplest. More recent algorithms are referenced in the Further Reading section.

The algorithm is recursive. Let there be N units in all (one original source and $N - 1$ receivers), of which up to m may be faulty. It is possible to show that interactive consistency can only be obtained when $N \geq 3m + 1$. If $N \leq 3m$, no algorithm can be constructed that satisfies the interactive consistency conditions.

The algorithm *Byz(N,m)* consists of the following three steps:

Step 1: The original source disseminates the information to each of the $N - 1$ receivers.

Step 2: If $m > 0$, each of the $N - 1$ receivers now acts as an original source to disseminate the value that it received in the previous step. To do this, each receiver runs the *Byz(N-1,m-1)* algorithm, and sends out its received value to the other $N - 2$ receivers. If a unit does not get a message from another unit, it assumes the default message was sent, and so enters the default into its records. If $m = 0$, this step is bypassed.

Step 3: At the end of the preceding step, each receiver has a vector containing the agreed values received (*a*) from the original source, and (*b*) from each of the other receivers (if $m > 0$). If $m > 0$, each receiver takes a vote over the values contained in its vector, and this is used as the value that was transmitted by the original source. If no majority exists, a default value is used. If $m = 0$, the receiver simply uses the value it received from the original source.

Note that we assume that all units have a timer available to them and a timeout mechanism to detect the absence (or loss) of a message. Otherwise, a faulty node could cause the entire system to be suspended indefinitely by remaining silent.

Let us consider some examples of this algorithm. We will use the following notations:

- If A and B are units, then $A.B(n)$ means that A sent B the message n.
- If U is a string of units $A_1, A_2, \cdots, A_m$, and B is a unit, then $U.B(n)$ means that B received the message n from A_m, who claims to have received it from A_{m-1}, and so on.
- A message that is not sent is denoted by φ. For example, $A.B(\varphi)$ means that the message that A was supposed to send B was never sent.

For example, $A.B.C(n)$ represents the fact that B told C that the value it received from A was n. Similarly, $A.B.C.D(n)$ means that D received the message n from C, who claims to have received it from B who, in turn, claims to have received it from A. The string of units thus represents a chain along which the given message n has passed. For example, Black.White.Green(341) means that Green received the message 341 from White, who claims to have received it from Black.

Example: Consider the degenerate case of the algorithm when $m = 0$, i.e., no fault tolerance is provided. In such a case, step 2 is bypassed, and the interactive consistency vector consists of a single value: the one that has been received from the original source.

Example: Consider now the case where $m = 1$. We must have at least $3m + 1 = 4$ units participating in this algorithm. Our model in this example consists of a sensor S and three receivers, R_1, R_2, and R_3. Suppose the sensor is faulty and sends out inconsistent messages to the receivers: $S.R_1(1)$, $S.R_2(1)$, $S.R_3(0)$. All the receivers are functional, and the default is assumed to be 1.

In the second step of the algorithm, R_1, R_2, and R_3 each acts as the source for the message it received from the sensor and runs *Byz(3,0)* on it. That is, the following messages are sent:

$S.R_1.R_2(1)$ $S.R_1.R_3(1)$
$S.R_2.R_1(1)$ $S.R_2.R_3(1)$
$S.R_3.R_1(0)$ $S.R_3.R_2(0)$

Define an interactive consistency vector (ICV) at receiver R_i as $(x_1^i, x_2^i, \cdots, x_{N-1}^i)$, where

$$x_j^i = \begin{cases} \text{Report of } R_j \text{ as determined by } R_i & \text{if } i \neq j \\ \text{Value received from the original source} & \text{if } i = j. \end{cases}$$

At the end of this step, the ICVs are each $(1, 1, 0)$ at every receiver. Taking the majority vote over this yields 1, which is the value used by each of them.

Example: Let $N = 7$, $m = 2$, but this time let receivers R_1 and R_6 be faulty and the other units (S, R_2, R_3, R_4, R_5) be functional. The messages sent out in the first round by S are consistent: $S.R_1(1)$, $S.R_2(1)$, $S.R_3(1)$, $S.R_4(1)$, $S.R_5(1)$, and $S.R_6(1)$. Each of the receivers now executes $Byz(6,1)$ in step 2 of the $Byz(7,2)$ algorithm.

Consider R_1 first. This unit is faulty and can send out any message it likes (or even nothing at all). Suppose it sends out the following messages in step 1 of the $Byz(6,1)$ algorithm for all receivers to agree on its value:

$$S.R_1.R_2(1) \quad S.R_1.R_3(2) \quad S.R_1.R_4(3) \quad S.R_1.R_5(4) \quad S.R_1.R_6(0).$$

In step 2 of this $Byz(6,1)$ algorithm, each of the remaining receivers (R_2, R_3, R_4, R_5, R_6) uses the $Byz(5,0)$ algorithm to disseminate the message it received from R_1. The following are the messages:

$$
\begin{array}{llll}
S.R_1.R_2.R_3(1) & S.R_1.R_2.R_4(1) & S.R_1.R_2.R_5(1) & S.R_1.R_2.R_6(1) \\
S.R_1.R_3.R_2(2) & S.R_1.R_3.R_4(2) & S.R_1.R_3.R_5(2) & S.R_1.R_3.R_6(2) \\
S.R_1.R_4.R_2(3) & S.R_1.R_4.R_3(3) & S.R_1.R_4.R_5(3) & S.R_1.R_4.R_6(3) \\
S.R_1.R_5.R_2(4) & S.R_1.R_5.R_3(4) & S.R_1.R_5.R_4(4) & S.R_1.R_5.R_6(4) \\
S.R_1.R_6.R_2(1) & S.R_1.R_6.R_3(8) & S.R_1.R_6.R_4(0) & S.R_1.R_6.R_5(\varphi)
\end{array}
$$

Note that R_6 being maliciously faulty is free to send out anything it likes.
The ICVs maintained at each of the receivers in connection with the $S.R_1(1)$ message are:

$$
\begin{aligned}
ICV_{S.R_1}(R_2) &= (1,2,3,4,1) \\
ICV_{S.R_1}(R_3) &= (1,2,3,4,8) \\
ICV_{S.R_1}(R_4) &= (1,2,3,4,0) \\
ICV_{S.R_1}(R_5) &= (1,2,3,4,0)
\end{aligned}
$$

$ICV_{S.R_1}(R_6)$ is irrelevant, since R_6 is faulty. Also, note that since R_5 received nothing from R_6, its value is recorded as the default, say 0.

When R_2, R_3, R_4, and R_5 examine their ICVs, they find no majority, and therefore assume the default value for $S.R_1$. This default is zero, and so each of these receivers records that the message that S sent R_1 is agreed to be 0.

Similarly, agreement can be reached on the message that S sent to each of the other receivers (the reader is encouraged to write out the messages). This completes the generation of the ICVs connected with the original $Byz(7,2)$ algorithm.

Let us now prove that algorithm Byz does indeed satisfy the interactive consistency conditions, IC1 and IC2 if $N \geq 3m + 1$. We proceed by induction on m. The induction hypothesis is that the theorem holds for all $m \leq M$, for some $M \geq 0$. We now consider two cases.

Case 1: The original source is nonfaulty.

We show by induction that whenever the original source is nonfaulty, algorithm $\text{Byz}(N, m)$ satisfies IC2 if there are more than $2k + m$ nodes, and at most k faulty elements. The proof is by induction on m. Assume the result holds for all $m \leq M$, and consider the case $m = M + 1$.

In the first step, the original source sends out its message to each of the other processors. Since the source is nonfaulty, all processors receive consistent messages.

In the second step, each processor runs $\text{Byz}(N - 1, m - 1)$ to disseminate the message it received from the original source. Since $N > 2k + m$, we have $N - 1 > 2k + m - 1$. Hence, by the induction hypothesis, executing $\text{Byz}(N - 1, m - 1)$ is sufficient to permit all correct processors to disseminate the messages they received.

Now, set $k = m$. Since there are at most m faulty elements, a majority of the processors is functional. Hence, the majority vote on the values disseminated will result in a consistent value being produced by each correct processor.

Case 2: The original source is faulty.

If the original source is faulty, at most $m - 1$ other processors can be faulty.

In step 1, the original source can send out any message it likes to each of the other processors. There are $N - 1 \geq 3(m - 1) + 1$ other processors. Hence, when these processors run *Byz(N-1,m-1)* among the $N - 1$ other processors, by the induction hypothesis, each processor will have consistent entries in its ICV for each of them. The only entry in the ICV that can differ is that corresponding to the original source. Therefore when the majority function is applied to each ICV, the result is the same, and the proof is completed.

We have shown that $N \geq 3m + 1$ is a sufficient condition for Byzantine agreement. We did this by construction, i.e., by presenting an algorithm that achieved consistency under these conditions. It also turns out that this condition is necessary. That is, under the condition of two-party messages and arbitrary failures, it is impossible for *any* algorithm to guarantee that conditions IC1 and IC2 will be met if $N < 3m$.

2.9.1 BYZANTINE AGREEMENT WITH MESSAGE AUTHENTICATION

The Byzantine generals problem is hard, because faulty processors could lie about the message they received. Let us now remove this possibility by requiring that messages be signed. That is, suppose each processor can append to its messages an unforgeable signature. Before forwarding a message, a processor appends its own signature to the message it received. The recipient can check the authenticity of each signature. Thus if a processor receives a message that has been forwarded through processors A and B, it can check to see whether the signatures of A and B have been appended to the message, and if they are valid. Once again, we assume that all processors have timers so that they can time out any (faulty) processor that remains silent.

In such a case, maintaining interactive consistency becomes very easy. Here is an algorithm that does so:

Algorithm *AByz(N,m)*

Step A1:   The original source signs its message ψ and sends it out to each of the processors.

Step A2:   Each processor i that receives a signed message $\psi : A$, where A is the set of signatures appended to the message ψ, checks the number of signatures in A. If this number is less than $m + 1$, it sends out $\psi : A \cup \{i\}$ (i.e., what it received plus its own signature) to each of the processors not in set A. It also adds this message ψ to its list of received messages.

Step A3:   When a processor has seen the signatures of every other processor (or has timed out), it applies some decision function to select from among the messages it has received.

Let us now show that the algorithm maintains Byzantine agreement for any number of processors. Clearly, if $N \le m + 2$, the problem becomes trivial.

As before, we consider two cases.

Case 1: The original source is functional. In such a case, an identical signed message (say, μ) is transmitted by the original source to every processor in the system. Since nobody can forge the original source's signature, no processor will accept any message other than μ in Step A2 (any corruption of a message will, by definition, be detected). As a result, it will correctly select μ as the message disseminated by the original source.

Case 2: The original source is faulty. In this case, different messages may be sent out to different processors, each with the original source's correct signature. We now show that the list of received messages (minus the signatures) is the same at each nonfaulty processor.

Let us proceed by contradiction. Suppose this is not true, and in particular, the sets at nonfaulty processors i and j (call them Ψ_i and Ψ_j) are different. Let ψ_1 be a message in Ψ_i, but not in Ψ_j.

Since processor i did not pass on ψ_1 to processor j, ψ_1 must have had at least $m + 1$ signatures appended to it. Let ℓ be one of these signatures. When processor ℓ received ψ_1, j's signature was not appended to ψ_1, and the list of signatures would have been less than $m + 1$ long. Hence, processor ℓ would have forwarded the message to j, and so $\psi_1 \in \Psi_j$, establishing the desired contradiction.

2.10 FURTHER READING

An excellent introduction to the basics of hardware fault tolerance can be found in [43]. Some basic definitions can be found in [4]. Hardware failure rate models are described in [48]. The topic of hardware/logic circuits testing is covered in many textbooks, e.g., [1,11]. The appendix to a recent PhD dissertation contains a useful table summarizing resilience techniques [37].

A general discussion of reliability evaluation, based on the most prominent hardware failure mechanisms, can be found in [2]; a book-length, detailed, treatment of the topic (covering each mechanism in detail) is [27]. Reliability handbooks, such as [21,40,44], are valuable sources of practical information.

See [14] for further information on time-dependent dielectric breakdown. NTBI is covered in detail in [15,19,38,49,50,52]; a model is presented in [9]. A comprehensive table of activation energies for various failure mechanisms can be found in [33].

An argument that calculating the aggregate MTTF by treating the various failure processes as independent results in an overly conservative estimate can be found in [57].

How to optimize circuits taking NBTI, HCI, and TDDB into account is the focus of a number of studies: see, for example, [12,13,32]. How to propagate the results of device models up the system hierarchy is described in [20].

Information on memory faults can be found in [51], whereas multithreaded techniques for protection against transient errors are surveyed in [34].

For a discussion of common-mode failures, see [3,28,29,46,56].

Readers who are weak in probability theory may have found some of the reliability derivations difficult to understand. A very readable source for the mathematical background associated with such probabilistic calculations is [47]. The textbook [8] is not recently written, but is still very useful as a detailed and advanced introduction to reliability models. [17] contains a description of reliability models in addition to a guide to statistical methods.

One approach to representing the dependence of overall system reliability on the health of individual modules is *fault trees*. For details, see [7,54].

Voting techniques have been the focus of some work in the literature: a good comprehensive reference is [24] with more recent work reported in [5,10,35]. Compensating faults in NMR structures were introduced in [42], and an analysis of hybrid redundancy with compensating faults appears in [22]. The sift-out modular redundancy is described in [45].

Various techniques for processor error checking by watchdog processors have been described in the literature. An excellent survey with an extensive list of references appears in [26]. The capabilities of watchdog processors were extended to include checking of memory accesses in [31]. Other signatures generation schemes for checking the program control flow, based on the use of m-out-of-n codes (see Chapter 3), have been described in [53]. The exploitation of multithreading techniques for fault tolerance is discussed in [30,39,41,55].

There is an extensive bibliography on Byzantine generals algorithms. See, for example, [16,18,23, 25,36]. A good survey can be found in [6].

2.11 EXERCISES

1. The lifetime (measured in years) of a processor is exponentially distributed, with a mean lifetime of 2 years. You are told that a processor failed sometime in the interval $[4, 8]$ years. Given this information, what is the conditional probability that it failed before it was 5 years old?

2. The lifetime of a processor (measured in years) follows the Weibull distribution, with parameters $\lambda = 0.5$ and $\beta = 0.6$.
   (a) What is the probability that it will fail in its first year of operation?
   (b) Suppose it is still functional after $t = 6$ years of operation. What is the conditional probability that it will fail in the next year?
   (c) Repeat parts (a) and (b) for $\beta = 2$.
   (d) Repeat parts (a) and (b) for $\beta = 1$.

3. To get a feel for the failure rates associated with the Weibull distribution, plot them for the following parameter values as a function of the time t:
   (a) Fix $\lambda = 1$, and plot the failure rate curves for $\beta = 0.5, 1.0, 1.5$.

(b) Fix $\beta = 1.5$, and plot the failure rate curves for $\lambda = 1,2,5$.

4. Write an expression for the reliability $R_{system}(t)$ of the series/parallel system shown in Fig. 2.22, assuming that each of the five modules has a reliability of $R(t)$.

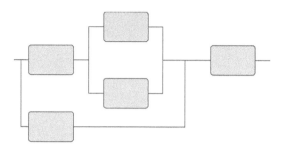

FIGURE 2.22

A 5-module series-parallel system.

5. The lifetime of each of the seven blocks in Fig. 2.23 is exponentially distributed with parameter λ. Derive an expression for the reliability function of the system $R_{system}(t)$, and plot it over the range $t = [0,100]$ for $\lambda = 0.02$.

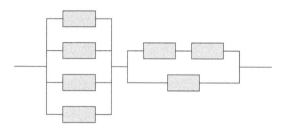

FIGURE 2.23

A 7-module series-parallel system.

6. Consider a triplex that produces a one-bit output. Failures that cause the output of a processor to be permanently stuck at 0 or stuck at 1 occur at constant rates λ_0 and λ_1, respectively. The voter never fails. At time t, you carry out a calculation, the correct output of which should be 0. What is the probability that the triplex will produce an incorrect result? (Assume that stuck-at faults are the only ones that a processor can suffer from, and that these are permanent faults; once a processor has its output stuck at some logic value, it remains stuck at that value forever).

7. Write the expression for the reliability of a 5MR system, and calculate its MTTF. Assume that failures occur as a Poisson process with rate λ per node, that failures are independent and permanent, and that the voter is failure-free.

8. Consider an NMR system that produces an eight-bit output. $N = 2m + 1$ for some m. Each processor fails at a constant rate λ, and the failures are permanent. A failed processor produces any of the 2^8 possible outputs with equal probability. A majority voter is used to produce the overall output, and the voter is assumed never to fail. What is the probability that, at time t, a majority of the processors produce the same incorrect output after executing some program?

9. Design a majority voter circuit out of two- and three-input logic gates. Assume that you are voting on one-bit inputs.

10. Derive an expression for the reliability of the voter you designed in the previous question. Assume that, for a given time t, the output of each gate is stuck-at-0 or stuck-at-1 with probability P_0 and P_1, respectively (and is fault-free with probability $1 - P_0 - P_1$). What is the probability that the output of your voter circuit is stuck-at-0 (stuck-at-1) given that the 3 inputs to the voter are fault-free, and do change between 000 and 111?

11. Show that the MTTF of a parallel system of N modules, each of which suffers permanent failures at a rate λ, is $\text{MTTF}_p = \sum_{k=1}^{N} \frac{1}{k\lambda}$.

12. Consider a system consisting of two subsystems in series. For improved reliability, you can build subsystem i as a parallel system with k_i units, for $i = 1, 2$. Suppose permanent failures occur at a constant rate λ per unit.
    (a) Derive an expression for the reliability of this system.
    (b) Obtain an expression for the MTTF of this system with $k_1 = 2$ and $k_2 = 3$.

13. List the conditions under which the processor/memory TMR configuration shown in Fig. 2.9 will fail, and compare them to a straightforward TMR configuration with three units, in which each unit consists of a processor and a memory. Denote by R_p, R_m, and R_v the reliability of a processor, a memory, and a voter, respectively, and write expressions for the reliability of the two TMR configurations.

14. Write expressions for the upper and lower bounds and the exact reliability of the following non-series/parallel system shown in Fig. 2.24 (denote by $R_i(t)$ the reliability of module i). Assume that D is a bidirectional unit.

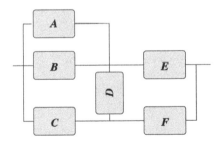

FIGURE 2.24

A 6-module nonseries/parallel system.

15. The system shown in Fig. 2.25 consists of a TMR core with a single spare a that can serve as a spare only for module 1. Assume that modules 1 and a are active. When either of the two modules 1 or a fails, the failure is detected by the perfect comparator C, and the single operational module is used to provide an input to the voter.
    (a) Assuming that the voter is perfect as well, which one of the following expressions for the system reliability is correct (where each module has a reliability R and the modules are independent).

(1) $R_{system} = R^4 + 4R^3(1 - R) + 3R^2(1 - R)^2$
(2) $R_{system} = R^4 + 4R^3(1 - R) + 4R^2(1 - R)^2$
(3) $R_{system} = R^4 + 4R^3(1 - R) + 5R^2(1 - R)^2$
(4) $R_{system} = R^4 + 4R^3(1 - R) + 6R^2(1 - R)^2$

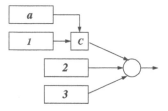

FIGURE 2.25

A TMR with a spare.

(b) Write an expression for the reliability of the system if instead of a perfect comparator for modules 1 and a, there is a coverage factor c (c is the probability that a failure in one module is detected, the faulty module is correctly identified, and the operational module is successfully connected to the voter that is still perfect).

16. A duplex system consists of two active units and a comparator. Assume that each unit has a failure rate of λ and a repair rate of μ. The outputs of the two active units are compared, and when a mismatch is detected, a procedure to locate the faulty unit is performed. The probability that upon a failure the faulty unit is correctly identified, and the fault-free unit (and consequently, the system) continues to run properly is the coverage factor c. Note that when a coverage failure occurs, the entire system fails, and both units have to be repaired (at a rate μ each). When the repair of one unit is complete, the system becomes operational and the repair of the second unit continues, allowing the system to return to its original state.

(a) Show the Markov model for this duplex system.

(b) Derive an expression for the long-term availability of the system, assuming that $\mu = 2\lambda$.

17. (a) Your manager in the Reliability and Quality Department asked you to verify her calculation of the reliability of a certain system. The equation that she derived is

$$\begin{aligned} R_{system} &= R_C[1 - (1 - R_A)(1 - R_B)][1 - (1 - R_D)(1 - R_E)] \\ &+ (1 - R_C)[1 - (1 - R_A R_D)(1 - R_B R_E)] \end{aligned}$$

However, she lost the system diagram. Can you draw the diagram based on the expression above?

(b) Write expressions for the upper and lower bounds on the reliability of the system, and calculate these values and the exact reliability for the case $R_A = R_B = R_C = R_D = R_E = R = 0.9$.

18. A duplex system consists of a switching circuit and two computing units: an active unit with a failure rate of λ_1 and a standby idle unit that has a lower failure rate $\lambda_2 < \lambda_1$ while idle. The switching circuit frequently tests the active unit, and when a fault is detected, the faulty unit is switched out, and the second unit is switched in, and becomes fully operational with a failure rate λ_1. The probability that upon a failure, the fault is correctly detected and the fault-free idle unit resumes the computation successfully is denoted by c (the coverage factor). Note that when a coverage failure occurs, the entire system fails.

(a) Show the Markov model for this duplex system (hint: three states are sufficient).

(b) Write the differential equations for the Markov model, and derive an expression for the reliability of the system.

19. You have a processor susceptible only to transient failures, which occur at a rate of λ per second. The lifetime of a transient fault (measured in seconds) is exponentially distributed with parameter μ. Your fault-tolerance mechanism consists of running each task twice on this processor, with the second execution starting τ seconds after the first. The executions take s seconds each ($\tau > s$). You can assume that the processor is functional when the first execution starts. Find the probability that the output of the first execution is correct, but that of the second execution is incorrect.

REFERENCES

[1] M. Abramovici, M.A. Breuer, A.D. Friedman, Digital Systems Testing and Testable Design (revised printing), IEEE Computer Society Press, 1995.

[2] R. Aitken, G. Fey, Z.T. Kalbarczyk, F. Reichenbach, M.S. Reorda, Reliability analysis reloaded: how will we survive?, in: Design, Automation and Test in Europe (DATE), 2013, pp. 358–367.

[3] S. Alcaide, C. Hernandez, A. Roca, J. Abella, DIMP: a low-cost diversity metric based on circuit path analysis, in: ACM/EDAC/IEEE Design Automation Conference (DAC), 2017, pp. 1–6.

[4] A. Avizienis, J.-C. Laprie, B. Randell, Dependability and its threats – a taxonomy, in: IFIP Congress Topical Sessions, August 2004, pp. 91–120.

[5] D.E. Bakken, Z. Zhan, C.C. Jones, D.A. Karr, Middleware support for voting and data fusion, in: International Conference on Dependable Systems and Networks, June 2001, pp. 453–462.

[6] M. Barborak, M. Malek, A. Dahbura, The consensus problem in fault-tolerant computing, ACM Computing Surveys 25 (June 1993) 171–220.

[7] R.E. Barlow, Reliability and Fault Tree Analysis, Society for Industrial and Applied Mathematics, 1982.

[8] R.E. Barlow, F. Proschan, Mathematical Theory of Reliability, Society of Industrial and Applied Mathematics, 1996.

[9] S. Bhardwaj, W. Wang, R. Vattikonda, Y. Cao, S. Vrudhula, Predictive modeling of the NBTI effect for reliable design, in: IEEE 2006 Custom Integrated Circuits Conference, 2006, pp. 9-3-1–9-3-4.

[10] D.M. Blough, G.F. Sullivan, Voting using predispositions, IEEE Transactions on Reliability 43 (December 1994) 604–616.

[11] M.L. Bushnell, V.D. Agrawal, Essentials of Electronic Testing for Digital, Memory, and Mixed-Signal VLSI Circuits, Kluwer Academic Publishers, 2000.

[12] F. Cacho, A. Gupta, A. Aggarwal, G. Madan, N. Bansal, M. Rizvi, V. Huard, P. Garg, C. Arnaud, R. Delater, C. Roma, A. Ripp, I/O Design Optimization Flow for Reliability in Advanced CMOS Nodes, paper 2D.1, 2014.

[13] J. Chen, S. Wang, M. Tehranipoor, Critical-reliability path identification and delay analysis, ACM Journal on Emerging Technologies in Computing Systems 10 (2) (February 2014) 12.

[14] M. Choudhury, V. Chandra, K. Mohanram, R. Aitken, Analytical model for TDDB based performance degradation in combinational logic, in: Design, Automation and Test in Europe (DATE), 2010, pp. 423–428.

[15] S. Corbetta, W. Fornaciari, Performance/reliability trade-off in superscalar processors for aggressive NBTI restoration of functional units, in: Great Lakes Symposium on VLSI, 2013, pp. 221–226.

[16] D. Dolev, The byzantine generals strike again, Journal of Algorithms 3 (1982) 14–30.

[17] C.E. Ebeling, An Introduction to Reliability and Maintainability Engineering, McGraw-Hill, 1997.

[18] M.J. Fischer, N.A. Lynch, A lower bound for the time to assure interactive consistency, Information Processing Letters 14 (June 1982) 183–186.

[19] H. Hong, J. Lim, H. Lim, S. Kang, Lifetime reliability enhancement of microprocessors: mitigating the impact of negative bias temperature instability, ACM Computing Surveys 48 (1) (September 2015) 9.

[20] V. Huard, N. Ruiz, F. Cacho, E. Pion, A bottom-up approach for system-on-chip reliability, Microelectronics and Reliability 51 (2011) 1425–1439.

[21] JEDEC Solid State Technology Association, Failure Mechanisms and Models for Semiconductor Devices, 2006.

[22] I. Koren, E. Shalev, Reliability analysis of hybrid redundancy systems, IEE Proceedings. Computers and Digital Techniques 131 (January 1984) 31–36.

[23] L. Lamport, R. Shostak, M. Pease, The byzantine generals algorithm, ACM Transactions on Programming Languages and Systems 4 (July 1982) 382–401.

[24] P.R. Lorczak, A.K. Caglayan, D.E. Eckhardt, A theoretical investigation of generalized voters for redundant systems, in: Nineteenth Fault Tolerant Computing Symposium, 1989, pp. 444–451.

[25] N.A. Lynch, M.J. Fischer, R.J. Fowler, A simple and efficient byzantine generals algorithm, in: 2nd Symposium on Reliability in Distributed Software and Database Systems, July 1982, pp. 46–52.

[26] A. Mahmood, E.J. McCluskey, Concurrent error detection using watchdog processors – a survey, IEEE Transactions on Computers 37 (February 1988) 160–174.

[27] J.W. McPherson, Reliability Physics and Engineering, Springer, 2010.

[28] S. Mitra, N.R. Saxena, E.J. McCluskey, Common-mode failures in redundant VLSI systems: a survey, IEEE Transactions on Reliability 49 (3) (September 2000) 285–295.

[29] S. Mitra, N.R. Saxena, E.J. McCluskey, Efficient design diversity estimation for combinatorial circuits, IEEE Transactions on Computers 53 (11) (November 2004) 1483–1492.

[30] S.S. Mukherjee, M. Kontz, S.K. Reinhardt, Detailed design and evaluation of redundant multithreading alternatives, in: International Symposium on Computer Architecture, 2002, pp. 99–110.

[31] M. Namjoo, E.J. McCluskey, Watchdog processors and capability checking, in: 12th International Symposium on Fault Tolerant Computing, 1982, pp. 245–248.

[32] F. Oboril, M.B. Tahoori, MTTF-balanced pipeline design, in: Design and Test in Europe (DATE), 2013, pp. 270–275.

[33] ON Semiconductor, Quality and Reliability Handbook, 2019.

[34] I. Oz, S. Arslan, A survey on multithreaded alternatives for soft error fault tolerance, ACM Computing Surveys 52 (2) (2019) 27.

[35] B. Parhami, Voting algorithms, IEEE Transactions on Reliability 43 (December 1994) 617–629.

[36] M. Pease, R. Shostak, L. Lamport, Reaching agreement in the presence of faults, Journal of the ACM 27 (April 1980) 228–234.

[37] G. Psychou, Stochastic Approaches for Speeding-Up the Analysis of the Propagation of Hardware-Induced Errors and Characterization of System-Level Mitigation Schemes, PhD Dissertation, Rheinisch-Westfalische Technische Hochschule Aachen, 2017.

[38] Z. Qi, M.R. Stan, NBTI resilient circuits using adaptive body biasing, in: Great Lakes Symposium on VLSI, 2008, pp. 285–290.

[39] S.K. Reinhardt, S.S. Mukherjee, Transient fault detection via simultaneous multithreading, in: International Symposium on Computer Architecture, 2000, pp. 25–36.

[40] Renesas Electronics, Semiconductor Reliability Handbook, 2017.

[41] E. Rotenberg, AR-SMT: a microarchitectural approach to fault tolerance in microprocessors, in: Fault-Tolerant Computing Systems Symposium, 1999, pp. 84–91.

[42] D.P. Siewiorek, Reliability modeling of compensating module failures in majority voting redundancy, IEEE Transactions on Computers C-24 (May 1975) 525–533.

[43] D.P. Siewiorek, R.S. Swarz, Reliable Computer Systems: Design and Evaluation, A.K. Peters, 1998.

[44] SONY, Seminconductors Quality and Reliability Handbook, 3rd edition, Chapter 4, available at https://www.sony-semicon.co.jp/products_en/quality/pdf/Handbook_e_201811.pdf, 2018.

[45] P.T. de Sousa, F.P. Mathur, Sift-out modular redundancy, IEEE Transactions on Computers C-27 (July 1978) 624–627.

[46] Z. Tang, J.B. Dugan, An integrated method for incorporating common cause failures in system analysis, in: Reliability and Maintainability Symposium (RAMS), 2004, pp. 610–614.

[47] K.S. Trivedi, Probability and Statistics with Reliability, Queuing, and Computer Science Applications, John Wiley, 2002.

[48] U. S. Department of Defense, Military Standardization Handbook: Reliability Prediction of Electronic Equipment, MIL-HDBK-217E, 1986.

[49] T. Siddiqua, A Multi-Level Approach to NBTI Mitigation in Processors, Ph.D. Dissertation, University of Virginia, 2012.

[50] T. Siddiqua, S. Gurumurthi, A multi-level approach to reduce the impact of NBTI on processor functional units, in: Great Lakes Symposium on VLSI, 2010, pp. 67–72.

[51] V. Sridharan, N. DeBardeleben, S. Blanchard, K.B. Ferreira, J. Stearley, J. Shalf, S. Gurumurthi, Memory errors in modern systems, in: ACM International Conference on Architectural Support for Programming Languages and Operating Systems (ASPLOS), 2015, pp. 297–310.

[52] J.H. Stathis, S. Zafar, The negative bias temperature instability in MOS devices: a review, Microelectronics-Review 46 (2006) 270–286.

[53] S. Upadhyaya, B. Ramamurthy, Concurrent process monitoring with no reference signatures, IEEE Transactions on Computers 43 (April 1994) 475–480.

[54] W.E. Vesely, Fault Tree Handbook, Nuclear Regulatory Commission, 1987.

[55] T.N. Vijaykumar, I. Pomeranz, K. Cheng, Transient-fault recovery using simultaneous multithreading, in: International Symposium on Computer Architecture, 2002, pp. 87–98.

[56] C. Wang, L. Xing, G. Levitin, Explicit and implicit methods for probabilistic common-cause failure analysis, Reliability Engineering & Systems Safety 131 (November 2014) 175–184.

[57] K.-C. Wu, M.-C. Lee, D. Marculescu, S.-C. Chang, Mitigating lifetime underestimation: a system-level approach considering temperature variations and correlations between failure mechanisms, in: Design and Test in Europe (DATE), 2012, pp. 1269–1274.

INFORMATION REDUNDANCY

Errors in data may occur when the data are being transferred from one unit to another, from one system to another, or even while the data are stored in a memory unit. To tolerate such errors, we introduce redundancy into the data: this is called *information redundancy*. The most common form of information redundancy is *coding*, which adds check bits to the data, allowing us to verify the correctness of the data before using it and, in some cases, even allowing the correction of the erroneous data bits. Several commonly used error-detecting and error-correcting codes are discussed in Section 3.1.

Introducing information redundancy through coding is not limited to the level of individual data words, but can be extended to provide fault tolerance for larger data structures. The best-known example of such a use is the redundant array of independent disks (RAID) storage system. Various RAID organizations are presented in Section 3.2, and the resulting improvements in reliability and availability are analyzed.

In a distributed system, where the same data sets may be needed by different nodes in the system, data replication may help with data accessibility. Keeping a copy of the data on just a single node could cause this node to become a performance bottleneck, and leave the data vulnerable to the failure of that node. An alternative approach would be to keep identical copies of the data on multiple nodes. Several schemes for managing the replicated copies of the same data are presented in Section 3.3.

We conclude this chapter with the description of *algorithm-based fault tolerance*, which can be an efficient information redundancy technique for applications that process large arrays of data elements.

3.1 CODING

Coding is an established area of research and practice, especially in the communication field, and many textbooks on this topic are available (see the Further Reading section). Here, we limit ourselves to a brief survey of the more common codes.

When coding, a d-bit data word is encoded into a c-bit *codeword*, which consists of a larger number of bits than the original data word, i.e., $c > d$. This encoding introduces information redundancy, that is, we use more bits than absolutely needed. A consequence of this information redundancy is that not all 2^c binary combinations of the c bits are valid codewords. As a result, when attempting to *decode* the c-bit word to extract the original d data bits, we may encounter an invalid codeword, and this will indicate that an error has occurred. For certain encoding schemes, some types of errors can even be corrected, and not just detected.

A code is defined as the set of all permissible codewords. Key performance parameters of a code are the number of erroneous bits that can be detected as erroneous, and the number of errors that can be corrected. The overhead imposed by the code is measured in terms of both the additional bits that are required, and the time needed to encode and decode.

An important metric of the space of codewords is the *Hamming distance*. The Hamming distance between two codewords is the number of bit positions, in which the two words differ. Fig. 3.1 shows the eight 3-bit binary words. Two words in this figure are connected by an edge if their Hamming distance is 1. The words 101 and 011 differ in two bit positions and therefore have a Hamming distance of 2; one

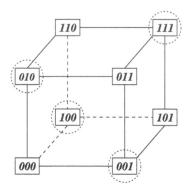

FIGURE 3.1

Hamming distances in the 3-bit word space.

has to traverse two edges in Fig. 3.1 to get from node 101 to node 011. Suppose two valid codewords differ in only the least significant bit position, for example, 101 and 100. In this case, a single error in the least significant bit in either one of these two codewords will go undetected, since the erroneous word is also an existing codeword. In contrast, a Hamming distance of two (or more) between two codewords guarantees that a single-bit error in any of the two words will not change it into the other.

The *code distance* is the minimum Hamming distance between any two valid codewords. The code that consists of the four codewords {001, 010, 100, 111}, marked by circles in Fig. 3.1, has a distance of 2 and is therefore capable of detecting any single-bit error. The code that consists only of the codewords {000, 111} has a distance of 3 and is therefore capable of detecting any single- or double-bit error. If double-bit errors are not likely to happen, this code can be used to *correct* any single-bit error. In general, to detect up to k bit errors, the code distance must be at least $k + 1$, whereas to correct up to k bit errors, the code distance must be at least $2k + 1$. The code {000, 111} can be used to encode a single data bit with 0 (for example) encoded as 000, and 1 as 111. This code is similar to the TMR redundancy technique, which was discussed in Chapter 2. In principle, many redundancy techniques can be considered as coding schemes. A duplex, for example, can be considered as a code, whose valid codewords consist of two identical data words. For a single data bit, the codewords will be 00 and 11.

The *rate* of a code is the fraction of bits that are nonredundant. That is, if a coder takes d-bit inputs and generates n-bit outputs, its rate will be d/n.

Another important property of codes is *separability*. A *separable* code has separate fields for the data and the check bits. Therefore decoding for a separable code simply consists of selecting the data bits and disregarding the check bits. The check bits must still be processed separately to verify the correctness of the data. A nonseparable code, on the other hand, has the data and check bits integrated together, and extracting the data from the encoded word requires some processing, thus incurring an additional delay. Both code types are covered in this chapter.

3.1.1 PARITY CODES

Perhaps the simplest codes of all are the parity codes. In its most basic form, a parity-coded word includes d data bits and an extra (check) bit that holds the parity. In an even (odd) parity code, this extra bit is set so that the total number of 1s in the whole $(d + 1)$-bit word (including the parity bit) is even (odd). The overhead fraction of the parity code is $1/d$.

A parity code has a Hamming distance of 2, and is guaranteed to detect all single-bit errors. If a bit flips from 0 to 1 (or vice versa), the overall parity will no longer be the same, and the error can be detected. However, simple parity cannot correct any bit errors.

Since the parity code is a separable code, it is easy to design parity encoding and decoding circuits for it. Fig. 3.2 shows circuits to encode and decode 5-bit data words. The encoder consists of a five-input

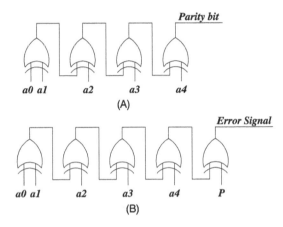

FIGURE 3.2

Even-parity encoding and decoding circuits. (A) Encoder. (B) Decoder.

modulo-2 adder, which generates a 0 if the number of 1s is even. The output of this adder is the parity signal for the even-parity code. The decoder generates the parity from the received data bits and compares this generated parity with the received parity bit. If they match, the output of the rightmost exclusive-or (*XOR*) gate is a 0, indicating that no error has been detected. If they do not match, the output is a 1, indicating an error. Note that double-bit errors cannot be detected by a parity check. However, all three (and in general, any odd number of) bit errors will be detected.

The choice of even parity or odd parity depends on which type of all-bits unidirectional error (i.e., all-0s or all-1s error) is more probable. If, for example, we select the even parity code, the parity bit generated for the all zeroes data word will be 0. In such a case, an all-0s failure will go undetected, because it is a valid codeword. Selecting the odd parity code will allow the detection of the all-0s failure. If, on the other hand, the all-1s failure is more likely than is the all-0s failure, we have to make sure that the all-1s word (data and parity bit) is invalid. To this end, we should select the odd parity code if the total number of bits (including the parity bit) is even, and vice versa.

Several variations of the basic parity code have been proposed and implemented. One of these is the parity-bit-per-byte technique. Instead of having a single parity bit for the entire data word, we assign a separate parity bit to every byte (or any other group of bits). This will increase the overhead from $1/d$ to m/d, where m is the number of bytes (or other equal-sized groups). On the other hand, up to m errors will be detected as long as they occur in different bytes. If the all-0s and all-1s failures are likely to happen, we can select the odd parity code for one byte and the even parity code for another byte. A variation of the above is the *byte-interlaced* parity code. For example, suppose that $d = 64$, and denote the data bits by $a_{63}, a_{62}, \cdots, a_0$. Use eight parity bits such that the first will be the parity bit of $a_{63}, a_{55}, a_{47}, a_{39}, a_{31}, a_{23}, a_{15}$ and a_7, i.e., all the most significant bits in the eight bytes. Similarly, the remaining seven parity bits will be assigned so that the corresponding groups of bits are interlaced. Such a scheme is beneficial when shorting of adjacent bits is a common failure mode. If, in addition, the parity type (odd or even) is alternated between the groups, the unidirectional errors (all-0s and all-1s) will also be detected.

An extension of the parity concept can render the code error correcting as well. The simplest such scheme involves organizing the data in a two-dimensional array as shown in Fig. 3.3. The parity bits

$$
\begin{array}{ccccccc}
0 & 0 & 0 & 1 & 1 & 1 & \mathbf{1} \\
1 & 0 & 1 & 0 & 1 & 1 & \mathbf{0} \\
1 & 1 & 0 & 0 & 0 & 0 & \mathbf{0} \\
0 & 0 & 0 & 1 & 1 & 1 & \mathbf{1} \\
1 & 1 & 1 & 1 & 1 & 1 & \mathbf{0} \\
\mathbf{1} & \mathbf{0} & \mathbf{0} & \mathbf{1} & \mathbf{0} & \mathbf{0} & \mathbf{0}
\end{array}
$$

FIGURE 3.3

Example of overlapping parity.

are shown in boldface. The bit at the end of a row represents the parity over this row; a bit at the bottom row is the parity bit for the corresponding column. The even parity scheme is followed for both rows and columns in Fig. 3.3. A single-bit error anywhere will result in a row and a column being identified as erroneous. Because every row and column intersect in a unique bit position, the erroneous bit can be identified and corrected.

The above was an example of *overlapping parity*, in which each bit is "covered" by more than one parity bit. We next describe the general theory associated with overlapping parity. Our aim is to be able to identify every single erroneous bit. Suppose there are d data bits in all. How many parity bits should be used, and which bits should be covered by each parity bit?

Let r be the number of parity bits (check bits) that we add to the d data bits resulting in codewords of size $d + r$ bits. Hence, there are $d + r$ error states, where in state i the ith bit of the codeword is erroneous (keep in mind that we are dealing only with single-bit errors: this scheme will not detect all double-bit errors). In addition, there is the state, in which no bit is erroneous, resulting in $d + r + 1$ states to be distinguished.

We detect faults by performing r parity checks, that is, for each parity bit, we check whether the overall parity of this parity bit and the data bits covered by it is correct. These r parity checks can generate up to 2^r different check outcomes. Hence, the minimum number of parity bits is the smallest

r that satisfies the following inequality:

$$2^r \geq d + r + 1. \tag{3.1}$$

How do we decide which data bits will be covered by each parity bit? We associate each of the $d + r + 1$ states with one of the 2^r possible outcomes of the r parity checks. This is best illustrated by an example.

Example: Suppose we have $d = 4$ data bits, $a_3 a_2 a_1 a_0$. From Eq. (3.1), we know that $r = 3$ is the minimum number of parity bits, which we denote by $p_2 p_1 p_0$. There are $4 + 3 + 1 = 8$ states that the codeword can be in. The complete 7-bit codeword is $a_3 a_2 a_1 a_0 p_2 p_1 p_0$, i.e., the least significant bit positions 0, 1, and 2 are parity bits, and the others are data bits. Table 3.1 shows one possible assignment of parity check outcomes to the states, which is also illustrated in Fig. 3.4. The

State	Erroneous parity check(s)	Syndrome
No errors	None	000
Bit p_0 error	p_0	001
Bit p_1 error	p_1	010
Bit p_2 error	p_2	100
Bit a_0 error	p_0, p_1	011
Bit a_1 error	p_0, p_2	101
Bit a_2 error	p_1, p_2	110
Bit a_3 error	p_0, p_1, p_2	111

Table 3.1 Example of assignment of parity values to states.

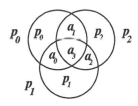

FIGURE 3.4

The assignment of parity bits in Table 3.1.

assignment of no errors in the parity checks to the "no errors" state is obvious, as is the assignment for the next three states, for which only one parity check is erroneous. The assignment of the bottom four states (corresponding to an error in a data bit) to the remaining four outcomes of the parity checks can be done in 4! ways. One of these is shown in Table 3.1 and Fig. 3.4. For example, if the two checks of p_0 and p_2 (and only these) are in error, that indicates a problem with bit position 4, which is a_1.

A parity bit will cover all bit positions, whose error is indicated by the corresponding parity check. Thus p_0 covers positions p_0, a_0, a_1, and a_3 (see Fig. 3.4), i.e., $p_0 = a_0 \oplus a_1 \oplus a_3$. Similarly,

$p_1 = a_0 \oplus a_2 \oplus a_3$, and $p_2 = a_1 \oplus a_2 \oplus a_3$. For example, for the data bits $a_3 a_2 a_1 a_0 = 1100$, the generated parity bits are $p_2 p_1 p_0 = 001$. Suppose now that the complete codeword 1100001 experiences a single-bit error and becomes 1000001. We recalculate the three parity bits, obtaining $p_2 p_1 p_0 = 111$. Calculating the difference between the new generated values of the parity bits and their previous values (by performing a bitwise *XOR* operation) yields 110. This difference, which is called the *syndrome*, indicates which parity checks are in error. The syndrome 110 indicates, based on Table 3.1, that bit a_2 is in error, and the correct data should be $a_3 a_2 a_1 a_0 = 1100$. This code is called a $(7,4)$ Hamming single error correcting (SEC) code.

The syndrome (which is the result of the parity checks) can be calculated directly from the bits $a_3 a_2 a_1 a_0 p_2 p_1 p_0$ in one step. This is best represented by the following matrix operation, in which all the additions are modulo-2. The matrix below is called the *parity check matrix*.

$$
\begin{array}{c}
a_3\,a_2\,a_1\,a_0\,P_2\,P_1\,P_0 \\
\begin{bmatrix} 1 & 1 & 1 & 0 & 1 & 0 & 0 \\ 1 & 1 & 0 & 1 & 0 & 1 & 0 \\ 1 & 0 & 1 & 1 & 0 & 0 & 1 \end{bmatrix}
\end{array}
\begin{bmatrix} a_3 \\ a_2 \\ a_1 \\ a_0 \\ P_2 \\ P_1 \\ P_0 \end{bmatrix}
= \begin{bmatrix} s_2 s_1 s_0 \end{bmatrix}
$$

For all the syndromes generated this way (see Table 3.1), except for 011 and 100, we can subtract 1 from the calculated syndrome to obtain the index of the bit in error. We can modify the assignment of states to the parity check outcomes, so that the calculated syndrome will for all cases (except, clearly, the no error case) provide the index of the bit in error after subtracting 1. For the example above, the order $a_3 a_2 a_1 p_2 a_0 p_1 p_0$ will provide the desired syndromes. If we modify the bit position indices so that they start with 1, and thus avoid the need to subtract a 1, we obtain the following parity check matrix:

$$
\begin{array}{c}
\begin{bmatrix} 1 & 1 & 1 & 1 & 0 & 0 & 0 \\ 1 & 1 & 0 & 0 & 1 & 1 & 0 \\ 1 & 0 & 1 & 0 & 1 & 0 & 1 \end{bmatrix} \\
7\ 6\ 5\ 4\ 3\ 2\ 1 \\
a_3\,a_2\,a_1\,P_2\,a_0\,P_1\,P_0
\end{array}
$$

Note that now the bit position indices of all the parity bits are powers of 2 (i.e., 1, 2, and 4), and the binary representations of these indices form the parity check matrix.

If $2^r > d + r + 1$, we need to select $d + r + 1$ out of the 2^r binary combinations to serve as syndromes. In such a case, it is best to avoid those combinations that include a large number of 1s. This will result in a parity check matrix that includes fewer 1s, leading to simpler circuits for the encoding and decoding operations. For example, for $d = 3$, we set $r = 3$, but only seven out of the eight 3-bit binary combinations are needed. Fig. 3.5 shows two possible parity check matrices: (a) uses the combination 111, whereas (b) does not. As a result, the encoding circuit for the matrix in (a) will require a single *XOR* gate for generating p_1 and p_2, but two *XOR* gates for generating p_0. In contrast, the encoding circuit for the matrix in (b) needs a single *XOR* gate for generating each parity bit.

$$
\begin{array}{c}
a_2\,a_1\,a_0\,P_2\,P_1\,P_0 \\
\begin{bmatrix}
1\ 0\ 1\ 1\ 0\ 0 \\
1\ 1\ 0\ 0\ 1\ 0 \\
1\ 1\ 1\ 0\ 0\ 1
\end{bmatrix}
\end{array}
\qquad
\begin{array}{c}
a_2\,a_1\,a_0\,P_2\,P_1\,P_0 \\
\begin{bmatrix}
0\ 1\ 1\ 1\ 0\ 0 \\
1\ 0\ 1\ 0\ 1\ 0 \\
1\ 1\ 0\ 0\ 0\ 1
\end{bmatrix}
\end{array}
$$

(A)   (B)

FIGURE 3.5

Two possible parity check matrices for $d = 3$.

The code in Table 3.1 is capable of correcting a single-bit error, but cannot detect a double-error. For example, if two errors occur in 1100001, yielding 1010001 (a_2 and a_1 are erroneous), the resulting syndrome is 011, indicating erroneously that bit a_0 should be corrected. One way to improve the error detection capabilities is to add an extra check bit that will serve as the parity bit of all the other data and check bits. The resulting code is called an $(8,4)$ single-error correcting/double-error detecting (SEC/DED) Hamming code. The generation of the syndrome for this code is shown below.

$$
\begin{array}{c}
a_3\,a_2\,a_1\,a_0\,P_3\,P_2\,P_1\,P_0 \\
\begin{bmatrix}
1\ 1\ 1\ 1\ 1\ 1\ 1\ 1 \\
1\ 1\ 1\ 0\ 0\ 1\ 0\ 0 \\
1\ 1\ 0\ 1\ 0\ 0\ 1\ 0 \\
1\ 0\ 1\ 1\ 0\ 0\ 0\ 1
\end{bmatrix}
\end{array}
\begin{bmatrix}
a_3 \\ a_2 \\ a_1 \\ a_0 \\ P_3 \\ P_2 \\ P_1 \\ P_0
\end{bmatrix}
=
\begin{bmatrix} s_3\,s_2\,s_1\,s_0 \end{bmatrix}
$$

As before, the last three bits of the syndrome indicate the bit in error to be corrected, as long as the first bit s_3 is equal to 1. Since p_3 is the parity bit of all the other data and check bits, a single-bit error changes the overall parity, and as a result, s_3 must be equal to 1. If s_3 is zero and any of the other syndrome bits is nonzero, a double or greater error is detected. For example, if one error occurs in 11001001 yielding 10001001, the calculated syndrome is 1110, indicating, as before, that a_2 is in error. If, however, two errors occur, resulting in 10101001, the calculated syndrome is 0011, indicating that an uncorrectable error has occurred. In general, an even number of errors is detectable, whereas an odd (and larger than 1) number of errors is indistinguishable from a single-bit error, leading to an erroneous correction.

Current memory circuits that have SEC/DED support (not all do) use either a $(39,32)$ or a $(72,64)$ Hamming code. Since errors in two or more physically adjacent memory cells are quite likely, the bits in a single memory word are often assigned to nonadjacent memory cells to reduce the probability of an uncorrectable double error in the same word.

A disadvantage of the above SEC/DED Hamming code is that the calculation of the additional check bit, which is the parity bit of all other check and data bits, may slow down encoding and decoding. One way to avoid this penalty, but still have the ability to detect double errors, is to assign to the data and check bits only syndromes that include an odd number of 1s. Note that in the original SEC Hamming code, each parity bit has a syndrome that includes a single 1. By restricting ourselves to the use of syndromes that include an odd number of 1s (for any single-bit error), a double error will result in a syndrome with an even number of 1s, indicating an error that cannot be corrected. A possible parity check matrix for such an $(8, 4)$ SEC/DED Hamming code is shown below.

$$
\begin{array}{c}
a_3\, a_2\, a_1\, a_0\ P_3\ P_2\ P_1\ P_0 \\
\begin{bmatrix}
0 & 1 & 1 & 1 & 1 & 0 & 0 & 0 \\
1 & 0 & 1 & 1 & 0 & 1 & 0 & 0 \\
1 & 1 & 0 & 1 & 0 & 0 & 1 & 0 \\
1 & 1 & 1 & 0 & 0 & 0 & 0 & 1
\end{bmatrix}
\end{array}
$$

Limiting ourselves to odd syndromes implies that we use only 2^{r-1} out of the 2^r possible combinations. This is equivalent to saying that we need an extra check bit beyond the minimum required for a SEC Hamming code, and the total number of check bits is the same as for the original SEC/DED Hamming code.

If the number of data bits is very large, the probability of having an error that is not correctable by an SEC code increases. To reduce this probability, we may partition the D data bits into, say, D/d equal slices (of d bits each) and encode each slice separately using an appropriate $(d + r, d)$ SEC Hamming code. This, however, will increase the overhead r/d imposed by the SEC code. We have therefore a tradeoff between the probability of an uncorrectable error and the overhead. If f is the probability of a bit error and if bit errors occur independently of one another, the probability of more than one bit error in a field of $d + r$ bits is given by

$$
\begin{aligned}
\Phi(d, r) &= 1 - (1 - f)^{d+r} - (d + r)f(1 - f)^{d+r-1} \\
&\approx \frac{(d + r)(d + r - 1)}{2}f^2 \quad \text{if } f \ll 1.
\end{aligned} \tag{3.2}
$$

The probability that there is an uncorrectable error in any one of the D/d slices is given by

$$
\begin{aligned}
\Psi(D, d, r) &= 1 - (1 - \Phi(d, r))^{D/d} \\
&\approx (D/d)\Phi(d, r) \quad \text{if } \Phi(d, r) \ll 1.
\end{aligned} \tag{3.3}
$$

Some numerical results illustrating the tradeoff are provided in Table 3.2.

3.1.2 CHECKSUM

Checksum is primarily used to detect errors in data transmission through communication channels. The basic idea is to add up the block of data that is being transmitted and to transmit this sum as well. The receiver then adds up the data it received and compares this sum with the checksum it received. If the two do not match, an error is indicated.

There are several variations of checksums. Assume the data words are d bits long. In the *single-precision* version, the checksum is a modulo-2^d addition. In the *double-precision* version, it is a modulo-2^{2d} addition. Fig. 3.6 shows an example of each. In general, the single-precision checksum catches fewer errors than the double-precision version, since we only keep the rightmost d bits of the sum. The *residue* checksum takes into account the carry out of the dth bit as an end-around carry (i.e., the carryout is added to the least significant bit of the checksum), and is therefore somewhat more reliable. The *Honeywell* checksum, by concatenating words together into pairs for the checksum calculation (performed modulo-2^{2d}), guards against errors happening in the same position. For example,

Table 3.2 The overhead versus probability of an uncorrectable error tradeoff for an overlapping parity code with a total of $D = 1024$ data bits, and a bit error probability of $f = 10^{-11}$.

d	r	Overhead r/d	$\Psi(D, d, r)$
2	3	1.5000	0.5120E-16
4	3	0.7500	0.5376E-16
8	4	0.5000	0.8448E-16
16	5	0.3125	0.1344E-15
32	6	0.1875	0.2250E-15
64	7	0.1094	0.3976E-15
128	8	0.0625	0.7344E-15
256	9	0.0352	0.1399E-14
512	10	0.0195	0.2720E-14
1024	11	0.0107	0.5351E-14

```
0000            0000            0000
0101            0101            0101
1111            1111            1111          00000101
0010            0010            0010          11110010
0110          00010110          0111          11110111
(A)             (B)             (C)             (D)
```

FIGURE 3.6

Variations of checksum coding (boxed quantities are the computed checksums). (A) Single-precision. (B) Double-precision. (C) Residue. (D) Honeywell.

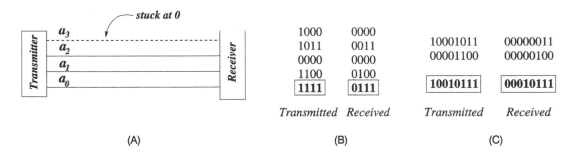

```
                    stuck at 0
a₃  - - - - - ↓           1000    0000      10001011    00000011
a₂                        1011    0011      00001100    00000100
a₁                        0000    0000
a₀                        1100    0100      10010111    00010111
                          1111    0111

                        Transmitted Received   Transmitted  Received
        (A)                    (B)                    (C)
```

FIGURE 3.7

Honeywell versus single-precision checksum (boxed quantities indicate transmitted/received checksum). (A) Circuit. (B) Single-precision. (C) Honeywell.

consider the situation in Fig. 3.7. Because the line carrying a_3 is stuck at 0, the receiver will find that the transmitted checksum and its own computed checksum match in the single-precision checksum. However, the Honeywell checksum, when computed on the received data, will differ from the received checksum, and the error will be detected. All the checksum schemes allow error detection, but not error location, and the entire block of data must be retransmitted if an error is detected.

3.1.3 M-OF-N CODES

The M-of-N code is an example of a unidirectional error-detecting code. As the term implies, in unidirectional errors all the affected bits change in the same direction, either from 0 to 1 or from 1 to 0, but not in both directions.

In an M-of-N code, every N-bit codeword has exactly M bits that are 1, resulting in $\binom{N}{M}$ codewords. Any single-bit error will change the number of 1s to either $M + 1$ or $M - 1$ and will be detected. Unidirectional multiple errors would also be detected. A simple example of an M-of-N code is the 2-of-5 code, which consists of 10 codewords, and can serve to encode the decimal digits. An example of a 2-of-5 code is shown in Table 3.3. There are 10! different ways of assigning the 10 codewords to the decimal digits. The assignment shown in the table preserves the binary order. The main advantage

Table 3.3 A 2-of-5 code for decimal digits.	
Digit	**Codeword**
0	00011
1	00101
2	00110
3	01001
4	01010
5	01100
6	10001
7	10010
8	10100
9	11000

of M-of-N codes is their conceptual simplicity. However, encoding and decoding become relatively complex operations, because such codes are, in general, nonseparable, unlike the parity and checksum codes.

Still, separable M-of-N codes can be constructed. For example, an M-of-2M code can be constructed by adding M check bits to the given M data bits so that the resulting 2M-bit codeword has exactly M 1s. Such codes are easy to encode and decode, but have a greater overhead (100% or more) than do the nonseparable ones. For example, to encode the 10 decimal digits, we start with 4 bits per digit, leading to a 4-of-8 code, which has a much higher level of redundancy than does the 2-of-5 code.

3.1.4 BERGER CODE

The M-of-2M code for detecting unidirectional errors is a separable code, but has a high level of information redundancy. A unidirectional error detecting code that is separable and has a much lower overhead is the Berger code. To encode, count the number of 1s in the word, express this count in binary representation, complement it, and append this quantity to the data. For example, suppose we are encoding 11101. There are four 1s in it, which is 100 in binary. Complementing results in 011 and the codeword will be 11101011.

The overhead of the Berger code can be computed as follows: If there are d data bits, then there can be at most d 1s in it, which can take up to $\lceil \log_2(d+1) \rceil$ bits to count. The overhead per data bit is therefore given by

$$\frac{\lceil \log_2(d+1) \rceil}{d}.$$

This overhead is tabulated for some values of d in Table 3.4. If $d = 2^k - 1$ for an integer k, then the number of check bits, denoted by r, is $r = k$, and the resulting code is called a maximum-length Berger code. For the unidirectional error detection capability provided, the Berger code requires the smallest number of check bits out of all known separable codes.

Table 3.4 Berger code overhead.		
d	r	Overhead
8	4	0.5000
15	4	0.2667
16	5	0.3125
31	5	0.1613
32	6	0.1875
63	6	0.0952
64	7	0.1094
127	7	0.0551
128	8	0.0625
255	8	0.0314
256	9	0.0352

3.1.5 CYCLIC CODES

In cyclic codes, encoding of data consists of multiplying (modulo-2) the data word by a constant number: the coded word is the product that results. Decoding is done by dividing by the same constant: if the remainder is nonzero, it indicates that an error has occurred. These codes are called cyclic, because for every codeword $a_{n-1}, a_{n-2}, \ldots, a_0$, its cyclic shift $a_0, a_{n-1}, a_{n-2}, \ldots, a_1$ is also a codeword. For example, the 5-bit code consisting of {00000, 00011, 00110, 01100, 11000, 10001, 00101, 01010, 10100, 01001, 10010, 01111, 11110, 11101, 11011, 10111} is cyclic.

Cyclic codes have been the focus of a great deal of research and are widely used in both data storage and communication. We will present only a small sampling of this work: the theory of cyclic codes rests on advanced algebra, which is outside the scope of this book. Interested readers are directed to the ample coding literature (see the Further Reading section).

Suppose k is the number of bits of data that we are seeking to encode. The encoded word of length n bits is obtained by multiplying the given k data bits by a number that is $n - k + 1$ bits long.

In cyclic coding theory, the multiplier is represented as a polynomial, called the *generator* polynomial. The 1s and 0s in the $(n - k + 1)$-bit multiplier are treated as the coefficients of an $(n - k)$-degree polynomial. For example, if the 5-bit multiplier is 11001, the generator polynomial is $G(x) = 1 \cdot X^4 + 1 \cdot X^3 + 0 \cdot X^2 + 0 \cdot X^1 + 1 \cdot X^0 = X^4 + X^3 + 1$. A cyclic code using a generator polynomial of degree $n - k$ and total number of encoded bits n is called an (n, k) cyclic code. An (n, k) cyclic code can detect all single errors and also all runs of adjacent bit errors, so long as these runs are shorter than $n - k$. These codes are therefore very useful in such applications as wireless communication, where the channels are frequently noisy and subject the transmission to bursts of interference that can result in runs of adjacent bit errors. For a polynomial of degree $n - k$ to serve as a generator polynomial of an (n, k) cyclic code, it must be a factor of $X^n - 1$. The polynomial $X^4 + X^3 + 1$ is a factor of $X^{15} - 1$, and can thus serve as a generator polynomial for a $(15, 11)$ cyclic code. Another factor of $X^{15} - 1$ is $X^4 + X + 1$, which can generate another $(15, 11)$ cyclic code. The polynomial $X^{15} - 1$ has five prime factors, namely,

$$X^{15} - 1 = (X + 1)(X^2 + X + 1)(X^4 + X + 1)(X^4 + X^3 + 1)(X^4 + X^3 + X^2 + X + 1).$$

Any one of these five factors and any product of two (or more) of these factors can serve as a generating polynomial for a cyclic code. For example, the product of the first two factors is $(X + 1)(X^2 + X + 1) = X^3 + 1$, and it can generate a $(15, 12)$ cyclic code. When multiplying $X + 1$ and $X^2 + X + 1$, note that all additions are performed modulo-2. Also note that subtraction in modulo-2 arithmetic is identical to addition, and thus, $X^{15} - 1$ is identical to $X^{15} + 1$.

The 5-bit cyclic code mentioned at the beginning of this section has the generator polynomial $X + 1$ satisfying $X^5 - 1 = (X + 1)(X^4 + X^3 + X^2 + X + 1)$ and is a $(5, 4)$ cyclic code. We can verify that $X + 1$ is the generator polynomial for the above $(5, 4)$ cyclic code by multiplying all 4-bit data words (0000 through 1111) by $X + 1$ or 11 in binary. For example, the codeword corresponding to the data word 0110 is 01010, as we now show. The data word 0110 can be represented as $X^2 + X$, and when multiplied by $X + 1$, results in $X^3 + X^2 + X^2 + X = X^3 + X$, which represents the 5-bit codeword 01010. The multiplication by the generator polynomial can also be performed directly in binary arithmetic, rather than using polynomials. For example, the codeword corresponding to the data word 1110 is obtained by multiplying 1110 by 11 in modulo-2 arithmetic as shown in Fig. 3.8. Note that this cyclic code is not separable. The data bits and check bits within the codeword 10010 are not separable.

$$
\begin{array}{r}
1110 \\
\times \quad 11 \\
\hline
1110 \\
1110 \\
\hline
10010
\end{array}
$$

FIGURE 3.8

Encoding the data word 1110.

One of the most significant reasons for the popularity of cyclic codes is the fact that multiplication and division by the generator polynomial can be implemented in hardware using simple shift registers and *XOR* gates. Such a simple implementation allows fast encoding and decoding. Let us start with an example: Consider the generator polynomial $X^4 + X^3 + 1$ (corresponding, as we have seen, to the multiplier 11001). See the circuit shown in Fig. 3.9, where the square boxes are delay elements, which hold their input for one clock cycle. The reader will find that this circuit does indeed multiply

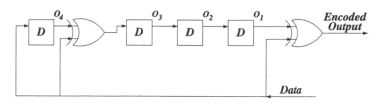

FIGURE 3.9

Encoding circuit for the $(15, 11)$ cyclic code with the generating polynomial $X^4 + X^3 + 1$.

```
            10001100101
  ×               11001
         _____
           10001100101
           00000000000
          00000000000
         10001100101
        10001100101
        _____
        110000100011101
```

FIGURE 3.10

Example of modulo-2 multiplication for encoding the 11-bit input 10001100101.

(modulo-2) serial inputs by 11001. To see why this should be, consider the multiplication shown in Fig. 3.10. Focus on the boxed column. It shows how the fifth bit of the product is the modulo-2 sum of the corresponding bits of the multiplicand shifted 0 times, 3 times, and 4 times. If the multiplicand is fed in serially, and we add the multiplicand shifted as shown above, we arrive at the product. It is precisely this shifting that is done by the delay elements of the circuit. Table 3.5 illustrates the operation of the encoding circuit, in which i_3 is the input to the O_3 delay element.

We now consider the process of decoding, which is done through division by the generator polynomial. Let us first illustrate the decoding process through division by the constant 11001, as shown in Fig. 3.11A. The final remainder is zero, indicating that no error has been detected. If a single error occurs and we receive 110000100111101 (the boldface **1** is the bit in error), the division will generate a nonzero remainder, as shown in Fig. 3.11B. To show that every single error can be detected, note that a single error in bit position i can be represented by X^i, and the received codeword that includes such an error can be written as $D(X)G(X) + X^i$, where $D(X)$ is the original data word, and $G(X)$ is the generator polynomial. If $G(X)$ has at least two terms, it does not divide X^i, and consequently dividing $D(X)G(X) + X^i$ by $G(X)$ will generate a nonzero remainder.

The above $(15, 11)$ cyclic code can be shown to have a Hamming distance of 3, thus allowing the detection of all double-bit errors irrespective of their bit positions. The situation is different when three-bit errors occur. Suppose first that the three-bit errors occur in nonadjacent bit positions, producing, for

Table 3.5 The operation of the encoder in Fig. 3.9 for the example in Fig. 3.10.

Shift clock	Input data	O_4	i_3	$O_3O_2O_1$	Encoded output
1	1	0	1	000	1
2	0	1	1	100	0
3	1	0	1	110	1
4	0	1	1	111	1
5	0	0	0	111	1
6	1	0	1	011	0
7	1	1	0	101	0
8	0	1	1	010	0
9	0	0	0	101	1
10	0	0	0	010	0
11	1	0	1	001	0
12	0	1	1	100	0
13	0	0	0	110	0
14	0	0	0	011	1
15	0	0	0	001	1

```
110000100011101 : 11001 = 10001100101          110000100111101 : 11001 = 10001100110
11001                                          11001
  10100                                          10100
  11001                                          11001
  11010                                          11011
  11001                                          11001
    11111                                          10111
    11001                                          11001
      11001                                          11100
      11001                                          11001
      00000                                          01011
```

(A)   (B)

FIGURE 3.11

Decoding through division. (A) Error-free. (B) A single-bit error (in boldface).

example, 11000 01110 10101 instead of 11000 01000 11101. Repeating the above division for this codeword results in the quotient and remainder shown in Fig. 3.12A. The final remainder is zero, and consequently the three-bit errors were not detected, although the final result is erroneous. If, however, the three-bit errors are adjacent, e.g., 11000 00110 11101, we obtain the quotient and remainder shown in Fig. 3.12B. The nonzero remainder indicates an error.

To implement a divider circuit, we should realize that division can be achieved through multiplication in the feedback loop. We illustrate this through the following example:

```
110000111010101 : 11001 =  10001101101          110000011011101 : 11001 =  10001110011
11001                                            11001
  10111                                            10011
  11001                                            11001
  11100                                            10100
  11001                                            11001
  10110                                            11011
  11001                                            11001
  11111                                            10110
  11001                                            11001
   11001                                            11111
   11001                                            11001
   11001                                            00110
   00000
```

            (A)   (B)

FIGURE 3.12

Decoding through division with three-bit errors. (A) Three nonadjacent errors (in boldface). (B) Three adjacent errors (in boldface).

Example: Let the encoded word be denoted by the polynomial $E(X)$, and use the previously defined notation of $G(X)$ and $D(X)$ for the generator polynomial and the original data word, respectively. If no bit errors exist, we will receive $E(X)$ and can calculate $D(X)$ from $D(X) = \frac{E(X)}{G(X)}$, and the remainder will be zero. In such a case, we can rewrite the division as

$$
\begin{aligned}
E(X) &= D(X) \cdot G(X) = D(X)\{X^4 + X^3 + 1\} \\
&= D(X)\{X^4 + X^3\} + D(X) \\
\text{thus } D(X) &= E(X) - D(X)\{X^4 + X^3\} \\
&= E(X) + D(X)\{X^4 + X^3\} \quad \text{(since addition = subtraction in modulo-2).}
\end{aligned}
$$

With this last expression, we can construct the feedback circuit for division (see Fig. 3.13). We start with all delay elements holding 0, produce first the seven quotient bits that constitute the data bits, and then the four remainder bits. If these remainder bits are nonzero, we know that an error has occurred. Table 3.6 illustrates the decode operation, in which i_3 is the input to the O_3 delay

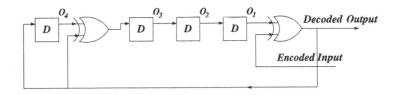

FIGURE 3.13

Decoding circuit for the $(15, 11)$ cyclic code with the generating polynomial $X^4 + X^3 + 1$.

element. The reader can verify that any error in the received sequence $E(X)$ will result in a nonzero remainder.

Table 3.6 The operation of the decoder in Fig. 3.13 for the input 110000100011101.

Shift clock	Encoded input	i_4	O_4	i_3	$O_3 O_2 O_1$	Decoded output
1	1	1	0	1	000	1
2	0	0	1	1	100	0
3	1	1	0	1	110	1
4	1	0	1	1	111	0
5	1	0	0	0	111	0
6	0	1	0	1	011	1
7	0	1	1	0	101	1
8	0	0	1	1	010	0
9	1	0	0	0	101	0
10	0	0	0	0	010	0
11	0	1	0	1	001	1
12	0	0	1	1	100	0
13	0	0	0	0	110	0
14	1	0	0	0	011	0
15	1	0	0	0	001	0

In many data transmission applications, there is a need to make sure that all burst errors of length 16 bits, or less, will be detected. Therefore cyclic codes of the type $(16+k, k)$ are used. The generating polynomial of degree 16 should be selected so that the maximum number of data bits is sufficiently large, allowing the use of the same code (and the same encoding and decoding circuits) for data blocks of many different sizes. Two generating polynomials of degree 16 are commonly used for this purpose. These are the CRC-16 polynomial (where CRC stands for cyclic redundancy check):

$$G(X) = (X+1)(X^{15}+X+1) = X^{16}+X^{15}+X^2+1,$$

and the CRC-CCITT polynomial,

$$G(X) = (X+1)(X^{15}+X^{14}+X^{13}+X^{12}+X^4+X^3+X^2+X+1) = X^{16}+X^{12}+X^5+1.$$

In both cases, the degree-16 polynomial divides $X^n - 1$ for $n = 2^{15} - 1$ (but not for any smaller value of n), and thus can be used for blocks of data of size up to $2^{15} - 1 = 32,767$ bits. Note that shorter blocks can still use the same cyclic code. Such blocks can be viewed as blocks of size $32,767$ bits with a sufficient number of leading 0s that can be ignored in the encoding or decoding operations. Also note that both CRC polynomials have only four nonzero coefficients, greatly simplifying the design of the encoding and decoding circuits.

The CRC-32 code, shown below, is widely used for data transfers over the Internet:

$$G(X) = X^{32}+X^{26}+X^{23}+X^{22}+X^{16}+X^{12}+X^{11}+X^{10}+X^8+X^7+X^5+X^4+X^2+X+1,$$

allowing the detection of burst errors, consisting of up to 32 bits for blocks of data of size up to $n = 2^{32} - 1$ bits.

For data transmissions of long blocks, it is more efficient to employ a separable encoding that will allow the received data to be used immediately without having to wait for all the bits of the codeword to be received and decoded. A separable cyclic code will allow the error detection to be performed independently of the data processing itself. Fortunately, there is a simple way to generate a separable (n, k) cyclic code. Instead of encoding the given data word $D(X) = d_{k-1}X^{k-1} + d_{k-2}X^{k-2} + \ldots + d_0$ by multiplying it by the generator polynomial $G(X)$ of degree $n - k$, we first append $(n - k)$ zeroes to $D(X)$ and obtain $\bar{D}(X) = d_{k-1}X^{n-1} + d_{k-2}X^{n-2} + \ldots + d_0X^{n-k}$. We then divide $\bar{D}(X)$ by $G(X)$, yielding

$$\bar{D}(X) = Q(X)G(X) + R(X),$$

where $R(X)$ is a polynomial of degree smaller than $n - k$. Finally, we form the codeword $C(X) = \bar{D}(X) - R(X)$, which will be transmitted. This n-bit codeword has $G(X)$ as a factor, and consequently, if we divide $C(X)$ by $G(X)$, a nonzero remainder will indicate that errors have occurred. In this encoding, $\bar{D}(X)$ and $R(X)$ have no terms in common, and thus the first k bits in $C(X) = \bar{D}(X) - R(X) = \bar{D}(X) + R(X)$ are the original data bits, whereas the remaining $n - k$ are the check bits, making the encoding separable.

Example: We illustrate the procedure described above through the $(5, 4)$ cyclic code that uses the same generator polynomial $X + 1$ as before. For the data word 0110, we obtain $\bar{D}(X) = X^3 + X^2$. Dividing $\bar{D}(X)$ by $X + 1$ yields $Q(X) = X^2$ and $R(X) = 0$. Thus the corresponding codeword is $X^3 + X^2$, or in binary 01100, where the first four bits are the data bits and the last one the check bit. Similarly, for the data word 1110, we obtain

$$\bar{D}(X) = X^4 + X^3 + X^2 = (X^3 + X + 1)(X + 1) + 1,$$

yielding the codeword 11101. The reader can verify that the same 16 codewords as before are generated, $\{00000, 00011, 00110, 01100, 11000, 10001, 00101, 01010, 10100, 01001, 10010, 01111, 11110, 11101, 11011, 10111\}$, but the correspondence between the data words and the codewords has changed.

3.1.6 ARITHMETIC CODES

Arithmetic error codes are those codes that are preserved under a set of arithmetic operations. This property allows us to detect any errors which may occur during the execution of an arithmetic operation in the defined set. Such concurrent error detection can obviously be attained by duplicating the arithmetic unit, but duplication is often too costly to be practical.

We say that a code is preserved under an arithmetic operation $\star$ if for any two operands X and Y, and the corresponding encoded entities X' and Y', there is an operation $\circledast$ for the encoded operands, satisfying

$$X' \circledast Y' = (X \star Y)'. \tag{3.4}$$

This implies that the result of the arithmetic operation $\circledast$, when applied to the encoded operands X' and Y', will yield the same result as encoding the outcome of applying the original operation $\star$ to the original operands X and Y. Consequently, the result of the arithmetic operation will be encoded in the same code as the operands.

We expect arithmetic codes to be able to detect all single-bit faults. Note, however, that a single-bit error in an operand or an intermediate result may well cause a multiple-bit error in the final result. For example, when adding two binary numbers, if stage i of the adder is faulty, all the remaining $(n - i)$ higher-order digits may become erroneous.

There are two classes of arithmetic codes: separable and nonseparable. The simplest nonseparable codes are the AN-codes, formed by multiplying the operands by a constant A. In other words, X' in Eq. (3.4) is $A \cdot X$, and the operations $\otimes$ and $\star$ are identical for addition and subtraction. For example, if $A = 3$, we multiply each operand by 3 (obtained as $2X + X$) and check the result of an add or subtract operation to see whether it is an integer multiple of 3. All error magnitudes that are multiples of A are undetectable. Therefore we should not select a value of A that is a power of the radix 2 (the base of the number system). An odd value of A will detect every single digit fault, because such an error has a magnitude of 2^i. Setting $A = 3$ yields the least expensive AN code that still enables the detection of all single errors.

For example, the number $0110_2 = 6_{10}$ is represented in the AN code with $A = 3$ by $010010_2 = 18_{10}$. A fault in bit position 2^3 may result in the erroneous number $011010_2 = 26_{10}$. This error is easily detectable, since 26 is not a multiple of 3.

The simplest separable codes are the residue code and the inverse residue code. In each of these, we attach a separable check symbol $C(X)$ to every operand X. For the residue code, $C(X) = X \bmod A = |X|_A$, where A is called the check modulus, i.e., $C(X)$ is the remainder (residue) when dividing X by A. For the inverse residue code, $C(X) = A - (X \bmod A)$. For both separable codes, Eq. (3.4) is replaced by

$$C(X) \otimes C(Y) = C(X \star Y). \tag{3.5}$$

This equality clearly holds for addition and multiplication, because the following equations apply:

$$\begin{aligned} |X + Y|_A &= ||X|_A + |Y|_A|_A, \\ |X \cdot Y|_A &= ||X|_A \cdot |Y|_A|_A. \end{aligned} \tag{3.6}$$

Example: If $A = 3$, $X = 7$, and $Y = 5$, the corresponding residues are $|X|_A = 1$ and $|Y|_A = 2$. When adding the two operands, we obtain $|7 + 5|_3 = 0 = ||7|_3 + |5|_3|_3 = |1 + 2|_3 = 0$. When multiplying the two operands, we get $|7 \cdot 5|_3 = 2 = ||7|_3 \cdot |5|_3|_3 = |1 \cdot 2|_3 = 2$.

For division, the equation $X - S = Q \cdot D$ is satisfied, where X is the dividend, D the divisor, Q the quotient, and S the remainder. The corresponding residue check is therefore

$$| |X|_A - |S|_A |_A = ||Q|_A \cdot |D|_A|_A.$$

Example: If $A = 3$, $X = 7$, and $D = 5$, the results are $Q = 1$ and $S = 2$. The corresponding residue check is $||7|_3 - |2|_3|_3 = ||5|_3 \cdot |1|_3|_3 = 2$. The subtraction in the left-hand-side term is done by adding the complement to the modulus 3, i.e., $|1 - 2|_3 = |1 + |3 - 2|_3|_3 = |1 + 1|_3 = 2$.

A residue code with A as a check modulus has the same undetectable error magnitudes as the corresponding AN code. For example, if $A = 3$, only errors that modify the result by some multiple of 3 will go undetected, and consequently, single-bit errors are always detectable. In addition, the checking algorithms for the AN code and the residue code are the same: in both we have to compute the residue of the result modulo-A. Even the increase in word length, $\lfloor \log_2 A \rfloor$, is the same for both codes. The most important difference is due to the property of separability. The arithmetic unit for the check symbol $C(X)$ in the residue code is completely separate from the main unit operating on X, whereas only a single unit (of a higher complexity) exists in the case of the AN code. An adder with a residue code is depicted in Fig. 3.14. In the error detection block shown in this figure, the residue modulo-A of the $X + Y$ result is calculated and compared to the result of the *Adder* mod A circuit. A mismatch indicates an error.

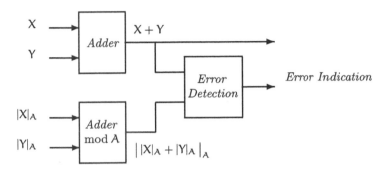

FIGURE 3.14

An adder with a separate residue check.

The AN and residue codes with $A = 3$ are the simplest examples of a class of arithmetic (separable and nonseparable) codes that use a value of A of the form $A = 2^a - 1$, for some integer a. This choice simplifies the calculation of the remainder when dividing by A (which is needed for the checking algorithm), and this is why such codes are called *low-cost* arithmetic codes. The calculation of the remainder when dividing by $2^a - 1$ is simple, because the equation

$$\left| z_i r^i \right|_{r-1} = |z_i|_{r-1}, \qquad r = 2^a \tag{3.7}$$

allows the use of modulo-$(2^a - 1)$ summation of the groups of size a bits that compose the number (each group has a value $0 \leq z_i \leq 2^a - 1$, see below).

Example: To calculate the remainder when dividing the number $X = 11110101011$ by $A = 7 = 2^3 - 1$, we partition X into groups of size 3, starting with the least significant bit. This yields $X = (z_3, z_2, z_1, z_0) = (11, 110, 101, 011)$. We then add these groups modulo-7; i.e., we "cast out" 7s and add the end-around-carry whenever necessary. A carry-out has a weight of 8, and because $|8|_7 = 1$, we must add an end-around-carry whenever there is a carry-out as illustrated below.

$$
\begin{array}{rl}
11 & z_3 \\
+\ 110 & z_2 \\
\hline
1\ \ \ 001 & \\
+\ \ \ \ \ 1 & \text{end-around carry} \\
\hline
010 & \\
+\ 101 & z_1 \\
\hline
111 & \\
+\ 011 & z_0 \\
\hline
1\ \ \ 010 & \\
1 & \text{end-around carry} \\
\hline
+\ 011 & \\
\end{array}
$$

The residue modulo-7 of X is 3, which is the correct remainder of $X = 1963_{10}$ when divided by 7.

Both separable and nonseparable codes are preserved when we perform arithmetic operations on unsigned operands. If we wish to include signed operands as well, we must require that the code be complementable with respect to R, where R is either 2^n or $2^n - 1$, and n is the number of bits in the encoded operand. The selected R will determine whether two's complement (for which $R = 2^n$) or one's complement (for which $R = 2^n - 1$) arithmetic will be employed. For the AN code, $R - AX$ must be divisible by A, and thus A must be a factor of R. If we insist on A being odd, it excludes the choice $R = 2^n$, and only one's complement can be used.

Example: For $n = 4$, R is equal to $2^n - 1 = 15$ for one's complement, and is divisible by A for the AN code with $A = 3$. The number $X = 0110$ is represented by $3X = 010010$, and its one's complement 101101 ($= 45_{10}$) is divisible by 3. However, the two's complement of 3X is 101110 ($= 46_{10}$) and is not divisible by 3. If $n = 5$, then for one's complement, R is equal to 31, which is not divisible by A. The number $X = 00110$ is represented by $3X = 0010010$, and its one's complement is 1101101 ($= 109_{10}$), which is not divisible by 3.

For the residue code with the check modulus A, the equation $A - |X|_A = |R - X|_A$ has to be satisfied. This implies that R must be an integer multiple of A, again allowing only one's complement arithmetic to be used. However, we may modify the procedure so that two's complement (with $R = 2^n$) can also be employed:

$$|2^n - X|_A = |2^n - 1 - X + 1|_A = |2^n - 1 - X|_A + |1|_A. \tag{3.8}$$

We therefore need to add a correction term $|1|_A$ to the residue code when forming the two's complement. Note that A must still be a factor of $2^n - 1$.

Example: For the residue code with $A = 7$ and $n = 6$, $R = 2^6 = 64$ for two's complement, and $R - 1 = 63$ is divisible by 7. The number $001010_2 = 10_{10}$ has the residue 3 modulo-7. The two's complement of 001010 is 110110. The complement of $|3|_7$ is $|4|_7$, and adding the correction term $|1|_7$ yields 5, which is the correct residue modulo-7 of 110110 ($= 54_{10}$).

A similar correction is needed when we add operands represented in two's complement, and a carry-out (of weight 2^n) is generated in the main adder. Such a carry-out is discarded according to the rules of two's complement arithmetic. To compensate for this, we need to subtract $|2^n|_A$ from the residue check. Since A is a factor of $(2^n - 1)$, the term $|2^n|_A$ is equal to $|1|_A$.

Example: If we add to $X = 110110$ (in two's complement) the number $Y = 001101$, a carry-out is generated and discarded. We must therefore subtract the correction term $|2^6|_7 = |1|_7$ from the residue check with the modulus $A = 7$, obtaining

$$
\begin{array}{ll}
\ 110110{=}X & \ 101{=}|X|_7 \\
+\ \underline{001101{=}Y} & +\ \underline{110{=}|Y|_7} \\
1\ \ 000011 & 1\ \ 011 \\
& \underline{1 \text{ end-around carry}} \\
& 100 \\
& -\ \underline{1 \text{ correction term}} \\
& 011
\end{array}
$$

where 3 is clearly the correct residue of the result 000011 modulo-7.

The above modifications result in an interdependence between the main arithmetic unit and the check unit that operates on the residues. Such an interdependence may cause a situation in which an error from the main unit propagates to the check unit and the effect of the fault is masked. However, it has been shown that the occurrence of a single-bit error is always detectable.

Error correction can be achieved by using two or more residue checks. The simplest case is the biresidue code, which consists of two residue checks A_1 and A_2. If n is the number of bits in the operand, select a and b such that n is the least common multiple of a, b. If $A_1 = 2^a - 1$ and $A_2 = 2^b - 1$ are two low-cost residue checks, then any single-bit error can be corrected.

3.1.7 LOCAL HARD AND SOFT DECISIONS

The rate of the Hamming codes (described in Section 3.1.1), that is defined as d/n, where $n = d + r$, increases with d, since the number of check bits r that must be added grows very slowly as $r \approx \log_2(n + 1)$. Thus the storage efficiency of the code increases with d, but then so does the complexity of the encode and decode operations, given that each parity check equation will include an increasing number of codeword bits. An obvious way to reduce the complexity of encoding and decoding is to restrict the number of codeword bits that participate in any given parity equation. This restriction, by itself, is insufficient. If a single codeword bit participates in a large number of parity equations, all of these equations will have to be considered when attempting to determine the value of that bit, so that all those parity equations will be satisfied. In terms of the corresponding parity check matrix, this implies restricting the number of 1s in each row of the matrix, as well as the number of 1s in each column. This leads to a sparse parity check matrix; the resulting parity codes are called low-density parity codes (LDPCs). There are two varieties of LDPC: regular and irregular; we focus here on the regular LDPCs. Regular LDPCs have the same number of 1s in each row, and the same number of 1s in each column. Denote the number of rows and columns of the parity check matrix by n_r and n_c, respectively, and denote the number of 1s per row by w_r, and the number of 1s per column by w_c.

We must have $n_r \cdot w_r = n_c \cdot w_c$, since both sides of this equation equal the total number of 1s in the matrix.

Clearly such low-density parity codes will need more check bits and will have a reduced code rate. For example, an LDPC with $n_r = 512$, $n_c = 4608$, $w_r = 54$, and $w_c = 6$ has a code rate of $R_{LDPC} = (n_c - n_r)/n_c = 1 - \frac{n_r}{n_c} = 1 - \frac{w_c}{w_r} = 0.889$, whereas a Hamming code for $d = 4096$ would require $r = 13$ parity bits, yielding a code rate of $R_{Hamming} = 4096/4109 = 0.997$. On the other hand, having parity equations that contain only a small number of codeword bits allows us to consider, even exhaustively, all the possible bit errors that may result in an erroneous parity check. This allows us to make simple local decisions (that depend on only a small number of bits), even if the total number of bits is large.

Two kinds of local decision algorithms have been developed: hard decision and soft decision. To simplify the description of these two approaches, it is common to use a bipartite graph representation of the parity check matrix. (When used in LDPC, such graphs are also called *Tanner graphs*.) We illustrate this graph representation using the (7,4) Hamming code that was defined in Table 3.1. Fig. 3.15 shows

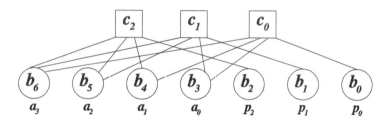

FIGURE 3.15

The bipartite (Tanner) graph for a (7,4) Hamming code.

the corresponding graph, where circles represent codeword bits, and squares represent parity check expressions. An edge connect a square (check) node c_i to a circle (bit) node b_j if the corresponding bit b_j participates in the parity check expression represented by c_i. The hard decision process is as follows:

- Each bit node b_i sends its bit value (0 or 1) to each check node it is connected to.
- Every check node c_j does the following: For each b_k it is connected to, it calculates the value that b_k should have to satisfy the parity equation that c_j represents, assuming that the values it receives from all the other bit nodes are correct, and sends this information to b_k.
- Each bit node b_i takes a majority vote on the values received from all check nodes it is connected to, and its own previous value. If the value reached by the majority vote is different from its previous value, b_i flips its bit value. For this reason, the hard decision process is sometimes called a bit-flipping algorithm.
- Until convergence is reached (i.e., no additional bit flipping, or in other words, the syndrome is 0), or some iteration limit is passed, the above steps are repeated.

Although the (7,4) Hamming code is not a low-density parity code, the hard decision algorithm can be used to correct bit errors (in this case, a single bit error) in regular Hamming codes. Figs. 3.16 and 3.17 illustrate the correction for the case, where the codeword $(b_6, b_5, b_4, b_3, b_2, b_1, b_0) =$

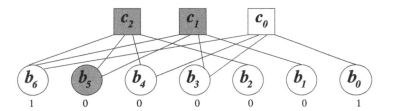

FIGURE 3.16

Step 1 of the hard decision algorithm for the (7,4) Hamming code.

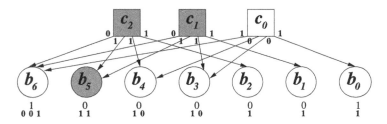

FIGURE 3.17

Step 2 of the hard decision algorithm for the (7,4) Hamming code.

$(a_3, a_2, a_1, a_0, p_2, p_1, p_0) = (1, 1, 0, 0, 0, 0, 1)$ has experienced a single-bit error, resulting in $(1, 0, 0, 0, 0, 0, 1)$. In Step 1, the bit nodes send their values to the check nodes as shown in Fig. 3.16, where the erroneous bit is indicated by a dark circle and the two parity checks that are not satisfied are indicated by dark squares. In Step 2, the check nodes send to all the bit nodes that are connected to them, the "proposed" bit values that will satisfy the parity equations, as shown in Fig. 3.17. Note, for example, that c_2 sends to the bit nodes b_6, b_5, b_4, and b_2 the opposite values that were sent to it by these four bit nodes, as it is unable to determine which of the four bits is erroneous.

Fig. 3.17 also shows all the values that each bit node receives from the check nodes connected to it, in addition to the bit node's original value. Out of the seven bit nodes only b_5 has a majority of incoming values that are different from its previous value, and it will therefore flip its value from 0 to 1. Once the modified bit values will be sent to the check nodes, all three parity check expressions will be satisfied, and the process will finish. For a Hamming code with a larger number of bits, the corresponding parity check matrix will be dense, resulting in a large number of iterations of the hard decision algorithm before it converges. In contrast, LDPCs have a very sparse parity check matrix, so a smaller number of iterations of the hard decision algorithm will be required.

The hard decision algorithm for LDPCs with long codewords may still require many iterations. A more efficient decoding (i.e., fewer iterations) can be achieved using a *soft decision* algorithm, which is based on the concept of belief propagation. The underlying approach of sending messages between the bit nodes and the check nodes in the Tanner graph is similar to that used in the hard decision algorithm. The main difference is that instead of sending a binary value (1 or 0), the probability, the belief that the codeword bit is 1 or 0, is sent. These probabilistic estimates will be progressively refined, based on the estimates of the other bits in the codeword.

We will need some notation to start with. Let $\mathbb{C}(b_i)$ be the set of check nodes that bit node b_i is connected to; let $\mathbb{B}(c_j)$ be the set of bit nodes that check node c_j is connected to.

The process starts with each bit node b_i transmitting the probability π_i that it holds a 1 to every check node it is connected to, i.e., to every element in $\mathbb{C}(b_i)$. This is the initial phase.

Next begins the iterative phase of the algorithm, which continues until a given stopping condition (to be described below) is satisfied. What we describe is a simplified version of the process; in practice, rather than the probabilities $\pi_i = \text{Prob}\{b_i = 1\}$, logarithms of the ratio $\frac{\text{Prob}(b_i=0)}{\text{Prob}(b_i=1)}$ are generally used. This is outside the scope of our discussion; see the pointers in the Further Reading section for details.

Each iteration consists of two steps:

Step 1: Each check node c_j receives the bit probability values from every element in $\mathbb{B}(c_j)$. Then, for each of these elements $b_i \in \mathbb{B}(c_j)$, it calculates a probability for $b_i = 1$ based on the values of the *other* bit nodes it is connected to. This is then sent to node b_i. How this calculation is done is best explained by means of an example.

Example: Consider a parity check matrix with the first row containing the entries: $0 \cdots 0\,0\,1\,0\,0\,1\,0\,0\,0\,1\,0$. The corresponding check node c_1 receives inputs from bit nodes b_1, b_5, and b_8, i.e., $\mathbb{B}(c_1) = \{b_8, b_5, b_1\}$. Let the received values be 0.1, 0.8, and 0.9, respectively. That is, b_8, b_5, b_1 each estimate their own probabilities (of holding a 1 logic value) as 0.1, 0.8, and 0.9, respectively.

Suppose we are implementing even parity, so that (if there are no errors) $b_8 \oplus b_5 \oplus b_1 = 0$. c_1 uses this fact to calculate updates of the probabilities associated with b_8, b_5, b_1. To satisfy even parity, the string $b_8 b_5 b_1$ must be one of the following: $000, 011, 101, 110$. Hence, for b_1 to have value 1, we must have $b_8 b_5 \in \{01, 10\}$. From this, c_1 calculates the following estimate for the probability that $b_1 = 1$:

$$(1 - \pi_5)\pi_8 + \pi_5(1 - \pi_8) = 0.2 \times 0.1 + 0.8 \times 0.9 = 0.74.$$

This information is sent back to bit node b_1. Similar calculations pertaining to b_5 and b_8 are sent by c_1 to those nodes. At the end of this step, every bit node has received such a probability estimate from each check node that it is connected to.

The central idea is that each check node c_j sends back to each of the bit nodes it is connected to (i.e., nodes in $\mathbb{B}(c_j)$) the probability for that bit node's value, *based on the values of the other bit nodes in* $\mathbb{B}(c_j)$. Assuming that even parity is used, if $b_i = 1$, then the number of the other bits that are 1 must be odd. Hence, the estimate, based on the values of these other bits, that $b_i = 1$, is the probability that there is an odd number of bits in the set $\mathbb{B}(c_j) - \{b_i\}$ that have value 1. This is the information that check node c_j propagates back to node b_i (and similarly to each of the other nodes in $\mathbb{B}(c_j)$).

Step 2: In Step 2 of each iteration, every bit node processes the information it received from all the check nodes it is connected to. In particular, for every $c_j \in \mathbb{C}(b_i)$, bit node b_i calculates and transmits to c_j the normalized product of the following estimates regarding its value: (a) Its own private value; (b) Its estimated value as transmitted to it by each check node in the set $\mathbb{C}(b_i) - \{c_j\}$, and a (c) Normalization constant. (Note that a different value is sent out to each check node it is connected to.) Again, an example is the best way to convey the process.

Example: Suppose that bit node b_1, in addition to being connected to check node c_1, is also connected to check nodes c_3 and c_9, i.e., $\mathbb{C}(b_1) = \{c_9, c_3, c_1\}$. Assume further that b_1 receives from c_9, c_3, and c_1 the values 0.79, 0.80, 0.74, respectively. These are the estimates of the probability of $b_1 = 1$, based on the values of the other bits. Recall that its own estimate was 0.9.
The following are the values it transmits to each of the check nodes in $\mathbb{C}(b_1)$:

Sent To c_1: $K_1 \times 0.90 \times 0.80 \times 0.79 = 0.5688 K_1$,

where $K_1 = \dfrac{1}{0.9 \times 0.8 \times 0.79 + (1 - 0.9) \times (1 - 0.8) \times (1 - 0.79)} = 1.7452$;

Sent To c_3: $K_3 \times 0.74 \times 0.90 \times 0.79 = 0.5261 K_3$,

where $K_3 = \dfrac{1}{0.74 \times 0.9 \times 0.79 + (1 - 0.74) \times (1 - 0.9) \times (1 - 0.79)} = 1.8811$;

Sent To c_9: $K_9 \times 0.74 \times 0.80 \times 0.9 = 0.5328 K_9$,

where $K_9 = \dfrac{1}{0.74 \times 0.8 \times 0.9 + (1 - 0.74) \times (1 - 0.8) \times (1 - 0.9)} = 1.8587$.

The normalization constants K_j are calculated so as to ensure that the probabilities add to 1. Consider, for example, the normalization constant K_1 in the above example. The estimate of b_1 being 1 is given by the product of K_1 together with each of the estimates of its being 1, namely $K_1 \times 0.9 \times 0.8 \times 0.79 = 0.5688 K_1$. The estimate of b_1 being 0 is given by the product of the estimates of its being 0, which are each the complement of its being 1. That is, the estimated probability of the bit being 0 is $K_1 \times (1 - 0.9) \times (1 - 0.8) \times (1 - 0.79) = 0.0042 K_1$. Since each bit must be either 0 or 1, adding the two must give 1, so that we have $(0.5688 + 0.0042) K_1 = 1$, solving which we get the value of K_1.
The values sent by b_1 are: 0.993, 0.989, and 0.990 to c_1, c_3, and c_9, respectively.

This iterative process continues until a stopping criterion is met. We typically stop when one of the following conditions is satisfied: (*a*) The value of the probability is sufficiently close to either 1 or 0, and (*b*) A specified upper limit on the number of iterations has been reached.
Note that multiplying the probabilities as we did in the iterative part of the algorithm rests on the assumption that these represent stochastically independent events. This is not strictly true. However, if the bipartite graph does not have short cycles, this is a reasonably good assumption. As a rule of thumb, ensuring that all cycles are of length greater than 6 has been found to work well.
The soft decision algorithm is well suited to deal with situations, where the values of some codeword bits may be ambiguous, and only an estimate of their value can be made. Take, for example, codewords stored in a NAND flash memory. When a logical 1 is stored in a flash memory cell, its voltage is not precisely equal to the nominal voltage V_1 associated with this logic level; in reality, it follows some probability distribution (often modeled as a normal distribution centered at V_1 with some given standard deviation). The same applies to logic level 0. These distributions can sometimes overlap meaningfully.

Example: Suppose the voltage associated with logic levels 0 and 1 are each normally distributed, with mean V_0 and V_1 volts and standard deviations both equal to some quantity, σ. Fig. 3.18 shows

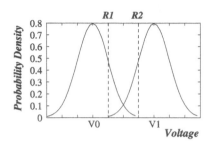

FIGURE 3.18

Threshold sensing of flash memory.

an example of probability density function of the output voltage associated with each of the two logic levels.

The cell is read by setting a word line to some voltage and determining whether or not the cell output is above or below this threshold. By repeatedly reading the cell with multiple voltage thresholds, we can determine which voltage range the output falls into. This can then be used along with our knowledge of the typical threshold density function to obtain a probability of the cell logic value.

Example: In Fig. 3.18, we show two voltage thresholds, R_1 and R_2. By carrying out readings with these two thresholds, we are able to determine which of the following ranges the voltage is in: $(-\infty, R_1)$; $[R_1, R_2)$; $[R_2, \infty)$. Associated with each, based on our knowledge of the device characteristics (i.e., of the probability density function), we can assign a probability of the logic level being 0 or 1. The designer selects the number and position of the thresholds; how this is done is outside the scope of our present discussion. A complicating factor in flash memory is that the voltage probability density functions associated with logic values can change as the device ages; these can also be affected by activity in neighboring cells.

In this example, we have implicitly assumed that a cell holds only one bit. However, there are multilevel cells available, which can hold multiple bits per cell. For example, in a two-bit cell, there will be additional nominal voltage levels specified to indicate each of the $2^2 = 4$ possible values of the cell contents, i.e., V_0, V_1, V_2, V_3.

We conclude our discussion of LDPC with a brief look at how to generate LDPC parity check matrices. There have been several approaches suggested for generating parity check matrices. The one we present here is perhaps the simplest.

We focus our coverage on *regular* parity-check matrices, where all rows have the same number w_r of 1s and similarly, all columns have the same number w_c of 1s. The approach we present here for generating an LDPC parity check matrix is due to Robert Gallager, who originated LDPC codes. This procedure works as follows: Start with populating the first $\eta = n_r/w_c$ rows of the matrix. The first row will consist of a string of w_r 1s, starting in the first column. The rest of the bits in that row are set to 0. The second row consists of another such string of w_r 1s, starting in column $w_r + 1$, all other bits on that row being 0. And so on. At the end of this process, we will have a matrix consisting of n_r/w_c rows and n_c columns; call this the first band of the matrix.

Next, construct the next η rows of the matrix by randomly permuting the columns of its first band. This is the second band.

Proceed in this manner, with each subsequent band of the matrix being a new random permutation of the columns of the first.

Example: Suppose we select $w_r = 4, w_c = 3$ in a 9×12 matrix. The first band of this matrix will consist of $9/3 = 3$ rows. It will be

$$111100000000$$
$$000011110000$$
$$000000001111.$$

To construct the second band, we randomly permute the columns of this first band. Suppose we end up with the permutation $6, 3, 11, 7, 8, 5, 1, 2, 4, 9, 10, 12$. (For example, the first column of the second band will be the 6th column of the first band.) The second band will thus be

$$010000111000$$
$$100101001000$$
$$001000000111.$$

Again, take a random permutation of the first band to obtain the third, and final, band. Suppose we obtain the permutation $10, 4, 5, 2, 9, 7, 3, 11, 6, 12, 1, 8$. This permutation of the rows of the first band yields

$$010100100010$$
$$001001001001$$
$$100010010100.$$

The overall matrix is therefore

$$\begin{pmatrix} 111100000000 \\ 000011110000 \\ 000000001111 \\ 010000111000 \\ 100101001000 \\ 001000000111 \\ 010100100010 \\ 001001001001 \\ 100010010100 \end{pmatrix}.$$

Techniques exist to make the encoding process faster by suitably transforming the parity check matrix; this is beyond the scope of our discussion; the interested reader should see the Further Reading section.

As noted earlier, low-density parity codes tend to not work well when the associated graph contains short cycles. To prevent this from happening, we can check, as we develop the parity check matrix, whether a short cycle is being formed, and pick a different random permutation if it is.

LDPC was introduced in the 1960s; however, due to the computational burden it imposes, it only became of practical interest in recent years. Analytical modeling of its performance is a subject of current research.

3.2 RESILIENT DISK SYSTEMS

An excellent example of employing information redundancy through coding at a higher level than individual data words is the RAID structure. RAID stands for redundant arrays of independent (or inexpensive) disks. We describe next five RAID structures.

3.2.1 RAID LEVEL 1

RAID1 consists of mirrored disks. In place of one disk, there are two disks, each being a copy of the other. If one disk fails, the other can continue to serve access requests. If both disks are working, RAID1 can speed up read accesses by dividing them among the two disks. Write accesses are, however, slowed down, because both disks must finish the update before the operation can complete.

Let us assume that the disks fail independently, each at a constant rate λ, and that the time to repair each is exponentially distributed with mean $1/\mu$. We will now compute the reliability and availability of a RAID1 system.

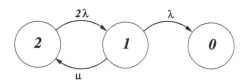

FIGURE 3.19

Markov chain for RAID1 reliability calculation.

To compute the reliability, we set up a three-state Markov chain, as shown in Fig. 3.19 (Markov chains are explained in Chapter 2). The state of the system is the number of disks that are functional: it can vary between 0 (failed system) and 2 (both disks up). The unreliability at time t is the probability of being in the failed state $p_0(t)$. The differential equations associated with this Markov chain are as follows.

$$\frac{dp_2(t)}{dt} = -2\lambda p_2(t) + \mu p_1(t);$$

$$\frac{dp_1(t)}{dt} = -(\lambda + \mu)p_1(t) + 2\lambda p_2(t);$$

$$p_0(t) = 1 - p_1(t) + p_2(t).$$

Solving these simultaneous differential equations with the initial conditions $p_2(0) = 1; p_0(0) = p_1(0) = 0$, we can obtain the probability that the disk system fails sometime before t. The expressions for the state probabilities are rather complex, and not very illuminating. We will make use of an approximation, whereby we compute the mean time to data loss (MTTDL), and then use the fact that $\mu \gg \lambda$ (the repair rate is much greater than the failure rate).

The MTTDL is computed in the following way: State 0 will be entered if the system enters state 1, and then makes a transition to state 0. If we start in state 2 at time 0, the mean time before state 1 is entered is $1/2\lambda$. The mean time spent staying in state 1 is $1/(\lambda + \mu)$. Following this, the system can either go back to state 2, which it does with probability $q = \mu/(\mu + \lambda)$ or to state 0, which it does with probability $p = \lambda/(\mu + \lambda)$. The probability that n visits are made to state 1 before the system transits to state 0 is clearly $q^{n-1}p$, because we would have to make $n - 1$ transitions from 1 to 2, followed by a transition from 1 to 0. The mean time to enter state 0 in this case is given by

$$T_{2\to0}(n) = n\left(\frac{1}{2\lambda} + \frac{1}{\lambda+\mu}\right) = n\,\frac{3\lambda+\mu}{2\lambda\,(\lambda+\mu)}.$$

Hence,

$$\begin{aligned}
\text{MTTDL} &= \sum_{n=1}^{\infty} q^{n-1}p\,T_{2\to0}(n) \\
&= \sum_{n=1}^{\infty} nq^{n-1}p\,T_{2\to0}(1) \\
&= T_{2\to0}(1)/p \\
&= \frac{3\lambda+\mu}{2\lambda^2}.
\end{aligned}$$

If $\mu \gg \lambda$, we can approximate the transition into state 0 by regarding the aggregate of states 1 and 2 as a single state, from which there is a transition of rate $1/\text{MTTDL}$ to state 0. Hence, the reliability can be approximated by the function

$$R(t) \approx e^{-t/\text{MTTDL}}. \tag{3.9}$$

Fig. 3.20 shows the unreliability of the system (probability of data loss) over time for a variety of mean disk lifetimes and mean disk repair times. It is worth noting the substantial impact of the mean repair time on the probability of data loss.

A calculation of the long-term availability of the disk system can be done based on a Markov chain identical to that shown in Fig. 2.16, yielding

$$A = \frac{\mu(\mu+2\lambda)}{(\lambda+\mu)^2}.$$

3.2.2 RAID LEVEL 2

Level 2 RAID consists of a bank of data disks in parallel with Hamming-coded disks. Suppose there are d data disks and r parity disks. Then, we can think of the ith bit of each disk as bits of a $(d + r)$-bit word. Based on the theory of Hamming codes, we know that we must have $2^r \geq d + r + 1$ to permit the correction of one bit per word.

We will not spend more time on RAID2, because other RAID designs impose much less overhead.

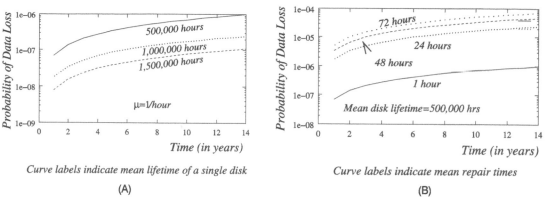

Curve labels indicate mean lifetime of a single disk

(A)

Curve labels indicate mean repair times

(B)

FIGURE 3.20

Unreliability of RAID1 system. (A) Impact of disk lifetime. (B) Impact of mean disk repair time.

3.2.3 RAID LEVEL 3

RAID3 is a modification of RAID2 and arises from the observation that each disk has error-correction coding per sector. Hence, if a sector is bad, we can identify it as such. RAID3 consists of a bank of d data disks together with one parity disk. The data are bit-interleaved across the data disks, and the ith position of the parity disk contains the parity bit associated with the bits in the ith position of each of the data disks. An example of a five-disk RAID3 system is shown in Fig. 3.21.

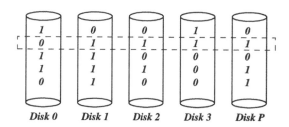

FIGURE 3.21

A RAID3 system with 4 data disks and an even parity disk.

For error-detection and error-correction purposes, we can regard the ith bit of each disk as forming a $(d + 1)$-bit word, consisting of d data and 1 parity bits. Suppose one such word has an incorrect bit in the jth bit position. The error-correcting code for that sector in the jth disk will indicate a failure, thus locating the fault. Once we have located the fault, the remaining bits can be used to restore the faulty bit.

For example, let the word be 01101, where 0110 are the data bits, and 1 is the parity bit. If even parity is being used, we know that a bit is in error. If the fourth disk (disk 3 in the figure) indicates an error in the relevant sector and the other disks show no such errors, we know that the word should be 01111, and the correction can be made appropriately.

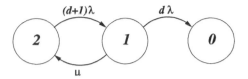

FIGURE 3.22

Markov chain for RAID3 reliability calculation.

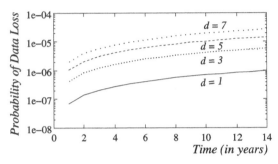

FIGURE 3.23

Unreliability of RAID3 system.

The Markov chains for the reliability and availability of this system are almost identical to those used in RAID1. In RAID1, we had two disks per group; here, we have $d + 1$. In both cases, the system fails (we have data loss) if two or more disks fail. Hence, the Markov chain for computing reliability is as shown in Fig. 3.22. The analysis of this chain is similar to that of RAID1: the mean time to data loss for this group is

$$\text{MTTDL} = \frac{(2d + 1)\lambda + \mu}{d(d + 1)\lambda^2}, \tag{3.10}$$

and the reliability is given approximately by

$$R(t) \approx e^{-t/\text{MTTDL}}. \tag{3.11}$$

Fig. 3.23 shows some numerical results for various values of d. The case $d = 1$ is identical to the RAID1 system. The reliability drops as d increases, as is to be expected.

3.2.4 RAID LEVEL 4

RAID4 is similar to RAID3, except that the unit of interleaving is not a single bit, but a block of arbitrary size, called a *stripe*. An example of a RAID5 system, with four data disks and a parity disk, is shown in Fig. 3.24. The advantage of RAID4 over RAID3 is that a small read operation may be

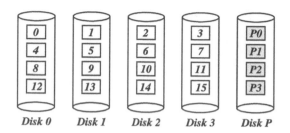

FIGURE 3.24

A RAID4 system with four data disks and a parity disk (each rectangle in the figure contains a block [stripe] of data).

contained in just a single data disk, rather than interleaved over all of them. As a result, small read operations are faster in RAID4 than in RAID3. A similar remark applies to small write operations: in such an operation, both the affected data disk and the parity disk must be updated. The updating of the parity is quite simple: the parity bit toggles if the corresponding data bit that is being written is different from the one being overwritten.

The reliability model for RAID4 is identical to that of RAID3.

3.2.5 RAID LEVEL 5

This is a modification of the RAID4 structure, and arises from the observation that the parity disk can sometimes be the system bottleneck: in RAID4, the parity disk is accessed in each write operation. To get around this problem, we can simply interleave the parity blocks among the disks. In other words, we no longer have a disk dedicated to carrying parity bits. Every disk has some data blocks and some parity blocks. An example of a five-disk RAID5 system is shown in Fig. 3.25.

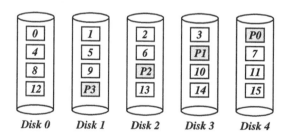

FIGURE 3.25

Distributed parity blocks in a five-disk RAID5 system.

The reliability model for RAID5 is obviously the same as for RAID4: it is only the performance model that is different.

An extension of RAID5 is RAID6. Here, the aim is to be able to resist not just one but two disk failures at the same time without losing any data. Additional code blocks are provided to do so.

3.2.6 HIERARCHICAL RAID

RAID structures can be organized hierarchically. Before explaining this organization, we introduce one level of RAID that does not include any redundancy: RAID level 0.

Level 0 is an arrangement, where the data are interleaved between two disks. There is no parity bit or other form of redundancy here, just parallelism. (In that sense the term RAID is misapplied here: the array of disks contains no redundancy.) The purpose is to increase data throughput to and from the disks by allowing parallel accesses.

Let us now consider hierarchical organization. The nomenclature for the level is *Level ij*, *Level i/j* or *Level i+j*, denoting that the disks consist of a RAID Level j organization of units, where each unit is organized as a RAID Level i entity.

Example: RAID level 50 (see Fig. 3.26) consists of a RAID level 0 organization of units, each unit consisting of a RAID level 5 structure. So, given a file consisting of segments $0, 1, 2, 3, \cdots$, we would assign segments $0, 2, 4, \cdots$ to be stored in one group of disks, whereas $1, 3, 5, \cdots$ would be stored in the other. Each of these two groups is organized as a RAID Level 5 structure.

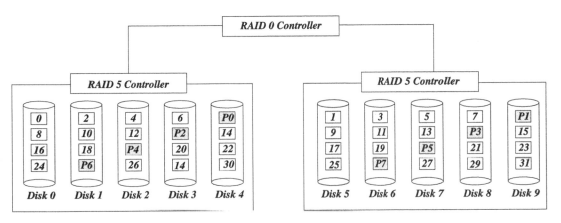

FIGURE 3.26

RAID50 structure.

Similarly, RAID31 consists of a RAID level 1 organization of units, each unit consisting of a Level 3 structure. The Level 1 organization is mirroring, so Level 31 consists of two mirrored RAID level 3 entities, i.e., two Level 3 entities, which are copies of each other. Each of these organizations has its own distinctive characteristics.

Example: Note that the striping is not directly "visible" from outside the RAID group. Thus for example, if a file is striped inside a RAID group, the individual stripes are not separately accessible from outside. This makes a difference in the speed with which recovery can be effected.

To see why, let us compare RAID10 and RAID01. Suppose each of these arrangements contains six disks in all. In RAID10 (Fig. 3.27), these six disks would be organized into three groups of mirrored disks (RAID 0 at the lower level; RAID 1 above). In RAID01 (Fig. 3.28), we would have two groups at the higher level mirroring each other; each of these groups consisting of three disks.

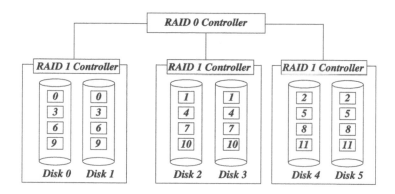

FIGURE 3.27

RAID10 structure.

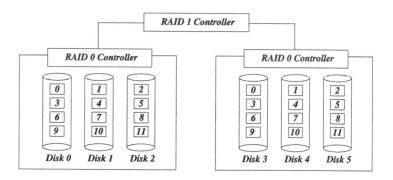

FIGURE 3.28

RAID01 structure.

Suppose Disk 0 fails in RAID01. The lower-level controller cannot, by itself, fix the problem, since it does not have any redundant data within its reach. It has, instead, to obtain the data from the controller of the other low-level group.

By contrast, suppose Disk 0 fails in the RAID10 configuration. The lower-level controller in charge of that disk can resolve the problem by itself: when a new disk is inducted into the system, this controller simply copies its (good) disk, i.e., Disk 1, into the new one. The volume of data copied is therefore much less in RAID10 than for RAID01. This translates into a quicker recovery from failure; note that the system is vulnerable to a second failure while it is still recovering from the first. As disk sizes increase and the recovery time increases, this difference may be significant.

3.2.7 MODELING CORRELATED FAILURES

In the analysis we have presented so far, we have assumed that the disks fail independently of one another. In this section, we will consider the impact of correlated failures.

Correlated failures arise, because power supply and control are typically shared among multiple disks. Disk systems are usually made up of *strings*. Each string consists of disks that are housed in one enclosure, and they share power supply, cabling, cooling, and a controller. If any of these items fails, the entire string can fail.

Let λ_{str} be the rate of failure of the support elements (power, cabling, cooling, control) of a string. If a RAID group is controlled by a single string, then the aggregate failure rate of the group is given by

$$\lambda_{total} = \lambda_{indep} + \lambda_{str}, \tag{3.12}$$

where λ_{indep} is approximately the inverse of the MTTDL, assuming independent disk failures. If the disk repair rate is much greater than the disk failure rate, data loss due to independent disk failures can be well modeled by Poisson processes. The sum of two Poisson processes is itself a Poisson process: we can therefore regard the aggregate failure process as Poisson with rate λ_{total}. The reliability is therefore given by

$$R_{total}(t) = e^{-\lambda_{total}t}. \tag{3.13}$$

The dramatic impact of string failures in a RAID1 system is shown in Fig. 3.29. (The impact for RAID3 and higher levels is similar). Figures of 150,000 hours for the mean string lifetime have been quoted in the literature, and at least one manufacturer claims mean disk lifetimes of 1,000,000 hours. Grouping together an entire RAID array as a single string therefore increases the unreliability by several orders of magnitude.

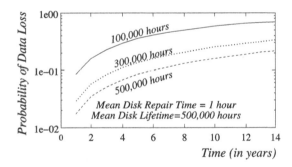

Curve labels indicate mean string lifetime

FIGURE 3.29

Impact of string failure rate on RAID1 system.

To get around this, one can have an orthogonal arrangement of strings and RAID groups, as depicted in Fig. 3.30. In such a case, the failure of a string affects only one disk in each RAID group. Because each RAID can tolerate the failure of up to one disk, this reduces the impact of string failures.

The orthogonal system can be modeled approximately as follows: Every data loss is caused by a sequence of events. If this sequence started with a single disk failure or by a string failure, we say the failure is *triggered* by an individual or string failure, respectively.

Since both string and disk failure rates are very low, we can, without significant error, model separately failures triggered by individual and string failures. We will find the (approximate) failure rate

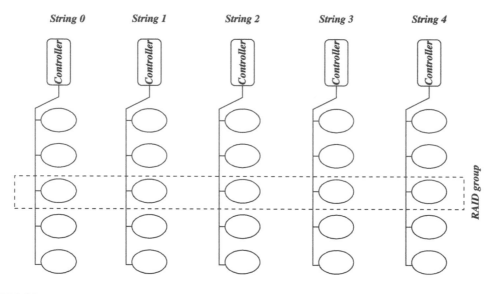

FIGURE 3.30

Orthogonal arrangement of strings and RAID groups ($d = 4$).

due to each. Adding these two failure rates will give us the approximate overall failure rate, which can then be used to determine the MTTDL, and the probability of data loss over any given time.

We next construct an approximate model that computes MTTDL and the reliability of the system at any time t. This model allows any general distribution for the repair times.

There is a total of $d + 1$ disks per RAID group, which in the orthogonal arrangement means $d + 1$ strings, and g groups of disks. The total number of disks is therefore $(d + 1)g$. Unlike our previous derivation, we will no longer assume that repair times are exponentially distributed: all we ask is that their distributions be known. Let $f_{disk}(t)$ denote the density function of the disk repair time.

The approximate rate at which individual failures trigger data loss in a given disk is given by $\lambda_{disk}\pi_{indiv}$, where λ_{disk} is the failure rate of a single disk, and π_{indiv} is the probability that a given individual failure triggers data loss. To calculate π_{indiv}, recall that it is the probability that another disk fails in the affected RAID group, whereas the previous failure has not yet been repaired. But this failure happens at the rate $d(\lambda_{disk} + \lambda_{str})$, since the second disk failure can happen either due to an individual disk, or string, failure. Let τ denote the (random) disk repair time. The probability of data loss conditioned on the event that the repair of the first disk takes τ time is

$$\text{Prob}\{\text{Data Loss} \mid \text{the repair takes } \tau\} = 1 - e^{-d(\lambda_{disk}+\lambda_{str})\tau}.$$

τ has the density function $f_{disk}(\cdot)$; hence, the unconditional probability of data loss is

$$\pi_{indiv} = \int_0^\infty \text{Prob}\{\text{Data Loss} \mid \text{the repair takes } \tau\} \cdot f_{disk}(\tau)d\tau$$

$$= \int_0^\infty \left(1 - e^{-d(\lambda_{disk}+\lambda_{str})\tau}\right) f_{disk}(\tau)d\tau$$

$$= \int_0^\infty f_{disk}(\tau)d\tau - \int_0^\infty e^{-d(\lambda_{disk}+\lambda_{str})\tau}f_{disk}(\tau)d\tau$$
$$= 1 - F_{disk}^*(d[\lambda_{disk} + \lambda_{str}]), \tag{3.14}$$

where $F_{disk}^*(\cdot)$ is the Laplace transform of $f_{disk}(\cdot)$. Since there are $(d+1)g$ data disks in all, the approximate rate at which data loss is triggered by individual disk failure is given by

$$\Lambda_{indiv} \approx (d+1)g\lambda_{disk}\{1 - F_{disk}^*(d[\lambda_{disk} + \lambda_{str}])\}. \tag{3.15}$$

Why is this approximate and not exact? Because we are assuming that $(d+1)g\lambda_{disk}$ is the rate at which individual disk failures occur *in a fault-free system*. Since the probability is very high that the system is entirely fault-free (if the repair times are much smaller than the time between failures, and the size of the system is not excessively large), this is usually a good approximation. It does have the merit of not imposing any limitations on the distribution of the repair time.

Let us now turn to computing Λ_{str}, the rate at which data loss is triggered by a string failure. The total rate at which strings fail (if all strings are up) is $(d+1)\lambda_{str}$. When a string fails, we have to repair the string itself and then make any necessary repairs to the individual disks, which may have been affected by the string failure. We will make the *pessimistic* approximation that failure can happen if another failure occurs in *any* of the groups or any of the disks before *all* of the groups are fully restored. This is pessimistic, because there are instances that are counted as causing data loss that, in fact, do not do so. For example, we will count as causing a data failure the occurrence of two string failures in the same string, the second occurring before the first has been repaired. We can also make the *optimistic* assumption that the disks affected by the triggering string failure are all immune to a further failure before the string and all its affected disks are fully restored. The difference between the failure rates predicted by these two assumptions will give us an idea of how tight the pessimistic bound happens to be.

Let τ be the (random) time taken to repair the failed string and all of its constituent disks that may have been affected by it. Let $f_{str}(\cdot)$ be the probability density function of this time. Then, under the pessimistic assumption, additional failures occur at the rate $\lambda_{pess} = (d+1)\lambda_{str} + (d+1)g\lambda_{disk}$. Under the optimistic assumption, additional failures occur at the rate $\lambda_{opt} = d\lambda_{str} + dg\lambda_{disk}$.

A data loss will therefore be triggered in the pessimistic model with the conditional (upon τ) probability $p_{pess} = 1 - e^{-\lambda_{pess}\tau}$, and in the optimistic model with the conditional (upon τ) probability $p_{opt} = 1 - e^{-\lambda_{opt}\tau}$. Integrating on τ, we obtain the unconditional pessimistic and optimistic estimates: $\pi_{pess} = 1 - F_{str}^*(\lambda_{pess})$, and $\pi_{opt} = 1 - F_{str}^*(\lambda_{opt})$, respectively, where $F_{str}^*(\cdot)$ is the Laplace transform of $f_{str}(\cdot)$. The pessimistic and optimistic rates at which a string failure triggers data loss are therefore given by

$$\begin{aligned} \Lambda_{str\_pess} &= (d+1)\lambda_{str}\pi_{pess}, \quad \text{and} \\ \Lambda_{str\_opt} &= (d+1)\lambda_{str}\pi_{opt}. \end{aligned} \tag{3.16}$$

The rate at which data loss happens in the system is therefore approximately

$$\Lambda_{data\_loss} \approx \begin{cases} \Lambda_{indiv} + \Lambda_{str\_pess} & \text{under the pessimistic assumption} \\ \Lambda_{indiv} + \Lambda_{str\_opt} & \text{under the optimistic assumption.} \end{cases} \tag{3.17}$$

From this, we immediately have

$$
\begin{aligned}
\text{MTTDL} &\approx \frac{1}{\Lambda_{\text{data\_loss}}} \\
R(t) &\approx e^{-\Lambda_{\text{data\_loss}} t}
\end{aligned}
\tag{3.18}
$$

as approximations of the MTTDL and reliability of the system, respectively.

3.2.8 RAID WITH SOLID-STATE DISKS

Flash memory has distinctive failure characteristics: write operations wear out flash memory cells. The issue we address here is how we should adjust RAID organization to take this into account. We assume here a proactive disk replacement policy. The disk writes are monitored, each disk has a lifetime specified in terms of the total number of writes it has taken. When it reaches this number of writes, it is replaced by a new device.

Let us focus on RAID levels 4 and 5. The basic approach is the same in both; the key difference is that, in Level 4, the parity blocks are all on one drive, whereas they are distributed evenly among the drives in Level 5. We can therefore regard them as two ends of a spectrum, ranging from high asymmetry with respect to parity blocks at one end (Level 4) to symmetry (Level 5). Other RAID arrangements can be envisaged within this spectrum.

If we denote the percentage of parity blocks being held at each drive by ϕ_i, the vector $\Phi = (\phi_1, \phi_2, \cdots, \phi_n)$ expresses the position within this spectrum of a RAID implementation. For example, for $n = 5$, $\Phi_a = (100, 0, 0, 0, 0)$ is RAID level 4 (with Φ_a being extremely asymmetric); $\Phi_b = (20, 20, 20, 20, 20)$ is RAID level 5 (Φ_b is extremely symmetric), whereas $\Phi_c = (40, 15, 15, 15, 15)$ is a RAID arrangement, whose symmetry falls somewhere between Φ_a and Φ_b.

As we have seen, the parity blocks are the ones most often written into. A solid-state disk, which holds more of them will therefore age faster than the others. For example, in an arrangement specified by Φ_c, the first drive will age faster than the rest. It is reasonable to approximate aging as directly proportional to the number of writes going to a disk. We can then write a simple approximate expression for the relative aging ratio of two disks, which hold $\phi_i\%$ and $\phi_j\%$ of the parity blocks, respectively, for a system consisting of a total of n disks:

$$
\rho_{i,j} = \frac{(n-1)\phi_i + 100 - \phi_i}{(n-1)\phi_j + 100 - \phi_j}.
$$

(The derivation is left to the reader as an exercise.) Thus in RAID level 4, the parity disk will age (approximately) n times faster than each of the other disks.

In RAID level 5, the disks age at roughly the same rate; all disks will hit their write limit at about the same time and be replaced when they do. In RAID level 4, the one parity disk will age the fastest; it will be replaced at a much faster rate than the other disks.

RAID levels 1 to 5 are resilient against the failure of any one disk; data loss may occur when a second disk failure occurs before recovery from the first is complete. Based on this, we can argue that reliability is enhanced by aging the disks in an unbalanced manner. In particular, we may prefer to have an arrangement, where one disk ages more rapidly than the others, rather than synchronously with the rest. That way, when a disk fails, there is a lower probability of a second disk failure during its replacement. Since the parity blocks are the ones most often updated, a disk holding a bigger fraction of the parity blocks is likely to age faster. Hence, the following policy, called *differential RAID*, has been suggested. At any point in time, allow one disk to have a bigger fraction of the parity blocks than the rest. As execution proceeds, shift this role of holding more parity blocks from disk to disk in a round-robin fashion. That is, suppose we start with disk A holding more of the parity blocks. It will age faster than the rest; when it comes time to replace it, do so and also move the parity-weighted role to the next disk, say disk B. Now, disk B will age faster; when it comes up for replacement, the parity-weighted role will be moved to the next disk, and so on. Simulation results have shown this approach to have reliability benefits.

3.3 DATA REPLICATION

Data replication in distributed systems is another example of how information redundancy can be used for improved fault tolerance at the system level. Data replication consists of holding identical copies of data on two or more nodes in a distributed system. As with a RAID system, a suitably managed data replication scheme can offer both fault tolerance and improved performance (because one can, for example, read data from nearby copies). However, it is important that the data replicates be kept consistent, despite failures in the system.

Consider, for example, a situation in which we keep five copies of the data: one copy on each of the five nodes of a distributed system, connected as shown in Fig. 3.31A. Suppose that a read or a write request may arrive to any of the five nodes on the bidirectional links in the figure. As long as all five copies are kept consistent, a read operation can be sent to any of the nodes. However, suppose two of the links fail, as shown in Fig. 3.31B. Then, node A is disconnected from nodes B and C. If a write operation updates the copy of the datum held in A, this write cannot be sent to the other nodes, and

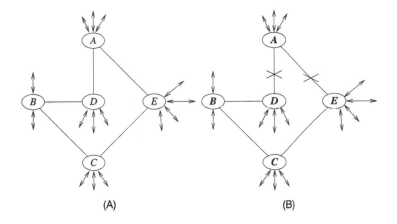

(A)   (B)

FIGURE 3.31

Disconnection endangers the correct operation of data replication. (A) Original network. (B) Disconnected network.

they will no longer be consistent with A. Any read of their data will therefore result in stale data being used.

In what follows, we describe two approaches to managing the replication of data through the assignment of weights (votes) to the individual copies: a nonhierarchical scheme and an hierarchical one. Such votes allow us to prefer copies that reside on more reliable and better connected nodes. We will assume that all faulty nodes can be recognized as such: no malicious behavior takes place.

3.3.1 VOTING: NONHIERARCHICAL ORGANIZATION

We next present a *voting* approach to handling data replication. To avoid confusion, we emphasize that we do not vote on multiple copies of data. If we read r copies of some data structure, we select one with the latest timestamp. We assume that data coding is used to detect/correct data errors in storage or transmission. Voting is not used for this purpose, but solely to specify minimum sets of nodes that need to be updated for a write operation, or that need to be accessed for a read operation to be completed.

The simplest voting scheme is the following: Assign v_i votes to copy i of that datum, and let S denote the set of all nodes with copies of the datum. Define v to be the sum of all the votes, $v = \sum_{i \in S} v_i$.

Define integers r and w with the following properties:

$$r + w \; > \; v;$$
$$w \; > \; v/2.$$

Let $V(X)$ denote the total number of votes assigned to copies in set X of nodes. The following strategy ensures that all reads are of the latest data:

> To complete a read, it is necessary to read from nodes of a set $R \subset S$ such that $V(R) \geq r$. Similarly, to complete a write, we must find a set $W \subset S$ such that $V(W) \geq w$, and execute that write on every copy in W.

This procedure works, because for any sets R and W such that $V(R) \geq r$ and $V(W) \geq w$, we must have $R \cap W \neq \emptyset$ (because $r + w > v$). Hence, any read operation is guaranteed to read the value of at least one copy, which has been updated by the latest write. Furthermore, for any two sets W_1, W_2 such that $V(W_1), V(W_2) \geq w$, we must have $W_1 \cap W_2 \neq \emptyset$. This prevents different writes to the same datum from being done concurrently, and guarantees that there exists at least one node that gets both updates.

Any set R such that $V(R) \geq r$ is said to be a *read quorum*, and any set W such that $V(W) \geq w$, is called a *write quorum*.

How would this system work for the example shown in Fig. 3.31? Assume we give one vote to each node: the sum of all votes is thus $v = 5$. We must have $w > 5/2$, so $w \in \{3, 4, 5\}$. Since $r + w > v$, we must have $r > v - w$. The following combinations are permissible:

$$(r, w) \in \{(1,5), (2,5), (3,5), (4,5), (5,5), (2,4), (3,4), (4,4), (5,4), (3,3)\}.$$

Consider the case $(r, w) = (1, 5)$. A read operation can be successfully completed by reading any one of the five copies; however, to complete a write, we have to update every one of the five copies. This ensures that every read operation gets the latest update of the data. If we pick $w = 5$, it makes no sense to set $r > 1$, which would needlessly slow down the read operation. In this case, we can still continue to read from each node even after the failures disconnect the network, as shown in Fig. 3.31B. However, it will be impossible to update the datum, since we cannot, from any source, reach all five copies to update them.

As another example, consider $(r, w) = (3, 3)$. This setting has the advantage of requiring just three copies to be written before a data update is successfully completed. However, read operations now take longer, because each overall read operation requires reading three copies, rather than one. With this system, after the network disconnection, read or write operations coming into node A will not be served. However, the four nodes that are left connected can continue to read and write as usual.

The selected values of r and w will affect the performance of the system. If, for instance, there are many more reads than writes, we may choose to keep r low to speed up the read operations. However, selecting $r = 1$ requires setting $w = 5$, which means that writes can no longer happen if even one node is disconnected. Picking $r = 2$ allows $w = 4$: the writes can still be done if four out of the five nodes are connected. We therefore have a tradeoff between performance and reliability.

The problem of assigning votes to nodes in such a way that availability is maximized is very difficult (the system availability is the probability that both read and write quorums are available). We therefore present two heuristics that usually produce good results (although not necessarily optimal). These heuristics allow us to use a general model that includes node and link failures. Assume that we know the availability of each node i: $a_n(i)$ and of each link j: $a_\ell(j)$. Denote by $L(i)$ the set of links incident on node i.

Heuristic 1: Assign to node i a vote $v(i) = a_n(i) \sum_{j \in L(i)} a_\ell(j)$ rounded to the nearest integer. If the sum of all votes assigned to nodes is even, give one extra vote to one of the nodes with the largest number of votes.

Heuristic 2: Let $k(i, j)$ be the node that is connected to node i by link j. Assign to node i a vote $v(i) = a_n(i) + \sum_{j \in L(i)} a_\ell(j) a_n(k(i, j))$ rounded to the nearest integer. As with Heuristic 1, if the sum of the votes is even, give one extra vote to one of the nodes with the largest number of votes.

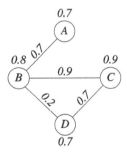

FIGURE 3.32

Vote assignment example (numbers indicate availabilities).

As an example, consider the system in Fig. 3.32. The initial assignment, due to Heuristic 1, is as follows:

$$v(A) \quad = \quad \text{round}(0.7 \times 0.7) = 0;$$

$$\begin{aligned}
v(B) &= \text{round}(0.8 \times 1.8) = 1; \\
v(C) &= \text{round}(0.9 \times 1.6) = 1; \\
v(D) &= \text{round}(0.7 \times 0.9) = 1.
\end{aligned}$$

Note that Heuristic 1 gives node A 0 votes. This means that A and its links are so unreliable compared to the rest that we may as well not use it. The votes add up to 3, and so the read and write quorums must satisfy the requirements

$$\begin{aligned}
r + w &> 3; \\
w &> 3/2.
\end{aligned}$$

Consequently, $w \in \{2, 3\}$. If we set $w = 2$, we have $r = 2$ as the smallest read quorum. The possible read quorums are therefore $\{BC, CD, BD\}$; these are also the possible write quorums.

If we set $w = 3$, we have $r = 1$ as the smallest read quorum. The possible read quorums are then $\{B, C, D\}$, and there is only one write quorum: BCD.

Under Heuristic 2, we have the following vote assignment:

$$\begin{aligned}
v(A) &= \text{round}(0.7 + 0.7 \times 0.8) = 1; \\
v(B) &= \text{round}(0.8 + 0.7 \times 0.7 + 0.9 \times 0.9 + 0.2 \times 0.7) = 2; \\
v(C) &= \text{round}(0.9 + 0.9 \times 0.8 + 0.7 \times 0.7) = 2; \\
v(D) &= \text{round}(0.7 + 0.2 \times 0.8 + 0.7 \times 0.9) = 1.
\end{aligned}$$

Since the votes add up to an even number, we give B an extra vote, so that the final vote assignment becomes: $v(A) = 1, v(B) = 3, v(C) = 2, v(D) = 1$. The votes now add up to 7, so that the read and write quorums must satisfy

$$\begin{aligned}
r + w &> 7; \\
w &> 7/2.
\end{aligned}$$

Consequently, $w \in \{4, 5, 6, 7\}$. Table 3.7 shows read and write quorums associated with $r + w = 8$. We invite the reader to augment the table by listing the availability associated with each given (r, w) pair: this is, of course, the probability that at least one read and one write quorum can be mustered despite node and/or link failures.

Table 3.7 Read and write quorums under Heuristic 2.

r	w	Read quorums	Write quorums
4	4	AB, BC, BD, ACD	AB, BC, BD, ACD
3	5	B, AC, CD	BC, ABD
2	6	B, C, AD	ABC, BCD
1	7	A, B, C, D	ABCD

We illustrate the process by solving the problem for $(r, w) = (4, 4)$. The availability in this case is the probability that at least one of the quorums AB, BC, BD, ACD can be used. We compute this probability by first calculating the availabilities of the individual quorums. Quorum AB can be used if A, B, and the single path connecting them are up. The probability of this occurring is

$$\text{Prob\{AB can be used\}} = a_n(A)a_n(B)a_l(l_{AB}) = 0.7 \cdot 0.8 \cdot 0.7 = 0.392,$$

where $a_l(l_{AB})$ is the availability of the link l_{AB} connecting the two nodes A and B. Quorum BC will be usable if B, C and at least one of the two paths connecting them are up. This probability can be calculated as follows:

$$\text{Prob\{BC can be used\}} = a_n(B)a_n(C)[a_l(l_{BC}) + a_l(l_{BD})a_n(D)a_l(l_{DC})(1 - a_l(l_{BC}))]$$

$$= 0.8 \cdot 0.9[0.9 + 0.2 \cdot 0.7 \cdot 0.7 \cdot 0.1] = 0.655.$$

Similarly, we can calculate the availabilities of the quorums BD and ACD. However, to compute the system availability, we cannot just add up the availabilities of the individual quorums, because the events "quorum i is up" are not mutually exclusive. Instead, we would have to calculate the probabilities of all intersections of these events, and then substitute them in the inclusion and exclusion formula, which is quite a tedious task. An easier and more methodical way of computing the system availability is to list all possible combinations of system components' states, and add up the probabilities of those combinations for which a quorum exists. In our example, the system has eight components (nodes and links), each of which can be in one of two states: "up" and "down," with $2^8 = 256$ system states in all. The probability of each state is a product of eight terms, each taking one of the following forms: $a_n(i)$, $(1 - a_n(i))$, $a_l(j)$, or $(1 - a_l(j))$. For each such state, we can establish whether a read quorum or a write quorum exists, and the availability of the system is the sum of the probabilities of the states in which both read and write quorums exist.

For $(r, w) = (4, 4)$, the lists of read quorums and write quorums are identical. For any other value of (r, w), these lists are different, and to calculate the availability of the system, we must take into consideration the relative frequencies of read and write operations, and multiply these by the probabilities that a read quorum and a write quorum exists, respectively.

A write quorum must consist of more than half the total number of votes. A system that is not easily or rapidly repaired, however, could degrade to the point at which no connected cluster exists that can muster a majority of the total votes. In such a case, no updates can be carried out to any data, even if a sufficiently large portion of the system remains operational.

This problem can be countered by dynamic vote assignment. Instead of keeping the read and write quorums static, we alter them to adjust to prevailing system conditions. In the discussion that follows, we assume that each node has exactly one vote. It is not difficult to relax this restriction.

For each datum, the algorithm consists of maintaining *version numbers* VN_i with each copy of that datum at each node i. Every time a node updates a datum, the corresponding version number is incremented. Assume that an update arrives at a node. This can only be executed if a write quorum can be gathered. The *update sites cardinality* at node i, denoted by SC_i, is the number of nodes that participated in the VN_ith update of that datum. When the system starts operation, SC_i is initialized to the total number of nodes in the system. The algorithm in Fig. 3.33 shows how the dynamic vote assignment procedure works.

The following example illustrates the algorithm. Suppose we start with seven nodes, all carrying copies of some datum. The state at time t_0 is as follows:

1. If an update request arrives at node i, node i computes the following quantities:

   - $M = \max\{VN_j, j \in S_i\}$ (where S_i is the set of nodes with which node i can communicate, including i itself), i.e., the maximum version number of the concerned datum among all the nodes with which node i can communicate.
   - $I = \{j | VN_j = M, j \in S_i\}$, i.e., the set of all nodes, whose version number is equal to the maximum.
   - $N = \max\{SC_j, j \in I\}$, i.e., the maximum update sites cardinality associated with all the nodes in I.

2. If $\|I\| > N/2$, then node i can raise a write quorum, and is allowed to carry out the update on all nodes in I; otherwise the update is not allowed. The update is carried out, and the version number of each copy of that datum in I is incremented, i.e., VN_i is incremented for each $i \in I$. Also, for each $i \in I$, we set $SC_i = \|I\|$. This entire step must be done atomically: all these operations must be done at each node in I, or none of them can be done.

FIGURE 3.33

Algorithm for dynamic vote assignment.

$$
\begin{array}{cccccccc}
 & A & B & C & D & E & F & G \\
VN & 5 & 5 & 5 & 5 & 5 & 5 & 5 \\
SC & 7 & 7 & 7 & 7 & 7 & 7 & 7
\end{array}
$$

Suppose now that at time t_0, a failure occurs in the system, disconnecting the system into two connected components: $\{A, B, C, D\}$ and $\{E, F, G\}$. No element in one component can communicate with any element in the other. Suppose E receives an update request at time $t_1 > t_0$. Since $SC_E = 7$, E has to find more than $7/2$ (i.e., four or more) nodes (including itself), to consummate that update. However, E can only communicate with two other nodes, F and G, and so the update request must be rejected.

At time $t_2 > t_0$, an update request arrives at node A, which is connected to three other nodes, and so the request can be honored. The update is carried out on A, B, C, and D, and the new state becomes the following:

$$
\begin{array}{cccccccc}
 & A & B & C & D & E & F & G \\
VN & 6 & 6 & 6 & 6 & 5 & 5 & 5 \\
SC & 4 & 4 & 4 & 4 & 7 & 7 & 7.
\end{array}
$$

At time $t_3 > t_2$, there is a further failure: the connected components of the network become $\{A, B, C\}, \{D\}, \{E, F, G\}$. At time $t_4 > t_3$, an update request arrives at C. The write quorum at C consists of just three elements now (i.e., the smallest number greater than $SC_C/2$), and so the update can be successfully completed at nodes A, B, and C. The state is now

$$
\begin{array}{cccccccc}
 & A & B & C & D & E & F & G \\
VN & 7 & 7 & 7 & 6 & 5 & 5 & 5 \\
SC & 3 & 3 & 3 & 4 & 7 & 7 & 7.
\end{array}
$$

What protocols must be followed to allow nodes to rejoin the components after having been disconnected from them? We leave their design to the reader.

3.3.2 VOTING: HIERARCHICAL ORGANIZATION

The obvious question that now arises is whether there is a way to manage data replication that does not require that $r + w > v$. If v is large (which can happen if a large number of copies is to be maintained), then data operations can take a long time. One solution is to have a hierarchical voting scheme as follows:

We construct an m-level tree in the following way. Let all the nodes holding copies of the data be the leaves at level $m - 1$. We then add virtual nodes at the higher levels up to the root at level 0. All the added nodes are only virtual groupings of the real nodes. Each node at level i will have the same number of children, denoted by ℓ_{i+1}. As an example, consider Fig. 3.34. In this tree, $\ell_1 = \ell_2 = 3$.

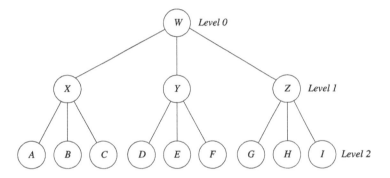

FIGURE 3.34

A tree for hierarchical quorum generation ($m = 3$).

We now assign one vote to each node in the tree and define the read and write quorum sizes, r_i and w_i, respectively, at level i to satisfy the inequalities

$$r_i + w_i > \ell_i;$$
$$w_i > \ell_i/2.$$

Then, the following algorithm is used to recursively assemble a read and write quorum at the leaves of the tree. *Read-mark* the root at level 0. Then, at level 1, read-mark r_1 nodes. When proceeding from level i to level $i + 1$, read-mark r_{i+1} children of each of the nodes read-marked at level i. It is not allowed to read-mark a node that does not have at least r_{i+1} nonfaulty children: if this was done, we need to backtrack and undo the marking of that node. Proceed like this until $i = m - 1$. The leaves that have been read-marked form a read-quorum. Forming a write-quorum is similar.

For the tree in Fig. 3.34, let us select $w_i = 2$ for $i = 1, 2$, and set $r_i = \ell_i - w_i + 1 = 2$. Starting at the root, read-mark two of its children, say X and Y. Now, read-mark two children for X and Y, say A, B for X, and D, E for Y. The read quorum is the set of read-marked leaves, namely, A, B, D, and E.

Suppose D had been faulty. Then, it cannot be part of the read-quorum, so we have to pick another child of Y, namely, F, to be in the read-quorum. If two of Y's children had been faulty, we cannot read-mark Y, and have to backtrack and try read-marking Z instead.

As an exercise, the reader should list read quorums generated by other values for r_i and w_i. For example, try $r_1 = 1, w_1 = 3, r_2 = 2, w_2 = 2$.

Note that the read quorum consists of just four copies. Similarly, we can generate a write quorum with four copies. If we had tried the nonhierarchical approach with one vote per node, our read and write quorums would have had to satisfy the conditions $r + w > 9$; $w > 9/2$. Hence, the write quorum in the nonhierarchical approach is of size at least 5, whereas that for the tree approach is 4.

Given each read and write quorum, the topology of the interconnection network, and the probability of node and link failures, we can, for each assignment of r_i and w_i, list the probability that read and write quorums will exist in any given system.

How can we prove that this approach does, in fact, work? We do so by showing that every possible read quorum has to intersect with every possible write quorum, in at least one node. This is not difficult to do, and we leave it as an exercise to the reader.

3.3.3 PRIMARY-BACKUP APPROACH

Another scheme for managing data replicas is the primary-backup approach, in which one node is designated as the primary, and all accesses are through that node. The other nodes are designated as backups. Under normal operation, all writes to the primary are also copied to the functional backups. When the primary fails, one of the backup nodes is chosen to take its place.

Let us now consider the details of this scheme. We start by describing how things work in the absence of failures. All requests from users (*clients* in the client-server terminology) are received by the primary server. It forwards the request to the copies and waits until it receives an acknowledgment from all of them. Once the acknowledgments are in, the primary fulfills the client's request.

All client requests must pass through the primary; it is the primary that serializes them, determining the order in which they are served. All messages from the primary are numbered, so that they can be processed by the backups in the order in which they are sent. This is extremely important, because changing the order in which requests are served could result in entering an incorrect state.

> **Example:** The primary receives a request, R_d, to deposit $1000 into Mr. Smith's bank account. This is followed by a request, R_t, to transfer $500 out of his account. He had $300 in his bank balance to begin with.
>
> Suppose the primary receives R_d first and then R_t. It forwards these messages in that order to each of the backups. Suppose backup B_1 receives R_d first, and then R_t. B_1 can process them in that order, leaving $800 in Mr. Smith's account. Now, suppose backup B_2 receives R_t first and then R_d. R_t cannot be honored: Mr. Smith does not have enough money in his account. Hence, the transfer request is denied in the copy of the account held by B_2. B_1 and B_2 are now no longer consistent.

In the absence of failures, it is easy to see that all the copies will be consistent if we follow this procedure. We now need to augment it to consider the case of failure. We will limit ourselves here to fail-stop failures, which are failures that result in silence. Byzantine failures (in which nodes can send back lying messages and do arbitrary things to their copies of the data) are not covered in detail; there are a few remarks about this failure at the end of the section.

Start by considering network failures. If the network becomes disconnected as a result of these failures, then it is only the component that is reachable by the primary that can take part in this algorithm. All others will fall out of date and will need to be reinitialized when the network is repaired.

Next, consider the loss of messages in the network. This can be handled by using a suitable communication algorithm, which retransmits messages until an acknowledgment is received. Hence, we can assume in what follows that if a message is transmitted, it will ultimately be received, unless we have a node failure.

Now, let us turn to node failures. Suppose one of the backups has failed and never returns an acknowledgment. The primary has to wait to receive an acknowledgment from each of the backups; if a backup fails, it may have to wait forever. This problem is easy to remedy: introduce a timeout feature. If the primary does not receive an acknowledgment from the backup within a specified period, the primary assumes the backup is faulty and proceeds to remove it from the group of backups. Obviously, the value that is used for the timeout depends on the interconnection network, and the speed of the processing.

Next, consider the failure of the primary itself, and let us see how this affects the processing of some request, R. How complicated it can be to handle this case depends on when the primary goes down. If it fails before forwarding any copies of R to any of its backups, there is no possibility of inconsistency among the backup copies: all we have to do then is to designate one of the backups as the new primary. This can be done by numbering the primary and each of the backups and always choosing the smallest-numbered functional copy to play the part of the primary.

If it fails after forwarding copies of R to all of its backups, then again there is no inconsistency among the backup copies: they have all seen identical copies of R. All that remains then is to choose one of the backups to be the new primary.

The third case is the most complex: if the primary fails after sending out messages to some, but not all, of its backups. Such a situation obviously needs some corrective action to maintain consistency among the backups. This is a little complicated and requires us to introduce the concept of a *group view*. To begin with, when the system starts with the primary and all backups fully functional and consistent, the group view consists of all of these copies. Each element in this set is aware of the group view, in other words, each backup knows the full set of backups to whom the primary is forwarding copies of requests. Call this initial group view G_0. At any point in time, there is a prevailing group view, which is modified as nodes fail and are repaired (as described below).

Messages as received by the backups are classified by them as either *stable* or *unstable*. A stable message is one that has been acknowledged by all the backups in the current group view. Until an acknowledgment has been observed, the message is considered to be unstable.

Suppose now that backup B_i detects that the primary has failed. We will discuss below how such failure might be detected. Then, B_i sends out a message announcing its findings to the other nodes in the current group view. A new group view is then constructed, from which the primary node is excluded, and a new primary is designated.

Before each node can install the new group view, it transmits to the other nodes in the old group view all the unstable messages in its buffer. This is followed by an `end-of-stream` message, announcing that all of its unstable messages have been sent. When it has received from every node in the new view an acknowledgment of these messages, it can proceed to assume that the new group view is now established.

What if another node fails when this is going on? This will result in a waited-for acknowledgment never being received: a timeout can be used to declare as faulty nodes that do not acknowledge messages, and the procedure of constructing yet another group view can be repeated.

This leaves us with the question of how the failure of a primary is to be discovered. There are many ways in which this can be done. For example, one may have each node run diagnostics on other nodes. Alternatively, we could require that the primary broadcast a message ("I am alive") at least once every T seconds, for some suitable T. If this requirement is not fulfilled, that could be taken as indicating that the primary is faulty.

We should mention that this procedure allows for nodes to be repaired. Such a node would make its database consistent with that of the nodes in the prevailing group view and announce its accession to the group through a message. The nodes would then go through the procedure of changing the group view to accommodate this returning node.

Finally, a brief comment about Byzantine failures. From Chapter 2, you will remember that these are much more complicated to deal with than fail-stop failures. One approach to dealing with these in a client-server framework is the Castro–Liskov algorithm. We only present a very brief outline of this algorithm; for details—and the proof that it does indeed work—we refer the reader to references in the Further Reading section.

The Castro–Liskov algorithm assumes a primary server node and additional replica nodes; each server node is modeled as a finite state machine. So long as each replica carries out the same operations in the same order, their state will be consistent. This has to be done in the face of up to m malicious failures, which can send spurious messages.

The client broadcasts its request to all the replicas; the primary server node is responsible for assigning a sequence number to it to ensure that requests are served by all replicas in the same order. Signatures and message digests are used to ensure protection against malicious events. A signed message allows a node to be confident that the purported sender of the message was the real sender, and not a spoofer. A message digest is the mapping $D(r)$ of message r such that given $D(r)$, it is computationally infeasible to find another message r' such that $D(r) = D(r')$. This allows a receiver to check for message bits (such as client requests) being tampered with along the way.

Replica nodes work on requests in the order of their sequence numbers. Prior to committing any state updates (i.e., finalizing actions in response to requests), there are rounds of communication to ensure that even if m malicious nodes send out spurious messages, the nonfaulty nodes will behave consistently and correctly. Similarly, if a node realizes the primary has been silent for a long time, or otherwise suspects it as having failed, it initiates a round of message exchanges to appoint another node as the new primary. Once again, these message exchanges are meant to protect against malicious nodes spuriously causing changes to the primary node.

Checkpoints (see Chapter 6) are used to save the system state every so often; garbage collection following checkpointing protects against excessive consumption of storage.

3.4 ALGORITHM-BASED FAULT TOLERANCE

Algorithm-based fault tolerance (ABFT) is an approach to provide fault detection and diagnosis through data redundancy. The data redundancy is not implemented at either the hardware or operating system software level. Instead, it is implemented at the application software level, and as a result, its exact implementation will differ from one class of applications to another. Implementing data re-dundancy is more efficient when applied to large arrays of data, rather than to many independent scalars. Consequently, ABFT techniques have been developed for matrix-based and signal processing applications, such as matrix multiplication, matrix inversion, LU decomposition, and the fast Fourier transform. We will illustrate the ABFT approach through its application to basic matrix operations.

Data redundancy in matrix operations is implemented using a checksum code. Given an $n \times m$ matrix A, we define the *column checksum matrix* A_C as

$$A_C = \begin{bmatrix} A \\ eA \end{bmatrix},$$

where $e = [1\ 1\ \dots 1]$ is a row vector containing n 1s. In other words, the elements in the last row of A_C are the checksums of the corresponding columns of A. Similarly, we define the *row checksum matrix* A_R as

$$A_R = [A\ \ Af],$$

where $f = [1\ 1\ \dots 1]^T$ is a column vector containing m 1s. Finally, the *full* $(n+1) \times (m+1)$ *checksum matrix* A_F is defined as

$$A_F = \begin{bmatrix} A & Af \\ eA & eAf \end{bmatrix}.$$

Based on the discussion in Section 3.1, it should be clear that the column or row checksum matrix can be used to detect a single fault in any column or row of A, respectively, whereas the full checksum matrix can be used to locate an erroneous single element of A. If the computed checksums are accurate (overflows are not discarded), locating the erroneous element allows us to correct it as well.

The above column, row, and full checksums can be used to detect (or correct) errors in various matrix operations. For example, we can replace the matrix addition $A + B = C$ by $A_C + B_C = C_C$, or $A_R + B_R = C_R$ or $A_F + B_F = C_F$. Similarly, instead of calculating $AB = C$, we may compute $AB_R = C_R$, or $A_C B = C_C$ or $A_C B_R = C_F$.

To allow locating and correcting errors, even if only a column or row checksum matrix is used (rather than the full checksum matrix), a second checksum value is added to each column or row, respectively. The resulting matrices, the following, are called column, row, and full-weighted matrices:

$$A_C = \begin{bmatrix} A \\ eA \\ e_wA \end{bmatrix} \quad A_R = [A\ Af\ Af_w] \ \ \text{and} \ \ A_F = \begin{bmatrix} A & Af & Af_w \\ eA & eAf & eAf_w \\ e_wA & e_wAf & e_wAf_w \end{bmatrix},$$

where $e_w = \begin{bmatrix} 1\ 2\ \dots\ 2^{n-1} \end{bmatrix}$ and $f_w = \begin{bmatrix} 1\ 2\ \dots\ 2^{m-1} \end{bmatrix}^T$.

This weighted-checksum code (WCC) can correct a single error, even if only two rows or two columns are added to the original matrix. For example, suppose that A_C is used and an error in column j is detected. Denote by $WCS1$ and $WCS2$ the values of the unweighted checksum eA and the weighted checksum e_wA in column j, respectively. We then calculate the error in the unweighted checksum $S_1 = \sum_{i=1}^n a_{i,j} - WCS1$, and the error in the weighted checksum $S_2 = \sum_{i=1}^n 2^{i-1}a_{i,j} - WCS2$. If only one of these two error syndromes S_1 and S_2 is nonzero, then the corresponding checksum value is erroneous. If both S_1 and S_2 are nonzero, $S_2/S_1 = 2^{k-1}$ implies that the element $a_{k,j}$ is erroneous, and can be corrected through $a'_{k,j} = a_{k,j} - S_1$.

The weighted checksum encoding scheme can be further extended to increase its error detection and correction capabilities by adding extra rows and/or columns with weights of the form $e_{w_d} = \begin{bmatrix} 1^{d-1} & 2^{d-1} & \dots & (2^{n-1})^{d-1} \end{bmatrix}$ and $f_{w_d} = \begin{bmatrix} 1^{d-1} & 2^{d-1} & \dots & (2^{m-1})^{d-1} \end{bmatrix}^T$. Note that for $d = 1$ and $d = 2$, we obtain the above two (unweighted and weighted) checksums. If all the weights for $d = 1, 2, \dots \nu$ are used, the resulting weighted checksum encoding scheme has a Hamming distance of $\nu + 1$, and as a result, is capable of detecting up to ν errors, and correcting up to $\lfloor \nu/2 \rfloor$. We will focus below only on the case of $\nu = 2$.

For large values of n and m, the unweighted and weighted checksums can become very large and cause overflows. For the unweighted checksum, we can use the single precision checksum scheme using two's complement arithmetic and discarding overflows. Discarding overflows implies that the sum will be calculated modulo-2^ℓ, where ℓ is the number of bits in a word. If only a single element of the matrix A is erroneous, the error cannot exceed $2^\ell - 1$, and the modulo-2^ℓ calculation performed for the single-precision checksum will provide the correct value of the syndrome S_1.

The weighted checksum uses the weights $[1 \ 2 \ \dots \ 2^{m-1}]$ and would need more than ℓ bits. We can reduce the largest value that the weighted checksum can assume by using a weight vector e_w with smaller weights. For example, instead of $\begin{bmatrix} 1 & 2 & \dots & 2^{n-1} \end{bmatrix}$, we can use $[1 \ 2 \ \dots \ n]$. For these weights, if both error syndromes S_1 and S_2 for column j are nonzero, $S_2/S_1 = k$ implies that the element $a_{k,j}$ is erroneous, and it can be corrected as before through $a'_{k,j} = a_{k,j} - S_1$.

If floating-point arithmetic is used for the matrix operations, an additional complexity arises. Floating-point calculations may have round-off errors that can result in a nonzero error syndrome S_1, even if all the matrix elements were computed correctly. Thus we must set an error bound δ such that $S_1 < \delta$ will not signal a fault. The proper value of δ depends on the type of data, the type of calculations performed, and the size of the matrix. Setting δ too low will lead to round-off errors misinterpreted as faults (causing false alarms), whereas setting it too high can reduce the probability of fault detection. One way to deal with this problem is to partition the matrix into submatrices and assign checksums to each submatrix separately. The smaller size of these submatrices will greatly simplify the selection of a value for δ, which will provide a good tradeoff between the probability of a false alarm and the probability of fault detection. Partitioning into submatrices will slightly increase the complexity of the calculations, but will allow the detection of multiple faults, even if only two (unweighted and weighted) checksums are used.

3.5 FURTHER READING

Many textbooks on the topic of coding theory are available. See, for example, [10–14,25,27,30,40,42, 44,46,51–53,60,64,65,67]. Cyclic codes are discussed in detail in [10,12,14,27,40,42,44,46,51–53,56, 60,64,65]. There are several websites that include descriptions of various codes, and even software implementations of some of them [36,47,68]. Arithmetic codes are discussed in [3,4,35,55], and unidirectional codes are covered in [15,56]. Detailed descriptions of residue codes appear in [59,61].

Low-density parity coding (LDPC) was introduced by Gallager [21]; its computational overhead originally prevented its use. Recently, however, the availability of faster processors has made it practical to use, especially in flash memory. Soft decisions in flash memory are covered, for example, in [66]. Irregular LDPC (not covered in this book) is studied in [58]. A good tutorial introduction can be found in [45]. In our presentation, we have omitted discussing methods to make the encoding process fast; for some details on this, again see [45]. Also covered in [45] are *turbo codes*, which we have not covered in this book.

Descriptions of RAID structures are widely available in textbooks on computer architecture. See also [17,28,50]. Using RAID with solid-state disks, and the concept of differential RAID, is treated in [7,39]. For an explanation of hierarchical RAID, see [5,38].

An excellent source for voting algorithms is [33]. Pioneering work in this area appears in [23] and [63]. Further key contributions are presented in [9,22]. Hierarchical voting is described in [37]. See also [54] for a discussion of the tradeoff between message overheads and data availability, and [26, 31,32] for dynamic vote assignment, as well as [1,43] on quorums when servers may suffer Byzantine faults. The tradeoff between the load of a quorum system and its availability has been studied in [49]. Partial quorums are discussed in [6]. The primary/backup approach to data-replica management can be found in [20,24,33,48,62]. The references also discuss another approach to replica management, where no single node is designated as the primary, but each copy can manage client requests. This is called *active replication* or the *state-machine approach*.

Algorithm-based fault tolerance was first proposed in [29] and further developed in [8,16,18,19,34]. Alternative weights for the checksum codes were presented in [2,41], and extending the approach to floating-point calculations was discussed in [57,69]. Round-off errors in floating-point operations are described in [35].

3.6 EXERCISES

1. Prove that it is possible to find at most 28 8-bit binary words such that the Hamming distance between any two of them is at least 3.
2. To an n-bit word with a single parity bit (for a total of $(n+1)$ bits), a second parity bit for the $(n+1)$-bit word has been added. How would the error detection capabilities change?
3. Show that the Hamming distance of an M-of-N code is 2.
4. Compare two parity codes for data words consisting of 64 data bits: (1) a $(72, 64)$ Hamming code and (2) a single parity bit per byte. Both codes require eight check bits. Indicate the error correction and detection capabilities, the expected overhead, and list the types of multiple errors that are detectable by these two codes.
5. Show that a code can detect all unidirectional errors if and only if no two of its codewords are ordered. Two binary N-bit words X and Y are *ordered* if either $x_i \leq y_i$ for all $i \in \{1, 2, \ldots, N\}$, or $x_i \geq y_i$ for all $i \in \{1, 2, \ldots, N\}$.
6. A communication channel has a probability of 10^{-3} that a bit transmitted on it is erroneous. The data rate is 12000 bps. Data packets contain 240 information bits, a 32-bit CRC for error detection, and 0, 8, or 16 bits for error correction coding (ECC). Assume that if eight ECC bits are added, all single-bit errors can be corrected, and if sixteen ECC bits are added all double-bit errors can be corrected.
   (a) Find the throughput in information bits per second of a scheme consisting of error detection with retransmission of bad packets (i.e., no error correction).

(b) Find the throughput if eight ECC check bits are used, so that single-bit errors can be corrected. Uncorrectable packets must be retransmitted.

(c) Finally find the throughput if sixteen ECC check bits are appended, so that two-bit errors can be corrected. As in (b), uncorrectable packets must be retransmitted. Would you recommend increasing the number of ECC check bits from 8 to 16?

7. Derive all codewords for the separable 5-bit cyclic code based on the generating polynomial $X + 1$, and compare the resulting codewords to those for the nonseparable code.

8. (a) Show that if the generating polynomial $G(X)$ of a cyclic code has more than one term, all single-bit errors will be detected.

(b) Show that if $G(X)$ has a factor with three terms, all double-bit errors will be detected.

(c) Show that if $G(X)$ has $X + 1$ as a factor, all odd numbers of bit errors will be detected. That is, if $E(X)$ contains an odd number of terms (errors), it does not have $X + 1$ as a factor. Also show that CRC-16 and CRC-CCITT contain $X + 1$ as a factor. What are the error detection capabilities of these cyclic codes?

9. Given that $X^7 - 1 = (X + 1)g_1(X)g_2(X)$, where $g_1(X) = X^3 + X + 1$

(a) Calculate $g_2(X)$.

(b) Identify all the $(7, k)$ cyclic codes that can be generated based on the factors of $X^7 - 1$. How many different such cyclic codes exist?

(c) Show all the codewords generated by $g_1(X)$, and their corresponding data words.

10. Given a number X and its residue modulo-3, $C(X) = |X|_3$, how will the residue change when X is shifted by one bit position to the left if the shifted-out bit is 0? Repeat this for the case, where the shifted-out bit is 1. Verify your rule for $X = 01101$ shifted five times to the left.

11. This question relates to soft decisions: recall that in such a case, each bit has a certain probability of being 1 or 0. In such a setting, show that for bits B_1, B_2,

$$2\text{Prob}(B_1 \oplus B_2 = 0) - 1 = (2\text{Prob}(B_1 = 1) - 1)(2\text{Prob}(B_2 = 1) - 1).$$

Extend this result to show that

$$2\text{Prob}(B_1 \oplus B_2 \oplus \cdots \oplus B_m = 0) = \prod_{\ell=1}^{m}(2\text{Prob}(B_\ell = 1) - 1).$$

12. Show that a residue check with the modulus $A = 2^a - 1$ can detect all errors in a group of $a - 1$ (or fewer) adjacent bits. Such errors are called *burst errors* of length $a - 1$ (or less), and they may occur when shifting an operand by several bit positions.

13. You have a RAID1 system, in which failures occur at individual disks at a constant rate λ per disk. The repair time of disks is exponentially distributed with rate μ. Suppose we are in an earthquake-prone area, where building-destroying earthquakes occur according to a Poisson process with rate λ_e. If the building is destroyed, so too is the entire RAID system. Derive an expression for the probability of data loss for such a system as a function of time. Assuming that the mean time between such earthquakes is 50 years, plot the probability of data loss as a function of time using the parameters $1/\lambda = 500,000$ hours and $1/\mu = 1$ hour.

14. For a RAID level 3 system with d data disks and one parity disk, as d increases the overhead decreases, but the unreliability increases. Suggest a measure for cost-effectiveness, and find the value of d, which will maximize your proposed measure.

15. Given a RAID level 5 system with an orthogonal arrangement of $d + 1$ strings and $g = 8$ RAID groups, compare the MTTDL for different values of d from 4 to 10. Assume an exponential repair time for single disks and for strings of disks with rates of 1/hour and 3/hour, respectively. Also assume failure rates for single disks and strings of disks of 10^{-6}/hour and $5 \cdot 10^{-6}$/hour, respectively.

16. Derive expressions for the reliability and availability of the network shown in Fig. 3.31A for the case $(r, w) = (3, 3)$, where a single vote is assigned to each node in the nonhierarchical organization. In this case, both read and write operations can take place if at least three of the five nodes are up. Assume that failures occur at each node according to a Poisson process with rate λ, but the links do not fail. When a node fails, it is repaired (repair includes loading up-to-date data), and the repair time is an exponentially distributed random variable with mean $1/\mu$. Derive the required expressions for the system reliability and availability using the Markov chains (see Chapter 2) shown in Fig. 3.35A and B, respectively, where the state is the number of nodes that are down.

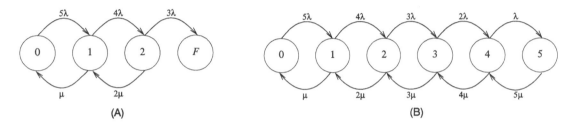

(A)   (B)

FIGURE 3.35

Markov chains for Question 16 $((r, w) = (3, 3))$. (A) Reliability chain. (B) Availability chain.

17. In Fig. 3.35, a Markov chain is provided for the case, in which nodes can be repaired in an exponentially distributed time. Suppose instead that the repair time was a fixed, deterministic time. How would this complicate the model?

18. For the model shown in Question 13, suppose $\lambda = 10^{-3}$ and $\mu = 1$. Calculate the reliability and availability of each of the following configurations: $(r, w) = (3, 3), (2, 4), (1, 5)$.

19. For the example shown in Fig. 3.36, the four nodes have an availability 1, whereas the links have the availabilities indicated in the figure. Use Heuristic 2 to assign votes to the four nodes, write down the possible values for w and the corresponding minimal values of r, and calculate the availability for each possible value of (r, w). Assume that read operations are twice as frequent as write operations.

20. Prove that in the hierarchical quorum generation approach in Section 3.3.2, every possible read quorum intersects with every possible write quorum in at least one node.

21. Consider the tree shown in Fig. 3.34. If p is the probability that a leaf node is faulty, obtain an expression for the probability that read and write quorums exist. Assume that $r_1 = r_2 = w_1 = w_2 = 2$, and that nodes at Levels 0 and 1 do not fail.

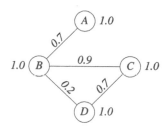

FIGURE 3.36

An example network (numbers indicate availabilities).

22. Show how checksums can be used to detect and correct errors in a scalar by matrix multiplication for the example that follows. Assume a 3×3 matrix

$$A = \begin{bmatrix} 1 & 2 & 3 \\ 4 & 5 & 6 \\ 7 & 8 & 9 \end{bmatrix}.$$

Show the corresponding column weighted matrix A_C, and assume that during the multiplication of A_C by the scalar 2, a single error has occurred resulting in the following output:

$$2 \cdot A = \begin{bmatrix} 2 & 4 & 6 \\ 8 & 10 & 12 \\ 14 & 17 & 18 \end{bmatrix}.$$

REFERENCES

[1] L. Alvisi, D. Malkhi, E. Pierce, M.K. Reiter, R.N. Wright, Dynamic byzantine quorum systems, in: International Conference on Dependable Systems and Networks (DSN '00), 2000, pp. 283–292.

[2] C.J. Anfinson, F.T. Luk, A linear algebraic model of algorithm-based fault tolerance, IEEE Transactions on Computers C-37 (December 1988) 1599–1604.

[3] A. Avizienis, Arithmetic error codes: cost and effectiveness studies for application in digital system design, IEEE Transactions on Computers C-20 (November 1971) 1322–1331.

[4] A. Avizienis, Arithmetic algorithms for error-coded operands, IEEE Transactions on Computers C-22 (June 1973) 567–572.

[5] S.H. Baek, B.W. Kim, E.J. Joung, C.W. Park, Reliability and performance of hierarchical RAID with multiple controllers, in: ACM Symposium on Principles of Distributed Computing, 2001, pp. 246–254.

[6] P. Bailis, S. Venkataraman, M.J. Franklin, J.M. Hellerstein, I. Stoica, Probabilistically bounded staleness for practical partial quorums, Proceedings of the VLDB Endowment 5 (8) (2012) 776–787.

[7] M. Balakrishnan, A. Kadav, V. Prabhakaran, D. Malkhi, Differential RAID: rethinking raid for SSD reliability, ACM Transactions on Storage 6 (2) (2010) 4.

[8] P. Banerjee, J.A. Abraham, Bounds on algorithm-based fault tolerance in multiple processor systems, IEEE Transactions on Computers C-35 (April 1986) 296–306.

[9] D. Barbara, H. Garcia-Molina, The reliability of voting mechanisms, IEEE Transactions on Computers C-36 (October 1987) 1197–1208.

[10] J. Baylis, Error-Correcting Codes, Chapman and Hall, 1998.

[11] E. Berlekamp (Ed.), Key Papers in the Development of Coding Theory, IEEE Press, 1974.

[12] E. Berlekamp, Algebraic Coding Theory, 2nd edition, Aegean Park Press, 1984.

[13] R. Blahut, Theory and Practice of Error Control Codes, Addison-Wesley, Reading, 1983.

[14] R. Blahut, Algebraic Codes for Data Transmission, Cambridge University Press, 2003.

[15] B. Bose, D.J. Lin, Systematic unidirectional error-detecting codes, IEEE Transactions on Computers C-34 (November 1985) 1026–1032.

[16] G. Bosilca, R. Delmas, J. Dongarra, J. Langou, Algorithm-based fault tolerance applied to high performance computing, Journal of Parallel and Distributed Computing 69 (4) (2009) 410–416.

[17] P.M. Chen, E.K. Lee, G.A. Gibson, R.H. Katz, D.A. Patterson, RAID: high-performance, reliable secondary storage, ACM Computing Surveys 26 (1994) 145–185.

[18] Z. Chen, J. Dongarra, Algorithm-based fault tolerance for fail-stop failures, IEEE Transactions on Parallel and Distributed Systems 19 (12) (2008) 1628–1641.

[19] Z. Chen, Online-ABFT: an online algorithm based fault tolerance scheme for soft error detection in iterative methods, ACM SIGPLAN Notices 48 (8) (2013) 167–176.

[20] A. Cherif, T. Katayama, Replica management for fault-tolerant systems, IEEE MICRO 18 (1998) 54–65.

[21] R. Gallager, Low-density parity-check codes, I.R.E. Transactions on Information Theory 8 (1) (1962) 21–28.

[22] H. Garcia-Molina, D. Barbara, How to assign votes in a distributed system, Journal of the ACM 32 (October 1985) 841–860.

[23] D.K. Gifford, Weighted voting for replicated data, in: Seventh ACM Symposium on Operating Systems, 1979, pp. 150–162.

[24] R. Guerraoui, A. Schiper, Software-based replication for fault tolerance, IEEE Computer 30 (April 1997) 68–74.

[25] R. Hamming, Coding and Information Theory, Prentice-Hall, 1980.

[26] M. Herlihy, Dynamic quorum adjustment for partitioned data, ACM Transactions on Database Systems 12 (1987).

[27] R. Hill, A First Course in Coding Theory, Oxford University Press, 1986.

[28] M. Holland, G.A. Gibson, D.P. Siewiorek, Architectures and algorithms for online failure recovery in redundant disk arrays, Distributed and Parallel Databases 2 (July 1994) 295–335.

[29] K.-H. Huang, J.A. Abraham, Algorithm-based fault tolerance for matrix operations, IEEE Transactions on Computers 33 (June 1984) 518–528.

[30] C.W. Huffman, V. Pless, Fundamentals of Error-Correcting Codes, Cambridge University Press, 2003.

[31] S. Jajodia, D. Mutchler, Dynamic voting, in: ACM SIGMOD International Conference on Management of Data, 1987, pp. 227–238.

[32] S. Jajodia, D. Mutchler, Dynamic voting algorithms for maintaining the consistency of a replicated database, ACM Transactions on Database Systems 15 (June 1990) 230–280.

[33] P. Jalote, Fault Tolerance in Distributed Systems, Prentice-Hall, 1994.

[34] J.Y. Jou, J.A. Abraham, Fault tolerant matrix arithmetic and signal processing on highly concurrent computing structures, Proceedings of the IEEE 74 (May 1986) 732–741.

[35] I. Koren, Computer Arithmetic Algorithms, A. K. Peters, 2002.

[36] I. Koren, Fault tolerant computing simulator, http://www.ecs.umass.edu/ece/koren/FaultTolerantSystems/simulator/.

[37] A. Kumar, Hierarchical quorum consensus: a new algorithm for managing replicated data, IEEE Transactions on Computers 40 (September 1991) 996–1004.

[38] J. Layton, Intro to nested-RAID: RAID01 and RAID10, Linux Magazine (2011).

[39] Y. Li, P.P. Lee, J.C. Lui, Stochastic analysis on RAID reliability for solid-state drives, in: IEEE 32nd International Symposium on Reliable Distributed Systems, 2013, pp. 71–80.

[40] S. Lin, D.J. Costello, Error Control Coding: Fundamentals and Applications, Prentice-Hall, 1983.

[41] F.T. Luk, H. Park, An analysis of algorithm-based fault tolerance techniques, Journal of Parallel and Distributed Computing 5 (1988) 172–184.

[42] F. MacWilliams, N. Sloane, The Theory of Error-Correcting Codes, North-Holland, 1977.

[43] D. Malkhi, M. Reiter, Byzantine Quorum Systems, Distributed Computing 11 (1998) 203–213.

[44] R. McEliece, The Theory of Information and Coding, 2nd edition, Cambridge University Press, 2002.

[45] S.J. Johnson, Iterative Error Correction: Turbo, Low-Density Parity-Check and Repeat-Accumulate Codes, Cambridge University Press, 2009.

[46] R.H. Morelos-Zaragoza, The Art of Error Correcting Coding, Wiley & Sons, 2002.

[47] R. Morelos-Zaragoza, The error correcting codes (ECC) home page, http://www.eccpage.com/.

[48] S. Mullender (Ed.), Distributed Systems, Addison-Wesley, 1993.

[49] M. Naor, A. Wool, The load, capacity, and availability of quorum systems, SIAM Journal on Computing 27 (1998) 423–447.

[50] D.A. Patterson, G.A. Gibson, R.H. Katz, A case for redundant arrays of inexpensive disks, in: International Conference on Management of Data, 1988, pp. 109–116.

[51] W. Peterson, E. Weldon, Error-Correcting Codes, 2nd edition, MIT Press, 1972.

[52] V. Pless, Introduction to the Theory of Error-Correcting Codes, 3rd edition, Wiley, 1998.

[53] O. Pretzel, Error-Correcting Codes and Finite Fields, Oxford University Press, 1992.

[54] S. Rangarajan, S. Setia, S.K. Tripathi, A fault tolerant algorithm for replicated data management, IEEE Transactions on Parallel and Distributed Systems 6 (December 1995) 1271–1282.

[55] T.R.N. Rao, Bi-residue error-correcting codes for computer arithmetic, IEEE Transactions on Computers C-19 (May 1970) 398–402.

[56] T.R.N. Rao, E. Fujiwara, Error-Control Coding for Computer Systems, Prentice-Hall, 1989.

[57] J. Rexford, N.K. Jha, Partitioned encoding schemes for algorithm-based fault tolerance in massively parallel systems, IEEE Transactions on Parallel and Distributed Systems 5 (June 1994) 649–653.

[58] T.J. Richardson, M.A. Shokrollahi, R.L. Urbanke, Design of capacity-approaching irregular low-density parity-check codes, IEEE Transactions on Information Theory 47 (2) (2001) 619–637.

[59] M.A. Soderstrand, W.K. Jenkins, G.A. Jullien, F.J. Taylor, Residue Number System Arithmetic Modern Application in Digital Signal Processing, IEEE Press, 1986.

[60] P. Sweeney, Error Control Coding: From Theory to Practice, Wiley, 2002.

[61] N.S. Szabo, R.I. Tanaka, Residue Arithmetic and Its Application to Computer Technology, McGraw-Hill, 1967.

[62] A.S. Tanenbaum, M. van Steen, Distributed Systems: Principles and Paradigms, Prentice-Hall, 2002.

[63] R.H. Thomas, A majority consensus approach to concurrency control for multiple copy databases, ACM Transactions on Database Systems 4 (June 1979) 180–209.

[64] L. Vermani, Elements of Algebraic Coding Theory, Chapman and Hall, 1996.

[65] A. Viterbi, J. Omura, Principles of Digital Communication and Coding, McGraw Hill, 1979.

[66] J. Wang, T. Courtade, H. Shankar, R.D. Wesel, Soft information for LDPC decoding in flash: mutual-information optimized quantization, in: IEEE GLOBECOM, 2011, pp. 1–6.

[67] D. Welsh, Codes and Cryptography, Oxford University Press, 1988.

[68] R. Williams, A painless guide to CRC error detection algorithms, http://www.ross.net/crc/crcpaper.html.

[69] S. Yajnik, N.K. Jha, Graceful degradation in algorithm-based fault tolerance multiprocessor systems, IEEE Transactions on Parallel and Distributed Systems 8 (February 1997) 137–153.

FAULT-TOLERANT NETWORKS

Interconnection networks are widely used today. The simplest example is a network connecting processors and memory modules in a shared-memory multiprocessor, in which processors perform read or write operations in the memory modules. Another example is a network connecting a number of processors (typically with their own local memory) in a distributed system, allowing the processors to communicate through messages, while executing parts of a common application. In these two types of network, the individual components (processors and memories) are connected through a collection of links and switchboxes, where a switchbox allows a given component to communicate with several other components without having a separate link to each of them.

A third type of network, called *wide-area networks*, connects large sets of processors that operate independently (and typically execute different and unrelated applications), allowing them to share various types of information. In such networks, the term *packet* is often used instead of message (a message may consist of several packets, each traversing the network independently), and they consist of more complicated switchboxes, called *routers*. The best known example of this kind of network is the Internet.

The network's links and switchboxes establish one or more paths between the sender of the message (the *source*) and its receiver (the *destination*). These links and switchboxes can be either unidirectional or bidirectional. The specific organization, or *topology*, of the network may provide only a single path between a given source and a given destination, in which case any fault in a link, or switchbox, along the path will disconnect the source-destination pair. Fault tolerance in networks is thus achieved by having multiple paths connecting source to destination, and/or spare units that can be switched in to replace the failed units.

Many existing network topologies contain multiple paths for some or all source-destination pairs, and there is a need to evaluate the resilience to faults provided by such redundancy, as well as the degradation in the network operation as faults accumulate.

We begin this chapter by presenting several measures of resilience/fault tolerance in networks. Then, we turn to several well-known network topologies used in distributed or parallel computing, analyze their resilience in the presence of failures, and describe ways of increasing their fault tolerance. We restrict ourselves in this chapter to networks meant for use in parallel and distributed computer systems (including networks-on-chip), and sensor networks. This field of network fault tolerance is large, and we will only be providing a brief sampling in this chapter. Pointers for further reading can be found toward the end.

There is a vast literature on adaptive routing and recovery from lost packets in the field of wide-area networks: for that material, the reader should consult one of the many available books on computer networks.

Fault-Tolerant Systems. https://doi.org/10.1016/B978-0-12-818105-8.00014-0

4.1 MEASURES OF RESILIENCE

To quantify the resilience of a network or its degradation in the presence of node and link failures, we need measures, several of which are presented in this section. We start with generic, graph-theoretical measures, and then list several measures specific to fault tolerance.

4.1.1 GRAPH THEORETICAL MEASURES

Representing the network as a graph, with processors and switchboxes as nodes, and links as edges, we can apply resilience measures used in graph theory. Two such measures are:

- **Node and link connectivity**: Perhaps the simplest consideration with respect to any network in the presence of faults is whether the network as a whole is still connected in spite of the failures, or whether some nodes are cut off and cannot communicate with the rest. The node (link) *connectivity* of a graph is defined as the minimum number of nodes (links) that must be removed from the graph to disconnect it: when a node is removed, all links incident on it are removed as well. Clearly, the greater the connectivity, the more resilient the network is to faults.
- **Diameter stability**: The *distance* between a source and a destination node in a network is defined as the smallest number of links that must be traversed to forward a message from the source to the destination. The *diameter* of a network is the longest distance between any two nodes. Even if the network has multiple paths for every source-destination pair, we must expect the distance between nodes to increase as links or nodes fail. *Diameter stability* focuses on how rapidly the diameter increases as nodes fail in the network (note that the term *nodes* refers not only to processors, but to switchboxes as well). A deterministic instance of such a measure is the *persistence*, which is the smallest number of nodes that must fail for the diameter to increase. For example, the persistence of a cycle graph is 1: the failure of just one node causes a cycle of n nodes to become a path of $n-1$ nodes, and the diameter jumps from $\lfloor n/2 \rfloor$ to $n-2$. A probabilistic measure of diameter stability is the vector

$$\mathbf{DS} = (p_{d+1}, p_{d+2}, \cdots),$$

where p_{d+i} is the probability that the diameter of the network increases from d to $d+i$ as a result of faults that occur according to some given probability distribution. In these terms, p_∞ is the probability of the diameter becoming infinite, namely, the graph being disconnected.

4.1.2 COMPUTER NETWORKS MEASURES

The following measures express the degradation of the dependability and performance of a computer network in the presence of faults better than the rather generic measures listed above:

- **Reliability**: We define $R(t)$, the network *reliability* at time t, as the probability that all the nodes are operational and can communicate with each other over the entire time interval $[0, t]$. If no redundancy exists in the network, $R(t)$ is the probability of no faults occurring up to time t. If the network has spare resources in the form of redundant nodes and/or multiple paths between source-destination pairs, the fact that the network is operational at time t means that any failed processing node has been successfully replaced by a spare, and even if some links failed, every source-destination pair can still communicate over at least one fault-free path.

If a specific source-destination pair is of special interest, we define the *path reliability*—sometimes called *terminal reliability*—as the probability that an operational path has existed for this source-destination pair during the entire interval $[0, t]$.

An important point to emphasize here is that the reliability (and for that matter, also the graph-theoretical measures listed above) does not include the option of repairing the network (other than switching in a spare), although the management of most actual networks involves the repair or replacement of any faulty component. The reason for that omission is that the reliability measure is intended to give an assessment of the resilience of the network, possibly compared to other similar networks. Also, in many cases, repair is not always possible or immediate and may be very expensive. If repair is an integral component of the system's management, *availability* (as defined in Chapter 2) can be used instead of reliability.

- **Bandwidth**: The meaning of *bandwidth* depends on its context. For a communications engineer, the bandwidth of a channel often stands for the range of frequencies that it can carry. The term can also mean the maximum rate at which messages can flow in a network (they are obviously related). For example, a particular link could be specified as being able to carry up to 10 Mbits per second. One can also use the term in a probabilistic sense: for a certain pattern of accesses to a file system, we can use the bandwidth to mean the average number of bytes per second that can be accessed by this system.

  The maximum rate at which messages can flow in a network (the theoretical upper bound of the bandwidth) usually degrades as nodes or links fail in a network. In assessing a network, we are often interested in how this expected maximum rate depends on the failure and repair rates.

- **Connectability**: The node and link connectivity, as defined above, are rather simplistic measures of network vulnerability and say nothing about how the network degenerates before it becomes completely disconnected. A more informative measure is *connectability*: the connectability at time t, denoted by $Q(t)$, is defined as the expected number at time t of source-destination pairs, which are still connected in the presence of a failure process. This measure is especially applicable to a shared memory multiprocessor, where $Q(t)$ denotes the expected number of processor-memory pairs that are still communicating at time t.

4.2 COMMON NETWORK TOPOLOGIES AND THEIR RESILIENCE

We present in this section examples of two types of networks. The first type connects a set of input nodes (e.g., processors) to a set of output nodes (e.g., memories) through a network composed only of switchboxes and links. As examples for this type, we use the multistage and crossbar networks with bandwidth and connectability as measures for their resilience. The second type is a network of computing nodes that are interconnected through links. No separate switchboxes exist in these networks; instead, the nodes serve as switches as well as processors, and are capable of forwarding messages that pass through them on the way to their final destination. The networks we use as examples for this type are mesh, hypercube and loop networks and the applicable measures for them are the reliability/path reliability, or the availability, if repair is considered.

4.2.1 MULTISTAGE AND EXTRA-STAGE NETWORKS

Multistage networks are commonly used to connect a set of input nodes to a set of output nodes through either unidirectional or bidirectional links. These networks are typically built out of 2×2 switchboxes. These are switches that have two inputs and two outputs each, and can be in any of the following four settings (see Fig. 4.1):

- Straight: The top input line is connected to the top output, and the bottom input line to the bottom output.
- Cross: The top input line is connected to the bottom output, and the bottom input line to the top output.
- Upper broadcast: The top input line is connected to both output lines.
- Lower broadcast: The bottom input line is connected to both output lines.

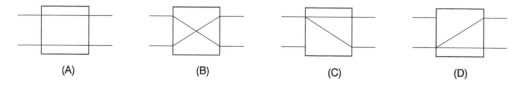

(A)   (B)   (C)   (D)

FIGURE 4.1

2×2 switchbox settings. (A) Straight. (B) Cross. (C) Upper broadcast. (D) Lower broadcast.

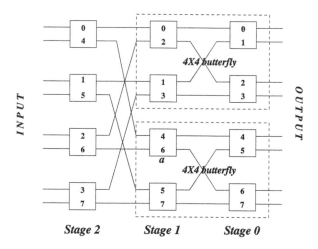

FIGURE 4.2

An 8×8 butterfly network.

A well-known multistage network is the *butterfly*. As an example, see the three-stage butterfly connecting eight inputs to eight outputs shown in Fig. 4.2. We have numbered each line in every switchbox such that a switchbox in stage i has lines numbered 2^i apart. Output line j of every stage goes into input line j of the following stage, for $j = 0, \cdots, 2^k - 1$. Such a numbering scheme is probably the easiest way to remember the butterfly structure.

A $2^k \times 2^k$ butterfly network connects 2^k inputs to 2^k outputs and is made up of k stages of 2^{k-1} switchboxes each. The connections follow a recursive pattern from the input end to the output. For example, the 8×8 butterfly network shown in Fig. 4.2 is constructed out of two 4×4 butterfly networks, plus an input stage consisting of four switchboxes. In general, the input stage of a k-stage butterfly ($k \geq 3$) has the top output line of each switchbox connected to the input lines of one $2^{k-1} \times 2^{k-1}$ butterfly, and the bottom output line of each switchbox connected to the input lines of another $2^{k-1} \times 2^{k-1}$ butterfly. The input stage of a two-stage butterfly (see the 4×4 butterfly in Fig. 4.2) has the top output line of each of its two switchboxes connected to one 2×2 switchbox, and the bottom output line to the second 2×2 switchbox.

An examination of the butterfly quickly reveals that the butterfly is not fault-tolerant: there is only one path from any given input to any specific output. In particular, if a switchbox in stage i were to fail, there would be 2^{k-i} inputs, which could no longer connect to any of 2^{i+1} outputs. The node and link connectivities are therefore each equal to 1. For example, if the switchbox in Stage 1 that is labeled a in Fig. 4.2 fails, the $2^{3-1} = 4$ inputs 0, 2, 4, and 6 will become disconnected from the $2^{1+1} = 4$ outputs 4, 5, 6, and 7.

One way to render the network fault-tolerant is to introduce an extra stage, by duplicating stage 0 at the input. In addition, bypass multiplexers are provided to route around switchboxes in the input and output stages. If a switchbox in these stages is faulty, such a multiplexer can be used to route around the failure. An 8×8 extra-stage butterfly is shown in Fig. 4.3. This network can remain connected, despite the failure of up to one switchbox anywhere in the system. Suppose, for example, that the stage-0 switchbox carrying lines 2, 3 fails. Then, whatever switching it would have done can be duplicated by the extra stage, whereas the failed box is bypassed by the multiplexer. Or, suppose that the switchbox in stage 2 carrying lines 0, 4 fails. Then, the extra stage can be set so that input line 0 is switched to

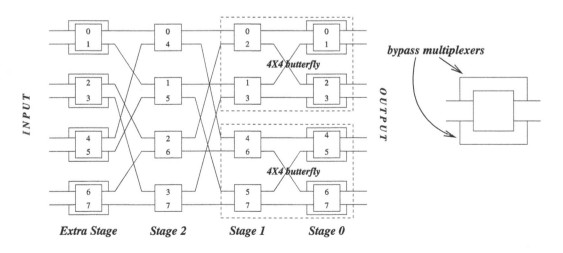

FIGURE 4.3

An 8×8 extra-stage butterfly network.

output line 1, and input line 4 to output line 5, thus bypassing the failed switchbox. Proving formally that this network can tolerate up to one switchbox failure is quite easy; this is left as an exercise for the reader. This proof is based on the fact that, because the line numbers in any stage-i box are 2^i apart, the numbers in any box other than at the output and extra stages are both of the same (even or odd) parity.

The network we have depicted connects a set of input nodes to a set of output nodes. The input and output nodes may be the same nodes, in which case node i provides data at line i of the input side and obtains data from line i of the output side. When the sets are disjoint (e.g., a set of processors is connected to a set of memory modules), we can have two networks, one in each direction. Fig. 4.4 illustrates these configurations.

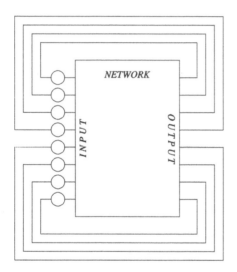
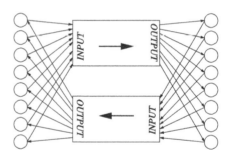

FIGURE 4.4

Two possible configurations for multistage networks.

Analysis of the butterfly network

In what follows we analyze the resilience of a k-stage butterfly interconnection network that connects $N = 2^k$ processors to $N = 2^k$ memory units in a shared-memory architecture.

Let us start by deriving the bandwidth of this network in the absence of failures. The bandwidth in this context is defined as the expected number of access requests from the processors that reach the memory modules. We will assume that every processor generates in each cycle, with probability p_r, a request to a memory module. This request is directed to any of the N memory modules with equal probability, $1/N$. Hence, the probability that a given processor generates a request to a specific memory module i ($i \in \{0, 1, \cdots, N-1\}$) is p_r/N. For simplicity, assume that each processor makes a request that is independent of its previous requests. Even if its previous request was not satisfied, the processor will generate a new, independent request. This is obviously an approximation: in practice, a processor will repeat its request until it is satisfied.

Because of the symmetry of the butterfly network and our assumption that all N processors generate requests to all N memories in a uniform fashion, all N output lines of a stage, say stage i, will carry a memory request with the same probability. Let us denote this probability by $p_r^{(i)}$, $i = 0, 1, \cdots, k-1$. We calculate this probability stage by stage, starting at the inputs (processors), where $i = k-1$ and working our way to the outputs (memories), where $i = 0$.

Starting from $i = k-1$, the memory requests of each processor (at a probability of p_r) will, on the average, be equally divided between the two output lines of the switchbox, to which the processor is connected. That is, the probability that a certain output line of a switchbox at stage $(k-1)$ will carry a request generated by one of the two processors is $p_r/2$. Because a request on that output line can be generated by either of the two processors, $p_r^{(k-1)}$ is the probability of the union of the two corresponding events (each with probability $p_r/2$). Using the basic laws of probability, we can write

$$p_r^{(k-1)} = p_r/2 + p_r/2 - (p_r/2)^2 = p_r - p_r^2/4.$$

Using a similar argument to derive an expression for $p_r^{(i-1)}$ when given $p_r^{(i)}$ yields the following recursive equation:

$$p_r^{(i-1)} = p_r^{(i)} - (p_r^{(i)})^2/4.$$

Here, too, we rely on the statistical independence of the requests carried by the two input lines to a switchbox, since the two routes they traverse are disjoint.

The bandwidth of the network is the expected number of requests that make it to the memory end, which is

$$BW = Np_r^{(0)}. \tag{4.1}$$

This approach can be extended to nonsymmetric access patterns, in which different memory modules are requested with differing probabilities.

We can now extend this analysis to include the possibility of faulty lines. Assume that a faulty line acts as an open circuit. For any link, let q_ℓ be the probability that it is faulty, and $p_\ell = 1 - q_\ell$ the probability that it is fault-free. Note that we have omitted the dependence on time to simplify the notation.

We assume that the failure probability of a switchbox is incorporated into that of its incident links, and thus in what follows we assume that only links can fail. The probability that a request at the input line to a switchbox at stage $(i-1)$ will propagate to one of the corresponding outputs in stage i is $p_\ell \, p_r^{(i)}/2$. The resulting recursive equation is therefore

$$p_r^{(i-1)} = p_\ell \, p_r^{(i)} - (p_\ell \, p_r^{(i)})^2/4.$$

Setting $p_r^{(k)} = p_r$, we now calculate $p_r^{(0)}$ recursively, and substitute it in Eq. (4.1).

Let us now turn to calculating the expected number of connected processor-memory pairs in a k-stage, $2^k \times 2^k$ network, which we call *network connectability*. We are focusing here on the properties of the network, and not on the health of the processors and memories. There are $k + 1$ links and k switchboxes that need to be traversed in a k-stage network. We make here a distinction between switchbox failures and link failure and denote by q_s the probability that a switchbox fails ($p_s = 1 - q_s$).

Because links and switchboxes are assumed to fail independently, and all $k+1$ links and all k switchboxes on the input-output path must be up for a given processor-memory pair to be connected, the probability that this happens is $(1-q_\ell)^{k+1}(1-q_s)^k = p_\ell^{k+1}p_s^k$. Since there are 2^{2k} input-output pairs, the expected number of pairs that are connected is given by

$$Q = 2^{2k}p_\ell^{k+1}p_s^k.$$

The network connectability measure does not provide any indication as to how many *distinct* processors and memories are still accessible. We say that a processor is *accessible* if it is connected to at least one memory; an *accessible* memory is defined similarly. To calculate the number of accessible processors, we obtain the probability that a given processor is able to connect to *any* memory. For this calculation, we again confine ourselves to link failures and assume that switchboxes do not fail. We can calculate this probability recursively, starting at the output stage. Denote by $\phi(i)$ the probability that at least one fault-free path exists from a switchbox in stage i to the output end of the network.

Consider $\phi(0)$. This is the probability that at least one line out of a switchbox at the output stage is functional: this probability is $1 - q_\ell^2$.

Now consider $\phi(i)$, $i > 0$. From any switchbox in stage i, we have links to two switchboxes in stage $(i-1)$. Consider the top outgoing link. A connection to the output end exists through this link if and only if that link is functional *and* the stage $(i-1)$ switchbox that it leads to is connected to the output end. The probability of this is $p_\ell\,\phi(i-1)$. Since the two outgoing links from any switchbox are part of link-disjoint paths to the output end, the probability of a stage i switchbox being disconnected from the output end is $(1 - p_\ell\,\phi(i-1))^2$. Hence, the probability that it is not disconnected is given by

$$\phi(i) = 1 - (1 - p_\ell\,\phi(i-1))^2.$$

The probability that a given processor can connect to the output end is therefore given by $p_\ell\,\phi(k)$. Since there are 2^k processors, the expected number of accessible processors that can connect to at least one memory, denoted by A_c, is thus

$$A_c = 2^k p_\ell\,\phi(k).$$

The butterfly network is symmetric, and so this is also the expression for the expected number of accessible memories.

In this analysis, we have focused on link failures and ignored switchbox failures. As an exercise, we leave to the reader the task of extending the analysis by accounting for the possibility of switchbox failures.

Analysis of the extra-stage network

The analysis of the nonredundant network was simplified by the independence between the two inputs to any switch. The incorporation of redundancy (in the form of additional switchboxes in the extra stage) into the multistage interconnection network in Fig. 4.3, resulting in two (or more) paths connecting any given processor-memory pair, introduces dependency among the links. The analysis is further complicated by the existence of the bypass multiplexers at the input and output stages. We will therefore not present here the derivation of an expression for the bandwidth of the extra-stage network. A pointer to such analysis is provided in the Further Reading section.

The derivation of an expression for the network connectability Q is, however, relatively simple and will be presented next. As in the previous section, Q is expressed as the expected number of connectable processor-memory pairs. We first have to obtain the probability that at least one fault-free path between a given processor-memory pair exists.

Each processor-memory pair in the extra-stage network is connected by two disjoint paths (except for both ends), hence

$$\text{Prob\{At least one path is fault-free\}} = \text{Prob\{First path is fault-free\}}$$
$$+ \text{Prob\{Second path is fault-free\}} - \text{Prob\{Both paths are fault-free\}}. \qquad (4.2)$$

This probability can assume one of the following two expressions (see, for example, the paths connecting processor 0 to memory 0, and the paths connecting processor 0 to memory 1 in Fig. 4.3):

$$A = (1 - q_\ell^2)p_\ell^k(1 - q_\ell^2) + p_\ell^{k+2} - p_\ell^{2k+2}(1 - q_\ell^2)^2;$$
$$B = 2(1 - q_\ell^2)p_\ell^{k+1} - p_\ell^{2k+2}(1 - q_\ell^2)^2,$$

where $(1 - q_\ell^2)$ is the probability that, for a switchbox with a bypass multiplexer, at least one out of the original horizontal link and its corresponding bypass link is operational. Since there are 2^{k+1} pairs, we can now write

$$Q = (A + B)2^{k+1}/2 = (A + B)2^k.$$

4.2.2 CROSSBAR NETWORKS

The structure of a multistage network limits the communication bandwidth between the inputs and outputs. Even if the processors (connected to the network inputs) attempt to access different memories (connected to the network outputs), they sometimes cannot all do so owing to the network's limitations. For example, if processor 0 (in Fig. 4.2) is accessing memory 0, processor 4 is unable to access any of the memories 1, 2, or 3. A crossbar, shown in Fig. 4.5A, offers a higher bandwidth. As can be seen from Fig. 4.5, if there are N inputs and M outputs, there is one switch associated with each of the NM input/output pairings. In particular, the switch in row i and column j is responsible for connecting the network input on row i to the network output on column j: we call this the (i, j) switchbox.

Each switchbox is capable of doing the following:

- Forward a message incoming from its left link to its right link (i.e., propagate it along its row).
- Forward a message incoming from its bottom link to its top link (i.e., propagate it along its column).
- Turn a message incoming from its left link to its top link.

Each link is assumed to be able to carry one message; each switch can process up to two messages at the same time. For example, a switchbox can be forwarding messages from its left to its right link at the same time as it forwards messages from its bottom link to its top link.

The routing strategy is rather obvious. For example, if we want to send a message from input 3 to output 5, we will proceed as follows: The input will first arrive to switchbox $(3, 1)$, which will forward it to $(3, 2)$, and so on, until it reaches switchbox $(3, 5)$. This switchbox will turn the message

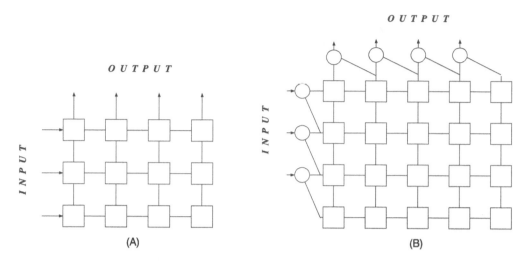

FIGURE 4.5

A 3 × 4 crossbar. (A) Not fault-tolerant. (B) Fault-tolerant.

into column 5 and forward it to box $(2,5)$, which will send it to box $(1,5)$, which will send it to its destination.

It is easy to see that any input-output combination can be realized, as long as there is no collision at the output (no two inputs are competing for access to the same output line.)

The higher bandwidth that results from this is especially desirable when both inputs and outputs are connected to high-speed processors, rather than relatively slow memories. This higher performance comes at a price: as mentioned above, an $N \times M$ crossbar with N inputs and M outputs needs NM switchboxes, whereas an $N \times N$ multistage network (where $N = 2^k$) requires only $\frac{N}{2} \log_2 N$ switchboxes.

It is obvious from Fig. 4.5A that the crossbar is not fault-tolerant: the failure of any switchbox will disconnect certain input-output pairs. Redundancy can be introduced to make the crossbar fault-tolerant: an example is shown in Fig. 4.5B. We add a row and a column of switchboxes and augment the input and output connections so that each input can be sent to either of two rows, and each output can be received on either of two columns. If any switch becomes faulty, the row and column to which it belongs are retired, and the spare row and column are pressed into service.

The connectability of the crossbar (the original structure and the fault-tolerant variation) can be analyzed to identify its dependence on the failure probabilities of the individual components. We demonstrate next the calculation of the connectability Q of the original crossbar, using the same assumptions and notation as for the multistage network. We assume that processors are connected to the inputs and memories to the outputs. As before, assume that q_ℓ is the probability that a link is faulty, $p_\ell = 1 - q_\ell$, and the switchboxes are fault-free. The probability of switchbox failures can be taken into account, if necessary, by suitably adjusting the link failure probabilities. Counting from 1, for input i to be connectable to output j, we have to go through a total of $i + j$ links. The probability that all of them are fault-free is p_ℓ^{i+j}. Hence,

$$Q = \sum_{i=1}^{N} \sum_{j=1}^{M} p_\ell^{i+j} = p_\ell^2 \, \frac{1-p_\ell^N}{1-p_\ell} \, \frac{1-p_\ell^M}{1-p_\ell}. \tag{4.3}$$

Calculating Q for the fault-tolerant crossbar and the bandwidth for both designs is more complicated; it is left as an exercise for the interested reader.

4.2.3 RECTANGULAR MESH AND INTERSTITIAL MESH

The multistage and crossbar networks discussed above are examples of networks constructed out of switchboxes and links and connecting a set of input nodes to a set of output nodes. A two-dimensional N × M rectangular mesh network is a simple example of a network topology, in which all the nodes are computing nodes, and there are no separate switchboxes (see Fig. 4.6). Most of the NM computing nodes (except the boundary nodes) have four incident links. To send a message to a node that is not an immediate neighbor, a path from the source of the message to its destination must be identified, and the message has to be forwarded by all the intermediate nodes along that path. As there is a large number of paths between any two nodes, the two-dimensional rectangular mesh can tolerate any single link failure and quite a few multiple link failures.

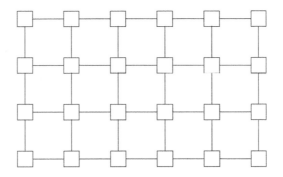

FIGURE 4.6

A 4 × 6 mesh network.

In contrast, the rectangular mesh network is unable to tolerate any faults in any of its nodes without losing the mesh property (that each internal node has four neighbors). We can introduce redundancy into the network and provide some tolerance to failures; one approach is shown in Fig. 4.7. The modified mesh includes spare nodes that can be switched in to take the place of any of their neighbors that have failed. The scheme shown in Fig. 4.7 is called a $(1,4)$ *interstitial redundancy*. In this scheme, each primary node has a single spare node, while each such spare node can serve as a spare for four primary nodes: the redundancy overhead is 25%. The main advantage of the interstitial redundancy is the physical proximity of the spare node to the primary node, which it replaces, reducing in this way the delay penalty resulting from the use of a spare.

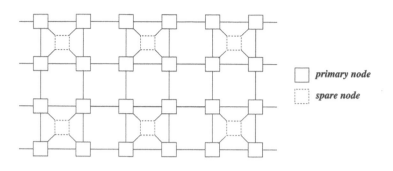

FIGURE 4.7

A mesh network with $(1, 4)$ interstitial redundancy.

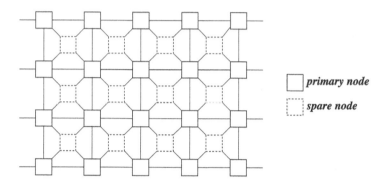

FIGURE 4.8

A mesh network with $(4, 4)$ interstitial redundancy.

Another version of interstitial redundancy is shown in Fig. 4.8. This is an example of a $(4, 4)$ interstitial redundancy, in which each primary node has four spare nodes, and each spare node can serve as a spare for four primary nodes. This scheme provides a higher level of fault tolerance at the cost of a higher redundancy overhead of almost 100%.

Let us now turn to the reliability of meshes. We will focus on the case, in which, as mentioned above, nodes are themselves processors engaging in computation, in addition to being involved in message-passing. In the context of this dual role of processors and switches, reliability no longer means just being able to communicate from one entry point of the network to another; it means instead the ability of the mesh, or a subset of it, to maintain its mesh property.

The algorithms that are executed by mesh-structured computers are often designed so that their communication structure matches that of the mesh. For example, an iterative algorithm designed for mesh structures and used to solve the differential equation (for some function $f(x, y)$)

$$\frac{\partial^2 f(x, y)}{\partial x^2} + \frac{\partial^2 f(x, y)}{\partial y^2} = 0$$

requires that each node iteratively average the values held by its neighbors. Thus if the mesh structure is disrupted, the system will not be able to efficiently carry out such mesh-structured computations. It is from this point of view that the reliability of the mesh is defined as the probability that the mesh property is retained.

The reliability of the $(1,4)$ interstitial scheme can be evaluated as follows: Let $R(t)$ be the reliability of every primary or spare node, and let the mesh be of size $N \times M$ with both N and M even numbers. In such a case, the mesh contains $N \cdot M/4$ clusters of four primary nodes with a single spare node. The reliability of a cluster, assuming that all links are fault-free, is

$$R_{cluster}(t) = R^5(t) + 5R^4(t)(1 - R(t)),$$

and the reliability of the $N \times M$ interstitial mesh is

$$R_{inter\_mesh}(t) = \left(R^5(t) + 5R^4(t)[1 - R(t)] \right)^{NM/4}.$$

This should be compared to the reliability of the original $N \times M$ mesh, which under the same assumptions, is $R_{mesh}(t) = R^{NM}(t)$. The assumption of fault-free links can be justified, for example, in the case where redundancy is added to each link, making the probability of its failure negligible compared to that of a computing node.

Other measures of dependability can be defined for the mesh network (or its variations). For example, suppose that an application that is about to run on the mesh requires an $n \times m$ submesh for its execution, where $n \le N$ and $m \le M$. In this case, the probability of being able to allocate an $n \times m$ fault-free submesh out of the $N \times M$ mesh in the presence of faulty nodes is of interest. Unfortunately, deriving a closed-form expression for this probability is very difficult, because of the need to enumerate all possible positions of a fault-free $n \times m$ submesh within an $N \times M$ mesh with faulty nodes. Such an expression can, however, be developed if the allocation strategy of submeshes is restricted. For example, suppose that only nonoverlapping submeshes within the mesh can be allocated. This strategy limits the number of possible allocations to $k = \left\lfloor \frac{N}{n} \right\rfloor \times \left\lfloor \frac{M}{m} \right\rfloor$ places. This now becomes a 1-of-k system (see Chapter 2), yielding

$$\text{Prob}\{A \text{ fault-free } n \times m \text{ submesh can be allocated}\} = 1 - [1 - R^{nm}(t)]^k,$$

where $R(t)$ is the reliability of a node. If nodes can be repaired, the availability is the more suitable measure. A Markov chain can be constructed to evaluate the availability of a node and, consequently, of a certain size submesh.

4.2.4 HYPERCUBE NETWORK

A hypercube network of n dimensions H_n consists of 2^n nodes and is constructed recursively as follows: A zero-dimension hypercube H_0 consists of just a single node. H_n is constructed by taking two H_{n-1} networks and connecting their corresponding nodes together. The edges that are added to connect corresponding nodes in the two H_{n-1} networks are called *dimension* $(n-1)$ edges. Fig. 4.9 shows some examples of hypercubes.

A node in a dimension n hypercube has n edges incident upon it. Sending a message from one node to another is quite simple if the nodes are named (numbered) in the following way: When the

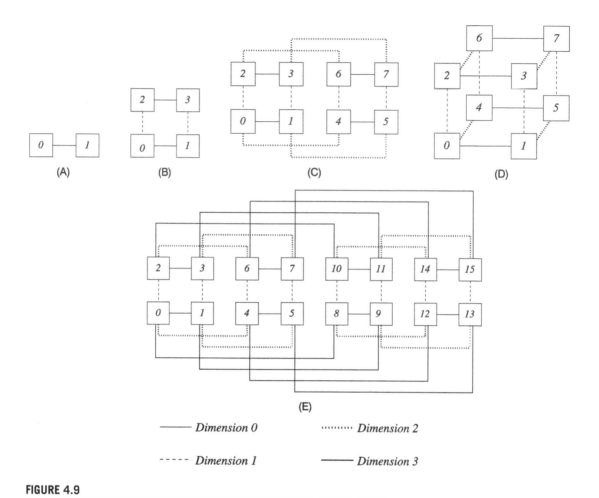

(E)

——— *Dimension 0*   ········· *Dimension 2*

‒ ‒ ‒ ‒ *Dimension 1*   ——— *Dimension 3*

FIGURE 4.9

Hypercubes. (A) H_1, (B) H_2, (C) and (D) H_3, and (E) H_4.

name is expressed in binary and nodes, i and j are connected by a dimension k edge, the names of i and j differ in only the kth bit position. Thus we know that, because nodes 0000 and 0010 differ in only bit position 1 (the least significant bit is in position 0), they must be connected by a dimension 1 edge.

This numbering scheme makes routing straightforward. Suppose a message has to travel from node 14 to node 2 in an H_4 network. Because 14 is 1110 in binary and 2 is 0010, the message will have to traverse one edge each in the dimensions in which the corresponding bit positions differ; in this case, dimensions 2 and 3. Thus if it first travels from node 1110 on a dimension 3 edge, it arrives at node 0110. Leaving this node on a dimension 2 edge, the message arrives at its destination, 0010. Clearly, another alternative is to go first on a dimension 2 edge arriving at 1010, and then on a dimension 3 edge to 0010.

More generally, if X and Y are the node addresses of the source and destination in binary, then the distance between them is the number of bits, in which their addresses differ. Going from X to Y can be accomplished by traveling once along each dimension in which they differ. More precisely, let $X = x_{n-1} \cdots x_0$ and $Y = y_{n-1} \cdots y_0$. Define $z_i = x_i \oplus y_i$, where $\oplus$ is the *XOR* operator. Then, the message must traverse an edge in every dimension i, for which $z_i = 1$. Thus $Z = z_{n-1} \cdots z_0$ is a routing vector that specifies which dimension edges have to be traversed to get to the destination.

H_n (for $n \geq 2$) can clearly tolerate link failures, because there are multiple paths from any source to any destination. However, node failures can disrupt the operation of a hypercube network. Several ways of adding spare nodes to a hypercube have been proposed. One way is to increase the number of communication ports of each node from n to $(n + 1)$, and connect these extra ports through additional links to one or more spare nodes. For example, if two spare nodes are used, each will serve as a spare for 2^{n-1} nodes, which are the nodes in an H_{n-1} subcube. Such spare nodes may require a large number of ports, namely, 2^{n-1}. This number of ports can be reduced by using crossbar switches, the outputs of which will be connected to the corresponding spare node. The number of ports of the spare node can thus be reduced to $n + 1$, which will also be the degree of all other nodes. Fig. 4.10 shows an H_4 hypercube with two spare nodes, and with all 18 nodes having five ports.

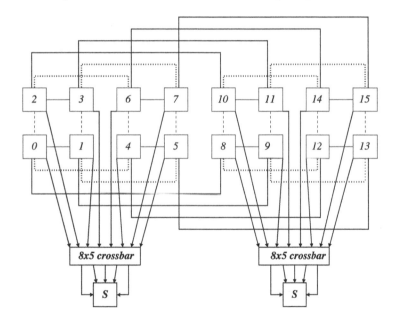

FIGURE 4.10

A hypercube with spare nodes.

Another way of incorporating node redundancy into the hypercube is by duplicating the processor in a few selected nodes. Each of these additional processors can serve as a spare, not only for the processor within the same node, but also for any of the processors in the neighboring nodes. For example, nodes 0, 7, 8, and 15 in H_4 (see Fig. 4.9E) can be modified to duplex nodes, so that every node in the hypercube has a spare at a distance no larger than 1. In this, and in the previous redundancy scheme, the replacement of a faulty processor by a spare processor will result in an additional communication delay that will be experienced by any node communicating with a spare node.

We now show how to calculate the reliability of this network. Assuming that the nodes and links fail independently of one another, the reliability of the H_n hypercube is the product of the reliabilities of the 2^n nodes, and the probability that every node can communicate with every other node, despite possible link failures. Since, for even moderately large n, multiple paths connect every source-destination pair in H_n, an exact evaluation of the latter probability would require a substantial enumeration.

Let us instead show how to obtain a good lower bound on the network reliability. We will start by assuming that the nodes are perfectly reliable: this will allow us to focus on link failures. Once the network reliability is obtained under this assumption, we can then introduce node failures by multiplying by the probability that all the nodes are functional.

As before, denote by q_c and q_ℓ the probability of a failure (before time t) of a node and a link, respectively (recall that t is omitted for expression simplicity). Denote the network reliability of H_n under these conditions by $NR(H_n, q_\ell, q_c)$. Throughout, we assume that the failures of individual components are independent of one another.

Our lower bound calculation will consist of listing three cases, under each of which the network is connected. These cases are mutually exclusive; we will add their probabilities to obtain our lower bound.

Our approach exploits the recursive nature of the hypercube. H_n can be regarded as two copies of H_{n-1}, with corresponding nodes connected by a link. Let us therefore decompose H_n in this way into two H_{n-1} hypercubes, A and B; H_n consists of these two networks, plus dimension $(n-1)$ links (the link dimensions of H_n are numbered 0 to $n-1$). We then consider the three mutually exclusive cases that follow, each of which results in a connected H_n. Keep in mind that we are assuming $q_c = 0$ to begin with. Also, when we say that a particular network is operational, we mean that all its nodes are functional and it is connected.

Case 1: Both A and B are operating, and at least one dimension-$(n-1)$ link is functional:

$$\text{Prob}\{\text{Case 1}\} = [NR(H_{n-1}, q_\ell, 0)]^2 \left(1 - q_\ell^{2^{n-1}}\right).$$

Case 2: One of $\{A, B\}$ is operating, and the other is not. All dimension $(n-1)$ links are functional:

$$\text{Prob}\{\text{Case 2}\} = 2NR(H_{n-1}, q_\ell, 0)[1 - NR(H_{n-1}, q_\ell, 0)] (1 - q_\ell)^{2^{n-1}}.$$

Case 3: One of $\{A, B\}$ is operating, and the other is not. Exactly one dimension $(n-1)$ link is faulty. This link is connected in the nonoperating H_{n-1} to a node that has at least one functional link to another node:

$$\text{Prob}\{\text{Case 3}\} = 2NR(H_{n-1}, q_\ell, 0) [1 - NR(H_{n-1}, q_\ell, 0)] 2^{n-1} q_\ell (1 - q_\ell)^{2^{n-2}}.$$

In the Exercises section, you are asked to show that each of these cases results in a connected H_n, and that the cases are mutually exclusive.

We therefore have

$$NR(H_n, q_\ell, 0) = \text{Prob}\{\text{Case 1}\} + \text{Prob}\{\text{Case 2}\} + \text{Prob}\{\text{Case 3}\}.$$

The base case is a hypercube of dimension 1: it consists of two nodes and one link, yielding

$$NR(H_1, q_\ell, 0) = 1 - q_\ell.$$

We may also start with a hypercube of dimension 2, for which

$$NR(H_2, q_\ell, 0) = (1 - q_\ell)^4 + 3q_\ell(1 - q_\ell)^3.$$

Finally, we consider the case $q_c \neq 0$. From the definition of network reliability, it follows immediately that

$$NR(H_n, q_\ell, q_c) = (1 - q_c)^{2^n} NR(H_n, q_\ell, 0). \tag{4.4}$$

4.2.5 CUBE-CONNECTED CYCLES NETWORKS

The hypercube topology has multiple paths between nodes and a low overall diameter of n for a network of 2^n nodes. However, these are achieved at the price of a high node degree. A node must have n ports, which implies that a new node design is required whenever the size of the network increases. An alternative is the cube-connected cycles (CCC), which keeps the degree of a node fixed at no more than three. A CCC network that corresponds to the H_3 hypercube (see Fig. 4.9D) is shown in Fig. 4.11. Each node of degree three in H_3 is replaced by a cycle consisting of three nodes. In general, each node

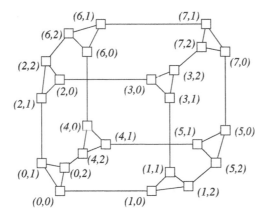

FIGURE 4.11

A CCC(3,3) Cube-connected cycles network.

of degree n in the hypercube H_n is replaced by a cycle containing n nodes, where the degree of every node in the cycle is 3. The resulting CCC(n, n) network has $n2^n$ nodes. In principle, each cycle may include k nodes with $k \geq n$, with the additional $k - n$ nodes having a degree of 2. This will yield a CCC(n, k) network with $k2^n$ nodes. The extra nodes of degree 2 have a very small impact on the properties that are of interest to us, and we will therefore restrict ourselves to the case $k = n$.

By extending the labeling scheme of the hypercube, we can represent each node of the CCC by $(i; j)$, where i (an n-bit binary number) is the label of the node in the hypercube that corresponds to the cycle, and j $(0 \leq j \leq n - 1)$ is the position of the node within the cycle. Two nodes, $(i; j)$ and $(i'; j')$, are linked by an edge in the CCC if and only if either

1. $i = i'$ and $j - j' = \pm 1 \mod n$, or
2. $j = j'$ and i differs from i' in precisely the jth bit.

The former case is a link along the cycle and the latter corresponds to the dimension j edge in the hypercube. For example, nodes 0 and 2 in H_3 (see Fig. 4.9D) are connected through a dimension 1 edge that corresponds to the edge-connecting nodes $(0, 1)$ and $(2, 1)$ in Fig. 4.11.

The lower degree of nodes in the CCC compared to the hypercube results in a bigger diameter. Instead of a diameter of size n for the hypercube, the diameter of the $CCC(n, n)$ is

$$2n + \left\lfloor \frac{n}{2} \right\rfloor - 2 \approx 2.5n.$$

The routing of messages in the CCC is also more complicated than that in hypercubes (discussed in Section 4.3.1). The fault tolerance of the CCC is, however, higher, because the failure of a single node in the CCC will only have an effect similar to that of a single faulty link in the hypercube. A closed form expression for the reliability of the CCC has not yet been derived.

4.2.6 LOOP NETWORKS

The cycle topology (also called loop network) that is replicated in the CCC network can serve as an interconnection network with the desirable properties of a simple routing algorithm, and a small node degree. However, an n-node loop with all its edges unidirectional has a diameter of $n - 1$, which means that a message from one node to the other will, on the average, have to be relayed by $n/2$ intermediate nodes. Moreover, a unidirectional loop network is not fault-tolerant; a single node or link failure will disconnect the network.

To reduce the diameter and improve the fault tolerance of the loop network, extra links can be added. These extra links are called *chords*, and one way of adding these unidirectional chords is shown in Fig. 4.12. Each node in such a chordal network has an additional backward link connecting it to a node at a distance s, called the *skip distance*. Thus node i $(0 \leq i \leq n - 1)$ has a forward link to node $(i + 1) \mod n$ and a backward link to node $(i - s) \mod n$. The degree of every node in this chordal network is 4, for any value of n.

Different topologies can be obtained by varying the value of s, and we can select s so that the diameter of the network is minimized. To this end, we need an expression for the diameter, denoted by D, as a function of the skip distance s. The diameter is the longest distance that a message must traverse from a source node i to a destination node j: it obviously depends on the routing scheme that is being used. Suppose we use a routing scheme that attempts to reduce the length of the path between i and j by using the backward chords (that allow skipping of intermediate nodes), as long as this is advantageous. If we denote by b the number of backward chords that are being used, then the number of nodes skipped is bs. If the maximum value of b, denoted by b', is reached, then the use of an additional backward chord will take us back to the source i (or even further). Thus b' should satisfy $b's + b' \geq n$. To calculate the diameter D, we therefore use b' backward chords, where

$$b' = \left\lfloor \frac{n}{s + 1} \right\rfloor.$$

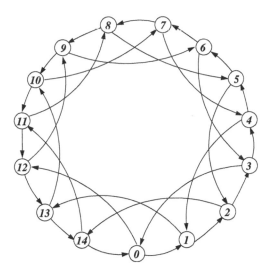

FIGURE 4.12

A 15-node chordal network with a skip distance of 3.

To these b' links, we may need to add a maximum of $s - 1$ forward links, and thus

$$D = \left\lfloor \frac{n}{s+1} \right\rfloor + (s-1). \tag{4.5}$$

We wish now to find a value of s that will yield a minimal D. Depending upon the value of n, there may exist several values of s that minimize D. The value $s = \lfloor \sqrt{n} \rfloor$ is optimal for most values of n, yielding $D_{opt} \approx 2\sqrt{n} - 1$. For example, if $n = 15$, as in Fig. 4.12, the optimal s that minimizes the diameter D is $s = \lfloor \sqrt{15} \rfloor = 3$ (the value that is used in the figure). The corresponding diameter is $D = \lfloor \frac{15}{4} \rfloor + 2 = 5$.

Analyzing the improvement in the reliability/fault tolerance of the loop network as a result of the extra chords is quite complicated. We can instead calculate the number of paths between the two farthest nodes in the network. If this number is maximized, it is likely that the reliability is close to optimal. We focus on the paths that are of the same length and consist of b' backward chords and $(s - 1)$ forward links, but use the backward chords and forward links in a different order. The number of such paths is

$$\binom{b' + s - 1}{s - 1}.$$

If we search for a value of s that will maximize the number of alternative paths of the minimum length between the two farthest nodes, we get $s = \lceil \sqrt{n} \rceil$. However, for most values of n, $s = \lfloor \sqrt{n} \rfloor$ also yields the same number of paths. In summary, we conclude that in most cases, the value of s that minimizes the diameter also maximizes the number of alternative paths, and thus improves the reliability of the network.

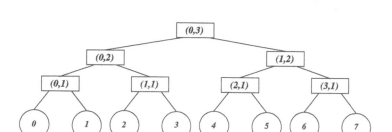

FIGURE 4.13

A simple binary tree connecting eight nodes.

4.2.7 TREE NETWORKS

A binary tree, like the one shown in Fig. 4.13, can allow every computing node to send a message to any other node, if all the links are bidirectional and operational. There is a single path from any node i to another node j. A message from i will be routed upwards to the switch at the common level for i and j, and then downwards to j. Switches are represented as two-tuples: switch (i, j) indicates switch number i at tree level j. (Leaves—which is where the computing nodes are—are at level 0.) For example, node 1 can send a message to node 3 through switches $(0, 1)$, $(0, 2)$, and $(1, 1)$. If node 1 wishes to send a packet to node 4, 5, 6, or 7, the packet must be forwarded to switch $(0, 3)$ before heading downwards to its destination.

Obviously, a simple binary tree with a single path from source to destination has very low communication bandwidth, and is not fault tolerant. A single link or switch failure will disconnect several nodes from the rest of the nodes. Increasing the communication bandwidth and improving the resilience can be achieved by adding communication links between switches and/or adding redundant switches. The various expanded tree networks are called *fat trees*.

Historically, the first proposal for a fat-tree design only doubled the number of parallel links at each level (also known as tier); see Fig. 4.14 for an example. These extra (bidirectional) links allow, for example, the four nodes 0, 1, 2, and 3 to send, in parallel, packets to the nodes 4, 5, 6, and 7. This approach increases the bandwidth, and many link failures can be tolerated, but a single switch failure will still disconnect the network.

There are multiple ways to add redundant switches to improve the resilience and communication bandwidth of the tree network. One such approach generates a k-ary, n-tree that includes n levels of switches with the same number of switches (k^{n-1}) and links at each level. Every switch in the levels $1, 2, \cdots, n-1$ has k upwards links and k downwards links. The switches at level 1 are connected to the processors. A 2-ary, 3-tree is shown in Fig. 4.15. In this multistage network, there are two paths that node 1 can use to send a packet to node 3, however routing in this 2-ary, 3-tree can still experience limited available paths. The message from node 1 can either be routed through switches $(0, 1)$ and $(0, 2)$, or through switches $(0, 1)$ and $(1, 2)$, but once this decision has been made, there is only one path downwards to the final destination. Such restrictions can degrade the bandwidth and fault tolerance. Obviously, increasing n and k will improve the bandwidth and resilience. Another way to extend the capabilities of the fat tree and increase its scalability is by adding extra links and allowing switches with different numbers of ports to be used in different stages of the tree network. Several such

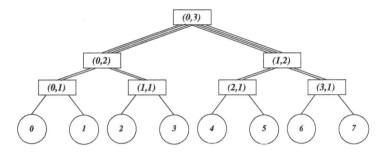

FIGURE 4.14

A fat tree connecting eight nodes.

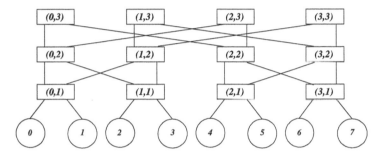

FIGURE 4.15

A 2-ary, 3-tree connecting eight nodes.

extended generalized fat-tree topologies have been proposed; references to them are provided in the Further Reading section.

The particular packet routing algorithm that is selected for a fat-tree network has a significant impact on the latency experienced by the packet, and the probability that it successfully reaches its destination in the presence of faulty links and switches. Two different routing approaches exist, i.e., source and distributed routing. In source routing the source node computes the path to the destination before sending the packet, and inserts the calculated path into the packet header. This scheme is often called deterministic routing. A simple routing strategy routes the packet upwards until it reaches a switch that is at the least common level (LCL) for the source and destination. Then, the packet is routed downwards towards its destination. In a k-ary, n-tree, there are multiple ways to transmit a packet to one of the switches in the corresponding LCL, but then there is only one path to the packet's destination.

In contrast, in distributed routing, the packet header generated by the source node only indicates the destination node, and every intermediate switch calculates the next link that should be used to forward the packet. This approach is also called adaptive routing. Dynamic local rerouting can be incorporated into distributed/adaptive routing to allow rerouting of the packet around faulty network components. This strategy is called dynamic local rerouting, since the rerouting decisions are made by the devices that are connected to the faulty component. Such a routing strategy supports fast recovery from network faults, but the resulting route may be suboptimal due to the local nature of the rerouting decisions.

In the upwards phase of packet transmission towards a switch in the LCL for the source and destination of the packet, tolerating failures is simple, as there are multiple upwards paths in the k-ary, n-tree. By contrast, tolerating failures in the downwards phase is more complicated and requires rerouting the packet on a path longer than the one selected for the fault-free case.

Several fault-tolerant routing algorithms that can route around faulty links and faulty switches and avoid deadlocks, for various generalized fat-tree topologies, have been proposed and pointers to them are provided in the Further Reading section.

4.2.8 AD HOC POINT-TO-POINT NETWORKS

The interconnection networks that we have considered so far have regular structures, and the resulting symmetry greatly simplified the analysis of their resilience. The computing nodes in a distributed computer system are quite often interconnected through a network that has no regular structure. Such interconnection networks, also called *point-to-point networks*, have typically more than a single path between any two nodes, and are therefore inherently fault-tolerant. For this type of network, we would like to be able to calculate the *path reliability*, defined as the probability that there exists an operational path between two specific nodes, given the various link failure probabilities.

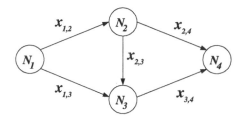

FIGURE 4.16

A four-node network.

Example: Fig. 4.16 shows a network of five directed links connecting four nodes. We are interested in calculating the path reliability for the source-destination pair $N_1 - N_4$. The network includes three paths from N_1 to N_4, namely, $\Pi_1 = \{x_{1,2}, x_{2,4}\}$, $\Pi_2 = \{x_{1,3}, x_{3,4}\}$ and $\Pi_3 = \{x_{1,2}, x_{2,3}, x_{3,4}\}$. Let $p_{i,j}$ denote the probability that link $x_{i,j}$ is operational, and define $q_{i,j} = 1 - p_{i,j}$. Note that here too we omit the dependence on time to simplify the notation. We assume that the nodes are fault-free; if the nodes can fail, we incorporate their probability of failure into the failure probability of the outgoing links. Clearly, for a path from N_1 to N_4 to exist, at least one of Π_1, Π_2, or Π_3 must be operational. We may not, however, simply add the three probabilities Prob$\{\Pi_i$ is operational$\}$, because some events will be counted more than once. The key to calculating the path reliability is to construct a set of *disjoint* (or mutually exclusive) events, and then add up their probabilities. For this example, the disjoint events that allow N_1 to send a message to N_4

are (a) Π_1 is up, (b) Π_2 is up, but Π_1 is down, and (c) Π_3 is up, but both Π_1 and Π_2 are down. The path reliability is thus

$$R_{N_1,N_4} = p_{1,2}p_{2,4} + p_{1,3}p_{3,4}\left[1 - p_{1,2}p_{2,4}\right] + p_{1,2}p_{2,3}p_{3,4}\left[q_{1,3}q_{2,4}\right].$$

For this simple network, it is relatively easy to identify the links that must be faulty, so that the considered paths are down and the events become disjoint. In the general case, however, the identification of such links can be very complicated, and using the inclusion and exclusion probability formula, detailed next, becomes necessary.

Suppose for a given source-destination pair, say N_s and N_d, m paths $\Pi_1, \Pi_2, \cdots \Pi_m$ exist from the source to the destination. Denote by E_i the event in which path Π_i is operational. The expression for the path reliability is

$$R_{N_s,N_d} = \text{Prob}\{E_1 \cup E_2 \cup \cdots \cup E_m\}. \tag{4.6}$$

The events $E_1, ..., E_m$ are not disjoint, but they can be decomposed into a set of disjoint events as follows:

$$E_1 \cup E_2 \cup \cdots \cup E_m = E_1 \cup \left(E_2 \cap \overline{E_1}\right) \cup \left(E_3 \cap \overline{E_1} \cap \overline{E_2}\right) \cup \cdots \cup \left(E_m \cap \overline{E_1} \cap \overline{E_2} \cap \cdots \cap \overline{E_{m-1}}\right), \tag{4.7}$$

where $\overline{E_i}$ denotes the event that path Π_i is faulty. The events on the right-hand side of Eq. (4.7) are disjoint, and their probabilities can therefore be added to yield the path reliability:

$$R_{N_s,N_d} = \text{Prob}\{E_1\} + \text{Prob}\{E_2 \cap \overline{E_1}\} + \cdots + \text{Prob}\{E_m \cap \overline{E_1} \cap \overline{E_2} \cap \cdots \cap \overline{E_{m-1}}\}. \tag{4.8}$$

This expression can be rewritten using conditional probabilities:

$$\begin{aligned} R_{N_s,N_d} = \text{Prob}\{E_1\} &+ \text{Prob}\{E_2\}\text{Prob}\{\overline{E_1}\,|\,E_2\} + \cdots \\ &+ \text{Prob}\{E_m\}\text{Prob}\{\overline{E_1} \cap \overline{E_2} \cap \cdots \cap \overline{E_{m-1}}\,|\,E_m\}. \end{aligned} \tag{4.9}$$

The probabilities $\text{Prob}\{E_i\}$ are easily calculated. The difficulty is in calculating the probabilities $\text{Prob}\{\overline{E_1} \cap \cdots \cap \overline{E_{i-1}}\,|\,E_i\}$. We can rewrite the latter as $\text{Prob}\{\overline{E_{1\,|\,i}} \cap \cdots \cap \overline{E_{i-1\,|\,i}}\}$, where $\overline{E_{j\,|\,i}}$ is the event, in which Π_j is faulty, given that Π_i is operational. To identify the links that must fail so that the event $\overline{E_{j\,|\,i}}$ occurs, we define the conditional set

$$\Pi_{j\,|\,i} = \Pi_j - \Pi_i = \{x_k\,|\,x_k \in \Pi_j \text{ and } x_k \notin \Pi_i\}.$$

We will illustrate the use of these equations through the following example:

Example: The six-node network shown in Fig. 4.17 has nine links, out of which six are unidirectional and three bidirectional. We are interested in calculating the path reliability for the pair $N_1 - N_6$. The list of paths leading from N_1 to N_6 includes the following:

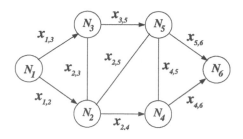

FIGURE 4.17

A six-node network.

$$\Pi_1 = \{x_{1,3}, x_{3,5}, x_{5,6}\};$$
$$\Pi_2 = \{x_{1,2}, x_{2,5}, x_{5,6}\};$$
$$\Pi_3 = \{x_{1,2}, x_{2,4}, x_{4,6}\};$$
$$\Pi_4 = \{x_{1,3}, x_{3,5}, x_{4,5}, x_{4,6}\};$$
$$\Pi_5 = \{x_{1,3}, x_{2,3}, x_{2,4}, x_{4,6}\};$$
$$\Pi_6 = \{x_{1,3}, x_{2,3}, x_{2,5}, x_{5,6}\};$$
$$\Pi_7 = \{x_{1,2}, x_{2,5}, x_{4,5}, x_{4,6}\};$$

$$\Pi_8 = \{x_{1,2}, x_{2,3}, x_{3,5}, x_{5,6}\};$$
$$\Pi_9 = \{x_{1,2}, x_{2,4}, x_{4,5}, x_{5,6}\};$$
$$\Pi_{10} = \{x_{1,3}, x_{2,3}, x_{2,4}, x_{4,5}, x_{5,6}\};$$
$$\Pi_{11} = \{x_{1,3}, x_{2,3}, x_{2,5}, x_{4,5}, x_{4,6}\};$$
$$\Pi_{12} = \{x_{1,3}, x_{3,5}, x_{2,5}, x_{2,4}, x_{4,6}\};$$
$$\Pi_{13} = \{x_{1,2}, x_{2,3}, x_{3,5}, x_{4,5}, x_{4,6}\}.$$

Note that these paths are ordered so that the shortest ones are at the top and the longest ones at the bottom. This simplifies the calculation of the path reliability, as will become apparent next.

The conditional set $\Pi_{1|2}$ is $\Pi_{1|2} = \Pi_1 - \Pi_2 = \{x_{1,3}, x_{3,5}\}$. The set $\{x_{1,3}, x_{3,5}\}$ must fail for Π_1 to be faulty, while Π_2 is working. The second term in Eq. (4.9) corresponding to Π_2 will thus be $p_{1,2}p_{2,5}p_{5,6}(1 - p_{1,3}p_{3,5})$.

For calculating the other terms in Eq. (4.9), the intersection of several conditional sets must be considered. For example, for Π_4, the conditional sets are $\Pi_{1|4} = \{x_{5,6}\}$, $\Pi_{2|4} = \{x_{1,2}, x_{2,5}, x_{5,6}\}$, and $\Pi_{3|4} = \{x_{1,2}, x_{2,4}\}$. Because $\Pi_{2|4}$ will fail when $\Pi_{1|4}$ fails, we can discard $\Pi_{2|4}$ and focus on $\Pi_{1|4}$ and $\Pi_{3|4}$. Both Π_1 and Π_3 must be faulty, while Π_4 is working. The fourth term in Eq. (4.9) corresponding to Π_4 will therefore be $p_{1,3}p_{3,5}p_{4,5}p_{4,6}(1 - p_{5,6})(1 - p_{1,2}p_{2,4})$.

A more complicated situation is encountered when calculating the third term in Eq. (4.9) for Π_3. Here, $\Pi_{1|3} = \{x_{1,3}, x_{3,5}, x_{5,6}\}$, $\Pi_{2|3} = \{x_{2,5}, x_{5,6}\}$, and the two conditional sets are not disjoint. Both Π_1 and Π_2 will be faulty if one of the following disjoint events occur: (1) $x_{5,6}$ is faulty, (2) $x_{5,6}$ is working, and either $x_{1,3}$ is faulty and $x_{2,5}$ is faulty, or $x_{1,3}$ is working, $x_{3,5}$ is faulty, and $x_{2,5}$ is faulty. The resulting expression is $p_{1,2}p_{2,4}p_{4,6}[q_{5,6} + p_{5,6}q_{1,3}q_{2,5} + p_{5,6}p_{1,3}q_{3,5}q_{2,5}]$. The remaining terms in Eq. (4.9) are similarly calculated, and the sum of all thirteen terms yields the required path reliability, R_{N_1, N_6}.

The alert reader would have noticed the similarity between the calculation of the path reliability and the computation of the availability for a given set of read and write quorums in a distributed system with data replication presented in Section 3.3. Here too, we have a number of components (links), each of which can be up or down, and we need to calculate the probability that certain combinations of such components are up. In the last example, we had 9 links, and we can enumerate all 2^9 states and calculate the probability of each state by multiplying nine factors of the form $p_{i,j}$ or $q_{i,j}$. We then add up the probabilities of all the states in which a path from node N_1 to node N_6 exists and obtain the path reliability R_{N_1,N_6}.

4.3 FAULT-TOLERANT ROUTING

We have already encountered fault-tolerant routing in fat trees. In this section, we will see that the same basic principle of exploiting redundant paths can be applied to other structures to render message routing fault-tolerant.

The objective of a fault-tolerant routing strategy is to get a message from source to destination, despite a subset of the network being faulty. The basic idea is simple: if no shortest or most convenient path is available, because of link or node failures, reroute the message through other paths to its destination.

The implementation of fault tolerance depends on the nature of the routing algorithm. In this section, we will focus on *unicast* routing in distributed computing. In a unicast, a message is sent from a source to just one destination. The problem of *multicast*, in which copies of a message are sent to a number of nodes, is an extension of the unicast problem.

Routing algorithms can be either centralized or distributed. Centralized routing involves having a central controller in the network that is aware of the current network state (which links or nodes are up, and which are down; which links are heavily congested) and lays out for each message the path it must take. A variation on this is to have the source act as the controller for that message, and specify its route. In distributed routing, there is no central controller: the message is passed from node to node, and each intermediate node decides which node to send it to next.

The route can be chosen either uniquely or adaptively. In the former approach, just one path can be taken for each source-destination pair. For instance, in a rectangular mesh, the message can move in two dimensions: horizontal and vertical. The rule may be that the message has to move along the horizontal dimension, until it is in the same column as the destination node, whereupon (if it is not already at the destination) it turns and moves vertically to reach the destination. In an adaptive approach, the path can be varied in response to network conditions. For instance, if a particular link is congested, the routing policy may avoid using it if at all possible.

Implementing fault tolerance in centralized routing is not difficult. A centralized router that knows the state of each link can use graph-theoretic algorithms to determine one or more paths that may exist from source to destination. Out of these, some secondary considerations (such as load balancing or number of hops) can be used to select the path to be followed.

In the rest of this section, we present routing approaches for two of the structures we have encountered before: the n-dimensional hypercube and the rectangular mesh.

4.3.1 HYPERCUBE FAULT-TOLERANT ROUTING

Although the hypercube network can tolerate link failures, we still must modify the routing algorithm so that it continues to successfully route messages in injured hypercubes, i.e., hypercubes with some faulty nodes or links. The basic idea is to list the dimensions along which the message must travel, and then traverse them one by one. As edges are traversed, they are crossed off the list. If, because of a link or a node failure, the desired link is not available, then another edge in the list, if any, is chosen for traversal. If no such edges are available (the message arrives at some node to find that all dimensions on its list are down), it backtracks to the previous node and tries again.

Before writing out the algorithm, we introduce some notation. Let TD denote the list of dimensions that the message has already traveled on, in the order in which they have been traversed. TD^R is the list TD reversed. $\oplus_{i=1}^{k}$ denotes the *XOR* operation carried out k times, sequentially. For example, $\oplus_{i=1}^{3} a_1 a_2 a_3$ means $(a_1 \oplus a_2) \oplus a_3$. If D is the destination and S the source, let $d = D \oplus S$, where $\oplus$ is a bitwise *XOR* operation on D and S. In general, $x \oplus y$ is called the relative address of node x with respect to node y. Let $SR(A)$ be the set of relative addresses reachable by traversing each of the dimensions listed in A, in that order. For example, if we travel along dimensions $1, 3, 2$ in a 4-dimensional hypercube, the set of relative addresses reachable by this travel would be: $0010, 1010, 1110$. Denote by e_n^i the n-bit vector consisting of a 1 in the ith bit position and 0 everywhere else, for example, $e_3^1 = 010$.

Messages are assumed to consist of (*a*) d: the list of dimensions that must be traversed from S to D, (*b*) the data being transmitted (the "payload"), and (*c*) TD: the list of dimensions taken so far.

By TRANSMIT(j) we mean "send the message $(d \oplus e^j,$ payload, $TD \odot j)$ along the jth-dimensional link from the present node," where $\odot$ denotes the "append" operation (e.g., $TD \odot x$ means "append x to the list TD").

The algorithm is shown in Fig. 4.18. When node V receives a message, the algorithm checks to see if V is its intended destination. If so, it accepts the message, and the message's journey is over. If V was not the intended final destination, the algorithm checks if the message can be forwarded so that it is one hop (or, equivalently, one dimension) closer to its destination. If this is possible, the message is forwarded along the chosen link. If not, we need to take a detour. To take a detour, we see if there is a link that this message has not yet traversed from V. If so, we send it along such a link (any such link will do: we are trying to move the message to some other node closer to the destination). If the message has traversed every such link, we need to backtrack and send the message back to the node from which V originally received it. If V happens to be the source node itself, then it means that the hypercube is disconnected, and there is no path from the source to the destination.

Example: We are given an H_3 with faulty node 011 (see Fig. 4.19). Suppose node $S = 000$ wants to send a message to $D = 111$. At 000, $d = 111$, so it sends the message out on dimension 0, to node 001. At node 001, $d = 110$ and $TD = (0)$. This node attempts to send it out on its dimension 1 edge. However, because node 011 is down, it cannot do so. Since bit 2 of d is also 1, it checks and finds that the dimension 2 edge to 101 is available. The message is now sent to 101, from which it makes its way to 111. What if both 011 and 101 had been down? We invite the reader to solve this problem.

How can we be confident that this algorithm will, in fact, find a way of getting the message to its destination (so long as a source-to-destination path exists)? The answer is that this algorithm implements a depth-first search strategy for graphs, and such strategies have been shown to be effective in finding a path if one exists.

```
If (d == 0 · · · 0)
    Accept message and Exit algorithm // Final destination has been reached.
else
    for j = 0 to (n − 1) step 1 do {
        if ((dⱼ == 1) && (jth dimension link from this node is nonfaulty)
            && (eₙʲ ∉ SR(TDᴿ)) { // Message gets one step closer to its destination.
            TRANSMIT(j)
            Exit algorithm
        }
    }
end if
// If we are not done at this point, it means there is no way of getting one
// step closer to the destination from this node: we need to take a detour.
if (there is a non-faulty link not in SR(TDᴿ)) // there is a link not yet attempted.
    Let h be one such link
else {
    Define g = max{m : ⊕ᵢ₌₁ᵐ eᵀᴰᴿ⁽ⁱ⁾ == 0 · · · 0}
    if (g==number of elements in SR(TD)) {
        Give up // Network is disconnected and no path exists to destination.
        Exit algorithm
    }
    else
        h = element (g + 1) in TDᴿ // Prepare to backtrack.
    end if
    TRANSMIT(h)
end
```

FIGURE 4.18

Algorithm for routing in hypercubes.

4.3.2 ORIGIN-BASED ROUTING IN THE MESH

The depth-first strategy described above has the advantage of not requiring any advance information about which nodes are faulty: it uses backtracking if it arrives at a dead-end. In this section, we describe a different approach, in which we assume that the faulty regions are known in advance. With this information available, no backtracking is necessary.

The topology we consider is a two-dimensional rectangular $N \times N$ mesh with at most $N - 1$ failures. The procedure can be extended to meshes of dimension three or higher, and to meshes with more than $N - 1$ failures. It is assumed that all faulty regions are square. If they are not, additional nodes are declared to have *pseudo_faults*, and are treated for routing purposes as if they were faulty, so that the regions do become square. Fig. 4.20 provides an example. Each node knows the distance along each direction (east, west, north, and south) to the nearest faulty region in that direction.

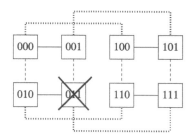

FIGURE 4.19

Routing in an injured hypercube.

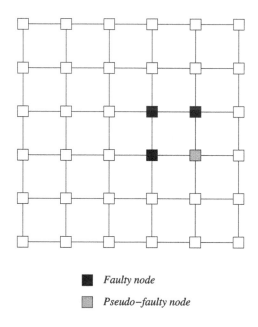

■ *Faulty node*

▨ *Pseudo–faulty node*

FIGURE 4.20

A faulty region in a mesh: Faulty regions must be square for the origin-based routing algorithm.

The idea of origin-based routing is to define one node as the origin. By restricting ourselves to the case in which there are no more than $N - 1$ failures in the mesh, we can ensure that the origin is chosen, so that its row and column do not have any faulty nodes. Suppose we want to send a message from node S to node D. The path from S to D is divided into an IN-path, consisting of edges that take the message closer to the origin, and an OUT-path, which takes the message farther away from the origin, ultimately reaching the destination. Here, distance is measured in terms of the number of hops along the shortest path. In degenerate cases, either the IN or the OUT paths can be empty.

Key to the functioning of the algorithm is the notion of an *outbox* associated with the destination node D. The outbox is the smallest rectangular region that contains within it both the origin and the destination. See Fig. 4.21 for an example.

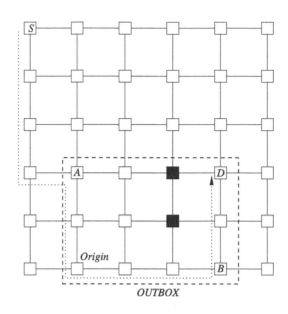

FIGURE 4.21

Example of an outbox.

Next, we need to define *safe nodes*. A node V is safe with respect to destination D and some set of faulty nodes $\mathcal{F}$ if both the following conditions are met:

- Node V is in the outbox for D.
- Given the faulty set $\mathcal{F}$, if neither V nor D is faulty, there exists a fault-free OUT-path from V to D.

Finally, we introduce the notion of a *diagonal band*. Denote by (x_A, y_A) the Cartesian coordinates of node A, then the diagonal band for a destination node D is the set of all nodes V in the outbox for D satisfying the condition that $x_V - y_V = x_D - y_D + e$, where $e \in \{-1, 0, 1\}$.

For example, $(x_D, y_D) = (3, 2)$ in Fig. 4.21, and $x_D - y_D = 3 - 2 = 1$. Thus any node V within the outbox of D such that $x_V - y_V \in \{0, 1, 2\}$ is in its diagonal band.

It is relatively easy to show, by induction, that the nodes of a diagonal band for destination D are safe nodes with respect to D. That is, once we get to a safe node, there exists an OUT-path from that node to D. Each step along an OUT-path increases the distance of the message from the origin: the message cannot therefore travel forever in circles.

The routing algorithm consists of three phases.

Phase 1. The message is routed on an IN path, until it reaches the outbox. At the end of phase 1, suppose the message is in node U.

Phase 2. Compute the distance from U to the nearest safe node in each direction, and compare this to the distance to the nearest faulty region in that direction. If the safe node is closer than the fault, route to the safe node. Otherwise, continue to route on the IN links.

Phase 3. Once the message is at a safe node U, if that node has a safe nonfaulty neighbor V that is closer to the destination, send it to V. Otherwise, U must be on the edge of a faulty region. In such a case, move the message along the edge of the faulty region toward the destination D, and turn toward the diagonal band when it arrives at the corner of the faulty square.

As an example, return to Fig. 4.21 and consider routing a message from node S at the northwest end of the network to D. The message first moves along the IN links, getting ever closer to the origin. It enters the outbox at node A. Since there is a failure directly east of A, it continues on the IN links until it reaches the origin. Then it continues, skirting the edge of the faulty region until it reaches node B. At this point, it recognizes the existence of a safe node immediately to the north and sends the message through this node to the destination.

For the case in which there are more than $N - 1$ failures in the mesh, we refer the reader to the Further Reading section for pointers to the literature.

4.4 NETWORKS ON A CHIP

Recent years have seen the proliferation of chips with a large number of processor cores. To support intrachip communication among the cores, we have networks-on-a-chip (NOCs). Early multicore designs had only a few cores and a simple ring (loop) network was deemed to provide sufficient bandwidth. As the number of cores increased, the loop networks have been commonly replaced by mesh networks. An example of a rectangular mesh is shown in Fig. 4.22. In our discussion, we will assume a rectangular mesh, with each internal node having neighbors at its east, west, north, and south. However, many other topologies are possible. For example, a hexagonal mesh would consist of each internal node having three neighbors that it is directly connected to. Each node of that mesh is a router (generally using a crossbar switch) connected to a processor core or memory module. Fault tolerance must consider protection against failures in each of the following areas:

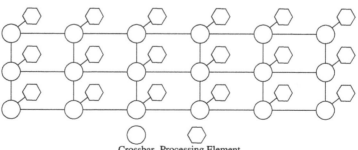

Crossbar Processing Element

FIGURE 4.22

A rectangular mesh.

- Router: The router includes a crossbar switch, buffers, arbitration logic, and links within the router.
- Links connecting one router to another.
- Through-silicon vias (TSVs) connecting one layer with another in the case of a 3-dimensional structure, involving the stacking of multiple layers.

One crosscutting issue is that caused by process variation. The chip manufacturing process is not deterministic, and there are variations between devices in different chips, and even within a single chip. Oxide thickness, gate length, and other parameters all tend to vary from one device to another. As a result, timing faults (caused by excessive signal delays) can arise, which manifest themselves in various ways. For instance, these can cause data corruption, incorrect arbitration of switching resources, misrouting, and loss of message bits. Running at a somewhat lower frequency can resolve timing problems by providing a suitable safety margin.

4.4.1 ROUTER FAULT TOLERANCE

A common routing technique in NOCs is *wormhole routing*, where messages (packets) are broken down into subunits called *flits*. This allows a large packet to be scattered among multiple switches at the same time, thereby reducing the storage requirements in each. (Buffers are a major consumer of power in NOCs.) Rather than a packet flowing switch-by-switch through the network, the flits belonging to a packet follow one another hop-by-hop much as the carriages in a railway train follow the engine. The routing is done at the head flit; the others follow in its wake, with the same switch settings, with the tail flit bringing the train to a close. A virtual circuit is usually set up by means of switch settings, which is constructed as the head flit moves from start to end; the other flits follow along this route. The virtual circuit comes to an end as the tail flit moves through the switches. Multiple virtual circuits may share the same physical circuit; this allows for more efficient resource utilization.

An incoming flit on a virtual circuit is buffered. If this is the header flit, then the control logic determines which output port on the router will be used. Then, a virtual circuit is allocated in the downstream router (i.e., the next hop along the journey). Flits that are not headers use the same virtual circuit as their predecessors, so these two initial steps are done only for headers. Following this, there is competition for access to the crossbar. A flit is only forwarded if there is space in the downstream buffers.

Deadlock is a danger in wormhole routing, and several schemes have been suggested to prevent it. One such set of rules goes as follows for a rectangular 2-dimensional mesh: Number the rows and columns of the mesh. At all times, forbid 180-degree turns (that is, reversing directions). In an even-numbered column, forbid any paths from turning from an eastwards (i.e., traveling towards the east) to either a northwards or southwards direction. In an odd-numbered column, forbid turns into a westwards direction from either a northwards or southwards direction. The above rules are sufficient to prevent deadlocks from occurring. Fig. 4.23 provides an illustration of forbidden turns.

The proof that these rules prevent deadlocks is as follows:

- Assume the result is not true and that these odd-even turn restrictions do not prevent deadlock.
- Then, there must be some set of packets $\pi_1, \pi_2, \cdots, \pi_n$, that are deadlocked. This means that π_2 blocks π_1 from progressing, π_3 blocks π_2, $\cdots$, and finally, π_1 blocks π_n.
- Since 180-degree turns are prohibited, the deadlocked route must consist of horizontal as well as vertical segments.

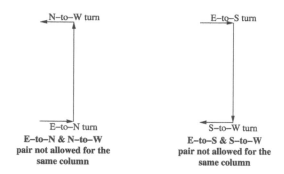

FIGURE 4.23

Odd-even turn rules: Illustration of forbidden turn pairs.

- Since there must be one or more vertical segments on the deadlocked route, pick the one that is furthest to the east (i.e., the right). This vertical segment (column) must be numbered either even or odd.
- The deadlock path along this vertical segment involves moving in either a north-south or south-north direction. Assume, without loss of generality, that it is a south-north direction of packet flow.
- At the bottom node of this segment, packets must be flowing from the west (i.e., from the left); at the top node of the segment, they must flow back towards the west—otherwise, it would not be a rightmost column.
- The above requires that there is a column at which packets are routed both eastwards to northwards (at the bottom of the segment) and northwards to westwards (at the top).
- However, such a routing is forbidden by the odd-even turn rules: you cannot have a column at which both eastward-to-northward and northward-to-westward turns can happen.
- The case of the north-south direction of packet flow along this column is similar.
- Hence, there is a contradiction, and no such column can exist. From this, it follows that deadlock cannot happen under the odd-even turn rules.

Fig. 4.24 shows the main subunits of a router. The inflow to the router are from each of its neighbors: for an interior node in a rectangular mesh, there are four. In addition, there is traffic from its host node. Buffers are provided to store such traffic prior to its being transmitted. The prioritization of traffic on each outgoing link is done by the control logic; this logic determines the crossbar settings (i.e., which inputs are pushed out on which outputs).

Fault tolerance can be applied at various levels of granularity. Connections (links and multiplexers) can be provided that allow the node to connect to additional routers. At the coarsest level, the entire router can be bypassed through these redundant connections: the node that it serves will then be directly connected to a neighboring router, which will add the bypassed router's duties to its own. Obviously, this will result in a potential bottleneck at this router. A variation on this approach is to provide each row and column of the mesh with spare routers, along with connections that allow them to take the place of failed routers. For instance, if we have one spare router per column together with the appropriate additional node-router links, then we can replace up to one failed router per column.

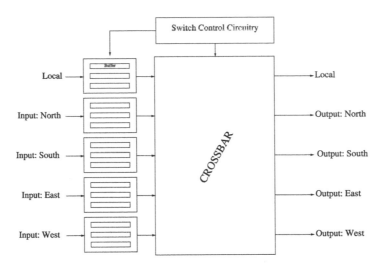

FIGURE 4.24

Router structure.

At a finer level of granularity, several approaches are possible. One approach is to break up the crossbar into two crossbars, one with a responsibility for output in the east-west direction and the other in the north-south direction. Inputs are copied to both these crossbars. If, for example, the north-south crossbar fails, we at least have switching capability to route traffic flowing out in the east-west direction, while the failed crossbar can be bypassed.

At an even finer level of granularity, we can deal with the failure of individual buffers. In Fig. 4.24, buffers are associated permanently with each of the input directions. However, with some additional circuitry, it is possible to connect the buffers in such a way that they can be dynamically assigned. For example, if several buffers associated with the east input have failed and we have heavy traffic incoming from that direction, we may remap buffers associated with the other inputs to take up this load.

Fault tolerance of the arbitration logic can be implemented by traditional redundancy. The logic that calculates the switch settings can be replicated; since this logic occupies only a small fraction of the total area of the switch and is critical to the correct functioning of the switch, the total area overhead of this approach is usually acceptable. The logic that resolves contention for the input and output lines of the crossbar, can be shared. For example, suppose the logic that arbitrates access to the top input line of the crossbar fails. Then, the arbitration circuitry of the bottom input line can take over that function as well. Note that the arbitration process is only needed for the header flit, so this is not a significant added burden. A similar remark applies to the logic that resolves any contention among crossbar inputs for the same crossbar output.

4.4.2 LINKS

Link faults can be either transient or permanent. Transients can be caused by coupling between nearby wires, or by noise; permanents by electromigration or other defects.

Error detection and correction codes of the type discussed in Chapter 3 are used to detect/correct a certain number of errors. Typically, one can detect more bit errors than one can correct; for instance, some codes can correct up to one bit error, and can detect up to two. Bit errors that are detected, but not corrected, by error-control coding are handled by retransmissions. Such retransmissions require that earlier transmissions be retained in memory for some time. For instance, if we do an error check every hop, there is one cycle latency to transmit a message along one hop, one cycle (at a minimum) to do the error checking, and one cycle to notify the sending node of the need to retransmit. Hence, messages must be held for at least three cycles following transmission. An alternative is to only do error checks at the destination node. This does away with the need to carry out checks at each hop; however, errors that are introduced early in the journey will be uncovered very late, meaning that recovery latency will be high. Furthermore, there is a greater chance that errors can accumulate to the point, where they are beyond the ability of the coding scheme to detect. Whether an end-to-end or hop-by-hop check is used depends on trading off the increased latency of error detection and response against the reduced overhead from no checking at intermediate nodes.

Note that when wormhole routing is used, the impact of undetected corruption of the header flit is considerable: it can result in the entire train of flits being misrouted. For this reason, we may choose to use a more resilient error-correcting code for header flits (at the cost of a somewhat increased number of bits and processing cycles).

Links are generally implemented as multiple parallel wires; if multiple wires of a link are affected, then multiplexing is worth considering. For example, if up to half of the wires comprising a link have failed, then the other half can take over the load of the failed wires, at the cost of doubling the time taken. This obviously requires additional circuitry. Whether or not this circuitry is worth the cost in terms of area and power consumption has to be determined at design time.

4.4.3 ROUTING IN THE PRESENCE OF FAILURE

There are many approaches to routing in the presence of failure; we present one here. Every node has a routing table indicating, for each destination, on which link to transmit the message. This routing table is built up recursively. Initially, a node fills up the routing table just for its immediate neighbors. For example, in a rectangular mesh, node (x, y) indicates that it has to use the east output link to go to (functional) node $(x + 1, y)$. Then, the nodes transmit this message to their neighbors. For example, node (x, y) tells its west neighbor $(x - 1, y)$ that it is transmitting to $(x + 1, y)$ using its east output link. This information is then used in the next step to build routes of length 2. For example, node $(x - 1, y)$ uses the information it received from (x, y) to use its east output link to go to $(x + 1, y)$. If a node is faulty, there is no entry for it in the routing table.

Note that such an approach to building up the routing table can easily take into account rules to avoid deadlock (one example being the odd-even rules mentioned earlier). A node will not transmit information to its neighbor if using that information would cause such rules to be broken. For example, if a left turn (say, turning from an eastward to a northward direction) is disallowed at a particular node (x, y), it will not tell its west neighbor $(x - 1, y)$ about accessing node $(x, y + 1)$ through (x, y)'s north output link.

4.5 WIRELESS SENSOR NETWORKS

4.5.1 BASICS

Sensor networks are used to monitor some designated environment. Body-area networks for monitoring patients, networks of particulate sensors for disseminating information about pollution levels, sensors attached to wildlife to study their migration habits, and sensor networks in forests to detect fires, are just some of the many examples.

Sensor networks consist of sensor nodes networked together. Individual sensor nodes are usually very small and light, consisting of one or more sensors, a processor, a radio for communication, and a store of energy (battery or supercapacitor). Some sensor nodes replenish their energy stores from the environment by using, for example, solar cells; this is called energy harvesting. Sensor nodes are highly resource-constrained in memory, processing power, and energy.

Sensor node placement is either deterministic or random. In deterministic placement, nodes are placed at predetermined locations. In random placement, practiced mostly in hard-to-reach locations, nodes might be scattered from a low-flying aircraft.

Sensors may be stationary or mobile. Mobility will obviously be constrained by topography and may be very limited in speed and range. Mobile sensors can be used to replace failed sensors or to act as *data mules*, downloading data dumps from other sensor nodes within a given area, consolidating, and then forwarding them. Providing mobility obviously increases the cost of a sensor node; furthermore, moving sensor nodes costs energy. Energy, as we shall see, is a major constraint in wireless sensor networks.

Once sensor nodes have been put in place, procedures exist for the nodes to form an ad hoc network. Nodes broadcast their existence to other nodes within transmission range and organize themselves into a network. Sensors can determine their location either by fairly accurate means like the global positioning system (GPS), or through less expensive approaches, such as sensing the strength of radio signals sent by other nodes. A sensor node can be assumed to know who its one-hop neighbors are, i.e., the nodes reachable by one hop of a radio transmission.

Sensor networks are often organized hierarchically. Clusters of nodes report their data to a local *cluster head*, which then collates the data and forwards them towards one of the *base stations*. These act as interfaces between the network and its users. In some cases, the cluster head does local processing to calculate some statistics of the raw data, and forwards these to a base station.

Energy is a significant constraint in sensor networks. A node may be powered, for example, by a single AA battery; when this runs out (if there is no energy harvesting), the node is as good as dead. Even if the node can harvest energy from the environment, energy inflow is usually highly variable, and sometimes not very predictable: think of a solar cell and the variation in its energy output over the course of a day.

Energy is consumed in acquiring, processing, and transmitting data. The dominant consumer is usually wireless communication: radio transmission (and reception) normally consumes far more energy than does data processing. For this reason, it is often best to do as much data reduction as possible within the node itself. Due to the cost of keeping the radio on, the radio is usually switched off for much of the time. These "sleeping" periods have to be coordinated, so that the receiving node and the transmitting node have their radios on at the same time.

The power required for reliable transmission depends on the data rate, the range required (i.e., the distance between the transmitter and receiver(s)), the modulation used, the topography, and the variable characteristics of the operating environment. Power is generally a superlinear function of the range required: to double the transmission range, we usually require well over double the transmission power. Radio channels (links) vary in quality by time-of-day and weather conditions. To achieve the same data rate in a degraded channel requires higher transmission power.

4.5.2 SENSOR NETWORK FAILURES

Sensor nodes can fail for a variety of reasons; they are subjected to hazards unknown in most other branches of computing. Sensor nodes scattered outdoors are subject to the vagaries of the weather. They are subject to vandalism if in an accessible populated area. If in the wild, small sensor nodes on the ground might be trodden on—or even eaten—by local wildlife.

In addition to hardware failures, sensor nodes also fail (as noted earlier) when they run out of energy. A sensor node may have such low levels of energy that it can sense, but not transmit data. If its energy level drops further, it may not even be able to keep the processor active. Even if energy harvesting is done, a node may have periods when it has run out of its stored energy and is awaiting favorable environmental conditions, under which it can replenish its energy stores.

Communication demands on a node depend on its tasks, and where it is in the information-relay chain. Usually, sensor networks are spread over a wide area, with outlying sensors far out of direct communication range from any base station. Transmissions from such sensors need to be relayed over multiple hops. Information is funneled towards a base station. Nodes close to a base station have not only to transmit their own data, but also act as relays for nodes farther away. This can lead to their energy being depleted quite quickly, unless this relaying activity can be spread over a large number of nodes, or such nodes are provided with additional energy reserves.

Also, as noted above, wireless channels vary in quality over time. Channel quality may be so bad over some interval of time that nodes are effectively cut off from all base stations. This is especially troublesome because the problem is usually correlated: all nodes within a given geographical area are faced with poor wireless conditions, and the network then becomes blind over that entire area. Furthermore, when detecting node failures, one has to always take into account that it may not be the node that has failed, but the radio channel from that node that is (temporarily) in poor condition.

The accuracy of sensor data can also change with time. A sensor may drift over time so that its output error is unacceptably high. We will describe in Chapter 7 how drift can be handled.

4.5.3 SENSOR NETWORK FAULT TOLERANCE

We will focus in this section on network connectivity. Degradation due to sensor aging and issues of sensor trustworthiness will be treated in Chapter 7.

When a node fails, it has two effects. One is the loss of sensing ability over a certain area that is covered exclusively by the failed node(s). The second is the loss of connectivity that may occur when the failed node can no longer relay messages between other nodes. We focus here on the second effect; the first can be dealt with by placing nodes in such a way that their sensing areas overlap sufficiently to be resilient against a certain number of failures.

Node connectivity (defined in Section 4.1.1) is the measure most often used for sensor networks. If the network turns out to be 1-connected, then there are one or more nodes, whose (single) failure will disconnect the network. The user might then analyze the topology of the disconnected components to see how critical it is to avoid such disconnection.

Table 4.1 Minimum-node-count structures out of set $\mathcal{P}$.

Condition	Best choice	Node connectivity
$1 < r_t/r_s < 3^{0.75}/2$	Hexagon	3
$3^{0.75}/2 \le r_t/r_s \le \sqrt{2}$	Square	4
$\sqrt{2} \le r_t/r_s \le \sqrt{3}$	Rhombus	4
$r_t/r_s > \sqrt{3}$	Triangle	6

There are three issues we will consider here. First, if sensors can be placed at will and fairly accurately, which regular structures should be chosen? Second, given a certain irregular structure, how do we deal with node failures and still maintain a certain amount of connectivity? Third, under conditions of spasmodic network connectivity, what can be done? In our discussion, we will assume that the communication range for each node is fixed and identical.

Regular structures

Let us start with the question of regular structures. There are two key parameters: the sensing range, r_s, of a sensor and its transmission range, r_t. We will make the simplifying assumption here that both are known in advance, are time-invariant, and have the same values for all sensors. This is obviously an approximation: for instance, the nature of the operating environment could well result in the ranges being different from one sensor to another. A sensor surrounded by metal filing cabinets in an office will have a different range as compared to one in an unobstructed corridor. Also, as noted earlier, transmission range can be adjusted by controlling the transmission power.

In all the regular structures considered, we will assume that nodes are placed at the vertices of regular structures with internode spacing adjusted to ensure that no "black holes" exist that are not sensed by any node, and that every node can communicate with each of its nearest neighbors. Our set of regular patterns are meshes composed of structures from the set $\mathcal{P} = \{\text{triangle, square, rhombus, hexagon}\}$.

A key metric is the area covered per node α_{node}. The expressions for the area per node for the four mesh structures are shown below (we omit the proofs):

$$\alpha_{node} = \begin{cases} \frac{3\sqrt{3}}{2}\left(\min\{r_s, \frac{r_t}{\sqrt{3}}\}\right)^2 & \text{for a triangle} \\ (\min\{r_t, 2r_s\cos(\theta/2)\})^2 \sin(\theta) & \text{for a rhombus} \\ 2\left(\min\{r_s, \frac{r_t}{\sqrt{2}}\}\right)^2 & \text{for a square} \\ \frac{3\sqrt{3}}{4}(\min\{r_t, r_s\})^2 & \text{for a hexagon,} \end{cases} \tag{4.10}$$

where θ denotes the acute angle of the rhombus (e.g., as $\theta \to \pi/2$, the rhombus approaches a square; as $\theta \to 0$, it approaches a straight line). Clearly, we wish to select θ to maximize α_{node}.

From this, we can determine which of these structures requires the smallest number of nodes to cover a given area. It turns out that this selection depends on the value of r_t/r_s, i.e., the ratio of transmission range to sensing range. The minimum node structure, for each of these r_t/r_s ratios, is shown in Table 4.1 for the case $r_t > r_s$, along with its node connectivity.

The associated proofs are based on rather involved geometrical arguments and are not provided here; interested readers should consult the Further Reading section. For the triangle-, square-, and hexagon-based meshes, if their middle point (centroid) can be sensed by the node at each vertex, then the entire area can be covered. As mentioned earlier, the node connectivity is a key measure of communication fault-tolerance.

Irregular structures

We turn now to considering irregular structures. These might result from, for example, the sensor placement procedure consisting of being thrown out of a low-flying drone, balloon, or aircraft. Placement is rather random in such cases; often, all we can do is to ensure a certain average number of nodes covering a given area. This average number should be high enough that the desired level of fault-tolerance is met to a sufficiently high probability.

Additional options become available if nodes are mobile. In such a case, nodes that go out of communication, because an intermediate node has failed, might be induced to move closer to one another. Note that this can result in setting off a chain reaction as other nodes, which were unaffected by the original failure are affected by this movement. These nodes will need to move as well, which can trigger another layer of nodes to move, and so on.

Sporadically connected networks

There are some applications, where, during normal execution, the network connectivity varies, and the sensor network is not connected all the time. This can happen for one or more of the following reasons:

- The nodes are mobile and go in and out of transmission range of one another. For example, the nodes could be on vehicles, or attached to migrating animals or birds.
- The network is very sparse and dependent on good radio channel conditions for connectivity. When channel conditions are poor, some nodes are disconnected from the rest of the network.
- Nodes may fail intermittently. This can happen, for example, if nodes depend largely on energy harvesting and have a very small energy store. For example, a node using solar cells may go silent towards the end of the night, or if it has faced too many very cloudy days, one after another.

Under such conditions, the user has to be *delay tolerant*. Nodes store messages until they have an opportunity to connect with certain other nodes, at which point they transmit.

One general approach to such a problem is to have an originating node generate L copies of its message m; when it comes within range of a "suitable" node that does not yet have a copy of m, it sends it to that node. When one of these nodes comes within range of a base station, it transmits m to the base station.

The number of copies L and the selection of nodes, to which a copy should be sent, depend on the mobility model. Node mobilities can vary. In many cases, nodes are restricted to wandering within a certain geographical area; in others, they may not be so constrained.

We will present one typical algorithm, called *binary spray and wait*. This algorithm is tuned for a random walk mobility model. That is, a node may travel up to a certain distance in unit time in any direction; nodes do not have preferred zones, to which they are confined. Buffer and energy limitations are not considered; it is implicitly assumed that no such limitations restrict its execution. Under such conditions, this simple algorithm works surprisingly well.

The binary spray-and-wait algorithm can be stated as follows:

- *Spray phase:* The originating node starts with L copies of the message m. When a node with n > 1 copies (n = 1, 2, ..., L) comes within range of another without any copies of m, it sends it ⌊n/2⌋ copies, keeping the rest for the moment. A node's involvement in this phase ends when it has either sent the message to its intended recipient (in which case, it obviously takes no further part in this algorithm), or it only has one copy left. In the latter case, it then switches to the wait phase with respect to message m.
- *Wait phase:* A node with only one copy of the message waits until it is within range of the intended recipient of m, at which point it transmits it.

Obviously, when we say that a node sends a multiple number of copies of messages, which can be implemented by sending one physical copy, plus the number of copies that it represents, it would waste energy and bandwidth to literally send multiple copies of messages.

4.6 FURTHER READING

A good general introduction to networks can be found in [19,20]; see also [33,51].

Graph-theoretic connectivity is described in textbooks on graph theory. See, for example, [13,26]. An MS thesis [72] provides more information on the use of connectivity in the study of network reliability. The notion of persistence was introduced in [12].

Several variations on the connectivity measure have been proposed. *Conditional connectivity* has been defined in [28] as follows: The node (link) conditional connectivity with respect to any network property P is the smallest number of nodes (links), which must be removed from the network, so that it is disconnected *and* every component that is left has some property P. An example for the property P is: "the component has at most k nodes." A variation on this connectivity measure was presented in [41].

Another measure, called *network resilience*, was introduced in [48]. Network resilience is defined with respect to some given probability threshold p. Let P(i) denote the probability that the network is disconnected exactly after the ith node failure (but not before that), and assume that nodes fail according to some given probability law. Then, the network resilience is the maximum ν such that

$$\sum_{i=1}^{\nu} P(i) \le p.$$

A third measure, called *toughness* was introduced in [17]. Toughness focuses on the number of components a network can be broken down into after a certain number of node failures. A network is said to have toughness t if the failure of any set of k of its nodes results in at most max{1, k/t} components. The greater the toughness, the fewer the components into which the graph splinters. Some related graph-theoretical work has been reported in [9,10]. A recent review of various measures of robustness and resilience of networks appears in [37].

The extra-stage network was described in [1]. The dependability analysis of the multistage and the extra-stage networks appears in [38–40]. Other fault-tolerant multistage networks are described in [2]. The bandwidth of multistage and crossbar networks was analyzed in [53]. The dependability of meshes was investigated extensively: see, for example, [47]. Interstitial redundancy for meshes was introduced in [62]. Several measures for hypercube reliability have been proposed and calculated. For a good summary, see [63]. The cube-connected cycles network was introduced in [57], and a routing algorithm for it was developed in [45], where an expression for the diameter is also presented. Several proposals for modifying this network to increase its reliability exist, e.g., [7,67]. Loop topologies have been studied extensively. The analysis that we present in this chapter is based on [60]. A more recent paper citing many past publications is [54]. Path (or terminal) reliability is studied in [29].

Fault-tolerant routing for hypercubes is presented in [11,15]. Such routing relies on a depth-first strategy: see any standard book on algorithms, e.g., [4,18]. The origin-based scheme for routing in meshes was introduced in [43]. The treatment there is more general, including the case in which there are N or more failures in the mesh.

The fat tree was first introduced in [42]. Many computing clusters, parallel machines, and data centers use some variation of fat trees (e.g., InfiniBand [46]) as their interconnection network. Multiple enhancements to the fat-tree topology have been proposed and various routing algorithms have been developed, see for example, [3,24,35,55,61]. A book focusing on fault-tolerant routing in fat trees was published in 2013 [25].

For a book on networks-on-chip, see [49]. Intel's ring and mesh NOC topologies are described in [31,32]. For accessible surveys on NOC fault-tolerance, consult [59,68]. Fault-tolerant routing is covered in [23] and error checking in [52]. The odd-even turn routing scheme is described in [16]. Through-silicon vias are discussed in [21], and virtual channel management in [50]. Routers are treated in [36,56,58]. We have limited ourselves here to traditional CMOS networks; for a survey of developments in on-chip optical networks see [8] (with some background on the underlying technology in [69]); crossbars based on nanotechnology are covered in [66].

A good survey of managing fault tolerance in sensor networks can be found in [71]. For a discussion of fault-tolerant sensor network protocols, see [34]. Adaptive wireless transmission power control is described in [44]. Data aggregation in sensor networks is covered in [5,65]; for relevant graph algorithms, see [22,27,30]. Coverage and connectivity in regular structures are analyzed in [6]. Some details on maintaining fault tolerance in irregular structures can be found in [14]. Moving nodes around to restore connectivity is treated in [70]. The spray-and-wait algorithm appears in [64].

4.7 EXERCISES

1. The node (link) connectivity of a graph is the minimum number of node-disjoint (link-disjoint) paths between any pair of nodes. Show that the node connectivity of a graph can be no greater than its link connectivity, and that neither the node nor the link connectivity can exceed the minimum node degree of the graph (the degree of a node is the number of edges incident on it). In particular, show that for a graph with ℓ links and n nodes, the minimum node degree can never exceed $\lfloor 2\ell/n \rfloor$.

2. In this problem, we will study the resilience of a number of networks using simulation (If you are unfamiliar with simulation, it may be helpful to skim through the chapter on simulation techniques). Assume that nodes fail with probability q_n and individual links with probability q_ℓ. All failures are independent of one another, and a node failure takes with it all the links that are incident on it. Vary q_n and q_ℓ between 0.01 and 0.25, and find the probability that the network is disconnected. Do this for each of the following networks:

   (a) $n \times n$ rectangular mesh, for $n = 10, 20, 30, 40$.

(b) $n \times n$ interstitial mesh with $(1,4)$ interstitial redundancy, for $n = 10, 20, 30, 40$.

(c) n-dimensional hypercube, for $n = 3, 4, 6, 8, 10, 12$.

3. For the networks listed above, find the diameter stability vector **DS**.

4. Consider an 8×8 butterfly network. Suppose that each processor generates a new request every cycle. This request is independent of whether or not its previous request was satisfied, and is directed to memory module 0 with probability $1/2$, and to memory module i with probability $1/14$, for $i \in \{1, 2, \cdots, 7\}$. Obtain the bandwidth of this network.

5. We showed how to obtain the probability, for a multistage network, that a given processor is unable to connect to *any* memory. In our analysis, only link failures were considered. Extend the analysis to include switchbox failures that occur with probability q_s. Assume that link and switchbox failures are all mutually independent of one another.

6. In a 4×4 multistage butterfly network, p_ℓ is the probability that a link is fault-free. Write expressions for the bandwidth BW, connectability Q, and the expected number of accessible processors. Assume that a processor generates memory requests with probability p_r. Also assume that switchboxes do not fail.

7. Prove that the extra-stage butterfly network can tolerate the failure of up to one switchbox and still retain connectivity from any input to any output. Assume that if the failed switchbox is either in the extra or the output stages, its bypass multiplexer is still functional.

8. Compare the reliability of an $N \times M$ interstitial mesh (with M and N both even numbers) to that of a regular $N \times M$ mesh, given that each node has a reliability $R(t)$ and links are fault-free. For what values of $R(t)$ will the interstitial mesh have a higher reliability?

9. Derive an approximate expression for the reliability of a square $(4, 4)$ interstitial redundancy array with 16 primary nodes and 9 spares. Denote the reliability of a node by R and assume that the links are fault-free.

10. A 3×3 crossbar has been augmented by adding a row and a column, and input demultiplexers and output multiplexers. Assume that a switchbox can fail with probability q_s and when it fails all the incident links are disconnected. Also assume that all links are fault-free, but multiplexers and demultiplexers can fail with probability q_m. Write expressions for the reliability of the original 3×3 crossbar and for the fault-tolerant crossbar. (For the purposes of this question, the reliability of the fault-tolerant crossbar is the probability that there is a functioning 3×3 crossbar embedded within the 4×4 system). Will the fault-tolerant crossbar always have a higher reliability than the original 3×3 crossbar?

11. Show that the three cases enumerated in connection with the derivation of the hypercube network reliability (Section 4.2.4) are mutually exclusive. Furthermore, show that H_n is connected under each of these cases. Assume that $q_c = 0$, i.e., that the nodes do not fail.

12. Obtain by simulation the network reliability of H_n for $n = 5, 6, 7$. Assume that $q_c = 0$. Compare this result in each instance with the lower bound that we derived.

13. The links in an H_3 hypercube are directed from the node with the lower index to the node with the higher index. Calculate the path reliability for the source node 0 and the destination node 7. Denote by $p_{i,j}$ the probability that the link from node i to node j is operational; assume that all nodes are fault-free.

14. All the links in a given 3×3 torus network are directed as shown in the diagram below. Calculate the terminal reliability for the source node 1 and the destination node 0. Denote by $p_{i,j}$ the proba-

bility that the link from node i to node j is operational and assume that all nodes are fault-free.

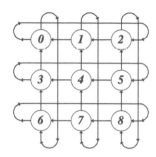

15. Generate random graphs in the following way: Start with n nodes; the probability that there is a (bidirectional) link connecting nodes i and j is p_e. Vary p_e between 0.2 and 0.8 in steps of 0.1, and answer the following for each value of p_e:
    (a) What fraction of these networks are connected?
    (b) Within the subset of connected networks, if links can fail with probability q_ℓ and nodes never fail, what is the diameter stability vector **DS** of the graph? Vary q_ℓ between 0.01 and 0.25.
16. Derive the node connectivity of each of the following meshes: triangular, rectangular, and hexagonal.
17. If, in a sensor network, the neighbors of a node do not hear from it for a specified amount of time τ they can declare it faulty. Briefly describe what factors you would take into account while determining an appropriate value of τ.
18. Provide an example of deadlock in wormhole routing. This is a situation in which there are multiple messages, which so interfere with one another that none of them can make any progress.
19. Consider a rectangular mesh. Suppose node A wishes to send a message to node B, which is d_x, d_y hops away in the x and y directions, respectively. Assuming no turn restrictions, what is the number of node-disjoint (shortest) paths that this message can take?
20. All the links in the given 5-node chordal network are directed (as shown in the diagram) while the 3 chords are bidirectional.

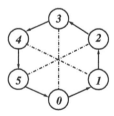

    (a) What is the diameter of the given network? Indicate one source-destination distance that equals the diameter.
    (b) Denote by d_l and d_c the transmission delay of a link and a chord, respectively. Calculate the average source-destination path delay assuming that $d_c = 2d_l$.
    (c) Denote by p_l the probability that a link is operational, and by p_c the probability that a chord is operational, and assume that links and chords fail independently and that all nodes are fault-free. Calculate the path reliability for the source node 0 and the destination node 1.

REFERENCES

[1] G.B. Adams III, H.J. Siegel, The extra stage cube: a fault-tolerant interconnection network for supersystems, IEEE Transactions on Computers 31 (May 1982) 443–454.

[2] G.B. Adams III, D.P. Agrawal, H.J. Siegel, Fault-tolerant multi-stage interconnection networks, IEEE Computer 28 (June 1987) 14–27.

[3] M. Adda, A. Peratikou, Routing and fault tolerance in Z-fat tree, IEEE Transactions on Parallel and Distributed Systems 28 (8) (August 2017) 2373–2386.

[4] A.V. Aho, J.E. Hopcroft, J.D. Ullman, The Design and Analysis of Computer Algorithms, Addison-Wesley, 1974.

[5] B. Ao, Y. Wang, L. Yu, R.R. Brooks, S.S. Iyengar, On precision bound of distributed fault-tolerant sensor fusion algorithms, ACM Computing Surveys 49 (1) (2016) 5.

[6] X. Bai, S. Kumar, D. Xuan, Z. Yun, T.-H. Lai, Deploying wireless sensors to achieve both coverage and connectivity, in: 7th ACM International Symposium on Mobile Ad Hoc Networking and Computing, ACM, 2006, pp. 131–142.

[7] P. Banerjee, The cubical ring connected cycles: a fault tolerant parallel computation network, IEEE Transactions on Computers 37 (May 1988) 632–636.

[8] J. Bashir, E. Peter, S.R. Sarangi, A survey of on-chip optical interconnects, ACM Computing Surveys 51 (6) (2019) 115.

[9] D. Bauer, E. Schmeichel, H.J. Veldman, Progress on tough graphs – another four years, in: Y. Alavi, A.J. Schwenk (Eds.), Graph Theory, Combinatorics, and Applications – Seventh Quadrennial International Conference on the Theory and Application of Graphs, 1995, pp. 19–34.

[10] D. Bauer, H.J. Broersma, E. Schmeichel, More Progress on Tough Graphs – the Y2K Report, Memorandum 1536, Faculty of Mathematical Sciences, University of Twente, 2000.

[11] D.M. Blough, N. Bagherzadeh, Near-optimal message routing and broadcasting in faulty hypercubes, International Journal of Parallel Programming 19 (October 1990) 405–423.

[12] F.T. Boesch, F. Harary, J.A. Kabell, Graphs as models of communication network vulnerability, Networks 11 (1981) 57–63.

[13] B. Bollobas, Modern Graph Theory, Springer-Verlag, 1998.

[14] J.L. Bredin, E.D. Demaine, M. Hajiaghayi, D. Rus, Deploying sensor networks with guaranteed capacity and fault tolerance, in: 6th ACM International Symposium on Mobile Ad Hoc Networking and Computing, ACM, 2005, pp. 309–319.

[15] M.-S. Chen, K.G. Shin, Depth-first search approach for fault-tolerant routing in hypercube multicomputers, IEEE Transactions on Parallel and Distributed Systems 1 (April 1990) 152–159.

[16] G.M. Chiu, The odd-even turn model for adaptive routing, IEEE Transactions on Parallel and Distributed Computing 11 (7) (2000) 729–738.

[17] V. Chvatal, Tough graphs and Hamiltonian circuits, Discrete Mathematics 2 (1973) 215–228.

[18] T.H. Cormen, C.E. Leiserson, R.L. Rivest, C. Stein, Introduction to Algorithms, MIT Press, 2001.

[19] W.J. Dally, B. Towles, Principles and Practices of Interconnection Networks, Morgan-Kaufman, 2004.

[20] J. Duato, S. Yalamanchili, L. Ni, Interconnection Networks: An Engineering Approach, Morgan-Kaufman, 2003.

[21] A. Eghbal, P.M. Yaghini, N. Bagherzadeh, M. Khayambashi, Analytical fault tolerance assessment and metrics for TSV-based 3d network-on-chip, IEEE Transactions on Computers 64 (12) (2015) 3591–3604.

[22] S. Even, Graph Algorithms, Cambridge University Press, 2011.

[23] D. Fick, A. DeOrio, G. Chen, V. Bertacco, D. Sylvester, D. Blaauw, A highly resilient routing algorithm for fault-tolerant NOCs, in: Conference on Design, Automation and Test in Europe, 2009, pp. 21–26.

[24] C. Gomez, M.E. Gomez, P. Lopez, J. Duato, An efficient fault-tolerant routing methodology for fat-tree interconnection networks, in: Parallel and Distributed Processing and Applications, ISPA 2007, in: LNCS, vol. 4742, Springer-Verlag, 2007, pp. 509–522.

[25] C. Gomez Requena, M.E. Gomez Requena, P. Lopez Rodriguez, Exploiting the Fat-Tree Topology for Routing and Fault-Tolerance, Scholar's Press, 2013.

[26] J.L. Gross, J. Yellen (Eds.), Handbook of Graph Theory, CRC Press, 2003.

[27] X. Han, P. Kelsen, V. Ramachandran, R. Tarjan, Computing minimal spanning subgraphs in linear time, SIAM Journal on Computing 24 (6) (1995) 1332–1358.

[28] F. Harary, Conditional connectivity, Networks 13 (1983) 346–357.

[29] S. Hariri, C.S. Raghavendra, SYREL: a symbolic reliability algorithm based on path and cutset methods, IEEE Transactions on Computers C-36 (October 1987) 1224–1232.

[30] M.R. Henzinger, S. Rao, H.N. Gabow, Computing vertex connectivity: new bounds from old techniques, Journal of Algorithms 34 (2) (2000) 222–250.

[31] Intel-64 and IA-32 architectures optimization reference manual, June 2016, available at https://www.intel.com/content/dam/www/public/us/en/documents/manuals/64-ia-32-architectures-optimization-manual.pdf.

[32] Intel Xeon processor scalable family technical overview, July 2017, available at https://software.intel.com/en-us/articles/intel-xeon-processor-scalable-family-technical-overview.

[33] P. Jalote, Fault Tolerance in Distributed Systems, Prentice-Hall, 1994.

[34] M.A. Kafi, J.B. Othman, N. Badache, A survey on reliability protocols in wireless sensor networks, ACM Computing Surveys 50 (2) (2017) 31.

[35] H. Kariniemi, J. Nurmi, Performance evaluation and implementation of two adaptive routing algorithms for XGFT networks, Computing and Informatics 23 (5–6) (2004) 415–435.

[36] J. Kim, C. Nicopoulos, D. Park, V. Narayanan, M.S. Yousif, C.R. Das, A gracefully degrading and energy-efficient modular router architecture for on-chip networks, ACM SIGARCH Computer Architecture News 34 (2) (2006) 4–15.

[37] G.W. Klau, R. Weiskircher, Robustness and resilience, in: U. Brandes, T. Erlebach (Eds.), Network Analysis: Methodological Foundations, in: Lecture Notes in Computer Science, vol. 3418, Springer-Verlag, 2005, pp. 417–437.

[38] I. Koren, Z. Koren, On the bandwidth of a multistage network in the presence of faulty components, in: Eighth International Conference on Distributed Computing Systems, June 1988, pp. 26–32.

[39] I. Koren, Z. Koren, On gracefully degrading multiprocessors with multistage interconnection networks, IEEE Transactions on Reliability 38 (Special Issue on "Reliability of Parallel and Distributed Computing Networks") (April 1989) 82–89.

[40] V.P. Kumar, A.L. Reibman, Failure dependent performance analysis of a fault-tolerant multistage interconnection network, IEEE Transactions on Computers 38 (December 1989) 1703–1713.

[41] S. Latifi, M. Hegde, M. Naraghi-Pour, Conditional connectivity measures for large multicomputer systems, IEEE Transactions on Computers 43 (February 1994) 218–222.

[42] C.E. Leiserson, Fat-trees: universal networks for hardware-efficient supercomputing, IEEE Transactions on Computers 34 (10) (October 1985) 892–901.

[43] R. Libeskind-Hadas, E. Brandt, Origin-based fault-tolerant routing in the mesh, in: IEEE Symposium on High Performance Computer Architecture, 1995, pp. 102–111.

[44] S. Lin, F. Miao, J. Zhang, G. Zhou, L. Gu, T. He, J.A. Stankovic, S. Son, G.J. Pappas, ATPC: adaptive transmission power control for wireless sensor networks, ACM Transactions on Sensor Networks 12 (1) (2016) 6.

[45] D.S. Meliksetian, C.Y.R. Chen, Optimal routing algorithm and the diameter of the cube-connected cycles, IEEE Transactions on Parallel and Distributed Systems 4 (October 1993) 1172–1178.

[46] Mellanox Technologies, Introduction to InfiniBand, available at https://www.mellanox.com/pdf/whitepapers/IB_Intro_WP_190.pdf.

[47] P. Mohapatra, C.R. Das, On dependability evaluation of mesh-connected processors, IEEE Transactions on Computers 44 (September 1995) 1073–1084.

[48] W. Najjar, J.-L. Gaudiot, Network resilience: a measure of network fault tolerance, IEEE Transactions on Computers 39 (February 1990) 174–181.

[49] C. Nicopoulos, V. Narayanan, C.R. Das, Network-on-Chip Architectures: A Holistic Design Exploration, vol. 45, Springer Science & Business Media, 2009.

[50] M. Oveis-Gharan, G.N. Khan, Efficient dynamic virtual channel organization and architecture for NOC systems, IEEE Transactions on Very Large Scale Integration (VLSI) Systems 24 (2) (2016) 465–478.

[51] K. Padmanabhan, D.H. Lawrie, Performance analysis of redundant-path networks for multiprocessor systems, ACM Transactions on Computer Systems 3 (May 1985) 117–144.

[52] D. Park, C. Nicopoulos, J. Kim, N. Vijaykrishnan, C.R. Das, Exploring fault-tolerant network-on-chip architectures, in: IEEE International Conference on Dependable Systems and Networks (DSN'06), 2006, pp. 93–104.

[53] J.H. Patel, Performance of processor-memory interconnections for multiprocessors, IEEE Transactions on Computers C-30 (October 1981) 771–780.

[54] J.M. Peha, F.A. Tobagi, Analyzing the fault tolerance of double-loop networks, IEEE/ACM Transactions on Networking 2 (August 1994) 363–373.

[55] F. Petrini, M. Vanneschi, K-ary N-trees: high performance networks for massively parallel architectures, in: Proc. 11th International Symposium on Parallel Processing (IPPS 97), 1997, pp. 87–93.

[56] P. Poluri, A. Louri, Shield: a reliable network-on-chip router architecture for chip multiprocessors, IEEE Transactions on Parallel and Distributed Systems 27 (10) (2016) 3058–3070.

[57] F.P. Preparata, J. Vuillemin, The cube-connected cycles: a versatile network for parallel computation, Communications of the ACM 24 (May 1981) 300–309.

[58] T. Putkaradze, S.P. Azad, B. Niazmand, J. Raik, G. Jervan, Fault-resilient NOC router with transparent resource allocation, in: 12th IEEE International Symposium on Reconfigurable Communication-Centric Systems-on-Chip (ReCoSoC), 2017, pp. 1–8.

[59] M. Radetzki, C. Feng, X. Zhao, A. Jantsch, Methods for fault tolerance in networks-on-chip, ACM Computing Surveys 46 (1) (2013) 8.

[60] C.S. Raghavendra, M. Gerla, A. Avizienis, Reliable loop topologies for large local computer networks, IEEE Transactions on Computers C-34 (January 1985) 46–55.

[61] F.O. Sem-Jacobsen, T. Skeie, O. Lysne, J. Duato, Dynamic fault tolerance in fat trees, IEEE Transactions on Computers 60 (4) (April 2011) 508–525.

[62] A.D. Singh, Interstitial redundancy: a new fault-tolerance scheme for large-scale VLSI processor arrays, IEEE Transactions on Computers 37 (November 1988) 1398–1410.

[63] S. Soh, S. Rai, J.L. Trahan, Improved lower bounds on the reliability of hypercube architectures, IEEE Transactions on Parallel and Distributed Systems 5 (April 1994) 364–378.

[64] T. Spyropoulos, K. Psounis, C.S. Raghavendra, Spray and wait: an efficient routing scheme for intermittently connected mobile networks, in: 2005 ACM SIGCOMM Workshop on Delay-Tolerant Networking, ACM, 2005, pp. 252–259.

[65] Y. Sun, H. Luo, S.K. Das, A trust-based framework for fault-tolerant data aggregation in wireless multimedia sensor networks, IEEE Transactions on Dependable and Secure Computing 9 (6) (2012) 785–797.

[66] O. Tunali, M. Altun, A survey of fault-tolerance algorithms for reconfigurable nano-crossbar arrays, ACM Computing Surveys 50 (6) (2017) 79.

[67] N.-F. Tzeng, P. Chuang, A pairwise substitutional fault tolerance technique for the cube-connected cycles architecture, IEEE Transactions on Parallel and Distributed Systems 5 (April 1994) 433–439.

[68] S. Werner, J. Navaridas, M. Lujan, A survey on design approaches to circumvent permanent faults in networks-on-chip, ACM Computing Surveys 48 (4) (2016) 59.

[69] S. Werner, J. Navaridas, M. Lujan, A survey on optical network-on-chip architectures, ACM Computing Surveys 50 (6) (2017) 89.

[70] M. Younis, S. Lee, A.A. Abbasi, A localized algorithm for restoring internode connectivity in networks of moveable sensors, IEEE Transactions on Computers 59 (12) (2010) 1669–1682.

[71] M. Younis, I.F. Senturk, K. Akkaya, S. Lee, F. Senel, Topology management techniques for tolerating node failures in wireless sensor networks: a survey, Computer Networks 58 (2014) 254–283.

[72] G.E. Weichenberg, High Reliability Architectures for Networks Under Stress, MS Thesis, MIT, 2003.

SOFTWARE FAULT TOLERANCE 5

Much has been written about why software is so defect-prone and about why the problem of designing and writing software is so intrinsically difficult. Researchers recognize both the *essential* and *accidental* difficulties of producing correct software. Essential difficulties arise from the inherent challenge of understanding a complex application and operating environment, and from having to construct a structure comprising an extremely large number of states, with very complex state-transition rules. Furthermore, software is subject to frequent modifications, as new features are added to adapt to changing application needs. In addition, as hardware and operating system platforms change with time, the software has to adjust appropriately. Finally, software is often used to paper over incompatibilities between interacting system components.

Accidental difficulties in producing good software arise from the fact that people make mistakes in even relatively simple tasks. Translating the detailed design into correctly working code may not require such advanced skills as creating a correct design in the first place, but is also mistake-prone.

A great deal of work has gone into techniques to reduce the defect rate of modern software. These techniques rely on extensive procedures to test software programs for correctness and completeness. However, testing can never conclusively verify the correctness of an arbitrary program. It is a reasonable assumption that any large piece of software that is currently in use contains defects.

Consequently, after doing everything possible to reduce the error rate of individual programs, we have to turn to fault-tolerance techniques to mitigate the impact of software defects (bugs). These techniques are the subject of this chapter.

5.1 ACCEPTANCE TESTS

As with hardware systems, an important step in any attempt to tolerate faults is to detect them. A common way to detect software defects is through acceptance tests. These are used in wrappers and in recovery blocks, both of which are important software fault-tolerance mechanisms; these will be discussed later.

If your thermometer were to read $-40°C$ on a sweltering midsummer day, you would suspect it was malfunctioning. This is an example of an *acceptance test*. An acceptance test is essentially a check of reasonableness. Most acceptance tests fall into one of the following categories:

Timing checks: One of the simplest checks is timing. If we have a rough idea of how long the code should run, a watchdog timer can be set appropriately. When the timer goes off, the system can assume that a failure has occurred (either a hardware failure or something in the software that caused the node to "hang"). The timing check can be used in parallel with other acceptance tests.

Fault-Tolerant Systems. https://doi.org/10.1016/B978-0-12-818105-8.00015-2

161

Verification of output: In some cases, the acceptance test is suggested naturally from the problem itself. That is, the nature of the problem is such that although the problem itself is difficult to solve, it is much easier to check that the answer is correct, and it is also less likely that the check itself will be incorrect. To take a human analogy, solving a jigsaw puzzle can take a long time; checking to see that the puzzle has been correctly put together is trivial and takes just a glance.

Examples of such problems are calculating the square root (square the result to check if you get the original number back), the factorization of large numbers (multiply the factors together), the solution of equations (substitute the supposed solution into the original equations), and sorting. Note that in sorting, it is not enough merely to check that the numbers are sorted: we have also to verify that all the numbers at the input are included in the output.

Sometimes, to save time, we will restrict ourselves to probabilistic checks. These do not guarantee that all erroneous outputs will be caught even if the checks are executed perfectly, but have the advantage of requiring less time. One example of such a check for the correctness of matrix multiplication is as follows:

Suppose we multiply two $n \times n$ integer matrices A and B to produce C. To check the result without repeating the matrix multiplication, we may select at random an $n \times 1$ vector of integers R, and carry out the operations $M_1 = A \times (B \times R)$ and $M_2 = C \times R$. If $M_1 \neq M_2$, then we know that an error has occurred. If $M_1 = M_2$, that still does not *prove* that the original result C was correct; however, it is very unlikely that the random vector R was selected such that $M_1 = M_2$, even if $A \times B \neq C$. To further reduce this probability, we may select another $n \times 1$ vector and repeat the check.

Range checks: In other cases, we do not have such convenient and obvious approaches to checking the correctness of the output. In such situations, range checks can be used. That is, we use our knowledge of the application to set acceptable bounds for the output: if it falls outside these bounds, it is declared to be erroneous. Such bounds may be either preset, or some simple function of the inputs. If the latter, the function has to be simple enough to implement, so that the probability of the acceptance test software itself being faulty is sufficiently low.

For example, consider a remote-sensing satellite that takes thermal imagery of the earth. We could obviously set bounds on the temperature range and regard any output outside these bounds as indicating an error. Furthermore, we could use spatial correlations, which means looking for excessive differences between the temperatures in adjacent areas, and flagging an error if the differences cannot be explained by physical features (such as volcanoes).

When setting the bounds on acceptance tests, we have to balance two parameters: *sensitivity* and *false alarm rate*. We have encountered these quantities before in Chapter 2: recall that sensitivity is the probability that the acceptance test catches an erroneous output. To be more precise, it is the conditional probability that the test declares an error, given the output is erroneous. The false alarm rate is the conditional probability that the test has declared an error, given that the tested entity is actually good.

An increase in sensitivity can be achieved by narrowing the acceptance range bounds. Unfortunately, this would at the same time increase the false alarm rate. In an absurdly extreme case, we could narrow the acceptance range to zero, so that every output flags an error. In such a case, the sensitivity would be 100%, but then every correct output would also be declared erroneous.

5.2 SINGLE-VERSION FAULT TOLERANCE

In this section, we consider ways by which individual pieces of software can be made more robust. We start by looking at *wrappers*, which are robustness-enhancing interfaces for software modules. Then, we discuss software rejuvenation, and finally, we describe the use of data diversity.

5.2.1 WRAPPERS

As its name implies, a wrapper is a piece of software that encapsulates the given program when it is being executed (see Fig. 5.1). We can wrap almost any level of software: examples include application software, middleware, and even an operating system kernel. Inputs from the outside world to the

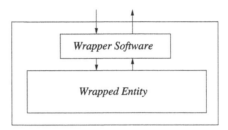

FIGURE 5.1

A wrapper.

wrapped entity are intercepted by the wrapper, which decides whether to pass them on, or to signal an exception to the system. Similarly, outputs from the wrapped software are also filtered by the wrapper.

Wrappers became popular when people started using commercial off-the-shelf (COTS) software components for high-reliability applications. COTS components are written for general-purpose applications, for which errors are an annoyance but not a calamity. Before such components can be used in applications requiring high reliability, they need to be embedded in some environment that reduces their error rate. This environment (the wrapper) has to head off inputs to the software that are either outside the specified range, or are known to cause errors; similarly, the wrapper passes the output through a suitable acceptance test before releasing it. If the output fails the acceptance test, this fact must be conveyed to the system, which then decides on an appropriate course of action.

Wrappers are specific to the wrapped entity and the system. Here are some examples of their use:

Dealing with buffer overflow: The C programming language does not perform range checking for arrays, which can cause either accidental or maliciously intended damage. Writing a large string into a small buffer causes buffer overflow; since no range checking is performed, a region of memory outside the buffer is overwritten. For example, consider the `strcpy()` function in C, which copies strings from one place to another. If one executes the call `strcpy(str1, str2)`, where `str1` is a buffer of size 5, and `str2` is a string of length 25, the resulting buffer overflow would overwrite a region of memory outside the `str1` buffer. Such overflows have been exploited by hackers to cause harm.

A wrapper can check to ensure that such overflows do not happen, for example, by checking that the buffer is large enough for the designated string to be copied. Violating this rule prevents the `strcpy()` function from being called; instead, the wrapper returns an error, or raises an exception.

Checking the correctness of the scheduler: Consider a wrapper around the task scheduler in a fault-tolerant, real-time system. Unlike general-purpose operating systems, such schedulers do not generally use round-robin scheduling. One real-time scheduling algorithm is *earliest deadline first* (EDF), in which, as the term implies, the system executes the task with the earliest absolute deadline among all the tasks that are ready to run. This is subject to constraints on preemptibility, because some tasks may not be preemptible in certain parts of their execution.

Such a scheduler can be wrapped by having the wrapper verify that the scheduling algorithm is being executed correctly, so that the scheduler always selects the ready task with the earliest deadline, and that any arriving task with an earlier deadline preempts the executing task (assuming the latter is preemptible). To do its job, the wrapper obviously needs information about which tasks are ready to run and their deadlines, and about whether the currently executing task is preemptible. To obtain this information, it may be necessary to get the vendor of the scheduler software to provide a suitable interface.

Using software with known bugs: Suppose we are using a software module with known bugs. That is, we have found, either through intensive testing or through field reports, that the software fails for a certain set of inputs, S. Suppose, furthermore, that the software vendor has not (yet) put out a version that corrects these bugs. Then, we can implement a wrapper that intercepts the inputs to that software and checks to see if those inputs are in the set S. If not, it forwards them to the software module for execution; if yes, it returns a suitable exception to the system. Alternatively, the wrapper can redirect the input to some alternative, custom-written, code that handles inputs in S.

Using a wrapper to check for correct output: Such a wrapper includes an acceptance test, through which every output is filtered. If the output passes the test, it is forwarded outside. If not, an exception is raised, and the system has to deal with a suspicious output.

Setting up multiple copies of critical variables A wrapper can be used to protect against transient faults in memory by automatically keeping multiple copies of the most critical variables. Deciding which variables are critical is based on the *spatial* and *temporal* impact of corrupted variable values. A measure of the spatial impact is the number of software modules that are ultimately affected by an error in a variable. That of the temporal impact is the duration of time for which the error persists (before being overwritten). Both impacts can be measured by a fault injection process (see the fault injection description in Section 9.6), or by a detailed analysis of the code. Coupled with the probability that a faulty value in a given variable propagates through to cause an incorrect output, we can define a suitable relative measure of the criticality of each variable value. Then, the designer can pick thresholds for triple- and double-redundancy of such variables. For example, the most critical 7% of the variables might be triple-redundant (meaning the wrapper automatically stores three copies of that variable whenever it is written), whereas the next most critical 10% of them might be dual-redundant. Experiments have shown such an approach to be quite effective in reducing failure rates (see the Further Reading section for a reference).

Facilitating retry under altered circumstances When a failure is detected, sometimes the success rate of a retry can be enhanced by altering some aspects of the execution. For example, memory deallocation (e.g., using a free() instruction in C) might be delayed, more memory may be allocated to buffers, allocated memory may be initialized to zero, message order may be reshuffled (so long as they relate to uncorrelated connections), and process scheduling can be altered. Wrappers can intercept calls to do such things and adjust them appropriately.

The idea behind this approach is the following: During normal testing prior to release, the software has already been made quite reliable; failure is therefore usually the outcome of some unfortunate combination of circumstances, which were not tested for during software development. By changing these circumstances, we make it much less likely that the same problem will recur.

Our ability to successfully wrap a piece of software depends on several factors:

- *Quality of the acceptance tests:* This is application-dependent and has a direct impact on the ability of the wrapper to stop erroneous outputs, where this is its function.
- *Availability of necessary information from the wrapped component:* Often, the wrapped component is a "black box," and all we can observe about its behavior is the output produced in response to a given input; in such cases, the wrapper will be somewhat limited. For example, our scheduler wrapper would be impossible to implement without information about the deadlines of the tasks waiting to run. Ideally, we would like complete access to the source code; where this is impossible for commercial or other reasons, we would like to have the vendors themselves provide well-defined interfaces, by which the wrapper can obtain relevant information from the wrapped software.
- *Extent to which the wrapped software module has been tested:* Extensively testing software allows us to identify regions of the input space, for which the software fails, and reduces the probability of contaminating the system with incorrect output.

5.2.2 SOFTWARE REJUVENATION

When your personal computer hangs, the obvious reaction is to reboot it. Rebooting is an example of *software rejuvenation.*

There are many software problems, which do not cause errors immediately, but trigger failure eventually. For example, as a process executes, it may keep getting allocated memory and file-locks without ever releasing them. Numerical errors may keep building up from one iteration to the next; data might get corrupted as uncorrected errors accumulate. A high degree of memory fragmentation may occur. If this goes on indefinitely, the process can become faulty and stop executing. To head this off, we can proactively halt execution, clean up its internal state, and then restart it. This is called software rejuvenation.

Two principal questions arise in connection with rejuvenation. First, at what level should rejuvenation occur? Second, how do we determine when to rejuvenate?

Rejuvenation level

There are several possible levels at which rejuvenation can occur. At the process level, we might, for example, terminate a process, clean it up by garbage collection, or reinitialize its data structures, and then restart it. If a task consists of multiple loosely-coupled subtasks, each with its own address space, and one of these subtasks is showing signs of aging effects, then rebooting might be focused on the affected subtasks, rather than on the whole. For this to work properly, it is best to ensure that data that need to be preserved across such microreboots (e.g., databases) are kept separately from the application, behind properly designed interfaces. Loose coupling between subtasks ensures that one can be rebooted without affecting the correctness of the others, and that it can be easily reintegrated into the system following a reboot.

At a higher level, the entire physical node might be rebooted. This involves a restart of the operating system on that node, which affects all the tasks running on it. All of these will be rejuvenated.

Recently, the concept of *virtualization* has become popular. A *hypervisor*, which is a thin layer of resource management software, is placed atop the hardware. It allows multiple virtual machines to be run on a single physical machine, with each virtual machine having its own "guest" operating system. Note that these guest operating systems may be different from one another, e.g., VM1 might be running Linux, while VM2 runs Windows. Virtualization is a very old concept, having been introduced in the IBM System/360 machines decades ago. The structure is illustrated in Fig. 5.2.

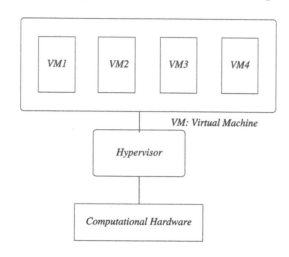

FIGURE 5.2

Virtual machine structure.

Rejuvenating such a system can be done at various levels. First, we can simply rejuvenate the hypervisor, and nothing else. (In other words, the virtual machines atop the hypervisor can have their state saved, and then restarted from that point once the hypervisor has been rejuvenated.) Second, the individual virtual machines might be rejuvenated, including everything they are executing. Third, we may concentrate on just a selection of the applications executing on one or more virtual machine. While rejuvenation is proceeding, one option (if there is sufficient hardware capacity) is to migrate a virtual machine from one hardware node to another. Which option we choose will depend on where the source of the problem (that triggered rejuvenation) is found to lie.

Rejuvenation imposes a performance penalty. First, there is the time for which the rejuvenation target is taken offline to be restarted. Second, if one or more (memory or file) caches are invalidated in the process, access times can become much longer, while the caches are warmed up—some approaches have been suggested to preserve cache contents to avoid this problem. In general, the performance penalty is smaller if the rejuvenation is carried out over a very restricted scope. For example, a microreboot carried out of an individual component of an application will cost less than will the rejuvenation of the entire application, which in turn will cost less than the rejuvenation of the entire node (as well as of all the applications running on that node).

Timing of rejuvenation

Software rejuvenation can be based on either time or prediction.

Time-based rejuvenation consists of rejuvenating at constant intervals. To determine the optimal inter-rejuvenation period, we must balance the benefits against the cost. Let us construct a simple mathematical model to do this. We use the following notation:

$\tilde{N}(t)$ Expected number of errors over an interval of length t (without rejuvenation);
C_e Cost of each error;
C_r Cost of each rejuvenation;
P Interrejuvenation period.

By adding up the costs due to rejuvenation and to errors, we obtain the overall expected cost of rejuvenation over a period P, denoted by $C_{rejuv}(P)$:

$$C_{rejuv}(P) = \tilde{N}(P)C_e + C_r.$$

The cost per unit time $C_{rate}(P)$ is then given by

$$C_{rate}(P) = \frac{C_{rejuv}(P)}{P} = \frac{\tilde{N}(P)C_e + C_r}{P}. \tag{5.1}$$

To get some insight into this expression, let us study three cases for $\tilde{N}(P)$. First, consider what happens if the software has a constant error rate λ throughout its execution, which implies that $\tilde{N}(P) = \lambda P$. Substituting this into Eq. (5.1), we have $C_{rate}(P) = \lambda C_e + C_r/P$. It is easy to see that to minimize $C_{rate}(P)$, we must set $P = \infty$. This implies that if the error rate is constant, software rejuvenation should not be applied at all. Rejuvenation is useful only to head off a potential increased error rate as the software executes.

Next, consider $\tilde{N}(P) = \lambda P^2$. From Eq. (5.1), we obtain $C_{rate}(P) = \lambda P C_e + C_r/P$. To minimize this quantity, we find P such that $dC_{rate}(P)/dP = 0$ (and $d^2C_{rate}(P)/dP^2 > 0$). Differentiating, we find the optimal value of the rejuvenation period, denoted by P^*, to be $P^* = \sqrt{\frac{C_r}{\lambda C_e}}$.

The third case is a generalization of the above: $\tilde{N}(P) = \lambda P^n$, $n > 1$. From Eq. (5.1), we have $C_{rate}(P) = \lambda P^{n-1}C_e + C_r/P$. Using elementary calculus, as before, we find the optimal value of the rejuvenation period to be

$$P^* = \left(\frac{C_r}{(n-1)\lambda C_e}\right)^{1/n}.$$

To set the period P appropriately, we need to know the values of the parameters C_r/C_e and $\tilde{N}(t)$. These can be obtained experimentally by running simulations on the software, or alternatively, the system could be made adaptive, with some default initial values being chosen to begin with. Over time, as we gather statistics reflecting the failure characteristics of the software, the rejuvenation period can be adjusted appropriately.

Prediction-based rejuvenation involves monitoring the system characteristics (amount of memory allocated, number of file locks held, and so on), and predicting when the system will fail. For example, if a process is consuming memory at a certain rate, the system can estimate when it will run out of memory. Alternatively, we might track the rate at which a node processes jobs and discover a consistent degradation in throughput. Rejuvenation then takes place just before the predicted crash.

The software that implements prediction-based rejuvenation must have access to enough state information to make such predictions. If it comes as part of the operating system, such information is easy to collect. If it is a package that runs atop the operating system with no special privileges, it will be constrained to using whatever interfaces are provided by the operating system to collect status information. For example, the Linux system provides the following utilities:

- `vmstat` provides information about processor utilization, memory and paging activity, traps, and I/O.
- `iostat` outputs the percentage CPU utilization at the user and system levels, as well as a report on the usage of each I/O device.
- `netstat` indicates network connections, routing tables, and a table of all the network interfaces.
- `nfsstat` provides information about network file server kernel statistics.

Once the appropriate status information has been collected, trends can be identified and a prediction made as to when these trends will cause errors to occur. For example, if we are tracking the allocation of memory to a process, we might do a least-squares fit of a polynomial to the memory allocations over some window of the recent past.

The simplest such fit is a straight line, or a polynomial of degree one, $f(t) = at + c$. More complex ones may involve a higher-degree polynomial, say of degree n. Suppose the selected window of the recent past consist of k time instances $t_1 < t_2 < \cdots < t_k$, where t_k is the most recent one. Given the measurements $\mu(t_1), \mu(t_2), \cdots, \mu(t_k)$, where $\mu(t_i)$ is the allocated memory at time t_i, we seek to find the coefficients of the polynomial

$$f(t) = a_n t^n + a_{n-1} t^{n-1} + \cdots + a_1 t + a_0$$

so as to minimize the quantity

$$\sum_{i=1}^{k} [\mu(t_i) - f(t_i)]^2.$$

This polynomial can then be used to extrapolate into the future, and predict when the process will run out of memory.

In the standard least-squares fit, each observed point $\mu(t_i)$ has the same weight in determining the fit. A variation of this procedure is the *weighted* least-squares fit, in which we seek to minimize the weighted sum of the squares. In our memory allocation example, we would choose weights $w_1, w_2, \ldots, w_k$, and then determine the coefficients of $f(t)$ such that the quantity

$$\sum_{i=1}^{k} w_i [\mu(t_i) - f(t_i)]^2$$

is minimized. Having weights allows us to give greater emphasis to certain points. For example, if we use $w_1 < w_2 < \cdots < w_k$, recent data will influence the fit more than older data.

The above curve-fitting approaches are all vulnerable to the impact of a few outlying points (points that are unusually high or low), which can have a distorting effect on the fit. Techniques are available to make the fit more robust by reducing the impact of such points; see the Further Reading section for a pointer to more information.

Yet another approach is to use machine learning (i.e., artificial intelligence) to track the behavior of the system. Historical data that allows one to correlate indicators, such as the amount of free memory, swap space, throughput, file handles, etc., with performance degradation and imminent failure, can be used to train a machine learning algorithm. Such an approach automatically adapts to changing circumstances, since new information can be integrated into the knowledge base to update the rejuvenation decision as the system operates. See the Further Reading section for more information.

Threshold-based approach: A threshold can be set for one or more indicators, such as free memory available, memory fragmentation, or swap space. When the indicator exceeds the threshold value, rejuvenation is carried out.

Combined approach: The approaches described above can be combined by rejuvenating at either the scheduled P or when a threshold is breached, or if there is prediction of imminent failure.

5.2.3 DATA DIVERSITY

The input space of a program is the space spanned by all possible inputs. This space can be divided into *failure* and *nonfailure* regions. The program fails if and only if an input from the failure region is applied. Data diversity can help in producing acceptable results, even when the input is in a failure region.

Failure regions come in every shape and size. Input spaces typically have a large number of dimensions, but we can visualize them only in the unrealistically simple case of a two-dimensional input space. Fig. 5.3 shows two arbitrarily drawn failure regions. In both cases, the failure region occupies the same fraction of the input area, but in Fig. 5.3A it consists of a number of relatively small islands, whereas in Fig. 5.3B it consists of a single large, contiguous, area. In both cases, the software will

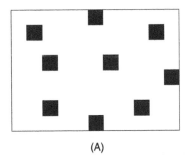 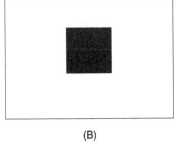

(A)   (B)

FIGURE 5.3

Failure regions. (A) Small, scattered fault regions. (B) Large, contiguous failure region.

fail for the same fraction of all possible inputs. The crucial difference is that in Fig. 5.3A, a small perturbation of the inputs is sufficient to move them out of a failure region to a nonfailure region.

Failure regions, such as in Fig. 5.3A, suggest a possible fault-tolerance approach: Consider perturbing the input slightly and hope that if the original input falls in a failure region, the perturbed input will fall in a nonfailure region. This general approach is called *data diversity*. How it is actually implemented depends on the error-detection mechanism. Suppose only one copy of the software is executed at any one time, and an acceptance test is used to detect errors. Then, upon detecting an error, we can recompute with perturbed inputs and recheck the resulting output. If massive redundancy is used, we may apply slightly different input sets to different versions of the program and vote on their output (see Section 5.3).

Perturbation of the input data can be done either explicitly or implicitly. Explicit perturbation consists of adding a small deviation term to a selected subset of the inputs. Implicit perturbation involves gathering inputs to the program in such a way that we can expect them to be slightly different. For example, suppose we have software controlling an industrial process, whose inputs are the pressure and temperature of some chemical reactor vessel. Every second, these parameters (p_i, t_i) are measured and then input to the controller. Now, from physical considerations, suppose we can expect that the pressure measured in sample i is not much different from that in sample $i-1$. Implicit perturbation, in this context, may consist of using (p_{i-1}, t_i) as an input alternative to (p_i, t_i). With luck, if (p_i, t_i) is in a failure region, (p_{i-1}, t_i) will not be, thus providing some resilience. Whether or not this is acceptable obviously depends on the dynamics of the application and the sampling rate. If, as is often the case, we sample at a higher rate than is absolutely necessary, this approach is likely to be useful.

Another approach is to reorder the inputs. A somewhat contrived example is the program that adds a set of three input floating-point numbers, a, b, c. If the inputs are in the order a, b, c, then it first computes $a+b$, and then adds c to this partial sum. Consider the case $a = 2.2E + 20$, $b = 5$, $c = -2.2E + 20$. Depending on the precision used (e.g., if the significand (mantissa) field of the floating-point number has room for fewer than 20 decimal digits, which is about 66 bits), it is possible that $a+b$—as calculated—will be $2.2E + 20$, so that the final result will be $a+b+c = 0$, which is incorrect. Now, change the order of the inputs; let it be a, c, b. Then, $a+c = 0$, so that $a+c+b = 5$.

There is one important difference between the two examples we have seen. Although in both cases we are reexpressing the inputs, the reactor vessel controller was an example of *inexact reexpression*, whereas the example of calculating $a+b+c$ is an instance of *exact reexpression*. In the first example, the software is attempting to compute some function, $f(p, t)$, of the pressure and temperature, yet for inputs (p, t) falling in a failure region, the actual output of the software will not equal $f(p, t)$; we are also likely to have $f(p_i, t_i) \neq f(p_{i-1}, t_i)$. In the second example, that of calculating $a+b+c$, we should—in theory—have $a+b+c = a+c+b$, and it is only the limitations of floating-point arithmetic that cause an error on this sequence a, b, c of inputs.

When exact reexpression is used, the associated output can be used as is (as long as it passes the acceptance test or the vote on the multiple versions of the program). If we have inexact reexpression, the output will not be exactly what was meant to be computed. Depending on the application and the amount of perturbation, we may or may not attempt to correct for the perturbation before using the output. If the application is somewhat robust, we may use the raw output as a somewhat degraded, but still acceptable, alternative to the desired output; if it is not, we must correct for the perturbation.

One way to correct the output for the perturbation is to use the Taylor expansion. Recall that for one variable (assuming that the function is differentiable to any degree), the Taylor expansion of $f(t)$ around the point t_0 is

$$f(t) = f(t_0) + \sum_{n=1}^{\infty} \frac{(t - t_0)^n f^{(n)}(t_0)}{n!},$$

where $f^{(n)}(t_0)$ is the value at $t = t_0$ of the nth derivative of $f(t)$ with respect to t.

In other cases, we may not have the desired function in analytic form, and must use other approaches to correct the output.

A related approach has been suggested for database fault tolerance. Suppose we have a transaction consisting of a string of operations. It is not hard to see that in many cases, we can *rephrase* these strings to arrive at the same final outcome. Interestingly, it has been observed that such "outcome equivalent" rephrasing can be resilient to faults. That is, consider two distinct strings of operations S_1, S_2, whose outcome is equivalent; S_2 is the same as S_1 except for rephrasing. Even if S_1 results in a fault being activated, it is often the case that S_2 will be run successfully. Detailed rules have been derived for such rephrasing: see the Further Reading section for a pointer.

5.2.4 SOFTWARE-IMPLEMENTED HARDWARE FAULT TOLERANCE (SIHFT)

Data diversity can be combined with time redundancy to construct techniques for software implemented hardware fault tolerance (SIHFT) with the goal of detecting hardware faults. A SIHFT technique can provide an inexpensive alternative to hardware and/or information redundancy techniques, and can be especially attractive when using COTS microprocessors, which often do not support error detection.

Suppose the program has all integer variables and constants. It can be transformed to a new program, in which all variables and constants are multiplied by a constant k (called the *diversity factor*), and whose final results are expected to be k times the results of the original program. When both the original and the transformed programs are executed on the same hardware (i.e., using time redundancy), the results of these two programs will be affected by hardware faults in different ways, depending on the value of k. By checking whether the results of the transformed program are k times the results produced by the original program, hardware faults can be detected.

How do we select a suitable value of k? The selected value should result in a high probability of detecting a fault, yet it should be small enough, so as not to cause an overflow or underflow, which may prevent us from correctly comparing the outputs of the two programs. Furthermore, if the original program includes logic operations, such as bit-wise *XOR* or *AND*, we should restrict ourselves to values that are of the form $k = 2^\ell$, with an integer ℓ, since in this case multiplication by k becomes a simple shift operation.

> **Example:** Consider an n-bit bus shown in Fig. 5.4, and suppose that bit i of the bus has a permanent stuck-at-0 fault. If the data sent over the bus has its ith bit equal to 1, the stuck-at fault will result in erroneous data being received at the destination. If a transformed program with $k = 2$ is executed on the same hardware, the ith bit of the data will now use line $(i + 1)$ of the bus, and will not be affected by the fault. The executions of the two programs will yield different results, indicating the presence of a fault.
>
> Obviously, the stuck-at-0 fault will not be detected if both bits i and $(i + 1)$ of the data that is forwarded on the bus are 0. Assuming that all 2^n possible values on the n-bit bus are equally likely, this event will occur with probability 0.25. If, however, the transformed program uses $k = -1$ (meaning that every variable and constant in the program undergoes a two's complement operation), almost all 0s in the original program will turn into 1s in the transformed program, greatly reducing the probability of an undetected fault.

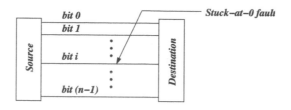

FIGURE 5.4

An n-bit bus with a permanent stuck-at-0 fault.

The risk of overflow while executing the transformed program exists even for small values of k. In particular, even $k = -1$ can generate an overflow if the original variable assumed the value of the largest negative integer number that can be represented using the two's complement scheme (for a 32-bit integer this is -2^{31}). Thus the transformed program should take appropriate precautions, for example, by scaling up the type of integer used for that variable. Range analysis can be performed to determine which variables must be scaled up to avoid overflows.

The actual transformation of the program, given the value of k, is quite straightforward and can be easily automated. The example in Fig. 5.5 shows the transformation for $k = 2$. Note that the result of the multiplication in the transformed program must be divided by k to ensure proper scaling of the variable y.

```
i = 0;
x = 3;
y = 1;
while (i < 5) {
     y = y * (x + i);
     i = i + 2;
}
z = y;
         (A)
```

```
i = 0;
x = 6;
y = 2;
while (i < 10) {
     y = y * (x + i)/2;
     i = i + 4;
}
z = y;
         (B)
```

FIGURE 5.5

An example of a program transformation for $k = 2$. (A) The original program. (B) The transformed program.

If floating-point variables are used in the program, some of the simple choices for k considered above are no longer adequate. For example, for $k = -1$, only the sign bit of the transformed variable will change (assuming the IEEE standard representation of floating-point numbers is followed, see the Further Reading section). Even selecting $k = 2^{\ell}$ for an integer ℓ is inappropriate, since multiplying by such a k will only affect the exponent field. The significand field will remain intact, and any error in it will not be detected. Both the significand field and the exponent field must therefore be multiplied, possibly by two different values of k.

To select value(s) of k for a given program such that the SIHFT technique will provide a high coverage (detect a large fraction of the hardware faults), we can carry out experimental studies by injecting faults into a simulation of the hardware (see Section 9.6 for a discussion of fault injection) and determine the fault-detecting capability for each candidate value of k.

Recomputing with shifted operands (RESO)

The recomputing with shifted operands (RESO) approach is similar to SIHFT, with the main difference being that the hardware is modified to support fault detection. In this approach, each unit that executes either an arithmetic or a logic operation is modified, so that it first executes the operation on the original operands, and then reexecutes the same operation on transformed operands. The same issues that had to be resolved for the SIHFT technique exist for the RESO technique as well. Here, too, the transformations of the operands are limited to simple shifts, which correspond to k being of the form $k = 2^\ell$, with ℓ an integer. Avoiding an overflow when executing the transformed computation is easier for RESO than for SIHFT, since the datapath of the modified hardware unit can be extended to include some extra bits. Fig. 5.6 shows an ALU (arithmetic and logic unit capable of executing addition, subtraction, and bitwise logic operations) that has been modified to support the RESO technique. In the first step, the two original operands X and Y are, for example, added without being shifted, and the result Z stored in the register. In the next step, the two operands are shifted by ℓ bit positions, and then added. The result of this second addition is then shifted by the same number of bit positions, but in the opposite direction, and then compared with the contents of the register, using the checker circuit.

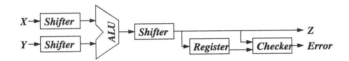

FIGURE 5.6

Example of the use of recomputing with shifted operands.

5.3 N-VERSION PROGRAMMING

In this approach to software fault tolerance, N independent teams of programmers develop software to the same specifications. These N versions of software are then run in parallel, and their output is voted on. The hope is that if the programs are developed independently, it is very unlikely that they will fail on the same inputs. Indeed, if the bugs are assumed to be statistically independent and each has the same probability q of occurring, then the probability of software failure of an N-version program can be computed in a way similar to that of an NMR cluster (see Chapter 2), that is, the probability of no more than m defective versions out of N versions, under the defect/bug independence assumption, is

$$p_{ind}(N, m, q) = \sum_{i=0}^{m} \binom{N}{i} q^i (1 - q)^{N-i}.$$

N-version programming is far from trivial to implement. We start our discussion by showing how difficult it can be to even arrive at a consensus among *correctly* functioning versions.

5.3.1 CONSISTENT COMPARISON PROBLEM

Consider N independently written software versions, $V_1, \cdots, V_N$, for some application. Suppose the overall structure of each version involves computing some quantity x and comparing it with a constant c. Let x_i denote the value of x as computed by version V_i. The comparison with c is said to be *consistent* if either $x_i \geq c$ for all $i = 1, \cdots, N$, or $x_i < c$ for all $i = 1, \cdots, N$.

Consider the following specified activity:

```
if (f(p,t)<c)
    take action A1
else
    take action A2
end if
```

Here, f(p,t) is some function of parameters p,t that is being called; the actions that are taken depend on the value that it returns. The job of each version of this activity is to output the action to be taken. In such a case, we clearly want all functional versions to be consistent in their comparisons.

Since the versions are written independently and may actually use different algorithms to compute the function $f(p, t)$, we expect that their respective calculations may yield values for $f(p, t)$ that differ slightly. To take a concrete example, let $c = 1.0000$ and $N = 3$. Suppose the versions V_1, V_2, and V_3 output values 0.9999, 0.9998, and 1.0001, respectively. Then, $x_1 < c$, $x_2 < c$, but $x_3 > c$: the comparisons are not consistent. As a result, V_1 and V_2 will order action A_1 to be taken, and V_3 will order action A_2, *even though all three versions are functioning correctly.*

Such inconsistent comparisons can occur, even if the precision is so high that the version outputs deviate by very little from one another: there is no way to guarantee a general solution to the consistent comparison problem. We can establish this by showing that any algorithm which guarantees that any two n-bit integers, which differ by less than 2^k will be mapped to the same ℓ-bit output (where $m + \ell \leq n$) must be the trivial algorithm that maps every input to the same number. Suppose we have such an algorithm: we start the proof with $k = 1$. 0 and 1 differ by less than 2^k, so the algorithm will map both of them to the same number, say α. Similarly, 1 and 2 differ by less than 2^k, so they will also be mapped to α. Proceeding in this way, we can easily show that $3, 4, \cdots$ will all be mapped by this algorithm to α, which means that this must be the trivial algorithm that maps all integers to the same number, α.

The above discussion assumes that it is integers that are being compared; however, it is easy to prove a similar result holds for real numbers of finite precision that differ even slightly from one another.

This problem may arise whenever the versions compare a variable with a given threshold. Given that the software may involve a large number of such comparisons, the potential exists for each version to produce distinct, unequal results, even if no errors have occurred, so long as even minor differences exist in the values being calculated. Such differences cannot usually be removed, because each version may use a different algorithm, and in any case is programmed independently.

Why is this a problem? After all, if nonfailing versions can differ in their output, it is reasonable to suppose that the output of any of them would be acceptable to the application. Although this is true, the system has no means to determine whether the outputs are in disagreement, because they are erroneous or because of the consistent comparison problem. Note that it is possible for the nonfailing versions to disagree due to this problem, whereas multiple failed versions produce identical wrong outputs (due to a common bug). The system would then most likely select the wrong output.

One can, in principle, bypass the consistent comparison problem completely, by having the versions decide on a consensus value of the variable before carrying out the comparison, that is, before checking if some variable $x > c$, the versions run an algorithm to agree on which value of x to use. However, this would add the requirement that, where there are multiple comparisons, the order of comparisons be specified. Restricting the implementation of the versions in this way can reduce version diversity, thus increasing the potential for correlated errors. Also, if the number of such comparisons is large, a significant degradation of performance could occur, because a large number of synchronization points would be created. Versions that arrive at the comparison points early would have to wait for the slower ones to catch up.

Another approach that has been suggested is to use confidence signals. While carrying out the "$x > c$?" comparison, each version should consider the difference $|x - c|$. If $|x - c| < \delta$ for some pre-specified δ, the version announces that it has low confidence in its output, because there is the potential for it to disagree with the other versions. The function that votes on the version outputs could then ignore the low-confidence versions, or give them a lower weight. Unfortunately, if one functional version has $|x - c| < \delta$, chances are quite high that this will also be true of other functional versions, whose outputs will also be devalued by the voter. In addition, it raises the possibility of an incorrect result that is far from c, outvoting multiple correct results, which are (correctly) close to c.

The frequency with which the consistent comparison problem arises, and the length of time for which it lasts, depend on the nature of the application. In applications where historical state information is not used (e.g., if the calculation depends only on the latest input values and is not a function of past values), the consistent comparison problem may occur infrequently and go away fairly quickly.

5.3.2 VERSION INDEPENDENCE

Correlated errors between versions can increase the overall error probability by orders of magnitude. For example, consider the case $N = 3$, which can tolerate up to one failed version for any input. Suppose that the probability that a version produces an incorrect output is $q = 10^{-4}$, that is, on the average, each of these versions produces an incorrect output once every 10,000 runs. If the versions are stochastically independent, then the error probability of the three-version system is

$$q^3 + 3q^2(1 - q) \approx 3 \times 10^{-8}.$$

Now, suppose stochastic independence does not hold, and there is one defect mode that is common to two of the three versions, and is exercised on the average once every million runs (that is, about one in every 100 bugs of a version is due to a common mistake). Every time this bug is exercised, the system will fail. The error probability of the three-version system now increases to over 10^{-6}, which is significantly greater than the error probability of the uncorrelated system.

Let us explore the issue of correlation a little further. Quite often, the input space (the space of all possible input patterns) can be subdivided into regions according to the probability that an input from that region will cause a version to fail. Thus, for example, if there is some numerical instability in a given subset of the input space, the error rate for that subspace may be greater than the average error rate over the entire space of inputs. Suppose that versions are stochastically independent *in each subspace*, that is,

Prob{V_1, V_2 both fail | input is from subspace S_i} =
$$\text{Prob}\{V_1 \text{ fails} \mid \text{input is from } S_i\} \times \text{Prob}\{V_2 \text{ fails} \mid \text{input is from } S_i\}.$$

According to the total probability formula, the unconditional probability of failure of an individual version is

$$\text{Prob}\{V_j \text{ fails}\} = \sum_i \text{Prob}\{V_j \text{ fails} \mid \text{input is from } S_i\} \times \text{Prob}\{\text{Input is from } S_i\} \quad (j = 1, 2).$$

The unconditional probability that both V_1 and V_2 will fail is

$$\text{Prob}\{V_1, V_2 \text{ both fail}\} = \sum_i \text{Prob}\{V_1 \text{ fails} \mid S_i\} \times \text{Prob}\{V_2 \text{ fails} \mid S_i\} \times \text{Prob}\{\text{Input is from } S_i\}.$$

Let us consider two numerical examples. For ease of exposition, we will assume the input space consists of only two subspaces S_1 and S_2, and that the probability of the input being from S_1 or S_2 is 0.5.

Example: Suppose the conditional failure probabilities are as follows:

Version	S_1	S_2
V_1	0.010	0.001
V_2	0.020	0.003

The unconditional failure probabilities for the two versions are

$$\begin{aligned}
\text{Prob}\{V_1 \text{ fails}\} &= 0.01 \times 0.5 + 0.001 \times 0.5 = 0.0055; \\
\text{Prob}\{V_2 \text{ fails}\} &= 0.02 \times 0.5 + 0.003 \times 0.5 = 0.0115.
\end{aligned}$$

If the two versions were stochastically independent, the probability of both failing for the same input would be

$$\text{Prob}\{V_1 \text{ fails}\} \cdot \text{Prob}\{V_2 \text{ fails}\} = 0.0055 \times 0.0115 = 6.33 \times 10^{-5}.$$

The actual joint failure probability, however, is somewhat greater:

$$P(V_1, V_2 \text{ both fail}) = 0.01 \times 0.02 \times 0.5 + 0.001 \times 0.003 \times 0.5 = 1.02 \times 10^{-4}.$$

The reason is that the two versions' failure propensities are positively correlated: they are both much more prone to failure in S_1 than in S_2.

Example: Suppose the failure probabilities are now as follows:

Version	S_1	S_2
V_1	0.010	0.001
V_2	0.003	0.020

The unconditional failure probabilities of the individual versions are identical to those in the previous example. However, the joint failure probability is now

$$\text{Prob}\{V_1, V_2 \text{ both fail}\} = 0.01 \times 0.003 \times 0.5 + 0.001 \times 0.02 \times 0.5 = 2.5 \times 10^{-5}.$$

This is about a five-fold decrease from the corresponding number in the previous example, and less than half of what it would have been if the versions had been stochastically independent.

The reason is that now the propensities to failure of the two versions are negatively correlated: V_1 is better in S_1 than in S_2, whereas the opposite is true for V_2. Intuitively, V_1 and V_2 make up for each other's deficiencies.

Ideally, we would therefore like the multiple versions to be negatively correlated; realistically, we expect most correlations to be positive, because the versions are ultimately all addressing the same problem. In any event, the focus in N-version programming has historically been on making the versions as stochastically independent as possible, rather than on making them negatively correlated.

The stochastic independence of versions can be compromised by a number of factors:

- Common specifications: If programmers work off the same specification, errors in these specifications will propagate to the software.
- Intrinsic difficulty of the problem: The algorithms being programmed may be far more difficult to implement in one subset of the input space than in others. Such a correlation in difficulty can translate into multiple versions having defects that are triggered by the same input sets.
- Common algorithms: Even if the implementation of the algorithm is correct, the algorithm itself may contain instabilities in certain regions of the input space. If the different versions are implementing the same algorithm, then these instabilities will be replicated across the versions.
- Cultural factors: Programmers who are trained to think in similar ways can make similar (or the same) mistakes quite independently. Furthermore, such correlation can result in ambiguous specifications being interpreted in the same erroneous way.
- Common software and hardware platforms: The operating environment comprises the processors on which the software versions are executed and the operating system. If we use the same hardware and operating system, faults/defects within these can trigger a correlated failure. Strictly speaking, this would not constitute a correlated *application software* failure; however, from the user's point of view, this would still be a failure. Common compilers can also cause correlated failures.

Independence among the versions can be gained by either *incidental diversity* or *forced diversity*. Incidental diversity is the by-product of forcing the developers of different modules to work independently of one another. Teams working on different modules are forbidden to directly communicate with one another. Questions regarding ambiguities in the specifications, or any other issue, have to be addressed to some central authority, which makes any necessary corrections and updates all the teams. Inspection of the software must be carefully coordinated, so that the inspectors of one version do not directly or indirectly leak information about another version.

Forced diversity is a more proactive approach and forces each development team to follow some approach that is believed to increase the chances of diversity. Here are some of the ways in which this can be forced:

Use diverse specifications: Several researchers have remarked that the majority of software bugs can be traced to the requirements specification. Some even claim that two-thirds of all bugs can be laid at the door of faulty specifications! This is one important motivation for using diverse specifications, that is, rather than working on a common specification, diversity can begin at the specification stage. The specifications may be expressed in different formalisms. The hope is that specification errors will not coincide across versions, and each specification version will trigger a different implementation error profile. It is beginning to be accepted that the specifications impact how one thinks about a problem: the *same* problem, if specified differently, may well pose a different level of difficulty to the implementor.

We may also decide to make the various versions have differing capabilities. For example, in a three-version system, one of the versions may be more rudimentary than the other two, providing a less accurate—but still acceptable—output. The hope is that the implementation of a simpler algorithm will be less error-prone and more robust (experience less numerical instability). In most cases, the two other versions will run correctly and provide good performance. In the (hopefully rare) instances when they do not, the third version can save the system (or at least help determine which of the two disagreeing other versions is correct). If the third version is very simple, then formal methods may be considered to actually *prove* that it is correct. A similar approach of using a simpler version is often used in recovery blocks, which are discussed in Section 5.4.

Use diverse programming languages: Anyone experienced in programming knows that the programming language can significantly impact the quality of the software that is produced. For example, we would expect a program written in assembly language to be more bug-prone than is one in a higher-level language. The nature of the bugs can also be different. In our discussion of wrappers (in Section 5.2.1), we saw that it is possible to get programs written in C to overflow their allocated memory. Such bugs would be impossible in a language that strictly manages memory. Errors arising from an incorrect use of pointers, not uncommon in C programs, will not occur in Fortran, which has no pointers.

Diverse programming languages may have diverse libraries and compilers, which the user hopes will have uncorrelated (or, even better, negatively correlated) bugs.

Certain programming languages may be more attuned to a given problem than others. For example, many would claim that Lisp is a more natural language, in which to code some artificial intelligence (AI) algorithms, than are C or Fortran. In other words, Lisp's expressive power is more congruent to some AI problems than that of C or Fortran. In such a case, an interesting problem arises. Should all versions use the language that is well-attuned to the problem, or should we force some versions to be written in other languages that are less suited to the application? If all the versions are written in the most suitable language, we can hope that their individual error rate will be lower; on the other hand, the different versions may experience correlated errors. If they are written in diverse languages, the individual error rates of the versions written in the "poorer" languages may be greater, but the *overall* error rate of the N-version system may be lower if these bugs do not give rise to as many correlated errors. A similar comment applies to the use of diversity in other dimensions, such as development environments or tools. This trade-off is difficult to resolve without extensive—and expensive—experimental work.

Use diverse development tools and compilers: This may make possible "notational diversity" and thereby reduce the extent of positive correlation between bugs. Since tools can themselves be faulty, using diverse tools for different versions may allow for greater reliability.

A similar remark applies to compilers. In addition, compiler diversity may provide some protection against hardware faults. That is, two different compilations, C_1 and C_2, of the same source code, generated by different compilers (or the same compiler with different levels of optimization selected), may exercise slightly different elements of the hardware. Thus there might be some hardware faults that are exercised by C_1, but not exercised also by C_2, or vice versa.

Use cognitively diverse teams: By *cognitive diversity*, we mean diversity in the way that people reason and approach problems. If teams are constituted to ensure that different teams have different approaches to reasoning and different mental maps, this can *potentially* give rise to software that has fewer correlated bugs. However, this is difficult to do in practice; it is therefore not normal practice to explicitly implement cognitive diversity for industrial software development.

5.3.3 OTHER ISSUES IN N-VERSION PROGRAMMING

Back-to-back testing: Having multiple versions that solve the same problem gives us the opportunity to test them back-to-back. The testing process consists of comparing their outputs for the same input, which helps identify noncoincident bugs.

In addition to comparing the overall outputs, designers have the option of comparing corresponding intermediate variables. Fig. 5.7 shows an idealized example. We have three versions V1, V2, V3. In

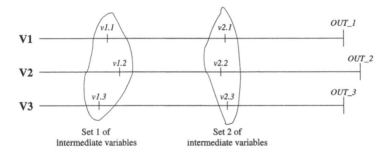

FIGURE 5.7

Example of intermediate variables in back-to-back testing.

addition to their final outputs, the designers have identified two points during their execution when corresponding variables are generated. These can be compared to provide additional back-to-back checks.

Using intermediate variables can provide increased observability into the behavior of the programs, and may identify defects that are not easily observable at the outputs. However, defining such variables constrains the developers to producing these variables, and may reduce program diversity.

Using diverse hardware and operating systems: The output of the system depends on the interaction between the application software and its platform, mainly comprising the operating system and the processor. Both processors and operating systems are notorious for the bugs they contain. It is therefore a good idea to complement software design diversity with hardware and operating system diversity, by running each version on a different processor type and operating system.

Cost of N-version programming: Software is expensive to develop, and creating N versions, rather than one, is more expensive still. Very little information is publicly available about the cost of developing N versions: for a pointer to a case study, see the Further Reading section. According to that study, the overhead of developing an additional version varies from 25% to 134% of the single-version cost. This is an extremely wide range!

A first-order estimate is that developing N versions is N times as expensive as developing a single version. However, some parts of the development process may be common. For instance, if all versions work off the same specifications, only one set of specifications needs to be developed. On the other hand, the management of an N-version project imposes overheads not found in traditional software development. Still, costs can be kept under control by carefully identifying the most critical portions of the code, and only developing N versions for these.

Producing a single good version versus many versions: Given a total time budget, consider two choices: (*a*) develop a single version (over which we lavish the entire allocated time), and (*b*) develop N versions. Unfortunately, software reliability modeling is not yet sufficiently advanced for us to make an effective estimate, of which would be better and under what circumstances.

Experimental results: A few experimental studies have been carried out into the effectiveness of N-version programming. Published results are generally only available for work carried out in universities, and it is not clear how the results obtained by using student programmers would change if professional and experienced programmers were used.

One typical study was conducted by the University of Virginia and the University of California at Irvine. The study had a total of 27 students write code for an antimissile application. The students ranged from some with no prior industrial experience to others with over ten years experience. All versions were written in Pascal and run on a Prime machine at the University of Virginia and a DEC VAX 11/750 at the University of California at Irvine. A total of 93 correlated bugs were identified by standard statistical hypothesis-testing methods: if the versions had been stochastically independent, we would have expected no more than about five. Interestingly, no correlation was observed between the quality of the programs produced and the experience of the programmer. A similar conclusion—that versions were not stochastically independent—was drawn from another experiment, conducted under NASA auspices, by North Carolina State University, the University of California at Santa Barbara, the University of Virginia, and the University of Illinois.

Another experiment was conducted at the City University of London. The purpose was to investigate whether diversity amongst existing commercial or open-source database management systems (DBMS) was sufficient for meaningful fault tolerance. They selected four DBMSs and used available bug repositories associated with each. Applying inputs known to cause bugs in one of them to the others, they observed that out of 273 bug scripts, only 5 caused undetectable failures in two DBMSs; none of them caused failure in more than two. Whereas, as the authors themselves stress, one must be cautious in drawing too definitive a conclusion from this (their bug repositories were far from comprehensive), this is a very encouraging indication of the usefulness of diversity for fault tolerance.

Our final example is the most recent study, using the UVa Online Judge website (`https://uva.onlinejudge.org` at the time of writing). This is a website containing a set of programming problems. Programmers are encouraged to submit their solutions to these problems; their submitted programs form a rich (and inexpensive!) source of data related to software diversity. The obvious caveat here is that these programs are not written under commercial conditions of inspection and testing, especially for ultra-reliable software. The programs under consideration are fairly small and far from the complexity of million-line software. One example is the $3n + 1$ problem, whose pseudocode is the following very short stretch:

```
input n;
output n;
while (n != 1) {
    if (n is ODD)
        n=3*n+1;
    else
        n=n/2;
    output n;
}
```

Thousands of programs were analyzed; these were (apparently) independently written and in multiple languages: C, C++, and Pascal. Upon detailed analysis, it was found that given two highly reliable programs (i.e., programs failing on an extremely small fraction of the input space), the probability that *both* would fail on the same input was roughly 100 times smaller than the probability of their individual failure. If they failed independently, the failure rate would have been much lower; there is thus positive failure correlation between the versions. For less reliable programs, in this case, programs with a failure probability greater than 5×10^{-3}, the pair behaved roughly independently, i.e., the probability of both programs failing on the same input was roughly the product of their individual failure probabilities. Faults were analyzed and categorized into "equivalence classes." The programming language did have an impact on the fault classes, i.e., the fault classes for Pascal were populated differently from those for C and C++. For example, Pascal programs contained significantly fewer loop errors. This indicates that language diversity does play a role in enhancing failure resilience. We should reiterate that these programs were not developed under commercial conditions, and that they are orders of magnitude shorter than typical commercial software packages, so we must be cautious when drawing conclusions. However, these results are suggestive of reliable programs not necessarily failing independently of one another, and of the diversity imposed implicitly by using diverse programming languages being useful.

5.4 RECOVERY BLOCK APPROACH

Similarly to N-version programming, the recovery block approach also uses multiple versions of software. The difference is that in the latter, only one version runs at any one time. If this version should be declared as failing, execution is switched to a backup.

5.4.1 BASIC PRINCIPLES

Fig. 5.8 illustrates a simple implementation of this method. There is a primary version and three secondary versions in this example. Only the primary is initially executed. When it completes execution, it passes along its output to an acceptance test, which checks to see if the output is reasonable. If it is, then the output is accepted by the system. If not, then the system state is rolled back to the point at which the primary started computation, and secondary 1 is invoked. If this succeeds (the output passes the acceptance test), the computation is over. Otherwise, we roll the system back to the beginning of the computation, and then invoke secondary 2. We keep going until either the outcome passes an acceptance test, or we run out of secondaries. In the latter case, the recovery block procedure will have failed, and the system must take whatever corrective action is needed in response (e.g., the system may be put in a "safe" state, such as a reactor being shut down).

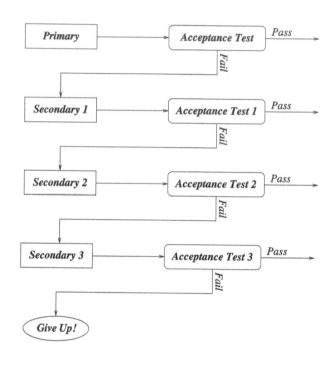

FIGURE 5.8

Recovery block structure with three secondaries.

The success of the recovery block approach depends on: (*a*) the extent to which the primary and various secondaries fail on the same inputs (correlated bugs), and (*b*) the quality of the acceptance test. These clearly vary from one application to the next.

5.4.2 SUCCESS PROBABILITY CALCULATION

Let us set up a simple mathematical model for the success probability of the recovery block approach, under the assumption that the different versions fail independently of one another. We can use this model to determine which parameters most affect the software failure probability. We use the following notation:

E   the event that the output of a version is actually erroneous;
T   the event that the test reports that the output is wrong;
f   the failure probability of a version;
s   the test sensitivity;
σ probability that the output is actually erroneous when the test flags it as such;
n the number of available software versions (primary plus secondaries).

   Thus

$$f = P\{E\}; \quad s = P\{T|E\}; \quad \sigma = P\{E|T\}.$$

For the scheme to succeed, it must succeed at some stage i, $1 \le i \le n$. This will happen if the test fails stages $1, ..., i-1$ (causing the scheme to go to the next version), and at stage i, the version's output is correct, and it passes the test. We now have

$$\text{Prob\{Success in stage } i\} = [P\{T\}]^{i-1} P\{\bar{E} \cap \bar{T}\}$$

$$\text{Prob\{Scheme is successful\}} = \sum_{i=1}^{n} [P\{T\}]^{i-1} P\{\bar{E} \cap \bar{T}\} \tag{5.2}$$

$$P\{E \cap T\} = P\{T|E\}P\{E\} = sf$$

$$P\{T\} = \frac{P\{E \cap T\}}{P\{E|T\}} = \frac{sf}{\sigma} \tag{5.3}$$

$$P\{\bar{E}|T\} = 1 - P\{E|T\} = 1 - \sigma$$

$$P\{\bar{E} \cap T\} = P\{\bar{E}|T\}P\{T\} = \frac{sf(1 - \sigma)}{\sigma}$$

$$P\{\bar{E}\} = 1 - P\{E\} = 1 - f$$

$$P\{\bar{E} \cap \bar{T}\} = P\{\bar{E}\} - P\{\bar{E} \cap T\} = (1-f) - \frac{sf(1 - \sigma)}{\sigma}. \tag{5.4}$$

Substituting Eqs. (5.3) and (5.4) into Eq. (5.2) yields

$$\text{Prob\{Scheme is successful\}} = \sum_{i=1}^{n} \left[\frac{sf}{\sigma} \right]^{i-1} \left[(1-f) - \frac{sf(1-\sigma)}{\sigma} \right]$$

$$= \frac{1 - \left(\frac{sf}{\sigma} \right)^n}{1 - \frac{sf}{\sigma}} \left[(1-f) - \frac{sf(1-\sigma)}{\sigma} \right]. \tag{5.5}$$

Eq. (5.5) can be examined to determine the effect of the various parameters on the success probability of the scheme. One such analysis is shown in Fig. 5.9 for a recovery block structure, with one primary and two secondaries ($n = 3$).

5.4.3 DISTRIBUTED RECOVERY BLOCKS

The structure of the *distributed recovery block* is shown in Fig. 5.10, where we consider the special case with just one secondary version. The two nodes carry identical copies of the primary and secondary.

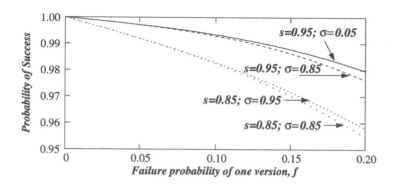

FIGURE 5.9

Success probability of the recovery block structure for $n = 3$.

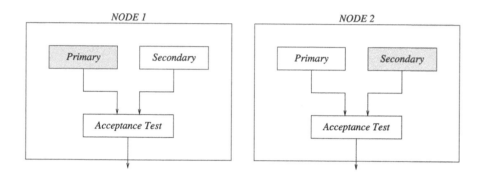

FIGURE 5.10

Distributed recovery block structure.

Node 1 executes the primary, while, in parallel, node 2 executes the secondary. If node 1 fails the acceptance test, the output of node 2 is used (provided that it passes the acceptance test). The output of node 2 can also be used if there is a watchdog timer and node 1 fails to produce an output within a prespecified time.

Once the primary copy fails, the roles of the primary and secondary copies are reversed. Node 2 continues to execute its copy, which is now treated as the primary. The execution by node 1 of what was previously the primary copy is used as a backup. This continues until the execution by node 2 is flagged as erroneous, in which case the system toggles back to using the execution by node 2 as a backup.

Because the secondary is executed in parallel with the primary, we do not have to wait for the system to be rolled back and the secondary to be executed: the execution is overlapped with that of the primary. This saves time, and is useful when the application is a real-time system with tight task deadlines.

Our example has included just two versions; the scheme can obviously be extended to an arbitrary number of versions. If we have n versions (primary plus $n-1$ secondaries), we will run all n in parallel, one on each processor.

5.5 PRECONDITIONS, POSTCONDITIONS, AND ASSERTIONS

Preconditions, postconditions, and assertions are forms of acceptance tests that are widely used in software engineering to improve software reliability. The *precondition* of a method (or function, or subroutine, depending on the programming language) is a logical condition that must be true when that method is called. For example, if we are operating in the domain of real numbers and invoke a method to calculate the square root of a number, an obvious precondition is that this number must be nonnegative.

A *postcondition* associated with a method invocation is a condition that must be true when we return from a method. For example, if a natural logarithm method was called with input X, and the method returns Y, we must have $e^Y = X$ (within the limits of the level of precision being used).

Preconditions and postconditions are often interpreted in contractual terms. The function invoking a method agrees to ensure that the preconditions are met for that method: if they are not, there is no guarantee that the invoked method will return the correct result. In return, the method agrees to ensure that the postconditions are satisfied upon returning from it.

Assertions are a generalization of preconditions and postconditions. An assertion tests for a condition that must be true at the point at which that assertion is made. For example, we know that the total node degree of an undirected graph must be an even number (since each edge is incident on exactly two nodes). So, we can assert at the point of computation of this quantity that it must be even. If it turns out not to be, an error has occurred; the response to the failure of an assertion is usually to notify the user, or carry out some other appropriate action.

Preconditions, postconditions, and assertions are used to catch errors before they propagate too far. The programmer has the opportunity to provide for corrective action to be taken if these conditions are violated.

5.6 EXCEPTION HANDLING

An *exception* is raised to indicate that something has happened during execution that needs attention, e.g., an assertion has been violated, due to either hardware or software failure. When an exception is raised, control is generally transferred to a corresponding *exception-handler*, which is a routine that takes the appropriate action. For example, if we have an arithmetic overflow when executing the operation $y = a * b$, then the result as computed will not be correct. This fact can be signaled as an exception, and the system must react appropriately.

Effective exception-handling can make a significant contribution to system fault tolerance. For this reason, a substantial fraction of the code in many current programs is devoted to exception handling. Throughout this discussion, we will assume that an exception is triggered in some routine that is invoked by some other routine, or by an operator external to the system.

Exceptions can be used to deal with (*a*) domain or range error, (*b*) an out-of-the-ordinary event (not failure) that needs special attention, or (*c*) a timing failure.

Domain and range errors: A domain error happens when an illegal input is used. For example, if X and Y are defined as real numbers and the operation $X = \sqrt{Y}$ is attempted with $Y = -1$, a domain error will have occurred, the value of Y being illegal. On the other hand, if X and Y are complex numbers, this operation will be perfectly legal.

A range error occurs when the program produces an output or carries out an operation that is seen to be incorrect in some way. Examples include the following:

- Reading from a file, and encountering an end-of-file, whereas we should still be reading data;
- Producing a result that violates an acceptance test embedded within the program;
- Trying to print a line that is too long;
- Generating an arithmetic overflow or underflow.

Out-of-the-ordinary events: Exceptions can be used to ensure special handling of rare, but perfectly normal, events. For example, if we are reading a list of items from a file and the routine has just read the last item, it may trigger an exception to notify the invoker that this was the last item, and that nothing further is available to be read.

Timing failures: In real-time applications, tasks have deadlines associated with them. Missing a deadline can trigger an exception. The exception-handler then decides what to do in response: for instance, it may switch to a backup routine.

5.6.1 REQUIREMENTS FROM EXCEPTION HANDLERS

What do we look for in an exception-handling system? First, it should be easy to program and use. It should be modular, and thus easily separable from the rest of the software. It should certainly not be mixed in with the other lines of code in a routine: that would obscure the purpose of the code and render it hard to understand, debug, and modify.

Second, exception handling should not impose a substantial overhead on the normal functioning of the system. We expect exceptions to be, as the term suggests, invoked only in exceptional circumstances: most of the time they will not be raised. The well-known engineering principle that the common case must be made fast requires that the exception-handling system not inflict too much of a burden in the usual case when no exceptional conditions exist.

Third, exception handling must not compromise the system state, that is, we must be careful not to render the system state inconsistent during exception handling. This is especially important in the exception-resume approach, which we discuss in the next section.

5.6.2 BASICS OF EXCEPTIONS AND EXCEPTION HANDLING

When an exception occurs, it is said to be *thrown*, *raised*, or *signaled*. Some authors distinguish between the raising and the signaling of an exception: the former is when the exception notification is to the module within which it occurred; the latter when this notification propagates to another module.

Exceptions can be either *internal* or *external*. An internal exception is one which is handled within the very same module in which it is raised. An external exception, on the other hand, *propagates* elsewhere. For example, if a module is called in a way that violates the specifications of its interface, an interface exception is generated, which has to be dealt with outside the called module.

Propagation of exceptions

Fig. 5.11 provides an example of exception propagation. Here, module A calls module B, which executes normally, until it encounters exception c. B does not have the handler for this exception, so it propagates the exception back to its calling module A, which executes the appropriate handler. If no handler can be found, the execution is terminated.

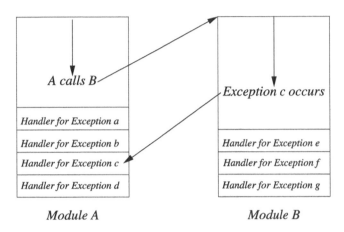

FIGURE 5.11

Example of exception propagation.

Automatically propagating exceptions can violate the principle of information hiding. Information hiding involves the separation of the interface definition of a routine (method, function, subroutine) from the way it is actually designed and implemented. The interface is public information; in contrast, the caller of the routine does not need to know the details of the design and implementation of every routine being called. Not only does this reduce the burden on the caller, it also makes it possible to improve the implementation without any changes having to be propagated to outside the routine.

The invoker (the calling routine) is at a different level of abstraction from the invoked routine. In the example just considered, suppose that some variable X in the invoked routine violated its range constraint. This variable may not even be visible to the invoker.

To get around this problem, we may replace automatic propagation with explicit propagation, in which the propagated information is modified to be consonant with scope rules. For example, if the variable X is invisible to the invoker, it may be told that there was a violation of a range constraint within the invoked routine. It will then have to make the best use it can of this information.

Exception-terminate and exception-resume

Exceptions may be classified into the *exception-terminate* (ET) and *exception-resume* (ER) categories. If an ET is generated while executing some module M, then execution of M is terminated, the appropriate exception handler is executed, and control is returned to the routine that called module M.

However, if an ER is generated, the exception-handling routine attempts to patch up the problem and returns control to M, which resumes execution.

Exception-terminates are much simpler to handle than are exception-resumes. Suppose, for example, that module A calls module B. While executing, module B encounters an exception. If the exception-terminate approach is taken, B will restore its state to what it was at its invocation, signal the exception, and terminate. Control is handed back to A. A thus has to deal only with the following two possibilities: either B executes without exceptions and returns a result, or B encounters an exception and terminates *with its state unchanged from before it was called.*

By contrast, if the exception-resume approach is taken, B will suspend execution, and control is transferred to the appropriate exception handler. After the handler finishes its task, it has the option of returning control to B, which can then resume from the instruction following the one which triggered the exception. Alternatively, the handler could send control elsewhere (it depends on the semantics of the handler). Following this, control returns to A. Thus when A gets back control after a call to B, we have the following three possibilities: The first is an exception-free execution of B, which poses no difficulties. The second is that an exception was encountered, which was dealt with by the exception handler, after which control was returned to B, which resumes and finishes execution. The third possibility is that the exception handler transfers control elsewhere in an attempt to handle the exception. After all this, control is handed back to A, possibly with B being in an inconsistent state. This third possibility requires that the programmer who wrote A knows the semantics of the exception handler, which may not be realistic.

After the exception has been handled and control has been returned to the invoking routine, several options are available, based on what kind of exception occurred:

- Domain error: We may choose to reinvoke, with corrected operands. If this is not possible, the entire computation may have to be abandoned.
- Range error: There are cases in which some acceptable value may be substituted for the incorrect one which triggered the exception, and the execution resumed. For example, if we have an underflow, we may choose to replace that result by 0 and carry on. If we have additional versions of the software, we may invoke alternatives, or we may just retry the whole operation, hoping that it arose from some transient failure, which has since gone away, or from some combination of concurrent events that is unlikely to recur.
- Out-of-the-ordinary events: These must be identified by the programmer and handled on a case-by-case basis.
- Timing failures: If the routine is iterative, we may simply use the latest value. For example, if the invoked routine was searching for the optimum value of some function, we may decide to use the best one it has found so far. Alternatively, we may switch to another version of the software (if available) and hope that it will not suffer from the same problem. If we are using the software in a real-time system that is controlling some physical device (e.g., a valve), we may leave the setting unchanged, or switch to a safety position.

It is important to stress that many exceptions can only be properly dealt with in context: it is the context that determines what the appropriate response should be. For example, suppose we encounter an arithmetic overflow in a floating-point computation. In some applications, it may be perfectly acceptable to set the result to ∞ and carry on. In others, it may not, and may require a far more involved response.

5.6.3 LANGUAGE SUPPORT

Older programming languages generally have very little built-in exception handling support. By contrast, more recent languages such as C++ and Java have extensive exception-handling support. For example, in Java, the user can specify exceptions that are *thrown* if certain conditions occur (such as the temperature of a nuclear reactor exceeding a prespecified limit). Such exceptions must be *caught* by an exception-handling routine, which deals with them appropriately (by raising an alarm or printing some output).

5.7 SOFTWARE RELIABILITY MODELS

As opposed to the well-established analytical models of hardware reliability, the area of modeling error rates and software reliability is relatively young and often controversial. There are many models in the literature, which sometimes give rise to contradictory results. Our inability to accurately predict the reliability of software is a matter of great concern, since software is often the major cause of system unreliability.

In this section, we briefly describe some software reliability models. Unfortunately, there is not yet enough evidence to determine which model would be best for what type of software. Models are useful in providing general guidance as to what the software *quality* is; they should not be used as the ultimate word on the actual numerical reliability of any piece of software.

In what follows, we distinguish between a *defect* (or a bug) that exists in the software when it is written and an *error* that is a deviation of the program operation from its exact requirements (as the result of a defect), and occurs only when the program is running (or is being tested). Once an error occurs, the bug causing it can be corrected; however, other bugs may still remain. An accepted definition of software reliability is *the probability of error-free operation of a computer program in a specified environment for a specified time.* To calculate this probability, the notion of *software error rate* must be introduced. Software reliability models attempt to predict this error rate as a function of the number of bugs in the software, and their purpose is to determine the length of testing (and subsequent correcting) required until the predicted future error rate of the software goes below some predetermined threshold (and the software can be released).

Note that the error rate is a function of two things: the bugs in the code and the rate at which inputs are presented, which activate those bugs.

Software reliability models typically make the following assumptions: The software has initially some unknown number of bugs. It is tested for a period of time, during which time some of the bugs cause errors. Whenever an error occurs, the bug causing it is fixed (fixing time is negligible) without causing any additional bugs, thus reducing the number of existing bugs by one. The models differ in their modeling of $\lambda(t)$, the software error rate at time t, and consequently, in the software reliability prediction.

5.7.1 JELINSKI–MORANDA MODEL

This model assumes that at time 0, the software has a fixed (and finite) number $N(0)$ of bugs, out of which $N(t)$ bugs remain at time t. The error process is a nonhomogeneous Poisson process, i.e., a Poisson process with a rate $\lambda(t)$ that may vary with time. The error rate $\lambda(t)$ at time t is assumed to be proportional to $N(t)$,

$$\lambda(t) = cN(t) \quad \text{(for some constant } c\text{)}.$$

Note that $\lambda(t)$ in this model is a step function; it has an initial value of $\lambda_0 = \lambda(0) = cN(0)$, decreases by c whenever an error occurs and the bug that caused it is corrected, and is constant between errors. The (testing, not including fixing) time between consecutive errors (say i and $i+1$) is exponentially distributed with parameter $\lambda(t_i)$, where t_i is the time of the ith error. The reliability at time t, or the probability of an error-free operation during $[0, t]$ is therefore

$$R(t) = e^{-\lambda_0 t}. \tag{5.6}$$

Given an error occurred at time τ, the conditional future reliability, or the conditional probability that the following interval of length t, namely $[\tau, \tau + t]$ will be error-free is

$$R(t \mid \tau) = e^{-\lambda(\tau)t}. \tag{5.7}$$

As the software runs for longer and longer, more bugs are caught and purged from the system, and so the error rate declines and the future reliability increases.

The obvious objection to this model is that it assumes that all bugs contribute equally to the error rate, as expressed by the constant of proportionality c. Actually, not all bugs are created equal: some of them are exercised more often than others. Indeed, the more troublesome bugs are those that are not exercised often: these are extremely difficult to catch during testing.

5.7.2 LITTLEWOOD–VERRALL MODEL

Similarly to the previous model, this model assumes a fixed and finite number $N(0)$ of initial bugs, out of which $N(t)$ remain at time t. The difference is that this model considers $M(t)$—the number of bugs discovered and corrected during $[0, t]$—rather than $N(t)$ ($M(t) = N(0) - N(t)$).

The errors occur according to a nonhomogeneous Poisson process with rate $\lambda(t)$, but $\lambda(t)$, rather than being deterministic, is considered a random variable with a gamma density function. The gamma density function has two parameters, α and ψ, where the parameter ψ is a monotonically increasing function of $M(t)$,

$$f_{\lambda(t)}(\ell) = \frac{[\psi(M(t))]^\alpha \ell^{\alpha-1} e^{-\psi(M(t))\ell}}{\Gamma(\alpha)}, \tag{5.8}$$

where $\Gamma(x) = \int_0^\infty e^{-y} y^{x-1} \, dy$ is the gamma function (defined in Section 2.2)

The gamma density function was chosen for practical reasons. It lends itself to analysis, and its two parameters provide a wide range of differently shaped density functions, making it both mathematically tractable and flexible. The expected value of the gamma density function in Eq. (5.8) is $\frac{\alpha}{\psi(M(t))}$, so that the predicted error rate will decrease, and the reliability will increase as the software is run for longer periods of time and more bugs are discovered.

Calculating the reliability requires some integrations, which we omit; see the Further Reading section for a pointer to the analysis. After such analysis, we obtain the following expressions for the software reliability:

$$R(t) = \left(1 + \frac{t}{\psi(0)}\right)^{-\alpha},$$
(5.9)

and

$$R(t \mid \tau) = \left(1 + \frac{t}{\psi(M(\tau))}\right)^{-\alpha}.$$
(5.10)

5.7.3 MUSA–OKUMOTO MODEL

This model assumes an infinite (or at least very large) number of initial bugs in the software, and similarly to the previous model, uses $M(t)$—the number of bugs discovered and corrected during time $[0, t]$. We use the following notation:

λ_0 the error rate at time 0;

c   a constant of proportionality;

$\mu(t)$ the expected number of errors experienced during $[0, t]$ $(\mu(t) = E(M(t)))$.

Under this model, the error rate after testing for a length of time t is given by

$$\lambda(t) = \lambda_0 e^{-c\mu(t)}.$$

The intuitive basis for this model is that, when testing first starts, the "easiest" bugs are caught quite quickly. After these have been eliminated, the bugs that still remain are more difficult to catch, either because they are harder to exercise, or because their effects get masked by subsequent computations. As a result, the rate at which an as-yet-undiscovered bug causes errors drops exponentially as testing proceeds.

From the definition of $\lambda(t)$ and $\mu(t)$, we have

$$\frac{d\mu(t)}{dt} = \lambda(t) = \lambda_0 e^{-c\mu(t)}.$$

The solution of this differential equation is

$$\mu(t) = \frac{\ln(\lambda_0 ct + 1)}{c},$$

and

$$\lambda(t) = \frac{\lambda_0}{\lambda_0 ct + 1}.$$

The reliability $R(t)$ can now be calculated as

$$R(t) = e^{-\int_0^t \lambda(z)dz} = e^{-\mu(t)} = (1 + \lambda_0 ct)^{-\frac{1}{c}},$$

and the conditional reliability $R(t \mid \tau)$ is

$$R(t \mid \tau) = e^{-\int_{\tau}^{\tau+t} \lambda(z)dz} = e^{-(\mu(\tau+t)-\mu(\tau))} = \left(1 + \frac{\lambda_0 ct}{1 + \lambda_0 c\tau}\right)^{-\frac{1}{c}}.$$

In Fig. 5.12, we show how the error rate varies with time for the Musa–Okumoto model. Note the very slow decay of the error rate. To get the error rate of software down to a sufficiently low point (following this model) clearly requires a significant amount of testing.

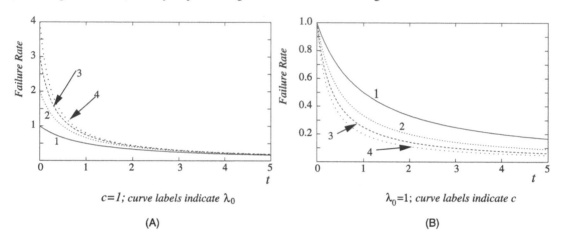

c=1; curve labels indicate λ_0

(A)

λ_0=1; curve labels indicate c

(B)

FIGURE 5.12

Error rates according to the Musa–Okumoto model. (A) Dependence on λ_0. (B) Dependence on c.

5.7.4 OSTRAND–WEYUKER–BELL (OWB) FAULT MODEL

The purpose of the OWB model is to predict which files in a software system are likely to have the most bugs. Development teams may then choose to focus more of their testing time on such files.

This model grew out of an evaluation, at AT&T Labs, of a number of large pieces of software. Based on empirical observations, its developers concluded that the following parameters were of use in making fault (i.e., bug) predictions concerning each file that was part of the software:

- File size;
- Whether the file is new or based on a previous release. If the latter, whether it has been changed since the previous edition;
- Age of the file;
- If a previous release existed, the number of faults in that release;
- Programming language.

They postulated a *negative binomial regression model* for fault estimation. In particular, the faults in file F_i are regarded as the outcome of a Poisson process with rate $\lambda_i = \gamma_i e^{\beta_1 x_1 + \cdots + \beta_n x_n}$, where γ_i is a gamma-distributed random variable with mean 1 and standard deviation σ_i, and $x_1, \cdots, x_n$ are the variables assumed to affect the fault behavior. The quantities σ_i and $\beta_1, \cdots, \beta_n$ are obtained by using the maximum likelihood method (see Section 9.2.3). The probability of k faults in the file is then given by $P_{faults}(k) = e^{-\lambda_i} \frac{\lambda_i^k}{k!}$.

Remark: The variables x_i fall into two classes: The first class consists of variables taking numerical values. The second are *categorical* variables, indicating membership of a class. For example, the number of lines of code in a file is a variable belonging to the first class. The programming language is a categorical variable.

Dealing with categorical variables is not difficult. If there are only two classes into which the quantity can fall (e.g., if there are only two programming languages used), then the values 0 and 1 can be assigned. For example, if the only two languages used in some project are C++ and Java, then the categorical variable $x_{language}$ can be assigned value 0 (to denote the language C++) and 1 (to denote Java). If, on the other hand, the class consists of more than two members, then the categorical variable can be encoded using multiple binary *dummy* variables. For instance, if we have some other project using the three languages C++, Java, and Python, the categorical variable $x_{language}$ is expressed through two dummy variables $x_{language,1}$ and $x_{language,2}$. For instance C++ could be represented by $x_{language,1} = 0, x_{language,2} = 0$, Java by $x_{language,1} = 0, x_{language,2} = 1$, and Python by $x_{language,1} = 1, x_{language,2} = 0$.

Traditionally, a categorical variable indicating membership in one of n categories is broken down into $n - 1$ binary dummy variables, with each being an indicator of membership in exactly one category. Returning to the three-language example above, $x_{language,1} = 1$ if and only if the language is Python, whereas $x_{language,2} = 1$ if and only if it is Java. If neither is 1, then the category is interpreted as C++.

In the OWB model regression, two variables are modified before being used: The log of the file size is used rather than the file size itself, whereas the square root of the number of faults in the previous edition is used, rather than the number of faults. This decision was based on empirical observations of the impact of these parameters on the number of faults.

5.7.5 MODEL SELECTION AND PARAMETER ESTIMATION

Anyone planning to use a reliability model has two problems: First, which of the many available models would be appropriate? Second, how are the model parameters to be estimated?

Selecting the appropriate model is not easy. The American Institute of Aeronautics and Astronautics (AIAA) recommends using one of the following four models, three of which we covered in this chapter: the Jelinski–Moranda, Littlewood–Verrall, Musa–Okumoto, and Schneidewind models. However, as mentioned earlier, no comprehensive and openly accessible body of experimental data is available to guide the user. This is in sharp contrast to hardware reliability modeling, where a systematic data collection effort formed the basis for much of the theory. Software reliability models are based on plausibility arguments. The best that one can suggest is to study the error rate as a function of testing, and guess which model it follows. For example, if the error rate seems to exhibit an exponential dependence on the testing time, then we may consider using the Musa–Okumoto model. Once a suitable model is selected, the parameters can be estimated by using the maximum likelihood method, which is outlined in Chapter 9.

5.8 FAULT-TOLERANT REMOTE PROCEDURE CALLS

A remote procedure call (RPC) is a mechanism by which one process can call another process executing on some other processor. RPCs are widely used in distributed computing.

We will describe next two ways of making RPCs fault tolerant: both are based on replication and bear similarities to the problem of managing replicated data. Throughout, we will assume that processes are fail-stop, i.e., they stop instantly upon failure and lose the contents of all internal state and volatile storage connected to them.

5.8.1 PRIMARY-BACKUP APPROACH

Each process is implemented as primary and backup processes, running on separate nodes. RPCs are sent to both copies, but normally only the primary executes them. If the primary should fail, the secondary is activated and completes the execution.

The actual implementation of this approach depends on whether the RPCs are *retryable* or *nonretryable*. A retryable RPC is one which can be executed multiple times without violating correctness. One example is the reading of some database. A nonretryable RPC should be completed exactly once. For example, incrementing somebody's bank balance is a nonretryable operation.

If the system is running only retryable operations, then implementation of the primary-backup approach is quite straightforward. On the other hand, if nonretryable operations may be involved, it is important to ensure that these be completed exactly once, even if multiple processes are used for fault tolerance. This can be done by the primary process checkpointing its operations on the backup. Should the primary fail while executing the RPC, the backup can pick up from the last checkpoint (see Chapter 6).

5.8.2 THE CIRCUS APPROACH

The *circus* approach also involves the replication of processes. Client and server processes are each replicated. Continuing the circus metaphor, these replicate sets are called *troupes*.

This system is best described through an example. Fig. 5.13 shows four replicates of a client process, making identical calls to four replicates of a server process. Each call has a *sequence number* associated with it that uniquely identifies the call.

A server waits until it has received identical calls from each of the four client copies, or the waiting times out, before executing the RPC. The results are then sent back to each of the clients. These replies are also marked by a sequence number to uniquely identify them.

A client may wait until receiving identical replies from each of the server copies before accepting the input (subject to a timeout to prevent it from waiting forever for a failed server process). Alternatively, it could simply take the first reply it gets and ignore the rest.

An additional complication must be taken care of: it is possible for multiple client troupes to be sending concurrent calls to the same server troupe. In such a case, each member of the server troupe must, to ensure correct functioning, serve the calls in exactly the same order.

There are two ways of ensuring that this order is preserved, called the *optimistic* and *pessimistic* approaches. In the optimistic approach, we make no special attempt to ensure preservation of the order. Instead, we let everything run freely and then check to see if they preserved order. If so, we accept the

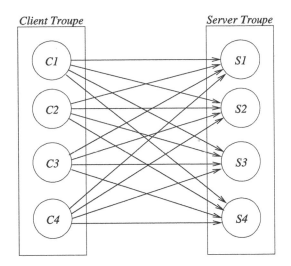

FIGURE 5.13

Example of a circus.

outputs, otherwise, we abort the operations and try again. This approach will perform very poorly if ordering is frequently not preserved.

The pessimistic approach, on the other hand, has built-in mechanisms that ensure that order is preserved.

Let us now present a simple optimistic scheme. Each member of the server troupe receives requests from one or more client troupes. When a member completes processing and is ready to commit, it sends a `ready_to_commit` message to each element of the client troupe. It then waits until *every* member of the client troupe acknowledges this call before proceeding to commit. On the client side, a similar procedure is followed: The client waits until it has received the `ready_to_commit` message from every member of the server troupe, before acknowledging the call. Once the server receives an acknowledgment from each member of the client troupe, it commits.

This approach ensures correct functioning by forcing deadlock if the serial order is violated. For example, let C_1 and C_2 be two client troupes making concurrent RPCs ρ_1 and ρ_2 to a server troupe consisting of servers S_1 and S_2. Let us see what happens if S_1 tries to commit ρ_1 first and then ρ_2, while S_2 works in the opposite order.

Once S_1 is ready to commit ρ_1, it sends a `ready_to_commit` message to each member of C_1, and waits to receive an acknowledgment from each of them. Similarly, S_2 gets ready to commit ρ_2, and sends a `ready_to_commit` message to each member of C_2. Now, members of each client troupe will wait until hearing a `ready_to_commit` from both S_1 and S_2. Since members of C_1 will not hear from S_2 and members of C_2 will not hear from S_1, there is a deadlock. Algorithms exist to detect such deadlocks in distributed systems. Once the deadlock is detected, the operations can be aborted before being committed, and then retried.

5.9 FURTHER READING

An excellent introduction to the intrinsic difficulties of making software run correctly can be found in [10,11]. A contrary view, arguing that complexity can be successfully encapsulated in software modules to render it invisible to users of those modules (human or software routines that call these modules) is presented in [19].

[45] is regarded as a classic in the field of software safety. Other excellent, general references for software fault tolerance are [31,74].

Wrappers are motivated in [79]. Systematic design procedures for wrappers are discussed in [63, 65]. In [70], the authors describe how to wrap a kernel. In [24], wrappers are used to prevent heap-smashing attacks. [30] describes the wrapping of Windows NT software.

Leeke *et al.*, present an approach to have wrappers maintain multiple copies of the most critical variables [44]. See their paper for detailed experimental results showing reliability improvements using their approach.

The idea of facilitating retry under altered circumstances was presented in [75]. The authors provide a good list of failure types that can be defended against by wrappers.

A good case study of the use of wrappers in an automotive software application is presented in [52] and in cloud computing in [53]. Wrapper inconsistencies are discussed in [23].

Software rejuvenation has a long history. People were rebooting their computers when they failed, or hung long before it was called rejuvenation. However, its formal use to enhance software reliability is fairly new. The basics of software aging are described well in [32]; some interesting empirical data from space missions is outlined in [33]. A good introduction to the rejuvenation idea can be found in [18,26,35], and a case study in [84]. Rejuvenation in virtualized systems is described in [12,54,62]. The use of software rejuvenation, including a tool to implement it, is described in [16]. A method by which to estimate the rate of software aging (and hence to determine when to rejuvenate) is provided in [27]. The application of rejuvenation to cluster systems, including a discussion of the relative merits of time-based and prediction-based approaches, can be found in [76], and the smoothing approach they use for prediction was proposed in [17]. For microreboots, involving reboots of individual components, see [15,43]. Machine learning approaches are described in [3]. An experimental study of the overhead associated with various levels of rejuvenation is presented in [1]. The *IEEE International Workshops on Software Aging and Rejuvenation* is a good source for reports of recent developments in the field.

Data diversity is described in some detail in [2], where experimental results are provided of a radar-tracking application. For the use of rephrasing in databases, see [28]. A good reference to SIHFT techniques, which also includes a detailed overview of related schemes appears in [59]. The IEEE floating-point number representation and the precision of floating-point operations are discussed in many books, e.g., [40]. The RESO technique is described in [61].

A good introduction to N-version programming can be found in [5]; for a more general discussion of dependable software, see [72]. A design paradigm is provided in [4]. The observation that requirements specifications are the cause of most software bugs is stated in multiple places, for example, see [8,45,78]. See [29] for a description of the four-version DBMS experiment conducted at the City University of London, and [64,77] for analyses of programs submitted to the UVa Online Judge website.

A survey of modeling software design diversity can be found in [50]. This chapter draws on the foundational work of the authors of [22]. An excellent description of the ways by which forced diversity among versions can be obtained can be found in [47]. An experiment in design diversity is described in [9]. Experiments to determine if the versions are stochastically independent, or not, have not been without some controversy; see [41] regarding some early experiments in this field. A study of the impact of specification language diversity on the diversity of the resulting software was published in [83]. An investigation into whether the results from different inspectors of software are independent of one another appears in [55].

Cognitive diversity among teams has been explored in the field of organizational behavior and psychology; for example, see [46,56].

The cost of creating multiple versions has not been systematically surveyed; an interesting initial study appears in [39]. An efficient N-version execution framework is presented in [34]. A survey of recent developments in software diversity appears in [6].

A comprehensive description of recovery blocks appears in [66].

An introduction to exceptions and exception handling can be found in [20], and a useful survey appears in [13]. A discussion of the comparative merits of exception-terminate and exception-resume is in [51]. The exception-handling mechanism in individual languages is generally treated in some detail in their language manuals and books; for example, see [7]. Exception handling in object-oriented systems is surveyed in [25], and in real-time software in [42]. A good outline of issues in distributed systems can be found in [82]. See [73] for preconditions and postconditions.

The notion of *failure-oblivious computing*, where the system may continue to perform acceptably, despite certain erroneous outputs, is emerging; see, for example, [21,68,69].

There is a substantial literature on software reliability models (also called software reliability growth models). A useful survey appears in [80]. A Bayesian approach is presented in [67]. The models discussed in this chapter have been presented in [38,48,49,57,58,60]. A comparison of modeling methods for software reliability appears in [81]; whether models meet industry perceptions is dealt with in [37]. See [14] for an argument as to why it is infeasible to expect to be able to quantify the failure probability of extremely reliable software.

A good discussion of fault-tolerant remote procedure calls can be found in [36]. Fail-stop failure modes are defined in [71].

5.10 EXERCISES

1. Join $N-1$ other people ($N=3,4,5$ are probably the best choices) to carry out an experiment in writing N-version programs. Write software to solve a set of differential equations, using the Runge–Kutta method. Programs for doing so are widely available and can be used to check the correctness of each version produced. Pick one of these, and compare the output of each version against this reference program for a large number of test cases. Identify the number of bugs in each version, and the extent to which they are correlated.

2. The correct output z of some system has as its probability density function the truncated exponential function (assume L is some positive constant)

$$f(z) = \begin{cases} \frac{\mu e^{-\mu z}}{1 - e^{-\mu L}} & \text{if } 0 \leq z \leq L \\ 0 & \text{otherwise} \end{cases}.$$

If the program fails, it may output any value over the interval $[0, L]$ with equal probability. The probability that the program fails on some input is q.

The penalty for putting out an incorrect value is π_{bad}; the penalty for not producing any output at all is π_{stop}.

We want to set up an acceptance test in the form of a range check, which rejects outputs outside the range $[0, \alpha]$. Compute the value of α, for which the expected total penalty is minimized.

3. Suggest measures to evaluate the spatial and temporal impact of errors in a variable (as used by a wrapper to determine if that variable is to be duplicated or triplicated).

4. In this problem, we will use simulation to study the performance of a bug removal process after an initial debugging (see Chapter 9).

Assume you have a program that has N possible inputs. There are b bugs in the program, and bug i is activated whenever any input in the set F_i is applied. It is not required that $F_i \cap F_j = \emptyset$, and so the bug sets may overlap, that is, the same input may trigger multiple bugs. If F_i has k elements in it, the elements of F_i are obtained by randomly drawing k different elements from the set of possible inputs.

Assume that you have a test procedure that applies inputs to the program. These inputs are randomly chosen from among the ones that have not been applied so far. Also assume that when an input is applied, which triggers one or more bugs, those bugs are immediately removed from the program. Plot the number of software bugs remaining in the program as a function of the number of inputs applied. Use the following parameters in your simulation:

(i) $N = 10^8$, and the number of elements in F_i is uniformly distributed over the set $\{1, 2, \ldots, n\}$.
   (a) The total number of bugs is $b = 1000$. $n = 50$, and a total of 10^6 randomly chosen test inputs are applied.
   (b) Repeat (a) for $n = 75$.
   (c) Repeat (a) for $n = 100$.
(ii) $N = 10^8$, and the number of elements in F_i has the following probability mass function:

$$\text{Prob}\{F_i \text{ has k elements})\} = \frac{p(1-p)^{k-1}}{1-(1-p)^n}, \text{ where } k = 1, \cdots, n.$$

Apply 10^6 randomly chosen test vectors in all. As before, assume there are $b = 1000$ software bugs.
   (a) $n = 50$; $p = 0.1$.
   (b) $n = 75$; $p = 0.1$.
   (c) $n = 100$; $p = 0.1$.
   (d) Repeat (a) to (c) for $p = 0.2$.
   (e) Repeat (a) to (c) for $p = 0.3$.

Discuss your results.

5. For an expected number of errors $\tilde{N}(P) = \lambda P^2$ over a rejuvenation period P, the optimal rejuvenation period is $P_{opt} = \sqrt{\frac{C_r}{\lambda C_e}}$, where C_r is the cost of each rejuvenation, and C_e is the cost of each error. On a certain computer system it has been decided to double the frequency of rejuvenation.

- (a) By how much would the rejuvenation cost increase (or decrease) with this rejuvenation period compared to the cost with the optimal rejuvenation period?
- (b) By how much would the rejuvenation cost per time unit increase (or decrease) with this rejuvenation period compared to the cost per time unit with the optimal rejuvenation period?

6. In this problem, we will use Bayes's law to provide some indication of whether bugs still remain in the system after a certain amount of testing. Suppose you are given that the probability of uncovering a bug (given that at least one exists) after t seconds of testing is $1 - e^{-\mu t}$. Your belief at the beginning of testing is that the probability of having at least one bug is q. (Equivalently, you think that the probability that the program was completely bug-free is $p = 1 - q$.) After t seconds of testing, you fail to find any bugs at all. Bayes's law gives us a concrete way in which to use this information to refine your estimate of the chance that the software is bug-free. Find the probability that the software is actually bug-free, *given that you have observed no bugs at all, despite t seconds of testing.*
Let us use the following notation:

- A is the event that the software is actually bug-free;
- B is the event that no bugs were caught, despite t seconds of testing.

(*a*) Show that

$$\text{Prob}\{A|B\} = \frac{p}{p + qe^{-\mu t}}.$$

(*b*) Fix $p = 0.1$, and plot curves of $\text{Prob}\{A|B\}$ against t for the following parameter values: $\mu = 0.001, 0.01, 0.1, 0 \leq t \leq 10000$.
(*c*) Fix $\mu = 0.01$, and plot curves of $\text{Prob}\{A|B\}$ against t for the following parameter values: $p = 0.1, 0.3, 0.5$.
(*d*) What conclusions do you draw from your plots in (*b*) and (*c*) above?

7. This question relates to recovery blocks. Based on the concepts of test sensitivity s and false alarm rate ρ_{fa}, derive an expression for the fraction of alarms that are false (for a single stage). The unconditional probability that an output of this stage is good is known to be p_g.
8. In the context of the SIHFT technique, the term *data integrity* has been defined as the probability that the original and the transformed programs will not both generate identical incorrect results. Show that if the only faults possible are single stuck-at faults in a bus (see Fig. 5.4), and k is either -1 or 2^{ℓ} with ℓ an integer, then the data integrity is equal to 1. Give an example when the data integrity will be smaller than 1. (Hint: Consider ripple-carry addition with $k = -1$.)
9. Compare the use of the *AN* code (see Chapter 3) to the RESO technique. Consider the types of faults that can be detected and the overheads involved in both cases.

REFERENCES

[1] J. Alonso, R. Matias, E. Vicente, A. Maria, K.S. Trivedi, A comparative experimental study of software rejuvenation overhead, Performance Evaluation 70 (3) (2013) 231–250.
[2] P.E. Ammann, J.C. Knight, Data diversity: an approach to software fault tolerance, IEEE Transactions on Computers 37 (April 1988) 418–425.

[3] J. Alonso, L. Belanche, D. Avresky, Predicting software anomalies using machine learning techniques, in: IEEE International Symposium on Network Computing and Applications (NCA '11), 2011, pp. 163–170.

[4] A. Avizienis, The methodology of N-version programming, in: M. Liu (Ed.), Software Fault Tolerance, Wiley, 1995, pp. 23–46.

[5] A. Avizienis, J. Kelly, Fault tolerance by design diversity: concepts and experiments, IEEE Computer 17 (August 1984) 67–80.

[6] B. Baudry, M. Monperrus, The multiple facets of software diversity: recent developments in year 2000 and beyond, ACM Computing Surveys 48 (1) (September 2015) 16.

[7] J.G.P. Barnes, Programming in ADA, Addison-Wesley, 1994.

[8] J.P. Bowen, V. Stavridou, Safety-critical systems, formal methods and standards, IEE/BCS Software Engineering Journal 8 (July 1993) 189–209.

[9] S. Brilliant, J.C. Knight, N.G. Leveson, Analysis of faults in an N-version software experiment, IEEE Transactions on Software Engineering 16 (February 1990) 238–247.

[10] F.P. Brooks Jr., No silver bullet – essence and accidents of software engineering, IEEE Computer 20 (April 1987) 10–19.

[11] F.P. Brooks Jr., The Mythical Man-Month: Essays on Software Engineering, Addison-Wesley, 1995.

[12] D. Bruneo, F. Longo, A. Puliafito, M. Scarpa, S. Distefano, Software rejuvenation in the cloud, in: ICST Conference on Simulation Tools and Techniques (SIMUTOOLS), 2012, pp. 8–16.

[13] A. Burns, A. Wellings, Real-Time Systems and Programming Languages, Addison-Wesley Longman, 1997.

[14] R.W. Butler, G.B. Finelli, The infeasibility of quantifying the reliability of life-critical software, IEEE Transactions on Software Engineering 19 (1) (January 1993) 3–12.

[15] G. Candea, S. Kawamoto, Y. Fujiki, G. Friedman, A. Fox, Microreboot – a technique for cheap recovery, in: Symposium on Operating System Design and Implementation, 2004, pp. 31–44.

[16] V. Castelli, R.E. Harper, P. Heidelberger, S.W. Hunter, K.S. Trivedi, K. Vaidyanathan, W.P. Zeggert, Proactive management of software aging, IBM Journal of Research and Development 45 (March 2001) 311–332.

[17] W.S. Cleveland, Robust locally weighted regression and smoothing scatterplots, Journal of the American Statistical Association 74 (December 1979) 829–836.

[18] D. Cotroneo, R. Natella, R. Pietrantuono, S. Russo, A survey of software aging and rejuvenation studies, ACM Journal on Emerging Technologies in Computing Systems 10 (1) (January 2014) 8.

[19] B. Cox, No silver bullet revisited, American Programmer 8 (November 1995).

[20] F. Cristian, Exception handling and tolerance of software faults, in: M. Liu (Ed.), Software Fault Tolerance, Wiley, 1995, pp. 81–107.

[21] T. Durieux, Y. Hamadi, Z. Yu, B. Baudry, M. Monperros, Exhaustive exploration of the failure-oblivious design space, in: IEEE International Conference on Software Testing, Verification, and Validation, 2018, pp. 139–149.

[22] D.E. Eckhardt, L.D. Lee, A theoretical basis for the analysis of multiversion software, IEEE Transactions on Software Engineering SE-11 (December 1985) 1511–1517.

[23] H. Femmer, D. Ganesan, M. Lindvall, D. McComas, Detecting inconsistencies in wrappers: a case study, in: Software Engineering in Practice (ICSE), 2013, pp. 1022–1031.

[24] C. Fetzer, Z. Xiao, Detecting heap smashing attacks through fault containment wrappers, in: 20th Symposium on Reliable Distributed Systems, 2001, pp. 80–89.

[25] A.F. Garcia, C.M.F. Rubira, A. Romanovsky, J. Xu, A comparative study of exception handling mechanisms for building dependable object oriented software, The Journal of Systems and Software 59 (2001) 197–222.

[26] S. Garg, Y. Huang, C. Kintala, K.S. Trivedi, Minimizing completion time of a program by checkpointing and rejuvenation, in: ACM SIGMetrics, 1996, pp. 252–261.

[27] S. Garg, A. van Moorsell, K. Vaidyanathan, K. Trivedi, A methodology for detection and elimination of software aging, in: Ninth International Symposium on Software Reliability Engineering, 1998, pp. 282–292.

[28] I. Gashi, P. Popov, Rephrasing rules for off-the-shelf SQL database servers, in: Sixth European Dependable Computing Conference, 2006, pp. 139–148.

[29] I. Gashi, P. Popov, L. Strigini, Fault tolerance via diversity for off-the-shelf products: a study with SQL database servers, IEEE Transactions on Dependable and Secure Computing 4 (4) (2007) 280–294.

[30] A.K. Ghosh, M. Schmid, F. Hill, Wrapping windows NT software for robustness, in: Fault-Tolerant Computing Symposium, FTCS-29, 1999, pp. 344–347.

[31] R. Gilreath, P. Porter, C. Nagy, Advanced Software Fault Tolerance Strategies for Mission Critical Spacecraft Applications, Task 3 Interim Report, NASA Ames Research Center, 1999.

[32] M. Grottke, R. Matias, K. Trivedi, The fundamentals of software aging, in: IEEE International Conference on Software Reliability Engineering Workshops, 2008.

[33] M. Grottke, A. Nikora, K. Trivedi, An empirical investigation of fault types in space mission system software, in: International Conference on Dependable Systems and Networks, 2010, pp. 447–456.

[34] P. Hosek, C. Cadar, Varan the unbelievable: an efficient N-version execution framework, in: International Conference on Architectural Support for Programming Languages and Operating Systems (ASPLOS), 2015, pp. 339–353.

[35] Y. Huang, C. Kintala, N. Kolettis, N.D. Fulton, Software rejuvenation: analysis, module and applications, in: Fault Tolerant Computing Symposium, FTCS-25, 1995, pp. 381–390.

[36] P. Jalote, Fault Tolerance in Distributed Systems, Prentice-Hall, 1994.

[37] S.L. Joshi, B. Deshpande, S. Punnekkat, Do software reliability prediction models meet industrial perceptions?, in: Innovations in Software Engineering Conference (ISEC), 2017, pp. 66–73.

[38] Z. Jelinski, P. Moranda, Software reliability research, in: W. Freiberger (Ed.), Statistical Computer Performance Evaluation, Academic Press, 1972, pp. 465–484.

[39] K. Kanoun, Cost of software diversity: an empirical evaluation, in: International Symposium on Software Reliability, 1999, pp. 242–247.

[40] I. Koren, Computer Arithmetic Algorithms, A. K. Peters, 2002.

[41] J.C. Knight, N.G. Leveson, A reply to the criticisms of the knight and leveson experiment, ACM SIGSoft Software Engineering Notes 15 (January 1990) 24–35.

[42] J. Lang, D.B. Stewart, A study of the applicability of existing exception-handling techniques to component-based real-time software technology, ACM Transactions on Programming Languages and Systems 20 (March 1998) 274–301.

[43] M. Le, Y. Tamir, Applying microreboot to system software, in: IEEE Conference on Software Security and Reliability, 2012, pp. 11–20.

[44] M. Leeke, A. Jhumka, An automated wrapper-based approach to the design of dependable software, in: DEPEND 2011: Fourth International Conference on Dependability, 2011.

[45] N.G. Leveson, Software safety: why, what, and how, ACM Computing Surveys 18 (February 1991) 34–46.

[46] L.L. Levesque, J.M. Wilson, D.R. Wholey, Cognitive divergence and shared mental models in software development project teams, Journal of Organizational Behavior 22 (2) (2001) 135–144.

[47] B. Littlewood, L. Strigini, A Discussion of Practices for Enhancing Diversity in Software Designs, DISPO Technical Report LS_DI_TR-04_v1_1d, November 2000.

[48] B. Littlewood, J.L. Verrall, A Bayesian reliability growth model for computer software, Applied Statistics 22 (1973) 332–346.

[49] B. Littlewood, J.L. Verrall, A Bayesian reliability model with a stochastically monotone failure rate, IEEE Transactions on Reliability R-23 (June 1974) 108–114.

[50] B. Littlewood, P. Popov, L. Strigini, Modeling software design diversity – a review, ACM Computing Surveys 33 (June 2001) 177–208.

[51] B. Liskov, A. Snyder, Exception handling in CLU, IEEE Transactions on Software Engineering SE-5 (June 1979) 546–558.

[52] C. Lu, J.-C. Fabre, M.-O. Killijan, Robustness of modular multi-layered software in the automotive domain: a wrapping-based approach, in: IEEE Conference on Emerging Technologies and Factory Automation, 2009, pp. 1–9.

[53] Q. Lu, X. Xu, L. Bass, L. Zhu, A tail-tolerant cloud API wrapper, IEEE Software 32 (1) (January/February 2015) 76–82.

[54] F. Machida, V. Nicola, K.S. Trivedi, Modeling and analysis of software rejuvenation in a server virtualized system, in: IEEE International Workshop on Software Aging and Rejuvenation, 2010.

[55] J. Miller, On the independence of software inspectors, The Journal of Systems and Software 60 (January 2002) 5–10.

[56] S. Mohammed, L. Ferzandi, K. Hamilton, Metaphor no more: a 15-year review of the team mental model construct, Journal of Management 36 (4) (2010).

[57] J.D. Musa, Software Reliability: Measurement, Prediction, Application, McGraw-Hill, 1987.

[58] J.D. Musa, K. Okumoto, A logarithmic Poisson execution time model for software reliability measurement, in: Seventh International Conference on Software Engineering (ICSE'84), 1984, pp. 230–238.

[59] N. Oh, S. Mitra, E.J. McCluskey, ED4I: error detection by diverse data and duplicated instructions, IEEE Transactions on Computers 51 (February 2002) 180–199.

[60] T.J. Ostrand, E.J. Weyuker, R.M. Bell, Predicting the location and number of faults in large software systems, IEEE Transactions on Software Engineering 31 (4) (April 2005) 340–355.

[61] J.H. Patel, L.Y. Fung, Concurrent error detection in ALU's by recomputing with shifted operands, IEEE Transactions on Computers C-31 (July 1982) 589–595.

[62] R. Pietrantuono, S. Russo, Software aging and rejuvenation in the cloud: a literature review, in: IEEE International Symposium on Software Reliability Engineering Workshops (Workshop on Software Aging and Rejuvenation), 2018, pp. 257–263.

[63] P. Popov, S. Riddle, A. Romanovsky, L. Strigini, On systematic design of protectors for employing OTS items, in: 27th EuroMicro Conference, 2001, pp. 22–29.

[64] P. Popov, V. Stankovic, L. Strigini, An empirical study of the effectiveness of forcing diversity based on a large population of diverse programs, in: IEEE International Symposium on Software Reliability, 2012, pp. 41–50.

[65] P. Popov, L. Strigini, S. Riddle, A. Romanovsky, Protective wrapping of OTS components, in: 4th ICSE Workshop on Component-Based Software Engineering: Component Certification and System Prediction, 2001.

[66] B. Randell, J. Xu, The evolution of the recovery block concept, in: M. Lyu (Ed.), Software Fault Tolerance, Wiley, 1995, pp. 1–21.

[67] N.E. Rallis, Z.F. Lansdowne, Reliability estimation for a software system with sequential independent reviews, IEEE Transactions on Software Engineering 27 (December 2001) 1057–1061.

[68] M. Rinard, C. Cadar, D. Dumitran, D.M. Roy, T. Leu, W.S. Beebee, Enhancing server availability and security through failure-oblivious computing, in: Symposium on Operating Systems Design and Implementation, 2004, pp. 303–316.

[69] M. Rinard, C. Cadar, H.H. Nguyen, Exploring the acceptability envelope, in: Conference on Object-Oriented Programming, Systems, Languages, and Applications (OOPSLA), 2005, pp. 21–29.

[70] F. Salles, M. Rodrigues, J.-C. Fabre, J. Arlat, Metakernels and fault containment wrappers, in: IEEE Fault-Tolerant Computing Symposium, FTCS-29, 1999, pp. 22–29.

[71] R.D. Schlichting, F.B. Schneider, Fail-stop processors: an approach to designing fault-tolerant computing systems, ACM Transactions on Computer Systems 1 (3) (August 1983) 222–238.

[72] L. Strigini, Fault tolerance against design faults, in: H. Diab, A. Zomaya (Eds.), Dependable Computing Systems: Paradigms, Performance Issues, and Applications, John Wiley and Sons, 2005, pp. 213–241.

[73] S.M. Sutton Jr., Preconditions, Postconditions, and Provisional Execution in Software Processes, CMPSCI Technical Report 95-77, Department of Computer Science, University of Massachusetts at Amherst, 1995.

[74] W. Torres-Pomales, Software Fault-Tolerance: A Tutorial, NASA Technical Memorandum TM-2000-210616, 2000.

[75] F. Qin, J. Tucek, J. Sundaresan, Y. Zhou, Rx: treating bugs as allergies—a safe method to survive software failures, ACM SIGOPS Operating Systems Review 39 (5) (2005) 235–248.

[76] K. Vaidyanathan, R.E. Harper, S.W. Hunter, K.S. Trivedi, Analysis and implementation of software rejuvenation in cluster systems, ACM SIGMETRICS Performance Evaluation Review (June 2001) 62–71.

[77] J.P. van der Meulen, Miguel Revilla, The effectiveness of software diversity in a large population of programs, IEEE Transactions on Software Engineering 34 (6) (2008) 753–764.

[78] A. Villemeur, Reliability, Availability, Maintainability and Safety Assessment, Wiley, 1991.

[79] J. Voas, J. Payne, COTS software failures: can anything be done?, in: IEEE Workshop on Application-Specific Software Engineering and Technology, March 1988.

[80] D. Wallace, C. Coleman, Application and Improvement of Software Reliability Models, Report of Task 323-08, NASA Software Assurance Technology Center, 2001.

[81] E.J. Weyuker, T.J. Ostrand, R.M. Bell, Comparing the effectiveness of several modeling methods for fault prediction, Empirical Software Engineering 15 (3) (2010) 277–295.

[82] J. Xu, A. Romanovsky, B. Randell, Concurrent exception handling and resolution in distributed object systems, IEEE Transactions on Parallel and Distributed Systems 11 (October 2000) 1019–1032.

[83] C.S. Yoo, P.H. Seong, Experimental analysis of specification language diversity impact of NPP software diversity, The Journal of Systems and Software 62 (May 2002) 111–122.

[84] J. Zhao, Y. Jin, K.S. Trivedi, R. Marias Jr., Y. Wang, Software rejuvenation scheduling using accelerated life testing, ACM Journal on Emerging Technologies in Computing Systems 10 (1) (January 2014) 9.

CHECKPOINTING

Computers today are thousands of times faster than they were just a few decades ago. Despite this, many important applications take days, or more, of computer time. Indeed, as computing speeds increase, computational problems that were previously dismissed as intractable become practical. Here are some applications that take a very long time to execute, even on today's fastest computers:

(1) Fluid-flow simulation: Many important physics applications require the simulation of fluid flows. These are notoriously complex, consisting of large assemblages of three-dimensional cells, interacting with one another. Examples include weather and climate modeling.

(2) Optimization: Optimally deploying resources is often very complex. For example, airlines must schedule the movement of aircraft and their crews, so that the correct combination of crews and aircraft are available, with all the regulatory constraints (such as flight crew rest hours, aircraft maintenance, and the aircraft types that individual pilots are certified for) satisfied.

(3) Astronomy: N-body simulations that account for the mutual gravitational interactions of N bodies, the formation of stars during the merger of galaxies, the dynamics of galactic cluster formation, and the hydrodynamic modeling of the universe are problems that can require huge amounts of time on even the fastest computers.

(4) Biochemistry: The study of protein folding holds the potential for tailoring treatments to an individual patient's genetic makeup and disease. This problem is sufficiently complex to require petaflops of computing power.

When a program takes very long to execute, the probability of failure during execution, as well as the cost of such a failure, become significant.

To illustrate this problem, we introduce the following analytical model, which we will use throughout this chapter: Consider a program that takes T hours to execute if no failures occur during its execution. Suppose the system suffers transient failures according to a Poisson process at a rate of λ failures per hour. Here, to simplify the derivation, we assume that transients are point failures, i.e., they induce an error in the system and then go away immediately. All the computation done by the program prior to the error is lost; the system takes negligible time to recover from the failure. Some of these simplifying assumptions are removed in Section 6.3.

Let E be the expected execution time, including any computational work lost to failures. To calculate E, we follow standard conditioning arguments. We list all the possible cases, systematically work through each one, weight each case with its probability of occurrence, and sum them all up to get the overall expected execution time.

It is convenient to break the problem down into two cases: either (Case 1) there are no failures during the execution, or (Case 2) there is at least one. If there are no failures during execution, the

Fault-Tolerant Systems. https://doi.org/10.1016/B978-0-12-818105-8.00016-4

execution time is (by definition) T. The probability of no failures happening over an interval of duration T is $e^{-\lambda T}$, so the contribution of Case 1 to the average execution time is $Te^{-\lambda T}$.

If failure does occur, things get a bit more complicated. Suppose that the first failure to hit the execution occurs τ seconds into the execution time T. Then, we have lost these τ seconds of work and will have to start all over again. In such an event, the expected execution time will be $\tau + E$. The probability that the first failure falls in the infinitesimal interval $[\tau, \tau + d\tau]$ is given by $\lambda e^{-\lambda \tau} d\tau$.

τ may be anywhere in the range $[0, T]$. Hence, we remove the conditioning on τ to obtain the contribution of Case 2 to the average execution time:

$$\int_{\tau=0}^{T} (\tau + E)\lambda e^{-\lambda \tau} d\tau = \frac{1}{\lambda} + E - e^{-\lambda T}\left\{\frac{1}{\lambda} + T + E\right\}.$$

Adding the contributions of Cases 1 and 2, we have

$$E = Te^{-\lambda T} + \frac{1}{\lambda} + E - e^{-\lambda T}\left\{\frac{1}{\lambda} + T + E\right\}. \tag{6.1}$$

Solving this equation for E, we obtain the (surprisingly simple) expression

$$E = \frac{e^{\lambda T} - 1}{\lambda}. \tag{6.2}$$

We can see that the average execution time E is very sensitive to T; indeed, it increases exponentially with T. The penalty imposed by the failure process can be measured by $E - T$, the extra time wasted due to failures. When normalizing $E - T$ by the failure-free execution time T, we obtain η, a dimensionless metric of this penalty,

$$\eta = \frac{E - T}{T} = \frac{E}{T} - 1 = \frac{e^{\lambda T} - 1}{\lambda T} - 1. \tag{6.3}$$

Note that η depends only on the product λT, the number of failures expected to strike the processor over the duration of an execution.

Fig. 6.1 plots η as a function of λT, showing that η starts quite small, but then goes up rapidly.

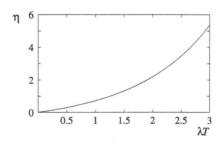

FIGURE 6.1

η as a function of the expected number of failures.

6.1 WHAT IS CHECKPOINTING?

Let us start with an example to which almost everyone who has balanced a checkbook can relate. We have a long list of numbers to add up using a hand calculator. As we do the addition, we record on a slip of paper the partial sum so far for, say, every five additions. Suppose we hit the Clear button by mistake after adding up the first seven numbers. To recover, all we need to do is to add to the partial sum recorded after five additions, the sixth, and seventh terms (see Table 6.1). We have been saved the labor of redoing all six additions: only two need to be done to recover. This is the principle of checkpointing: the partial sums are called *checkpoints*.

Table 6.1 Example of checkpointing.

Item	Amount	Checkpoint
1	23.51	
2	414.78	
3	147.20	
4	110.00	
5	326.68	1022.17
6	50.00	
7	215.00	
8	348.96	
9	3.89	
10	4.55	1644.57
11	725.95	

In general, a *checkpoint* is a snapshot of the entire state of the process at the moment it was taken. It represents all the information that we would need to restart the process from that point. We record the checkpoint on *stable storage*, i.e., a storage in whose reliability we have sufficient confidence. Disks are the most commonly used medium of stable storage: they can hold data even if the power supply is interrupted (so long as there is no physical damage to the disk surface), and enormous quantities of data can be stored very cheaply. This is important, because a checkpoint can be very large: tens or hundreds of megabytes (or more) is not uncommon. Recently, solid-state disks (flash memory) have become increasingly common; these are much faster to access, while remaining nonvolatile. Thus checkpointing to flash memory takes much less time. However, flash memory remains more expensive than traditional disks.

Occasionally, standard memory (RAM), which is rendered (relatively) nonvolatile by the use of a battery backup, is also used as stable storage. When choosing a stable storage medium, it is important to keep in mind that nothing is perfectly reliable. When we use a particular device as stable storage, we are making the judgment that its reliability is sufficiently high for the application at hand.

Two more terms are worth defining at this point. Taking a checkpoint increases the application execution time: this increase is defined as the *checkpoint overhead. Checkpoint latency* is the time needed to save the checkpoint. In a very simple system, the overhead and latency are identical. However, in systems that permit some part of the checkpointing operation to be overlapped with application execution, the latency may be substantially greater than the overhead. For example, suppose a process checkpoints by writing its state into an internal buffer. Having done so, the CPU continues executing the process, while another unit handles writing out the checkpoint from the buffer to disk. Once this is done, the checkpoint has been stored and is available for use in the event of failure.

The checkpointing latency obviously depends on the checkpoint size. This can vary from program to program, as well as with time, during the execution of a single program. For example, consider the following contrived piece of C code:

```
for (i=0; i<1000000; i++)
  if (f(i)<min) {min=f(i); imin=i;}
for (i=0; i<100; i++) {
  for (j=0; j<100; j++) {
    c[i][j] += i*j/min;
  }
}
```

This program fragment consists of two easily distinguishable portions. In the first, we compute the smallest value of $f(i)$ for $0 < i < 1,000,000$, where $f()$ is some function specified in the program. In the second portion, we do a matrix multiplication followed by a division.

A checkpoint taken when the program is executing the first portion need not be large. In fact, all we need to record are the program counter and the variables min and imin—the system will usually record all the registers, but most of them will not actually be relevant here. A checkpoint taken when the second portion is being executed must include the array c[i][j] as it has been computed so far.

The size of the checkpoint is therefore program-dependent. It may be as small as a few kilobytes or as large as several terabytes.

6.1.1 WHY IS CHECKPOINTING NONTRIVIAL?

From the preceding discussion, the reader may be wondering why checkpointing merits a full chapter in this book. Surely the concept as outlined above is quite trivial. Unfortunately, in checkpointing (as in so much else), the devil is in the detail. Here are some of the issues that arise and that we spend most of this chapter discussing:

1. At what level (user or kernel) should we checkpoint: what are the pros and cons of each level? How transparent to the user should the checkpointing process be?
2. How many checkpoints should we have?
3. At which points during the execution of a program should we checkpoint?
4. How can we reduce checkpointing overhead?
5. How do we checkpoint distributed systems, in which there may or may not be a central controller, and in which messages pass between individual processes?

In addition to these issues, there is the question of how to restart the computation at a different node if that becomes necessary. A program does not exist in isolation: it interacts with libraries and the operating system. Its page tables may need to be adjusted to reflect any required changes to the virtual-to-physical address translation. In other words, we have to be careful to ensure, when restarting on processor B a task checkpointed on processor A, that the execution environment of B is sufficiently aligned with that of A to allow this restart to proceed correctly.

In addition, program interactions with the outside world should be carefully considered, because some of them cannot be undone. For example, if the system has printed something, it cannot unprint it. A missile, once launched, cannot be unlaunched. Such outputs must therefore not be delivered before the system is certain that it will not have to undo them.

6.2 CHECKPOINT LEVEL

Checkpointing can be done at the kernel, application, or the user level.

- Kernel-level checkpointing: If checkpointing procedures are included in the kernel, checkpointing is transparent to the user, and generally no changes are required to programs to render them checkpointable. When the system restarts after failure, the kernel is responsible for managing the recovery operation.

  In a sense, every modern operating system takes checkpoints. When a process is preempted, the system records the process state, so that execution can resume from the interrupted point without loss of computational work. However, most operating systems provide little or no checkpointing explicitly for fault tolerance.
- User-level checkpointing: In this approach, a user-level library is provided to do the checkpointing. To checkpoint, application programs are linked to this library. As with kernel-level checkpointing, this approach generally requires no changes to the application code; however, explicit linking is required with the user-level library. The user-level library also manages recovery from failure.
- Application-level checkpointing: Here, the application is responsible for carrying out all the checkpointing functions. Code for checkpointing and managing recovery from failure must therefore be written into the application. This approach provides the user with the greatest control over the checkpointing process, but is expensive to implement and debug.

Note that the information available to each level may be different. For example, if the process consists of multiple threads, some kernels are not aware of them: they have to be managed at the user level. Similarly, the user and application levels do not have access to information held at the kernel level. Nor can they ask, upon recovery, that a recovering process be assigned a particular process identifying number. As a result, a single program could have multiple process identifiers over the course of its life. This may or may not be a problem, depending on the application. Similarly, the user and application levels may not be allowed to checkpoint parts of the file system: in such cases, we may have to store the names and pointers to the appropriate files instead.

6.3 OPTIMAL CHECKPOINTING: AN ANALYTICAL MODEL

We next provide a model which quantifies the impact of overhead on the optimal placement of checkpoints. We have already mentioned that in a modern system, the checkpointing overhead may be much smaller than the checkpointing latency. Briefly, the overhead is that part of the checkpointing activity that is not hidden from the application; it is the part that is not done in parallel with the application execution.

FIGURE 6.2

Checkpointing latency and overhead (squares represent latency and the shaded portions represent overhead).

Let us begin by introducing some notation with the aid of Fig. 6.2. Denoting the latency by T_{lt}, it is the time interval between when the checkpointing operation starts (e.g., t_0 in the figure) and when it ends (t_2 in the figure). To simplify the expressions below, we assume that this time interval is of a fixed size; in other words, $T_{lt} = t_2 - t_0 = t_5 - t_3 = t_8 - t_6$. The three checkpoints that are shown in Fig. 6.2 represent the state of the system at t_0, t_3, and t_6, respectively. The overhead, denoted by T_{ov}, is that part of the T_{lt} interval, during which the system is blocked from executing, due to the checkpointing process. Here too, for simplicity, we assume that this is a fixed-size interval, and, in the figure, $T_{ov} = t_1 - t_0 = t_4 - t_3 = t_7 - t_6$.

If a failure occurs some time during the latency interval T_{lt}, we assume that the checkpoint being taken is useless, and that the system must roll back to the previous checkpoint. For example, if failure occurs anytime in the interval $[t_3, t_5]$ in Fig. 6.2, we have to roll back to the preceding checkpoint that contains the state of the process at time t_0.

In the previous simpler model, we assumed that recovery from failure was instantaneous. Here, we make the more realistic assumption that the recovery time has an average of T_r; that is, if a transient failure hits a process at time τ, the process becomes active again only at an expected time of $\tau + T_r$. This recovery time includes the time spent in a faulty state, plus the time it takes to recover to a functional state (e.g., the time it takes to complete rebooting the processor).

Let us consider the interval of time between when the ith checkpoint has been completed (and is ready to be used, if necessary), and when the $i + 1$st checkpoint is complete, and denote its expected value by E_{int}. Let T_{ex} be the amount of time spent executing the application over this period; that is, if N checkpoints are placed uniformly through the program's execution time T, then $T_{ex} = T/(N + 1)$. Thus if there is no failure, the total execution time over one intercheckpoint interval, plus the checkpointing overhead, will be equal to $T_{ex} + T_{ov}$.

What happens if there is a failure τ seconds into the interval $T_{ex} + T_{ov}$? First, we lose all the work that was done during the time τ. Second, it takes an average of T_r seconds to recover from this failure and restart computations. Hence, the total amount of extra time, due to a failure that occurs τ seconds into the interval, is $\tau + T_r$.

6.3.1 TIME BETWEEN CHECKPOINTS—A FIRST-ORDER APPROXIMATION

In the first-order approximation, we assume that, at most, one failure strikes the system between successive checkpoints. To calculate the expected time between two successive checkpoints, we follow the same conditioning strategy as before: we look at two cases, find the contribution of each case to the expected time, and add up the weighted contributions.

Case 1 involves no failure between successive checkpoints. Since the intercheckpoint interval is $T_{ex} + T_{ov}$, the probability of Case 1 is $e^{-\lambda(T_{ex}+T_{ov})}$, and the weighted contribution of Case 1 to the expected interval length is

$$(T_{ex} + T_{ov})e^{-\lambda(T_{ex}+T_{ov})}.$$

Case 2 involves one failure during the intercheckpoint interval: this happens with a probability that can be approximated by $1 - e^{-\lambda(T_{ex}+T_{ov})}$. This is actually the probability of *at least* one failure over an interval of length $T_{ex} + T_{ov}$, but if we assume that fault arrivals follow a Poisson process, then the probability of experiencing n failures over the interval $T_{ex} + T_{ov}$ drops very rapidly with n when $\lambda(T_{ex} + T_{ov}) \ll 1$ (as is usually the case). We therefore assume that the probability of more than one failure between checkpoints is negligible. The amount of additional time taken due to the failure is $\tau + T_r$; the average value of τ is $(T_{ex} + T_{ov})/2$. Hence, the expected amount of *additional* time is $(T_{ex} + T_{ov})/2 + T_r$. This time period is spent on top of the basic time needed for (re-)execution and checkpointing $T_{ex} + T_{ov}$, and thus the total expected contribution of Case 2 is approximately

$$\left(1 - e^{-\lambda(T_{ex}+T_{ov})}\right)\left\{T_{ex} + T_{ov} + \frac{T_{ex} + T_{ov}}{2} + T_r\right\}$$

$$= \left(1 - e^{-\lambda(T_{ex}+T_{ov})}\right)\left\{\frac{3(T_{ex} + T_{ov})}{2} + T_r\right\}$$

Adding up the contributions of Cases 1 and 2, we obtain the expected length of the intercheckpoint interval, E_{int}:

$$E_{int} \approx \frac{3}{2}(T_{ex} + T_{ov}) + T_r - \left(\frac{(T_{ex} + T_{ov})}{2} + T_r\right)e^{-\lambda(T_{ex}+T_{ov})}. \tag{6.4}$$

6.3.2 OPTIMAL CHECKPOINT PLACEMENT

The above analysis focused on calculating the expected length of the intercheckpoint interval, E_{int}, given a specific number N of equally spaced checkpoints, such that we execute the program for $T_{ex} = T/(N + 1)$ time units between any two consecutive checkpoints (where T is the execution time of the program, not including checkpointing and recovery from failures.) One of the main problems of checkpointing is the need to decide on the value of T_{ex} or, in other words, determine how many checkpoints to schedule during the execution of a long program.

The problem of determining the optimal number of checkpoints is known as the *checkpoint placement problem*, and its objective is to select N (or equivalently, T_{ex}), so as to minimize the expected total execution time of the program or, equivalently, to minimize the figure of merit

$$\eta = \frac{E_{int}}{T_{ex}} - 1.$$

We show next how to determine the optimal value of T_{ex} for the simple model described above. Simplifying Eq. (6.4) by using the first-order approximation

$$e^{-\lambda(T_{ex}+T_{ov})} \approx 1 - \lambda(T_{ex} + T_{ov}),$$

we obtain

$$
\begin{aligned}
\eta &= \frac{\frac{3}{2}(T_{ex} + T_{ov}) + T_r - \left(\frac{(T_{ex}+T_{ov})}{2} + T_r\right)(1 - \lambda(T_{ex} + T_{ov}))}{T_{ex}} - 1 \\
&= \frac{(T_{ex} + T_{ov})\left[1 + \lambda\left(\frac{T_{ex}+T_{ov}}{2} + T_r\right)\right]}{T_{ex}} - 1.
\end{aligned} \tag{6.5}
$$

To select T_{ex} so as to minimize η, we differentiate Eq. (6.5) with respect to T_{ex}, and equate the derivative to zero, yielding

$$
T_{ex}^{opt} = \sqrt{\frac{2T_{ov}}{\lambda} + T_{ov}(2T_r + T_{ov})}. \tag{6.6}
$$

Based on the value of T_{ex}^{opt}, we can calculate the number of checkpoints to minimize η,

$$
N_{opt} = \frac{T}{T_{ex}^{opt}} - 1.
$$

Since N must be an integer, if the above equation does not result in an integer, the normal practice is to calculate the value of η for the nearest two integers to N_{opt}, as calculated above, and select whichever number of checkpoints N results in a lower value. In this calculation, the value of T_{ex} to be used should be $T_{ex} = T/(N+1)$, rather than that calculated from Eq. (6.6).

Keep in mind that the above result is correct only for the simplified model, with at most one failure during the intercheckpoint interval. We relax this assumption in the next section, where a more accurate model is presented.

The alert reader may have been somewhat surprised by the appearance of T_r in the above expression for N_{opt}. T_r is the cost of recovering from a failure and, intuitively, is not expected to affect the optimal number of checkpoints. Indeed, T_r disappears from the expression for N_{opt} in the more exact model, as we will see below. In the exercises, we invite the reader to find an intuitive reason for the presence of T_r in the expression for N_{opt} for the approximate model.

Note that we arrived at this result while deciding to place the checkpoints uniformly along the time axis. Is uniform placement optimal? If the checkpointing cost is the same, irrespective of when the checkpoint is taken, the answer is "yes." If the checkpoint size—and hence the checkpoint cost—varies greatly from one part of the execution to the other, the answer is often "no," and depends on the extent to which the checkpoint size varies.

6.3.3 TIME BETWEEN CHECKPOINTS: A MORE ACCURATE MODEL

To relax the assumption that there is at most one failure in an intercheckpoint interval, we go back to the conditioning on the time of the first failure, but now deal more accurately with Case 2. As before, Case 1, in which there are no failures between successive checkpoints contributes

$$
(T_{ex} + T_{ov})e^{-\lambda(T_{ex}+T_{ov})}
$$

to the average intercheckpoint time E_{int}.

In Case 2, suppose a failure occurred at time τ ($\tau < T_{ex} + T_{ov}$), an event that has a probability of $\lambda e^{-\lambda \tau} d\tau$. The amount of time wasted due to the failure is $\tau + T_r$, after which the computation will resume, and will take an added average time of E_{int}. The contribution of Case 2 is therefore

$$\int_{\tau=0}^{T_{ex}+T_{ov}} (\tau + T_r + E_{int}) \lambda e^{-\lambda \tau} d\tau = E_{int} + T_r + \frac{1}{\lambda}$$
$$- \left(T_{ex} + T_{ov} + T_r + \frac{1}{\lambda} + E_{int} \right) e^{-\lambda(T_{ex}+T_{ov})}.$$

Adding the two cases results in the following equation for E_{int}:

$$E_{int} = (T_{ex} + T_{ov})e^{-\lambda(T_{ex}+T_{ov})} + E_{int} + T_r + \frac{1}{\lambda}$$
$$- \left(T_{ex} + T_{ov} + T_r + \frac{1}{\lambda} + E_{int} \right) e^{-\lambda(T_{ex}+T_{ov})},$$

whose solution is

$$E_{int} = \left(T_r + \frac{1}{\lambda} \right) \left(e^{\lambda(T_{ex}+T_{ov})} - 1 \right). \tag{6.7}$$

Consider again the figure of merit

$$\eta = \frac{E_{int}}{T_{ex}} - 1,$$

which should be minimized to ensure that the normalized cost of checkpointing is minimal. Using the expression in Eq. (6.7), we obtain

$$\eta = \frac{(T_r + \frac{1}{\lambda})(e^{\lambda(T_{ex}+T_{ov})} - 1)}{T_{ex}} - 1, \tag{6.8}$$

which reduces to the expression in Eq. (6.3) when $T_r = T_{ov} = 0$. Suppose we look for a T_{ex} that minimizes η: this is obviously the value of T_{ex}, for which $\partial\eta/\partial T_{ex} = 0$ and $\partial^2\eta/\partial T_{ex}^2 > 0$. It is easy to show that the optimal value of T_{ex} is one that satisfies the equation

$$e^{\lambda(T_{ex}+T_{ov})} = \frac{1}{1 - \lambda T_{ex}}. \tag{6.9}$$

Thus the optimal value T_{ex}^{opt} does not depend on the recovery time T_r, just the overhead T_{ov}. Once the value of T_{ex}^{opt} is known, we can calculate the corresponding optimal number of checkpoints: $N_{opt} = \frac{T}{T_{ex}^{opt}} - 1$. Note that after selecting an integer value for N, T_{ex} must be recalculated.

6.3.4 REDUCING OVERHEAD

The most obvious way to reduce checkpointing overhead is to use a buffer. The system writes the checkpoint into a part of its main memory, and then returns to executing the application. Direct memory access (DMA) is then used to copy the checkpoint from main memory to disk. DMA in most modern machines only requires CPU involvement at the beginning and at the end of the operation.

A refinement of this approach is called *copy-on-write* buffering. The idea is that if large portions of the process state have remained unchanged since the last checkpoint, it is a waste of time to copy the unchanged pages to disk all over again. Avoiding the recopying of the unaltered pages is facilitated by exploiting the memory protection bits provided by most memory systems. Briefly, each page of the physical main memory is provided with protection bits that can indicate whether the page is read-write, read-only, or inaccessible. To implement copy-on-write buffering, the protection bits of the pages belonging to the process are all set to read-only when the checkpoint is taken. The application continues running while the checkpointed pages are transferred to disk. Should the application attempt to update a page, an access violation is triggered. The system is then supposed to respond by buffering the appropriate page, following which the permission on that page can be set to read-write. The buffered page is, in due course, copied to disk. (Clearly, the user-specified status of a page has to be saved elsewhere, to prevent a read-only or inaccessible page being written into.)

The advantage of copy-on-write over simple buffering is that if the process does not update the main memory pages too often, most of the work involved in copying the pages to a buffer area can be avoided. This is an example of *incremental checkpointing*, which consists of simply recording the changes in the process state, since the previous checkpoint was taken. If these changes are few, the size of the incremental checkpoints will be quite small, and much less will have to be saved per checkpoint.

The obvious drawback of incremental checkpointing is that the process of recovery is more complicated. It is no longer a matter of simply loading the latest checkpoint and resuming computation from there; one has to build the system state by examining a succession of incremental checkpoints.

Another approach to lowering the checkpointing overhead attempts to reduce the amount of information that must be stored in a checkpoint. There are two types of variables that are unnecessary to record in a checkpoint: those that have not been updated since the last checkpoint, and those that are "dead." A dead variable is one whose present value will never again be used by the program. There are two kinds of dead variables: those that will never again be referenced by the program, and those for which the next access will be a write. The challenge is to accurately identify such variables.

The address space of a process has four segments: code, global data, heap, and stack. Finding some dead variables in the code and stack is not difficult. Because self-modifying code is no longer used, we can regard the code segment in memory as read-only, which need not be checkpointed. The stack segment is equally simple: the contents of addresses held in locations below the stack pointer are obviously dead. (The virtual address space usually has the stack segment at the top, growing downward: locations below the stack pointer represent memory not currently being used by the stack.) As far as the heap segment is concerned, many languages allow the programmer to explicitly allocate and deallocate memory (e.g., the malloc() and free() calls in C). The contents of the free list are dead by definition. Finally, some user-level checkpointing packages (e.g., libckpt) provide the programmer with procedure calls (such as include_bytes(), exclude_bytes()) that specify regions of the memory that should be included in, or excluded from, checkpoints.

6.3.5 REDUCING LATENCY

Checkpoint compression has been suggested as one way to reduce latency. The smaller the checkpoint, the less has to be written onto disk. How much, if anything, is gained through compression depends on the following:

- The extent of the compression. This is application-dependent: in some cases, the compression reduces checkpoint size by over 50%; in others, it barely makes a difference.
- The work required to execute the compression algorithm. This usually has to be done by the CPU, and thus contributes to the checkpointing overhead.

In simple sequential checkpointing, where the CPU does not execute until the checkpoint has been committed to disk, compression is beneficial whenever the reduction in disk write time more than compensates for the execution time of the compression algorithm. In more efficient systems, where $T_{ov} < T_{lt}$, the usefulness of this approach is questionable, and must be carefully assessed before being used.

Another way of reducing latency is the incremental checkpointing technique mentioned earlier.

6.4 CACHE-AIDED ROLLBACK ERROR RECOVERY (CARER)

Reducing checkpointing overhead allows us to increase the checkpointing frequency, thereby reducing the penalty of a rollback upon failure. The cache-aided rollback error recovery (CARER) approach is a scheme that seeks to reduce the time required to take a checkpoint by marking the process footprint in main memory and cache as parts of the checkpointed state. This, of course, assumes that the memory and cache are far less prone to failure than is the processor itself, and are therefore reliable enough to store checkpoints. If not, the probability of the checkpoint itself being corrupted would be unacceptably high, and the CARER approach cannot be used.

The checkpoint consists of the processes' footprint in main memory, together with any lines of the cache which may be marked as being part of the checkpoint. This approach requires a hardware modification to be made to the system, in the form of an extra checkpoint bit associated with each cache line. When this bit is 1, it indicates the corresponding line is *unmodifiable*, which means that the line is part of the latest checkpoint, and so the processor may not update any word in that line without being forced to take a checkpoint immediately after that update. If the bit is 0, the processor is free to modify the word.

Because all of the process footprint in the main memory and the marked lines in the cache do double duty as both memory and part of the checkpoint, we have less freedom in deciding when checkpoints have to be taken. The general rule is that a checkpoint is forced whenever the system needs to update anything in a cache line whose checkpoint bit is 1, or in the main memory. If a checkpoint is not taken at such a time, then, upon a fault occurring afterwards, the system will not rollback to the old values of the processor registers, but to modified contents of the memory and/or cache. The above implies that checkpoints are also forced when an external interrupt occurs or an I/O instruction is executed (since either could update the memory). To summarize, we are forced to take a checkpoint every time one of the following happens:

- A cache line marked *unmodifiable* is to be updated.
- The main memory is to be updated.
- An I/O instruction is executed or an external interrupt occurs.

Taking a checkpoint involves (*a*) saving the processor registers in memory, and (*b*) setting to 1 the checkpoint bit associated with each valid cache line. By definition, therefore, a line in the cache, whose checkpoint bit is 1 was last modified before the latest checkpoint was taken.

As a result, the checkpoint consists of the footprint of the process in the main memory, together with all the cache lines that are marked unmodifiable and the register copies. Rolling back to the previous checkpoint is now very simple: just restore the registers from their copies in memory and mark as invalid all the lines in the cache, whose checkpoint bit is 0.

This approach is not without its costs. The hardware of the cache has to be modified to introduce the checkpoint bit, and every write-back of any cache line into main memory involves taking a checkpoint.

6.5 CHECKPOINTING IN DISTRIBUTED SYSTEMS

A distributed system consists of a set of processors and their associated memories, connected by means of an interconnection network (see Chapter 4). Each processor usually has local disks, and there can also be a network file system equally accessible to all the processors.

Logically, we will consider a distributed system to consist of a number of *processes* connected together by means of directional *channels*. Channels can be thought of as point-to-point connections from one process to another. Unless otherwise specified, we will assume that each channel is error-free and delivers all messages in the order in which it received them.

We start by providing some details about the system model underlying the analysis that follows. The state of a process has the obvious meaning: the state of the channel at time t is the set of messages carried by this channel up to time t (together with the order in which they were received). The state of the distributed system is the aggregate of the states of the individual processes, and of the channels.

The state of a distributed system is said to be *consistent* if, for every message delivery recorded in the state, there is a corresponding message-sending event. A state that violated this constraint would, in effect, be saying that we could have a message delivered that had not yet been sent. This violates causality, and such a message is called an *orphan*. Note that the converse need not be the case; it is perfectly consistent to have the system state reflect the sending of a message, but not its receipt.

Fig. 6.3 provides an illustration. Here, we have two processes, P and Q, each of which has two checkpoints (CP_1, CP_2, and CQ_1, CQ_2, respectively), taken over the duration shown here. Message m is sent by P to Q.

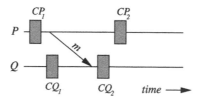

FIGURE 6.3

Consistent and inconsistent states.

The following sets of checkpoints represent a consistent system state:

- $\{CP_1, CQ_1\}$: Neither checkpoint has any information about m.
- $\{CP_2, CQ_1\}$: CP_2 records that m was sent; CQ_1 has no record of receiving m.
- $\{CP_2, CQ_2\}$: CP_2 records that m was sent; CQ_2 records that it was received.

In contrast, the set $\{CP_1, CQ_2\}$ does *not* represent a consistent system state. CP_1 has no record of m being sent, whereas CQ_2 records that m was received. m is therefore an orphan message in this set of checkpoints.

A set of checkpoints that represents a consistent system state is said to form a *recovery line*. We can roll the system back to any available recovery line and restart from there:

- $\{CP_1, CQ_1\}$: Rolling back P to CP_1 undoes the sending of m, and rolling back Q to CQ_1 means that Q does not have any record of having received m. Thus restarting from these checkpoints, P will again send out m, which Q will receive in due course.
- $\{CP_2, CQ_1\}$: Rolling back P to CP_2 means that it will not retransmit m; however, rolling back Q to CQ_1 means that now Q has no record of ever having received m. In this case, the system managing the recovery has to be able to play back m to Q. This can be done by using the checkpoint of P, or by having a separate message log recording everything received by Q. We will discuss message logs later.
- $\{CP_2, CQ_2\}$: The checkpoints record the sending, and receipt, of m.

Sometimes, checkpoints may be placed in such a way that they will never form part of a recovery line. Fig. 6.4 provides such an example. CQ_2 records the receipt of m_1, but not the sending of m_2. $\{CP_1, CQ_2\}$ cannot be consistent (since otherwise m_1 would become an orphan); similarly $\{CP_2, CQ_2\}$ cannot be consistent (since otherwise m_2 would become an orphan).

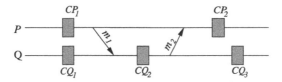

FIGURE 6.4

CQ_2 is a useless checkpoint.

6.5.1 THE DOMINO EFFECT AND LIVELOCK

If we do not coordinate checkpoints either directly (through message passing) or indirectly (by using synchronized clocks), a single failure could cause a sequence of rollbacks that send every process back to its starting point. This is called the *domino effect*.

In Fig. 6.5, we have a distributed system consisting of two processors, P and Q, sending messages to each other. The checkpoints are positioned as shown. When P suffers a transient failure, it rolls back to checkpoint CP_3. However, because it sent out a message m_6 after CP_3 was taken, Q has to roll back to before it received this message (otherwise Q would have recorded a message that was officially never sent: an *orphan* message). Consequently, Q must roll back to CQ_2. But this will trigger a rollback of P to CP_2, because Q sent a message m_5 to P, and P has to move back to a state in which it never received

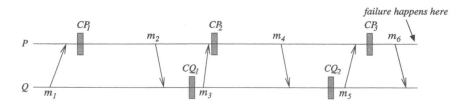

FIGURE 6.5

Example of the domino effect.

this message. This continues until all of the processes have rolled back to their starting positions. This sequence of rollbacks is called a *domino effect*.

It is the interaction between the processes in the form of messages being passed between them that gives rise to the domino effect. The problem arises when we insist on the checkpoints forming a consistent distributed state in which no orphan messages exist. There is a somewhat weaker problem that arises when messages are lost due to rollback, illustrated in Fig. 6.6. Suppose Q rolls back to

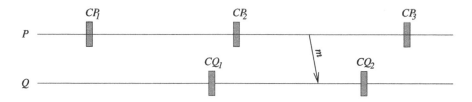

FIGURE 6.6

Example of a lost message.

CQ_1 after receiving message m from P. When it does so (unless inter-processor messages are stored somewhere safe), all activity associated with having received that message is lost. If P does not roll back to CP_2, then the situation is as if P had sent a message, which was never received by Q. This is not as severe a problem as orphan messages, because lost messages do not violate causality. They can be treated as any messages that may be lost due to network problems, for example, by retransmission. Note, however, that if Q had sent an acknowledgment of that message to P before rolling back, then that acknowledgment would be an orphan message unless P rolls back to CP_2.

There is another problem that can arise in distributed checkpointed systems, that of *livelock*. Consider the situation shown in Fig. 6.7. Q sends P a message m_1, and P sends Q message m_2. Then, P fails at the point shown, *before receiving* m_1. To prevent m_2 from being orphaned, Q must roll back to CQ_1. In the meantime, P recovers, rolls back to CP_2, sends another copy of m_2, and then receives the copy of m_1 that was sent before all the rollbacks began. However, because Q has rolled back, this copy of m_1 is now orphaned, and so P has to repeat its rollback. This in turn orphans the second copy of m_2 as well, forcing Q to also repeat its rollback. This dance of the rollbacks may continue indefinitely, unless there is some outside intervention.

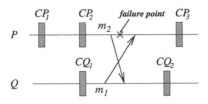

FIGURE 6.7

Example of livelock.

6.5.2 A COORDINATED CHECKPOINTING ALGORITHM

We have seen that if checkpointing is uncoordinated, distributed systems can suffer the domino effect or livelock. In this section, we outline one approach to checkpoint coordination.

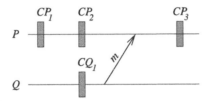

FIGURE 6.8

P taking CP_3 forces Q to checkpoint.

Consider Fig. 6.8 and suppose that P wants to establish a checkpoint at CP_3. This checkpoint will record, among other things, that message m was received from Q. As a result, to prevent this message from ever being orphaned, Q must checkpoint as well, that is, if we want to prevent m from ever becoming an orphan message, the fact that P establishes a checkpoint at CP_3 forces Q to take a checkpoint to record the fact that m was sent.

Let us now describe an algorithm that carries out such coordinated checkpointing. There are two types of checkpoint in this algorithm, *tentative* and *permanent*. When a process P wants to take a checkpoint, it records its current state in a tentative checkpoint. P then sends a message to all other processes from whom it received a message since taking its last checkpoint. Call this set $\hat{P}$. This message tells each process Q the last message m_{qp} that P received from it before the tentative checkpoint was taken. If sending message m_{qp} has not been recorded in a checkpoint by Q, then to prevent m_{qp} from being orphaned, Q will be asked to take a tentative checkpoint recording of the sending of m_{qp}. If all the processes in $\hat{P}$ that need to confirm taking a checkpoint as requested do so, then all the tentative checkpoints can be converted to permanent checkpoints. If, for some reason, one or more members of $\hat{P}$ are not able to checkpoint as requested, P and all other members of $\hat{P}$ abandon their tentative checkpoints, instead of making them permanent.

Note that this process can set off a chain reaction of checkpoints. If P initiates a round of checkpointing among processes in $\hat{P}$, each member of $\hat{P}$ can itself potentially spawn a set of checkpoints among processes within its corresponding set.

6.5.3 TIME-BASED SYNCHRONIZATION

Orphan messages cannot happen if each process checkpoints at exactly the same global time. However, this is practically impossible, because clock skews and message communication times cannot be reduced to zero. Time-based synchronization can still be used to facilitate checkpointing: we just have to take account of nonzero clock skews in doing so.

In time-based synchronization, we checkpoint the processes at previously agreed times. For example, we may ask each process to checkpoint when its local clock reads a multiple of 100 seconds. By itself, such a procedure is not enough to avoid orphan messages, see Fig. 6.9. Here, each process is

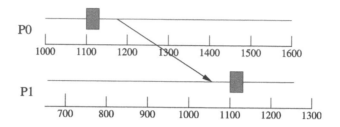

FIGURE 6.9

Creation of an orphan message in time-based synchronization.

checkpointing at time 1100 (where time is read off the local clock). Unfortunately, the skew between the two clocks is such that process P_0 checkpoints much earlier (in real time) than does process P_1. As a result, P_0 sends out a message to P_1 after its checkpoint, which is received by P_1 before its checkpoint. This message is a potential orphan.

If clock skews can be bounded, it is easy to prevent such orphan messages from being generated. Suppose the maximum skew between any two clocks in the distributed system is δ, and that each process is asked to checkpoint when its local clock reads τ. Following this checkpoint, a process P_0 should not send out messages to any process P_1, until it is certain that P_1's local clock reads later than τ. Because the skews are upper-bounded by δ, this means that P_0 should remain silent over the duration $[\tau, \tau + \delta]$ (as measured by P_0's local clock).

We can shorten this interval of silence if there is a lower bound on the interprocess message delivery time. If this time is ϵ, then it is clearly enough for process P_0 to remain silent over the duration $[\tau, \tau + \delta - \epsilon]$ to prevent the formation of orphan messages—if $\epsilon > \delta$, this interval is of zero length, and there is no need for such an interval of silence.

Yet another variation is for a process that receives a message to not include it in its checkpoint, and not act upon it if the message could possibly become an orphan. Suppose message m is received by process P_1 when its clock reads t. Message m must have been sent (by, say, process P_0) no later than ϵ units earlier, before P_1's clock reads $t - \epsilon$. Because the clock skew is upper-bounded by δ, at this time, P_0's clock should have read at most $t - \epsilon + \delta$. If $t - \epsilon + \delta < \tau$, then the sending of this message would have been recorded in P_0's checkpoint, and as a result, the message cannot be an orphan. Hence, if message m is received by P_1 when its clock reads at least $\tau - \delta + \epsilon$, it cannot be an orphan. Thus another way to avoid orphan messages is for a receiving process not to act upon any message received in a window of time $[\tau - \delta + \epsilon, \tau]$ (neither use it nor include it in its checkpoint at time τ) until after taking its own checkpoint at time τ (time as told by the receiving process's local clock).

6.5.4 DISKLESS CHECKPOINTING

Main memory is volatile and is, by itself, often unsuitable as a medium in which to store a checkpoint. However, with extra processors, we can borrow some techniques from RAID (see Section 3.2) to permit checkpointing in main memory. By avoiding disk writes, checkpointing can be made much faster. Diskless checkpointing is probably best used as one level in a two-level checkpointing scheme, which is mentioned in the Further Reading section.

Diskless checkpointing is implemented by having redundant processors using RAID-like techniques to deal with failure. For example, suppose we have a distributed system consisting of six executing, and one extra, processors. Each executing processor stores its checkpoint in its own memory; the extra processor stores in its memory the parity of these checkpoints. Thus if any one of the executing processors were to fail, its checkpoint can be reconstructed from the remaining five checkpoints, plus the parity checkpoint.

We can similarly use other levels of RAID as analogs. For example, RAID level 1 involves disk mirroring. By analogy, we can mirror the checkpoints; in other words, hold in two separate main memory modules identical copies of each checkpoint. Such a system can obviously withstand up to one failure.

In such systems, the interprocessor network must have enough bandwidth to cope with the sending of checkpoints. Also, hotspots can develop that will slow down the whole system. For example, suppose we have multiple executing, and one checkpointing, processors. If all the executing processors send their checkpoints to the checkpointing processor to have the parity calculated, the result will be a potentially debilitating hotspot. We can alleviate the problem by distributing the parity computations, as shown in Fig. 6.10.

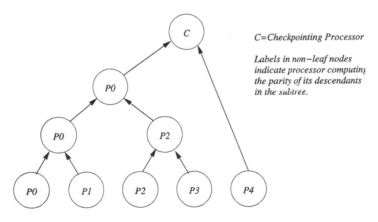

C=Checkpointing Processor

Labels in non−leaf nodes indicate processor computing the parity of its descendants in the subtree.

FIGURE 6.10

Distributing the parity computations.

6.5.5 MESSAGE LOGGING

Recovery consists of rolling back to the latest checkpointing and taking up the computation from that point. In a distributed system, however, to continue the computation beyond the latest checkpoint, the recovering process may require all the messages it received since that checkpoint, played back in the same order as it originally got them. If coordinated checkpointing is used, each process can be rolled back to its latest checkpoint and restarted: those messages will automatically be resent during the reexecution. However, if we want to avoid the overhead of coordination and decide to let processes checkpoint independently of one another, logging messages into stable storage is an option.

We will consider two approaches to message logging: *pessimistic* and *optimistic*. Pessimistic message logging ensures that rollback will not spread to other processes; if a process fails, no other process will need to be rolled back to ensure consistency. In contrast, in optimistic logging, we may have a situation in which a process failure can trigger the rollback of other processes as well.

Throughout this section, we will assume that to recover a process, it is sufficient to roll it back to some checkpoint, and then replay to it the messages it received since that point, in the order in which they were originally received.

Pessimistic message logging

Several pessimistic message logging algorithms exist. Perhaps the simplest is for the receiver of a message to stop whatever it is doing when it receives a message, log the message onto stable storage, and then resume execution. Recovering a process from failure is extremely simple: just roll it back to its latest checkpoint and play back to it the messages it received since that checkpoint, in the right order. No orphan messages will exist in the sense that every message will have been either received before the latest checkpoint, or explicitly saved in the message log. As a result, rolling back one process will not trigger the rollback of any other process.

The requirement that a process must log messages into its stable storage (as opposed to a volatile storage) can impose a significant overhead. If we are designing the system to be able to withstand at most one isolated failure at any one time, then the above-mentioned basic algorithm is overkill, and a *sender-based message logging* can be used instead.

As its name implies, the sender of a message records it in a log. To save time, this log is stored initially in a high-speed buffer; when required, the log can be read to replay the message. This scheme is implemented as follows. Each process has a send-counter and a receive-counter, which increments every time the process sends or receives a message, respectively. Each message has a send sequence number (SSN), which is the value of the send-counter at the node when it is transmitted. When a process receives a message, it allocates it a receive sequence number (RSN), which is the value of the receive-counter (at the receiver end) when it was received. The receiver also sends out an acknowledgment to the sender, including the RSN it has allocated to the message. Upon receiving this acknowledgment, the sender acknowledges the acknowledgment in a message to the receiver. Between the time that the receiver receives the message and sends its acknowledgment, and when it receives the sender's acknowledgment of its own acknowledgment, the receiver is forbidden to send any messages to any other processes. This, as we shall see, is essential to maintaining correct functioning upon recovery.

A message is said to be *fully logged* when the sending node knows both its SSN and its RSN; it is *partially logged* when the sending node does not yet know its RSN.

When a process rolls back and restarts computation from the latest checkpoint, it sends out to the other processes a message listing the SSN of their latest message that it recorded in its checkpoint. When this message is received by a process, it knows which messages are to be retransmitted, and does so.

The recovering process now has to use these messages in the same order as they were used before it failed. This is easy to do for fully-logged messages, because their *RSNs* are available, and they can be sorted by this number. The only remaining problem is the partially-logged messages, whose *RSNs* are not available. Partially-logged messages are those that were sent out, but whose acknowledgment was never received by the sender. This could be either a) because the receiver failed before the message could be delivered to it, or b) because it failed after receiving the message, but before it could send out the acknowledgment. However, recall that the receiver is forbidden to send out messages of its own to other processes between receiving the message and sending out its acknowledgment. As a result, receiving the partially-logged messages in a different order the second time cannot affect any other process in the system, and correctness is preserved. Clearly, this approach is only guaranteed to work if there is at most one failed node at any time.

Optimistic message logging

Optimistic message logging has a lower overhead than pessimistic logging; however, recovery from failure is much more complex. At the moment, optimistic logging is probably not much more than of theoretical interest, and so we only provide here a brief outline of the technique.

When messages are received, they are written into a high-speed volatile buffer. Then, at a suitable time, the buffer is copied into stable storage. Process execution is not disrupted, and so the logging overhead is very low. The problem is that upon failure, the contents of the buffer can be lost. This can lead to multiple processes having to be rolled back. For this method to work, we need a scheme to compute the recovery line. See the Further Reading section for a pointer to such a scheme.

Staggered checkpointing

Many checkpointing algorithms can result in a large number of processes taking checkpoints at nearly the same time. If they are all writing to a shared stable storage, such as a set of disks equally available to all processes through a network, this surge can lead to congestion at the disks or network, or both. To avoid this problem, we can take one of the following two approaches:

The first is to write the checkpoint into a local buffer and then stagger the *writes* of this buffer into stable storage. This assumes that we have a buffer of sufficiently large capacity.

The second approach is to try staggering the checkpoints in time. Staggering can be done as follows. Ensure that, at any time, at most one process is taking its checkpoint. These checkpoints may not be consistent, meaning that there may well be orphan messages in the system. To avoid this, have a coordinating phase, in which each process logs in stable storage all messages it sent out since its previous checkpoint. The message-logging phase of the processes will overlap in time; however, if the volume of messages sent is smaller than the size of the individual checkpoints, the disk system and the network will see a much reduced surge.

If a process fails, it can be restarted after rolling it back to its last checkpoint. All the messages that are stored in the message log can be played back to it. As a result, the process can be recovered up to the point just before τ, the time when it first received a message that was not logged. It is as if a checkpoint was taken just prior to τ; we call this combination of checkpoint and message log a *logical* checkpoint. The staggered checkpointing algorithm guarantees that all the logical checkpoints form a consistent recovery line.

Let us now state in a more precise manner the algorithm for a distributed system consisting of the n processors $P_0, P_1, \cdots, P_{n-1}$. The algorithm consists of two phases: a checkpointing and a message-logging phase. The first phase is as follows:

```
/* Checkpointing Phase */
for (i=0; i<=n-1; i++){
      Pi takes a checkpoint.
      Pi sends a message to P(i+1) mod n, ordering the
      latter to take a checkpoint.
}
```

The second phase begins at the end of the above loop when P_0 gets a message from P_{n-1} ordering P_0 to take a checkpoint: this is the cue for P_0 not to take another checkpoint, but to initiate the second phase. It does this by sending out a *marker* message on each of its outgoing channels. When a process P_i ($i \neq 0$) receives a marker message, it does the following:

```
/* Message Logging Phase */
if (no previous marker message was received in this round by Pi) then {
      Pi sends a marker message on each of its outgoing channels.
      Pi logs all messages received by it after the preceding checkpoint
      and before the marker was received.
}
else
      Pi updates its message log by adding all the messages received by it
      since the last message log and before the marker was received.
end if
```

Consider the system shown in Fig. 6.11A: It consists of three processes, P_0, P_1, and P_2, each of which can communicate with the others. Process P_0 acts as the checkpointing coordinator; it starts the first phase of the algorithm by taking a checkpoint and sending out a take_checkpoint order to P_1 to do so. P_1 sends such an order to P_2 after taking its own checkpoint. P_2 sends a take_checkpoint order back to P_0. When P_0 receives this take_checkpoint order, it knows the first phase has completed: each of the processes has taken a checkpoint and the second phase of the algorithm can begin. P_0 sends a message_log order on each of its outgoing channels, to P_1 and P_2, asking them to log onto stable storage the (application) messages they received since they recorded the checkpoint. P_1 does so; P_2 has no such message to log. In each case, they send out similar message_log orders. When, for example, P_0 receives such an order from P_1, it checks if it has received any messages between the last time it logged messages and when it received this order, and discovers that it has nothing to log. A little time later, it receives such an order from P_2; it responds to this by logging m_5.

Each time such a message is received, the process logs the messages; if it is the first time such a message_log order is received by it, the process sends out marker messages on each of its outgoing channels.

We are proceeding on the assumption that given the checkpoint and the messages received, a process can be recovered. Hence, each process can be recovered up to the point when it receives a message that is not logged (this is the logical checkpoint position indicated in Fig. 6.11B).

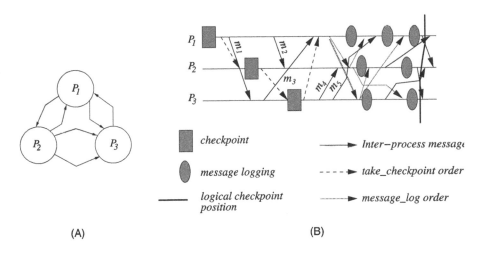

P_1

P_2 P_3

(A)

P_1

P_2

m_1 m_2 m_3 m_4 m_5

P_3

▮ *checkpoint*   ──────▶ *Inter–process message*

⬭ *message logging*   - - - -▶ *take_checkpoint order*

── *logical checkpoint position*   ·········▶ *message_log order*

(B)

FIGURE 6.11

Example for the staggering algorithm. (A) System model. (B) System operation.

Note that in this algorithm, we may have orphan messages with respect to the physical checkpoints that are taken in the first phase. However, orphan messages will not exist with respect to the latest (in time) logical checkpoints that can be generated using the physical checkpoint and the message log.

6.6 CHECKPOINTING IN SHARED-MEMORY SYSTEMS

We now describe a variant of the CARER scheme for shared-memory bus-based multiprocessors, in which each processor has its own private cache. This scheme involves changing the algorithm used to maintain cache coherence among the multiple caches in a multiprocessor. In this variant, in place of the single bit that marked a line as unmodifiable, we have a multibit identifier: we associate a checkpoint identifier C_{id} with each cache line. A checkpoint counter C_{count} keeps track of the current checkpoint number. To take a checkpoint, we increment this counter. Thus any line that was modified before this instant will have a C_{id} field, which is smaller than the value of the counter. Whenever a line is updated, we set $C_{id} = C_{count}$. If a line has been modified since being brought into the cache and $C_{id} < C_{count}$, this line is part of the checkpoint state, and is therefore *unmodifiable*. Any *writes* into such a line must wait until the line is first written into the main memory.

If the counter has k bits, it rolls over to 0 after reaching $2^k - 1$. When it reaches $2^k - 1$ and a checkpoint is to be taken, each modified line has its C_{id} set to 0.

6.6.1 BUS-BASED COHERENCE PROTOCOL

Let us first consider a cache coherence algorithm without checkpointing. We will then see how it can be modified to take account of checkpointing.

The algorithm is for bus-based multiprocessors: all the traffic between caches and memory must travel on this bus. This means that all the caches can watch the traffic on the bus.

A cache line can be in one of the following states: *invalid, shared unmodified, exclusive modified,* and *exclusive unmodified. Exclusive* means that this is the only valid copy in any of the caches; *modified* means that the line has been modified since it was brought into the cache from the main memory. Fig. 6.12 shows the state diagram associated with this algorithm. If the line is in *shared unmodified*

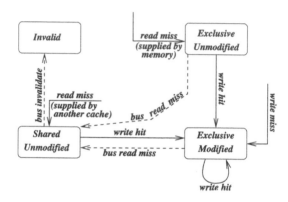

FIGURE 6.12

Original bus-based cache coherence algorithm.

state and the processor wishes to update it, it moves into the *exclusive modified* state. (All other caches holding the same line must invalidate their copies, since these are no longer current.) When in the *exclusive modified* or *exclusive unmodified* states, another cache puts out a read request on the bus, this cache must service that request (since it holds the only current copy of that line). As a by-product of this action, the memory is also updated if necessary. After doing so, the state moves from *exclusive modified* to *shared unmodified*. A write miss is handled by considering it to be a read miss followed by a write hit. Hence, when there is a write miss, the line is brought into the cache and its state becomes *exclusive modified*, because it is modified upon the write, and this cache holds the only current copy of that line. The other transitions are reasoned similarly.

How can we modify this protocol to account for checkpointing? The original *exclusive modified* state now splits into two: *exclusive modified* and *unmodifiable*. The state diagram for this algorithm is shown in Fig. 6.13. When a line becomes part of the checkpoint, it is marked *unmodifiable* to keep it stable. Before this line can be changed, it must first be copied to memory so that it will be retained for use in the event of a rollback.

6.6.2 DIRECTORY-BASED PROTOCOL

In this approach to cache coherence, a directory is maintained centrally, which records the status of each line. We can regard this directory as being controlled by some shared-memory controller. This controller handles all read and write misses and all other operations that change line state. For example, if a line is in the *exclusive unmodified* state and the cache holding that line wants to modify it, it notifies

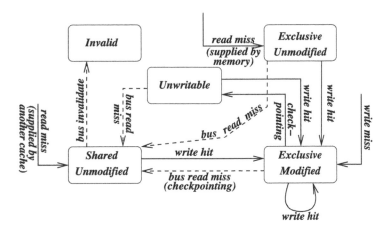

FIGURE 6.13

Bus-based cache coherence and checkpointing algorithm.

the controller of its intention. The controller can then change the state to *exclusive modified*. It is then a simple matter to implement this checkpointing scheme atop such a protocol.

6.7 CHECKPOINTING IN REAL-TIME SYSTEMS

A real-time system is characterized by the need to meet deadlines. In *hard* real-time systems, missing a deadline can be very costly; process control is one such example. In *soft* real-time systems, on the other hand, missed deadlines may lower the quality of service provided, but are not catastrophic. Most multimedia systems are soft real-time systems. However, it is ultimately the application that determines whether the system is hard or soft. A multimedia system that is used for the remote control of a vehicle is a hard real-time system; the more common case in which it is used to watch movies over the Internet is soft real-time.

The performance of a real-time system is related to the probability that the system will meet all its critical deadlines. Therefore the goal of checkpointing in a real-time system is to maximize this probability and not to minimize the mean execution time. Indeed, checkpointing in a real-time system may well *increase* the average execution time: this is a price worth paying if the probability of missing a deadline decreases sufficiently.

We present next an analytical model very similar to the one presented in Section 6.3, but one that calculates the *density function* of the execution time of a task instead of the *average* execution time. Similarly to the previous model, we place a checkpoint after every T_{ex} seconds of useful work; each checkpoint takes T_{ov} seconds in overhead. We are assuming here that checkpoint latency and overhead are identical: the system is so simple that the CPU has no other unit to which to delegate the checkpointing task. Transient faults occur at a constant rate λ. When a transient failure hits the processor, it goes down for T_r seconds (including rebooting if necessary).

Let $f_{int}(t)$ be the probability density function of the time taken between successive initiations of checkpoints. We proceed by the same conditioning argument as before. There are two cases. In *Case 1*, there is no failure over the interval $T_{ex} + T_{ov}$; in *Case 2*, there is at least one failure.

If Case 1 occurs (which it does with probability $e^{-\lambda(T_{ex}+T_{ov})}$), the interval between checkpoint initiations will be $T_{ex} + T_{ov}$. In Case 2, the time will be greater than $T_{ex} + T_{ov}$. To analyze Case 2, let us condition on the epoch of the first failure. Suppose the first failure hits τ seconds into the interval. Then, we lose all τ seconds of computation. Furthermore, we take T_r seconds to recover. Hence, $\tau + T_r$ seconds later, the processor is ready to restart execution of this interval. Following such a restart, the density function of the rest of the execution of this interval will be identical to the unconditional density function. Therefore the conditional density function of the execution time, conditioned on the first failure happening τ seconds into the interval, is $f_{int}(t - [\tau + T_r])$. The probability of the first failure happening in the interval $[\tau, \tau + d\tau]$ is $\lambda e^{-\lambda\tau} d\tau$. Thus

$$f_{int}(t) = \int_{\tau=0}^{T_{ex}+T_{ov}} \lambda e^{-\lambda\tau} f_{int}(t - [\tau + T_r]) d\tau \quad \text{if } t > T_{ex} + T_{ov} + T_r. \tag{6.10}$$

Clearly, the execution time can never be less than $T_{ex} + T_{ov}$, nor can it fall in the interval $(T_{ex} + T_{ov}, T_{ex} + T_{ov} + T_r)$, because a failure takes T_r seconds to recover from. Furthermore, it will be exactly equal to $T_{ex} + T_{ov}$ in the (common) case that there is no failure. This is represented by a Dirac delta function at that point of magnitude $e^{-\lambda(T_{ex}+T_{ov})}$. (For those unfamiliar with the term, a Dirac delta function $\delta(t)$ has the property that for any density function $f(t)$ and some constant a, $\int_{-\infty}^{\infty} f(t)\delta(t-a)dt = f(a)$. It is an impulse function).

To summarize, we can now write the density function as

$$f_{int}(t) = \begin{cases} e^{-\lambda(T_{ex}+T_{ov})}\delta(t - [T_{ex} + T_{ov}]) & \text{if } t = T_{ex} + T_{ov} \\ 0 & \text{if } t \neq T_{ex} + T_{ov} \text{ and } t \leq T_{ex} + T_{ov} + T_r \\ \int_{\tau=0}^{T_{ex}+T_{ov}} \lambda e^{-\lambda\tau} f_{int}(t - [\tau + T_r]) d\tau & \text{if } t > T_{ex} + T_{ov} + T_r. \end{cases}$$

$$\tag{6.11}$$

Such an equation can be solved numerically.

If we take N checkpoints, the density function of the overall execution time is the $(N+1)$-fold convolution of the density function per intercheckpoint interval: $f_{exec}(t) = f_{int}^{*(N+1)}(t)$. The average time taken is calculated as shown in Section 6.3.1. If the real-time deadline is t_d, the probability of missing it is given by

$$p_{miss} = \int_{t=t_d}^{\infty} f_{exec}(t)dt.$$

To demonstrate the tradeoff, let us consider a specific numerical example. Let $T = 0.15$ seconds and $\lambda = 10^{-3}$ per second. The recovery time is $T_r = 0.1$ second. In Fig. 6.14, the probability of missing a deadline is plotted for two cases: $T_{ov} = 0.015$ and $T_{ov} = 0.025$. Table 6.2 shows the average execution time as a function of the number of checkpoints. For the parameters used, the expected execution time actually worsens as we increase the number of checkpoints: this is to be expected, because the

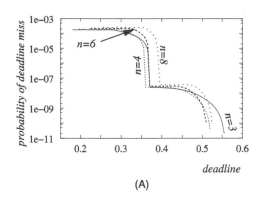
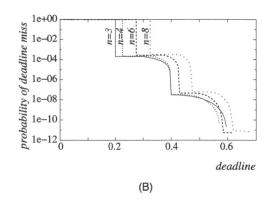

FIGURE 6.14

Probability of missing a deadline (n is the number of checkpoints). (A) $T_{ov} = 0.015$ and (B) $T_{ov} = 0.025$.

Table 6.2 Average execution time for different numbers of checkpoints.		
Number of checkpoints, n	$T_{ov} = 0.015$	$T_{ov} = 0.025$
1	0.180	0.200
2	0.195	0.225
3	0.210	0.250
4	0.225	0.275
5	0.240	0.300
6	0.255	0.325
7	0.270	0.350
8	0.285	0.375

probability of failure during execution is less than 1%. However, when we focus on the probability of missing a deadline, the situation is more complicated, see Fig. 6.14. For tight deadlines, when there is little available slack, increasing the number of checkpoints can make things worse. When deadlines are further into the future, thereby making more slack available, a greater number of checkpoints improves matters. For example, for a deadline of 0.5 and $T_{ov} = 0.015$, using six checkpoints is significantly better than using three. By contrast, for a deadline of 0.3, having three checkpoints is better than six. In every case, the deadline-missing probabilities are small: however, there are real-time applications, where such probabilities have to be very low indeed.

The reader should compare the results for $T_{ov} = 0.025$ with those for $T_{ov} = 0.015$, and obtain an intuitive explanation for the differences seen.

6.8 CHECKPOINTING WHILE USING CLOUD COMPUTING UTILITIES

Cloud computing utilities have become widely available over the past few years. Rather than purchase their own computing hardware, users have the option of buying processing time and nonvolatile storage from vendors, such as Amazon, IBM, or Microsoft.

In many instances, charges for a unit of processing time vary with time depending on current demand. The *spot pricing* model, for instance has the following characteristics:

- Processing charges per unit time ("spot price") vary with time, depending on demand.
- The current spot price is public information; users may track it at will.
- Several processing platform types or instances exist for users to select from; each has its own spot price.
- Users have the option of bidding for processing time on selected platforms. Their workload will be processed so long as their bid does not fall below the current spot price. If, however, the spot price rises above the bid, their workload is terminated without warning and any unsaved work is lost. We term this "bid failure."
- Charges are made for discrete units of time, say in hours. At the end of each unit, the charges are updated. If a workload finishes successfully within a given unit, the full price for that unit (according to that unit's spot price) is charged; if it suffers failure within that unit, no charges are made *for that final unit.*
- In addition to processing time, users can buy nonvolatile, persistent storage. The price for such storage is very low, amounting typically to pennies to the Gbyte per month.

A user has the option of checkpointing at any time. This is user-level checkpointing; they will be charged for the processing time incurred in taking the checkpoint. Nonvolatile storage costs are usually negligible, except for truly enormous checkpoints.

Note the similarities between this problem and the traditional checkpointing problem as described in earlier pages. Failure, defined as the enforced termination of ongoing computation, can here occur not just due to traditional software or hardware failure, but also due to the spot price going above the user's bid. The same issues of deciding where to place checkpoints arise here, too. However, such an optimization problem is much more complicated when bid failure has to be taken into account. Recall that in earlier sections, we assumed that failures occur according to a Poisson process. This is often a reasonable approximation as long as only hardware and software failures are considered. On the other hand, bid failure is unlikely to follow a Poisson process. The spot price varies with demand; demand depends on customer price elasticity. Demand may depend considerably on time-of-day. There is a growing literature on the subject, see the Further Reading section for a few recent pointers.

6.9 EMERGING CHALLENGES: PETASCALE AND EXASCALE COMPUTING

Supercomputer systems are today created by putting together a very large number of nodes. This trend is likely to continue. We can envisage systems consisting of hundreds of thousands of compute nodes, each node consisting of hundreds of processing cores along with associated memory and I/O support. For example, one recent study evaluated a system consisting of 204,800 nodes, each node having 768 cores.

With an increase in the number of nodes, there comes an increase in the failure rate. The supercomputers of today typically have a mean time between failure of less than 40 hours. Large-scale and long-lived workloads, involving thousands of nodes and running for hundreds of hours or more, require checkpointing to make meaningful progress in such an environment. However, such workloads also generate large-sized checkpoints, with significant time and energy overheads. For example, one recent study (on the French Grid'5000 distributed computational platform) found that checkpointing on a node cost between 2520 and 3570 Joules per GByte (note the wide variation in energy consumption per node despite all the nodes being supposedly similar to one another). Checkpoints can be enormous in many applications that run on such systems. To cite two extreme cases, a checkpoint size of 160 TBytes has been quoted for the astrophysics application CHIMERA (used to simulate the core collapse of a supernova) and 20 TBytes in GTC (used in the study of plasmas for nuclear fusion). Storing such checkpoints can take considerable time; techniques to reduce such overheads are urgently required.

It is likely that a combination of approaches will be needed to reduce checkpointing overheads in such systems to manageable levels. First, faster nonvolatile memory is becoming available. Traditional disks are being replaced by flash drives, which allow for much faster access. The development of memristor and phase-change memories is proceeding apace. Second, as much checkpointing activity as possible can be overlapped with regular processing. Incremental checkpointing can be used, where just the information changed since the previous checkpoint is stored. Compiler analysis of data structures could identify "dead" data, which will never again be accessed by the workload: clearly, such data need not be included in the checkpoint. Furthermore, as we have already mentioned in this chapter, data can be compressed before being stored as a checkpoint; obviously compression will incur its own overhead. To reduce intercore synchronization overhead, coordinated checkpointing could be considered within individual sets of tightly coupled nodes, whereas message logging could be used for messages between loosely coupled nodes. Finally, some researchers have suggested a combined application of redundant calculation (using one or more shadow nodes to duplicate the activity of each "primary" node) and checkpointing to reduce the pressure on the checkpointed system.

Experimental results from actual supercomputer facilities will drive the optimal checkpointing policy, as some common assumptions may be observed to be untrue. We already noted above the wide disparity in energy consumption for taking checkpoints between supposedly similar nodes. To take another example, workers at the Oak Ridge National Laboratory recently reported that failures on their supercomputer were temporally correlated. Failures occurred not randomly over time, but bunched: one failure was soon followed by another. By the same token, a long period without a failure was likely to indicate that failure was less likely to occur in the near future. An obvious response to this is to lengthen the intercheckpoint interval if a failure has not been observed for some considerable time.

6.10 OTHER USES OF CHECKPOINTING

Fault tolerance is but one application of checkpoints. Here, briefly, are two others:

- Process migration: Since a checkpoint represents a process state, migrating a process from one processor to another simply involves moving the checkpoint, after which computation can resume on the new processor. The nature of the checkpoint determines whether the new processor must be of the same kind, and run the same operating system as the old one.

Process migration can be used to recover from permanent or intermittent faults. Another use is in load balancing, to achieve overall better utilization of a distributed system, by ensuring that the computational load is appropriately shared among the processors.

- Debugging: Checkpointing can be used to provide the programmer with snapshots of the program state at discrete epochs. Such snapshots can be extremely useful to study the change of variable values over time and to get a deeper understanding of program behavior.

6.11 FURTHER READING

A good discussion of the various levels at which checkpointing can be done appears in [41]. Application-level checkpointing is analyzed in [31]. The distinction between checkpointing latency and overhead, and the greater impact of overhead, was pointed out in [54]. Copy-on-write for faster checkpointing is discussed in [35], and memory exclusion in [43]. A recent study of the feasibility of incremental checkpointing for scientific applications can be found in [45]. Checkpoint compression is discussed in [27,28].

Checkpoint placement for general-purpose systems has a large literature associated with it: some examples are [9,21,33,48,61,62]. An early performance model for checkpointing is presented in [50]. CARER is described in [3,26]. A more recent work on using caches in checkpointing can be found in [51].

There is an excellent survey of distributed checkpointing issues with a comprehensive bibliography in [18]. A slightly more theoretical treatment can be found in [6]. Two widely cited early works in checkpointing in distributed systems are the algorithms which appeared in [10], and in [32] (described in Section 6.5.2). The staggered checkpointing algorithm is presented in [55]. A good reference for the use of synchronized clocks to avoid explicit coordination during checkpointing is [39]. Uncoordinated checkpointing is described in [23]. Diskless checkpointing using approaches similar to that in RAID is discussed in detail in [24,40,42]. Two-level recovery is considered in [53]. This paper contains a detailed performance model of a two-level recovery scheme. A more recent multilevel scheme is presented in [37].

There is substantial literature on message logging, including optimistic and pessimistic algorithms [5,18], sender-based message logging [29], optimistic recovery schemes [30,49,56], and the drawbacks of optimistic algorithms [25]. Coordinated local checkpointing of distributed systems is discussed in [2].

When discussing message logging, we assumed that process recovery would follow if we rolled back the affected process to a checkpoint and then replayed the messages that it received beyond that point. This is not always true: it is possible for the process to take a different execution path if something in the operating environment is different (e.g., the amount of available swap space in the processor is different). For a discussion on this, see [11].

The bus-based coherence protocol is covered in [58].

Checkpointing in real-time systems is discussed in [34,48]. Checkpointing for mobile computers is a topic of growing interest, given the proliferation of mobile applications. For some algorithms, see [1,4,12,38,44]. Other applications of checkpointing (besides fault tolerance) are discussed in [57].

User-level checkpointing in commercial cloud computing facilities has gathered increasing interest in recent years. For a good introduction, see [22,60]. An approach to optimization in such a setup is presented in [13].

Checkpointing in supercomputers has also attracted considerable research interest over recent years. For a good introduction to fault tolerance in supercomputers, see [7,8,16]; for studies of failures and fatal events in such systems, see [14,47]. Given the substantial checkpoint size in many supercomputer applications, attention has been paid to reducing checkpointing overhead; examples include [46,52]. The often considerable impact of reliability considerations on supercomputers has been termed the *reliability wall* in [59]. The energy implications of checkpointing are explored in [15,19,36]. Data and models associated with a supercomputer at the Oak Ridge National Laboratory can be found in [52]. As supercomputers increase in size, checkpointing costs can increase to the point where, under certain circumstances, it is better to obtain reliability through replicated computation rather than through checkpointing; see [17,20].

6.12 EXERCISES

1. In Section 6.3.1, we derived an approximation for the expected time between checkpoints as a function of the checkpoint parameters.
   (a) Calculate the optimum number of checkpoints, and plot the approximate total expected execution time as a function of T_{ov}. Assume that $T = 1$, $T_{lt} = T_{ov}$ and $\lambda = 10^{-5}$. Vary T_{ov} from 0.01 to 0.2.
   (b) Plot the approximate total expected execution time as a function of λ. Fix $T = 1$, $T_{ov} = 0.1$, and vary λ from 10^{-7} to 10^{-1}.
2. In Section 6.3.1, we derived an expression for N_{opt}, the optimal number of checkpoints. We noted that this term includes T_r, the recovery time per failure. In particular, N_{opt} tends to decrease as T_r increases.
   Explain why the assumption that there can be no more than one failure in any intercheckpoint interval contributes to the presence of T_r in this expression.
3. You have a task with execution time T. You take N checkpoints, equally spaced through the lifetime of that task. The overhead for each checkpoint is T_{ov} and $T_{lt} = T_{ov}$. Given that during execution, the task is affected by a total of k point failures (i.e., failures from which the processor recovers in negligible time). Answer the following questions:
   (a) What is the maximum execution time of the task?
   (b) Find N such that this maximum execution time is minimized. It is fine to get a noninteger answer (say x): in practice, this will mean that you will pick the better of $\lfloor x \rfloor$ and $\lceil x \rceil$.
4. Solve Eq. (6.9) numerically, and compare the calculated T_{ex}^{opt} to the value obtained in Eq. (6.6) for the simpler model. Assume $T_r = 0$ and $T_{lt} = T_{ov} = 0.1$. Vary λ from 10^{-7} to 10^{-2}.
5. A certain program executing on a given computer has an expected total execution time of $T = 5$ hours (in a fault-free case). The computer experiences transient faults at a constant rate of $\lambda = 5 \times 10^{-6}/sec$.
   (a) What is the probability that the program will complete its execution successfully?
   (b) To increase the probability of successful completion, checkpointing has been incorporated with an overhead of $T_{ov} = 5sec$ each time a checkpoint is taken. Upon a fault, the pro-

gram is rolled back, and the recovery process takes $T_r = 10$ sec. Using the first-order approximation, according to which the intercheckpoint interval is given by (see Eq. (6.5)) $E_{int} \approx (T_{ex} + T_{ov}) \left[1 + \lambda \left(\frac{T_{ex} + T_{ov}}{2} + T_r \right) \right]$, and the optimal T_{ex} is given by Eq. (6.6), calculate the average total time the program will execute on the given computer in the presence of faults and checkpointing.

(c) The given program goes through twenty phases of computing, each lasting 20 minutes, and at the end of such a phase, the size of the program state that needs to be checkpointed is drastically reduced so that $T_{ov} = 1$ sec. If instead of the optimal placement of checkpoints as in (b), a checkpoint is taken every 20 minutes, what would be the average total time the program will execute in the presence of faults?

6. In this problem, we will look at checkpointing for real-time systems. You have a task with an execution time of T and a deadline of D. N checkpoints are placed equidistantly through the lifetime of the task. The overhead for each checkpoint is T_{ov}. Point transient failures occur at a constant rate λ.

(a) Derive a first-order model for the probability of missing a deadline by conditioning on the number of failures over $[0, T + NT_{ov}]$. Start by calculating the probability of missing a deadline if there is exactly one failure over $[0, T + NT_{ov}]$. Then, find lower and upper bounds for the probability of missing a deadline if there is more than one failure over $[0, T + NT_{ov}]$. Use the total probability formula to derive expressions for lower and upper bounds of this probability.

(b) Plot the upper bound of the deadline-missing probability as a function of N, where N varies from 0 to $\min(20, \lfloor (P - T)/T_{ov} \rfloor)$.

  (b1) Set $\lambda = 10^{-5}$, $P = 1.0$, $T_{ov} = 0.05$, and plot curves for the following values of T: 0.5, 0.6, 0.7.

  (b2) Set $\lambda = 10^{-5}$, $P = 1.0$, $T = 0.6$, and plot curves for the following values of T_{ov}: 0.01, 0.05, 0.09.

  (b3) Set $P = 1.0$, $T = 0.6$, $T_{ov} = 0.05$, and plot curves for the following values of λ: 10^{-3}, 10^{-5}, 10^{-7}.

7. In this problem, we will study what happens if the checkpoint overheads are not constant over time, but vary, that is, there are times when the size of the process state is small and others when they are substantial. Suppose you are given this information, namely, you have a function $T_{ov}(t)$, which is the checkpointing overhead t seconds into the task execution.

(a) Devise an algorithm to place checkpoints in such a way that the expected overall overhead is approximately minimized—you may want to consult reference works on optimization for this. You can assume that if the execution time is T and failure occurs at constant rate λ, $\lambda T \ll 1$.

(b) Let $T_{ov}(t) = 10 + \sin(t)$. For $T = 1000$ and failure rate $\lambda = 10^{-5}$, run your algorithm to place the checkpoints appropriately.

8. Identify all the consistent recovery lines in the following execution of two concurrent processes:

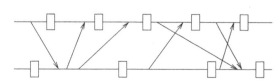

9. Suppose you are designing a checkpointing scheme for a distributed system specified to be single-fault tolerant, that is, the system needs only to guarantee successful recovery from any one failure: a second failure before the system has recovered from the first one is assumed to be of negligible probability. You decide to take checkpoints and carry out message logging. Show that it is sufficient for each processor to simply record the messages it sends out in its volatile memory; by volatile memory, we mean memory that will lose its contents in the event of a failure.

10. We have seen that checkpointing distributed systems is quite complex, and that uncoordinated checkpointing can give rise to a domino effect. In this problem, we will run a simulation to get a sense of how likely it is that a domino effect will happen.

    You have N processors, each of which has its own clock. A processor checkpoints when its clock reads nT for $n = 1, 2, \cdots$. If t is the time told by a perfect clock, the time told by any of these clocks is given by $t + \epsilon$, where ϵ is uniformly distributed over the range $[-\Delta, \Delta]$. The clocks are therefore synchronized with a maximum skew between any two clocks of 2Δ.

    The messages sent out by the processors can be modeled as follows. Each processor generates messages according to a Poisson process with rate μ; any message can be to any of the $N - 1$ other processors with equal probability.

    Failures strike processors according to a Poisson process with rate λ, and processors fail independently of one another.

    Write a simulation program to evaluate the probability that the domino effect happens in this system. (If you are not familiar with how to write such simulations, look in Chapter 9.) Study the impact of varying N, Δ, λ, and μ. Comment on your results.

REFERENCES

[1] A. Acharya, B.R. Badrinath, Checkpointing distributed applications on mobile computers, in: International Conference on Parallel and Distributed Information Systems (PDIS), September 1994, pp. 73–80.

[2] R. Agarwal, P. Garg, J. Torrellas, Rebound: scalable checkpointing for coherent shared memory, in: International Symposium on Computer Architecture (ISCA), 2011, pp. 153–164.

[3] R.E. Ahmed, R.C. Frazier, P.N. Marinos, Cache-aided rollback error recovery (CARER) algorithms for shared-memory multiprocessor systems, in: Fault-Tolerant Computing Symposium (FTCS), 1990, pp. 82–88.

[4] J. Ahn, S.G. Min, C.S. Hwang, A causal message logging protocol for mobile nodes in mobile computing systems, Future Generations Computer Systems 20 (4) (2004) 663–686.

[5] L. Alvisi, K. Marzullo, Message logging: pessimistic, optimistic, causal, and optimal, IEEE Transactions on Software Engineering 24 (2) (February 1998) 149–159.

[6] O. Babaoglu, K. Marzullo, Consistent global states of distributed systems: fundamental concepts and mechanisms, in: S. Mullender (Ed.), Distributed Systems, ACM Press, 1993, pp. 55–96.

[7] G. Bosilca, A. Bouteiller, E. Brunet, F. Cappello, J. Dongarra, A. Guermouche, T. Herault, Y. Robert, F. Vivien, D. Zaidouni, Unified model for assessing checkpointing protocols at extreme-scale, Concurrency and Computation: Practice and Experience 26 (17) (2014) 2772–2791.

[8] F. Cappello, Fault tolerance in petascale/exascale systems: current knowledge, challenges, and research opportunities, The International Journal of High Performance Computing Applications 23 (3) (2009) 212–226.

[9] K.M. Chandy, J.C. Browne, C.W. Dissly, W.R. Uhrig, Analytic models for rollback and recovery strategies in data base systems, IEEE Transactions on Software Engineering SE-1 (1) (March 1975) 100–110.

[10] K.M. Chandy, L. Lamport, Distributed snapshots: determining global states of distributed systems, ACM Transactions on Computer Systems 3 (1) (August 1985) 63–75.

[11] E. Cohen, Y.-M. Wang, G. Suri, When piecewise determinism is almost true, in: Pacific Rim Symposium on Fault-Tolerant Systems (PRFTS), 1995, pp. 66–71.

[12] P.J. Darby III, N.-F. Tzeng, Decentralized QoS-aware checkpointing arrangement in mobile grid computing, IEEE Transactions on Mobile Computing 9 (8) (2010) 1173–1186.

[13] S. Di, Y. Robert, F. Vivien, D. Kondo, C.L. Wang, F. Cappello, Optimization of cloud task processing with checkpoint-restart mechanism, in: International Conference on High Performance Computing, Networking, Storage and Analysis (SC), 2013, 64.

[14] S. Di, H. Guo, R. Gupta, E.R. Pershey, M. Snir, F. Cappello, Exploring properties and correlations of fatal events in a large-scale HPC system, IEEE Transactions on Parallel and Distributed Systems 30 (2) (February 2019) 361–374.

[15] M. Diouri, O. Glück, L. Lefevre, F. Cappello, Energy considerations in checkpointing and fault tolerance protocols, in: IEEE/IFIP International Conference on Dependable Systems and Networks (DSN) Workshops, 2012, pp. 1–6.

[16] I.P. Egwutuoha, D. Levi, B. Selic, S. Chen, A survey of fault tolerance mechanisms and checkpoint/restart implementations for high performance computing systems, Journal of Supercomputing 65 (3) (2013) 1302–1326.

[17] J. Elliott, K. Kharbas, D. Fiala, F. Mueller, K. Ferreira, C. Engelmann, Combining partial redundancy and checkpointing for HPC, in: IEEE International Conference on Distributed Computing Systems (ICDCS), 2012, pp. 615–626.

[18] E.N. Elnozahy, L. Alvisi, Y.M. Wang, D.B. Johnson, A survey of rollback-recovery protocols in message-passing systems, ACM Computing Surveys 34 (3) (September 2002) 375–408.

[19] N. El Sayed, B. Schroeder, To checkpoint or not to checkpoint: understanding energy-performance I/O tradeoffs in HPC checkpointing, in: IEEE International Conference on Cluster Computing, 2014, pp. 93–102.

[20] K. Ferreira, J. Stearley, J.H. Laros III, R. Oldfield, K. Pedretti, R. Brightwell, R. Riesen, P.G. Brieges, D. Arnold, Evaluating the viability of process replication reliability for exascale systems, in: International Conference for High Performance Computing, Networking, Storage and Analysis (SC), 2011, 44.

[21] E. Gelenbe, On the optimum checkpoint interval, Journal of the ACM 26 (April 1979) 259–270.

[22] Y. Gong, B. He, A.C. Zhou, Monetary cost optimizations for MPI-based HPC applications on Amazon clouds: checkpoints and replicated execution, in: International Conference for High Performance Computing, Networking, Storage and Analysis (SC), 2015, pp. 1–12.

[23] A. Guermouche, T. Ropars, E. Brunet, M. Snir, F. Cappello, Uncoordinated checkpointing without domino effect for send-deterministic MPI applications, in: IEEE International Parallel & Distributed Processing Symposium (IPDPS), 2011, pp. 989–1000.

[24] D. Hakkarinen, Z. Chen, Multilevel diskless checkpointing, IEEE Transactions on Computers 62 (4) (2013) 772–783.

[25] Y. Huang, Y.M. Wang, Why optimistic message logging has not been used in telecommunications systems, in: Fault-Tolerant Computing Symposium (FTCS), 1995, pp. 459–463.

[26] D.B. Hunt, P.N. Marinos, A general purpose cache-aided rollback error recovery (CARER) technique, in: Fault-Tolerant Computing Symposium (FTCS), 1987, pp. 170–175.

[27] D. Ibtesham, D. Arnold, P.G. Bridges, K.B. Ferreira, R. Brightwell, On the viability of compression for reducing the overheads of checkpoint/restart based fault tolerance, in: IEEE International Conference on Parallel Processing (ICPP), 2012, pp. 148–157.

[28] D. Ibtesham, K.B. Ferreira, D. Arnold, A checkpoint compression study for high-performance computing systems, The International Journal of High Performance Computing Applications (HPCA) 29 (4) (2015) 387–402.

[29] D.B. Johnson, W. Zwaenepoel, Sender-based message logging, in: Fault-Tolerant Computing Symposium (FTCS), July 1987, pp. 14–19.

[30] D.B. Johnson, W. Zwaenepoel, Recovery in distributed systems using optimistic message logging and checkpointing, in: ACM Symposium on Principles of Distributed Computing (PODC), August 1988, pp. 171–181.

[31] A. Kokolis, A. Mavrogiannis, D. Rodopoulos, C. Strydis, D. Soudris, Runtime interval optimization and dependable performance for application-level checkpointing, in: Design, Automation & Test in Europe (DATE), 2016, pp. 594–599.

[32] R. Koo, S. Toueg, Checkpointing and rollback recovery for distributed systems, IEEE Transactions on Software Engineering SE-13 (1) (January 1987) 23–31.

[33] I. Koren, Z. Koren, S.Y.H. Su, Analysis of a class of recovery procedures, IEEE Transactions on Computers C-35 (8) (August 1986) 703–712.

[34] C.M. Krishna, K.G. Shin, Y.-H. Lee, Optimization criteria for checkpointing, Communications of the ACM 27 (10) (October 1984) 1008–1012.

[35] K. Li, J.F. Naughton, J.S. Plank, Low-latency, concurrent checkpointing for parallel programs, IEEE Transactions on Parallel and Distributed Systems 5 (August 1994) 874–879.

[36] B. Mills, R.E. Grant, K.B. Ferreira, R. Riesen, Evaluating energy savings for checkpoint/restart, in: First International Workshop on Energy Efficient Supercomputing, 2013, pp. 6.1–6.8.

[37] A. Moody, G. Bronevetsky, K. Mohror, B.R. De Supinski, Design, modeling and evaluation of a scalable multi-level check-pointing system, in: ACM/IEEE International Conference for High Performance Computing, Networking, Storage and Analysis (SC), 2010, pp. 1–11.

[38] N. Neves, W.K. Fuchs, Adaptive recovery for mobile environments, Communications of the ACM 40 (1) (January 1997) 68–74.

[39] N. Neves, W.K. Fuchs, Coordinated checkpointing without direct coordination, in: IEEE International Computer Performance & Dependability Symposium (IPDS), September 1998, pp. 23–31.

[40] J.S. Plank, Improving the performance of coordinated networks of workstations using RAID techniques, in: IEEE Symposium on Reliable Distributed Systems (SRDS), 1996, pp. 76–85.

[41] J.S. Plank, An Overview of Checkpointing in Uniprocessor and Distributed Systems, Focusing on Implementation and Performance, Technical Report UT-CS-97-372, University of Tennessee, 1997.

[42] J.S. Plank, K. Li, M.A. Puening, Diskless checkpointing, IEEE Transactions on Parallel and Distributed Systems 9 (October 1998) 972–986.

[43] J.S. Plank, Y. Chen, K. Li, M. Beck, G. Kingsley, Memory exclusion: optimizing the performance of checkpointing systems, Software, Practice & Experience 29 (2) (February 1999) 125–142.

[44] D.K. Pradhan, P. Krishna, N.H. Vaidya, Recovery in mobile applications: design and tradeoff analysis, in: Fault-Tolerant Computing Symposium (FTCS), June 1996, pp. 16–25.

[45] J.C. Sancho, F. Pertini, G. Johnson, J. Fernandez, E. Frachtenberg, On the feasibility of incremental checkpointing for scientific computing, in: Parallel and Distributed Processing Symposium (IPDPS), 2004, pp. 58–67.

[46] K. Sato, N. Maruyama, K. Mohror, A. Moody, T. Gamblin, B.R. de Supinski, S. Matsuoka, Design and modeling of a non-blocking checkpointing system, in: International Conference on High Performance Computing, Networking, Storage and Analysis (SC), 2012, pp. 19.1–19.10.

[47] B. Schroeder, G.A. Gibson, Understanding failures in petascale computers, Journal of Physics. Conference Series 78 (2007) 012022.

[48] K.G. Shin, T.-H. Lin, Y.-H. Lee, Optimal checkpointing of real-time tasks, IEEE Transactions on Computers 36 (11) (November 1987) 1328–1341.

[49] R.B. Strom, S. Yemeni, Optimistic recovery in distributed systems, ACM Transactions on Computer Systems 3 (3) (April 1985) 204–226.

[50] A.N. Tantawi, M. Ruschitzka, Performance analysis of checkpointing strategies, ACM Transactions on Computer Systems 2 (2) (May 1984) 123–144.

[51] R. Teodorescu, J. Nakano, J. Torrellas, SWICH: a prototype for efficient cache-level checkpointing and rollback, IEEE MICRO 26 (5) (September 2006) 28–40.

[52] D. Tiwari, S. Gupta, S.S. Vazhkudai, Lazy checkpointing: exploiting temporal locality in failures to mitigate checkpointing overheads on extreme-scale systems, in: International Conference on Dependable Systems and Networks (DSN), 2014, pp. 25–36.

[53] N.H. Vaidya, A case for two-level distributed recovery schemes, in: ACM SIGMETRICS Conference on Measurement and Modeling of Computer Systems, May 1995, pp. 64–73.

[54] N.H. Vaidya, Impact of checkpoint latency on overhead ratio of a checkpointing scheme, IEEE Transactions on Computers 46 (8) (August 1997) 942–947.

[55] N.H. Vaidya, Staggered consistent checkpointing, IEEE Transactions on Parallel and Distributed Systems 10 (7) (July 1999) 694–702.

[56] Y.-M. Wang, W.K. Fuchs, Optimistic message logging for independent checkpointing in message passing systems, in: Symposium on Reliable Distributed Systems (SRDS), October 1992, pp. 147–154.

[57] Y-M. Wang, Y. Huang, K-P. Vo, P-Y. Chung, C. Kintala, Checkpointing and its applications, in: Fault-Tolerant Computing Symposium (FTCS), June 1995, pp. 22–31.

[58] K.-L. Wu, W.K. Fuchs, J.H. Patel, Error recovery in shared memory multiprocessors using private caches, IEEE Transactions on Parallel and Distributed Systems 1 (2) (April 1990) 231–240.

[59] X. Yang, Z. Wang, J. Xue, Y. Zhou, The reliability wall for exascale supercomputing, IEEE Transactions on Computers 61 (6) (June 2012) 767–779.

[60] S. Yi, A. Andrzejak, D. Kondo, Monetary cost-aware checkpointing and migration on Amazon cloud spot instances, IEEE Transactions on Services Computing 5 (4) (August 2012) 512–524.

[61] J.W. Young, A first order approximation to the optimum checkpoint interval, Communications of the ACM 17 (9) (September 1974) 530–531.

[62] A. Ziv, J. Bruck, An online algorithm for checkpoint placement, IEEE Transactions on Computers 46 (9) (September 1997) 976–985.

CYBER-PHYSICAL SYSTEMS

Any system consisting of a computer tightly embedded in a physical system is a cyber-physical system (CPS). CPSs have proliferated in the past decade; every year, new applications emerge for them. Let us consider a few examples.

- *Fly-by-wire aircraft:* Modern aircraft automate most aviation functions. Computers adjust engine thrust and control surface settings in response to pilot commands and changes in environmental conditions, such as turbulence. Computers have taken over to the extent that many modern aircraft are difficult to fly without their assistance. (Some also argue that the increased role played by computers has reduced hand-flying experience and therefore eroded piloting skills.) Pilots of large commercial aircraft are essentially system managers; low-level actuator settings are often mediated by the computer system. We also have unmanned aerial vehicles (UAVs) used in surveillance and rescue operations, which may take navigation decisions autonomously.
- *Automobiles:* Modern cars have dozens of processors, controlling almost all activity. For example, traction control involves the computer automatically sensing when a wheel is skidding and altering torque appropriately. Antilock braking consists of identifying when braking results in wheel slip exceeding a certain threshold, and then releasing/reapplying brakes suitably. The aim is to keep wheel slip close to the point at which friction is maximized. Collision warning senses obstacles in the projected vehicle path and warns the driver, or applies brakes autonomously. Self-driving cars are on the horizon: the computer has to carry out steering and speed control operations in response to detected traffic, obstacles, speed limits, traffic lights, road conditions, and other criteria.
- *Power distribution grid:* The conventional model of power distribution is to have a small number of powerful generating units distributing electrical power to a large number of consuming nodes (homes, factories, etc.). This model is changing rapidly. Solar and wind generation units numbering in their tens of thousands provide energy that is mostly consumed locally, but may also be injected into the grid for distribution. Power production must be balanced with power consumption in a situation where power storage is expensive and solar and wind generation capacity is highly variable (based on environmental conditions). Incentives, such as differential energy pricing (where electricity prices vary with the production/demand ratio), must be integrated into the management system.
- *Chemical plants:* Computers control the operation of chemical plants. The state of chemical reactors is monitored. Valves are controlled to adjust flows appropriately and maintain safety. Energy inputs are managed. Input feeds are provided, and outputs from the plant drawn at suitable intervals.

The central feature distinguishing fault tolerance in CPSs from those in general-purpose systems is the existence of deadlines for computational task completion. The cyber (computational) part of a CPS is usually in the feedback loop of a controlled plant. Delay in the feedback loop contributes to a reduction in the quality of control; indeed, beyond a certain delay, the plant may become uncontrollable (think, for example, of what would happen if a vehicle braking system took 10 seconds to recognize that the car in front of it has slowed or stopped). Fault tolerance in a CPS consists of ensuring that, despite failures, there is enough computational capacity to meet all safety-critical task deadlines.

7.1 STRUCTURE OF A CYBER-PHYSICAL SYSTEM

Every CPS is unique; however, most CPSs share certain broad characteristics, and are made up of the following interacting elements:

- *Controlled plant:* This is the application. Controlled plants vary in their complexity. They may be centralized or distributed. Their dynamics are generally well known; we rely on our knowledge of the plant dynamics to obtain task deadlines (as we shall see).
- *Cyber part (Controller):* The cyber part comprises the processors that make up the computational platform and the associated systems, middleware, and applications software. As we mentioned earlier, the focus of fault tolerance is to ensure that computational deadlines are met. The cyber part may consist of a centralized unit, or be distributed across the controlled plant.
- *Operating environment:* The operating environment affects the controlled plant state. For example, turbulence has an impact on an aircraft, and rain has an impact on the distance required for a car to stop.
- *Sensors:* The state of the controlled plant and that of the operating environment are estimated through sensors. These regularly provide inputs to the control tasks being run by the cyber system.
- *Actuators:* Actuators are used by the computer or operator to adjust the state of the controlled plant. For example, an aircraft actuators include the rudder, elevator, speedbrakes, and ailerons.
- *Operators:* There is usually one or more human operators. The extent of their involvement varies with the application. Here are three examples, ranging from low-level to high-level control: At one extreme, the driver of a traditional car, for instance, is in fairly low-level control, managing steering, accelerating, and braking from second to second. An intermediate example is a remote-controlled drone, which can fly on autopilot most of the time, but requires human intervention for certain actions (like recognizing and attacking a target). At the other extreme, a Mars rover is so far away, and signals from Earth take so long to reach it that a substantial part of its decision-making has to be done autonomously.

In a nutshell, a CPS typically operates as follows: Sensors regularly report data to the computer. Control tasks are triggered by (*a*) sensor values crossing a threshold, (*b*) a timer expiring, or (*c*) operator input. These control tasks are scheduled to run on the computational platform in such a way that their deadlines are met. The control task outputs are sent to the actuators and to the operator display (if one exists). The actuators are then set according to these commands (e.g., an aircraft elevator is moved to a specified setting), as a result of which the controlled plant functions appropriately. The process is summarized in Fig. 7.1.

Where does fault tolerance enter the picture? Processors are subject to transient, intermittent or permanent failure. Such a failure (and recovery from a transient or intermittent fault) can lead to a disruption in processing. Disruptions must be managed to ensure that hard deadlines continue to be

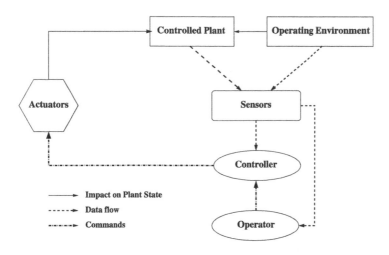

FIGURE 7.1

Structure of a generic cyber-physical system.

met (to an acceptably high probability). The software implementations of some complex control tasks may have bugs, and there have been several aviation disasters that were caused by software bugs.

Equally, sensors may fail as well. Such a failure may be obvious, as when a sensor simply stops sending data, or reports data that are obviously absurd. On the other hand, there may be subtle failure, as when it drifts out of calibration and sends increasingly erroneous values. We need some mechanism to stop erroneous data from fatally impairing the CPS.

Sidebar: Human factors

There is another source of vulnerability to CPS that deserves careful consideration. This is the interaction of the CPS with its human operator(s). Not enough is known about how to ensure that such interactions are trouble-free. A potentially dangerous occurrence is when the cyber system encounters a problem it cannot resolve and abruptly hands back control to the operator. This may result in an urgent demand upon the operator for low-level directives; a startled, incompetent or over-stressed operator can then make serious errors that endanger the CPS.

For example, if the pitot tubes (measuring flow velocity) of an aircraft are blocked, and inconsistent airspeed indications are fed to the cyber system, it may react by no longer providing automatic stall protection and handing back stall-avoidance duties to the pilot. If the pilot does not react correctly and in a timely fashion, the aircraft can then stall and crash. This is not a made-up example: see the report on the Air France 447 crash mentioned in the Further Reading section.

How to set up such transfer of control in a safe manner without placing unreasonable demands on the operator is a matter for industrial psychology and human factors engineering. A related issue is how to set up displays so that operators can be presented with relevant data, and not be overwhelmed (human bandwidth in dealing with data is notoriously limited). Despite these issues being outside the scope of our book, readers should always keep them in mind.

With this background, we are ready to turn to some basics. We will start by looking at where task deadlines come from. To do this, we need to properly define what we mean by "failure." After all, the purpose of fault tolerance is to ensure that despite the failure of one or more computational components (hardware or software), the overall system should not fail. We will then cover approaches used to protect against faults in the sensor and processor subsystems. Unlike in general-purpose systems, real-time considerations play a key part; for this reason, we will consider fault-tolerant task scheduling in detail.

7.2 THE CONTROLLED PLANT STATE SPACE

Failure in a CPS is best defined by reference to the application. The user or application specialist can specify what the controlled plant needs to do (or not do) for it to be defined as not failing. Since the plant is a physical entity, the state space in which it operates is also physical. One can define a subset of this state space as "allowed." So long as the controlled plant is within this allowed state space, it is defined as not failing; failure occurs upon departure from the allowed state space. There are variations on this basic approach. The controlled plant may operate in one of several phases; the allowed state space may be separately specified for each. For example, the allowed state space may be different for a space probe about to land on Mars than it is during its cruise phase, in space. As another example, when an aircraft is on its landing flare and less than fifty feet off the ground, its allowed deviation from its reference trajectory may be quite different from the allowed deviation when it is cruising at 30,000 feet.

> **Example:** Consider an aircraft during its landing phase. It has a desired optimal trajectory; it is considered to function satisfactorily so long as it is within a certain specified deviation from its optimal values along the following dimensions: angle of attack, vertical and horizontal position (deviation of position from the optimal), airspeed, sink rate, pitch angle, roll angle, and flight-path angle.

> **Example:** A chemical reactor vessel is managed to ensure that its temperature, pressure, and chemical concentrations are each within a given range of their optimal value.

The purpose of fault tolerance in CPS is therefore to prevent faults within the cyber system from contributing to the controlled plant leaving its allowed state space. In some cases, the controlled plant may be so deep within its allowed state space that no fault tolerance needs to be applied at the moment. This happens when the state of the plant is such that even if the worst-case erroneous output is applied to one or more actuators for a certain limited period of time, the plant will not become unsafe.

An important point to keep in mind is that the controlled plant behavior in a CPS is usually much more precisely known than in a general-purpose application. When the application is an aircraft or land vehicle, for example, its dynamics are defined by a set of simultaneous differential equations, whose numerical coefficients are known quite accurately. It is from an analysis of these plant dynamics that everything else flows.

Given the task of controlling a physical entity, control-theoretic algorithms are executed to determine how the actuators are to be set. How optimal control algorithms are obtained is outside the scope of this book; we invite the interested reader to some sources in the Further Reading section. Suffice it to say that the control engineer would have selected a repertoire of algorithms, whose execution constitutes the control workload of the cyber system.

Based on the dynamics of the controlled plant and the selected control algorithms, we can now proceed to determine task deadlines. We will start with a simple approach before proceeding to explore its limitations and extending it.

Return to the comment that we made at the beginning of this chapter that the cyber system is in the feedback loop of the controlled plant. Now, it is common sense (and this can be readily backed up and quantified by control-theoretic analysis of the controlled plant) that an increased delay in the feedback loop contributes to a worsening in the quality of control. Our first attempt to specify a task deadline is to define it as the delay, beyond which we can no longer ensure that the controlled plant stays within its allowed state space.

A little thought raises two complicating issues associated with this definition. First, the feedback delay beyond which the controlled plant leaves its allowed state space, depends on its current state. That is, if it is deep within its allowed state space, it may be able to survive a substantial feedback delay. On the other hand, if it is on the margins of its allowed state space, then even a small delay may suffice to drive it out. The obvious implication of this is that deadlines are dependent on the state of the controlled plant. Since we cannot specify a different deadline for each possible state (there is usually an infinite number of them), we need to take a practical approach, that is, breaking up the allowed state space into subspaces, and specifying a certain deadline that works everywhere within that subspace. How many subspaces are to be created depends on how rapidly the deadline varies as a function of the plant state; it is a job for the control engineer and lies outside our purview. Another related issue is that of the age of the data used by the control algorithm. In other words, the algorithm is working off data reported by the sensors. Since these data are being updated at only a finite rate, and the actual data can change from one moment to the next, this also has an impact. The extent of this impact depends on the control algorithm.

The second issue is more complicated. We do not, except in the simplest applications, have just a single control task. There are often dozens of control tasks. They all impact the controlled plant; it therefore stands to reason that the performance of one affects the demands on another.

> **Example:** Consider a control system that is trying to handle a vehicle on a slippery road. Such a system applies torque/braking force to each wheel as well as steering the vehicle. The quality of the steering algorithm and the delay in executing it will affect the impact on safety of the torque/braking task on each wheel.

Therefore where multiple interacting control tasks are concerned, one cannot specify the deadline of a task in isolation; one has to supply a vector of deadlines. Furthermore, relaxing the deadline of one task may force us to reduce the deadline of another, to compensate. One can consider the cyber system as being required to operate within a response-time space, i.e., a space with one dimension for each output; a subset of that space can be carved out to form a deadline-satisfying subspace. So long as the task response times are within this space, no deadlines are violated. Again, note that this deadline-satisfying subspace is a function of the state of the controlled plant and of the operating environment. To avoid having an infinity of these subspaces (one for each point in the controlled plant state space), we can divide the controlled plant state space into a set of subspaces, and specify a deadline-satisfying cyber response time subspace associated with each.

The purpose of the foregoing has been to emphasize the inherent complexity of the problem of assigning deadlines to tasks. For practical reasons, a heuristic approach is often followed, which is sufficient to maintain safety by overfulfilling the true deadline requirements. One approach is to have a cyber workload consisting solely of periodic control tasks, whose deadlines are equal to their respective periods. A periodic task τ_i releases a new iteration every P_i seconds. We must finish executing one iteration of a task before the subsequent iteration is released. By analysis of the controlled plant dynamics, the control engineer obtains a set of task periods, which satisfy the plant's safety requirements (over a given subset of the controlled plant's state space).

7.3 SENSORS

Sensors are the means by which the CPS determines the state of both the controlled plant and the operating environment. Failure of the sensing system can obviously have catastrophic consequences for the CPS, and so fault tolerance is required.

Sensors estimate accessible physical parameters. Quite often, sensors come with some processing capability bundled with them and deliver processed output. Sensor output is typically passed on to an *estimator*, which is responsible for estimating the controlled plant state based on these inputs. The estimated state is then passed along to the software computing the individual control settings. Fig. 7.2 summarizes this process.

FIGURE 7.2

From sensor data to actuator inputs.

Estimator design is an important topic in control theory and the interested reader should look up any standard book on feedback control. The control law may involve complex calculations (e.g., model predictive control), or simply consist of a weighted sum of the estimated states, for example, actuator setting $u_i = -w_{i,1}\hat{x}_1 - w_{i,2}\hat{x}_2 - \cdots - w_{i,n}\hat{x}_n$, where $w_{i,j}$ are precalculated weights, and $(\hat{x}_1, \hat{x}_2, \cdots, \hat{x}_n)$ is the estimated plant state vector.

Note that all state variables are not always equally important, and as a result, the weights $w_{i,j}$ will usually be nonidentical. Also, the impact of different control signals on the plant may be quite different from one another; the plant may be highly sensitive to one, but much less to another.

The quality of the estimator and the dynamics of the controlled plant (these, incidentally, are related: the estimator design is based in part on the plant dynamics) together determine the role of each sensed variable and the sensitivity of the quality of control to how accurately it is measured.

In many cases, if the error in a sensed value exceeds some bounds, it may be better to drop that value altogether in calculating the plant state estimate. Two options exist in such an instance. The first is to use a *reduced-order* estimator, which does not require that variable. Obviously, control based on such a reduced-order estimator may be somewhat degraded. The second option is to change the control objectives. For example, an aircraft, which has just suffered significant sensor failures, may be diverted to land at the nearest suitable airport. A self-driving car may warn that it can no longer function autonomously and hand back control to the driver. (Abruptly handing back control comes with dangers: recall the comments about this earlier in this chapter.)

Redundancy is the standard approach to ensuring sensor fault tolerance. Both explicit sensor redundancy and implicit data redundancy can be exploited. The former consists of using redundant sensors (e.g., multiple thermometers or angle-of-attack sensors) and running an agreement algorithm on their value. The latter consists of using the physical dependencies between sensed variables (e.g., if pressure and temperature are both measured in a boiler, they can be expected to be highly correlated).

In the discussion that follows, we will make two assumptions about a redundant set of sensors, each of which senses the same variable.

- A1. The sensors are physically positioned in such a way that they can expect to face very nearly the same value of the sensed variable.
- A2. The sensing epochs are synchronized quite tightly in time, i.e., the sensors sample the environment almost simultaneously.

Both assumptions ensure that the ground truth faced by redundant sensors is almost identical; they allow us to simplify fault detection and handling. In other words, if two sensors s_1, s_2 measure the same quantity, the values they measure around some time t can be modeled as $v_i(t) = v_{true}(t) + n_i(t)$, $i = 1, 2$, where $v_{true}(t)$ is the ground truth of the measured quantity at time t, and $n_i(t)$ is a noise parameter. No sensor is perfectly accurate; typically, sensors are specified with a given error tolerance. For example, a temperature sensor may be rated as accurate to $\pm 0.5^\circ C$, meaning that there is a zone of tolerance around the true temperature of $0.5^\circ C$ in each direction.

If assumptions A1 and A2 do not hold, then additional models will be required to correlate the sensor measurements as functions of geographical position and time. That is beyond the scope of our discussion in this chapter.

The questions we have to address with respect to sensors are the following:

- Given a redundant set of sensors, how do we determine which are likely to be faulty?
- Even functional sensors can drift out of calibration over time. How can we recalibrate the system on the fly?
- Given a set of data from supposedly functional sensors, how do we obtain a voted output value representing our estimate of the sensed variable?

Fig. 7.3 shows the flow of sensor data. Data produced by redundant sensors are first analyzed to remove outliers. The remaining data are then voted on to arrive at a result. Throughout, we can use stored historical data from the sensors, not just the latest data reported, for both fault detection and recalibration.

FIGURE 7.3

Flow of sensor data.

7.3.1 CALIBRATION

We start by considering what it means for a sensor to be faulty. The trivial answer is that any sensor, which reports a significantly incorrect value of the sensed parameter, is faulty. However, that is an excessively restricted definition. It is much better to regard a sensor as faulty only when it no longer produces information of sufficiently good quality.

What is the difference between these two definitions? The second is a generalization of the first. It is certainly the case that a sensor producing accurate readings is producing data of good quality. However, accuracy is not necessary: what is required is sufficient consistency and responsiveness to the sensed variable.

To see this more clearly, consider a light sensor. Suppose that it is not accurate, but generates the plot shown in Fig. 7.4. Most of the inaccuracy from this sensor arises from a fixed, positive, bias, which we can easily correct for, that is, it is possible to recalibrate it so that its output can be translated to a correct reading.

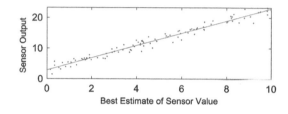

FIGURE 7.4

Light sensor output.

Recalibration involves storing the best estimate of the sensed parameter as a function of time and comparing it with the value that the sensor reports. Standard regression techniques can then be used to derive an expression for the interpreted value as a function of the reported value (linear functions are often used). The quality of the regression can be tested by evaluating its root mean square error for each of the reported data points. There can be a threshold (either absolute or relative) for declaring the regression unacceptable; in such a case, the sensor can be regarded as behaving too erratically to depend upon.

> **Example:** Our best estimates of a certain parameter collected as a time series (i.e., at distinct points in time) are as follows: 1, 5, 4, 7, 4, 5, 6, 2. Our sensor reports the following values: 2, 7, 4, 8, 3, 6, 8, 3 for these sampling epochs. Suppose we want a linear function $v_{estimated} = m \cdot v_{sensed} + c$, where $v_{estimated}$ is the estimated value when the sensor returns a reading of v_{sensed}. Standard regression techniques can then be used to obtain m and c; in this case, we have $m = 0.75; c = 0.39$. The root mean square error can be used as an index of the quality of the regression.

The value v_{sensed} reported by the sensor cannot be assumed to be identical to the true value of the measured parameter. Instead, it is, in general, the sum of three terms: $v_{sensed} = v_{true} + v_{bias} + v_{noise}$. These terms are the true value of the parameter, the sensor bias, and the sensor noise, respectively. Inaccuracy arises as a result of sensor bias and sensor noise. The difference between these two quantities is that bias is either effectively constant, or changes only very slowly over time. Noise, on the other hand, tends to fluctuate rapidly; furthermore, sensor failure could also manifest itself as noise. As long as the bias term is only slowly changing, and the noise amplitude is relatively small, we can continue to use the information provided by the sensor by estimating, and correcting for, the bias. If the noise amplitude exceeds a certain limit, we may declare the sensor as faulty. We can do so, for example, by making an estimate $v_{estimate}$ of v_{true} by combining the outputs of multiple redundant sensors, and then tracking the value of $v_{estimated} - v_{sensed}$ over time for each individual sensor.

The more accurate our estimate, the better the calibration. In an ideal case, a sensor can be calibrated against a trusted reference, which is known to be highly accurate (e.g., in a standards laboratory): this can be done prior to deployment. In the field, such references do not exist; the estimate is then based on the aggregated data obtained by the collection of sensors (this is sometimes called *blind* or *macro* calibration).

7.3.2 DETECTING FAULTY SENSORS

Detecting a faulty sensor can be done in a variety of ways. First, if the sensor is *self-validating*, there will be a fault check internal to the sensor itself. Self-validation is useful when the sensor has access to much more data than it actually transmits. For instance, the sensor might only transmit data at specified intervals, but collect those data either continuously or at a much higher rate. Such a sensor might, for example, calculate the frequency spectrum of its internal high-rate measurements; if this shows a deviation from the expected values, a fault might be suspected. To take another case, a sensor might in fact measure multiple parameters $\eta_1, \eta_2, \cdots, \eta_n$ internally, and then carry out a computation to estimate the value of some desired quantity as a function of these parameters $v = f(\eta_1, \eta_2, \cdots, \eta_n)$. The transmitted values are updated estimates of v; the parameters η_i are internal to the sensor, and not sent out. The sensor is therefore the only entity aware of its measurements of η_i; it can look for inconsistencies within this set to indicate the possibility that it is faulty. As sensors become more intelligent, with more processing capability present at the sensors themselves, such an approach becomes more feasible.

Another approach is to use a redundant set of sensors to measure the same quantity, and then carry out some processing to obtain an agreed-upon result. As mentioned earlier, sensor data come with uncertainty intervals; typically, these are modeled as a window centered on the reported value and having a specified half-width, that is, if a sensor reports a data value of v with a half-width of Δ, we can say with a sufficiently high confidence that the true value lies somewhere in the interval $[v - \Delta, v + \Delta]$. One rule of thumb is to declare two sensor values as being in agreement if their difference is less than the root mean square of their uncertainty half-widths. Alternatively, one might define agreement not in 0–1 terms, but along a continuum; for example, the inverse of the absolute difference between data values might be used.

With sensor data at hand, outlier detection can be done. An outlier is a datum, whose value is significantly different from the picture painted by the data as a whole. There are three kinds of outliers: *global*, *contextual*, and *collective*.

- *Global outliers:* A datum is a global outlier if it differs significantly from the bulk of the redundant data set. For example, consider four pitot tubes that measure airspeed. Suppose the results returned are $\{150, 155, 153, 290\}$. The 290 datum is a global outlier, and is likely to be erroneous.

- *Contextual outliers:* Contextual outliers are those data that are at variance from the overall picture as sensed by the data. For example, an altimeter that reads the altitude as 10 feet when the aircraft is at cruise and was last measured to be at 30,000 feet, is a contextual outlier.
- *Collective outliers:* It is possible for a subset of the data to be clustered together, but to collectively report false, unrepresentative, or unusual data. For example, suppose we have multiple temperature sensors, which each report a temperature in the neighborhood of $40^\circ C$ at the North Pole in December. This is obviously not likely to be a problem affecting an individual sensor; it might reflect a fire nearby, or an intruder deliberately feeding false data into the system.

Of these, global and contextual outliers are the most relevant as fault indicators.

There are several, rather similar, ways to identify global outliers; we present a representative technique here. Let us start with the notion of *distance*. Geographical distance is easy to understand intuitively. The notion of distance can be generalized considerably; indeed, it is understood that any function $d(x, y)$ can be used as a distance measure (between points x and y in some space) if it satisfies the following basic properties:

- D1. A distance is never negative.
- D2. The distance between a point and itself is zero, i.e., $d(x, x) = 0$.
- D3. Distance is a symmetric measure, i.e., $d(x, y) = d(y, x)$.
- D4. Distance obeys the triangle inequality, i.e., for any three points x, y, z,

$$d(x, z) \le d(x, y) + d(y, z).$$

When determining which sensors generate outlier values, we first have to select a distance measure. If we are basing our outlier detection on just one real data value, then the difference in absolute value is sufficient: $d(x, y) = |x - y|$. However, we do not usually diagnose a sensor as faulty based on just one outlier reading. We base it on the last N readings it has produced, and how that compares to those of other similar and nearby sensors.

Three issues now arise:

- How should we select the value of N?
- What is an appropriate distance measure to use?
- What is the threshold for deciding when two sensors are in disagreement?

The selection of N involves resolving a tradeoff. If N is very large, then very old readings will continue to play a part in deciding whether a sensor output deviates significantly from those of its colleagues. Equally, newer, highly deviant readings from a sensor that has recently failed may be drowned out by old, coincident, readings, thereby delaying detection. On the other hand, if N is very small, short-lived transient failures, or the passing impact of noise, can cause an essentially good sensor to be labeled as bad. N must therefore be selected based on what would be a good resolution of this tradeoff. Alternatively, the contribution of old readings to the distance measure might be devalued.

Example: One example of devaluing older readings, based on how long ago they were taken, is *exponential smoothing*. Suppose we have readings from sensor s_k together with time stamps indicating when they were taken. Denote s_k's reading at time t_i by $v_{k,i}$, $i = 1, 2, \cdots$. Define some real number $0 < \rho < 1$. If the current time is t, then the weight assigned to the i'th reading is

$w(t_i, t) = \rho^{t-t_i}$. The weighted average of the readings is then given by

$$\frac{\sum_i w(t_i, t) \cdot v_{k,i}}{\sum_i w(t_i, t)} = \frac{\sum_i \rho^{t-t_i} \cdot v_{k,i}}{\sum_i \rho^{t-t_i}}.$$

Thus the weight assigned to any datum drops as its age increases. The smaller the value of ρ, the greater is the rate at which this weight declines.

The distance measure that is selected is also of importance. Not all distance measures are equally sensitive to the same underlying characteristics. In some cases, distance measures may flag a problem that may simply indicate the need for recalibration.

Let us consider two measures to illustrate this point: one is the Euclidean distance between two vectors, say $\vec{A} = (a_1, a_2, \cdots, a_n)$ and $\vec{B} = (b_1, b_2, \cdots, b_n)$, and the other, the cosine distance between them. The Euclidean distance is defined as $D_2(\vec{A}, \vec{B}) = \sqrt{\sum_{\ell=1}^{n}(a_\ell - b_\ell)^2}$, whereas the cosine distance is defined as 1 minus the cosine of the angle between these vectors; it is calculated as $D_{cos}(\vec{A}, \vec{B}) = 1 - \frac{\vec{A} \cdot \vec{B}}{\|\vec{A}\|\|\vec{B}\|}$, where $\|\vec{A}\|$ denotes the Euclidean norm of vector $\vec{A}$, i.e., its absolute magnitude given by $\sqrt{\sum_{\ell=1}^{n} a_\ell^2}$, and $\vec{A} \cdot \vec{B}$ is the dot product of the two vectors, i.e., $\sum_{\ell=1}^{n}(a_\ell \cdot b_\ell)$.

To make things concrete, consider the two vectors $\vec{A} = (1, 1, 1, 1, 1)$ and $\vec{B} = (2, 2, 2, 2, 2)$. The Euclidean distance between them is easily calculated to be $\sqrt{5}$. However, the cosine distance between them is 0. Which of them is right? They both are, since each measures a different thing. The Euclidean distance tells us the deviation between the two points in absolute terms. The cosine distance tells us that the two vectors are along the same direction; hinting that the difference between them may be due to a miscalibration involving scaling that can be corrected.

The threshold for deciding whether two sensor values are in agreement or not has to be selected on a case-by-case basis. As already mentioned, a good rule of thumb is to say that agreement exists if two outputs are within the root mean square of the accuracy half-widths of each sensor; however, the user may decide to select either a more rigorous or a more relaxed rule, depending on the circumstances.

We model each datum from the set of redundant data (i.e., data reported by multiple sensors each measuring the same physical quantity) as a node in a complete graph (i.e., an edge exists between every two nodes). The weight of the edge between nodes i and j is the distance between the data represented by these nodes. The distance measure used, e.g., either the Euclidean or the cosine, is selected by the designer. Each distance measure has its own characteristics, which should be thoroughly understood before being selected. If a node has no (or very few) neighbors at a distance less than a given threshold, we can label it an outlier. As mentioned earlier, one choice for a threshold might be the root mean square of the error limits associated with the sensors reporting those data.

Example: We have n temperature sensors, with sensor s_i having an error halfwidth of Δ_i. We decide to define two sensors as being essentially in agreement if their reported temperatures differ by no more than the root mean square of their error half-widths, that is, the threshold for sensors s_i and s_j will be $\sqrt{\frac{\Delta_i^2 + \Delta_j^2}{2}}$. We then build a complete graph of n nodes. An edge is deleted if its endpoints are not in agreement. Nodes with fewer than a given number of neighbors in this reduced graph are declared to represent outlier temperatures; the sensors that generated these outlier numbers are then suspected of having failed.

Another approach to sensor fault detection uses Bayesian analysis.[1] Such an approach requires the following information:

- The probability density function of the outputs generated by a faulty sensor.
- The probability density function of the outputs generated by a nonfaulty sensor, given any additional contextual information we may have.
- The probability that a given sensor is faulty.

We make here the assumptions that sensors fail independently of one another, and that data are available on sensor failure rates. For a redundant set K of n sensors, $K = \{s_1, s_2, \cdots, s_n\}$, define the sensor status vector by $\vec{\phi} = (\phi_1, \cdots, \phi_n)$. Here, $\phi_i = 0$ if sensor s_i is nonfaulty; it is 1 otherwise. Denote by $\vec{V} = (v_1, v_2, \cdots, v_n)$ the vector of data values received from these sensors: the i'th element of this vector is the value reported by s_i. Note that to simplify the notation, we suppress the subscript and use v to denote the value reported by a sensor, previously denoted by $v_{estimated}$. Let ξ denote any contextual information we may have from other sources. For example, we may know from physical considerations that the state variables are constrained to be in some subspace. Then, we have from Bayes's Law that

$$P(\vec{\phi} = \vec{j} | \vec{V}, \xi) = \frac{f(\vec{V} | \vec{\phi} = \vec{j}, \xi) P(\vec{\phi} = \vec{j} | \xi)}{f(\vec{V} | \xi)} = \frac{f(\vec{V} | \vec{\phi} = \vec{j}, \xi) P(\vec{\phi} = \vec{j} | \xi)}{\sum_{\vec{i} \in \Theta} f(\vec{V} | \vec{\phi} = \vec{i}, \xi) P(\vec{\phi} = \vec{i} | \xi)}, \qquad (7.1)$$

where

- $f(\vec{V} | \vec{\phi} = \vec{j}, \xi)$ is the probability density function of the data vector reported by redundant sensor set K, given that the functionality of this sensor set $\vec{\phi}$ is equal to $\vec{j}$ and any additional contextual information ξ.
- $P(\vec{\phi} = \vec{j} | \xi)$ is the probability that the functionality of the sensor set $\vec{\phi}$ is equal to $\vec{j}$, given the additional information ξ.
- $f(\vec{V} | \xi)$ is the probability density function of this sensor set generating a vector of outputs $\vec{V}$, given the additional information ξ.
- Θ is the set of all 2^n possible values that $\vec{\phi}$ can assume.

We use Eq. (7.1) to calculate the probability of each of the 2^n possible functionality status vectors. Pick whichever such vector that maximizes this value. Given how rapidly 2^n grows with n, this approach is obviously only feasible for small redundant sensor sets.

A second approach evaluates the *trustworthiness* of each sensor, based on an analysis of the data that this sensor and its redundant colleagues have generated. This approach is most applicable when there is a reasonably large number of redundant sensors. (Readers familiar with data mining may notice similarities with algorithms used in evaluating the trustworthiness of online data sources; those

---

[1] This part should be skipped by readers without much knowledge of probability, especially of Bayes's Law of conditional probability.

familiar with Markov chains will notice mathematical similarities.) The idea is that if a sensor is highly trustworthy, i.e., it is believed to produce very good data, it is likely to agree closely with those of its colleagues, which also produce very good data. Hence, its outputs will likely correlate closely with other highly trusted sensors. We can use this concept to iteratively build a trust rank of a sensor.

First, we have to determine the *similarity* between the most recent N outputs of any two sensors s_i, s_j, where N is selected by the user. Let $\vec{v_k} = (v_{k,1}, \cdots, v_{k,N})$ denote the vector of the past N values generated by sensor s_k. The similarity between the outputs $\vec{v_i}$ and $\vec{v_j}$ of the sensors s_i and s_j increases as the *distance* between $\vec{v_i}$ and $\vec{v_j}$ decreases. There are several similarity measures we can select. One is the *extended Jaccard similarity*, which is defined as follows:

$$J(\vec{v_i}, \vec{v_j}) = \frac{\vec{v_i} \cdot \vec{v_j}}{\|\vec{v_i}\|^2 + \|\vec{v_j}\|^2 - \vec{v_i} \cdot \vec{v_j}}. \tag{7.2}$$

The extended Jaccard similarity is a normalized measure, whose magnitude ranges in the interval $[0, 1]$. Two identical vectors will have similarity 1. (Note that this similarity measure will not work if one or both vectors is all zeros: in such a case, some other measure will be required.)

Example: Let $\vec{v_1} = (1, 1, 2, 1, 1), \vec{v_2} = (1, 2, 3, 1, 0)$; these represent the last five values reported by sensors s_1, s_2, respectively. Then, their dot product is given by $\vec{v_1} \cdot \vec{v_2} = 1 \times 1 + 1 \times 2 + 2 \times 3 + 1 \times 1 + 1 \times 0 = 10$. $\|\vec{v_1}\| = \sqrt{1^2 + 1^2 + 2^2 + 1^2 + 1^2} = \sqrt{8} = 2.83$; $\|\vec{v_2}\| = \sqrt{1^2 + 2^2 + 3^2 + 1^2 + 0^2} = \sqrt{15} = 3.87$. The extended Jaccard similarity is $J(\vec{v_1}, \vec{v_2}) = \frac{10}{8+15-10} = 0.77$.

In what follows, we will denote by $\sigma(\vec{v_i}, \vec{v_j})$ the similarity between $\vec{v_i}$ and $\vec{v_j}$ using whichever similarity measure has been selected.

Now, define auxiliary variables $q_{i,j}$ as follows:

$$q_{i,j} = \frac{\sigma(\vec{v_i}, \vec{v_j})}{\sum_{s_k \in K} \sigma(\vec{v_i}, \vec{v_k})},$$

where K denotes the set of redundant sensors to which s_k belongs. Clearly, $q_{i,j}$ is in the range $[0, 1]$.

We now proceed accordingly: Define the trustworthiness *rank* of a sensor s_i, denoted by R_i, as follows:

$$R_i = \sum_{s_j \in K - \{s_i\}} R_j q_{j,i}. \tag{7.3}$$

Note that this equation has an infinite number of solutions for the R_i's; to obtain a unique solution, we will need to normalize it, for instance by requiring that the trust ranks sum to 1. When this is done, if there are n sensors in the redundant set, the average trust rank will always be $1/n$. (Alternatively, multiply all trust ranks by n, in which case the average trust rank will always be 1.)

Example: Consider a set of five redundant sensors; the window over which comparisons are made is six long, that is, we base our similarity and trustworthiness rank calculations over the past six outputs. The outputs of the sensors are as follows:

$$\vec{v_1} = (1, 2, 2, 2, 1, 1) \qquad \vec{v_2} = (1, 3, 2, 2, 1, 1) \qquad \vec{v_3} = (2, 2, 2, 2, 1, 1)$$

$$\vec{v}_4 = (1,2,3,4,5,5) \qquad \vec{v}_5 = (2,2,9,2,9,8).$$

The resulting trust ranks are, in order of sensor number: $0.234, 0.232, 0.231, 0.183, 0.121$. (If we decide to normalize them so that their average score is 1, we would multiply each of these trust ranks by 5.) The standard deviation of these outputs is 0.049, and the coefficient of variation (defined as the standard deviation divided by the mean) of the trust ranks is 0.24. No two sensors have the same history of reported values; however, based on closeness within the group, sensor s_1 has the highest rank, and s_5 the lowest. We can use these numbers to weight a voting process; alternatively, sensors with a trust rank below some threshold can be regarded as suspicious.

Example: Consider five sensors reporting the following values:

$$\vec{v}_1 = (1,1,1,1,1) \qquad \vec{v}_2 = (1,1,1,1,1) \qquad \vec{v}_3 = (1,1,1,1,1)$$
$$\vec{v}_4 = (1,1,1,1,1) \qquad \vec{v}_5 = (2,9,8,15,9).$$

The trust ranks are now given by $0.242, 0.242, 0.242, 0.242$, and 0.032, respectively. Note the very low trust accorded the fifth sensor.

Suppose we are calculating some function, say $U(v_1, v_2, \cdots, v_n)$ of the reported sensor readings $v_1, v_2, \cdots, v_n$. (For example, v_1 might be the speed of a vehicle, and v_2 the prevailing temperature.) Suppose the uncertainty half-width associated with sensor input v_i is Δ_i. Then, *if the sensed values are (reasonably) independent of one another*, we can state the uncertainty half-width of $U(v_1, v_2, \cdots, v_n)$ as follows:

$$\Delta u \approx \sqrt{\sum_{i=1}^{n} \left(\frac{\partial U(v_1, \cdots, v_n)}{\partial v_i} \right)^2 \Delta_i^2}. \tag{7.4}$$

This expression assumes that the relative uncertainties of each of the sensor values are sufficiently small, that higher-order terms (i.e., exponents greater than 2) can be safely ignored. This expression provides some guidance as to where high-quality data are required, and for which variables a rough estimate is sufficient.

Example: Suppose $U(v_1, v_2) = w_1 v_1 + w_2 v_2$. Then, we have the half-width of the estimate of $U(.,.)$ as $\sqrt{w_1^2 \Delta_1^2 + w_2^2 \Delta_2^2}$; the half-width relative to the estimate of $U(\cdot, \cdot)$ is $\frac{\sqrt{w_1^2 \Delta_1^2 + w_2^2 \Delta_2^2}}{w_1 v_1 + w_2 v_2}$. Note how the weights affect both the absolute and relative half-widths; in particular, if $w_1 v_1$ and $w_2 v_2$ have different signs so that the denominator is small, the relative error may be substantial. This needs to be taken into consideration during the design process, when the sensor specifications are being determined.

7.3.3 CONFIDENCE MEASURES FOR INTERVALS

Let I_i, α_i be the report of sensor s_i in some redundant set K: I_i is the interval reported, and α_i the attendant confidence in that report, that is, sensor s_i is reporting with confidence α_i that the true value of the sensed parameter is in the interval I_i.

Confidence should not be confused for probability, although many of the mathematical operations carried out on the two are similar. The true value of the sensed parameter, say $v_{i,true}$, exists even if we do not know it. It is not a random variable once it has happened; it is a deterministic quantity. So, in reality, either $v_{i,true} \in I_i$ or it is not; there is no probability as such attached to it. Our confidence measure is just a way of saying what level of certainty we wish to attach to that interval.

Define the intervals $\gamma_i^{(j)}$ as follows: $\gamma_i^{(0)} = I_i$ and $\gamma_i^{(1)} = \bar{I}_i$, the complement of I_i. For example, if $I_i = [3,4]$, $\gamma_i^{(0)} = [3,4]; \gamma_i^{(1)} = (-\infty, 3) \cup (4, \infty)$. (We are assuming in our treatment that the sensors report scalars.)

Define a binary string $M = \mu_1 \mu_1 \cdots \mu_n$ as representing the intersection $\gamma_1^{(\mu_1)} \cap \gamma_2^{(\mu_2)} \cdots \cap \gamma_n^{(\mu_n)}$, where $\mu_i \in \{0, 1\}$. Call M a *legal* string if it represents a nonempty intersection. For example, if $I_1 = [3,4]$, $I_2 = [4,5]$, the string $\mu_1 \mu_2 = 00$ is not legal (I_1 and I_2 do not overlap), whereas the string 01 is legal (and represents the interval $[3,4]$ since the complement of I_2 includes all of I_1). Define by $\mathcal{L}$ the set of all legal strings representing intersections of intervals reported by sensors in set K.

Define $\psi(M) = \prod_{i=1}^{n} (\alpha_i 1_{\mu_i=0} + (1-\alpha_i) 1_{\mu_i=1})$. (For those unfamiliar with the symbolism: 1_X is an *indicator function*, which is 1 if the logical condition X is true, and 0 if it is false.) Then, a measure of the confidence we have in an interval represented in the string $\mu_1 \mu_2 \cdots \mu_n$ is the following:

$$\kappa(M) = \frac{\psi(M)}{\sum_{m \in \mathcal{L}} \psi(m)}.$$

Let us turn now to fault tolerance. Suppose we are told that f is the maximum number of sensors in redundant set K that can be faulty at any given time. (That is, the system specifications require only that it be reliable if no more than f sensors have failed.) We can integrate this fact into the framework above by considering only intervals that are the intersection of $n - f + 1$ or more sensor reports. This way, we can be sure that at least one of the intervals involved in the intersection is the output of a nonfaulty sensor. In other words, we define a string $M = \mu_1 \cdots \mu_n$ as *FT legal* only if $\mu_1 + \cdots + \mu_n \leq f$. Confidence is then calculated only over intervals represented by an FT legal string. Defining $\mathcal{L}^{(FT)}$ as the set of all FT legal strings representing the redundant sensor set, we obtain the following measure of confidence:

$$\kappa^{(FT)}(M) = \frac{\psi(M)}{\sum_{m \in \mathcal{L}^{(FT)}} \psi(m)}.$$

Example: Assume we have a set of three redundant sensors, i.e., $n = 3$. Assume $f = 1$. The outputs of these three sensors for some sampling instant are the following: $I_1 = [5,7]; I_2 = [4,6]; I_3 = [5.5, 8]$. The corresponding confidences are $\alpha_1 = 0.9; \alpha_2 = 0.8; \alpha_3 = 0.8$. Since $f = 1$, all legal strings representing an intersection of these intervals must contain at most one 1. Table 7.1 contains our calculations. Since $0.576 + 0.144 + 0.144 = 0.864$, the confidences are found by dividing the product of the individual confidence values by this normalizing quantity.

Table 7.1 Interval calculations for three redundant sensors.

String	Interval	$\psi(\cdot)$	Confidence
000	[5.5,6]	$0.9 \times 0.8 \times 0.8 = 0.576$	0.667
001	[5,5.5]	$0.9 \times 0.8 \times 0.2 = 0.144$	0.167
010	[6,7]	$0.9 \times 0.2 \times 0.8 = 0.144$	0.167

Strings 011, 101, 110, and 111 are not FT-legal; 100 is the empty interval.

7.4 THE CYBER PLATFORM

Fault tolerance within the computational, or cyber, platform, can be implemented using the approaches mentioned in the rest of this book. In addition, however, the real-time nature of CPS applications raises the issue of overruns and how to provide temporal (time) redundancy to reliably deal with them.

The computational workload of a CPS is typically very well-profiled in advance. The individual tasks are tested and evaluated in depth. Their worst-case execution requirements are estimated; real-time scheduling algorithms try to ensure that task deadlines are met. Each scheduling algorithm comes with its own schedulability test, i.e., given the workload there is a mathematical check that reports whether there is sufficient computational capacity to meet all deadlines.

> **Example:** Suppose we have a set of periodic tasks $\{\tau_1, \cdots, \tau_n\}$ assigned to execute on a single processor, that is, each task τ_i is released for execution every P_i seconds; it requires a maximum of c_i seconds to execute. Its deadline equals its period, i.e., we require that each iteration of a task complete before the next iteration of the same task is released. Clearly, $c_i \leq P_i$. Assume that tasks can be preempted, are independent of one another (i.e., no task needs the output of any other task), and that preemption costs are negligible.
>
> The earliest deadline first (EDF) scheduling algorithm schedules tasks by executing whichever unfinished task has the earliest absolute deadline; ties (if any) are broken arbitrarily. Suppose an iteration of task τ_i is released every P_i seconds, and it has to be completed before the subsequent iteration of τ_i is released, that is, its relative deadline equals its period. Then a mathematical analysis of EDF shows that all deadlines will be met so long as the following condition holds:
>
> $$\sum_{i=1}^{n} \frac{c_i}{P_i} \leq 1.$$

However, occasionally, task overruns can occur, that is, sometimes tasks can take longer to run than their estimated worst-case time. This can occur for a number of reasons: the estimate may be incorrect and the code may have been presented with an unusual set of inputs for which it takes longer to run; there may be a brief transient failure, during which the processor hangs, or there may be a previously undetected problem in the software. Whereas every effort should be made to avoid overruns in the first place, an ultra-reliable system must provide some effective response when they do (hopefully, very rarely) occur. The reason is that a task overrun does not affect just the overrunning task: by occupying the processor for longer than it should, it can trigger a cascade of delays that cause other tasks to miss deadlines as well. It is not difficult to construct examples, where a single overrunning task causes the current iteration of *every* other task on that processor to miss its deadline.

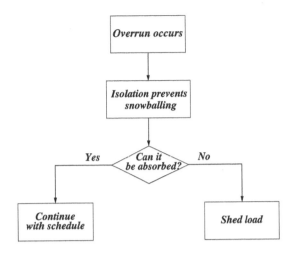

FIGURE 7.5

Approaches to handling task overruns.

There are three approaches to task overruns. They are complementary, meaning that they can be used together in any combination. One is *isolation*, to ensure that the overrun of one task (or group of tasks) does not trigger excessive delays of others. The second is *load shedding* by abandoning the execution of low-criticality tasks. The third is *absorption*, where the system is given some reserve capacity, by which up to a certain amount of overrun can be absorbed.

Fig. 7.5 summarizes how these approaches work together. When an overrun occurs, isolation techniques prevent that overrun from snowballing and affecting all the tasks assigned to that processor. The system detects the overrun (by using a timer) and determines if the overrun can be absorbed. If so, execution can proceed with just further monitoring, and no changes to the workload. If the overrun cannot be absorbed, load must be shed. We now look at each of these techniques in turn.

7.4.1 ISOLATION

Individual tasks or groups of tasks on a particular processor can be isolated from one another by assigning them to virtual servers running on the processor. The processor is time-multiplexed between these servers. For example, we may have these servers gain access to the processor in a round-robin order: server 1 for ξ_1 time, then switching to server 2 for ξ_2 time, and so on. To each server we assign one task or task group. A task is confined to executing only within its assigned server. As a result, an overrunning task cannot affect the tasks assigned to other servers, and overrun isolation is provided.

These servers can be modeled by associating each of them with a *supply function*.[2] The supply function associated with server j, $Z_j(t)$, is the total minimum time guaranteed to the server by the

---

[2] To make it simpler to explain and to understand, we will assume that the processor clock frequency is kept constant; it is not difficult to relax this assumption.

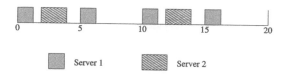

FIGURE 7.6

Periodic server for overrun isolation.

processor over *any* interval of duration t. Define $\beta_j = \lim_{t\to\infty} \frac{Z_j(t)}{t}$ and $\delta_j = \sup_{t\geq 0}\left\{t - \frac{Z_j(t)}{\beta_j}\right\}$. β_j is the long-term average time provided to server j per unit time. We can show (see the Exercises) that the maximum time between activity on the processor by server j is δ_j; i.e., this is the maximum time between the end of one time slice allocated to server j and the beginning of the next.

$Z_j(t)$ is used to determine schedulability for task sets constrained to work within the confines of server j.

> **Example:** We have a processor that is supporting two servers. See Fig. 7.6. Server 1 occupies the processor for 1 ms every 5 ms, starting at time 0. This server delivers a long-term average, $\beta_1 = 0.2$ seconds per second. The duration between the end of one Server-1 time-slice and the next is $\delta_1 = 4$ ms. Server 2 occupies the processor for 1.8 ms every 10 ms starting at time 2 ms; it thus delivers a long-term average $\beta_2 = 0.18$ seconds per second with the duration between the end of one Server-2 time-slice and the next being $\delta_2 = 8.2$ ms. An overrun of a task assigned to Server 1 is limited to running just while this server is in operation; it cannot encroach on the time assigned to a task assigned to Server 2.

> **Remark:** The reader should be mindful that there are other ways besides processor occupation, which may cause one task to affect the function of another. To take the above example, if all tasks running on a given processor share its cache, a task assigned to Server 1 can affect the contents of the cache. For example, it may cause the eviction of material required by a task assigned to Server 2; when Server 2 returns to execution, such material may need to be brought back into the cache, thus incurring delays. This is an example of how tasks may interfere with one another through the process of sharing resources.
>
> To avoid such interference, we may reserve one portion of the cache for the exclusive use of Server 1 and another for Server 2. However, this is not without its drawbacks: the cache available for use by each server now drops, and thus can lead to a higher cache miss rate.

Deriving the full scheduling analysis is outside the scope of our coverage here, see the Further Reading section for pointers to the literature on the subject. Simple expressions exist to check for schedulability. For instance, for the EDF scheduling algorithm, given a periodic task set with the properties mentioned above, the task set is schedulable on server j if for all time $t > 0$,

$$\sum_{i=1}^{n} \left\lfloor \frac{t}{P_i} \right\rfloor c_i \leq Z_j(t). \tag{7.5}$$

Isolation ensures that overrunning tasks cannot do damage beyond their assigned servers. However, we do need to detect an overrun when it occurs, so that we may then respond to it. This is not difficult to do: a timer can track how long each task has been running at a known clock frequency, and an interrupt can be triggered when the task exceeds its estimated execution bound.

7.4.2 LOAD SHEDDING

Once an overrun has been detected, the system must respond appropriately. If the overrun cannot be absorbed (see below), we must shed some of the assigned load to make up for the additional time that has unexpectedly been consumed. We will present two approaches to reduce system load.

Multicriticality: When deciding which tasks to abandon to reduce the computational burden, we must take their criticality into account. Not all tasks are equally important to the application. For example, steering and stability control in a car are much more critical than operating the navigation or climate control system. To save highly critical tasks, we can simply sacrifice tasks of lower criticality.

The algorithm is quite simple; we will describe the situation where there are just two levels of criticality. The system works in two modes: normal and abnormal. In the normal mode, all tasks are executed. When any of the low-critical tasks overrun, we can simply drop it. If a high-critical task overruns, the system switches to abnormal mode. In this mode, all low-critical tasks are abandoned, and only critical tasks are executed. When the system becomes idle at some point in the future (i.e., with all pending high-criticality work completed), it can switch back to normal mode. This is summarized in Fig. 7.7. Extensive work has been done on calculating schedulability in such a setup; the reader will find pointers to the literature in the Further Reading section.

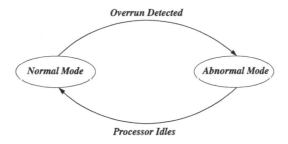

FIGURE 7.7

Switching between modes.

Substituting tasks: Another option to reduce computational load is to substitute a task by another, which performs the same overall function (albeit at a lower quality), but imposes a lower burden. For example, suppose we are calculating the appropriate setting for the actuators of some physical plant. There are several control algorithms to choose from. One is *model predictive control*, where we select the appropriate control action by evaluating the future state-space trajectory of the plant as a function of the current action taken. The horizon to which we evaluate this trajectory will affect both the quality of the control provided as well as the computational burden; if it is well into the future, both will be high; if we look ahead just a short interval, both will be low. Alternatively, we may switch from using computationally expensive model-predictive control to a cheaper (and potentially lower-quality) one calculated by linearly combining the controlled plant state variables, that is, the control will be a function of $w_1 x_1 + w_2 x_2 + \cdots + w_n x_n$, where w_i, x_i are weights and plant state variables, respectively.

7.4.3 OVERRUN ABSORPTION

We can design a system to continue undisturbed even if up to a certain number of tasks overrun. This involves providing enough processing redundancy to absorb the additional work.

One approach is to require a certain amount of slack to be provided in the schedule to begin with. This approach can be integrated into the periodic server outlined earlier. To make this concrete, consider EDF scheduling introduced earlier in this chapter. Suppose the *maximum* total workload that has to be completed in *any* interval of time t, and assigned to server j, is given by a *demand bound function*, $dbf_j(t)$.

> **Example:** Suppose our workload consists of just a single task; this is a periodic task with a worst-case execution time of 2 ms and a period of 5 ms. The worst-case demand of such a task over any interval of time t can be calculated by releasing such a task at the start of this interval and determining how many executions have to be completed before time t. Then, simply multiply this number by the worst-case execution time per iteration (2 ms in this case). In this case therefore the demand bound function would be $dbf(t) = 2 \lfloor t/5 \rfloor$.

Then, so long as $dbf_j(t) \leq Z_j(t)$ for all time $t > 0$, all deadlines can be satisfied. The difference $Z_j(t) - dbf_j(t)$ introduces slack in the schedule to allow for a certain limited amount of overrun.

A related approach is to remap tasks onto another processor that has enough spare capacity to meet all deadlines. It may be necessary to preload the task object code into these backup processors' memories to avoid the delay of moving code from one processor's memory to the backup.

A second approach involves dynamic voltage and frequency scaling. It is well known that increasing the supply voltage to a processor (up to a certain limit) decreases circuit delays, and therefore permits it to be clocked at a higher frequency (again, up to a limit). Such an upclocking is not cost-free: it entails significantly increased power consumption and thermal stress (which can shorten processor lifetime). However, in an emergency, and for a short time, increasing clocking rate may be considered the least bad option to deal with an overrun.

7.5 ACTUATORS

We have already seen how faults within redundant sensor sets can be identified. We now consider fault detection and identification for the actuators. To do so, we exploit information redundancy, that is, we compare what the controlled plant does in response to an actuator command to what we expect it to do.

A simple example will illustrate this. The controlled plant here is an overhead water tank. The actuator is a pump you use to fill the tank. Your tank is empty, and you turn on the pump. Half an hour later, you return to find the tank still empty. There is no leak detected (via sensors, namely your eyes); the obvious conclusion is that something went wrong with the pumping process. You now have

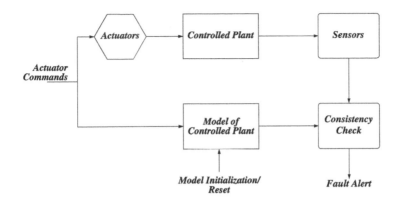

FIGURE 7.8

Fault detection process.

an indication that something is faulty, but do not yet know what is wrong. There are at least three possibilities leading to this anomaly: the pump is faulty, the power supply to the pump is disconnected, or the source of water for the pump is dry. Here, you are comparing what is expected of the state of the water tank (containing at least some water) to what is actually observed. Some further obvious manual checks should suffice to identify the source of the problem.

Fault detection and identification for actuators follows the same approach, which is illustrated in Fig. 7.8. We have a mathematical model for the controlled plant that tells us how its state evolves as a function of the actuator inputs (and noise inputs from the operating environment). These commands are copied to a model of the plant. The anticipated output of the plant can then be calculated based on this model. We then carry out a consistency check, based on comparing this anticipated output with the actual output. Note that such a consistency check may not limit itself to just the *current* anticipated and actual outputs, but may also take into account a long history of *past* anticipated and actual output pairs.

Fault detection and identification is a substantial topic in control theory, and requires an extensive background in this field to understand. We will limit ourselves here to providing a high-level overview requiring only some linear algebra to follow; the Further Reading section contains pointers to some of the relevant literature.

Let us consider a controlled plant that can be modeled as a linear discrete-time system, that is, if we denote the state of the plant by the vector $\vec{x}$, we can model its behavior over time by the following linear equation:

$$\vec{x}(k+1) \quad = \quad \mathbf{A}\vec{x}(k) + \mathbf{B}\vec{u}(k) + \vec{n}(k) \tag{7.6}$$

$$\vec{y}(k) \quad = \quad \mathbf{C}\vec{x}(k), \tag{7.7}$$

where $\mathbf{A}, \mathbf{B}, \mathbf{C}$ are matrices that define the system, $\vec{u}$ is the plant input (applied via the actuator settings), and $\vec{y}$ is the plant output (assessed usually via sensor outputs). States, inputs, and outputs are specified at sampling instants of time, which are multiples of some time interval, ΔT, that is, $\vec{x}(k)$, $\vec{u}(k)$, and $\vec{y}(k)$ correspond to the state, input, and output vectors at time $k\Delta T$, respectively. The final term, $\vec{n}(k)$, is noise; it is often well-modeled as a Gaussian random variable with mean $\vec{0}$ and some given variance vector.

Corresponding model states and outputs are denoted by $\hat{x}(k)$ and $\hat{y}(k)$, respectively. We have $\hat{y}(k) = C\hat{x}(k)$.

We carry out an estimate of the state as follows:

$$\hat{x}(k+1) = A\hat{x}(k) + B\vec{u}(k) + L(\vec{y}(k) - \hat{y}(k)). \tag{7.8}$$

Here, L is a matrix, whose function will become apparent shortly.

The error in the estimate (assuming no faults) is given by

$$
\begin{aligned}
\vec{e}(k+1) &= \vec{x}(k+1) - \hat{x}(k+1) \\
&= (A - LC)\vec{e}(k) + \vec{n}(k). \tag{7.9}
\end{aligned}
$$

If we initialize the model so that its state accurately reflects the initial plant state, we have the initial condition $\vec{e}(0) = \vec{0}$; otherwise we will start with some initial error. However, if $A - LC$ is suitably chosen (by carefully selecting the matrix L), the impact of this initial error will decay to zero with time. How L is selected is beyond the scope of our discussion: the interested reader should consult one of the control theory references in the Further Reading section of this chapter. (We are also assuming that the dynamics of the controlled plant are quite accurately known.)

Notice that the estimated error in the fault-free case is only a function of noise (whose statistics are assumed known) and the initial error, not of the actual inputs applied. It can be computed for the noise-free case; the function of the matrix L is to ensure that the value of $A - LC$ is such that the dynamics of the difference Equation (7.9) are convenient (e.g., the error does not blow up over time).

Now, the consistency check has as its inputs the outputs of the (actual) plant and of the plant model, that is, it has both $\vec{y}(k)$ and $\hat{y}(k)$. The difference between them is given by $C\vec{e}(k)$, plus a noise term.

What happens if an actuator is faulty? Then, the actually applied control is not necessarily the same as the commanded control. In Eq. (7.9), we did not have a term representing control inputs, because we assumed that the actuators were fault-free; hence the terms representing inputs in both the physical plant and the model canceled each other when we carried out the subtraction to get Eq. (7.9). This will no longer be true if there is an actuator fault; in such a case, the plant's input will be different from that used by the model. This will become apparent upon tracking the behavior of $\vec{e}(k)$ over time. In particular, if the applied control diverges meaningfully from the commanded control, $\vec{e}(k)$ will no longer be close to $\vec{0}$, and can be taken to be indicative of a problem.

Example: Consider the elevator control of an aircraft. The elevator deflection affects aircraft pitch. The relevant aircraft state variables are the aircraft angle of attack x_1, its pitch angle rate x_2, and the pitch angle x_3. Assume the elevator control task has a period of 2 ms, i.e., the elevator setting is updated every 2 ms. Furthermore, suppose we are given that the aircraft is *approximately* modeled as a linear discrete-time system according to the following equations:

$$
\begin{aligned}
x_1(k+1) &= 0.9936x_1(k) + 1.1252x_2(k) + 0.0049u(k); \\
x_2(k+1) &= -0.0003x_1(k) + 0.9907x_2(k) + 0.0004u(k); \\
x_3(k+1) &= -0.0002x_1(k) + 1.1287x_2(k) + x_3(k) + 0.0002u(k).
\end{aligned}
$$

(This approximation assumes the other aircraft variables, such as speed and altitude, do not meaningfully change. This removes the need to model such issues as drag.) Suppose the output is $y(k) = x_3$, i.e., our sensors allow us to observe the pitch angle only.

Thus we have $\mathbf{A} = \begin{pmatrix} 0.9936 & 1.1252 & 0 \\ -0.0003 & 0.9907 & 0 \\ -0.0002 & 1.1287 & 1 \end{pmatrix}$, $\mathbf{B} = (0.0049\ 0.0004\ 0.0002)^T$, and $\mathbf{C} = (0\ 0\ 1)$.

(The superscript T indicates transpose, i.e., for convenience we have written out the transpose of the column vector $\mathbf{B}$.) The selection of $\mathbf{L}$ is done so that $\mathbf{A}$-$\mathbf{LC}$ has "good" properties as discussed below.

Let the control input (i.e., the elevator deflection to achieve a target aircraft pitch of x_3^{target}) be calculated as $u(k+1) = g \cdot x_3^{target}(k) - w_1 x_1(k) - w_2 x_2(k) - w_3 x_3(k)$, where $w_1 = -0.6559$, $w_2 = 202.995$, and $w_3 = 9.603$. $g = 10$ is a suitable scaling factor. (These constants were calculated using standard control-theoretic techniques; simply take them as given here.) This is the deflection the system commands of the elevator. Since we do not know the exact values of $x_i(k)$, we will use their estimated values $\hat{x}_i(k)$ instead, in making this calculation.

Suppose the elevator is malfunctioning; its actual deflection differs from the commanded deflection by an amount $u_e(k)$. Then, we will have

$$\vec{\epsilon}(k+1) = (\mathbf{A} - \mathbf{LC})\vec{\epsilon}(k) + \vec{n}(k) + Bu_e(k). \qquad (7.10)$$

Now, the difference between what was expected at the output, and what was actually observed, is given by

$$\hat{y}(k) - \vec{y}(k) = \mathbf{C}\vec{\epsilon}(k). \qquad (7.11)$$

If $u_e(k)$ is sufficiently large, this difference error will quickly be noticed.

The threshold at which such divergence becomes indicative of a fault obviously depends on the level of noise. In most instances, noise can be modeled as a stochastic process, whose parameters are known (from experience and measurement).

The role of $\mathbf{L}$ should be apparent from an examination of Eq. (7.10). It influences the trajectory of the estimation error as well as the response of the system state variables to control inputs.

7.6 FURTHER READING

An accessible survey of cyber-physical systems can be found in [18]. An important application, drive-by-wire cars, is presented in [13]. A look at the Air France 447 crash is provided in [26]. A detailed description of the *Curiosity* Mars rover is provided in [17].

An extensive survey of scheduling issues, including handling overruns appears in [4]. Fault-tolerant scheduling for real-time systems is surveyed in [15]. The standard reference for mixed-criticality systems is [3]. For a discussion of the controlled plant state space and its role in adaptive fault tolerance, see [16,29].

We have had to pass lightly over details requiring a knowledge of control theory; there are many excellent books on the subject, e.g., [1,24]. See [5] for a widely-used approach to optimal control. Estimator design is also covered in a large number of places, such as [20].

Sensor calibration is covered extensively in the technical literature. Some useful references are [2] for blind calibration, and [22] for self-calibration. For self-validating sensors, see [11]. Papers on assessing the quality of sensors include [14,23,28]. Combining sensor results is treated in [21,25]; measures of agreement between sensors are surveyed in [6]. Outlier analysis is a major topic in data analytics; see [10,19,30].

Fault diagnosis is treated well in [9,12,25]. An example of flight actuator fault detection can be found in [27].

Finally, the importance of integrating safety analysis into each phase of system development is stressed in [8]. Many failures in complex systems arise from the interaction of individual modules rather than from within these modules themselves; an approach to dealing with this problem is explored in [7].

7.7 EXERCISES

1. You have a controlled plant with just one state variable, $x(t)$. Its dynamics are given by the differential equation

$$\frac{dx(t)}{dt} = -5x(t) + 3u(t),$$

where the actuator input is specified by the scalar $u(t)$. The plant's allowed state space is $-5 \leq x(t) \leq 5$. Assume the time units for the differential equations are in seconds.

Zero-order hold is used with period 0.1 second, that is, the control is updated every 0.1 second, with the actuator setting being held constant throughout that period. The actuator is physically limited to the range $-1 \leq u(t) \leq 1$. No matter what the computer may demand, it cannot deliver a control output outside that range.

Determine if fault tolerance is needed for the cyber platform if the current state is

- (a) $x(0) = 0$.
- (b) $x(0) = 2$.
- (c) $x(0) = -4.8$.
- (d) $x(0) = 4$.

2. You have points in some 4-dimensional space. Define $x = (x_1, x_2, x_3, x_4)$, $y = (y_1, y_2, y_3, y_4)$ as two points in that space, and $A = \{1, 2, 3, 4\}$. Which of the following functions satisfies the properties of a distance measure:

- (a) $d(x, y) = \min_{i \in A} \{x_i - y_i\}$.
- (b) $d(x, y) = \max_{i \in A} \{x_i - y_i\}$.
- (c) $d(x, y) = \max_{i \in A} \{x_i\} - \max_{i \in A} \{y_i\}$.
- (d) $d(x, y) = |x_1 - y_1|$.

3. A set of ten redundant sensors $K = \{s_1, s_2, \cdots, s_{10}\}$ is measuring temperature. The error half-width of each measurement is $1°C$. The reported temperatures are $100, 101, 104, 105, 106, 110, 105, 106, 117, 103$, respectively. Execute the edge-deletion approach, and draw the re-

sulting graph. If the threshold for outlier detection is for a node to have fewer than three neighbors, indicate the outlier nodes. (These will be suspected as having suffered at least transient failure.)

4. You have a set of six sensors reporting the following values over the past several sampling periods:

$$\vec{v}_1 \ : \ \{100, 103, 105, 103, 101, 100, 150, 152\};$$
$$\vec{v}_2 \ : \ \{100, 102, 104, 100, 100, 100, 140, 139\};$$
$$\vec{v}_3 \ : \ \{100, 103, 105, 103, 101, 100, 153, 147\};$$
$$\vec{v}_4 \ : \ \{100, 107, 105, 108, 101, 100, 149, 157\};$$
$$\vec{v}_5 \ : \ \{100, 103, 105, 103, 101, 100, 150, 157\};$$
$$\vec{v}_6 \ : \ \{100, 103, 105, 103, 201, 200, 250, 252\}.$$

Calculate the trust rank of each sensor.

5. A CPS calculates the function $f(v_1, v_2, v_3) = v_1^3 + v_2 v_3 - v_1 v_2 v_3$ based on sensor reported values it receives for v_1, v_2, v_3. These are: $v_1 = 5 \pm 1; v_2 = 4 \pm 3; v_3 = 1 \pm 0.1$. Calculate the uncertainty half-width of $f(v_1, v_2, v_3)$ for these data.

6. The approach to dealing with task overruns can also be used for providing reserve capacity to run additional tasks if a processor fails, and its assigned tasks have to be transferred to others. Discuss how this can be done.

7. Derive Eq. (7.1) using Bayes's Law, explicitly showing each step in the process.

8. Construct a set of periodic tasks by selecting their period, nominal execution time, and deadline so that the overrun of an iteration of one task leads to the overrun of at least one iteration of every other task.

9. Show that under the isolation approach described in Section 7.4.1, the maximum time between activity on a processor by server i is δ_i.

10. In the aircraft example in Section 7.5, suppose we pick $\mathbf{L} = (-65.0 \quad 1.5 \quad 2.6)^T$. Consider the case where noise is negligible, and where the elevator is stuck at 0.1 radians. A command to set the elevator at 0 radians is sent out. Plot the quantity $\hat{y}(k) - \vec{y}(k)$ as a function of k; this is the difference between what was expected at the observed pitch angle, and what was observed. Assume any reasonable initial state of the aircraft.

REFERENCES

[1] Karl J. Åström, Björn Wittenmark, Computer-Controlled Systems: Theory and Design, Courier Corporation, 2013.
[2] Laura Balzano, Robert Nowak, Blind calibration of sensor networks, in: Proceedings of the 6th International Conference on Information Processing in Sensor Networks, 2007, pp. 79–88.
[3] Alan Burns, Robert I. Davis, A survey of research into mixed criticality systems, ACM Computing Surveys (CSUR) 50 (6) (2017) 82.
[4] Giorgio C. Buttazzo, Hard Real-Time Computing Systems: Predictable Scheduling Algorithms and Applications, Springer Science & Business Media, 2011.
[5] Eduardo F. Camacho, Carlos Bordons Alba, Model Predictive Control, Springer Science & Business Media, 2013.
[6] Gregory Duveiller, Dominique Fasbender, Michele Meroni, Revisiting the concept of a symmetric index of agreement for continuous datasets, Scientific Reports 6 (2016) 19401.
[7] C.H. Fleming, Safety-Driven Early Concept Analysis and Development, PhD Dissertation, Massachusetts Institute of Technology, 2015.

[8] C.H. Fleming, N.G. Leveson, Early concept development and safety analysis of future transportation systems, IEEE Transactions on Intelligent Transportation Systems 17 (12) (December 2016) 3512–3523.

[9] Zhiwei Gao, Carlo Cecati, Steven X. Ding, A survey of fault diagnosis and fault-tolerant techniques part I: fault diagnosis with model-based and signal-based approaches, IEEE Transactions on Industrial Electronics 62 (6) (June 2015) 3757–3767.

[10] Jiawei Han, Jian Pei, Micheline Kamber, Data Mining: Concepts and Techniques, Elsevier, 2011.

[11] M.P. Henry, D.W. Clarke, The self-validating sensor: rationale, definitions and examples, Control Engineering Practice 1 (4) (August 1993) 585–610.

[12] Rolf Isermann, Fault-Diagnosis Systems: An Introduction From Fault Detection to Fault Tolerance, Springer Science & Business Media, 2006.

[13] Rolf Isermann, Ralf Schwarz, Stefan Stolzl, Fault-tolerant drive-by-wire systems, IEEE Control Systems 22 (5) (October 2002) 64–81.

[14] Farinaz Koushanfar, Miodrag Potkonjak, Alberto Sangiovanni-Vincentelli, On-line fault detection of sensor measurements, in: Sensors, 2003, vol. 2, 2003, pp. 974–979.

[15] C.M. Krishna, Fault-tolerant scheduling in homogeneous real-time systems, ACM Computing Surveys (CSUR) 46 (4) (April 2014) 48.

[16] C.M. Krishna, Ameliorating thermally accelerated aging with state-based application of fault-tolerance in cyber-physical computers, IEEE Transactions on Reliability 64 (1) (January 2015) 4–14.

[17] E. Lakdawalla, The Design and Engineering of Curiosity, Springer, 2018.

[18] E.A. Lee, S.A. Seshia, Introduction to Embedded Systems: A Cyber-Physical Systems Approach, MIT Press, 2016.

[19] Jure Leskovec, Anand Rajaraman, Jeffrey David Ullman, Mining of Massive Datasets, Cambridge University Press, 2014.

[20] F.L. Lewis, Optimal Estimation: With an Introduction to Stochastic Control Theory, Wiley, 1986.

[21] R.J. Moffat, Contributions to the theory of single-sample uncertainty analysis, Journal of Fluids Engineering 104 (2) (June 1982) 250–258.

[22] Randolph L. Moses, Robert Patterson, Self-calibration of sensor networks, in: Unattended Ground Sensor Technologies and Applications IV, vol. 4743, International Society for Optics and Photonics, 2002, pp. 108–120.

[23] Kevin Ni, Greg Pottie, Bayesian selection of non-faulty sensors, in: IEEE International Symposium on Information Theory, ISIT 2007, 2007, pp. 616–620.

[24] K. Ogata, Discrete-Time Control Systems, Prentice Hall, 1995.

[25] R.J. Patton, P.M. Frank, R.N. Clarke, Fault Diagnosis in Dynamic Systems: Theory and Application, Prentice-Hall, 1989.

[26] P.M. Salmon, G.H. Walker, N.A. Stanton, Pilot error versus sociotechnical systems failure: a distributed situation awareness analysis of air France 447, Theoretical Issues in Ergonomics 17 (1) (January 2016) 64–79.

[27] A. Varga, D. Ossmann, LPV model-based robust diagnosis of flight actuator faults, Control Engineering Practice 31 (October 2014) 135–147.

[28] X.-Y. Xiao, W.-C. Peng, C.-C. Hung, W.-C. Lee, Using SensorRanks for in-network detection of faulty readings in wireless sensor networks, in: ACM International Workshop on Data Engineering for Wireless and Mobile Access, 2007, pp. 1–8.

[29] Y. Xu, I. Koren, C.M. Krishna, AdaFT: a framework for adaptive fault tolerance for cyber-physical systems, ACM Transactions on Embedded Computing Systems 16 (3) (July 2017) 79.

[30] Y. Zhang, N. Meratnia, P.J.M. Havinga, Outlier detection techniques for wireless sensor networks: a survey, IEEE Communications Surveys and Tutorials 12 (2) (April 2010) 159–170.

CASE STUDIES

8

The purpose of this chapter is to illustrate the practical use of methods described previously in this book, by highlighting the fault-tolerant aspects of several computer systems used in applications requiring high reliability. We do not aim at providing a comprehensive, low-level description of each design; for that, the interested reader should consult the references mentioned in the Further Reading section.

8.1 AEROSPACE SYSTEMS

Computers in aerospace systems are a prime example of designs that must support fault tolerance. First, aerospace applications are life-critical, where passengers or astronauts are involved. Second, aerospace systems must operate fault-free for many hours, in the case of airplanes, and for several years, or even decades, in the case of space missions (for example, the two Voyager spacecraft are still transmitting data more than forty years after launch). Third, high altitude aircraft and deep space vehicles operate in harsh environments replete with flows of elementary charged particles. (The Sun is a major—and highly variable—source of such flows: it ejects, on the average, over a million tonnes of such elementary charged particles every second.) The rate of these particle hits goes up drastically with altitude. Airplanes still experience a sufficiently low rate of particle hits that can, in most cases, be tolerated by conventional fault tolerance techniques. Spacecraft, on the other hand, are exposed to considerably higher levels of radiation and require more extensive protection from particle hits. Finally, aerospace applications are big-budget items, which can justify, and afford to pay, the often considerable costs of fault tolerance.

8.1.1 PROTECTING AGAINST RADIATION

As we have seen earlier in this book, radiation is a prominent cause of hardware failure. When energetic charged particles pass through a memory cell, they can cause its state to flip. They may even cause permanent damage to semiconductor devices.

Two approaches are taken to protect against high levels of radiation. The first is to provide shielding to attenuate radiation. A good example of this is the *Juno* spacecraft, which arrived at Jupiter in 2016. *Juno* has a radiation vault consisting of a hollow cube of Titanium, with walls about 1 cm thick, weighing 200 kg. This massive shield reduces radiation by a factor of about 800: just over 0.1% of the radiation gets through the shield. Inside this vault are the principal command, data handling and power-control circuitry of the spacecraft.

Fault-Tolerant Systems. https://doi.org/10.1016/B978-0-12-818105-8.00018-8

The second approach is to use radiation-hardened devices, specifically designed to withstand high doses of radiation without losing functionality. *Juno* uses RAD750 processors, which are a radiation-hardened version of the PowerPC 750. It runs at up to 133 MHz, consuming about 5 watts. It replaces much of the dynamic circuitry in critical areas of the PowerPC with static circuitry, which is far more resistant to radiation. This causes some loss of performance and a substantial increase in chip area, which is accepted as a necessary price to pay. In addition, phase-locked loops used in clock distribution were hardened and circuitry modified to compensate effectively for temperature variations.

8.1.2 FLIGHT CONTROL SYSTEM: BOEING 777

The extensive deployment of fault-tolerant computing in aviation was triggered by the introduction of fly-by-wire (FBW) flight control. Traditional flight controls have employed hydraulic actuators and valves, directly controlled through mechanical cables connected to the pilot controls. Such a cable-heavy system is complex and requires frequent periodic maintenance. In an FBW flight control system, the actuators are instead controlled by electrical signals (transmitted through wires) generated by digital flight control computers. The pilot's control inputs command the desired outcome, whereas the FBW computers calculate the inputs to the actuators at each flight control surface as required to achieve that outcome, implementing a closed loop (feedback) control system. Besides the pilot's inputs, the flight control system also receives readings from sensors measuring acceleration, angle of attack, air pressure, and other relevant parameters. As the FBW computers directly control all the flight actuators, they have to provide extremely high levels of functional integrity and reliability. The Boeing 777 had the requirement that the probability of any fault impacting the functional integrity and availability of the airplane must be less than 10^{-10} per flight hour. Traditional hydraulic and mechanical flight controls systems fail gradually. In contrast, a system-wide failure of the FBW computer may rapidly render the airplane uncontrollable. Therefore an FBW computing system must be designed to tolerate and even mask a wide variety of faults, including hardware faults, power failures, software bugs, and Byzantine faults.

Airbus designed the first large commercial airplanes with an FBW system. The Airbus A320 (circa 1988) and A340 (circa 1992) had four computers in their FBW system. Two computers form a command/monitor pair, and upon an error detection it is replaced by the second command/monitor pair. Errors in a computer pair operation were detected primarily through a mismatch between the commands (to the actuators) that they output, but also using control sequence checking by a watchdog unit and self-test when the computers are powered on. The second computer pair uses a different hardware processor (than the first pair), and different software. Together such diversity protects against common mode failures.

A different approach to fault tolerance has been employed by the Boeing company, whose first commercial airliner with FBW control was the Boeing 777 (circa 1995). The Boeing 777 provides continuous fault masking by making extensive use of triple modular redundancy for all its hardware resources, namely, the computing system, electrical power supply, hydraulic power, and communication paths. The design goal has been to tolerate component failures, power failures, electromagnetic interference, in general, and specifically for the flight control processor, to tolerate common mode failures, design faults, software bugs, and Byzantine faults.

Fig. 8.1 shows a block diagram of the primary flight computer (PFC) system. It is a triple-triple redundancy design that consists of three identical channels (left, center, and right), where each channel

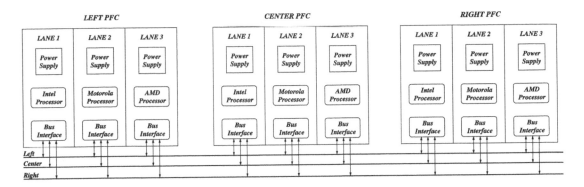

FIGURE 8.1

Block diagram of the Boeing 777 flight control system.

includes three dissimilar computing lanes. Each lane has its own power supply. The three channels are isolated, physically and electrically, from each other, and are connected to three (left, center, and right) digital autonomous terminal access communication (DATAC) buses (also known as ARINC 629 data buses). Each such bus is isolated, both physically and electrically, from the other two. All communications over the buses are checked using a cyclic redundancy check (CRC) code that uses the generating polynomial $X^{16} + X^{12} + X^5 + 1$. The three lanes within each PFC channel contain different microprocessors (from Intel, AMD, and Motorola) and execute control programs that were compiled by three different compilers. The purpose of such hardware and software design diversity is to protect against common mode failures and (microprocessor and software) design errors.

Note that a 3-version programming approach was not used. Originally, Boeing had three separate teams of programmers develop three different versions of the control program. However, these teams ended up having to ask the system designers so many questions to clarify software requirements that the management decided that the independence of the three teams was irreparably compromised. Consequently, a decision to revert to the customary approach of developing a single version of the ADA control program was made.

The three computing lanes do not operate as a TMR. Instead, one of them serves as the command processor, while the other two monitor the outputs generated by the designated command processor. Although all three lanes interface with all three data buses using dedicated hardware, only the command processor is communicating through the data buses with the remaining two channels; it transmits its proposed flight surface command to the other two channels. Thus each command lane receives three values of the proposed commands, and performs a median value select to determine what is called the "selected" surface command. A complete agreement among the three channels is not necessary, and the median value is selected to better handle Byzantine faults. The monitoring lanes in each channel then compare the output of their command lane to the selected value and, in case of discrepancy, the output of the command lane will be inhibited.

Pilot inputs are applied using conventional controls (yoke, rudder pedals, etc.). One objective was to make the feel of the controls (including the physical, tactile, feedback from them) as close to traditional aircraft as possible. Transducers in the actuator control electronics units (ACEs) convert the analog pilot control signals into digital ones and transmit them to the PFCs through the data buses. These transducers are continuously monitored for short and open circuit faults. In addition to the converted pilot inputs, the PFCs receive airplane inertial and outside air data (through multiple sensors), and then determine the control surface commands. These commands, in digital form, are converted to analog by the ACEs, and are then applied to the various actuators controlling the airplane. The analog signals are also converted back to digital form and compared to the original digital signals to validate the digital to analog conversion. In addition, if the ACEs detect an invalid command from the PFCs, the direct mode is activated, where the ACEs use the pilot's inputs directly, thus ignoring the PFC outputs. The same direct mode can be selected manually by the pilot.

Note that the PFC design contains one level of redundancy beyond that required to achieve the airplane's functional integrity. Consequently, replacement of faulty units can be deferred to a convenient time and place, resulting in a reduction of flight delays or cancellations. Indeed, facilitating deferred maintenance was one of the objectives of the Boeing 777 design.

Besides the flight control computing system, the Boeing 777 includes an airplane information management system (AIMS) that executes computations required for flight management, display, data communication, airplane condition monitoring, maintenance, and flight data recording. AIMS is highly fault-tolerant. There are two such separate, independent, and identical systems with each one of them consisting of four core processors and four I/O modules that can operate with one faulty core processor and one faulty I/O module.

Extensive fault masking may create unintended risks if it causes faults to be overlooked by the maintenance crew. In 2005, a Boeing 777 had a major upset while climbing after takeoff from Perth, Australia. It had a faulty accelerometer that had generated erroneous outputs for over two years. However, because backups were available, it did not have to be replaced right away, and the plane was allowed to keep flying (quite legally) with this faulty unit in place. The software simply disregarded it and used instead outputs received from other accelerometers. During the 2005 flight, a second accelerometer failed as well, causing the system to switch to accepting inputs from the previously failing accelerometer. (The power cycling between flights apparently caused the in-flight system to lose track of the fact that the first accelerometer was faulty.) The result was conflicting indications to the pilots: that the aircraft was about to stall and at the same time that it was approaching overspeed conditions. Resolving such problems with incomplete system status information (the pilots could not identify the cause of the problem) in real-time under extreme stress is very hard. Fortunately, in the 2005 event, no lives were lost: the pilots were able to successfully return to Perth.

8.2 NONSTOP SYSTEMS

Several generations of NonStop systems have been developed since 1976, by Tandem Computers (since acquired by Hewlett Packard). The main use for these fault-tolerant systems has been in online transaction processing, where a reliable response to inquiries in real-time must be guaranteed. The fault-tolerance features implemented in these systems have evolved through several generations, taking advantage of better technologies and newer approaches to fault tolerance. In this section, we present the main (although not all) fault-tolerance aspects of the NonStop designs.

8.2.1 ARCHITECTURE

The NonStop systems have followed four key design principles, listed below.

- *Modularity:* The hardware and software are constructed of modules of fine granularity. These modules constitute units of failure, diagnosis, service, and repair. Keeping the modules as decoupled as possible reduces the probability that a fault in one module will affect the operation of another.
- *Fail-fast operation:* A fail-fast module either works properly or stops. Thus each module is self-checking and stops upon detecting a failure. Hardware checks (through error-detecting codes; see Chapter 3) and software consistency tests (see Chapter 5) support fail-fast operation.
- *Single-failure tolerance:* When a single module (hardware or software) fails, another module immediately takes over. For processors, this means that a second processor is available. For storage modules, it means that the module and the path to it are duplicated.
- *Online maintenance:* Hardware and software modules can be diagnosed, disconnected for repair, and then reconnected, without disrupting the entire system's operation.

We next discuss briefly the original architecture of the NonStop systems, focusing on the fault-tolerance features. In the next two sections, the maintenance aids and software support for fault tolerance are presented. Finally, we describe the modifications which have been made to the original architecture.

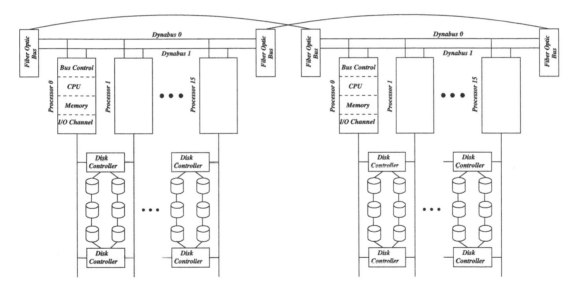

FIGURE 8.2

Original NonStop system architecture.

Although there have been several generations of NonStop systems, many of the underlying principles remain the same and are illustrated in Fig. 8.2. The system consists of clusters of computers: a cluster may include up to 16 processors. Each custom-designed processor has a CPU, a local memory containing its own copy of the operating system, a bus control unit, and an I/O channel. The CPU differs from standard designs in its extensive error detection capabilities to support the fail-fast mode of operation. Error detection on the datapath is accomplished through parity checking and prediction, whereas the control part is checked using parity, detection of illegal states, and specially designed self-checking logic (the description of which is beyond the scope of this book, but a pointer to the literature is provided in the Further Reading section). In addition, the design includes several serial-scan shift registers, allowing fast testing to isolate faults in field-replaceable units.

The memory is protected with a Hamming code capable of single-error correction and double-error detection (see Section 3.1). The address is protected with a single-error-detection parity code.

The cache has been designed to perform retries to take care of transient faults. There is also a spare memory module that can be switched in if permanent failures occur. The cache supports a write-through policy, guaranteeing the existence of a valid copy of the data in the main memory. A parity error in the cache will force a cache miss, followed by refetching of the data from the main memory.

Parity checking is not limited to memory units, but is also used internally in the processor. All units that do not modify the data, such as buses and registers, propagate the parity bits. Other units that alter the data, such as arithmetic units and counters, require special circuits that predict the parity bits based on the data and parity inputs. The predicted parity bits can then be compared to the parity bits generated out of the produced outputs, and any mismatch between the two will raise a parity error indication. This technique is very suitable to adders, but extending it to multipliers would result in a very complicated circuit, and consequently, a different technique to detect faults in the multiplier has been followed. After each multiply operation, a second multiplication is performed with the two operands exchanged, and one of them shifted prior to the operation. Since the correlation between the results of the two multiplications is trivial, a simple circuit can detect faults in the multiply operation. Note that even a permanent fault will be detected, because the same multiplication is not repeated. This error detection scheme is similar to the recomputation with shifted operands technique for detecting faults in arithmetic operations (see Section 5.2.4).

Note the absence of a shared memory in Fig. 8.2. A shared memory can simplify the communication among processors, but may become a single point of failure. The 16 (or fewer) processors operate independently and asynchronously and communicate with each other through messages sent over the dual Dynabuses. The Dynabus interface is designed such that a single processor failure will not disable both buses. Similar duplication is also followed in the I/O systems, in which a group of disks is controlled by dual-ported controllers, which are connected to I/O buses from two different processors. One of the two ports is designated as the primary. If the processor (or its associated I/O bus) that is connected to the primary port fails, the controller switches to the secondary/backup port. With dual-ported controllers and dual-ported I/O devices, four separate paths run to each device. All data transfers are parity-checked, and a watchdog timer detects if a controller stops responding, or if a nonexistent controller was addressed.

The above design allows the system to continue its operation despite the failure of any single module. To further support this goal, the power, cabling, and packaging were also carefully designed. Parts of the system are redundantly powered from two different power supplies, allowing them to tolerate a power supply failure. In addition, battery backups are provided so that the system state can be preserved in case of a power failure.

The controllers have a fail-fast requirement similar to the processors. This is achieved through the use of dual lock-stepped microprocessors (executing the same instructions in a fully synchronized manner) with comparison circuits to detect errors in their operation, and self-checking logic to detect errors in the remaining circuitry within the controller. The two independent ports within the controller are implemented using physically separated circuits to prevent a fault in one from affecting the other.

The system supports disk mirroring (see Section 3.2), which, when used, provides eight paths for data read and write operations. Disk mirroring is further briefly discussed in Section 8.2.3. The disk data is protected by end-to-end checksums (see Section 3.1). For each data block, the processor calculates a checksum and appends it to the data written to the disk. This checksum is verified by the processor when the data block is read from the disk. The checksum is used for error detection, whereas the disk mirroring is used for data recovery.

8.2.2 MAINTENANCE AND REPAIR AIDS

Special effort has been made to automatically detect errors, analyze them, and report the analysis to remote support centers, and then track related repair actions. The system includes a maintenance and diagnostic processor, which communicates with all the processors in the system and with a remote service center. This maintenance processor collects failure-related information and allows engineers at the remote center to run diagnostic tests. It is also capable of reconfiguring the system in response to detected faults.

Internally, each computing processor module has a diagnostic unit, which monitors the status of the computing processor and the associated logic, including the memory, the Dynabus interface, and the I/O channel. It reports to the central maintenance processor any errors that are detected. In addition, the diagnostic unit, upon a request received from the remote service center (through the central maintenance processor), can force the computing processor to run in a single-step mode and collect diagnostic information obtained through the scan paths. It can also generate pseudorandom tests, and run them on the various components of the computing processor module.

The central maintenance processor is capable of some automatic fault diagnosis through the use of a knowledge database that includes a large number of known error values. It also controls and monitors a large number of sensors for power supply voltages, intake and outlet air temperatures, and fan rotation.

8.2.3 SOFTWARE

As should be clear by now, the amount of hardware redundancy in the original NonStop system was quite limited, and massive redundancy schemes, such as triple modular redundancy, were avoided. Almost all redundant hardware modules that do exist (such as redundant communication buses) contribute to the performance of the fault-free system. Most of the burden of the system fault tolerance is borne by the operating system (OS) software. The OS detects failures of processors or I/O channels and performs the necessary recovery. It manages the process pairs that constitute the primary fault-tolerance scheme used in NonStop. A process pair includes a primary process and a passive backup process that is ready to become active when the primary process fails. When a new process starts, the OS generates a clone of this process on another processor. This backup process goes immediately into passive mode and waits for messages from either its corresponding primary, or the OS. At certain points during the execution of the primary process, checkpoints are taken (see Chapter 6), and a checkpointing message containing the process state is sent by the primary to the backup. The process state of the backup is updated by the OS, while the backup process itself remains passive. If the primary process fails, the OS orders the backup to start execution from the last checkpoint.

Processors continuously check on each other's health by sending "I am alive" messages once every second to all other processors (over the two interprocessor buses) and to themselves (to verify that the bus send and receive circuits are working). Every two seconds, each processor checks whether it has received at least one "I am alive" message from every other processor. If such a message is missing, the corresponding processor is declared faulty and all outstanding communications with it are canceled. All processors operate as independent entities, and no master processor exists that could become a single point of failure.

An important component of the OS is the disk access process, which provides reliable access to the data on the disks, despite any failure in a processor, channel, controller, or the disk module itself. This process is also implemented as a (primary/backup) process pair, and it manages a pair of mirrored disks that are connected through two controllers and two I/O channels, providing eight possible paths to the data. As was indicated in Section 3.2, mirrored disks provide better performance through shorter read times (by preferring the disk with the shorter seek time) and support of multiple read operations. Disk write operations are more expensive, but not necessarily much slower, since the two writes are done in parallel.

Because transaction processing has been the main market for NonStop systems, special care has been taken to ensure reliable transactions. A transaction monitoring module (of the OS) controls all the steps from the beginning of the transaction to its completion, going through multiple database accesses and multiple file updates on several disks. This module guarantees that each transaction will have the standard so-called *ACID* properties required of databases:

- *Atomic:* Either all, or none, of the database updates are executed.
- *Consistent:* Every successful transaction preserves the consistency of the database.
- *Isolated:* All events within a transaction are isolated from other transactions, which may execute concurrently to allow any failing transaction to be reset.
- *Durable:* Once a transaction commits, its results survive any failure.

Any failure during the execution of a transaction will result in an abort-transaction step, which will undo all database updates.

Most of the above techniques focus on tolerating hardware failures. To deal with software failures, numerous consistency checks are included in every software module, and upon the detection of a problem, the processor is halted, resulting in the backup process being initiated. These consistency checks stop the process when a system data structure becomes contaminated, reducing considerably the chances of a database contamination. They also make system software errors very visible, allowing their correction, thus resulting in high-quality software.

8.2.4 MODIFICATIONS TO THE NONSTOP ARCHITECTURE

Numerous modifications have been integrated into the hardware and software design of the NonStop systems as they evolved over time. We describe in what follows only the most significant of these.

The original NonStop architecture relied heavily on custom-designed processors with extensive use of self-checking techniques to allow processors to follow the fast-fail design principle. With the rapid increase in the cost of designing and fabricating custom processors, the original approach was no longer economically viable, and the architecture was modified to use commercial microprocessors. Such microprocessors do not support the level of self-checking that is required for the fast-fail

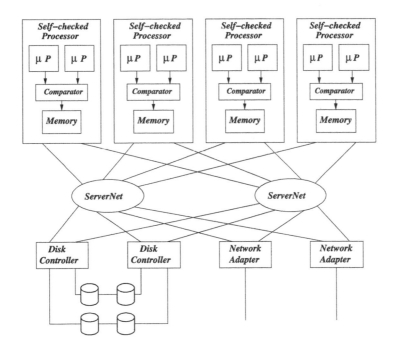

FIGURE 8.3

Modified NonStop system architecture.

operation, and consequently, the design was changed to a scheme based on tight lock-stepping of pairs of microprocessors, as shown in Fig. 8.3. A memory operation will not be executed unless the two separate requests are identical; if they are not, the self-checked processor will stop executing its task.

Another significant modification to the architecture is the replacement of the I/O channels and the interprocessor communication links (through the Dynabuses: see Fig. 8.2) by a high-bandwidth, packet-switched network called *ServerNet*, shown in Fig. 8.3. As the figure shows, this network is comprised of two independent fabrics so that a single failure can disrupt the operation of at most one fabric. Both fabrics are used by all the processors; each processor decides independently which fabric to use for a given message.

The ServerNet provides not only high bandwidth and low latency, but also better support for detection and isolation of errors. Each packet transferred through the network is protected with a cyclic redundancy check (CRC; see Section 3.1). Every router that forwards the packet checks the CRC and appends either a "This packet is bad" or "This packet is good" flag to the packet, allowing easy isolation of link failures.

Current trends in commercial microprocessors are such that achieving self-checking through lock-step operation is no longer viable: guaranteeing that two microprocessors will execute a task in a fully synchronous manner is very difficult. The reasons for this include (1) the fact that certain functional units within microprocessors use multiple clocks and asynchronous interfaces; (2) the need to deal with soft errors (which become more likely as VLSI feature sizes become smaller) leads to low-level fix-up routines that may be executed on one microprocessor, and not the other, and (3) the use of variable frequencies by power/temperature management techniques. Moreover, most high-end microprocessors have multiple processor cores running multiple tasks. A failure in one processor running a single task in a lock-stepped mode will disrupt the operation of multiple processors—an undesirable event.

To address the above, the NonStop system architecture has been further modified, moving from tight lock-step to loose lock-step operation. Instead of comparing the outputs of every memory operation of each processor, only the outputs of I/O operations are compared. As a result, variations due to soft-error corrections, cache retries, and the like, are more likely to be tolerated, and not result in mismatches. Furthermore, the modified NonStop architecture also allows triple modular redundancy (TMR; see Chapter 2) configurations. The standard NonStop configuration of dual redundancy can only detect errors, whereas the TMR configuration allows uninterrupted operation, even after a failure or a mismatch due to asynchronous executions of the copies of the same task. An additional benefit of the TMR configuration is that it is capable of protecting applications that do not follow the recommended implementation as primary/backup process pairs.

8.3 STRATUS SYSTEMS

The Stratus fault-tolerant system has quite a few similarities to the NonStop system described above. Every unit in both systems is replicated (at least twice) to avoid single points of failure. This includes the processors, memory units, I/O controllers, disk and communication controllers, buses, and power supplies. The main difference between the two types of system is that the NonStop fault-tolerance approach focuses mainly on the software, whereas the Stratus design achieves its fault tolerance mainly through hardware redundancy. As a result, off-the-shelf software need not be modified to consist of primary/backup process pairs before running it on a Stratus server.

Stratus systems use the pair-and-spare principle described in Section 2.5.6, in which each pair consists of two processors operating in lock-step mode. The architecture of a single pair is shown in Fig. 8.4. Upon a mismatch between the two CPUs, the pair will declare itself faulty and will no longer be involved in producing results. The second pair will continue to execute the application.

As discussed in the previous section, modern off-the-shelf microprocessors have asynchronous behavior. For this reason, enforcing a tight lock-step operation that requires a match for every memory operation would drastically decrease performance. Consequently, in more recent designs of Stratus servers (as shown in Fig. 8.4), only the I/O outputs from the motherboards are compared, and a mismatch will signal an error. A motherboard consists of a standard microprocessor, a standard memory unit, and a custom unit that contains the I/O interface and interrupt logic.

Similarly to NonStop systems, current Stratus systems can be configured to use TMR structures with voting to detect or mask failures. If such a TMR configuration suffers a processor or memory failure, it can be reconfigured to a duplex, until the failed unit has been repaired or replaced.

Unlike NonStop systems, the memory unit is also duplicated, allowing the contents of the main memory to be preserved through most system crashes. The I/O and disks are duplicated as well, with redundant paths connecting individual I/O controllers and disks to the processors. The disk systems

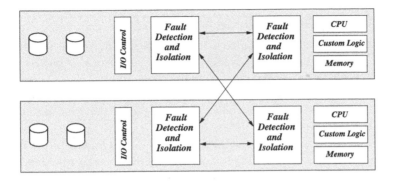

FIGURE 8.4

A single pair in a Stratus system.

use disk mirroring (see Section 3.2). A disk utility checks for bad blocks on the disks and repairs them by copying from the other disk.

The processors, memories, and I/O units have hardware error-checking, and the error signals that they generate are used by the system software, which includes extensive detection and recovery capabilities for both transient and permanent faults. Hardware components judged to have failed permanently are removed, and the provided redundancy ensures that in most cases the system can continue to function, despite the removal of the failed component. A component that was hit by a transient fault, but has since recovered, is restarted and rejoins the system.

Device drivers that cause a significant fraction of operating system crashes are hardened to reduce their failure rate. Such hardening takes the form of (*a*) reducing the chances that a device will malfunction, (*b*) promptly detecting the malfunctioning of a device, and (*c*) dealing with any such malfunctioning locally, as much as possible, to contain its effects and prevent it from propagating to the operating system.

I/O device malfunctioning probability can be reduced, for example, by running sanity checks on the input, thus protecting the device from an obviously bad input. Prompt detection can be carried out by using timeouts to detect device hangs and to check the value returned by the device for obvious errors. In some cases, it may be possible—when the device is otherwise idle—to make it carry out some test actions.

Upon a system crash, an automatic reboot is carried out. One of the CPUs is kept offline to dump its memory to disk: such a dump can be analyzed to diagnose the cause of the failure. Once this dump has been completed, the offline CPU can be resynchronized with its functioning counterpart(s) and rejoin the system. If the reboot is unsuccessful, the system is powered down, and then powered up again, followed by another reboot attempt.

Every fault detected by the system is reported to a remote Stratus support center, allowing service engineers to continuously monitor the system and if necessary, troubleshoot and resolve problems online. If permanent faults are detected, hot-swappable replacement parts are automatically ordered and shipped to the customer.

8.4 CASSINI COMMAND AND DATA SUBSYSTEM

The Cassini spacecraft was designed to explore Saturn and its satellites. Launched in 1997, it reached Saturn in 2004 and continued working remarkably productively for over a dozen years, until, at the end of its mission, it was deliberately crashed into Saturn in September 2017.

Computational activity level was relatively low until the spacecraft reached Saturn: since then, it launched the Huygens probe to study the satellite Titan, and carried out detailed studies of Saturn, its rings, and several of its satellites.

The spacecraft had three mission modes: *normal*, which took up most of the mission; *mission-critical*, during three critical stages of the mission: launch, Saturn orbit insertion, and Titan probe relay; and *safing*, when the satellite suffered a fault and had to be placed in a configuration that was safe and appropriate for manual intervention from Earth.

The command and data subsystem (CDS) issued commands to the other subsystems, and controls the buffering and formatting of data for sending back to Earth. In particular, it had the following functions:

- *Communications:* Management of commands from the ground and of telemetry to send data from the spacecraft to Earth. Also, communication with the spacecraft's engineering and science subsystems (such as the attitude and articulation control (AACS) and the radio frequency (RFS) subsystems).
- *Command sequencing:* Storing and playing out command sequences to manage given activities, such as launch and Saturn orbit insertion.
- *Time keeping:* Maintaining the spacecraft time reference, to coordinate activity and facilitate synchronization.
- *Data handling:* Buffering data as needed if the data collection rate is greater than the downlink transmission rate.
- *Temperature control:* Monitoring and managing spacecraft temperatures.
- *Fault protection:* Running algorithms, which react to faults detected either outside or in the CDS.

Because the spacecraft was meant to operate for about 20 years without any chance of hardware replacement or repair, the CDS needed to be fault tolerant. Such fault tolerance is provided by a dual-redundant system.

Fig. 8.5 provides a block diagram of the CDS. The heart of the CDS was a pair of flight computers, each with very limited memory: 512 KWords of RAM and 8 KWords of PROM. For storage of data meant for transmission to Earth, there were two solid-state recorders, each of 2 GBit capacity. Each flight computer was connected to both recorders. Communication was by means of a dual-redundant 1553B bus. The 1553B bus was introduced in the 1970s and consists of a cable (plus couplers and connectors), a bus controller that manages transmissions on the bus (all traffic on the bus either originates with the bus controller or is in response to a bus controller command), and a remote terminal at each flight computer, to allow it to communicate with the other computer. Sensors connected to the bus provided the flight computers with state information, such as temperature, pressure, and voltage levels. One flight computer was the primary at any given time; the other a backup. The bus controller of the backup computer was inhibited: that of the primary being the only one active.

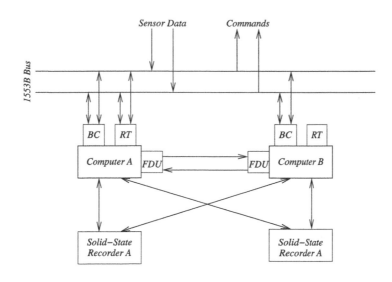

FIGURE 8.5

Cassini CDS block diagram. *FDU* (Fault Detection Unit): manages CDS redundancy. *RT* (Remote Terminal): permits communication with the other computer. *BC* (Bus Controller): 1553B controller. Only one is active at any time.

The CDS was designed under the assumption that the system would never have to cope with multiple faults at any given time. Apart from a specified set of failures, the system was supposed to be protected against any single failure. This exception set included stuck bits in the interface circuitry that took the CDS to an uncommanded state, design faults, and the issuing of wrong commands from Earth.

Errors were classified according to the location of the corresponding fault (central vs. peripheral), their impact (noninterfering vs. interfering), and their duration (transient vs. permanent). Central faults were those that occur in one of the flight computers; faults occurring in other units, such as the solid-state recorders, bus, or the sensor units, were classified as peripheral.

Noninterfering faults were, as the term implies, faults that do not affect any service that is necessary to the current mission phase. For some such faults, it was sufficient to log them for future analysis; for others, some corrective action may have needed to be taken. Interfering faults were those that affected a service that was important to the current mission phase. Transient faults could be allowed to die away, following which the system was restored to health; permanent faults required either automatic switching to a redundant entity or placing the spacecraft in a safe mode to await instructions from ground control. As a general rule, if a fault could be handled by ground control, it was so handled: the philosophy was to carry out autonomous recovery only if ground-based intervention was not practical.

If the CDS itself failed for a substantial period of time, this was detected by the AACS, which then placed the spacecraft in a default "safe mode" to wait for the CDS to recover. The AACS also had the ability to recognize some obviously unsafe operating configurations, and could reject orders to configure the system in an unsafe way.

8.5 IBM POWER8

The IBM POWER8 has extensive error detection and isolation capabilities, allowing analysis of faults and generation of a suitable response to permanent and transient faults. Incorporated redundant hardware (e.g., a spare data lane on each bus) allows tolerating many permanent faults. The processor's functions are continuously monitored and fault information is collected in fault isolation registers, and reported to a dedicated service processor integrated into the system. This service processor determines the course of action to be taken for each fault, as is detailed below.

If transient errors are detected within a computation unit (mostly through the use of residue checking) while executing an instruction, an instruction retry is initiated. If an instruction retry occurs multiple times without success, the fault is considered to be permanent. In such a case, the power virtual machine (PowerVM) attempts to migrate the workload running on the failing processor to an alternative processor. This is accomplished by migrating the processor state to the replacement processor. Obviously, this requires that there is sufficient spare capacity in the system. If not, the PowerVM can terminate a lower priority task.

Retry techniques are also used in other parts of the system. If a fault is detected on the memory bus that connects the memory controllers to the memory units, the transmission is retried. Bus errors are detected using a CRC. The bus also has a spare data lane that can replace a failing bus lane. The memory controller has a replay buffer that allows memory transfers to be retried following the detection of certain faults.

The L2 and L3 cache units use single error correction/double error detection error control codes (SEC/DED ECC). Transient errors that are detected in the L1 caches can be corrected by a fast retry operation that is handled by the hardware. SEC/DED ECC is also used in all processor buses and in other data arrays that are not directly visible to the programmer. Correctable permanent errors in L2 or L3 caches are handled by deleting a cache line that exhibits a persistent error, or by replacing a column of an L3 cache dynamically with a spare. Note that a single permanent fault can be corrected by the ECC. However, doing so runs the risk that a transient error subsequently occurring in the same word will yield an uncorrectable error situation. To avoid such situations, permanently faulty components are replaced by spares.

Not all processor faults can be corrected by the above-mentioned techniques. If an uncorrectable error (called a checkstop) occurs, the service processor attempts to isolate the root cause of the checkstop, and allow the system to reboot with the failed component disconnected. The auto-restart option, when enabled, can reboot the system automatically following such an unrecoverable error.

For each memory port, there are eight dynamic random access memory (DRAM) modules, another DRAM module for the error correction check bits, and a spare module. To prevent a failure of any single memory module from affecting multiple bits in a codeword, the bits of the codeword are distributed across multiple memory modules, allowing error correction despite the complete failure of a single memory module. (This is called the chipkill correction). The spare DRAM modules are used to replace DRAM modules that have experienced a chipkill event.

In addition to the ECC and spare modules, the memory subsystem also implements scrubbing of memory contents to identify and correct single bit errors. *Memory scrubbing* consists of regularly reading the memory, word by word, and correcting any bit errors encountered. This way, transient memory errors are corrected before they accumulate and their number exceeds the correction capabilities of the SEC/DED code. The hypervisor (also known as the virtual machine monitor, i.e., the software that allows multiple virtual machines to run alongside each other and share physical resources) is informed of single-cell permanent faults for deallocation of the corresponding memory page.

The POWER8 processor also supports fault tolerance in the I/O subsystem. Device drivers are allowed to perform a retry after certain nonfatal I/O events (e.g., transient errors) to avoid a failover to an alternate device or I/O path. Device drivers are also allowed to terminate an I/O operation if there is a hard error or another unrecoverable error, to protect against reliance on data that cannot be corrected. This is accomplished by freezing the access to the faulty I/O subsystem.

The service processor is powered separately from the main application processing cores and it runs its own operating system. The service processor is always working, regardless of the state of the main cores, monitoring and managing the system hardware resources. For example, it monitors the built-in temperature sensors and sends commands to the fans to increase their speed when the ambient temperature is above the normal operating range. The service processor can also initiate an orderly system shutdown if the temperature exceeds the critical level, or the input voltages are out of operational specification.

The service processor monitors the operation of the firmware during the boot process, and also monitors the hypervisor for termination. The hypervisor, in turn, monitors the service processor, and can perform a reset and reload if it detects the loss of the service processor.

8.6 IBM G5

The IBM G5 processor makes extensive use of fault-tolerance techniques to recover from transient faults that constitute the majority of hardware faults (see Chapter 1). Fault tolerance is provided for the processor, memory, and I/O systems. In the processor and I/O systems, this takes the form of physical replication; in memory, extensive use is made of error detection and correction codes of the type described in Section 3.1. In addition, extensive hardware support is provided for rollback recovery from transient failures.

Traditional redundancy methods are used to implement fault tolerance in the I/O subsystem. There are multiple paths from the processor to the I/O devices: these can be dynamically switched as necessary to route around faults. Inline error checking is provided, and the channel adapters are designed to prevent interface errors from propagating into the system.

The G5 processor pipeline includes an I-unit, which is responsible for fetching instructions, decoding them, generating any necessary addresses, and placing pending instructions in an instruction queue. There is an E-unit, which executes the instructions and updates the machine state. Both the I- and E-units are duplicated: they work in lock-step, which allows the results of their activity to be compared. A successful comparison indicates that all is well; a divergence between the two instances indicates an error.

In addition, the processor has an R-unit, which consists of 128 32-bit and 128 64-bit registers. The R-unit is used to store the checkpointed machine state to facilitate rollback recovery: this includes general-purpose, status word, and control registers. The R-unit registers are protected by an error-correcting code (ECC), and the R-unit is updated whenever the duplicate E-units generate identical results.

The processor has an ECC-protected store buffer, into which pending stores can be written. When a store instruction commits, the relevant store buffer entry can be written into cache.

All writes to the L1 cache are also written through to the L2 cache: as a result, there is always a backup copy of the L1 contents. The L2 cache and the main memory, as well as the buses connecting the processor to the L2 cache and the L2 cache to main memory, are protected using ECC (a $(72, 64)$ SEC/DED Hamming code, see Section 3.1), whereas errors in L1 are detected using parity. When an L2 line is detected as erroneous, it is invalidated in the cache. If this line is dirty (i.e., was modified since being brought in from main memory), the line is corrected if possible, and the updated line is stored in the main memory. If it is not possible to correct the error, the line is invalidated in cache, and steps are taken to prevent the propagation of the erroneous data.

Special logic detects the same failures happening repeatedly in the same storage location in the L2 cache. Such repeated identical failures are taken to indicate a permanent fault: the affected cache line is then retired from use.

The data in the main memory are protected by the same $(72, 64)$ SEC/DED code, and the address bus is protected using parity bits, one parity bit for every 24 bits. *Memory scrubbing* is used to prevent transient memory errors from accumulating. Spare DRAM is also provided, which can be switched in to replace a malfunctioning memory chip.

G5 systems have a variety of responses to errors. Localized data errors in the registers or the L2 cache can be corrected by means of an ECC. Errors in the L1 cache are detected by means of parity and corrected by using the corresponding copy in the L2 cache. If a processor operation results in an erroneous output (detected by disagreeing outputs from the duplicated I or E-units), the system retries the instruction, in the hope that the error was caused by a transient fault. Such a retry is started by freezing the checkpointed state: updates to the R-unit are not permitted. Pending writethroughs to the L2 cache from instructions that have already been checkpointed are completed. The checkpointed state held in the R-unit is loaded into the appropriate machine registers, and the machine is restarted from the checkpointed state. Note that this is not a system checkpointing process (which, upon a failure, reexecutes a large section of the application) of the type that has been described in Chapter 6. Instead, it is a hardware-controlled process for *instruction retry* and is transparent even to the operating system.

There may be instances in which recovery fails. For example, a permanent fault that results in repeated errors may occur. In such an event, the checkpoint data are transferred to a spare processor (if available) and execution continues on that processor.

Unless the system runs out of spares to deal with permanent failures, or the checkpointed data are found to have been corrupted, a failure and the subsequent recovery will be transparent to the operating system and the application: the recovery process is generally handled rapidly in hardware.

8.7 IBM SYSPLEX

The IBM sysplex is a multinode system that offers some fault-tolerance protection for enterprise applications. The system is configured as shown in Fig. 8.6. A number of computing nodes (up to 32) are interconnected; each node is either a single- or multiple-processor entity. The system includes a global timer, which provides a common time reference to unambiguously order the events across nodes. A storage director connects this cluster of processors to a shared storage, in the form of multiple disk systems. This storage is equally shared: every node has access to any part of it. Connection between the computing nodes and the storage devices is made fault tolerant through redundant connections. The storage itself can be made sufficiently reliable through coding or replication. The existence of truly

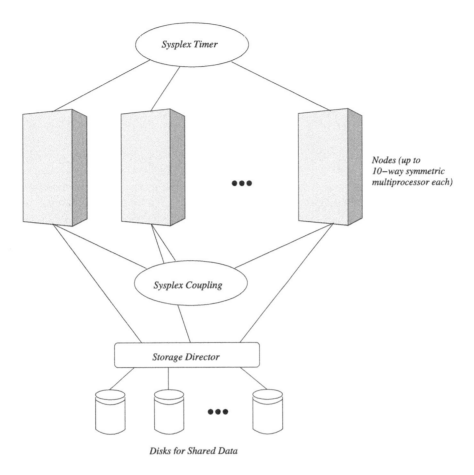

Nodes (up to 10–way symmetric multiprocessor each)

Disks for Shared Data

FIGURE 8.6

IBM sysplex configuration.

shared disk storage makes it possible for applications running on one node to be easily restarted on another.

Processes indicate, through a registration service, whether a restart may be required. When a process is completed, it deregisters itself, to indicate that it will no longer require restart.

When the system detects a node failure, it must (*i*) try to restart that node and (*ii*) restart the applications that were running on that node. Failure detection is through a heartbeat mechanism: the nodes periodically emit heartbeats or "I am alive" messages. If a sufficiently long sequence of heartbeat messages is missed from a node, it is declared to have failed. False alarms can arise, because it is possible under some circumstances for functional nodes to miss sending out heartbeats at the right time. The heartbeat mechanism must therefore be carefully tuned to balance the need to catch failures against the need to keep the false alarm rate sufficiently low.

When a node failure is detected, the automatic restart manager (ARM) takes charge of restarting the affected tasks. The ARM has access to the global system state: it is aware of the loading of each node, and can carry out load balancing while in the process of migrating affected tasks to other nodes. The ARM is also aware of task affinity groups, which are tasks that must be assigned together to the same node (e.g., because they have a heavy amount of intercommunication), and of any sequencing constraints (e.g., that task P should be restarted only after task Q has done so). Also provided is the maximum number of restart attempts, both on the original node and on other nodes, as well as the amount of memory required.

When restarting tasks on other nodes, care has to be taken that the supposedly failed node is really down. This is necessary to avoid the possibility of two copies of the same task—the original and restarted versions—both being active. Such duplicates may be no more than a harmless waste of computational resources in some applications; in other cases, however, duplication may result in erroneous results (e.g., incorrect updates may occur in databases). Similarly, care must be taken when a node's access to the global shared state is lost, to ensure that erroneous events do not occur. For example, if node x loses access to the global state and decides to recover application α, it may well be that some other node y is restarting α as well, thus resulting in two copies of α. Sysplex deals with such problems by disallowing restarts on nodes which have lost access to the global state. To implement such a policy, an array of system sequence numbers, is used. The system sequence number associated with a node is incremented every time access to global shared state is lost and then reestablished. Every process P on a given node x is labeled with the value of the system sequence number at the time it registers for the restart service (notifies the system that it should be restarted if there is a failure). Should access to the shared state now be lost, and then be restored, process P's sequence number will no longer equal the latest value of the system sequence number. P will then be deregistered from the recovery service.

ARM also provides support for the hot-standby mode. In such a mode, there are primary and secondary servers for a given application: if the primary fails, the output of the secondary can be used. The switchover from primary to secondary is much faster than when hot-standby is not used.

8.8 INTEL SERVERS

8.8.1 ITANIUM

Intel's Itanium is a 64-bit processor meant for use in high-end servers and similar applications. It is an explicitly parallel instruction computer (EPIC) capable of executing up to six instructions per cycle, which are bundled by the compiler so that data dependencies are avoided. It has several built-in features for fault tolerance to enhance availability.

The Itanium makes extensive use of parity and error-correcting coding in its data buses (where a single-bit error can be corrected), and in its three levels of cache. There are separate data (L1D) and instruction (L1I) caches at the L1 level, whereas L2 and L3 are unified caches.

L1I and L1D (both the tag and data arrays) are protected by error-detecting parity. When an error is detected, the entire cache is invalidated. L1D has byte-wise parity to facilitate load/store operations of granularity finer than a word. Since faults tend to be spatially correlated (meaning that if a particular location is suffering a transient fault, it is more likely that physically neighboring locations will be affected as well), bits from adjacent cache lines are physically interleaved on silicon. This reduces the probability of a (potentially undetectable) multiple-bit error in a given cache line.

The L2 cache has its data array protected by an error-correcting code (a $(72, 64)$ SEC/DED Hamming code), and its tag array by error-detecting parity (one parity bit for no more than 24 bits). Errors correctable by coding are usually automatically corrected; other (more wide-ranging) responses are outlined below.

Both the tag and data arrays of L3 are protected by similar error-correcting codes. Single-bit data errors are silently corrected when the data are written back. Upon a tag array error, all four ways of the relevant entry in the tag array are scrubbed.

When an error in any level of the cache is detected, the system corrects it if possible, sends out a "corrected machine check interrupt" to indicate that such a correction has occurred, and resumes its normal operation. An exception to this is when an error is "promoted," as is described later.

Suppose the error is not hardware-correctable. If it requires hardware error containment to prevent it from spreading, a bus reset is carried out. A bus reset clears all pending memory and bus transactions and all the internal state machines. All architectural state is preserved (meaning that the register files, caches and TLBs (translation lookaside buffers) are not cleared).

If hardware error containment is not required, a machine check abort (MCA) is signaled. An MCA may be either local or global. If local, it is restricted to the processor or thread encountering the error: information about this is not sent out to any other processors in the system. In contrast, all the processors will be notified of a global MCA.

Error handling is done layer by layer. We have already seen that the hardware will correct such errors if it can. Above the hardware layer are the processor abstraction (PAL) and the system abstraction (SAL) layers, whose job it is to hide lower-level implementation concerning, respectively, the processor and the system external to the processor (such as the memory or the chipset) from higher-level entities (such as the operating system). Error handling is attempted by these layers in turn. If either layer can successfully handle the error, error handling can end there, once information about the error has been sent to the operating system. If neither of these abstraction layers can deal with the error, the operating system gets into the act. For example, if an individual process is identified as the error source, the operating system can abort it.

There are instances in which the error is impossible to successfully handle at any level. In such an instance, a reboot and I/O reinitialization may be necessary. Such a reboot may be local to an individual processor or involve the entire system, depending on the nature of the error.

In some cases, an error may be "promoted," and a higher-level response than is strictly necessary may be employed. For example, suppose the processor is being used in a duplex, or some other redundant architecture in which multiple processors are executing the same code, off identical inputs, and to the beat of a synchronized clock. The cycle-by-cycle output of the redundant processors can then be compared to detect faults. In such a setup, taking a processor out of lock-step to carry out a hardware error correction may not be the most appropriate response: instead, it may be best to signal a global MCA, and let some higher-scope entity handle the problem.

When erroneous data are detected (but not corrected), the usual response is to reboot the entire system (or at least the affected node if the system has multiple processors). The Itanium offers a more focused approach. Erroneous data are marked as such (something that is called *data poisoning*), and any process that tries to use such data is aborted. The effect of erroneous data is therefore less pronounced, especially if used by only a small number of processes. Data poisoning is carried out at the L2 cache level, and the rules for implementing it are as follows:

- Any store to a poisoned cache line is ignored.

- If a poisoned line is removed from the cache (to make room for a new line), it is written back to main memory, and a flag is raised at that location, to indicate that the contents are poisoned.
- Any process that attempts to fetch a poisoned line triggers an MCA.

As mentioned before, once an error has been detected, information about it is passed on to the operating system. This can be done through an interrupt. Alternatively, the operating system may choose to mask out such interrupts and, from time to time, poll lower layers for this information. Such information can be used to better manage the system. For example, if a particular page frame in main memory is observed to suffer from a high error rate, the operating system could decide to stop mapping anything into it.

Due to the extensive set of fault-tolerance mechanisms implemented in the Itanium (compared to most previous commercial microprocessors), it has been used as a building block in several fault-tolerant multiprocessors, including the NonStop systems. More recent implementations of the HP's NonStop systems and Stratus servers use the Xeon processor, described in the next section.

8.8.2 XEON

A more recent Intel processor with fault-tolerance support is the Xeon, which has a more traditional x86 architecture. The Xeon processor was designed to support continuous self-monitoring and self-healing. The processor actively monitors for errors, all the interconnects, data buffers, and data paths. Self-healing means that the processor not only repairs many errors when they occur, but also attempts to proactively reduce the number of potential future errors. Furthermore, the processor supports a high level of availability through the use of multiple levels of redundancy and OS-assisted recovery from certain uncorrectable errors.

Memory is protected using a single error correction, double error detection (SEC/DED) Hamming code. The memory address is protected using a simple parity code. To prevent a failure of any single memory chip from affecting multiple bits in a codeword, the bits of a Hamming codeword are scattered across multiple memory chips. This allows the reconstruction of the memory contents, despite the complete failure of a single memory chip. To deal with a faulty memory chip, dynamic bit-steering is employed: if a memory chip fails completely (or has exceeded a threshold of bit errors that have been corrected), it is replaced by a spare memory chip. Such a replacement is done on-the-fly. If higher data availability is desired, the Xeon processor allows the user to request mirroring of some portions of its application to prevent data loss, even if a memory component suffers an uncorrectable error. Obviously, memory mirroring reduces the storage capacity available to the application. As the memory is the most likely part of the processor to experience transient error, the Xeon processor uses scrubbing to limit the accumulation of bit errors in a any codeword. Furthermore, as the rate of memory bit flips goes up considerably with the temperature, memory thermal throttling is employed. When the temperature goes beyond a predetermined threshold, the frequency of the memory operation is lowered to reduce the probability of transient bit flips.

Failures can also occur in internal data paths and in the memory channel address lines. Soft errors in the internal communication fabric are handled by retries and hard errors are handled by having extra *failover* lanes in the data paths, which are activated upon the detection of such errors.

At the CPU level, the Xeon processor uses error-correcting codes to protect the registers from transient faults. The execution units include error-detection circuits using residue and parity codes. If an error is detected, the instruction is retried. If the retry fails, a fatal error signal is generated. The internal multicore communication network, called quick path interconnect, (QPI) which connects each core to any other core in the system and to the I/O, is protected using a cyclic redundancy check. When a transmission error is detected, QPI initiates a packet retry. If the error persists the QPI's self-healing feature reduces the width of the specific QPI link (from 20 to 10, and even 5 signals) to keep the system running (at an obvious cost to performance). The QPI protocol also enables dynamic processor sparing and migration in the case of a faulty processor.

At the highest level, the processor interacts with the operating system (OS), virtual machine manager, and application software to support recovery from errors that the hardware was unable to correct. The Xeon processor (like the Itanium described earlier) uses a machine check architecture mechanism, through which the processor reports to the OS hardware errors, such as system bus errors, ECC errors, parity errors, cache errors, and translation-look-aside buffer (TLB) errors. Reporting the hardware-corrected errors allows analysis of error symptoms that can be used to predict failures before they actually occur. Based on this analysis the OS can decide on memory or core migration allowing self-healing in the presence of processor and memory faults.

When a correctable hardware error is detected, the internal error-correction mechanisms automatically repair the error and inform the OS that a correctable error occurred. The OS can then log the error for further analysis. If an uncorrectable error is detected, a machine check signal is sent to the OS. If the OS determines that the memory page, where the uncorrectable memory error occurred is not in use, then that page is removed from the storage space and marked for repair. If the faulty memory page is in use, the OS informs the application that is using that page that an unrecoverable error has happened, and the location of the error within the page. The application can then attempt to recover from the data error. If the affected data can be reconstructed, the application reconstructs the data in a different memory page. If however, the corrupted data cannot be reconstructed, the OS system will terminate the application.

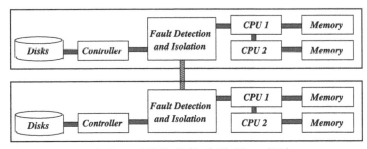

Lockstepped CPUs; Multipath I/O; Mirrored Disks

FIGURE 8.7

Two lockstepped NEC servers with mirrored hard drives.

Xeon processors have been used in the NonStop and Stratus systems and in several NEC servers. Two NEC servers operate in lockstep and are connected to hard drives that are mirrored in a RAID 1 configuration, as shown in Fig. 8.7. The two servers operate as one, and present themselves as a single server to the user. NEC engineers have compared their lockstep implementation to an alternative design that relies instead on the fault-tolerant VMware vSphere fault-tolerance package. The benchmarks used were on-line transaction processing ones. They have concluded that when running a single virtual machine (VM), the hardware-based fault-tolerant server outperformed the software-base solution by 28.9%. With a higher number of VMs, the advantage of the hardware solution increased until, with eight VMs, the hardware-based fault-tolerant server executed 2.48 times the number of transactions per second that the software-based solution achieved.

8.9 ORACLE SPARC M8 SERVER

The SPARC M8 server design has reliability enhancement features at the processor hardware and operating system levels. At the processor level, SEC/DED code is used by all integer and floating-point architectural registers and in the L2 and L3 cache units. These two cache units also have spare cache lines to replace faulty ones. The L1 cache units only have parity protection and upon an error, a retry is performed, and if unsuccessful the corresponding line in L2 is accessed. All cache units use parity code for the address lines. The ALUs are either parity or residue protected. The on-chip network (connecting the 12 to 32 cores, the memory, and the I/O) uses CRC, allowing a retry upon a detected error and supports single lane failover using a spare lane.

The main memory uses a single-error correction, triple-error detection code. In addition, memory module sparing (that is transparent to the application) is supported, as described below. The memory system connected to a single SPARC M8 can include up to 16 memory modules that are organized as a 16-way interleaved memory; it can also support a 15-way interleaved configuration. This capability allows automatic memory module sparing: when a faulty module is detected (or when a module experiences a persistent recoverable transient error), it can be disconnected and its contents remapped to the remaining 15 modules. Clearly, the user should leave sufficient capacity of each module unused in the initial configuration to allow such remapping. If persistent recoverable errors are localized to a specific address, only the corresponding page will be retired. Like other servers the SPARC M8 performs periodic memory scrubbing to prevent accumulation of errors.

To support high availability, the SPARC M8 includes redundant, hot-swappable power supply and fan units, as well as two independent clock sources for each board that can continue to operate with a single clock source.

The fault-tolerance features are managed by the fault management architecture (FMA) layer of the Solaris operating system and by a redundant pair of service processors (SPs) with automatic active/standby failover. When the active SP fails, the standby SP takes over with no impact on the ability to monitor and manage the system. The SP and FMA collaboratively and continuously monitor the system for errors. System health diagnostics are also recorded by the SP and forwarded to a remote center for further analysis. Periodic component status checks are performed to detect signs of an impending fault, and then recovery mechanisms are triggered to prevent system failure. The service processor has diagnostic capabilities and all detected error events are sent to the FMA, which, in turn, can decide whether to have the system continue to operate in a degraded mode. Alternatively, it might reboot with the failing component automatically configured out of the system. Such components include cores, threads, and memory pages that experience a large number of correctable errors.

A software watchdog periodically checks for the operation of the software running on the computation cores, including the operating system.

The Solaris file system regularly checks its data; any errors are detected and automatically repaired using a RAID implementation that uses parity coding and striping.

The open-source SPARC instruction set architecture (ISA) was originally developed by the SUN Microsystem corporation that was later acquired by Oracle. Fujitsu also designed and manufactured several generations of SPARC servers. Most of the fault-tolerance features in the Fujitsu servers have been similar to those implemented in the Oracle servers. Some of the differences include the support that the Fujitsu SPARC64 X+ server has had for dynamic degradation of the number of associative ways of the L1 and L2 cache units. In addition, the Fujitsu servers support instruction retry: each instruction is checked upon commit, and retried if an error was detected.

In 2017 Oracle and Fujitsu launched together the SPARC M12 server with up to 384 cores and 32TB RAM. The server is based on the SPARC64 XII processor that implements (in addition to all the above mentioned fault-tolerance features) an instruction retry mechanism for correcting single-bit errors occurring in the ALUs or registers. When such an error is detected, all instructions that are currently in the execution pipeline are aborted. Then, the instruction that caused the error is reexecuted alone to increase the possibility of successful execution. If the instruction commits successfully, the processor resumes normal pipelined execution.

8.10 CLOUD COMPUTING

Cloud computing has become increasingly important in recent years. The idea is to have a service provider, such as Microsoft, Google, or Amazon, set up extensive computing infrastructure, and then sell computational services to users in academia and business. These users are then spared the burden of administering their own computational platforms, and can simply buy as much computational service as they need. The infrastructure typically consists of a very large number of computing nodes interconnected together. These nodes are typically spread over multiple widely separated geographical sites.

A cloud is thus a very large distributed computational platform. Many of the same problems inherent to distributed computing naturally emerge here as well. Among these is the need for fault tolerance: with a very large number of commodity machines, failures are often observed. Fault tolerance in cloud computing is an active area of research. What follows is a sampling of ideas that have been suggested in recent years.

8.10.1 CHECKPOINTING IN RESPONSE TO SPOT PRICING

The service provider wishes to make as much money as possible selling cloud services; the buyer wishes to get as much computational work done as possible for a given sum of money. The former sets up a pricing scheme to meet their goal; the latter then responds.

Typically, users have on-demand versus spot pricing. In the on-demand market, one can buy the services of a set of virtual machines at a fixed price per unit time. Much cheaper, though, is *spot pricing*, where the service provider attempts to sell, at a lower price, computational capacity that would otherwise go unused.

Spot pricing works as follows: The buyer puts forth a bid B, which is the maximum they are willing to pay. Based on current demand, there is a spot price S, which the service provider charges for computation. (The user is billed S, rather than B, per unit of service; B is the user's maximum stated limit.) The spot price is recalculated at regular intervals, for instance, updated on the hour, every hour. So long as $B \geq S$, the user continues to get computational access. The moment the spot price rises so that $B < S$, the user's computational job is abruptly killed, without warning. Any computational work that is not checkpointed is therefore lost.

The issue is then when to checkpoint. Note that the user has no advance warning of spot price changes; all they have is historical information about prices in the past that they can use as a projection in deciding when to take a checkpoint.

Note the essential similarity to the traditional checkpointing problem. In both cases, computational results that are not saved are lost when the thread of computation is abruptly terminated. In traditional fault tolerance, the termination is due to failure. In spot pricing, the termination is due to an increase of the spot price beyond the user's bid. The objective of checkpoint placement is the same in both cases: to account for the cost of checkpointing in scheduling these checkpoints.

8.10.2 PROACTIVE VIRTUAL MACHINE MIGRATION

The physical platform on which virtual machines execute can deteriorate with time. Such deterioration can be detected by mining node event logs. These logs maintain information about when each failure-related event occurred in the node. Events may be classified as hardware, software, or undetermined. They may be listed as irrecoverable or recoverable after a certain number of attempts. This information is first processed to remove duplicates (i.e., the same underlying issue being recorded multiple times, as events spaced a short duration apart). Data mining techniques are then used to study these logs, with a view to identifying pending failure "signatures," that is, we look for sets of events in the log, which typically indicate that a significant failure is about to occur. (Obviously, no prediction is perfect, so there will be false alarms as well as failures that were not predicted.) If such an indication occurs, the resource manager can migrate virtual machines running on that physical node to other nodes.

8.10.3 FAULT TOLERANCE AS A SERVICE

Just as computational cycles are bought as a service from the provider, fault tolerance can be purchased as well. The user specifies certain capabilities that need to be replicated for fault tolerance. The service provider then matches available resources to such incoming demands from the user. The provider must also continually monitor the functioning of these resources so that the appropriate service level is maintained. Sometimes, this requires the remapping (reassignment) of resources to users.

The user may decide that it is too expensive to replicate everything related to their application. Instead, replication may be purchased for just the most critical components. The question is how to determine which components are the most critical. One suggestion is to use an approach that draws its inspiration from the well-known *page rank algorithm* used to identify important web pages. The idea is that a component which is invoked often is likely to be more important. A directed graph is created, with individual components being the nodes and directed edges denoting an invocation relationship, that is, if component a invokes a service on component b, then there is an edge $e_{a,b}$ connecting the nodes n_a, n_b in the system graph. Let $\phi_{a,b}$ be the frequency with which component a invokes a service on component b. Then, the weight of the edge $e_{a,b}$ is calculated as $w_{a,b} = \frac{\phi_{a,b}}{\sum_j \phi_{a,j}}$. If a node invokes no other component, we create an edge from this node to every node in the system (including itself); the weight of each such edge is then set to $1/m$, where m is the number of nodes in the system. Note that the weights of the edges leaving a node always sum to 1.

Let $N(a)$ denote all the nodes which have a link from node n_a. Define a parameter $d \in [0, 1]$, whose meaning will be described in a moment. Now, define the following equation of the significance level of component a:

$$U(a) = \frac{1-d}{n} + d \sum_{k \in N(a)} U(k)w_{k,i}. \qquad (8.1)$$

To obtain a solution to this recursion, we start with random values for the $U(k)$, and then iteratively apply the recursion until it converges. The values $U(a)$ can then be treated as the relative importance of component a.

Let us now turn to the value of d and the role it plays. Note that if $d = 1$, then $U(a) = 1/n$ for each component a, and there is no need for a recursion; each component is equally important. If $d = 0$, then the importance of component a stems entirely from its relationship to the other components.

Secondly, note that the system of Eqs. (8.1) are dependent. To obtain absolute values for them, we will need to add a boundary condition: $\sum_a U(a) = A$, where A is some suitable value (often taken as 1).

Note that apart from the invocation frequency of one component by another, we have not included any domain knowledge in our model. This is not difficult to include: see the Further Reading section for a pointer.

The user can then assign redundancy to components in line with their significance.

8.11 FURTHER READING

Most books on fault tolerance include descriptions of existing fault-tolerant systems, for example [20, 30,34].

Details of the systems mentioned in this chapter can be found in the references that follow; our description and figures are based on these.

The fly-by-wire system in the Boeing 777 has been presented in [40–42]. The 2005 failing Boeing accelerometer event is described in [21].

Further details on the original Tandem systems can be found at [2,23,38]. The Itanium-based design of the NonStop system is described in [5]. The more recent Xeon-based implementation is presented in [12]. Self-checking logic, which was used in the early designs of some NonStop processors is described in [22]. Design of self-checking checkers is presented in [1]. The shifted operands technique for detecting errors in arithmetic units appears in [29,36].

The Stratus systems are described in white papers published by Stratus Technologies and available at `https://www.stratus.com/resources/solution-brief/`. Hardening drivers to make them more resilient is discussed in [13].

The Cassini spacecraft CDS is described in [8]; information about the Cassini AACS can be found in [7]. NASA has published a primer on fault-tolerance techniques that have been used in spacecraft [9]. A more recent presentation on NASA's fault-tolerant systems appears in [14]. The design of the space shuttle is described in [11].

Further details about the IBM Power processors and their fault-tolerance features are available at [10,32]. A radiation hardened version of IBM's PowerPC 750 processor that was designed by BAE Systems and used in several space mission, is described in [4].

The main source for the IBM G5 processor is the 1999 September/November special issue of the IBM *Journal of Research and Development*. An overview of the fault-tolerance techniques used in G5 is provided in [37]. Another good introduction can be found in [35]. The G5 cache and the I/O system are described in [39] and [15], respectively.

The main reference for the IBM S/390 Sysplex is the Volume 36, No. 2, issue of the *IBM Systems Journal*, for an overview, see [27], and for a description of high-availability, see [6]. A very informative comparison of the IBM and HP/Tandem NonStop designs is included in [3].

Information about the Intel Itanium processor is widely available. Excellent introductions can be found in the September/October 2000 issue of *IEEE Micro*, which contains several relevant papers, and in [24]. Another good source is the Intel Corporation website, especially [16,17]. The Itanium has been used in several designs of fault-tolerant systems, including IBM, NEC, Fujitsu, and Hewlett-Packard's NonStop [5,33].

Intel's Xeon processor design and its fault-tolerance support are described in [18]. Its use in an NEC server is covered in [26]. A detailed description of the reliability enhancing features of the SPARC M8 appears in [28].

Cloud computing is the focus of much current research. A good overall outline is provided in [19]. Fault tolerance in mobile ad hoc clouds is covered in [44]. Exploiting redundancy to help satisfy time-constrained computations in a cloud platform is the subject of [25]. A cloud may consist of components of widely varying reliability. Fault-tolerance and reliability issues connected with this are covered in [31,43].

REFERENCES

[1] M.J. Ashjaee, S.M. Reddy, On-totally self-checking checkers for separable codes, IEEE Transactions on Computers C-26 (Aug. 1977) 737–744.

[2] W. Bartlett, B. Ball, Tandems approach to fault tolerance, Tandem Systems Review 8 (February 1988) 84–95.

[3] W. Bartlett, L. Spainhower, Commercial fault tolerance: a tale of two systems, IEEE Transactions on Dependable and Secure Computing 1 (1) (January 2004) 87–96.

[4] R. Berger, et al., The RAD750 – a radiation-hardened PowerPC processor for high performance spaceborne applications, in: IEEE Aerospace Conference, 2001.

[5] D. Bernick, B. Bruckert, P. Del-Vigna, D. Garcia, R. Jardine, J. Klecka, J. Smullen, NonStop advanced architecture, in: Dependable Systems and Networks Symposium (DSN'05), 2005, pp. 12–21.

[6] N.S. Bowen, J. Antognini, R.D. Regan, N.C. Matsakis, Availability in parallel systems: automatic process restart, IBM Systems Journal 36 (1997) 284–300, available at: www.research.ibm.com/journal/sj/362/antognini.html.

[7] G.M. Brown, D.E. Bernard, R.D. Rasmussen, Attitude and articulation control for the Cassini spacecraft: a fault tolerance overview, in: 14th Annual Digital Avionics Systems Conference, 1995, pp. 184–192.

[8] T.K. Brown, J.A. Donaldson, Fault protection design for the command and data subsystem on the Cassini spacecraft, in: 13th Annual Digital Avionics Systems Conference, 1994, pp. 408–413.

[9] R.W. Butler, A Primer on Architectural Level Fault Tolerance, NASA Report (NASA/TM-2008-215108), 2008, available at: https://ntrs.nasa.gov/search.jsp?R=20080009026.

[10] A.B. Caldeira, B. Grabowski, V. Haug, M.-E. Kahle, A. Laidlaw, C.D. Maciel, M. Sanchez, S.Y. Sung, IBM power system S822: technical overview and introduction, available at: https://www.redbooks.ibm.com/redpapers/pdfs/redp5102.pdf.

[11] G. Chapline, P. Sollock, P.O. Neill, A. Hill, T. Fiorucci, J. Kiriazes, Avionics, navigation, and instrumentation, available at: https://www.nasa.gov/centers/johnson/pdf/584731main_Wings-ch4e-pgs242-255.pdf, 2007.

[12] V. Cooper, K. Charters, NonStop X system overview, available at: https://dan-lewis-fns9.squarespace.com/s/NonStop-X-Overview-V3.pdf, 2015.

[13] S. Graham, Writing drivers for reliability, robustness fault tolerant systems, in: Microsoft Windows Hardware Engineering Conference, April 2002.

[14] M.B. Goforth, NASA avionics architectures for exploration (AAE) and fault tolerant computing, in: Fault-Tolerant Space-borne Computing Employing New Technologies, 2014, Presentation available at: https://ntrs.nasa.gov/archive/nasa/casi.ntrs.nasa.gov/20140008709.pdf.

[15] T.A. Gregg, S/390 CMOS server I/O: the continuing evolution, IBM Journal of Research and Development 41 (July/September 1997) 449–462.

[16] Intel Corporation, Intel Itanium processor family error handling guide, Document 249278-003, available at: http://application-notes.digchip.com/027/27-45868.pdf.

[17] Intel Corporation, Intel Itanium2 processor, available at: https://www.intel.com/pressroom/kits/itanium2/.

[18] Intel Corporation, Intel Xeon processor E7 family: reliability, availability, and serviceability, available at: https://www.intel.com/content/dam/www/public/us/en/documents/white-papers/xeon-e7-family-ras-server-paper.pdf.

[19] R. Jhawar, V. Piuri, M. Santambrogio, Fault tolerance management in cloud computing: a system-level perspective, IEEE Systems Journal 7 (2) (November 2012) 288–297.

[20] B.W. Johnson, Design and Analysis of Fault-Tolerant Digital Systems, Addison-Wesley, 1989.

[21] C.W. Johnson, C.M. Hollow, The dangers of failure masking in fault-tolerant software: aspects of a recent in-flight upset event, in: The 2nd Institution of Engineering and Technology Conference on System Safety, 2007, pp. 60–65.

[22] P.K. Lala, Self-Checking and Fault-Tolerant Digital Design, Morgan Kaufmann, 2000.

[23] I. Lee, R.K. Iyer, Software dependability in the Tandem Guardian system, IEEE Transactions on Software Engineering 8 (May 1995) 455–467.

[24] T. Luck, Machine check recovery for Linux on Itanium processors, in: Linux Symposium, July 2003, pp. 313–319.

[25] A. Marathe, R. Harris, D. Lowenthal, B.R. De Supinski, B. Rountree, M. Schulz, Exploiting redundancy for cost-effective, time-constrained execution of HPC applications on Amazon EC2, in: International Symposium on High-Performance Parallel and Distributed Computing, 2014, pp. 279–290.

[26] N.E.C. Corporation, Fault tolerance performance and scalability comparison: NEC hardware-based FT vs. software-based FT, available at: https://www.nec-enterprise.com/Newsroom/Fault-Tolerance-ease-of-set-up-comparison-NEC-hardware-based-FT-vs-software-based-FT-482, 2015.

[27] J.M. Nick, B.B. Moore, J.-Y. Chung, N.S. Bowen, S/390 cluster technology: parallel sysplex, IBM Systems Journal 36 (1997) 172–201, available at: https://ieeexplore.ieee.org/document/5387195.

[28] Oracle Corporation, Oracle's SPARC T8 and SPARC M8 server reliability, availability, and serviceability, White Paper, available at: https://community.oracle.com/docs/DOC-1017903.

[29] J.H. Patel, L.Y. Fung, Concurrent error detection in ALUs by recomputing with shifted operands, IEEE Transactions on Computers 31 (July 1982) 589–595.

[30] D.K. Pradhan (Ed.), Fault Tolerant Computer System Design, Prentice-Hall, 1996.

[31] W. Qiu, Z. Zheng, X. Wang, X. Yang, M.R. Lyu, Reliability-based design optimization for cloud migration, IEEE Transactions on Services Computing 7 (2) (August 2013) 223–236.

[32] P.N. Sanda, K. Reick, S. Swaney, J.W. Kellington, P. Kudva, Sustaining error resiliency: the IBM POWER6 microprocessor, in: Hot Chips 19, 2007, also in: 2nd Workshop on Dependable and Secure Nanocomputing, 2008, available at: http://webhost.laas.fr/TSF/WDSN08/2ndWDSN08(LAAS)_files/Slides/WDSN08S-01-Sanda.pdf, 2008.

[33] Y. Shibata, Fujitsu's chipset development for high-performance, high-reliability mission-critical IA servers PRIMEQUEST, Fujitsu Science and Technology Journal 41 (October 2005) 291–297, available at: www.fujitsu.com/downloads/MAG/vol41-3/paper03.pdf.

[34] D.P. Siewiorek, R.S. Swarz, Reliable Computer Systems: Design and Evaluation, A.K. Peters, 1998.

[35] T.J. Slegel, R.M. Averill III, M.A. Check, B.C. Giamei, B.W. Krumm, C.A. Krygowski, W.H. Li, J.S. Liptay, J.D. Mac-Dougall, T.J. McPherson, J.A. Navarro, E.M. Schwarz, K. Shum, C.F. Webb, IBM's S/390 G5 microprocessor design, in: IEEE Micro, March/April 1999, pp. 12–23.

[36] G.S. Sohi, M. Franklin, K.K. Saluja, A study of time-redundant fault-tolerance techniques for high performance pipelined computers, in: Fault-Tolerant Computing Symposium, 1989, pp. 436–443.

[37] L. Spainhower, T.A. Gregg, IBM S/390 parallel enterprise server G5 fault tolerance: a historical perspective, IBM Journal of Research and Development 43 (September/November 1999) 863–873.

[38] HPE integrity NonStop, Technical Reports, available at: https://www.hpe.com/us/en/servers/nonstop.html.

[39] P.R. Turgeon, P. Mak, M.A. Blake, C.B. Ford III, P.J. Meaney, R. Seigler, W.W. Shen, The S/390 G5/G6 binodal cache, IBM Journal of Research and Development 43 (September/November 1999) 661–670.

[40] Y.C. Yeh, Triple-triple redundant 777 primary flight computer, in: IEEE Aerospace Applications Conference, vol. 1, February 1996, pp. 293–307.

[41] Y.C. Yeh, Design considerations in Boeing 777 fly-by-wire computers, in: Third IEEE International High-Assurance Systems Engineering Symposium, Nov. 1998.

[42] Y.C. Yeh, Safety critical avionics for the 777 primary flight controls system, in: The 20th Digital Avionics Systems Conference, vol. 1, October 2001, pp. 1C2/1–1C2/11.

[43] Z. Zheng, T.C. Zhou, M.R. Lyu, T. King, Component ranking for fault-tolerant cloud applications, IEEE Transactions on Services Computing 5 (4) (July 2011) 540–550.

[44] B. Zhou, R. Buyya, A group-based fault tolerant mechanism for heterogeneous mobile clouds, in: EAI International Conference on Mobile and Ubiquitous Systems: Computing, Networking and Services, 2017, pp. 373–382.

SIMULATION TECHNIQUES

9

This chapter introduces the reader to statistical simulation approaches for evaluating the reliability and associated attributes of fault-tolerant computer systems.

Simulation is frequently used when analytical approaches are either not feasible or not sufficiently accurate. Simulation, in general, has a deep theoretical foundation in statistics that can take years to master, and to which many books have been devoted. However, learning to write a basic simulation program and to use the fundamental statistical tools for analyzing the output data is much easier. These basic techniques are what we concentrate on in this chapter. Having said that, this chapter is meant primarily for readers with a reasonably strong understanding of probability theory.

We start by explaining how to write a simulation program. We then show how the output can be analyzed to deduce the system attributes. We then consider ways in which the results can be made more accurate by reducing the variance of the simulation output. We end the chapter by considering a different kind of simulation – fault injection, which is an experimental technique to characterize a system's response to faults.

9.1 WRITING A SIMULATION PROGRAM

When faced with the need to construct a simulation model, the engineer has three options:

- Write a program in a high-level general programming language, such as Python, C, Java, or C++.
- Use a special-purpose simulation language, such as SIMPSCRIPT, GPSS, or SIMAN.
- Use or modify an available simulation package that has been designed to simulate such systems. Examples include SimpleScalar for computer architectures and OPNET for network simulation.

In this section, we will focus on the first option. Readers wishing to follow one of the other approaches should consult the user's manual of the chosen language or package.

The most common form of simulation programs is a *discrete-event* simulation, in which the events of interest (changes in the state variables) occur at discrete instants of time. Most events of interest in fault-tolerant computing, such as the arrival of jobs at a computer system, error occurrence, the failure of a processor, and its recovery or replacement, are discrete events. By contrast, the flow of water out of a leaky bucket is an example of a continuous-event system: the state variable (water level) is a continuous function of time at the macrolevel. Of course, if one were to consider it at an atomic level, this would become a discrete-event system, as the molecules of water leak one by one out of the bucket. This is an example of a situation in which what is continuous at one level of granularity turns out to be discrete at a finer level.

Fault-Tolerant Systems. https://doi.org/10.1016/B978-0-12-818105-8.00019-X

Let us illustrate the simulation process by an example, after which we will extract some general principles of the approach.

Example: Suppose we wish to simulate the mean time to data loss (MTTDL) of a RAID level 1 disk system. This system is so simple that good analytical models exist for its analysis, and we do not really need a simulation model to obtain the MTTDL. Still, this will be a good warm-up exercise in writing simulation programs. Also, simulation can be used when the analytical model breaks down due to its limiting assumptions that do not always apply in practice (e.g., when the failures deviate significantly from a Poisson process). It is easy to take care of this in simulation by generating random variables according to whichever distribution is found to best represent reality.

RAID level 1 systems have been covered in Chapter 3: recall that the system consists of two mirrored disks, and that data loss occurs when the second disk fails before the first failed disk has been repaired.

We start by identifying the events of interest to us: these are *failures* and *repair actions*. Suppose failures occur as a Poisson process with rate λ, and repair time is a random variable r with a known probability density function $f_r(\cdot)$. Assuming that the parameters of the failure process and repair time distributions are known to us, we can generate failure and repair times using a random number generator, as described later in Section 9.5. We show in Section 9.2 how the input parameters can be estimated if they are not given to us.

The key data structure in the simulation is a linked list called the *event chain*, which holds the scheduled events (in this case, disk failure and repair instants) in temporal (meaning time) order. We also define a variable called *the clock*, which keeps the current simulated time and has an initial value of 0. The simulation consists of advancing the clock from one event to the next, recording statistics as we go. The flowchart for the simulation is shown in Fig. 9.1. One point of detail is worth mentioning. Since the granularity of the time being measured is not infinitely fine (owing to the finite word length of the computer), it is possible – although highly improbable – that we will have two events: a disk failure and a repair completion (of the other disk) scheduled for the same instant in the event chain. In this case, we must decide in which order the events will be inserted in the event chain. For example, we may decide that the failure event goes in first and the repair completion next. Let us illustrate the operation of the algorithm in Fig. 9.1. We begin by generating first-failure epochs for the two disks: suppose they happen at times 28 and 95 seconds, respectively. At time 0, the system state is (Up, Up), representing the condition of the two disks. The event chain now is

$$(28, \mathrm{d1}, \mathrm{F}) \leftrightarrow (95, \mathrm{d2}, \mathrm{F}),$$

where the three elements in the 3-tuple indicate the epoch of the event, the disk in question (d1 or d2), and the event (F for failure and C for repair completion).

The clock is now advanced to the next event in the event chain, which occurs at time 28 seconds. The event is the failure of the first disk, and the system state now is (Down, Up). Generate a repair time for this disk: suppose the length of the generated repair time is 10 seconds, and the disk will be up again at time 38 seconds. Remove the event that we just processed from the event chain, and insert the repair event into the event chain:

$$(38, \mathrm{d1}, \mathrm{C}) \leftrightarrow (95, \mathrm{d2}, \mathrm{F}).$$

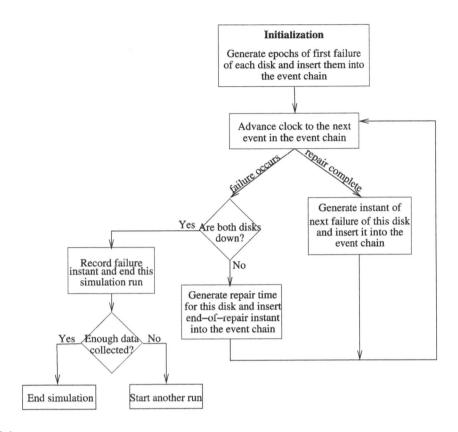

FIGURE 9.1

Simulation of a RAID level 1 system.

Advance to the next event in the chain, at time 38 seconds. At this point, the first disk is back up, so the state of the system is (Up, Up). Generate the next failure time of this disk: suppose this failure is 68 seconds into the future, which means that the failure will happen at time $38 + 68 = 106$ seconds. The event chain is now

$$(95, d2, F) \leftrightarrow (106, d1, F).$$

Advance to the next event at time 95 seconds. The system state now is (Up, Down). Generate the repair time of this disk: suppose it is 14 seconds, so that this disk will come up at time $95 + 14 = 109$ seconds. The event chain is now

$$(106, d1, F) \leftrightarrow (109, d2, C).$$

Advance to the next event, at time 106 seconds. The system state is now (Down, Down), representing data loss. For this simulation run, time to data loss (TTDL) is 106 seconds, and a new simulation run can begin. After all the runs are completed, the MTTDL of the system is estimated by calculating the average of the TTDLs of all the runs. If desired, a confidence interval for the MTTDL can be constructed, as shown later in Section 9.2.5.

More complex simulations require more work, but the principle is the same. We create an event chain that is ordered temporally and advances from one event to the next, recording statistics appropriately. One has to be extremely careful to ensure that all events are captured in the event chain, and that the simulation does not skip over any of them.

The following are the key steps to follow when writing a simulation program:

- Thoroughly understand the system being simulated. Not doing so can result in a wrong system being modeled.
- List the events of interest.
- Determine the dependencies between events, if any.
- Understand the state transitions.
- Correctly estimate the distributions of the various input random variables.
- Identify the statistics to be gathered.
- Correctly analyze the output statistics to extract the required system attributes.

9.2 PARAMETER ESTIMATION

To run a simulation program, the values of certain input parameters are needed, such as failure and repair rates. In addition, we need a way of analyzing the simulation output and extracting parameters, such as reliability and mean time to system failure. In this section we will see how such parameter values can be estimated. We will distinguish between point estimation and interval estimation, describe three methods by which to obtain point estimates of parameter values, and show how a confidence interval for the parameter can be constructed. Most of our discussion assumes that we know the underlying shape of the distribution that the data will follow, and that this shape depends on one or more parameters whose exact value is unknown to us. For example, we may believe that processors fail according to a Poisson process, which we can characterize by estimating the rate λ of this process. In some cases, we will estimate parameters even without knowledge of the exact shape of the distribution, using approximating formulas (most notably, the central limit theorem).

9.2.1 POINT VERSUS INTERVAL ESTIMATION

Suppose we are given a random variable X with a known distribution function characterized by a parameter θ. To estimate θ, we either sample from experimental observations or simulate the underlying system (whose parameters are known) to generate n independent observations of X, denoted by $X_1, ..., X_n$, and use a suitable function $T(X_1, ..., X_n)$ as an estimator of θ. Since we will very likely not obtain the exact value of θ, we denote the estimate $\hat{\theta}$. Note that $\hat{\theta}$ is a random variable and will have a different value if a different sample $X_1, ..., X_n$ is selected.

In what follows, we denote the expectation of a random variable X by $E(X)$ and its variance by $Var(X)$. Recall that the standard deviation of X (commonly denoted by $\sigma(X)$) is the square root of the variance. We would like an estimator to be *unbiased*.

Definition: An estimator $\hat{\theta} = T(X_1, ..., X_n)$ is called an *unbiased estimator* of a parameter θ if $E(\hat{\theta}) = E(T(X_1, ..., X_n)) = \theta$.

Even if the estimator of a continuous variable is unbiased, the chance that our point estimate is exactly equal to the real parameter is practically zero, although the difference between the two is likely to diminish as n increases. We can characterize the confidence in our estimate by calculating an interval in which the parameter is expected to lie. This is *interval estimation*, and the resulting interval is called a *confidence interval*. The wider the interval, the greater is the confidence that it includes the actual parameter, but the less informative it is. The next three sections discuss methods of obtaining point estimators, and Section 9.2.5 deals with constructing confidence intervals.

9.2.2 METHOD OF MOMENTS

Suppose we want to estimate the values of k parameters of the probability distribution of some random variable X. We define the jth *distribution moment* as $E(X^j)$ $(j = 1, 2, ...)$. We then sample or simulate n independent observations of X, namely, $X_1, ..., X_n$ and define the jth *sample moment* m_j as

$$m_j = \frac{\sum_{i=1}^{n} X_i^j}{n}.$$

We now equate the first k distribution moments with the first k sample moments:

$$\hat{E}(X^j) = m_j \quad (j = 1, ..., k).$$

The left hand sides include the k estimators as unknowns, and so we have k equations, the solution of which yields estimators of the k parameters.

Let us consider some examples.

Example: Suppose we believe that the running time X of a task has a normal distribution with two parameters μ and σ^2 whose values we do not know. We execute the task n times and record the running times $X_1, ..., X_n$. Since $\mu = E(X)$ and $\sigma^2 = var(X) = E(X - \mu)^2 = E(X^2) - (E(X))^2$, we can use the method of moments to write the two equations for our estimators, $\hat{\mu}$ and $\hat{\sigma}^2$, of the mean and variance, respectively:

$$\hat{\mu} = \overline{X} = \frac{X_1 + X_2 + \cdots + X_n}{n},$$

and

$$\hat{\sigma}^2 = \frac{\sum_{i=1}^{n} X_i^2}{n} - \hat{\mu}^2 = \frac{\sum_{i=1}^{n} X_i^2}{n} - \overline{X}^2 = \frac{\sum_{i=1}^{n} (X_i - \overline{X})^2}{n}.$$

Although $\overline{X}$ is an unbiased estimate of μ, $\hat{\sigma}^2$ is not an unbiased estimate of σ^2. As shown in almost any basic book on statistics, a small correction will result in an unbiased estimator for σ^2:

$$\hat{\sigma}^2 = \frac{\sum_{i=1}^{n} (X_i - \overline{X})^2}{n - 1}. \tag{9.1}$$

When n is large (as it is in most engineering experiments), there is no significant numerical difference between dividing by n or by $n-1$.

Example: Suppose we know that the lifetime X of a processor is exponentially distributed, but do not know the value of the parameter λ of that distribution. The density function for the processor lifetime is

$$f(x) = \lambda e^{-\lambda x}.$$

We have one unknown, and therefore need just one equation. We start with n processors and run them until they all fail. Let X_i be the lifetime of processor i. Then, our estimate of the first moment of the processor lifetime (its mean value) is the sample average $\overline{X}$. Since $E(X) = 1/\lambda$, we end up with the equation

$$\frac{1}{\lambda} = \overline{X},$$

and therefore,

$$\hat{\lambda} = \frac{1}{\overline{X}}.$$

Although $\overline{X}$ is an unbiased estimator of $1/\lambda$, $1/\overline{X}$ is *not* an unbiased estimator of λ. Still, it is often a good estimate.

Example: Suppose, instead, that X follows a Weibull distribution. Recall that X has the density function

$$f(x) = \lambda \beta x^{\beta-1} e^{-\lambda x^\beta} \qquad (x \geq 0). \tag{9.2}$$

The two parameters of this distribution are λ and β, so we need two equations to solve for these two unknowns. We obtain these equations by writing out expressions for the first two moments: $E(X)$ and $E(X^2)$:

$$
\begin{aligned}
E(X) &= \lambda^{-1}\Gamma(1+1/\beta), \\
E(X^2) &= \lambda^{-2}\Gamma(1+2/\beta),
\end{aligned}
$$

where $\Gamma(x) = \int_0^\infty t^{x-1} e^{-t} dt$ is the gamma function (see Section 2.2). We can therefore write

$$
\begin{aligned}
\hat{\lambda}^{-1}\Gamma(1+1/\hat{\beta}) &= \overline{X}, \\
\hat{\lambda}^{-2}\Gamma(1+2/\hat{\beta}) &= \frac{\sum_{i=1}^{n} X_i^2}{n}.
\end{aligned}
$$

We have two equations in the two unknowns λ and β, which we can solve to obtain the estimates $\hat{\lambda}$ and $\hat{\beta}$.

The method of moments is a fairly simple approach, which often works reasonably well, although, as we have seen, it does not always result in unbiased estimators. Still, we can generalize and say that the sample average $\overline{X}$ can be used as an estimate for the expected value $E(X)$.

9.2.3 METHOD OF MAXIMUM LIKELIHOOD

The maximum likelihood method determines parameter values for which the *given observations* would have the highest probability (or, in the case of a continuous random variable, the highest density function). Given a set of observations, we set up a *likelihood function* as a function of the parameter values. We then find those values of the parameters for which this function is maximized.

Example: We believe that the intervals between failures of a certain system are exponentially distributed, with parameter λ. Furthermore, these intervals are independent of one another. From experimental observation of the system, we obtain the following five values for the interfailure intervals: $10, 5, 11, 12, 15$ seconds.

The joint density function of these five observations is the product of the density function value at each of the individual observations, since these were made independently of one another. This joint density, conditioned on the parameter being λ, is the likelihood function $L(\lambda)$:

$$L(\lambda) = \lambda e^{-10\lambda} \cdot \lambda e^{-5\lambda} \cdot \lambda e^{-11\lambda} \cdot \lambda e^{-12\lambda} \cdot \lambda e^{-15\lambda} = \lambda^5 e^{-53\lambda}.$$

We now seek that value of λ, which will maximize $L(\lambda)$. We can do this using basic calculus:

$$\frac{dL(\lambda)}{d\lambda} = \left(5\lambda^4 - 53\lambda^5\right) e^{-53\lambda} = 0.$$

Solving for λ yields $\lambda = 0, \; 5/53$.

Clearly, $\lambda = 0$ is a minimum, whereas $\lambda = 5/53$ is a maximum. Hence, our estimate of λ, based on this set of observations, is $\hat{\lambda} = 5/53$. (Note that this is equal to the method of moments estimate for the same parameter, which is $\hat{\lambda} = 1/\overline{X} = 1/(53/5) = 5/53$.)

Example: Suppose now that we believe that the interfailure times are distributed according to the Weibull distribution, which has the probability density function shown in Eq. (9.2), and we have to estimate the two parameters λ and β, using the same five observations as in the previous example. The likelihood function is now given by

$$
\begin{aligned}
L(\lambda, \beta) &= f(10) \cdot f(5) \cdot f(11) \cdot f(12) \cdot f(15) \\
&= \lambda^5 \beta^5 10^{\beta-1} 5^{\beta-1} 11^{\beta-1} 12^{\beta-1} 15^{\beta-1} e^{-\lambda(10^\beta + 5^\beta + 11^\beta + 12^\beta + 15^\beta)}.
\end{aligned}
$$

When attempting to maximize a function like this, it is easier to proceed by maximizing $\ln(L(\lambda, \beta))$, rather than $L(\lambda, \beta)$ itself. Since $\ln(x)$ is a monotonically increasing function of x, this will lead to the same values for $\hat{\lambda}, \hat{\beta}$. Now,

$$
\begin{aligned}
\ln(L(\lambda, \beta)) &= 5\ln(\lambda) + 5\ln(\beta) + (\beta - 1)(\ln(99000)) - \lambda\left(10^\beta + 5^\beta + 11^\beta + 12^\beta + 15^\beta\right) \\
&= 5\ln(\lambda) + 5\ln(\beta) + 11.5(\beta - 1) - \lambda\left(10^\beta + 5^\beta + 11^\beta + 12^\beta + 15^\beta\right).
\end{aligned}
$$

To find $\hat{\lambda}, \hat{\beta}$, we differentiate the log-likelihood with respect to λ and β, and equate the derivatives to zero:

$$\frac{\partial \ln(L(\lambda, \beta))}{\partial \lambda} = 0,$$

$$\frac{\partial \ln(L(\lambda, \beta))}{\partial \beta} = 0.$$

This yields the equations

$$5\lambda^{-1} = 10^\beta + 5^\beta + 11^\beta + 12^\beta + 15^\beta,$$
$$5\beta^{-1} + 11.5 = \lambda\left(10^\beta \ln(10) + 5^\beta \ln(5) + 11^\beta \ln(11) + 12^\beta \ln(12) + 15^\beta \ln(15)\right).$$

These equations can now be solved to obtain the values of $\hat{\lambda}$ and $\hat{\beta}$.

We now turn to the issue of experiments that are concluded before they are truly complete. For instance, suppose we are conducting experiments to obtain processor lifetime data. We may have a certain time limit to our experiment: at that point, we terminate data collection even if not all the processors under test have failed yet. When using such experiments to estimate parameter values, we have to take into account the premature termination of the experiment. We do this by multiplying the joint density of the completed observations by the probability that the nonfailed units have lifetimes exceeding the experimental time limit.

Example: We carry out experiments to estimate the lifetime of a processor. We believe that the processor lifetime (measured in hours) follows an exponential distribution, with parameter μ whose value we are seeking to estimate. The density function for the processor lifetime is

$$f(x) = \mu e^{-\mu x},$$

and the cumulative probability distribution function is

$$F(x) = 1 - e^{-\mu x}.$$

We start with a total of 10 processors and impose a time limit of 1000 hours on our experiment, that is, our experiment will end when 1000 hours have elapsed, or all the processors have failed (whichever occurs sooner).

Suppose our observations are that four failures occurred before the experiment is terminated, at times $700, 800, 900, 950$ hours, respectively. The remaining six processors have lifetimes exceeding 1000 hours.

The likelihood function for the whole sample is given by

$$\begin{aligned} L(\mu) &= f(700)f(800)f(900)f(950)\,(1 - F(1000))^6 \\ &= \mu^4 e^{-\mu(700+800+900+950)} e^{-6000\mu} \\ &= \mu^4 e^{-9350\mu}. \end{aligned}$$

We find $\hat{\mu}$, which maximizes the likelihood function by getting the derivative of L and equating it to zero:

$$\frac{dL(\mu)}{d\mu} = \left(4\mu^3 - 9350\mu^4\right) e^{-9350\mu} = 0,$$

which results in $\mu = 0$, 4.3×10^{-4}.
The maximum likelihood estimate is therefore $\hat{\mu} = 4.3 \times 10^{-4}$.

If we terminate the experiment prematurely, we lose information and the quality of the estimate is likely to suffer. This is shown in the following example:

Example: Consider again the previous example, except that we decide to set the time limit of our experiment at some relatively small T, say $T = 500$ hours. Based on the measurements in the previous example, no failures will have occurred over this interval. Applying the maximum likelihood method, we seek the value of μ, which maximizes

$$L(\mu) = (1 - F(T))^{10} = \left(e^{-\mu T}\right)^{10} = e^{-10\mu T}.$$

The maximum likelihood estimate resulting from our experiment is $\hat{\mu} = 0$, which translates to a prediction that the processor lifetimes are infinite. This result is, of course, ludicrous; however, it is the best that we can extract from the maximum likelihood approach and the observation that no failures have occurred.

The maximum likelihood approach can also be used when the data are not observed exactly, but are only known to lie in some interval. Once again, this is probably best explained through an example.

Example: Similarly to the previous examples, we have 10 processors whose lifetime of X days is exponentially distributed with an unknown parameter μ. The units operate in some remote location, and we can only check on their status at 11 AM every day. We observe the first failure on the 50th day, the second on the 120th day, and the third on the 200th day, at which point the experiment concludes.
When we observe a failure at 11 AM on day i, it means that the lifetime of the processor was greater than $i - 1$ days, but less than i days. The probability of such a failure is therefore equal to

$$q_i = F(i) - F(i-1) = e^{-(i-1)\mu} - e^{-i\mu}.$$

The likelihood function associated with our observations is then given by

$$L(\mu) = q_{50} q_{120} q_{200} \left(e^{-200\mu}\right)^7.$$

We can now find the value of μ, which maximizes this likelihood function.

The greater these sampling intervals, the worse is likely to be our estimate. Indeed, if the time-intervals are too coarse, the maximal likelihood method will make ridiculous predictions. Consider the following modification to our previous example:

Example: Consider a situation in which the processors are checked every T days, for some large T (say $T = 300$). Suppose we find, on the very first check, that all 10 processors have failed: this means that all 10 have had lifetimes less than T days.

The likelihood function associated with this observation is

$$L(\mu) = (F(T))^{10} = \left(1 - e^{-\mu T}\right)^{10}.$$

The value of μ that maximizes this function is $\hat{\mu} = \infty$; our estimate is thus that the average processor lifetime is zero! What this means is that T was set so high that we were not able to obtain much information from checking after T days.

9.2.4 THE BAYESIAN APPROACH TO PARAMETER ESTIMATION

The Bayesian approach relies on Bayes's formula for reversing conditional probability, and it works as follows: We start with some *prior* knowledge of the parameter we are estimating, expressed through a probability or density function of the parameter values. We then collect experimental or observational data of the random variable, and construct a *posterior* probability or density of the parameter, based on both our prior knowledge and the observations. The parameter estimate is the expected value of this posterior probability.

Example: We believe that a processor fails according to a Poisson process with rate λ, which is the parameter we wish to estimate. Suppose we know that λ is somewhere in the range $[10^{-4}, 2 \times 10^{-4}]$ per second, and we express this knowledge by considering λ to be a random variable uniformly distributed over that range. Thus

$$f_{prior}(\lambda) = \begin{cases} 10^4 & \text{if } \lambda \in [10^{-4}, 2 \times 10^{-4}] \\ 0 & \text{otherwise.} \end{cases}$$

The current estimate for λ is its expected value, $\hat{\lambda} = 1.5 \times 10^{-4}$/second.

Suppose now that we run the processor for τ hours without observing a failure. The posterior density of λ, which incorporates the information gleaned from this experiment is as follows:

$$
\begin{aligned}
f_{posterior}(\lambda) &= f_{prior}(\lambda \mid \text{lifetime} \geq \tau) \\
&= \frac{\text{Prob}\{\text{Lifetime} \geq \tau \mid \text{Failure rate} = \lambda\} f_{prior}(\lambda)}{\int_{\ell=10^{-4}}^{2 \cdot 10^{-4}} \text{Prob}\{\text{Lifetime} \geq \tau \mid \text{Failure rate} = \ell\} f_{prior}(\ell) d\ell} \\
&= \frac{e^{-\lambda\tau} f_{prior}(\lambda)}{\int_{\ell=10^{-4}}^{2 \cdot 10^{-4}} e^{-\ell\tau} f_{prior}(\ell) d\ell} \\
&= \begin{cases} \dfrac{10^4 e^{-\lambda\tau}}{10^4 \int_{\ell=10^{-4}}^{2 \cdot 10^{-4}} e^{-\ell\tau} d\ell} & \text{if } \lambda \in [10^{-4}, 2 \times 10^{-4}] \\ 0 & \text{otherwise} \end{cases} \\
&= \begin{cases} \dfrac{\tau e^{-\lambda\tau}}{e^{-0.0001\tau} - e^{-0.0002\tau}} & \text{if } \lambda \in [10^{-4}, 2 \times 10^{-4}] \\ 0 & \text{otherwise.} \end{cases}
\end{aligned}
$$

The estimate of λ is now given by the expected value of this new density:

$$\hat{\lambda} = \int_{\lambda=10^{-4}}^{2\cdot10^{-4}} \lambda\, f_{posterior}(\lambda)\, d\lambda = \frac{(1+0.0001\tau)e^{-0.0001\tau} - (1+0.0002\tau)e^{-0.0002\tau}}{\tau\left(e^{-0.0001\tau} - e^{-0.0002\tau}\right)}.$$

Fig. 9.2 plots the estimate of λ based on observed values of τ. Note that as τ increases, λ tends to the lower bound of the $[0.0001, 0.0002]$ interval; it can never go outside this interval, however.

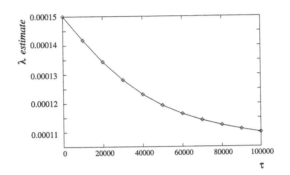

FIGURE 9.2

Estimate of λ based on observed τ.

The Bayesian approach is controversial, because it depends on the existence of prior information about the parameter being estimated. In some cases, this information may not be difficult to derive. For instance, if we are asked to evaluate an unknown coin, we can assume that the probability of getting a "head" is uniformly distributed over the entire possible range of $[0, 1]$. In other cases, it may not be possible to do so with any confidence.

   Note also that if the prior density is zero over any given parameter interval, it will remain zero for that interval, no matter what the experimental results are. In our earlier example, we started with a prior density that was nonzero only over the interval $[0.0001, 0.0002]$ per second. Since the posterior densities are constructed by multiplying this prior density by some additional terms, all posterior densities will also be nonzero over this interval only. When the prior density is zero over some interval I, it means that we already *know* that the parameter cannot fall in that interval. Since this knowledge is assumed to be correct, no amount of posterior information can result in the probability of falling in I being anything, but zero.

9.2.5 CONFIDENCE INTERVALS

Definition: A *confidence interval* with *confidence level* $1 - \alpha$ for a parameter θ is an interval $[a, b]$ calculated as a function of a sample of size n, $X_1, ..., X_n$, in such a way that if we calculate similar intervals based on a large number of samples of size n, a fraction $1 - \alpha$ out of these intervals will actually include the real parameter θ.

$1 - \alpha$ is usually selected to be 0.95 or 0.99, also expressed as 95% or 99%.

The most common use of confidence intervals in engineering applications is that of calculating a confidence interval for the expectation μ of some random variable, and this is discussed next. Our treatment rests on a fundamental result of probability theory: the central limit theorem. We state it here without proof.

Central limit theorem: *Suppose $X_1, X_2, \cdots, X_n$ are independent and identically distributed random variables with mean μ and standard deviation σ. Consider the average of these variables, $\overline{X} = \frac{X_1 + X_2 + \cdots X_n}{n}$. In the limit, as $n \to \infty$, $\overline{X}$ follows the normal distribution, with mean μ and standard deviation $\sigma/\sqrt{n}$: this means that for a large n,*

$$F_{\overline{X}}(x) = \text{Prob}\{\overline{X} \leq x\} \approx \frac{1}{\sqrt{2\pi}\sigma/\sqrt{n}} \int_{-\infty}^{x} e^{-\frac{1}{2}\left(\frac{y-\mu}{\sigma/\sqrt{n}}\right)^2} dy.$$

Stated slightly differently, for a large sample size n,

$$\text{Prob}\left\{\frac{\overline{X} - \mu}{\sigma/\sqrt{n}} \leq z\right\} \approx \Phi(z), \tag{9.3}$$

where

$$\Phi(z) = \frac{1}{\sqrt{2\pi}} \int_{-\infty}^{z} e^{-y^2/2} dy$$

is the probability distribution function of a standard normal random variable (with mean 0 and standard deviation 1). We should stress that this is an approximate result; it is exact only in the limit as $n \to \infty$.

Let us now define Z_p to be the number for which $\Phi(Z_p) = p$. Then, we have from Expression (9.3) that, in the limit as $n \to \infty$,

$$\text{Prob}\left\{\frac{\overline{X} - \mu}{\sigma/\sqrt{n}} \leq Z_{1-\frac{\alpha}{2}}\right\} = 1 - \frac{\alpha}{2},$$

and

$$\text{Prob}\left\{\frac{\overline{X} - \mu}{\sigma/\sqrt{n}} > Z_{1-\frac{\alpha}{2}}\right\} = 1 - \left(1 - \frac{\alpha}{2}\right) = \frac{\alpha}{2}.$$

Since $\Phi(z)$ is symmetric about $z = 0$,

$$\text{Prob}\left\{\frac{\overline{X} - \mu}{\sigma/\sqrt{n}} \leq -Z_{1-\frac{\alpha}{2}}\right\} = \frac{\alpha}{2},$$

and therefore

$$\text{Prob}\left\{-Z_{1-\frac{\alpha}{2}} \leq \frac{\overline{X} - \mu}{\sigma/\sqrt{n}} \leq Z_{1-\frac{\alpha}{2}}\right\} = 1 - \alpha,$$

or stated differently,

$$\text{Prob}\left\{\overline{X} - Z_{1-\frac{\alpha}{2}}\frac{\sigma}{\sqrt{n}} \leq \mu \leq \overline{X} + Z_{1-\frac{\alpha}{2}}\frac{\sigma}{\sqrt{n}}\right\} = 1 - \alpha. \tag{9.4}$$

The interval

$$[a, b] = \left[\overline{X} - Z_{1-\frac{\alpha}{2}}\frac{\sigma}{\sqrt{n}}, \overline{X} + Z_{1-\frac{\alpha}{2}}\frac{\sigma}{\sqrt{n}}\right] \tag{9.5}$$

is called a $1 - \alpha$ confidence interval. $1 - \alpha$ is called the *confidence level* of the interval. So long as the experiment has not yet been conducted and $\overline{X}$ remains a random variable, there is a probability of $1 - \alpha$ that the true mean μ will be included in the interval. Once we have calculated $\overline{X}$ (based on simulation or experimentation), it is no longer a random variable; it is a fixed number. Since μ is also a fixed number, it will either be inside this interval or outside it. The level of confidence $1 - \alpha$ is therefore not the probability that the true mean lies within the calculated interval; it is rather the confidence we have in the method of calculation that was used to generate the interval – it is successful in $1 - \alpha$ of the cases. This is a subtle technical point, which does not affect how we use confidence intervals.

Example: Suppose we wish to estimate the mean lifetime (in months) μ of a device, by constructing for it a 95% confidence interval. In a sample of $n = 50$ such devices, we obtained an average lifetime of $\overline{X} = 37$ months, with a standard deviation of $\sigma = 5$ months. Looking up a table of the standard normal distribution, we find that $Z_{0.975} = 1.96$. Hence, the 95% confidence interval for μ is

$$[a, b] = \left[37 - 1.96 \cdot \frac{5}{\sqrt{50}}, 37 + 1.96 \cdot \frac{5}{\sqrt{50}}\right] = [35.61, 38.39].$$

We now say to a confidence of 95% that the expected lifetime of a device of the type analyzed is between 35.6 months and 38.4 months.

Example: Suppose the confidence interval obtained in the previous example is too wide for our requirements; we need a 95% interval that is not wider than 1 month. Since we have no control over σ and $Z_{1-\frac{\alpha}{2}}$, the only way to make the interval narrower is by increasing the sample size n. We require that

$$2 \times Z_{1-\frac{\alpha}{2}}\sigma/\sqrt{n} \leq 1,$$

or

$$2 \times 1.96 \times 5/\sqrt{n} \leq 1,$$

which results in

$$n \geq (2 \times 1.96 \times 5)^2 = 384.16.$$

We therefore need a sample of at least 385 devices to obtain the required accuracy in estimating μ.

Example: A given system either fails during the day, or it does not. We want to estimate the probability p that it does fail, using a 99% confidence interval. To estimate p based on n experiments or simulation runs (where each experiment represents one day), we define

$$X_i = \begin{cases} 1 & \text{if the system fails in experiment } i \\ 0 & \text{otherwise.} \end{cases}$$

Since $E(X) = p$, our estimate of p is

$$\hat{p} = \overline{X} = \frac{\sum_{i=1}^{n} X_i}{n};$$

$\hat{p}$ is actually the fraction of days on which the system failed. To get a confidence interval for p, note that $Var(X) = p(1-p)$, and $\sigma(X) = \sqrt{p(1-p)}$. Relying once more on the central limit theorem, and using $\hat{p}$ instead of the unknown p, we obtain the approximate confidence interval for p at confidence level $1 - \alpha$:

$$[a, b] = \left[\hat{p} - Z_{1-\frac{\alpha}{2}} \sqrt{\frac{\hat{p}(1-\hat{p})}{n}} \ , \ \hat{p} + Z_{1-\frac{\alpha}{2}} \sqrt{\frac{\hat{p}(1-\hat{p})}{n}} \right].$$

Suppose we conducted $n = 200$ experiments, out of which the system failed in 12 cases, resulting in $\hat{p} = 0.06$. From tables of the normal distribution, we can determine that $Z_{0.995} = 2.57$. Our 99% confidence interval is therefore

$$\left[0.06 - 2.57\sqrt{\frac{0.06 \times 0.94}{200}} \ , \ 0.06 + 2.57\sqrt{\frac{0.06 \times 0.94}{200}} \right] = [0.017 \ , \ 0.103].$$

We can say with a confidence of 99% that the failure probability is somewhere between 0.017 and 0.103.

The last interval has a width of 0.086 and is clearly not informative enough for most applications. To get a more accurate result we need to increase n. Say, for example, that we require the width of the confidence interval to be no larger than 0.002 (which implies that the estimate will be at a remove of at most 0.001 from the real failure probability, with a confidence of 99%). What should the number of experiments (or simulation runs) be? Based on our "pilot study," we have $\hat{p} = 0.06$, and therefore n must satisfy

$$2 \times 2.57 \frac{\sqrt{0.06 \times 0.94}}{\sqrt{n}} \leq 0.002,$$

which results in

$$n \geq \frac{4 \times 2.57^2 \times 0.06 \times 0.94}{0.002^2} = 3.7 \times 10^5.$$

In most instances, it will be impractical to conduct so many experiments.

The last example has highlighted a major problem in high-reliability systems: in most cases, we will need a substantial amount of data to validate statistically the high reliability of the system. Suppose we are trying to validate by experiment that the true failure probability p of a life-critical system is 10^{-8}. For such a low failure probability to be validated, we need a very high level of confidence indeed, say 99.999999% (or even higher), requiring a truly astronomical volume of data. We explore this matter further in the Exercises.

9.3 VARIANCE REDUCTION METHODS

As is evident from Eq. (9.5), the width of a confidence interval is inversely proportional to $\sqrt{n}$, where n is the number of simulation runs or experiments, and proportional to the standard deviation of the random variable under study. The brute-force way to shrink the confidence interval of an estimate is obviously to increase n. However, in the interest of efficiency, we should also consider the option of somehow reducing the variance (and, consequently, the standard deviation) of the estimate. In this section, we consider several schemes for doing so.

The first two approaches rely on the following facts from elementary statistics:

$$
\begin{aligned}
E(X+Y) &= E(X)+E(Y), \\
\text{and} \quad Var(X+Y) &= Var(X)+Var(Y)+2Cov(X,Y), \\
\text{where} \quad Cov(X,Y) &= E\{[X-E(X)][Y-E(Y)]\} \text{ is called the covariance of X and Y.}
\end{aligned}
$$

9.3.1 ANTITHETIC VARIABLES

Suppose we run simulations to estimate some parameter (for example, mean time to data Loss (MTTDL) in a RAID system). In traditional simulation, we would run n independent simulations and use the results. If Z_1, Z_2 are the outputs from two independent runs, we can expect that

$$
Cov(Z_1, Z_2) = 0
$$

so that

$$
Var\left(\frac{Z_1+Z_2}{2}\right) = \frac{Var(Z_1)+Var(Z_2)}{4}.
$$

When the method of antithetic variables is used, we try to run simulations in pairs, coupled together in such a way that their results (any parameter that is estimated by the simulation, be it reliability, waiting time, etc.) are negatively correlated, and then treat $Y = (Z_1 + Z_2)/2$ as the output from this pair of runs. If the simulation pair produces the outputs Z_1, Z_2 such that $Cov(Z_1, Z_2) < 0$, the variance of Y will be *smaller* than it would be if the two runs were independent, and not coupled.

A good way to couple pairs of simulation runs is to couple the random variables used by them. Suppose the output of the simulation is a monotonic function of the random variables, and the first run of the pair uses uniform random variables $U_1, U_2, \cdots, U_n$, then the second run can use $1-U_1, 1-U_2, \cdots, 1-U_n$. The corresponding random variables in the two sequences are negatively correlated: if U_i is large, $1-U_i$ is small, and vice versa. This applies even when the distributions of the random variables used in the simulation are not uniform. We are assuming that to generate such random variables, we will ultimately need to call uniform random number generators (URNGs), described later in Section 9.5.1. We can apply the coupling on the output of these URNGs. For example, if we need to generate exponentially distributed random variables by using $X = -(1/\mu)\ln U$, the coupled simulations will generate U, and then use $X_1 = -(1/\mu)\ln U$ and $X_2 = -(1/\mu)\ln(1-U)$, respectively (see Section 9.5.3).

In other words, if we can write the simulation output as being a monotone function of the uniform random variables used, then it is possible to show that the simulation outputs will indeed be negatively correlated when the method of antithetic variables is used. Showing this is outside the scope of this book, see the Further reading section for details on where to find the proof.

Example: Consider a structure composed of k elements. Denote by S_i the state of component i: a functional component is denoted by $S_i = 1$, whereas if it is down we have $S_i = 0$. A *structure function* $\phi(S_1, S_2, \ldots, S_k)$ is an indicator function (assumes the values $0, 1$), which expresses the dependence of the functionality of the system on the functionality of its components: it is equal to 1 if the system is functional for given values of $S_1, \ldots, S_k$, and to 0 if it is not.
For instance, if the system consists of k elements connected in series, we have

$$\phi(S_1, S_2, \cdots, S_k) = S_1 \times S_2 \times \cdots \times S_k.$$

If it is a triplex system with a perfect voter, and S_i denotes the state of the ith processor, then

$$\phi(S_1, S_2, S_3) = \begin{cases} 1 & \text{if } S_1 + S_2 + S_3 \geq 2 \\ 0 & \text{otherwise.} \end{cases}$$

Now suppose we want to simulate the reliability R, for some given length of time t, of a system with a very complex structure function that cannot easily be analyzed. Using traditional methods, we would run a simulation by generating random variables that would determine whether individual components were up or not, and then determine whether the overall system was functional during $[0, t]$. Using antithetic variables, we will run the simulations in pairs, with the random variables coupled, as described above. If Y_i is the average of the values of the structure function from the two simulation runs in pair i, and we run a total of $2n$ simulations (or n pairs), then the estimated reliability of the system is

$$\hat{R} = \frac{Y_1 + Y_2 + \cdots + Y_n}{n}.$$

Furthermore, the variance of the estimate is likely to be far lower than would be obtained if we ran $2n$ independent simulations.
It is important to note that the Y_is are independent of one another, that is, although each run consists of paired simulations, there is no coupling between one pair and another. This allows us to use traditional statistical analysis on the Y_i values.

By how much can we expect the variance of the estimate to drop? This depends on the covariance of the two outputs in each pair of runs. In the Exercises, you are invited to determine the usefulness of this approach in a variety of cases.

9.3.2 USING CONTROL VARIABLES

When simulating to estimate the mean value $E(X)$ of a random variable X, select some other random variable Y whose expectation is known or can be calculated precisely to be θ_Y. Consider the random variable

$$Z = X + k(Y - \theta_Y).$$

Z has the properties

$$
\begin{aligned}
E(Z) &= E(X), \\
Var(Z) &= Var(X) + k^2 Var(Y) + 2k Cov(X, Y).
\end{aligned}
$$

Hence, if we can pick k suitably, we can exploit any correlation between X and Y to reduce the variance of the estimate of $E(Z)$ (which is equal to $E(X)$), and then use simulation to estimate $E(Z)$, rather than $E(X)$. Because $Var(Z) \le Var(X)$, this will result in a narrower confidence interval. Y is called the *control variable* or *control variate*.

It is easy to show that $Var(Z)$ is minimized when

$$k = -\frac{Cov(X, Y)}{Var(Y)}.$$

For this value of k,

$$Var(Z) = Var(X) - \frac{(Cov(X, Y))^2}{Var(Y)}.$$

If $Cov(X, Y)$ and $Var(Y)$ are not known in advance, we can estimate them by running n simulations (for some initial small n), generating X_i, Y_i for $i = 1, ..., n$ and using the following estimates:

$$\widehat{Cov}(X, Y) = \frac{\sum_{i=1}^{n} (X_i - \overline{X})(Y_i - \overline{Y})}{n - 1},$$

and

$$\widehat{Var}(Y) = \frac{\sum_{i=1}^{n} (Y_i - \overline{Y})^2}{n - 1},$$

where $\overline{X} = \frac{\sum_{i=1}^{n} X_i}{n}$ and $\overline{Y} = \frac{\sum_{i=1}^{n} Y_i}{n}$.

Example: We are interested in estimating the reliability (at time t) of a complex system that uses processor redundancy without repair. To help reduce variance, we can use as a control variable the number of processors that are up at that time.

9.3.3 STRATIFIED SAMPLING

Another approach to reducing variance is through the method of stratified sampling. This approach is probably best introduced through an example.

Example: A computer system runs daily from 9 AM to 5 PM and is available for repair only after 5 PM. We wish to simulate the system and estimate the probability π that the system survives through a randomly selected day. Because the failure rates of the processors are different on weekdays and on weekends due to different utilizations, the system has two different survival probabilities: π_1 on a weekday, and π_2 on a weekend day.

The conventional way to do a simulation experiment is the following: For each run, first select the day at random (weekday with probability $p_1 = 5/7$, weekend with probability $p_2 = 2/7$), apply the appropriate failure rate for that type of day, and then simulate for the behavior of the system over that day. If it fails during run i, set $X_i = 0$; if it survives, set $X_i = 1$. Make n runs for a sufficiently large n, and then estimate the survival probability as $\hat{\pi} = (X_1 + X_2 + \cdots + X_n)/n$.

A better approach, which uses the method of stratified sampling, is to carry out two sets of runs. Set 1 consists of n_1 runs in which the system is simulated under weekday conditions (with the failure rates set appropriately), and set 2 consists of n_2 runs (where $n_1 + n_2 = n$) with the failure rates set according to weekend conditions. Then, if the survival probability estimated from set i is $\hat{\pi}_i$ ($i = 1, 2$), the overall survival probability is estimated as

$$\hat{\pi} = (5/7)\hat{\pi}_1 + (2/7)\hat{\pi}_2.$$

Denoting

$$V_1 = \mathrm{Var}(X|\text{Weekday}) = \pi_1(1 - \pi_1),$$

and

$$V_2 = \mathrm{Var}(X|\text{Weekend}) = \pi_2(1 - \pi_2),$$

we obtain

$$\mathrm{Var}(\hat{\pi}) = \frac{(5/7)^2 V_1}{n_1} + \frac{(2/7)^2 V_2}{n_2}.$$

We claim that this second approach can be expected to yield estimates with a smaller variance if n_1 and n_2 are chosen appropriately. There are two ways of choosing n_1 and n_2:

- The most straightforward way is to set $n_i = np_i$.
- A better approach is to use a pilot simulation to obtain a rough estimate of V_1 and V_2, and select n_i to minimize the variance of the estimate under the constraint $n_1 + n_2 = n$.

In general, suppose we are running a simulation to estimate the mean value $E(X)$ of some random variable X, and that this mean value depends on some parameter, $Q \in \{q_1, q_2, \cdots, q_\ell\}$. Suppose we can accurately calculate $p_i = \mathrm{Prob}\{Q = q_i\}, i = 1, 2, \cdots, \ell$.

Using the stratified sampling approach, we first run n_i simulations to estimate $E(X)$ conditioned on the event $\{Q = q_i\}$, for every $i = 1, \cdots, \ell$. Then, we estimate $E(X)$ by unconditioning on each of these events, using the total expectation formula, that is,

$$E(X) = E[E(X|Q)] = E(X|Q = q_1)p_1 + E(X|Q = q_2)p_2 + \cdots + E(X|Q = q_\ell)p_\ell.$$

The effectiveness of the stratified sampling approach is based on the identity that you are invited to prove in the Exercises:

$$Var(X) = E_Q[Var(X|Q)] + Var_Q[E(X|Q)].$$

Here, the subscript Q refers to the fact that the expectation and variance are being computed based on the probability distribution of Q.

The actual amount of variance reduction will depend on the extent of the correlation between X and Q. In effect, we are using our knowledge of $Prob\{Q = q_i\}$ to reduce the variance, since Q itself does not need to be simulated any more, and the variability introduced by simulating it is eliminated.

9.3.4 IMPORTANCE SAMPLING

In the importance sampling approach to simulation, we simulate a modified system in which the chance of failure has been artificially boosted, and then correct for that boost. A detailed development of the theory is beyond the scope of this book: we have limited ourselves to providing just an introduction to it. There are three reasons for this:

- Importance sampling is a temperamental technique. If not carefully used, it can end up actually *increasing* the variance of the simulation.
- It is not yet a mature technique. It is, rather, the focus of much current research.
- It (as well as the splitting technique which follows it) is more mathematically complicated than anything else encountered in this book.

The importance sampling approach is based on the following reasoning. Suppose we want to estimate by simulation some parameter $\theta = E[\phi(X)]$, where $\phi(\cdot)$ is some function, and X is a random variable with probability density function $f(x)$.

Assume that $g(x)$ is a probability density function with the property that $g(x) > 0$ for all x, for which $f(x) > 0$. Then,

$$
\begin{aligned}
E[\phi(X)] &= \int \phi(x)f(x)\,dx \\
&= \int \frac{\phi(x)f(x)}{g(x)} g(x)\,dx \\
&= \int \psi(x)g(x)\,dx,
\end{aligned}
\tag{9.6}
$$

where $\psi(x) = \frac{\phi(x)f(x)}{g(x)}$. Now, $\int \psi(x)g(x)\,dx$ is equal to $E[\psi(Y)]$, where Y is a random variable with probability density function $g(\cdot)$. This suggests that we estimate $E[\psi(Y)]$, rather than $E[\phi(X)]$ (although both are equal to θ).

More precisely, the standard approach to estimating $\theta = E(\phi(X))$ would be to obtain a sample of X, namely, $X_1, X_2, \cdots, X_n$, and estimate θ as

$$\hat{\theta} = \overline{\phi(X)} = \frac{1}{n}\sum_{i=1}^{n} \phi(X_i).$$

The importance sampling approach is to obtain a sample of Y (with density function $g(y)$), denoted by $Y_1, Y_2, \cdots, Y_n$, and then estimate θ as

$$\hat{\theta} = \overline{\psi(Y)} = \frac{1}{n} \sum_{i=1}^{n} \psi(Y_i).$$

For this method to be beneficial, it is necessary that

$$\text{Var}(\psi(Y)) < \text{Var}(\phi(X)).$$

This will happen if we select some $g(x)$ with the property that $f(x)/g(x)$ is small whenever $\phi(x)$ is large, and vice versa. The choice of $g(x)$ is crucial to the reduction of variance: an incorrect choice can render the method of importance sampling counterproductive by actually increasing the variance.

> **Example:** Consider two random variables A and B, each exponentially distributed with parameter μ, that is, their density functions are each of the form $f(x) = \mu e^{-\mu x}$, for $x \geq 0$. Then, suppose we want to use simulation to estimate the parameter $\theta = \text{Prob}\{A + B > 100\}$. Assume that $\mu \gg 1/50$, so that it is unlikely that $A + B > 100$ (and θ is therefore very small).
>
> We could obviously solve this problem analytically, without any need for simulation. However, let us use it as a vehicle to explain how the principles of importance sampling could be used here.
>
> Using the conventional approach, we would generate two samples of size n for A and B: $a_1, a_2, \cdots, a_n$ and $b_1, b_2, \cdots, b_n$, respectively. Define
>
> $$\phi(a_i, b_i) = \begin{cases} 1 & \text{if } a_i + b_i > 100 \\ 0 & \text{otherwise.} \end{cases}$$
>
> Because $\theta = E(\phi(A, B))$, we can estimate
>
> $$\hat{\theta} = \frac{1}{n} \sum_{i=1}^{n} \phi(a_i, b_i).$$
>
> As we saw in Section 9.2.5, we will need a very large number of observations to accurately estimate a very small value of θ. In the importance sampling approach, we change the density function so that larger values of A and B are more likely. In particular, let us use the density function $g(x) = \gamma e^{-\gamma x}$ for some $\gamma \ll \mu$. Using this density function, we generate values of A and B denoted by $a_1', a_2', \cdots, a_n'$ and $b_1', b_2', \cdots, b_n'$. We then use the estimate
>
> $$\hat{\theta} = \frac{1}{n} \sum_{i=1}^{n} \phi(a_i', b_i') \frac{f(a_i')}{g(a_i')} \frac{f(b_i')}{g(b_i')} = \frac{1}{n} \sum_{i=1}^{n} \phi(a_i', b_i') \left(\frac{\mu}{\gamma}\right)^2 e^{-(\mu-\gamma)(a_i'+b_i')}.$$
>
> It now remains for us to obtain a suitable value of γ to reduce the variance of the estimate. Denoting the ith term of the above sum by S_i, we note that if $a_i' + b_i' \leq 100$, $S_i = 0$. Also, if $a_i' + b_i' > 100$, then
>
> $$S_i = \left(\frac{\mu}{\gamma}\right)^2 e^{-(\mu-\gamma)(a_i'+b_i')} \leq \left(\frac{\mu}{\gamma}\right)^2 e^{-100(\mu-\gamma)}.$$

Selecting γ to minimize

$$\left(\frac{\mu}{\gamma}\right)^2 e^{-100(\mu-\gamma)}$$

will minimize the maximum possible value of S_i, and thereby reduce the variance of S_i. Simple calculus shows that $\gamma = 0.02$ minimizes the above quantity.

Thus the importance sampling approach to this problem is as follows:

- Generate a_i', b_i' according to the density function $g(x) = 0.02e^{-0.02x}$, for $i = 1, 2, \cdots, n$.
- Define $\phi(a_i', b_i') = 1$ if $a_i' + b_i' > 100$ and 0 otherwise.
- Estimate θ by

$$\hat{\theta} = \frac{1}{n} \sum_{i=1}^{n} \phi(a_i' + b_i') \left(\frac{\mu}{0.02}\right)^2 e^{-(\mu-0.02)(a_i'+b_i')}.$$

Simulating continuous-time Markov chains: mean time between system failures

Suppose the system we are analyzing can be described by a Markov chain (see Chapter 2) with continuous time t, also called a CTMC (continuous-time Markov chain). Let λ_{ij} be the rate of transition from state i to state j, then, $\lambda_i = \sum_{j \neq i} \lambda_{ij}$ is the total rate of departure from state i. The sojourn time of the system in each state (the time it stays in a state before leaving it) is exponentially distributed with parameter λ_i for state i.

Now, suppose that all the transitions in the chain are either *component failure* or *repair* transitions. A subset of the states, these in which the system is considered to have failed, are called *system-failure* states.

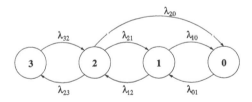

FIGURE 9.3

A continuous time Markov chain.

Example: Consider a system of three processors that can fail and be repaired, and suppose the system behaves according to the Markov chain depicted in Fig. 9.3. The state is the number of processors that are functional. Suppose the only failure transitions in this system are $3 \rightarrow 2$, $2 \rightarrow 1$, $2 \rightarrow 0$, and $1 \rightarrow 0$. The repair transitions are $2 \rightarrow 3$, $1 \rightarrow 2$, and $0 \rightarrow 1$. The rates of transition are as shown on the arrow labels. From this, we can write

$$\lambda_3 = \lambda_{32},$$
$$\lambda_2 = \lambda_{21} + \lambda_{20} + \lambda_{23},$$

$$
\begin{aligned}
\lambda_1 &= \lambda_{10} + \lambda_{12}, \\
\lambda_0 &= \lambda_{01}.
\end{aligned}
$$

Suppose the system is operational as long as at least one processor is operational, then the set of system-failure states is $\{0\}$.

Going back to the general failure-repair Markov chain, we are interested in finding the mean time between system failures (MTBF). Because repair time is usually much shorter than time between component failures, the chain makes a large number of transitions before it enters one of the system-failure states, and thus the simulation will have to run for a very long time to measure the time until the system fails. We can use importance sampling to speed up the simulation as follows:

Let us define state N as the initial state with all components functional, and let $t = 0$ be the time at which the simulation starts. By definition, there are no repair transitions out of state N; there can only be failure transitions. Let F be the set of system-failure states. Since we are considering systems with repair, there will be one or more repair transitions out of all states with any failed components. Ultimately, the system will return to state N. Let this time of return be τ_R, the *system regeneration* time. (At this point, the system is as good as new). Let τ_F be the time until the system first enters a system failure state. Then, you are invited in the Exercises to show that

$$
E[\tau_F] = \frac{E[\min(\tau_R, \tau_F)]}{\text{Prob}\{\tau_F < \tau_R\}}. \tag{9.7}
$$

In most systems, where repair rates are much greater than failure rates, we can expect that $E[\min(\tau_R, \tau_F)]$ will be only slightly smaller than $E(\tau_R)$, since the system can be expected to return to state N many times before it enters a system-failure state. We can expect the system to return to state N fairly quickly. So, traditional simulation can be used to estimate $E[\min(\tau_R, \tau_F)]$: just calculate the average length of time it takes the system to return from state N to state N.

Estimating $\theta = \text{Prob}\{\tau_F < \tau_R\}$, on the other hand, should be done using importance sampling, because $\tau_F < \tau_R$ is the rare event in which the system fails before returning to state N. Notice that we no longer need to keep track in our simulations of the time it takes to make the transitions, or of how long τ_F or τ_R may be; all we need to record is the number of times that $\tau_F < \tau_R$. This means that we do not need to change the sojourn time of the system in any of its states, just the transition probabilities.

The technique we will follow to implement importance sampling is called *balanced failure biasing*. Before presenting it, we have to introduce some notation. Each transition out of any state represents either a failure or a repair event. In state N, since everything is functional, there can only be failure events. Conversely, in a state in which everything is down, there can only be repair events. Let $n_F(i)$ be the number of failure transitions (the number of outgoing transitions in the Markov chain denoting component failure events) out of state i.

Since we are not interested in finding out the amount of time the system spends in each state, we need only simulate a discrete-time Markov chain (DTMC) embedded into the continuous-time chain. This is a DTMC that studies just the progress of the system from one state to the next, without recording the sojourn time in each state.

Example: Suppose we have a CTMC that has the following events: It starts from state N, moves to state i_1 at time t_1, to state i_2 at time t_2, etc. The sample path for the corresponding embedded discrete-time Markov chain will be N, then i_1, then i_1, etc.

We now define a probability transition function p_{ij} for the DTMC, which is the probability that the system moves to state j given that it was in state i. It can be shown that

$$p_{ij} = \begin{cases} 0 & \text{if } i = j \\ \frac{\lambda_{ij}}{\sum_{k \neq i} \lambda_{ik}} & \text{if } i \neq j. \end{cases}$$

Intuitively, the probability that the system will transit from state i to state j is the rate of going from i to j as a fraction of the total rate of leaving state i.

Define by $p_R(i)$ the probability of making a repair transition out of state i. Now, pick some p^* (usually 0.2 to 0.4 works well), and define a new DTMC characterized by transition probabilities $\tilde{p}_{ij}$, defined as follows:

- *Case 1:* $i = N$

$$\tilde{p}_{ij} = \begin{cases} \frac{1}{n_F(i)} & \text{if } i \to j \text{ is a failure transition and } p_{ij} > 0 \\ 0 & \text{otherwise.} \end{cases}$$

- *Case 2:* i is neither N nor a system-failure state, and $p_R(i) > 0$,

$$\tilde{p}_{ij} = \begin{cases} \frac{p^*}{n_F(i)} & \text{if } i \to j \text{ is a failure transition and } p_{ij} > 0 \\ \frac{(1-p^*)p_{ij}}{p_R(i)} & \text{if } i \to j \text{ is a repair transition and } p_{ij} > 0 \\ 0 & \text{otherwise.} \end{cases}$$

- *Case 3:* i is not a system-failure state, but $p_R(i) = 0$,

$$\tilde{p}_{ij} = \begin{cases} \frac{1}{n_F(i)} & \text{if } p_{ij} > 0 \\ 0 & \text{otherwise.} \end{cases}$$

- *Case 4:* i is a system-failure state

$$\tilde{p}_{ij} = p_{ij}.$$

We have only modified transition probabilities out of states that are not system-failure states. For these, we have done the following:

- The total probability of making a failure transition is now p^*.
- This probability is equally divided among all the failure transitions.

We now perform n simulation runs of the modified system, recording for each the likelihood ratio of the sample path (where the sample path is the sequence of states that are visited). The likelihood ratio for simulation run k, L_k, is defined as

$$L_k = \frac{\text{Probability of the original DTMC having this sample path}}{\text{Probability of the modified DTMC having this sample path}}.$$

Let

$$I_k = \begin{cases} 1 & \text{if simulation run } k \text{ ends with system failure} \\ 0 & \text{if simulation run } k \text{ ends with the system back in state N.} \end{cases}$$

Then, we estimate the probability that $\tau_F < \tau_R$ as follows:

$$\hat{\theta} = \frac{\sum_{k=1}^{n} I_k L_k}{n}.$$

Let us now relate this to Eq. (9.6). The transition probabilities that we use to simulate the system (the $\tilde{p}_{ij}$ values) are a realization of $g(x)$. L_k is a realization of $f(x)/g(x)$. Finally, I_k is a realization of $\phi(x)$. Because failure is a discrete event, we replace the integral in Eq. (9.6) by a sum.

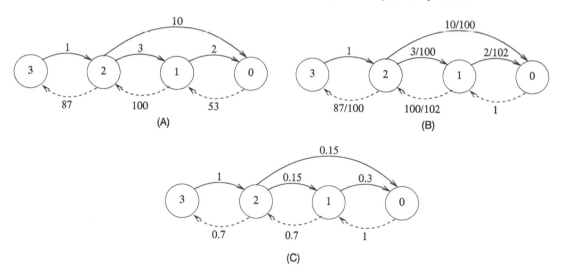

FIGURE 9.4

A continuous-time Markov chain and its embedded and modified discrete-time Markov chains. Solid lines indicate failure transitions; dashed lines indicate repair transitions. (A) Continuous-time Markov chain. (B) Embedded discrete-time Markov chain. (C) Modified discrete-time Markov chain.

Example: Consider the system shown in Fig. 9.4A: its embedded DTMC is shown in Fig. 9.4B. The labels for the CTMC arrows are the transition rates, and those for the embedded DTMC arrows the transition probabilities. By definition, the transition probabilities out of each state must add up

Table 9.1 Three sample paths and the associated likelihood ratios.

Run no.	Sample path	Likelihood ratio	$\tau_F < \tau_R$?
1	$3, 2, 3$	$L_1 = \frac{1 \times 0.87}{1 \times 0.7}$	No
2	$3, 2, 1, 2, 1, 0$	$L_2 = \frac{1 \times (3/100) \times (100/102) \times (3/100) \times (2/102)}{1 \times 0.7 \times 0.15 \times 0.7 \times 0.15 \times 0.7 \times 0.3}$	Yes
3	$3, 2, 1, 2, 3$	$L_3 = \frac{1 \times (3/100) \times (100/102) \times (87/100)}{1 \times 0.15 \times 0.7 \times 0.7}$	No

to 1. (In a general DTMC, it is permissible for a state to transit to itself; this will never happen here since each transition represents either a failure or a repair event). State 0 is the only system-failure state.

Now, suppose we select $p^* = 0.3$. Consider the transitions out of each state, one by one:

- State 3: There is only one transition out of this state, to state 2. We therefore have $\tilde{p}_{32} = 1$.
- State 2: There is one repair transition out of state 2, and $n_F(2) = 2$ failure transitions. Each of these failure transitions will have probability $p^*/2 = 0.15$ of happening; the single repair transition will happen with probability $1 - p^* = 0.7$.
- State 1: There is one repair transition and one failure transition out of this state: $n_F(1) = 1$, the failure transition will happen with probability $p^* = 0.3$, and the repair transition with probability $1 - p^* = 0.7$.
- State 0: This is a system-failure state: there is no change to the transition probabilities out of this state.

Fig. 9.4C depicts the modified DTMC. We will now simulate this chain, to estimate $\text{Prob}\{\tau_F < \tau_R\}$ under the new transition probabilities. Suppose we decide to make a total of three simulation runs, and average them to find an estimate for this probability. (In reality, one would carry out perhaps thousands or even millions of such simulation runs, but we are just illustrating the technique here.) We will simulate the system, starting from state 3. The simulation will end when the system enters either state 3 (in which case, we have $\tau_F > \tau_R$), or the system-failure state 0 (in which case, $\tau_F < \tau_R$). Table 9.1 shows possible results for these runs.

Consider the first of the three runs: The sequence of states is $3 \to 2 \to 3$. The probability of such a sequence of transitions taking place in the modified DTMC is $\tilde{p}_{32} \times \tilde{p}_{23} = 1 \times 0.7$; the corresponding probability for the original DTMC is $p_{32} \times p_{23} = 1 \times 0.87$. The likelihood ratio is therefore $\frac{1 \times 0.87}{1 \times 0.7}$. (Recall that this is the factor that corrects for our modification of the transition probabilities to get $\tilde{p}_{ij}$).

Similarly for the remaining runs:

Run 2 of the three simulation runs is the only one that has resulted in the event $\tau_F < \tau_R$. Therefore $I_1 = 0, I_2 = 1, I_3 = 0$, and our simulation estimate is

$$\hat{\theta} = \widehat{\text{Prob}}\{\tau_F < \tau_R\} = \frac{0 \times L_1 + 1 \times L_2 + 0 \times L_3}{3} = \frac{L_2}{3} = 0.0025.$$

Simulating continuous-time Markov chains: reliability

To find reliability by simulation, the conventional way is to run the system until it enters a system-failure state, and then find the total elapsed time to system failure. From these times we can obtain the probability distribution function of the time-to-first-failure whose complement is the reliability function.

Balanced failure biasing can be used for shortening the simulation time for this case as well. There is, however, an important difference between calculating the reliability function and estimating the MTBF that we showed in the previous section. For the latter, we were able to avoid the task of actually storing durations and just counted the number of times the system failed before getting back to state N. In our present case, we have to maintain time information in our simulation. Also, we would like to force at least one transition out of state N.

Doing the latter is quite simple. In a conventional simulation, we would use the density function $f(t) = \lambda_N e^{-\lambda_N t}$ for simulating the sojourn time of the system in state N. In the forcing technique, we use instead the density function

$$\tilde{f}(t) = \begin{cases} \dfrac{\lambda_N e^{-\lambda_N t}}{1 - e^{-\lambda_N T}} & \text{if } 0 \leq t \leq T \\ 0 & \text{otherwise} \end{cases}$$

for some predetermined T. This forces at least one transition out of N prior to time T.

The likelihood ratio associated with this choice is obviously $f(t)/\tilde{f}(t)$. In practice, we will combine forcing with balanced failure biasing, in which case the overall likelihood ratio will be the product of the likelihood ratios of the two.

It is important to note that the forcing technique should only be used if $1 - e^{-\lambda_N T}$ is a relatively small quantity, and transitions out of state N are rare over the interval $[0, T]$.

9.4 SPLITTING

As with importance sampling, the mathematics behind splitting is beyond the scope of this book; our only purpose here is to provide the reader with an introductory taste of this approach. The more mathematically sophisticated reader, and those wishing to use it in practice, should consult the references in the Further reading section for details.

Consider a system characterized by transitions among a given set of states S. Its state at time t is denoted by $\mathsf{SysState}(t)$. It makes transitions from one state to another; denote by τ_σ the epoch of the first transition (beyond time 0) into the set of states σ. To avoid confusion, note that if there is a transition at time t, then $\mathsf{SysState}(t)$ represents the state immediately following that transition (purists might prefer to notate this by $\mathsf{SysState}(t^+)$).

Example: Let $S = \{s_1, s_2, \cdots, s_8\}$ be the set of states for some discrete-state system. Define $\sigma = \{s_1, s_2\}$. Suppose the system is in state s_1 to begin with, at time 0. It makes transitions at time $18, 26, 57, 58, \cdots$, and we have $\mathsf{SysState}(18) = s_3$, $\mathsf{SysState}(26) = s_5$, $\mathsf{SysState}(57) = s_1$, $\mathsf{SysState}(58) = s_2$. Then, $\tau_\sigma = 57$.

Now, consider a stochastic system with two disjoint sets of states, S_{common} and S_{rare}. We start the system from some given initial state s_{start}, and wish to know the probability $P(\tau_{S_{rare}} < \tau_{S_{common}} | s_{start})$. Suppose, as the notation implies, the system is rarely in a state in S_{rare}; it is much more likely to be found in one of the states of S_{common}. If $P(\tau_{S_{rare}} < \tau_{S_{common}}|s_{start})$ is extremely small, obtaining it by traditional brute-force simulation may take a long time; splitting is one way of accelerating the simulation process.

The splitting approach for rare-event simulation is based on conditional probability. Consider a sequence of sets $S_1, S_2, \cdots, S_M$, such that $S_{rare} = S_M \subset S_{M-1} \subset \cdots \subset S_1$, and that $S_1 \cap S_{common} = \emptyset$.

Define the event E_i as occurring if $\tau_{S_i} < \tau_{S_{common}}$. Then, directly from the laws of conditional probability, we can write

$$P(E_M|s_{start}) = P(E_M|E_{M-1})P(E_{M-1}|E_{M-2})\cdots P(E_2|E_1)P(E_1|s_{start}). \qquad (9.8)$$

If $P(E_M) \ll 1$, directly simulating for this probability will take a long time. Instead, we could simulate to obtain the terms on the RHS of the above equation, each of which is not as small as $P(E_M)$, and for which statistics can therefore be obtained more easily.

There are many variants of the splitting approach; we describe just one of them here. Simulate to obtain $P(E_1)$ from the given starting state s_{start}.

The simulation starts from the starting state and ends when a transition takes the system into either S_1 or S_{common}, whichever happens earlier. If S_{common} is entered first, that simulation run ends and indicates $\tau_{S_{common}} < \tau_{S_{rare}}$, which is not the event we are looking for. If, on the other hand, S_1 is entered first, we record the state at which it enters, say $s_{1,1}$. We repeat this process n_1 times, recording the entry state if any; assume it enters S_1 first a total of m_1 times. Let the states of entry into S_1 be $s_{1,1}, s_{1,2}, \cdots, s_{1,m_1}$. Note that some of these states could be the same, i.e., it is possible that $s_{1,i} = s_{1,j}$, even if $i \neq j$. The probability $P(E_1|s_{start})$ is estimated to be $\pi_1 = m_1/n_1$.

Now, obtain $P(E_2|E_1)$ by simulation. Make a total of n_2 simulation runs. The starting state for each of these simulations will be selected at random (with replacement) from the states $s_{1,1}, s_{1,2}, \cdots, s_{1,m_1}$. Again, end the simulation run the moment that it enters either S_2 or S_{common}. Let m_2 be the number of such runs in which S_2 is entered; our estimate of $P(E_2|E_1)$ is then $\pi_2 = m_2/n_2$.

Continue in this manner to find estimates $\pi_3, \pi_4, \cdots, \pi_M$, of $P(E_3|E_2), P(E_4|E_3), \cdots, P(E_M|E_{M-1})$, respectively. Multiply them to obtain an estimate of $P(E_M|s_{start})$, i.e.,

$$P(E_M|s_{start}) \approx \pi_1 \pi_2 \cdots \pi_M = \frac{m_1}{n_1}\frac{m_2}{n_1}\cdots\frac{m_M}{n_M}. \qquad (9.9)$$

Fig. 9.5 illustrates the process. To avoid cluttering the diagram, let us pick $n_i = 3$ (a far smaller number than we would, in practice) for each i. Let $M = 3$ (again, in practice, this would usually be bigger). We launch $n_1 = 3$ simulations from s_{start}. One ends up in S_{common}, the other two enter S_1. The first simulation is halted the moment either a state in S_{common} or in S_1 is entered. For simplicity, in the figure, we have shown s_{start} to be outside S_{common}; there is obviously nothing to prevent us from selecting a starting state within S_{common}. It is the transitions occurring beyond time 0 that we are concerned with.

We therefore have two starting points for simulations starting in S_1. We start three simulations from this pair of points; only one of them makes it to S_2, the other two are terminated upon entry into S_{common}.

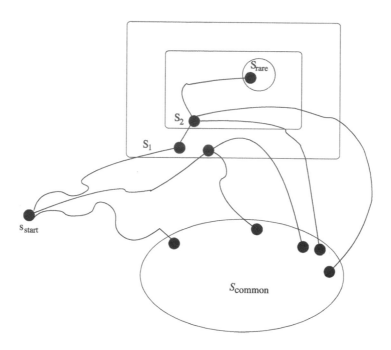

FIGURE 9.5

Example of splitting.

Finally, we start three simulations from this one point in S_2, one of which reaches S_{rare}. Thus we have $m_1 = 2$, $m_2 = m_3 = 1$, so that $\pi_1 = 2/3; \pi_2 = \pi_3 = 1/3$. Hence, our estimate of the probability $P(\tau_{S_{rare}} < \tau_{S_{common}} | s_{start})$ is $\frac{2}{3}\frac{1}{3}\frac{1}{3} = \frac{2}{27}$.

We remind the reader that, in practice, we would pick a far larger number than 3 for the number of simulations at each level.

To speed up our simulation at the cost of some accuracy, we might terminate a run prematurely if it wanders off too far in the "wrong" direction. For example, if we have 10 levels, and we are evaluating $\pi_9 = P(E_9|E_8)$, if the simulation that starts in S_8 goes into the set $S_3 - S_2$, then we may judge that it is very unlikely that it will turn around and head back to S_9 before first entering S_{common}, and so terminate it right away to save time.

All this sounds simple enough, but the devil is in the detail. Two implementation issues arise. First, how should we pick the sequence of nested subspaces $S_1, S_2, \cdots S_M$? Second, how many simulation runs should we make for each step, i.e., what should n_i be? To answer these questions, we have to solve an optimization problem, i.e., minimize the variance of the estimate of $P(E_M)$, given a certain amount of simulation effort. Such an analysis falls well outside the scope of our coverage in this book; pointers to the (active) literature on the subject can be found in the Further reading section. However, one can have some guidelines. $\pi_i = m_i/n_i$ is an *estimate* of the true probability p_i^{true} of going from S_{i-1} to S_i without first entering S_{common}. The following rule of thumb works well in many cases:

Select $S_1, S_2, \cdots, S_M$ so that

$$\pi_1 \approx \pi_2 \approx \cdots \pi_M \approx e^{-2} \approx 0.14. \tag{9.10}$$

From this, using $P(\tau_{S_{rare}} < \tau_{S_{common}} | s_{start}) \approx \pi_1 \cdots \pi_M$, we can also obtain the number of levels M.

We now have a circular process. To obtain the various subspaces S_i, we need to know π_i. But then, if we knew what these quantities were, we would not need to run any simulations to begin with!

A practical approach to this quandary is to make some preliminary, exploratory pilot runs, and adjust the subsets S_i based on that (imperfect, high-variance) simulation information. We could use splitting for such pilot runs with the S_i selected intuitively. If Eq. (9.10) is satisfied and the simulation time required at each level is roughly the same, then an equal number of simulations is carried out at each level. The actual number will depend on the total simulation budget.

A variation of this involves not insisting on Eq. (9.10) being satisfied. Instead, suppose we pick the subsets S_i intuitively, and again run pilot simulations to obtain preliminary values for π_i (i.e., rough estimates of p_i^{true}). Then, the following rule of thumb has been suggested: select n_i so that

$$\frac{n_1}{\sqrt{\frac{1-\pi_1}{\xi_1 \pi_1}}} \approx \frac{n_2}{\sqrt{\frac{1-\pi_2}{\xi_2 \pi_2}}} \approx \frac{n_M}{\sqrt{\frac{1-\pi_M}{\xi_M \pi_M}}} \tag{9.11}$$

where ξ_i is the average effort (e.g., simulation time) required to complete one of the n_i simulation runs for $P(E_i | E_{i-1})$. If we have a fixed simulation budget B then the constraint

$$\xi_1 n_1 + \xi_2 n_2 + \cdots + \xi_M n_M = B \tag{9.12}$$

must be satisfied.

In general, the splitting approach becomes more difficult to implement as the dimensionality of the underlying state space increases.

Example: Suppose we are simulating a power grid to study the probability that tripping a particular branch of it causes a snowball effect, which ultimately results in more than 50% of the system capacity being lost (before repair is completed). The probability of such a major loss tends to rise exponentially with the probability of the failure of a single branch of the grid. Suppose we pick S_1 as the subset of states in which at least 2% of the grid capacity is lost. Then, we will run n_1 simulations, starting from the initial branch failure to a point where S_1 occurs, or repair is completed. Record the system state at each of these S_1 entry points: call them $x_1, \cdots, x_k$. Then, selecting n_2 of these points (sampling at random, with replacement from the points $x_1, \cdots, x_k$), run n_2 simulations, starting from these points to when either the system has been repaired, or 50% of the capacity has been lost.

Example: Consider an energy-harvesting sensor network. Each node has a supercapacitor energy store, which is charged by a solar cell. Energy is depleted as sensing and communication activities occur. If the energy store is depleted beyond a certain point, the node will no longer be able to communicate (for all practical purposes suffer transient failure until sufficient recharging occurs), and will drop out of the network.

Given that the supercapacitor is charged to capacity at time T_0, we wish to find the probability that it is depleted to failure before being charged to capacity again. If this probability is high enough, then traditional simulation will suffice. However, if it is small, then splitting may be useful.

The levels $S_1, \cdots, S_M$ will indicate different levels of energy storage; i.e., we will define energy levels $L_1 > L_2 > \cdots > L_M$, such that S_i denotes the condition in which the energy level is no more than L_i, for $i = 1, \cdots, M$. The starting state s_{start} is that corresponding to a fully charged supercapacitor. Let us define here S_{common} as the fully charged state, and S_{rare} as representing the set of states in which the system has insufficient energy to function.

Suppose we decide to use the rule of thumb $\pi_i \approx e^{-2}$ that was mentioned previously. A few pilot runs will be carried out to determine an appropriate level for L_1, such that the probability of going from the initial state to L_1 (rather than going back to the starting state s_{start} before first entering L_1) is about e^{-2}. Similarly, starting from each of these "entry" states into L_1, we use pilot runs to select L_2, and so on.

With the pilot runs complete, we are ready for the main simulation. Suppose our total simulation budget is about B seconds of computer time; based on our pilot simulation runs, we conclude that each simulation, starting from L_i, costs ξ_i of time. Then, we use Eqs. (9.11) and (9.12) to obtain the appropriate number of runs n_i at each stage.

Example: Consider again a sensor network, which relays fixed-size packets from node to node for delivery to a base station. Each node has a limited number of buffers. When a buffer is full, any message directed to its node is lost. The initial state is S_0 when a buffer is entirely empty. We wish to find the probability that the buffer is unable to accept an incoming packet before it becomes completely empty again.

The similarity of this problem with the previous one should be obvious. The relevant state is the number of empty slots at the buffer when a packet arrives. Again, we can define levels $L_1 > L_2 > \cdots > L_M = 0$ and sets $S_1, \cdots, S_M$, where S_i is defined as the set of states in which the number of slots at a moment of packet arrival is no greater than L_i. We can then proceed as in the previous example.

Where does this approach not work well? Look at Eq. (9.9). If we cannot define $S_1, \cdots, S_{M-1}$ such that the probability of going from S_i to S_{i+1} (before going to S_{common}) is large enough, then we need to seek some other approach. In other words, in the splitting approach, we are replacing a rare-event simulation by a sequence of simulations looking for relatively commonplace events (i.e., where $P(E_{i+1}|E_i)$ is not very small). When such a chain of commonplace events is not available, this approach should not be used.

Example: Consider a system of 10 processors each of which can be swiftly repaired but where the processor failure rate is very low. Suppose system failure happens when more than 3 processors are down at the same time. This is our rare event. Define S_{common} as the state where all processors are up and S_{rare} as that when more than 3 processors are down. Now, to use splitting to evaluate the probability $P(\tau_{S_{rare}} < \tau_{S_{common}})$, we can define levels $L_i = i$ such that level i indicates i failed processors. S_i is then the set of states where at least L_i processors are down. However, under the conditions described here, the probability of going from S_i to S_{i+1} before first going to S_{common} will be very small. Splitting is therefore not a good choice for such a problem.

9.5 RANDOM NUMBER GENERATION

At the heart of any simulation of probabilistic events is the random number generator whose job it is to generate independent and identically distributed (*i.i.d.*) random variables, according to some specified probability distribution function. The quality of such a generator is often critical to the accuracy of the results that the simulation produces, so that choosing a good generator is of considerable practical importance. We discuss in this section how to create random number generators, and how to test their quality.

When faced with the need to generate a stream of *i.i.d.* random numbers according to some probability distribution function, we usually proceed in two steps. In the first step, we generate a stream of *i.i.d.* random numbers that are uniformly distributed in the range [0, 1]; in the second, we transform these to fit the desired probability distribution.

9.5.1 UNIFORMLY DISTRIBUTED RANDOM NUMBER GENERATORS

In an ideal world, we would be able to generate truly random numbers that were both distributed uniformly over [0, 1] and statistically independent of one another. If we can identify some physical process that displays the appropriate stochastic properties, we could simply take measurements of that process. For example, one commercially available generator amplifies the shot noise, plus the thermal noise in transistors, and then uses a thresholding function to convert that noise to bits (if the noise is above the threshold, it is a 1, otherwise it is a 0). This stream of bits is then processed to produce a sequence of numbers that satisfy quite stringent tests of randomness.

In most instances, however, we have to make do with random numbers generated by a computer program. Herein lies a fundamental contradiction. Typically, such a sequence of random numbers $X_1, X_2, \cdots$ satisfies some function $f(\cdot)$, such that $X_{i+1} = f(X_i)$. Given the *seed* X_0, we can therefore predict what the numbers are going to be: there is nothing truly random about them. This is why numbers generated in such a way are called *pseudorandom*. We hope when we generate them that they look sufficiently random that we can get away with using them, rather than truly random numbers in our simulations. In effect, we are trying a variation of the well-known Turing test for intelligence on the random number sequences. The Turing test for artificial intelligence is as follows: Have people interact with either a computer or a human being, without being told which. If they cannot make out from the responses they get to questions whether they are talking to a computer or a human, then the computer has intelligence. The variation that applies to random number sequences states that if we generate a pseudorandom sequence and give it to a statistician without telling her how it was obtained, she should not be able to distinguish between such a sequence and one generated truly randomly. This is an extremely stringent test, and one that most generators will fail. All that is realistic to hope for is that the pseudorandom numbers generated will be sufficiently close to the real thing to make our simulations sufficiently accurate for our purposes. A major source of error in simulations is using poor quality random number generators. Later in this section, we will see how to test such sequences to determine if they satisfy statistical properties of randomness.

A commonly used set of URNGs use the *linear congruential* method:

$$X_{i+1} = (aX_i + c) \mod m, \quad 0 \le a, c < m,$$

where a, c, m are constants. m is called the modulus of the generator, a the multiplier, and c the increment. If $c = 0$, this is known as a multiplicative generator. We start this iterative process by specifying X_0, the seed of this sequence. The properties of the generator depend on the values of these constants. Given such a sequence of integers (which must clearly be in the set $\{0, 1, \cdots, m-1\}$), we define the sequence of fractions $U_i = X_i/m$, which are supposed to be uniformly distributed and mutually independent in the range $[0, 1]$.

Because the sequence $X_1, X_2, \ldots$ must consist of numbers from a finite set, the sequence will repeat with time, that is, given any such generator, there always exists some M such that $X_i = X_{i+M}$. The smallest such M is called the *period*, P, of the generator, and clearly $P \leq m$.

Example: Consider the generator $X_{n+1} = (aX_n + c) \mod 8$. (We use an unrealistically small modulus just for illustration: in practice as we will see, very large moduli are used). We will show that the values of a and c are critical to the functioning of the generator.
Start by considering the following set of results:

seed	0	1	2	3	4	5	6	7
X_1	1	4	7	2	5	0	3	6
X_2	4	5	6	7	0	1	2	3
X_3	5	0	3	6	1	4	7	2
X_4	0	1	2	3	4	5	6	7
X_5	1	4	7	2	5	0	3	6
X_6	4	5	6	7	0	1	2	3
X_7	5	0	3	6	1	4	7	2
			$a=3; c=1; m=8$					

Note that for this sequence, every value of the seed results in a sequence of numbers with period 4. Let us now try another set of constants:

seed	0	1	2	3	4	5	6	7
X_1	2	4	6	0	2	4	6	0
X_2	6	2	6	2	6	2	6	2
X_3	6	6	6	6	6	6	6	6
X_4	6	6	6	6	6	6	6	6
X_5	6	6	6	6	6	6	6	6
X_6	6	6	6	6	6	6	6	6
X_7	6	6	6	6	6	6	6	6
			$a=2; c=2; m=8$					

The result is quite disastrous: a very nonrandom and correlated stream of numbers. This generator gets trapped into producing a stream of 6s, irrespective of the seed. Let us try yet another set of constants:

seed	0	1	2	3	4	5	6	7
X_1	1	6	3	0	5	2	7	4
X_2	6	7	0	1	2	3	4	5
X_3	7	4	1	6	3	0	5	2
X_4	4	5	6	7	0	1	2	3
X_5	5	2	7	4	1	6	3	0
X_6	2	3	4	5	6	7	0	1
X_7	3	0	5	2	7	4	1	6
$a = 5; c = 1; m = 8$								

For these values of a and c, we have, for every seed, a sequence of numbers with the maximum period of 8. We should caution that it does not automatically follow that this is a good generator: just that it passes a basic sanity check.

The linear congruential generator (LCG) has a period of m if and only if each of the following properties hold:

- c and m are relatively prime (their highest common factor is 1).
- For every prime number p that divides m, $a - 1$ is a multiple of p.
- If m is a multiple of 4, then $a - 1$ is also a multiple of 4.

The proof of this result is outside the scope of this book, see the Further reading section for where to find it.

Since random number generators are so important in simulation, many researchers have carried out extensive searches in the parameter space to find generators with good properties. One widely used generator with fairly good statistical properties uses the parameters $a = 16807$, $m = 2^{31} - 1$, $c = 0$.

The periods of LCGs are limited by m, and that can be a problem for running very long simulations. In simulating fault-tolerant systems in which a very large number of events must be generated for each system failure that is encountered, the periods of such generators are often much too small. For example, in the generator mentioned above, $m = 2^{31} - 1 = 2,147,483,647$, and it is entirely possible to have in a simulation more than two billion calls to a random number generator. Because we want the number of calls to be much less than the generator period, we can use combined generators. One way of doing this is to select parameters a_{ij}, m_1, m_2, k, and define

$$X_{1,n} = (a_{11}X_{1,n-1} + a_{12}X_{1,n-2} + \cdots + a_{1k}X_{1,n-k}) \mod m_1;$$
$$X_{2,n} = (a_{21}X_{2,n-1} + a_{22}X_{2,n-2} + \cdots + a_{2k}X_{2,n-k}) \mod m_2.$$

Now, if these parameters are carefully chosen, the sequence

$$U_n = (X_{1,n}/m_1 - X_{2,n}/m_2) \mod 1$$

(the fractional part of this expression) will have properties close to those of *i.i.d.* uniformly distributed random variables.

After a long computer search for suitable parameters for such a generator, the following has been recommended as having good statistical properties: $k = 3$, $m_1 = 2^{32} - 209$, $(a_{11}, a_{12}, a_{13}) =$

$(0, 1403580, -810728)$, $m_2 = 2^{32} - 22853$, $(a_{21}, a_{22}, a_{23}) = (527612, 0, -1370589)$. Such a generator has main cycles of length approximately 2^{191}. See the Further reading section for details.

9.5.2 TESTING UNIFORM RANDOM NUMBER GENERATORS

All tests for URNGs ask the following question: how faithfully does the output of the URNG follow the properties of a uniformly distributed stream of random numbers that are statistically independent of one another? To answer this question, we must first identify some of the key properties of interest.

The most obvious property is that of uniformity, that is, we would like to calculate the extent to which the output is uniformly distributed over the range $[0, 1]$. Suppose we generate 1000 numbers and find that all of them are in the range $[0, 0.7]$. Now, it is *not impossible* that a set of 1000 numbers selected independently and uniformly from the unit interval should all fall in the range $[0, 0.7]$: the probability of this event is $0.7^{1000} = 1.25 \times 10^{-155}$, which, although very small, is certainly not zero. Thus if we get such a sequence from the URNG that we are testing, we cannot say *for sure* that the URNG is bad: all we can say is that it is *unlikely* that a good generator will produce a sequence like that, and consequently we declare the generator bad.

We present next some ways of testing the goodness of a URNG.

The χ^2 Test

Use the URNG to generate a large sequence of numbers. Define $a_0, a_1, a_2, \ldots, a_{k-1}, a_k$ for some suitable k such that

$$0 = a_0 < a_1 < a_2 < \cdots < a_{k-1} < a_k = 1,$$

and define intervals $I_i = [a_i, a_{i+1})$ for $i = 0, 1, \cdots, k-1$. Then, let O_i and E_i be the observed and expected frequencies, respectively, of generated numbers to fall within interval I_i, and define the quantity S, which measures the deviation of the observed frequencies from the expected ones, as

$$S = \sum_{i=0}^{k-1} \frac{(O_i - E_i)^2}{E_i}.$$

Clearly, a good URNG will result in a small value of S. It can be shown (the Further reading section has a pointer to where you can find this derivation) that if the random numbers were the output of a perfect URNG, and we have a large number of them (with at least five expected to fall within each of the intervals I_i), S approximately follows the χ^2 distribution with $k - 1$ degrees of freedom. It is easy to find tables of the χ^2 distribution in books on statistics, or on the Internet. We reject the URNG if S is so large that the probability that a true URNG would generate such a deviation (or a larger one) is very small.

Example: Let us break up the interval $[0, 1]$ into ten equal subintervals, each of length 0.1. Thus $I_i = [0.1i, 0.1i + 0.1)$, for $i = 0, 1, \ldots, 9$. Suppose that after generating 1000 random numbers, we get the results shown in Table 9.2. Let us pick 0.05 as our significance level; this means that we will reject the URNG if it results in a sum S, such that the probability of an ideal URNG generating such a sum, or larger, is less than 0.05. Referring to a χ^2 table with 9 degrees of freedom, we see that, at a significance level of 0.05, we should reject the URNG if $S > 16.9$. Because in this example, we

Table 9.2 Illustrating the χ^2 test.

i	O_i	E_i	$(O_i - E_i)^2$	$(O_i - E_i)^2/E_i$
0	15	100	7225	72.25
1	100	100	0	0.00
2	200	100	10000	100.00
3	88	100	144	1.44
4	100	100	0	0.00
5	100	100	0	0.00
6	90	100	100	1.00
7	80	100	400	4.00
8	27	100	5329	53.29
9	200	100	10000	100.00
	1000	1000	TOTAL	331.98

have $S = 331.98$, we reject this generator – it deviates too much from the expected behavior. There is a very small probability (much smaller than 0.05) that a good URNG will produce a sequence of numbers like this one.

Serial test

To test whether a URNG produces uniformly distributed random numbers is necessary, but certainly not sufficient. To see why, consider the following generator (this is an extreme, contrived example whose sole purpose is to make a point). Generate $Y_1, Y_2, \cdots, Y_n$ using any URNG that closely follows the uniform distribution. Then, generate a sequence $Z_1, Z_2, \cdots, Z_n$, such that for some $k > 1$,

$$Z_1 = Z_2 = \cdots = Z_k = Y_1;$$
$$Z_{k+1} = Z_{k+2} = \cdots = Z_{2k} = Y_2;$$
$$\vdots$$
$$Z_{(n-1)k+1} = Z_{(n-1)k+2} = \cdots = Z_{nk} = Y_n.$$

If $Y_1, \cdots, Y_2$ follows the uniform distribution sufficiently closely, the sequence Z_i will pass the χ^2 Test. However, the Z_is would certainly not be acceptable, because they are highly correlated. So, we need to test for lack of correlation as well, in the expectation that such lack of correlation will look like statistical independence of successive numbers. Such an independence is really a fake: the nth random number is a function of the $(n-1)$st. All that we are really testing for is whether the sequence of generated numbers *looks* like an independent sequence. Similarly, it is entirely possible (though unlikely) that we would independently generate random numbers that *appear* correlated. The best we can realistically do is ask the question: is the probability sufficiently high that such a sequence of numbers would be generated by an ideal generator that produced numbers independently of one another?

To test for correlation between successive numbers, we can use the serial test. In k dimensions, the test is as follows: Generate a sequence of random numbers and then group them together into k-tuples as follows:

$$
\begin{aligned}
G_1 &= (X_1, X_2, \cdots, X_k); \\
G_2 &= (X_{k+1}, X_{k+2}, \cdots, X_{2k}); \\
G_3 &= (X_{2k+1}, X_{2k+2}, \cdots, X_{3k});
\end{aligned}
$$
$$
\vdots
$$

Then, divide the k-dimensional unit cube into n equal subcubes, count the number of k-tuples that fall into each of the subcubes, and check (using the χ^2 test) whether the k-tuples are uniformly distributed among the subcubes.

Example: Suppose we are testing for correlation in two dimensions. To do this, we generate pairs $(X_1, X_2), (X_3, X_4), \ldots$. We then subdivide the two-dimensional unit cube (the unit square) into, say, 100 squares (call them mini squares), each of area 0.01. We count the number n_i of pairs that fall into mini square i, and use the χ^2 test to check if these pairs are uniformly spread through the unit square. If correlation exists, some of the mini squares will have a significantly higher concentration of pairs than the others (see Fig. 9.6).

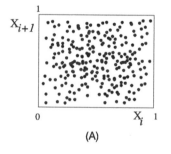 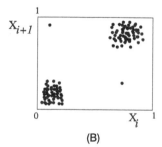

(A)   (B)

FIGURE 9.6

Comparing two generators. (A) URNG A and (B) URNG B.

Permutation test
Given a certain sequence of numbers, divide them into nonoverlapping subsequences, each of a chosen length k. Each of these subsequences can be in one of k! possible orderings. If the URNG is good, we expect these orderings to be equally likely to occur, which can be checked using the χ^2 test.

Example: Consider the case $k = 3$. Denote a subsequence by u_1, u_2, u_3. This subsequence has $3! = 6$ possible orderings: $u_1 \leq u_2 \leq u_3$; $u_1 \leq u_3 \leq u_2$; $u_2 \leq u_1 \leq u_3$; $u_2 \leq u_3 \leq u_1$; $u_3 \leq u_1 \leq u_2$, and $u_3 \leq u_2 \leq u_1$. If we generate a large number of such sequences, we expect a good URNG to generate each of these six orderings with a frequency of $1/6$. If the frequency of at least one ordering differs significantly from $1/6$ (as measured by the χ^2 test), the URNG will fail this test.

The spectral test

This is probably the most powerful test available. The approach followed by the spectral test is perhaps easiest to understand in two-dimensional space. Let us try to draw parallel lines in such a way that each point in the scatter plot is on one of these lines. Then, find the maximum distance between any two adjacent parallel lines. Let d_2 be the maximum of this quantity, taken over all possible ways in which such parallel lines can be drawn (the subscript refers to the fact that we are working in two dimensions). We define $v_2 = 1/d_2$ as the two-dimensional accuracy of the URNG. The larger this quantity, the better: the intuition behind this is that for large values of v_2, the points are spread out more "randomly" in two-dimensional space.

This approach can be generalized to higher dimensions. In k-dimensional space (where we would plot $(X_i, X_{i+1}, \cdots, X_{i+k-1})$), we can replace the parallel lines by $k-1$-dimensional parallel hyperplanes, and repeat the distance calculation. The quantity $v_k = 1/d_k$ (where d_k is defined for k dimensions as d_2 was for two) is the k-dimensional accuracy of the URNG.

It has been recommended to study the scatter up to about six dimensions, and require that $v_i \geq 2^{30/i}$ for $i = 2, 3, 4, 5, 6$ to accept a generator as good.

The only issue left is how to compute v_i. The theory behind this is beyond the scope of this book; the user can download routines for running the spectral test from the Internet.

9.5.3 GENERATING OTHER DISTRIBUTIONS

Given a URNG, we can easily generate random numbers that follow other distributions. There are a handful of standard methods for doing this.

Inverse transform technique

This technique is based on the fact that if a random variable X has a probability distribution function $F_X(\cdot)$, the random variable $Y = F_X(X)$ is uniformly distributed over $[0, 1]$. This can be easily proved as follows:

Denote by F_X^{-1} the inverse function of F_X, that is, $F_X^{-1}(F_X(y)) = y$. (If the inverse does not exist, because there are multiple such quantities y, use the smallest such y.) Then, for $0 \leq y \leq 1$,

$$\text{Prob}\{Y \leq y\} = \text{Prob}\{F_X(X) \leq y\}$$
$$(\text{because } F_X(\cdot) \text{ is non-decreasing}) = \text{Prob}\{X \leq F_X^{-1}(y)\}$$
$$= F_X(F_X^{-1}(y))$$
$$= y.$$

Therefore if we generate random numbers $Y_1, Y_2, \ldots$ that are uniformly distributed over $[0, 1]$, we will get random variables distributed according to $F_X(\cdot)$ by solving $X_i = F_X^{-1}(Y_i)$.

Example: Suppose we want to generate instances of X, an exponentially distributed random variable with parameter μ. The probability distribution function of X is

$$F_X(x) = 1 - e^{-\mu x}, \quad x \geq 0.$$

Now, define

$$Y = F_X(X) = 1 - e^{-\mu X}$$

and

$$e^{-\mu X} = 1 - Y,$$

hence

$$-\mu X = \ln(1 - Y),$$

and finally

$$X = -(1/\mu)\ln(1 - Y).$$

Thus to generate exponentially distributed random numbers, generate uniformly distributed random numbers y over $[0, 1]$, and then output $x = -(1/\mu)\ln(1 - y)$. The computation can be speeded up a little by recognizing that $-(1/\mu)\ln y$ will also work, see the Exercises for details.

Working with discrete random variables is similar, as shown by the following example:

Example: We are asked to generate a discrete-valued random variable V with the following probability mass function:

$$\text{Prob}\{V = v\} = \begin{cases} 0.1 & \text{if } v = 1 \\ 0.3 & \text{if } v = 2 \\ 0.6 & \text{if } v = 2.25 \\ 0 & \text{otherwise.} \end{cases}$$

The only values that V can take are $1, 2, 2.25$. The corresponding probability distribution function is clearly

$$F(v) = \text{Prob}\{V \leq v\} = \begin{cases} 0.0 & \text{if } v < 1 \\ 0.1 & \text{if } 1 \leq v < 2 \\ 0.4 & \text{if } 2 \leq v < 2.25 \\ 1.0 & \text{if } v \geq 2.25. \end{cases}$$

This distribution function has jumps at $v = 1, 2$, and 2.25, and is flat otherwise. Now, generate a uniformly distributed random variable U over the interval $[0, 1]$, and output

$$V = \begin{cases} 1 & \text{if } 0 \leq U \leq 0.1 \\ 2 & \text{if } 0.1 < U \leq 0.4 \\ 2.25 & \text{if } 0.4 < U \leq 1.0. \end{cases}$$

Example: Suppose we are asked to generate a *nonhomogeneous Poisson process*. This is a generalization of the well-known Poisson process: the only difference is that the rate of event occurrences is not a constant λ, but a function of the time t, denoted by $\lambda(t)$. The probability of an occurrence during the interval $[t, t + dt]$ is given by $\lambda(t)dt$. Nonhomogeneous Poisson processes are useful in modeling components with failure rates that change with age.

Our task now is to generate times, at which events occur in such a process. We will do so by generating the time of the first event, then the time of the second event based on the time of the first event, and so on.

To do this with the inverse transform technique, we first need to compute the probability distribution function of the time between successive event occurrences. The probability of *no* event occurrence in the time interval $[t_1, t_2]$ is given by

$$e^{-\int_{t_1}^{t_2} \lambda(\tau)d\tau}.$$

Therefore if the ith event occurred at time t_i, the interval to the next event occurrence has the following probability distribution function:

$$F(x \mid t_i) = 1 - e^{-\int_{t_i}^{x+t_i} \lambda(\tau)d\tau}.$$

Suppose, as an example, that $\lambda(t) = at$, which means that the failure rate increases linearly as a function of time. Then, the distribution function of the time interval between the ith and $(i+1)$st events will be

$$F(x \mid t_i) = 1 - e^{-\int_{t_i}^{x+t_i} a\tau d\tau} = 1 - e^{-a[x^2 + 2xt_i]/2}.$$

To use the inverse transform technique, we set

$$u = 1 - e^{-a[x^2 + 2xt_i]/2}.$$

Solving for x,

$$x = -t_i + \sqrt{t_i^2 - 2\ln(1-u)/a}.$$

This is the length of the interval separating t_i and t_{i+1}. Thus we will generate event times as follows: Generate $U_1, U_2, \cdots$, uniformly distributed over $[0, 1]$.

1. Set $t_1 = \sqrt{-2\ln(1-U_1)/a}$;

2. Set $t_2 = t_1 - t_1 + \sqrt{t_1^2 - 2\ln(1-U_2)/a} = \sqrt{t_1^2 - 2\ln(1-U_2)/a}$;

3. Set $t_3 = t_2 - t_2 + \sqrt{t_2^2 - 2\ln(1-U_3)/a} = \sqrt{t_2^2 - 2\ln(1-U_3)/a}$,

and so on.

Example: Suppose we want to generate positive random variables distributed according to the Weibull distribution (see Eq. (9.2)), for which

$$F(x) = 1 - e^{-\lambda x^\beta} \quad \text{(for } x \geq 0\text{)}.$$

We now have

$$u = 1 - e^{-\lambda x^\beta},$$

and, consequently,

$$x = [-\ln(1-u)/\lambda]^{1/\beta}.$$

Rejection method

Suppose we are given a random number generator that produces random numbers according to a probability density function $g(\cdot)$, and would like to generate random numbers according to a probability density function $f(\cdot)$, such that $f(x) \leq cg(x)$ for all x and for some finite constant c. Then, the rejection method proceeds as follows:

1. Generate a random number Y according to the probability density function $g(\cdot)$.
2. Generate U, uniformly distributed over $[0, 1]$.
3. If $U \leq \frac{f(Y)}{cg(Y)}$, output Y; otherwise go back to step 1, and try again. The output has the required probability density function, $f(\cdot)$.

The role of the constant c is to ensure that the $f(Y)/cg(Y)$ is never greater than 1. We would like to select a function $g(\cdot)$ such that c is not very large. As you are invited to prove in the Exercises, the average number of times we have to loop through the above procedure to generate one output is c.

We next prove that this method produces the desired results:

$$\text{Prob}\{X \leq x\} = \text{Prob}\left\{Y \leq x \,\middle|\, U \leq \frac{f(Y)}{cg(Y)}\right\}$$

$$= \frac{\text{Prob}\left\{Y \leq x \text{ and } U \leq \frac{f(Y)}{cg(Y)}\right\}}{\text{Prob}\left\{U \leq \frac{f(Y)}{cg(Y)}\right\}};$$

$$\text{Prob}\left\{Y \leq x \text{ and } U \leq \frac{f(Y)}{cg(Y)}\right\} = \text{Prob}\left\{U \leq \frac{f(Y)}{cg(Y)} \,\middle|\, Y \leq x\right\} \text{Prob}\{Y \leq x\}$$

$$= \frac{F(x)}{c} \text{ (fill in the missing steps as an exercise);}$$

$$\text{Prob}\left\{U \leq \frac{f(Y)}{cg(Y)}\right\} = \frac{1}{c} \text{ (showing this is another exercise).}$$

$$\text{Hence, Prob}\{X \leq x\} = F(x), \text{ which completes the proof.}$$

Example: Suppose we want to generate random variables Z according to the normal distribution, with mean 0 and variance 1. The desired density function is

$$h(z) = \frac{1}{\sqrt{2\pi}} e^{-z^2/2}, \quad -\infty < z < \infty.$$

We need to find a suitable function $g(\cdot)$. A URNG will not do: its density function goes to 0 beyond a finite interval. However, we know how to generate an exponentially distributed random variable (with parameter 1): it has density $g(x) = e^{-x}$ for $x \geq 0$. The only problem is that the normal distribution is nonzero for both positive and negative z, and the exponential is only defined for $x \geq 0$.

This difficulty can be easily overcome: observe that $h(z)$ is symmetric about the origin and $h(z) = h(-z)$. Let us generate a random variable $X = |Z|$: it has twice the density of the normal over the nonnegative half of the interval. This results in the density function

$$f(x) = \frac{2}{\sqrt{2\pi}} e^{-x^2/2}, \quad 0 \leq x < \infty.$$

Then, we set $Z = X$ with probability 0.5, and set $Z = -X$ with probability 0.5.

We start by finding a c such that $f(x) \leq cg(x)$. To do this requires us to maximize $f(x)/g(x)$ over $x \geq 0$: simple calculus shows that this happens when $x = 1$, so we can use

$$c = \frac{f(1)}{g(1)} = \sqrt{\frac{2e}{\pi}}.$$

After some algebraic manipulation, we get

$$\frac{f(x)}{cg(x)} = e^{-(x-1)^2/2}.$$

Therefore to generate X, we carry out the following steps:

1. Generate Y, with probability density function $g_Y(y) = e^{-y}$.
2. Generate U_1 uniformly distributed over $[0, 1]$.
3. If $U_1 \leq e^{-(Y-1)^2/2}$, output $X = Y$; otherwise go back to step 1, and try again.

To generate Z from X, we do the following:

1. Generate U_2 uniformly distributed over $[0, 1]$.
2. If $U_2 \leq 0.5$, output $Z = X$, otherwise output $Z = -X$.

Composition method

When the random variable to be generated is the sum of other random variables, we can generate each of the latter, and then add them up.

Example: We want to generate a random variable Z, which is defined as $Z = V + X + Y$, where the following hold:

1. V is uniformly distributed over the interval $[0, 10]$.
2. X is exponentially distributed with parameter 16.
3. Y has the normal distribution, with mean 5 and variance 23.

We generate V and X using the inverse transform technique, and Y using the rejection method. We then add them up and output the result.

9.6 FAULT INJECTION

As mentioned previously in this chapter, simulating a system to obtain its reliability, or similar attributes, requires the knowledge of the parameters, such as the components' failure rates. These can be obtained either through lengthy observations, or much faster through fault injection experiments. In such experiments, various faults are injected either into a simulation model of the target system or a hardware-and-software prototype of the system. The behavior of the system in the presence of each fault is then observed and classified. Parameters that can be estimated based on such experiments include the probability that a fault will cause an error, and the probability that the system will perform successfully the actions required to recover from the error (the latter probability is often called *coverage factor*, see Chapter 2). These actions consist of detecting the fault, identifying the system component affected by the fault, and taking an appropriate recovery action, which may involve system reconfiguration. Each of these actions takes time that is not a constant, but may change from one fault to another and may also depend on the current workload. Thus fault injection experiments, in addition to providing estimates for the coverage factor, can also be used to estimate the distribution of the individual delay associated with each of the above actions.

In addition, fault injection experiments can be used to evaluate and validate the system dependability. For example, errors in the implementation of fault-tolerance mechanisms can be discovered, and system components whose failure is more likely to result in a total system crash, can be identified. Also, the effect of the system's workload on the dependability can be observed.

9.6.1 TYPES OF FAULT INJECTION TECHNIQUES

Initially, fault injection studies involved injection of physical faults into the hardware components of the system. This necessitates being able to modify the current value of almost every circuit node, thus mimicking a fault that may occur there. With the considerable increase in circuit density in current VLSI technologies and the associated reduction in device size, this technique is now limited in its capabilities, because only the pins of integrated circuits can be easily accessed.

Accessibility can be improved by taking advantage of scan chains, which connect a large number of internal circuit latches in a sequential manner, and are currently included in many designs of complex integrated circuits. Scan chains are normally constructed to simplify the debugging and manufacturing test of the circuit by allowing the user to shift out the current values (for observation purposes) and shift in new values. By shifting in erroneous bits, the scan chain can be used to inject faults as well.

Even so, injecting faults into all internal circuit nodes is not practically feasible, due to the very large number of circuit nodes in even a moderately complex system, which makes an exhaustive insertion prohibitive. Instead, a subset of these insertion points must be carefully selected.

Several alternative schemes have been developed to allow the injection of faults without having direct access to internal nodes. One such scheme is to subject the hardware to particle radiation (for example, heavy-ion radiation). Such radiation can clearly inject faults into otherwise inaccessible locations, but on the other hand it can only inject transient faults, because the effect of the particle hit will disappear after a brief delay. This technique has the additional advantage of closely resembling what might happen in real-life. As device feature sizes in current integrated circuits get smaller, errors due to neutron and alpha particle hits become more common. Such particle hits (also called soft errors or single event upsets) are abundant in space, but also appear at ground level, due to cosmic rays that bombard the earth, and as a result of radioactive atoms that exist in trace amounts in the packaging materials.

A different method for fault injection is through power supply disturbances. The supply voltage is briefly dropped to levels below the nominal range. Unlike the radiation method, which usually generates single event upsets, this scheme affects many nodes in the circuit simultaneously, producing multiple transient faults. Moreover, the exact location of these faults cannot be controlled. The effect of power supply disturbances does, however, resemble a real-life situation that may be experienced by computer systems in industrial applications.

Another approach to fault injection is through electromagnetic interference. The system is subjected to electromagnetic bursts, which can be either allowed to affect all components, or be restricted to individual ones. Here too, the injected faults are transient.

The above-mentioned physical injection techniques rely on having a working prototype of the target system. If the designers wish to test some fault-tolerance features in their design and modify them if the observed dependability is insufficient, then the use of a physical injection technique may prove to be too costly. An alternative would be to inject faults through the software layer. This technique, known as software implemented fault injection (SWIFI), can be applied either to a prototype of the target system, or to a simulation model of it. SWIFI also overcomes some of the problems with physical fault injection, such as repeatability and controllability. It provides easy access to many internal circuit nodes in the system (but not to all of them), and allows the control of the location, time, duration, and type of the injected faults much more easily than does physical injection. An important advantage of the SWIFI approach is that it is not restricted to hardware faults, but allows the injection of software faults as well. Such software faults can cause *data*, *interface*, and *code* errors.

A data error, as the term implies, involves corrupting some segment of memory (e.g., heap, stack, code section, etc.). A corresponding network error can be simulated by delaying, dropping, or corrupting messages.

An interface error involves corrupting the values being sent to a software module's input interface, or values from its output interface. Such errors are often generated by randomly flipping one or more bits, or using an incorrect data type to that specified.

Code errors involve changing instructions in the code. These may be replaced by nops (which do nothing), or by some other instructions. Such changes can be made either at the source code or machine code level.

Example: Typical injected code errors consist of changing constant values, branch conditions, or assignment statements. Others include altering dynamic memory allocation or deallocation. The following table provides a few examples:

Correct	Changed
`int i = 0;`	`int i=5;`
`if (j<55) ...`	`if (j>55) ...`
`i=j;`	`i=k;`
`free(ptr)`	`nop`

If SWIFI is applied to a simulation model of the target system rather than a prototype, then mixed-mode simulation techniques can be used, supporting several levels of system abstraction including architectural, functional, logical, and electrical. In mixed-mode simulation, the system is decomposed in a hierarchical manner, allowing us to simulate various components at different levels of abstraction. Thus an injected fault can be simulated at a low abstraction level and the propagation of its effect throughout the system can be simulated at higher abstraction levels, greatly reducing the simulation time. Although simulation-based fault injection has several desirable properties, injecting faults into a hardware-software prototype provides more realistic, credible, and accurate results.

Software fault injections can be performed either during compilation or during run time. To inject faults during compile time, the program instructions are modified and errors are injected into the source code, or assembly code, to emulate the effect of hardware (permanent or transient) and software faults. To inject faults during run time, one can use either timers (hardware or software) to determine the exact instant of the injection, or a software trap that will allow determining the exact time of the injection relative to some system event. This technique requires only minor modifications, if any, to the application program. A third method of timing the fault injection through software is by adding instructions to the application program. This will allow faults to be injected in predetermined time instances during the execution of the program.

9.6.2 FAULT INJECTION APPLICATION AND TOOLS

Fault injections have been applied for measuring the coverage and latency parameters, for studying error propagation, and for analyzing the relationship between the workload of the system and its fault handling capabilities. Another interesting application of fault injection schemes has been to evaluate the effect of transient faults on the availability of highly dependable systems. These systems were capable of recovering from the transient faults, but still had wasted time doing that, thus reducing the availability.

Various fault injectors have been developed and are currently in use. Some are mentioned in the Further reading section. Studies comparing several fault injectors have been conducted, concluding that two fault injectors may either validate each other, or complement each other. The latter happens if they cover different faults.

The different approaches to fault injection result in quite different properties of the corresponding tools. Some of these differences are summarized in Table 9.3.

All fault injection schemes require a well-defined fault model, which should represent as closely as possible the faults that one expects to see during the lifetime of the target system. A fault model must specify the types of faults, their location and duration, and, possibly, the statistical distributions of these characteristics. The fault models used in currently available fault injection tools vary considerably, from

Table 9.3 Comparing the properties of four approaches to fault injection.

Property	Hardware direct injection	Hardware indirect injection	Software during compilation	Software during runtime
Accessibility	low	high	low	low to medium
Controllability	high	low	high	high
Intrusiveness	none	none	low	high
Repeatability	high	low	high	high
Cost	high	high	low	low

very detailed device level faults (for example, a delay fault on a particular wire) to simplified functional level faults (such as an erroneous adder output).

9.7 FURTHER READING

Two textbooks on simulation [16,45], provide useful information on how to write simulation programs. Another, more elementary and limited, source is the operations research book [26]. A large number of topics related to simulation models can be found in [4]. Many simulations are written in special-purpose simulation languages, such as GPSS; for a good source for this language, see [47]. In our treatment, we did not discuss parallel simulation: this is a very promising approach to speeding up simulation. For details, see [18].

The topic of parameter estimation is covered in many books. See, for example, [12,49]. A readable section on the subject can be found in [51].

Perhaps the best sources for variance reduction methods are the two above-mentioned books [17, 45]. For importance sampling, see [22,25,40,41]. These also contain a useful bibliography. [37] provides an early source for the technique of forcing. A case study of the use of importance sampling in evaluating real-time system dependability is presented in [15]; another more recent reference is [9].

For splitting, good initial references are [19,32,36,46,48,55]. Useful references for analysis of splitting is provided in [20,21]. An example of splitting in network reliability analysis can be found in [39]. Our example on the use of splitting in power grid reliability is based on [58]. For examples of further work in this area, see [9,33]. Finally, importance sampling and splitting can be combined: see [34].

An excellent source of information about uniform random number generators is Volume 2 of [30]. You can find there a detailed mathematical treatment of the properties of the linear congruential generator, including the relationships that must hold to have $P = m$. Especially valuable is the detailed treatment of statistical tests of randomness that is provided. The theoretical basis for the χ^2 test is explained in detail, and the most powerful test of all – the spectral test – is covered extensively. This book also has an outstanding set of references to the literature. Additional sources of information on empirical statistical tests are [5] and [28].

The recent work in [31] is useful for good random number generators with extremely long periods.

Generating random numbers with distributions other than uniform is discussed in many books. For example, see [5,45]. A survey on Gaussian random number generation can be found in [38].

Several survey papers reviewing the uses of fault injectors and the various available tools have been published [11,27]. Some of the fault injection tools that have been developed rely on hardware fault injection, e.g., Messaline [2], FIST [23], Xception [10], and GOOFI [1]. Others are based on software fault injection, for example, Ferrari [29], FIAT [6], NFtape [50], and DOCTOR [24]. For how to assess fault-injection coverage, see [44].

Fault injection to evaluate software resilience is more difficult, since it is hard to determine what kinds of software faults are truly representative of reality; see, for example, the comprehensive recent survey [43] as well as [14,42]. A good comparison of several tools for evaluating the dependability of a fault-tolerant system was presented in [3]. Another use of software fault injection is to assess the risk involved in using a software product [56,57]. This scheme uses code that modifies the program state by injecting anomalies in the instructions to see how badly the software can behave.

An important issue associated with the data generated by simulation, or other means, is data visualization. The important question of how best to display data in a way that humans can grasp accurately and rapidly is the object of much research. For example, decisions need to be made as to what kind of plots are created (e.g., 2-D vs 3-D, color usage, scatter plots vs line plots or histograms, linear vs log axes, axis displacement values) and how the data are aggregated. A good overview can be found in [35]; also see [52–54] for book-length coverage.

Recent developments in virtual reality have opened up new vistas for presentation of data in an adaptive way; see, for example, [8,13].

9.8 EXERCISES

1. You are given a set of 10 processors that are believed to follow a Poisson failure process, with failure rate λ per hour per processor. You run the processors for a week, and obtain the following numbers of failures for each processor: 2, 4, 2, 1, 1, 2, 3, 2, 0, 2.
   (a) What is your estimate for the value of λ?
   (b) Construct a 95% confidence interval for λ using Eq. (9.1) to estimate the standard deviation.
   (c) Construct a 95% confidence interval for λ using the fact that for the Poisson distribution $E(x) = Var(x) = \lambda$.
   (d) Explain the difference between the results of parts (b) and (c).

2. You are given a set of 10 processors that are believed to follow a Poisson failure process, with failure rate λ per hour per processor. The prior density of λ is a uniform distribution over the range $[0.001, 0.002]$.
   (a) You run these processors for 100 hours without any of the processors failing. What is the best estimate for the value of λ (the mean of the posterior density of λ)?
   (b) You continue the experiment for a total of 10,000 hours without observing any failures. What is your best estimate for λ?
   (c) Suppose you were to run this experiment for a *very* long time without any processor failing. What do you think the posterior density function for λ would be?

3. This question follows up on our comments on the difficulty of validating the reliability of a life-critical system to a sufficiently high level of confidence.
   Suppose you were calculating the confidence interval for the reliability of a life-critical system whose true failure probability over a given interval of operation is 10^{-8}. (Of course, you do not *know* that this failure probability is 10^{-8}, which is why you are gathering statistics). Obtain an estimate of the number of observations you would require to show with 99.999999% confidence that the true failure probability is in the range $[0.9 \times 10^{-8}, 1.1 \times 10^{-8}]$.
   You will need for this question an algorithm to calculate the values of the normal distribution with sufficient accuracy. It should not be difficult to find one through an Internet search: see, for example, [7].

4. Evaluate RANDU, which was a routine widely used many years ago to generate uniform random numbers. Its recursive formula is $X_{n+1} = (65539 X_n) \mod 2^{31}$. Pick $X_0 = 23$, and use each of the testing methods described in Section 9.5.2. Software for the spectral test can be found on the Internet.

5. Repeat Problem 4 for the random number generator that is included in your favorite computer system or spreadsheet.

6. Given a uniform random number generator, obtain a generator for continuous-valued random variables with the following probability density functions (assume that the densities are 0 outside the specified ranges):
   (a) $f_1(x) = 0.25, \quad 16 \leq x \leq 20$.
   (b) $f_2(x) = 0.4\mu_1 e^{-\mu_1 x} + 0.6\mu_2 e^{-\mu_2 x}, x \geq 0$.
   (c) $f_3(x) = \frac{1}{24} x^4 e^{-x}, \quad x > 0$.
   (d) $f_4(x) = \begin{cases} x & \text{if } 0 \leq x \leq 1 \\ 2-x & \text{if } 1 \leq x \leq 2 \\ 0 & \text{otherwise.} \end{cases}$

7. Generate discrete random variables with the following probability mass functions (assume that the parameters have known values):
   (a) $\text{Prob}\{X = n\} = p(1-p)^{n-1}, \quad n = 1, 2, 3, \cdots; \quad 0 < p < 1$.
   (b) $\text{Prob}\{X = n\} = e^{-\lambda} \lambda^n / n!, \quad n = 0, 1, 2, \cdots; \lambda > 0$.
   (c) $\text{Prob}\{X = n\} = \begin{cases} 0.25 & \text{if } n = 1 \\ 0.50 & \text{if } n = 2 \\ 0.25 & \text{if } n = 3 \\ 0 & \text{otherwise.} \end{cases}$
   (d) $\text{Prob}\{X = n\} = 0.7 e^{-\lambda} \lambda^n / n! + 0.3 e^{-2\lambda}(2\lambda)^n / n!$.

8. When deriving the generator for exponentially distributed random variables, we showed that $-(1/\lambda)\ln(1-U)$ would work. However, we pointed out that $-(1/\lambda)\ln U$ would also yield exponentially distributed random variables. Prove that this is the case.

9. When proving the correctness of the rejection method, we omitted some steps. Complete the proof with these steps in place.

10. Write a simulation program to obtain the MTTF of the system shown in Fig. 9.4A.

11. Write a simulation program to find the MTTDL of a RAID level 3 system, consisting of eight data disks and one parity disk. The disks fail independently, according to a Poisson process with rate 10^{-4} per hour. The repair time (in hours) has an exponential density with mean 2 hours.
   (a) Estimate the mean time to data loss, MTTDL.
   (b) Derive the 99% confidence interval after running a total of 1000 simulation runs.
   (c) Determine how many runs are required to make the width of the 99% confidence interval less than 10% of the estimated MTTDL (from part (a)).
   (d) Vary the number of simulations from 1000 to 10000, and plot the width of the confidence interval over this range.

12. Repeat the above simulation using the method of antithetic variables. Compare the width of the 99% confidence interval you obtain with the two approaches for an identical total number of simulations, ranging from 1000 to 10000.

13. Repeat the above simulation using the method of importance sampling. Use the balanced failure biasing technique. Vary the value of p^* from 0.1 to 0.9 in steps of 0.1, and run 1000 simulations for each such value. Plot the width of the 99% confidence interval as a function of p^*.

14. Consider the example discussed in Section 9.3.3. Suppose you carry out a few runs to get a rough estimate of π_1 and π_2, and end up with $\hat{\pi}_1 = 0.9$ and $\hat{\pi}_2 = 0.98$. Your simulation time budget al-

lows you to carry out a total of 1000 simulation runs, so that $n_1 + n_2 = 1000$. What values should you select for n_1 and n_2 to minimize the variance of your estimate of the survival probability, π.

15. Consider the system shown in Fig. 9.7. Each block suffers failure independently of the others,

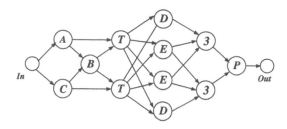

FIGURE 9.7

Non series-parallel system.

according to a Poisson process with rates $\lambda_A = 0.001$, $\lambda_B = 0.002$, $\lambda_C = 0.005$, $\lambda_D = 0.01$, $\lambda_E = 0.009$, $\lambda_T = 0.005$, and $\lambda_P = 0.00001$ per hour. The subscripts refer to the block labels. The blocks marked 3 are perfectly reliable and never fail. The nodes *In* and *Out* represent the input and output points, and not blocks: they do not fail.

Each node takes an exponentially distributed amount of time to repair: the mean time to repair is 1 hour for all nodes.

Failure happens when there is no longer a path from the *In* node to the *Out* node.

(a) Write a simulation program to obtain the mean time to failure for this system. Plot the width of the 99% confidence interval associated with simulation runs ranging from 500 to 10000.

(b) Use the method of control variables and repeat part (a).

(c) Repeat part (a) by using importance sampling with balanced failure biasing ($p^* = 0.2$).

16. Repeat part (a) of the previous problem, with the blocks now suffering failure according to a nonhomogeneous Poisson process in which the failure rates are increasing functions of time. Use $\lambda_i(t) = t^{1/3}\lambda_i$, for $i \in \{A, B, C, D, E, P, T\}$.

17. Derive Eq. (9.8).

18. (This problem requires a good background in probability theory.) Consider a three-level splitting simulation. If n_i, p_i^{true}, $i = 1, 2, 3$ are as defined in Section 9.4, derive an expression for the variance of the simulation result as a function of n_i, p_i^{true}. Assume that the simulations starting from each level are independent of those from any other level.

REFERENCES

[1] J.L. Aidemark, J.P. Vinter, P. Folkesson, J. Karlsson, GOOFI: a generic fault injection tool, in: Dependable Systems and Networks Conference (DSN-2001), 2001, pp. 83–88.

[2] J. Arlat, A. Costes, Y. Crouzet, J.C. Laprie, D. Powell, Fault injection and dependability evaluation of fault-tolerant systems, IEEE Transactions on Computers 42 (August 1993) 913–923.

[3] J. Arlat, Y. Crouzet, J. Karlsson, P. Folkesson, E. Fuchs, G.H. Leber, Comparison of physical and software-implemented fault injection techniques, IEEE Transactions on Computers 52 (September 2003) 1115–1133.

[4] J. Banks (Ed.), Handbook of Simulation, Wiley, 1998.

[5] J. Banks, J.S. Carson II, B.L. Nelson, D.M. Nicol, Discrete-Event System Simulation, Prentice-Hall, 2001.

[6] J.H. Barton, E.W. Czeck, Z. Segall, D.P. Siewiorek, Fault injection experiments using FIAT, IEEE Transactions on Computers 39 (April 1990) 575–582.

[7] B.D. Bunday, S.M.H. Bokhari, K.H. Khan, A new algorithm for the normal distribution function, Sociedad de Estadistica e Investigacion Operativa Test 6 (1997) 369–377.

[8] S. Butscher, S. Hubenschmid, J. Müller, J. Fuchs, H. Reiterer, Clusters, trends, and outliers: how immersive technologies can facilitate the collaborative analysis of multidimensional data, in: CHI Conference on Human Factors in Computing Systems, 2018, Paper 90.

[9] V. Caron, A. Guyader, M.M. Zuniga, B. Tuffin, Some recent results in rare event estimation, ESAIM Proceedings 44 (January 2014) 239–259.

[10] J. Carreira, H. Madeira, J.G. Silva, Xception: a technique for the experimental evaluation of dependability in modern computers, IEEE Transactions on Software Engineering 24 (February 1998) 125–136.

[11] J.A. Clark, D.K. Pradhan, Fault injection: a method for validating computer-system dependability, IEEE Computer 28 (June 1995) 47–56.

[12] A.C. Cohen, B.J. Whitten, Parameter Estimation in Reliability and Life Span Models, Marcel Dekker, 1988.

[13] C. Donalek, S.G. Djorgovski, A. Cioc, A. Wang, J. Zhang, E. Lawler, S. Yeh, A. Mahabal, M. Graham, A. Drake, S. Davidoff, Immersive and collaborative data visualization using virtual reality platforms, in: IEEE International Conference on Big Data (Big Data), 2014, pp. 609–614.

[14] J.A. Duraes, H.S. Madeira, Emulation of software faults: a field data study and a practical approach, IEEE Transactions on Software Engineering 32 (11) (2006) 849–867.

[15] G. Durairaj, I. Koren, C.M. Krishna, Importance sampling to evaluate real-time system reliability, Simulation 76 (March 2001) 172–183.

[16] G.S. Fishman, Discrete Event Simulation, Springer-Verlag, 2001.

[17] G.S. Fishman, A First Course in Monte Carlo, Duxbury, 2006.

[18] R.M. Fujimoto, Parallel and Distributed Simulation, Wiley, 2000.

[19] M.J.J. Garvels, The Splitting Method in Rare Event Simulation, Ph.D. Dissertation, University of Twente, 2000.

[20] M.J.J. Garvels, D.P. Kroese, A comparison of restart implementations, in: 1998 Winter Simulation Conference, vol. 1, IEEE, 1998, pp. 601–608.

[21] P. Glasserman, P. Heidelberger, P. Shahabuddin, T. Zajic, Multilevel splitting for estimating rare event probabilities, Operations Research 47 (4) (1999) 585–600.

[22] A. Goyal, P. Shahabuddin, P. Heidelberger, V.F. Nicola, P.W. Glynn, A unified framework for simulating Markovian models of highly dependable systems, IEEE Transactions on Computers 41 (January 1992) 36–51.

[23] U. Gunneflo, J. Karlsson, J. Torin, Evaluation of error detection schemes using fault injection by heavy-ion radiation, in: 19th IEEE International Symposium on Fault-Tolerant Computing (FTCS-19), June 1989, pp. 340–347.

[24] S. Han, K.G. Shin, H.A. Rosenberg, DOCTOR: an integrated software fault injection environment for distributed real-time systems, in: International Computer Performance and Dependability Symposium (IPDS'95), April 1995, pp. 204–213.

[25] P. Heidelberger, Fast simulation of rare events in queuing and reliability models, ACM Transactions on Modeling and Computer Simulation 5 (January 1995) 43–55.

[26] F.S. Hillier, G.J. Lieberman, Introduction to Operations Research, McGraw-Hill, 2001.

[27] M.C. Hsueh, T.K. Tsai, R.K. Iyer, Fault injection techniques and tools, IEEE Computer 30 (April 1997) 75–82.

[28] R. Jain, The Art of Computer Systems Performance Analysis, Wiley, 1991.

[29] G.A. Kanawati, N.A. Kanawati, J.A. Abraham, FERRARI: a flexible software-based fault and error injection system, IEEE Transactions on Computers 44 (February 1995) 248–260.

[30] D.E. Knuth, The Art of Computer Programming, vol. 2, Addison Wesley, 1998.

[31] P. L'Ecuyer, Random numbers, in: International Encyclopedia of Social and Behavioral Sciences, 2001.

[32] P. L'Ecuyer, V. Demers, B. Tuffin, Splitting for rare-event simulation, in: 2006 Winter Simulation Conference, 2006, pp. 137–148.

[33] P. L'Ecuyer, Z.I. Botev, D.P. Kroese, On a generalized splitting method for sampling from a conditional distribution, in: 2018 Winter Simulation Conference, 2018, pp. 1694–1705.

[34] D. Jacuemart-Tomi, J. Morio, F. Le Gland, A combined importance splitting and sampling algorithm for rare event simulation, in: 2013 Winter Simulation Conference, 2013, pp. 1035–1046.

[35] C. Kelleher, T. Wagener, Ten guidelines for effective data visualization in scientific publications, Environmental Modelling and Software 26 (2011) 822–827.

[36] A. Lagnoux, Rare event simulation, Probability in the Engineering and Informational Sciences 20 (2006) 45–66.

[37] E.E. Lewis, F. Bohm, Monte Carlo simulation of Markov unreliability models, Nuclear Engineering and Design 77 (1984) 49–62.

[38] J.S. Malik, A. Hemani, Gaussian random number generation: a survey on hardware architectures, ACM Computing Surveys 49 (3) (2016) 53.

[39] L. Murray, H. Cancela, G. Rubino, A splitting algorithm for network reliability estimation, IIE Transactions 45 (2) (2013) 177–189.

[40] M.K. Nakayama, Fast simulation methods for highly dependable systems, in: Winter Simulation Conference, 1994, pp. 221–228.

[41] M.K. Nakayama, A characterization of the simple failure-biasing method for simulations of highly reliable Markovian systems, ACM Transactions on Modeling and Computer Simulation 4 (January 1994) 52–86.

[42] R. Natella, D. Cotroneo, J.A. Duraes, H.S. Madeira, On fault representativeness of software fault injection, IEEE Transactions on Software Engineering 39 (1) (2013) 80–96.

[43] R. Natella, D. Cotronae, H.S. Madeira, Assessing dependability with software fault injection: a survey, ACM Computing Surveys 48 (3) (2016) 44.

[44] D. Powell, E. Martins, J. Arlat, Y. Crouzet, Estimators for fault tolerance coverage evaluation, IEEE Transactions on Computers 44 (February 1995) 261–274.

[45] S.M. Ross, Simulation, Academic Press, 2012.

[46] G. Rubino, T. Bruno (Eds.), Rare Event Simulation Using Monte Carlo Methods, John Wiley & Sons, 2009.

[47] T.J. Schriber, An Introduction to Simulation Using GPSS/H, Wiley, 1991.

[48] J.F. Shortle, C.-H. Chen, A preliminary study of optimal splitting for rare-event simulation, in: 2008 Winter Simulation Conference, 2008, pp. 266–272.

[49] H.W. Sorenson, Parameter Estimation: Principles and Problems, Marcel Dekker, 1980.

[50] D.T. Stott, G. Ries, M.-C. Hsueh, R.K. Iyer, Dependability analysis of a high-speed network using software-implemented fault injection and simulated fault injection, IEEE Transactions on Computers 47 (January 1998) 108–119.

[51] K.S. Trivedi, Probability and Statistics with Reliability, Queuing and Computer Science Applications, John Wiley, 2002.

[52] E.R. Tufte, The Visual Display of Quantitative Information, Graphics Press, 1983.

[53] E.R. Tufte, Beautiful Evidence, Graphics Press, 2006.

[54] E.R. Tufte, N.H. Goeler, R. Benson, Envisioning Information, Graphics Press, 1990.

[55] M. Villén-Altamirano, J. Villén-Altamirano, Restart: a straightforward method for fast simulation of rare events, in: 1994 Winter Simulation Conference, 1994, pp. 282–289.

[56] J.M. Voas, G. McGraw, Software Fault Injection, Wiley Computer Publishing, 1998.

[57] J. Voas, G. McGraw, L. Kassab, L. Voas, Fault-injection: a crystal ball for software liability, IEEE Computer 30 (June 1997) 29–36.

[58] S.-P. Wang, A. Chen, C.-W. Liu, C.-H. Chen, J. Shortle, Rare-event splitting simulation for analysis of power system blackouts, in: 2011 IEEE Power and Energy Society General Meeting, 2011, pp. 1–7.

DEFECT TOLERANCE IN VLSI CIRCUITS

10

With the continuing increase in the total number of devices in VLSI circuits (e.g., microprocessors) and in the density of these devices (due to the reduction in their size) has come an increasing need for defect tolerance. Some of the billions of submicron devices that are included in a VLSI chip are bound to have imperfections resulting in yield-reducing manufacturing defects, where yield is defined as the expected percentage of operational chips out of the total number fabricated.

Consequently, increasing attention is being paid to the development and use of defect-tolerance techniques for yield enhancement, to complement existing efforts at the manufacturing stage. Design stage yield-enhancement techniques are aimed at making the integrated circuit *defect tolerant*, or less sensitive to manufacturing defects, and these include incorporating redundancy into the design, modifying the circuit floorplan, and modifying its layout. We concentrate in this chapter on the first two, which are directly related to the focus of this book.

Adding redundant components to the circuit can help in tolerating manufacturing defects, and thus increase the yield. However, too much redundancy may reduce the yield since a larger-area circuit is expected to have a larger number of defects. Moreover, the increased area of the individual chip will result in a reduction in the number of chips that can fit in a fixed-area wafer. Successful designs of defect-tolerant chips must therefore rely on accurate yield projections to determine the optimal amount of redundancy to be added. We discuss several statistical yield prediction models and their application to defect-tolerant designs. Then, various yield-enhancement techniques are described, and their use illustrated.

10.1 MANUFACTURING DEFECTS AND CIRCUIT FAULTS

Manufacturing defects can be roughly classified into global defects (or gross area defects) and spot defects. Global defects are relatively large-scale defects, such as scratches from wafer mishandling, large area defects from mask misalignment, and over- and under-etching. Spot defects are random local and small defects from materials used in the process and from environmental causes, mostly the result of undesired chemical and airborne particles deposited on the chip during the various steps of the process.

Both defect types contribute to yield loss. In mature, well-controlled fabrication lines, gross area defects can be minimized and almost eliminated. Controlling random spot defects is considerably more difficult, and the yield loss, due to spot defects, is typically much greater than the yield loss due to global defects. This is especially true for large-area integrated circuits, since the frequency of global defects is almost independent of the die size, whereas the expected number of spot defects increases with the chip area. Consequently, spot defects are of greater significance when yield projection and enhancement are concerned, and are therefore the focus of this chapter.

Spot defects can be divided into several types according to their location and to the potential harm they may cause. Some cause missing patterns, which may result in open circuits, whereas others cause extra patterns that may result in short circuits. These defects can be further classified into intralayer and interlayer defects. Intralayer defects occur as a result of particles deposited during the lithographic processes; they are also known as photolithographic defects. Examples of these are missing metal (diffusion or polysilicon), and extra metal (diffusion or polysilicon). Also included are defects in the silicon substrate, such as contamination in the deposition processes. Interlayer defects include missing material in the vias between two metal layers, or between a metal layer and polysilicon, and extra material between the substrate and metal (diffusion or polysilicon) or between two separate metal layers. These interlayer defects occur as a result of local contamination, because of, for example, dust particles.

Not all spot defects result in structural faults, such as line breaks or short circuits. Whether or not a defect will cause a fault depends on its location, size, and the layout and density of the circuit (see Fig. 10.1). For a defect to cause a fault, it has to be large enough to connect two disjoint conductors, or to disconnect a continuous pattern. Out of the three circular missing-material defects appearing in the layout of metal conductors in Fig. 10.1, the two top ones will not disconnect any conductor, whereas the bottom defect will result in an open circuit fault.

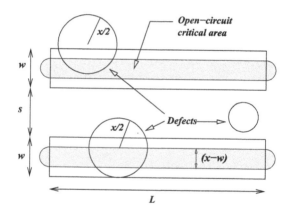

FIGURE 10.1

The critical area for missing-metal defects of diameter x.

We therefore make the distinction between physical *defects* and circuit *faults*. A defect is any imperfection on the wafer, but only those defects that actually affect the circuit operation are called faults: these are the only ones causing yield losses. Thus for the purpose of yield estimation, the distribution of faults, rather than that of defects, is of interest.

Some random defects that do not cause structural faults (also termed functional faults) may still result in parametric faults, that is, the electrical parameters of some devices may be outside their desired range, affecting the performance of the circuit. For example, although a missing-material photolithographic defect may be too small to disconnect a transistor, it may still affect its performance. Parametric faults may also be the result of global defects that cause variations in process parameters. This chapter does not deal with parametric faults; it concentrates instead on functional faults, against which fault-tolerance techniques can be used.

10.2 PROBABILITY OF FAILURE AND CRITICAL AREA

We next describe how the fraction of manufacturing defects that result in functional faults can be calculated. This fraction, also called the *probability of failure* (POF), depends on a number of factors: the type of the defect, its size (the greater the defect size, the greater the probability that it will cause a fault), its location, and circuit geometry. A commonly adopted simplifying assumption is that a defect is circular with a random diameter x (as shown in Fig. 10.1). Accordingly, we denote by $\theta_i(x)$ the probability that a defect of type i and diameter x will cause a fault, and by θ_i the average POF for type i defects. Once $\theta_i(x)$ is calculated, θ_i can be obtained by averaging over all defect diameters x. Experimental data lead to the conclusion that the diameter x of a defect has a probability density function $f_d(x)$ given by

$$f_d(x) = \begin{cases} kx^{-p} & \text{if } x_0 \leq x \leq x_M \\ 0 & \text{otherwise,} \end{cases} \tag{10.1}$$

where $k = (p-1)x_0^{p-1}x_M^{p-1}/(x_M^{p-1} - x_0^{p-1})$ is a normalizing constant, x_0 is the resolution limit of the lithography process, and x_M is the maximum defect size. The values of p and x_M can be determined empirically and may depend on the defect type. Typically, p ranges in value between 2 and 3.5. θ_i can now be calculated as

$$\theta_i = \int_{x_0}^{x_M} \theta_i(x) \, f_d(x) \, dx. \tag{10.2}$$

Analogously, we define the *critical area* $A_i^{(c)}(x)$ for defects of type i and diameter x as the area, in which the center of a defect of type i and diameter x must fall to cause a circuit failure, and by $A_i^{(c)}$ the average over all defect diameters x of these areas. $A_i^{(c)}$ is called the critical area for defects of type i, and can be calculated as

$$A_i^{(c)} = \int_{x_0}^{x_M} A_i^{(c)}(x) \, f_d(x) \, dx. \tag{10.3}$$

Assuming that given a defect, its center is uniformly distributed over the chip area, and denoting the chip area by A_{chip}, we obtain

$$\theta_i(x) = \frac{A_i^{(c)}(x)}{A_{chip}}, \tag{10.4}$$

and, consequently, from Eqs. (10.2) and (10.3),

$$\theta_i = \frac{A_i^{(c)}}{A_{chip}}. \tag{10.5}$$

Since the POF and the critical area are related through Eq. (10.5), any one of them can be calculated first. There are several methods of calculating these parameters. Some methods are geometry-based, and they calculate $A_i^{(c)}(x)$ first, others are Monte Carlo–type methods, where $\theta_i(x)$ is calculated first.

We illustrate the geometrical method for calculating critical areas through the VLSI layout in Fig. 10.1, which shows two horizontal conductors. The critical area for a missing-material defect of size x in a conductor of length L and width w is the size of the shaded area in Fig. 10.1, given by

$$A_{miss}^{(c)}(x) = \begin{cases} 0 & \text{if } x < w \\ (x-w)L + \frac{1}{2}(x-w)\sqrt{x^2 - w^2} & \text{if } x \geq w. \end{cases} \tag{10.6}$$

The critical area is a quadratic function of the defect diameter, but for $L \gg w$, the quadratic term becomes negligible. Thus for long conductors, we can use just the linear term. An analogous expression for $A_{extra}^{(c)}(x)$ for extra-material defects in a rectangular area of width s, between two adjacent conductors, can be obtained by replacing w by s in Eq. (10.6).

Other regular shapes can be similarly analyzed, and expressions for their critical area can be derived. Common VLSI layouts consist of many shapes in different sizes and orientations, and it is very difficult to derive the exact expression for the critical area of all, but very simple and regular layouts. Therefore other techniques have been developed, including several more efficient geometrical methods and Monte Carlo simulation methods. One geometrical method is the polygon expansion technique, in which adjacent polygons are expanded by x/2, and the intersection of the expanded polygons is the critical area for short-circuit faults of diameter x.

In the Monte Carlo approach, simulated circles representing defects of different sizes are placed at random locations of the layout. For each such "defect," the circuit of the "defective" IC is extracted and compared with the defect-free circuit to determine whether the defect has resulted in a circuit fault. The POF $\theta_i(x)$ is calculated for defects of type i and diameter x as the fraction of such defects that would have resulted in a fault. It is then averaged using Eq. (10.2) to produce θ_i, and $A_i^{(c)} = \theta_i A_{chip}$. An added benefit of the Monte Carlo method is that the circuit fault resulting from a given defect is precisely identified. Traditionally the Monte Carlo approach has been very time-consuming but efficient implementations have been developed, allowing this method to be used for large ICs.

Once $A_i^{(c)}$ (or θ_i) has been calculated for every defect type i, it can be used as follows: Let d_i denote the average number of defects of type i per unit area; then the average number of manufacturing *defects* of type i on the chip is $A_{chip} d_i$. The average number on the chip of circuit *faults* of type i can now be expressed as $\theta_i A_{chip} d_i = A_i^{(c)} d_i$.

In the rest of this chapter, we will assume that the defect densities are given, and the critical areas are calculated. Thus the average number of faults on the chip, denoted by λ, can be obtained using

$$\lambda = \sum_i A_i^{(c)} d_i = \sum_i \theta_i A_{chip} d_i, \qquad (10.7)$$

where the sum is taken over all possible defect types on the chip.

10.3 BASIC YIELD MODELS

To project the yield of a given chip design, we can construct an analytical probability model that describes the expected spatial distribution of manufacturing defects and, consequently, of the resulting circuit faults that eventually cause yield loss. The amount of detail needed regarding this distribution differs between chips that have some incorporated defect tolerance, and those which do not. In case of a chip with no defect tolerance, its projected yield is equal to the probability of no faults occurring anywhere on the chip. Denoting by X the number of faults on the chip, the chip yield, denoted by Y_{chip}, is given by

$$Y_{chip} = Prob\{X = 0\}. \qquad (10.8)$$

If the chip has some redundant components, projecting its yield requires a more intricate model that provides information regarding the distribution of faults over partial areas of the chip, as well as possible correlations among faults occurring in different subareas. In this section, we describe statistical yield models for chips without redundancy; in Section 10.4, we generalize these models for predicting the effects of redundancy on the yield.

10.3.1 THE POISSON AND COMPOUND POISSON YIELD MODELS

The most common statistical yield models appearing in the literature are the Poisson model and its derivative, the compound Poisson model. Although other models have been suggested, we will concentrate here on this family of distributions, due to the ease of calculation when using them, and the documented good fit of these distributions to empirical yield data.

λ denotes the average number of faults occurring on the chip, i.e., it is the expected value of the random variable X. Assuming that the chip area is divided into a very large number n of small statistically independent subareas, each with a probability λ/n of having a fault in it, we get the following binomial probability for the number of faults on the chip:

$$\begin{aligned} Prob\{X = k\} &= Prob\{k \text{ faults occur on chip}\} \\ &= \binom{n}{k}\left(\frac{\lambda}{n}\right)^k \left(1 - \frac{\lambda}{n}\right)^{n-k}. \end{aligned} \qquad (10.9)$$

Letting $n \to \infty$ in Eq. (10.9) results in the Poisson distribution

$$Prob\{X = k\} = Prob\{k \text{ faults occur on chip}\} = \frac{e^{-\lambda}\lambda^k}{k!}, \qquad (10.10)$$

and the chip yield is equal to

$$Y_{chip} = Prob\{X = 0\} = e^{-\lambda}. \qquad (10.11)$$

Note that we use here the *spatial* (area dependent) Poisson distribution, rather than the time-dependent Poisson process discussed in Chapter 2.

It has been known since the beginning of integrated circuit manufacturing that Eq. (10.11) is too pessimistic, and leads to predicted chip yields that are too low when extrapolated from the yield of smaller chips or single circuits. It later became clear that the lower predicted yield was caused by the fact that defects, and consequently faults, do not occur independently in the different regions of the chip, but rather tend to cluster more than is predicted by the Poisson distribution. Fig. 10.2 demonstrates how increased clustering of faults can increase the yield. The same six faults occur in both wafers, but the wafer on the right has a higher yield, due to the tighter clustering.

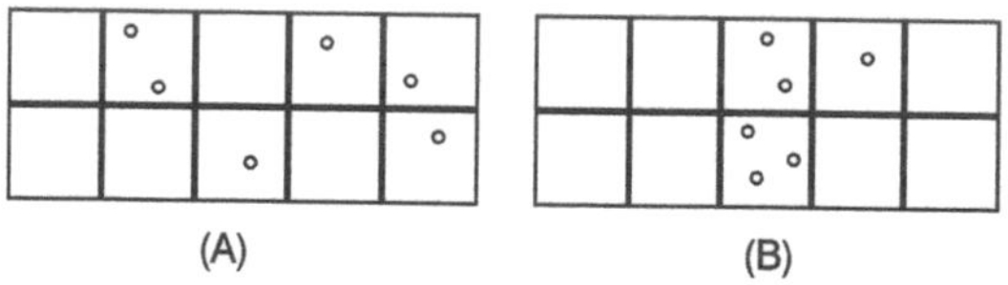

(A) (B)

FIGURE 10.2

Effect of clustering on chip yield. (A) Non-clustered faults, $Y_{chip} = 0.5$. (B) Clustered faults, $Y_{chip} = 0.7$.

Clustering of faults implies that the assumption that subareas on the chip are statistically independent, which led to Eq. (10.9) and, consequently, to Eqs. (10.10) and (10.11), is an oversimplification. Several modifications to Eq. (10.10) have been proposed to account for fault clustering. The most commonly used modification is obtained by considering the parameter λ in Eq. (10.10) as a random variable rather than a constant. The resulting *compound Poisson distribution* produces a distribution of faults, in which the different subareas on the chip are correlated, and which has a more pronounced clustering than that generated by the pure Poisson distribution.

Let us now demonstrate this compounding procedure. Let λ be the expected value of a random variable L with values ℓ and a density function $f_L(\ell)$, where $f_L(\ell)d\ell$ denotes the probability that the chip fault average lies between ℓ and $\ell + d\ell$. Averaging (or compounding) Eq. (10.10) with respect to this density function results in

$$\text{Prob}\{X = k\} = \int_0^\infty \frac{e^{-\ell}\ell^k}{k!} f_L(\ell)\, d\ell, \tag{10.12}$$

and the chip yield is

$$Y_{chip} = \text{Prob}\{X = 0\} = \int_0^\infty e^{-\ell} f_L(\ell)\, d\ell. \tag{10.13}$$

The function $f_L(\ell)$ in this expression is known as the *compounder* or *mixing function*. Any compounder must satisfy the conditions

$$\int_0^\infty f_L(\ell)d\ell = 1 \; ; \; E(L) = \int_0^\infty \ell f_L(\ell)d\ell = \lambda.$$

The most commonly used mixing function is the gamma density function with the two parameters, α and $\frac{\alpha}{\lambda}$,

$$f_L(\ell) = \frac{\alpha^\alpha}{\lambda^\alpha \Gamma(\alpha)} \ell^{\alpha-1} e^{-\frac{\alpha}{\lambda}\ell}, \tag{10.14}$$

where $\Gamma(y) = \int_0^\infty e^{-u} u^{y-1} du$ (see Section 2.2). Evaluating the integral in Eq. (10.12) with respect to Eq. (10.14) results in the widely used *negative binomial* yield formula

$$\text{Prob}\{X = k\} = \frac{\Gamma(\alpha + k)}{k! \, \Gamma(\alpha)} \frac{(\frac{\lambda}{\alpha})^k}{(1 + \frac{\lambda}{\alpha})^{\alpha+k}}, \tag{10.15}$$

and

$$Y_{\text{chip}} = \text{Prob}\{X = 0\} = \left(1 + \frac{\lambda}{\alpha}\right)^{-\alpha}. \tag{10.16}$$

This last model is also called *the large-area clustering* negative binomial model. It implies that the whole chip constitutes one unit, and that subareas within the same chip are correlated with regard to faults. The negative binomial yield model has two parameters, and is therefore flexible and easy to fit to actual data. The parameter λ is the average number of faults per chip, whereas the parameter α is a measure of the amount of fault clustering. Smaller values of α indicate increased clustering. Actual values for α typically range between 0.3 and 5. When $\alpha \to \infty$, Expression (10.16) becomes equal to Eq. (10.11), which represents the yield under the Poisson distribution, characterized by a total absence of clustering. (Note that the Poisson distribution does not *guarantee* that the defects will be randomly spread out: all it says is that there is no inherent clustering. Clusters of defects can still form by chance in individual instances.)

10.3.2 VARIATIONS ON THE SIMPLE YIELD MODELS

The large-area clustering compound Poisson model described above makes two crucial assumptions: the fault clusters are large compared with the size of the chip, and they are of uniform size. In some cases, it is clear from observing the defect maps of manufactured wafers that the faults can be divided into two classes – heavily clustered and less heavily clustered (see Fig. 10.3) – and clearly originate from two sources: systematic and random. In these cases, a simple yield model, as described above, will not be able to successfully describe the fault distribution. This inadequacy will be more noticeable when attempting to evaluate the yield of chips with redundancy. One way to deal with this is to include in the model a gross yield factor Y_0 that denotes the probability that the chip is *not* hit by a gross defect. Gross defects are usually the result of systematic processing problems that affect whole wafers, or parts of wafers. They may be caused by misalignment, over- or under-etching, or out-of-spec semiconductor parameters, such as threshold voltage. It has been shown that even fault clusters with very high fault densities can be modeled by Y_0. If the negative binomial yield model is used, then introducing a gross yield factor Y_0 results in

$$Y_{\text{chip}} = Y_0 \left(1 + \frac{\lambda}{\alpha}\right)^{-\alpha}. \tag{10.17}$$

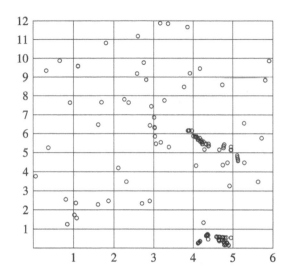

FIGURE 10.3

A wafer defect map.

As chips become larger, this approach becomes less practical, since very few faults will hit the entire chip. Instead, two fault distributions, each with a different set of parameters, may be combined. X, the total number of faults on the chip, can be viewed as $X = X_1 + X_2$, where X_1 and X_2 are statistically independent random variables, denoting the number of faults of type 1 and of type 2, respectively, on the chip. The probability function of X can be derived from

$$\text{Prob}\{X = k\} = \sum_{j=0}^{k} \text{Prob}\{X_1 = j\} \times \text{Prob}\{X_2 = k-j\} \qquad (10.18)$$

and

$$Y_{\text{chip}} = \text{Prob}\{X = 0\} = \text{Prob}\{X_1 = 0\} \times \text{Prob}\{X_2 = 0\}. \qquad (10.19)$$

If X_1 and X_2 are modeled by a negative binomial distribution with parameters λ_1, α_1, and λ_2, α_2, respectively, then

$$Y_{\text{chip}} = \left(1 + \frac{\lambda_1}{\alpha_1}\right)^{-\alpha_1} \left(1 + \frac{\lambda_2}{\alpha_2}\right)^{-\alpha_2}. \qquad (10.20)$$

Another variation on the simple fault distributions may occur in very large chips, in which the fault clusters appear to be of uniform size, but are much smaller than the chip area. In this case, instead of viewing the chip as one entity for statistical purposes, it can be viewed as consisting of statistically independent regions called *blocks*. The number of faults in each block has a negative binomial distribution, and the faults within the area of the block are uniformly distributed. The large-area negative binomial distribution is a special case, in which the whole chip constitutes one block. Another special case is the small-area negative binomial distribution, which describes very small independent fault clusters. Mathematically, the medium-area negative binomial distribution can be obtained, similarly to the large-area case, as a compound Poisson distribution, where the integration in Eq. (10.12) is performed independently over the different regions of the chip. Let the chip consist of B blocks with an average of ℓ faults. Each block will have an average of ℓ/B faults, and according to the Poisson distribution, the chip yield will be

$$Y_{chip} = e^{-\ell} = \left(e^{-\ell/B}\right)^B, \tag{10.21}$$

where $e^{-\ell/B}$ is the yield of one block.

When each factor in Eq. (10.21) is compounded separately with respect to Eq. (10.14), the result is

$$Y_{chip} = \left[\left(1 + \frac{\lambda/B}{\alpha}\right)^{-\alpha}\right]^B = \left(1 + \frac{\lambda}{B\alpha}\right)^{-B\alpha}. \tag{10.22}$$

It is also possible that each region on the chip has a different sensitivity to defects, and thus block i has the parameters λ_i, α_i, resulting in

$$Y_{chip} = \prod_{i=1}^{B}\left(1 + \frac{\lambda_i}{\alpha_i}\right)^{-\alpha_i}. \tag{10.23}$$

It is important to note that the differences among the various models described in this section become more noticeable when they are used to project the yield of chips with built-in redundancy.

To estimate the parameters of a yield model, the "window method" is regularly used in the industry. Wafer maps that show the location of functioning and failing chips are analyzed using overlays with grids or windows. These windows contain some adjacent chip multiples (e.g., one, two, and four), and the yield for each such multiple is calculated. Values for the parameters Y_0, λ, and α are then determined by means of curve fitting.

10.4 YIELD ENHANCEMENT THROUGH REDUNDANCY

In this section, we describe several techniques to incorporate redundancy in the design of VLSI circuits to increase the yield. We start by analyzing the yield enhancement due to redundancy, and then present schemes to introduce redundancy into memory and logic designs.

10.4.1 YIELD PROJECTION FOR CHIPS WITH REDUNDANCY

In many integrated circuit chips, identical blocks of circuits are often replicated. In memory chips, these are blocks of memory cells, which are also known as *subarrays*. In digital chips they are referred to as *macros*. We will use the term *modules* to include both these designations.

In very large chips, if the whole chip is required to be fault-free, the yield will be very low. The yield can be increased by adding a few spare modules to the design, and accepting those chips that have the required number of fault-free modules. However, adding redundant modules increases the chip area and reduces the number of chips that will fit into the wafer area. Consequently, a better measure for evaluating the benefit of redundancy is the *effective yield*, defined as

$$Y_{chip}^{eff} = Y_{chip} \frac{\text{Area of chip without redundancy}}{\text{Area of chip with redundancy}}. \tag{10.24}$$

The maximum value of Y_{chip}^{eff} determines the optimal amount of redundancy to be incorporated into the chip.

The yield of a chip with redundancy is the probability that it has enough fault-free modules for proper operation. To calculate this probability, a much more detailed statistical model than described earlier is needed, a model that specifies the fault distribution for any subarea of the chip, as well as the correlations among the different subareas of the chip.

Chips with one type of modules

For simplicity, let us first deal with projecting the yield of chips, whose only circuitry is N identical modules, out of which R are spares, and at least $M = N - R$ must be fault-free for proper operation. Define the following probability:

$$F_{i,N} = \text{Prob}\{Exactly\ i\ out\ of\ the\ N\ modules\ are\ fault\text{-}free\}.$$

Then the yield of the chip is given by

$$Y_{chip} = \sum_{i=M}^{N} F_{i,N}. \tag{10.25}$$

Using the spatial Poisson distribution implies that the average number of faults per module, denoted by λ_m, is $\lambda_m = \lambda/N$. In addition, when using the Poisson model, the faults in any distinct subareas are statistically independent, and thus

$$
\begin{aligned}
F_{i,N} &= \binom{N}{i} \left(e^{-\lambda_m}\right)^i \left(1 - e^{-\lambda_m}\right)^{N-i} \\
&= \binom{N}{i} \left(e^{-\lambda/N}\right)^i \left(1 - e^{-\lambda/N}\right)^{N-i},
\end{aligned} \tag{10.26}
$$

and the yield of the chip is

$$Y_{chip} = \sum_{i=M}^{N} \binom{N}{i} \left(e^{-\lambda/N}\right)^i \left(1 - e^{-\lambda/N}\right)^{N-i}. \tag{10.27}$$

Unfortunately, although the Poisson distribution is mathematically convenient, it does not match actual defect and fault data. If any of the compound Poisson distributions is to be used, then the different modules on the chip are not statistically independent, but rather correlated with respect to the number of faults. A simple formula, such as Eq. (10.27), which uses the binomial distribution, is therefore not appropriate. Several approaches can calculate the yield in this case, all leading to the same final expression.

The first approach applies only to the compound Poisson models, and is based on compounding the expression in Eq. (10.26) over λ_m (as shown in Section 10.3). Replacing λ/N by ℓ, expanding $\left(1 - e^{-\ell}\right)^{N-i}$ into the binomial series $\sum_{k=0}^{N-i}(-1)^k\binom{N-i}{k}\left(e^{-\ell}\right)^k$, and substituting into Eq. (10.26), results in

$$F_{i,N} = \binom{N}{i}\sum_{k=0}^{N-i}(-1)^k\binom{N-i}{k}\left(e^{-\ell}\right)^{i+k}. \qquad (10.28)$$

By compounding Eq. (10.28) with a density function $f_L(\ell)$, we obtain

$$F_{i,N} = \binom{N}{i}\sum_{k=0}^{N-i}(-1)^k\binom{N-i}{k}\int_0^\infty e^{-(i+k)\ell}f_L(\ell)\,d\ell.$$

Defining $y_n = \int_0^\infty e^{-n\ell}f_L(\ell)\,d\ell$ (y_n is the probability that a *given* subset of n modules is fault-free, according to the compound Poisson model) results in

$$F_{i,N} = \binom{N}{i}\sum_{k=0}^{N-i}(-1)^k\binom{N-i}{k}y_{i+k}, \qquad (10.29)$$

and the yield of the chip is equal to

$$Y_{chip} = \sum_{i=M}^{N}\sum_{k=0}^{N-i}(-1)^k\binom{N}{i}\binom{N-i}{k}y_{i+k}. \qquad (10.30)$$

The Poisson model can be obtained as a special case by substituting

$$y_{i+k} = e^{-(i+k)\lambda/N},$$

whereas for the negative binomial model

$$y_{i+k} = \left(1 + \frac{(i+k)\lambda}{N\alpha}\right)^{-\alpha}. \qquad (10.31)$$

The yield of the chip under this model is

$$Y_{chip} = \sum_{i=M}^{N}\sum_{k=0}^{N-i}(-1)^k\binom{N}{i}\binom{N-i}{k}\left(1 + \frac{(i+k)\lambda}{N\alpha}\right)^{-\alpha}. \qquad (10.32)$$

The approach described above to calculating the chip yield applies only to the compound Poisson models. A more general approach involves using the inclusion and exclusion formula to calculate the probability $F_{i,N}$:

$$F_{i,N} = \binom{N}{i} \sum_{k=0}^{N-i} (-1)^k \binom{N-i}{k} y_{i+k},$$ (10.33)

which is the same expression as in Eq. (10.29), which leads to Eq. (10.30).

Since Eq. (10.30) can be obtained from the basic inclusion and exclusion formula, it is quite general and applies to a larger family of distributions than the compound Poisson models. The only requirement for it to be applicable is that for a given n, any subset of n modules have the same probability of being fault-free, and no statistical independence among the modules is required.

As shown above, the yield for any compound Poisson distribution (including the pure Poisson) can be obtained from Eq. (10.30) by substituting the appropriate expression for y_n. If a gross yield factor Y_0 exists, it can be included in y_n. For the model, in which the defects arise from two sources and the number of faults per chip X, can be viewed as $X = X_1 + X_2$,

$$y_n = y_n^{(1)} y_n^{(2)},$$

where $y_n^{(j)}$ denotes the probability that a given subset of n modules has no type j faults ($j = 1, 2$). The calculation of y_n for the medium-size clustering negative binomial probability is slightly more complicated; a pointer to it is included in the Further Reading section.

More complex designs

The simple architecture analyzed in the preceding section is an idealization, because actual chips rarely consist entirely of identical circuit modules. The more general case is that of a chip with multiple types of modules, each with its own redundancy. In addition, all chips include support circuits, which are shared by the replicated modules. The support circuitry almost never has any redundancy and, if damaged, renders the chip unusable. In what follows, expressions for the yield of chips with two different types of modules, as well as some support circuits, are presented. The extension to a larger number of module types is straightforward, but cumbersome, and is therefore not included.

Denote by N_j the number of type j modules, out of which R_j are spares. Each type j module occupies an area of size a_j on the chip ($j = 1, 2$). The area of the support circuitry is a_{ck} (ck stands for chip-kill, since any fault in the support circuitry is fatal for the chip). Clearly, $N_1 a_1 + N_2 a_2 + a_{ck} = A_{chip}$.

Since each circuit type has a different sensitivity to defects, it has a different fault density. Let λ_{m_1}, λ_{m_2}, and λ_{ck} denote the average number of faults per type 1 module, type 2 module, and the support circuitry, respectively. Denoting by F_{i_1,N_1,i_2,N_2} the probability that exactly i_1 type 1 modules, exactly i_2 type 2 modules, and all the support circuits are fault-free, the chip yield is given by

$$Y_{chip} = \sum_{i_1=M_1}^{N_1} \sum_{i_2=M_2}^{N_2} F_{i_1,N_1,i_2,N_2},$$ (10.34)

where $M_j = N_j - R_j$ ($j = 1, 2$). According to the Poisson distribution,

$$F_{i_1,N_1,i_2,N_2} = \binom{N_1}{i_1} \left(e^{-\lambda_{m_1}}\right)^{i_1} \left(1 - e^{-\lambda_{m_1}}\right)^{N_1-i_1}$$

$$\times \binom{N_2}{i_2} \left(e^{-\lambda_{m_2}}\right)^{i_2} \left(1 - e^{-\lambda_{m_2}}\right)^{N_2-i_2} e^{-\lambda_{ck}}. \qquad (10.35)$$

To get the expression for F_{i_1,N_1,i_2,N_2} under a general fault distribution, we need to use the two-dimensional inclusion and exclusion formula

$$F_{i_1,N_1,i_2,N_2} = \sum_{k_1=0}^{N_1-i_1} \sum_{k_2=0}^{N_2-i_2} (-1)^{k_1}(-1)^{k_2} \binom{N_1}{i_1}\binom{N_1-i_1}{k_1}\binom{N_2}{i_2}\binom{N_2-i_2}{k_2} y_{i_1+k_1,i_2+k_2},$$

$$(10.36)$$

where y_{n_1,n_2} is the probability that a given set of n_1 type 1 modules, a given set of n_2 type 2 modules, and the support circuitry are all fault-free. This probability can be calculated using any of the models described in Section 10.3, with λ replaced by $n_1\lambda_{m_1} + n_2\lambda_{m_2} + \lambda_{ck}$.

Two noted special cases are the Poisson distribution, for which

$$y_{n_1,n_2} = \left(e^{-\lambda_{m_1}}\right)^{n_1} \left(e^{-\lambda_{m_2}}\right)^{n_2} e^{-\lambda_{ck}} = e^{-(n_1\lambda_{m_1} + n_2\lambda_{m_2} + \lambda_{ck})}, \qquad (10.37)$$

and the large-area negative binomial distribution, for which

$$y_{n_1,n_2} = \left(1 + \frac{n_1\lambda_{m_1} + n_2\lambda_{m_2} + \lambda_{ck}}{\alpha}\right)^{-\alpha}. \qquad (10.38)$$

Some chips have a very complex redundancy scheme that does not conform to the simple M-of-N redundancy. For such chips, it is extremely difficult to develop closed-form yield expressions for any model with clustered faults. One possible solution is to use Monte Carlo simulation, in which faults are thrown at the wafer according to the underlying statistical model, and the percentage of operational chips is calculated. A much faster solution is to calculate the yield using the Poisson distribution, which is relatively easy (although complicated redundancy schemes may require some nontrivial combinatorial calculations). This yield is then compounded with respect to λ using an appropriate compounder. If the Poisson yield expression can be expanded into a power series in λ, analytical integration is possible. Otherwise, which is more likely, numerical integration has to be performed. This very powerful compounding procedure was employed to derive yield expressions for interconnection buses in VLSI chips, for partially good memory chips, and for hybrid redundancy designs of memory chips.

10.4.2 MEMORY ARRAYS WITH REDUNDANCY

Defect-tolerance techniques have been successfully applied to many designs of memory arrays, due to their high regularity, which greatly simplifies the task of incorporating redundancy into their design. A variety of defect-tolerance techniques have been exploited in memory designs from the simple technique of using spare rows and columns (also known as word lines and bit lines, respectively), through the use of error-correcting codes. These techniques have been successfully employed by many semiconductor manufacturers, resulting in significant yield improvements, ranging from 30-fold increases in the yield of early prototypes to 1.5-fold, or even three-fold yield increases in mature processes.

The most common implementations of defect-tolerant memory arrays include redundant bit lines and word lines, as shown in Fig. 10.4. The figure shows a memory array that was split into two sub-

Spare	*Rows*

Memory Array | *Spare Columns* | *Spare Columns* | *Memory Array*

FIGURE 10.4

A memory array with spare rows and columns.

arrays (to avoid very long word and bit lines, which may slow down the memory read and write operations) with spare rows and columns. A defective row, for example, or a row containing one or more defective memory cells can be disconnected by blowing a fusible link at the output of the corresponding decoder, as shown in Fig. 10.5. The disconnected row is then replaced by a spare row, which has a programmable decoder with fusible links, allowing it to replace any defective row (see Fig. 10.5).

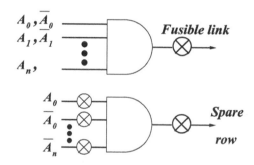

FIGURE 10.5

Standard and programmable decoders.

The first designs that included spare rows and columns relied on laser fuses that impose a relatively large area overhead and require the use of special laser equipment to disconnect faulty lines and connect spare lines in their place. Later, laser fuses have been replaced by CMOS fuses, which can be programmed internally, with no need for external laser equipment. Since any defect that may occur in the internal programming circuit will constitute a chip-kill defect, several memory designers have incorporated error-correcting codes into these programming circuits to increase their reliability.

To determine which rows and columns should be disconnected and replaced by spare rows and columns, respectively, we first need to identify all the faulty memory cells. The memory must be thoroughly tested, and for each faulty cell, a decision has to be made as to whether the entire row or column should be disconnected. In recent memory chip designs, the identification of faulty cells is done internally using built-in self-testing (BIST), thus avoiding the need for external testing equipment. In more advanced designs, the reconfiguration of the memory array, based on the results of the testing, is also performed internally. Implementing self-testing of the memory is quite straightforward and involves scanning sequentially all memory locations and writing and reading 0s and 1s into all the bits. The next step of determining how to assign spare rows and columns to replace all defective rows and columns is considerably more complicated, because individual defective cells can be taken care of by either replacing the cell's row, or the cell's column. An arbitrary assignment of spare rows and columns may lead to a situation where the available spares are insufficient, whereas a different assignment may allow the repair of the memory array.

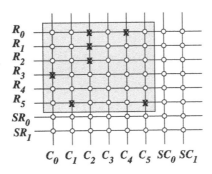

FIGURE 10.6

A 6×6 memory array with two spare rows, two spare columns, and seven defective cells (marked by **x**).

To illustrate the complexity of this assignment problem, consider the 6×6 memory array with two spare rows (SR_0 and SR_1) and two spare columns (SC_0 and SC_1), shown in Fig. 10.6. The array has 7 of its 36 cells defective, and we need to decide which rows and columns to disconnect and replace by spares to obtain a fully operational 6×6 array. Suppose we use a simple *row first* assignment algorithm that calls for using all the available spare rows first, and then the spare columns. For the array in Fig. 10.6, we will first replace rows R_0 and R_1 by the two spare rows and be left with four defective cells. Because only two spare columns exist, the memory array is not repaired.

To devise a better algorithm for determining which rows and columns should be switched out and replaced by spares, we can use the bipartite graph shown in Fig. 10.7. This graph contains two sets of vertices corresponding to the rows (R_0 through R_5) and columns (C_0 through C_5) of the memory array, and has an edge connecting R_i to C_j if the cell at the intersection of row R_i and column C_j is defective. Thus to determine the smallest number of rows and columns that must be disconnected (and replaced by spares), we need to select the smallest number of vertices in Fig. 10.7 required to cover all the edges (for each edge, at least one of the two incident nodes must be selected). For the simple example in Fig. 10.7, it is easy to see that we should select C_2 and R_5 to be replaced by a spare column and row, respectively, and then select one out of C_0 and R_3, and, similarly, one out of C_4 and R_0.

This problem is known as bipartite graph edge covering, and has been shown to be NP-complete. Therefore there is currently no algorithm of polynomial complexity to solve the spare rows and columns assignment problem. We could restrict our designs to have, for example, spare rows only, which would considerably reduce the complexity of this problem. If only spare rows are available, we must replace

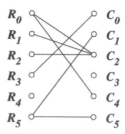

FIGURE 10.7

The bipartite graph corresponding to the memory array in Fig. 10.6.

every row with one or more defective cells by a spare row if one exists. This, however, is not a practical solution for two reasons. First, if two (or more) defects happen in a single column, we will need to use two (or more) spare rows instead of a single spare column (see, for example, column C_2 in Fig. 10.6), which would significantly increase the required number of spare rows. Second, a reasonably common defect in memory arrays is a completely defective column (or row), which would be uncorrectable if no spare columns (or rows) are provided.

As a result, many heuristics for the assignment of spare rows and columns have been developed and implemented. These heuristics rely on the fact that it is not necessary to find the minimum number of rows and columns that should be replaced by spares, but only to find a feasible solution for repairing the array with the given number of spares.

A simple assignment algorithm consists of two steps: The first identifies which rows (or columns) must be selected for replacement. A *must-repair* row is a row that contains a number of defective cells that is greater than the number of currently available spare columns. *Must-repair* columns are defined similarly. For example, column C_2 in Fig. 10.6 is a must-repair column, because it contains three defective cells, whereas only two spare rows are available. Once such must-repair rows and columns are replaced by spares, the number of available spares is reduced, and other rows and columns may become must-repair. For example, after identifying C_2 as a must-repair column and replacing it by, say SC_0, we are left with a single spare column, making row R_5 a must-repair row. This process is continued until no new must-repair rows and columns can be identified, yielding an array with sparse defects.

Although the first step of identifying must-repair rows and columns is reasonably simple, the second step is complicated. Fortunately, to achieve high performance, the size of memory arrays that have their own spare rows and columns is kept reasonably small (about 1 Mbit or less) and as a result, only a few defects remain to be taken care of in the second step of the algorithm. Consequently, even a very simple heuristic, such as the above-mentioned *row-first*, will work properly in most cases. In the example in Fig. 10.6, after replacing the must-repair column C_2 and the must-repair row R_5, we will replace R_0 by the remaining spare row, and then replace C_0 by the remaining spare column. A simple modification to the row-first algorithm that can improve its success rate is to first replace rows and columns with multiple defective cells, and only then address the rows and columns which have a single defective cell.

Even the yield of memory chips that use redundant rows and columns cannot be expected to reach 100%, especially during the early phases of manufacturing when the defect density is still high. Consequently, several manufacturers package and sell partially good chips instead of discarding them. Partially good chips are chips that have some, but not all, of their cell arrays operational, even after using all the redundant lines.

The embedding of large memory arrays in VLSI chips has become very common with the most well-known example of large cache units in microprocessors. These large embedded memory arrays are designed with more aggressive design rules compared with the remaining logic units and, consequently, tend to be more prone to defects. As a result, most manufacturers of microprocessors include some form of redundancy in the cache designs, especially in the second-level cache units, which normally have a larger size than the first level of caches. The incorporated redundancy can be in the form of spare rows, spare columns, or spare subarrays.

Advanced redundancy techniques

The conventional redundancy technique (using spare rows and columns) can be enhanced, for example, by using an error-correcting code (ECC). Such an approach has been applied in the design of a 16-Mb DRAM chip. This chip includes four independent subarrays with 16 redundant bit lines and 24 redundant word lines per subarray. In addition, for every 128 data bits, nine check bits were added to allow the correction of any single-bit error within these 137 bits (this is a (137,9) SEC/DED Hamming code; see Section 3.1). To reduce the probability of two or more faulty bits in the same word (e.g., due to clustered faults), every eight adjacent bits in the subarray were assigned to eight separate words. It was found that the benefit of the combined strategy for yield enhancement was greater than the sum of the expected benefits of the two individual techniques. The reason is that the ECC technique is very effective against individual cell failures, whereas redundant rows and columns are very effective against several defective cells within the same row or column, as well as against completely defective rows and columns. As mentioned in Chapter 3, the ECC technique is commonly used in large memory systems to protect against transient faults occurring while the memory is in operation, in order to increase its reliability. The reliability improvement, due to the use of ECC, was shown to be only slightly affected by the use of the check bits to correct defective memory cells.

Increases in the size of memory chips made it necessary to partition the memory array into several subarrays to decrease the current and reduce the access time, by shortening the length of the bit and word lines. Using the conventional redundancy method implied that each subarray has its own spare rows and columns, leading to situations, in which one subarray had an insufficient number of spare lines to handle local faults while other subarrays still had some unused spares. One obvious approach to resolve this problem is to turn some of the local redundant lines into global redundant lines, allowing for a more efficient use of the spares at the cost of higher silicon area overhead, due to the larger number of required programmable fuses.

Several other approaches for more efficient redundancy schemes have been developed. One such approach was followed in the design of a 1-Gb DRAM. This design used fewer redundant lines than the traditional technique, and the redundant lines were kept local. For added defect-tolerance, each subarray of size 256-Mb (a quarter of the chip) was fabricated in such a way that it could become part of up to four different memory ICs. The resulting wafer shown in Fig. 10.8 includes 112 such subarrays, out of which 16 (marked by a circle in the figure) would not be fabricated in an ordinary design, in which the chip boundaries are fixed.

To allow this flexibility in determining the chip boundaries, the area of the subarray had to be increased by 2%, but to keep the overall area of the subarray identical to that in the conventional

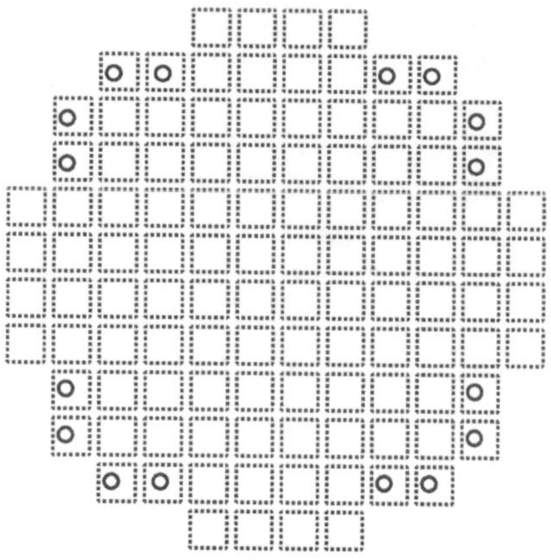

FIGURE 10.8

An 8" wafer containing 112 256-MByte subarrays. (The 16 subarrays marked with a circle would not be fabricated in an ordinary design.)

design, row redundancy was eliminated, thus compensating for this increase. Column redundancy was still implemented.

Yield analysis of the design in Fig. 10.8 shows that if the faults are almost evenly distributed and the Poisson distribution can be used, there is almost no advantage in using the new design compared to the conventional design with fixed chip boundaries, and use of the conventional row and column redundancy technique. There is however, a considerable increase in yield if the medium-area negative binomial distribution (described in Section 10.3) applies. The extent of the improvement in yield is very sensitive to the fabrication parameter values.

Another approach for incorporating defect-tolerance into memory ICs combines row and column redundancy with several redundant subarrays that are to replace those subarrays hit by chip-kill faults. Such an approach was followed by the designers of another 1-Gbit memory, which includes eight mats of size 128-Mbit each, and eight redundant blocks of size 1-Mbit each (see Fig. 10.9). The redundant block consists of four basic 256-Kbit arrays, and has an additional eight spare rows and four spare columns (see Fig. 10.10), the purpose of which is to increase the probability that the redundant block itself is operational, and can be used for replacing a block with chip-kill faults.

Every mat consists of 512 basic arrays of size 256-Kbit each, and has 32 spare rows and 32 spare columns. However, these are not global spares. Four spare rows are allocated to a 16-Mbit portion of the mat, and eight spare columns are allocated to a 32-Mbit portion of the mat.

The yield of this new design of a memory chip is compared to that of the traditional design with only row and column redundancy in Fig. 10.11, demonstrating the benefits of some amount of block redundancy. The increase in yield is much greater than the 2% area increase required for the redundant blocks. It can also be shown that column redundancy is still beneficial, even when redundant blocks are incorporated, and that the optimal number of such redundant columns is independent of the number of spare blocks.

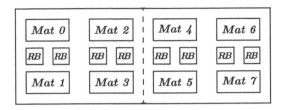

FIGURE 10.9

A 1-Gb chip with eight mats of size 128-Mbit each, and eight redundant blocks (*RB*) of size 1-Mbit each.

FIGURE 10.10

A redundant block, including four 256-Kbit arrays, eight redundant rows, and four redundant columns.

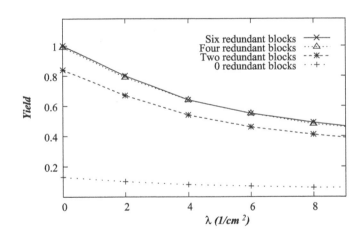

FIGURE 10.11

Yield as a function of λ for different numbers of redundant blocks per half chip (chip-kill probability $= 5 \times 10^{-4}$).

10.4.3 LOGIC INTEGRATED CIRCUITS WITH REDUNDANCY

In contrast to memory arrays, very few logic ICs have been designed with any built-in redundancy. Some regularity in the design is necessary if a low overhead for redundancy inclusion is desired. For completely irregular designs, duplication, and even triplication, are currently the only available redundancy techniques, and these are often impractical, due to their large overhead. Regular circuits, such as programmable logic arrays (PLAs) and arrays of identical computing elements, require less redundancy, and various defect-tolerance techniques have been proposed (and some implemented) to enhance their yield. These techniques, however, require extra circuits, such as spare product terms (for PLAs), reconfiguration switches, and additional input lines to allow the identification of faulty product terms. Unlike memory ICs, in which all defective cells can be identified by applying external test patterns, the identification of defective elements in logic ICs (even for those with regular structure) is more complex and usually requires the addition of some built-in testing aids. Thus testability must also be a factor in choosing defect-tolerant designs for logic ICs.

The situation becomes even more complex in random logic circuits, such as microprocessors. When designing such circuits, it is necessary to partition the design into separate components, preferably with each having a regular structure. Then, different redundancy schemes can be applied to the different components, including the possibility of no defect-tolerance in components, for which the cost of incorporating redundancy becomes prohibitive.

We describe next two examples of such designs: a defect-tolerant microprocessor and a wafer-scale design. These demonstrate the feasibility of incorporating defect tolerance for yield enhancement in the design of processors, and prove that the use of defect tolerance is not limited to the highly regular memory arrays.

The Hyeti microprocessor is a 16-bit defect-tolerant microprocessor that was designed and fabricated to demonstrate the feasibility of a high-yield defect-tolerant microprocessor. This microprocessor may be used as the core of an application-specific microprocessor-based system that is integrated on a single chip. The large silicon area consumed by such a system would most certainly result in low yield, unless some defect tolerance in the form of redundancy were incorporated into the design.

The data path of the microprocessor, contains several functional units, such as registers, an arithmetic and logic unit (ALU), and bus circuitry. Almost all the units in the data path have circuits that are replicated 16 times, leading to the classic bit-slice organization. This regular organization was exploited for yield enhancement by providing a spare slice that can replace a defective slice. Not all the circuits in the data path, though, consist of completely identical subcircuits. The status register, for example, has each bit associated with unique random logic, and therefore has no added redundancy.

The control part has been designed as a hardwired control circuit that can be implemented using PLAs only. The regular structure of a PLA allows a straightforward incorporation of redundancy for yield enhancement, through the addition of spare product terms. The design of the PLA has been modified to allow the identification of defective product terms.

Yield analysis of this microprocessor, has shown that the optimal redundancy for the data path is a single 1-bit slice, and the optimal redundancy for all the PLAs is one product term. A higher-than-optimal redundancy has, however, been implemented in many of these PLAs, because the floorplan of the control unit allows for the addition of a few extra product terms to the PLAs, with no area penalty. A practical yield analysis should take into consideration the exact floorplan of the chip and allow the addition of a limited amount of redundancy beyond the optimal amount. Still, not all the available area should be used up for spares, since this will increase the circuit area, which will, in turn, increase the chip-kill area. This greater chip-kill area can, at some point, offset the yield increase resulting from the added redundancy.

Fig. 10.12 depicts the effective yield (see Eq. (10.24)), without redundancy in the microprocessor, and with the optimal redundancy as a function of the area of the circuitry added to the microprocessor (which serves as a controller for that circuitry). The figure shows that an increase in yield of about 18% can be expected when the optimal amount of redundancy is incorporated in the design.

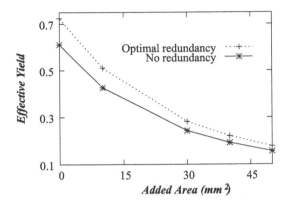

FIGURE 10.12

The effective yield as a function of the added area, without redundancy and with optimal redundancy, for the negative binomial distribution with $\lambda = 0.05/mm^2$ and $\alpha = 2$.

A second experiment with defect-tolerance in nonmemory designs is the 3-D computer, an example of a wafer-scale design. The 3-D computer is a cellular array processor implemented in wafer-scale integration technology. The most unique feature of its implementation is its use of stacked wafers. The basic processing element is divided into five functional units, each of which is implemented on a different wafer. Thus each wafer contains only one type of functional unit and includes spares for yield enhancement, as explained below. Units in different wafers are connected vertically through microbridges between adjacent wafers to form a complete processing element. The first working prototype of the 3-D computer was of size 32×32. The second prototype included 128×128 processing elements.

Defect tolerance in each wafer is achieved through an interstitial redundancy scheme (see Section 4.2.3), in which the spare units are uniformly distributed in the array and are connected to the primary units with local and short interconnects. In the 32×32 prototype, a $(1,1)$ redundancy scheme was used, and each primary unit had a separate spare unit. A $(2,4)$ scheme was used in the 128×128 prototype; each primary unit is connected to two spare units, and each spare unit is connected to four primary units, resulting in a redundancy of 50%, rather than the 100% for the $(1,1)$ scheme. The $(2,4)$ interstitial redundancy scheme can be implemented in a variety of ways. The exact implementation in the 3-D computer and its effect on the yield are further discussed in the next section.

Since it is highly unlikely that a fabricated wafer will be entirely fault-free, the yield of the processor would be zero if no redundancy were included. With the implemented redundancy, the observed yield of the 32×32 array after repair was 45%. For the 128×128 array, the $(1,1)$ redundancy scheme would have resulted in a very low yield (about 3%), due to the high probability of having faults in a primary unit and in its associated spare. The yield of the 128×128 array with the $(2,4)$ scheme was projected to be much higher.

10.4.4 MODIFYING THE FLOORPLAN

The floorplan of a chip is normally not expected to have an impact on its yield. This is true for chips that are small and have a fault distribution that can be accurately described by either the Poisson, or the compound Poisson yield models with large-area clustering (in which the size of the fault clusters is larger than the size of the chip).

The situation has changed with the introduction of integrated circuits with a total area of $2\ cm^2$, and up. Such chips usually consist of different component types, each with its own fault density, and have some incorporated redundancy. If chips with these attributes are hit by medium-sized fault clusters, then changes in the floorplan can affect their projected yield.

Consider the following example, depicted in Fig. 10.13, of a chip consisting of four equal-area modules (functional units), M_1, M_2, M_3, and M_4. The chip has no incorporated redundancy, and all four modules are necessary for the proper operation of the chip.

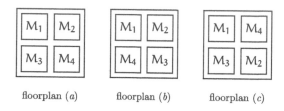

| floorplan (a) | floorplan (b) | floorplan (c) |

FIGURE 10.13

Three floorplans of a 2×2 array.

Assuming that the defect clusters are medium-sized relative to the chip size, and that the four modules have different sensitivities to defects, we use the medium-area negative binomial distribution (described in Section 10.3) for the spatial distribution of faults, with parameters λ_i (for module M_i) and α (per block), and $\lambda_1 \le \lambda_2 \le \lambda_3 \le \lambda_4$.

This chip has $4!=24$ possible floorplans. Since rotation and reflection will not affect the yield, we are left with three distinct floorplans, shown in Fig. 10.13. If small-area clustering (clusters smaller than or comparable to the size of a module) or large-area clustering (clusters larger than or equal to the chip area) is assumed, the projected yields of all possible floorplans will be the same. This is not the case, however, when medium-area clustering (with horizontal or vertical blocks of two modules) is assumed.

Assuming horizontal defect blocks of size two modules, the yields of floorplans (a), (b), and (c) are

$$Y(a) = Y(b) = (1 + (\lambda_1 + \lambda_2)/\alpha)^{-\alpha} (1 + (\lambda_3 + \lambda_4)/\alpha)^{-\alpha};$$

$$Y(c) = (1 + (\lambda_1 + \lambda_4)/\alpha)^{-\alpha} (1 + (\lambda_2 + \lambda_3)/\alpha)^{-\alpha}. \qquad (10.39)$$

A simple calculation shows that under the condition $\lambda_1 \le \lambda_2 \le \lambda_3 \le \lambda_4$, floorplans (a) and (b) have the higher yield. Similarly, for vertical defect blocks of size two modules,

$$Y(a) = Y(c) = (1 + (\lambda_1 + \lambda_3)/\alpha)^{-\alpha} (1 + (\lambda_2 + \lambda_4)/\alpha)^{-\alpha};$$

$$Y(b) = (1 + (\lambda_1 + \lambda_4)/\alpha)^{-\alpha} (1 + (\lambda_2 + \lambda_3)/\alpha)^{-\alpha}, \qquad (10.40)$$

and floorplans (a) and (c) have the higher yield. Thus floorplan (a) is the one which maximizes the chip yield for any cluster size. An intuitive explanation for the choice of (a) is that the less sensitive modules are placed together, the higher the chance that the chip will survive a cluster of defects.

If the previous chip is generalized to a 3×3 array (as depicted in Fig. 10.14), and $\lambda_1 \leq \lambda_2 \leq \cdots \leq \lambda_9$, then, unfortunately, there is no one floorplan that is always the best, and the optimal floorplan depends on the cluster size. However, the following generalizations can be made. For all cluster sizes,

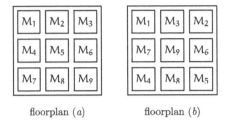

floorplan (a)   floorplan (b)

FIGURE 10.14

Two floorplans of a 3 × 3 array.

the module with the highest fault density (M_9) should be placed in the center of the chip, and each row or column should be rearranged so that its most sensitive module is in its center (such as, for example, floorplan (b) in Fig. 10.14). Note that we reached this conclusion without assuming that the boundaries of the chip are more prone to defects than its center. The intuitive explanation to this recommendation is that placing highly sensitive modules at the chip corners increases the probability that a single fault cluster will hit two or even four adjacent chips on the wafer. This is less likely to happen if the less sensitive modules are placed at the corners.

The next example is that of a chip with redundancy. The chip consists of four modules, M_1, S_1, M_2, and S_2, where S_1 is a spare for M_1, and S_2 is a spare for M_2. The three topologically distinct floorplans for this chip are shown in Fig. 10.15. Let the number of faults have a medium-area negative

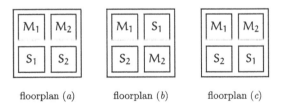

floorplan (a)   floorplan (b)   floorplan (c)

FIGURE 10.15

Three alternative floorplans for a chip with redundancy.

binomial distribution with an average of λ_1 for M_1 and S_1, and λ_2 for M_2 and S_2, and a clustering parameter of α per block. Assuming that the defect clusters are horizontal and of size two modules each, the yields of the three floorplans are the following:

$$
\begin{aligned}
Y(a) = Y(c) &= 2[1 + (\lambda_1 + \lambda_2)/\alpha]^{-\alpha} + 2[1 + \lambda_1/\alpha]^{-\alpha}[1 + \lambda_2/\alpha]^{-\alpha} \\
&- 2[1 + (\lambda_1 + \lambda_2)/\alpha]^{-\alpha}[1 + \lambda_1/\alpha]^{-\alpha} - 2[1 + (\lambda_1 + \lambda_2)/\alpha]^{-\alpha}[1 + \lambda_2/\alpha]^{-\alpha} \\
&+ [1 + (\lambda_1 + \lambda_2)/\alpha]^{-2\alpha};
\end{aligned}
$$
(10.41)

$$Y(b) = \left[2(1+\lambda_1/\alpha)^{-\alpha} - (1+2\lambda_1/\alpha)^{-\alpha}\right]$$
$$\times \left[2(1+\lambda_2/\alpha)^{-\alpha} - (1+2\lambda_2/\alpha)^{-\alpha}\right]. \quad (10.42)$$

It can be easily proved that for any values of λ_1 and λ_2, $Y(a) = Y(c) \geq Y(b)$.

If, however, the defect clusters are vertical and of size two modules, then clearly, $Y(a)$ is given by Eq. (10.42), and $Y(b) = Y(c)$ and are given by Eq. (10.41). In this case, $Y(b) = Y(c) \geq Y(a)$ for all values of λ_1 and λ_2. Floorplan (c) should therefore be preferred over floorplans (a) and (b). An intuitive justification for the choice of floorplan (c) is that it guarantees the separation between the primary modules and their spares for any size and shape of the defect clusters. This results in a higher yield, since it is less likely that the same cluster will hit both the module and its spare, thus killing the chip.

This last recommendation is exemplified by the design of the 3-D computer, described in Subsection 10.4.3. The (2,4) structure that has been selected for implementation in the 3-D computer is shown in Fig. 10.16A. This floorplan has every spare unit adjacent to the four primary units that it can replace.

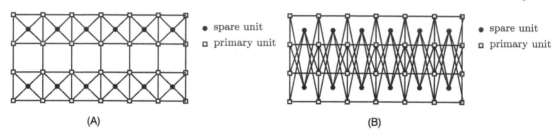

(A) (B)

FIGURE 10.16

The original and a alternative floorplans of a wafer in the 3-D computer. (A) the original floorplan. (B) an alternative floorplan.

This layout has short interconnection links between the spare and any primary unit that it may replace, and as a result, the performance degradation upon a failure of a primary unit is minimal. However, the close proximity of the spare and primary units results in a low yield in the presence of clustered faults, since a single fault cluster may cover a primary unit and all of its spares.

Several alternative floorplans can be designed that place the spare farther apart from the primary units connected to it (as recommended above). One such floorplan is shown in Fig. 10.16B. The projected yields of the 128×128 array using the original floorplan (Fig. 10.16A), or the alternative floorplan (Fig. 10.16B), are shown in Fig. 10.17. The yield has been calculated using the medium-area negative binomial distribution with a defect block size of two rows of primary units (see Fig. 10.16A). Fig. 10.17 clearly shows that the alternative floorplan, in which the spare unit is separated from the primary units that it can replace, has a higher projected yield.

10.5 FURTHER READING

Several books (e.g., [14,16,17]), an edited collection of articles [9], and journal survey papers (e.g., [11,26,31,32,36,42,44,45,54,63]) have been devoted to the topic of this chapter. More specifically, for

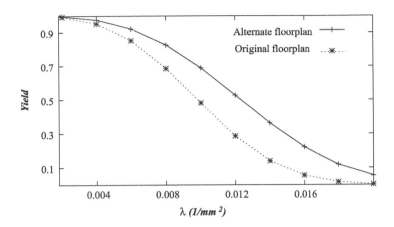

FIGURE 10.17

The yield of the original and alternate floorplans, depicted in Fig. 10.16, as a function of λ ($\alpha = 2$).

a detailed description of how critical areas and POFs can be calculated, see Chapter 5 in [17] as well as [60,67]. Two geometrical methods different from those mentioned in this chapter are the virtual artwork technique [43] and the Voronoi diagram approach [52]. Parametric faults resulting from variations in process parameters are described in [13,58].

Triangular and exponential density functions have been proposed as compounders in [47] and [56], respectively. The more commonly used (as a mixing function) gamma distribution has been suggested in [50] and [59]. The "window method" that is used to estimate the parameters of yield models is described in [31,50,53,56,61]. It has been extended in [34] to include estimation of the block size for the medium-area clustering yield model.

Simpler techniques for projecting the yield of an already manufactured chip when either moving the manufacturing to a different fabrication facility or changing the technology employed are described in [1].

Designs of defect-tolerant memories are described in [6,19,21,22,64,72,73]. The use of ECC is presented in [19]; the flexible chip boundaries scheme appears in [64], and the memory design with redundant subarrays is described in [73]. Some of these designs have been analyzed in [23,25,62]. Many techniques for assigning spare rows and columns to defective rows and columns in memory arrays have been developed, see for example [2,3,10,37,57].

Defect-tolerance techniques for logic circuits have been proposed (and some implemented) in [5, 29,30,33,38,40,48,69,74]. The Hyeti microprocessor is described and analyzed in [40], and the 3-D computer is presented in [74]. Techniques to improve the yield of multi-cores and systems on a chip appear in [39,46,51,55]. Defect tolerance in 3-D circuits is studied in [68,71]. Layout modification techniques (not covered in this chapter) have been reported in many papers, e.g., [8,12]. The impact of scaling on yield was analyzed in [28].

The designers of many modern microprocessors have incorporated redundancy into the design of the embedded cache units. To determine the type of redundancy to be employed in the cache units of the PowerPC microprocessors, row, column, and subarray redundancies were compared considering the area and performance penalties and the expected yield improvements [65]. Based on their analysis, the designers have decided to use row only redundancy for the level 1 cache unit and row and column redundancy for the level 2 cache unit.

Intel's Pentium Pro processor incorporated redundancy in its 512-KByte level 2 cache [18]. This cache unit consists of 72 subarrays of 64-K memory cells each, organized into four quadrants, and a single redundant subarray has been added to every quadrant. The reported increase in yield, due to the added redundancy, is 35%. This design includes a circuit for a BIST that identifies the faulty cells, and a flash memory circuit that is programmed to replace a defective subarray with a spare subarray.

The two 64-KBytes cache unit in Hewlett–Packard's PA7300LC microprocessor have been designed with redundant columns. Four spare columns are included in a spare block that can be used to replace a faulty four-column block using multiplexers that are controlled by programmable fuses. A BIST circuit is included to test the cache unit and identify the faulty block [35]. Different algorithms for built-in test and repair of memories are described in [20,49].

The spare rows and columns assignment algorithm used in the self-repair circuit for the embedded memory unit in an Alpha microprocessor is described in [2].

The effect of floorplanning on yield has been analyzed in [24,27].

The yield of analog and mixed-signal circuits was studied in [15,41]. Design for manufacturability of sub-65 nm CMOS circuits, considering lithography aspects, subwavelength patterning, stress proximity effects, and process variability is described in [7,70]. The unique defects that occur in post-CMOS cicuits (e.g., Nanowires and carbon nanotubes) and the corresponding yield estimations are described in [4,66].

10.6 EXERCISES

1. Derive an expression for the critical area $A_{miss}^{(c)}(u)$ for square $u \times u$ missing-material defects in a conductor of length L and width w. Assume that one side of the defect is always parallel to the conductor, and that $L \gg w$ so that the nonlinear edge effects can be ignored.

2. Use the polygon expansion technique to calculate approximately the critical area for circular short-circuit defects of diameter 3 for the 14×7 layout consisting of two conductors shown below.

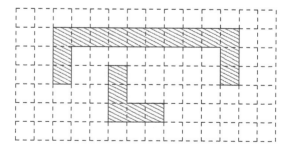

3. Find the average critical area $A_{miss}^{(c)}$ for circular missing-material defects in a single conductor of length L and width w using the defect size distribution in Eq. (10.1) with $p = 3$. Assume that $L \gg w$, and ignore the nonlinear term in Eq. (10.6).

4. (a) Derive an expression for the critical area $A_{miss}^{(c)}(x)$ of a circular missing-material defect with diameter x in the case of two conductors of length L, width w, and separation s (as shown in Fig. 10.1). Ignore the nonlinear terms and note that the expression differs for the three cases: $x < w$; $w \le x \le 2w + s$; and $2w + s < x \le x_M$.

(b) Find the average critical area $A_{miss}^{(c)}$ using the defect size distribution in Eq. (10.1) with $p = 3$. For simplicity, assume $x_M = \infty$.

5. A chip with an area of 0.2 cm^2 (and no redundancy) is currently manufactured. This chip has a POF of $\theta = 0.6$ and an observed yield of $Y_1 = 0.87$. The manufacturer plans to fabricate a similar, but larger, chip, with an area of 0.3 cm^2, using the same wafer fabrication equipment. Assume that there is only one type of defects, and that the yield of both chips follows the Poisson model $Y = e^{-\theta A_{chip} d}$, with the same POF θ and the same defect density d.

(a) Calculate the defect density d and the projected yield Y_2 of the second chip.

(b) Let the area of the second chip be a variable A. Draw the graph of Y_2, the yield of the second chip, as a function of A (for A between 0 and 2).

6. A chip of area A_{chip} (without redundancy, and with one type of defects) is currently manufactured at a yield of $Y = 0.9$. The manufacturer is examining the possibility of designing and fabricating two larger chips with areas of $2A_{chip}$ and $4A_{chip}$. The designs and layouts of the new chips will be similar to those of the current chip (i.e., same θ), and the defect density d will remain the same.

(a) Calculate the expected yields of the two new chips assuming a Poisson model.

(b) Calculate the expected yields of the two new chips assuming a negative binomial model with $\alpha = 1.5$.

(c) Discuss the difference between the results of (a) and (b).

7. A design consisting of ten identical modules has been manufactured and the observed yield was 0.1.

(a) What is the average number of faults λ assuming a Poisson yield model? What is λ if the negative binomial model with $\alpha = 2$ is assumed?

(b) To increase the yield a single spare module has been added. Ignoring the increase in the area of the chip, calculate the yield of the new design for the Poisson and the negative binomial models.

8. For a chip without redundancy assume that X, the number of faults on the chip, follows a compound Poisson distribution.

(a) Use as a compounder the triangular density function

$$f_L(\ell) = \begin{cases} \frac{\ell}{\lambda^2} & 0 \le \ell \le \lambda \\ \frac{2\lambda - \ell}{\lambda^2} & \lambda \le \ell \le 2\lambda, \end{cases}$$

and show that it results in the following expression for the chip yield:

$$Y_{chip} = \text{Prob}\{X = 0\} = \int_0^{2\lambda} e^{-\ell} f_L(\ell) \, d\ell = \left(\frac{1 - e^{-\lambda}}{\lambda} \right)^2. \qquad (10.43)$$

(b) Now use as a compounder the exponential density function

$$f_L(\ell) = \frac{e^{-\ell/\lambda}}{\lambda},$$

and show that it results in

$$Y_{chip} = Prob\{X = 0\} = \int_0^\infty e^{-\ell} f_L(\ell) \, d\ell = \frac{1}{1+\lambda}. \tag{10.44}$$

(c) Compare the yield expressions in Eqs. (10.43) and (10.44) to those for the Poisson and negative binomial models (for chips without redundancy) by drawing the graph of the yield as a function of λ for $0.001 \leq \lambda \leq 1.5$. For the negative binomial model, use three values of α, namely, $\alpha = 0.25, 2$, and 5.

9. Why does the spare row in Fig. 10.5 include a fusible link?

10. To a memory array with four rows and eight columns, a single spare row and two spare columns have been added. The testing of the memory array has identified four defective cells indicated by an x in the diagram below.

$$
\begin{bmatrix}
x & 0 & 0 & 0 & 0 & 0 & 0 & 0 \\
0 & 0 & 0 & 0 & 0 & x & 0 & 0 \\
0 & 0 & 0 & 0 & 0 & 0 & 0 & 0 \\
0 & x & 0 & 0 & 0 & x & 0 & 0
\end{bmatrix}
$$

(a) List two ways to reconfigure the memory array, i.e., which rows and columns will be disconnected and replaced by spares.

(b) Show a distribution of the four defective cells within the array, for which the available spares will be insufficient. How many such distributions of four defective cells exist?

(c) Given that there are four defective cells, and that they are randomly distributed over the array, what is the probability of such an irreparable distribution?

11. A 6×6 memory array with two spare rows and two spare columns is shown in Fig. 10.18. Show the corresponding bipartite graph, identify all the must-repair rows and columns, and select additional rows/columns to cover the remaining defective cells. Will the column-first (row-first) algorithm, if applied after replacing the must-repair rows (must-repair columns), be able to repair the memory array?

12. A chip consists of five modules, out of which four are needed for proper operation, and one is a spare. Suppose the fabrication process has a fault density of 0.7 faults/cm², and the area of each module is 0.1 cm².

(a) Calculate the expected yield of the chip using the Poisson model.

(b) Calculate the expected yield of the chip using the negative binomial model with $\alpha = 1$.

(c) For each of the two models in parts (a) and (b), is the addition of the spare module to the chip beneficial from the point of view of the effective yield?

(d) Discuss the difference in the answer to (c) between the two models.

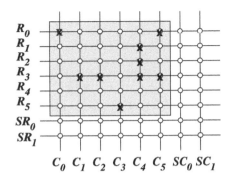

FIGURE 10.18

A 6×6 memory array with two spare rows, two spare columns, and nine defective cells (marked by an **x**).

REFERENCES

[1] A. Ahmadi, H.-G. Stratigopoulos, K. Huang, A. Nahar, B. Orr, M. Pas, J.M. Carulli, Y. Makris, Yield forecasting across semiconductor fabrication plants and design generations, IEEE Transactions on Computer-Aided Design of Integrated Circuits and Systems (TCAD) 36 (12) (2017) 2120–2133.

[2] D.K. Bhavsar, An algorithm for row-column self-repair of RAMs and its implementation in the alpha 21264, in: International Test Conference (ITC'99), 1999, pp. 311–318.

[3] D. Blough, Performance evaluation of a reconfiguration algorithm for memory arrays containing clustered faults, IEEE Transactions on Reliability 45 (June 1996) 274–284.

[4] S. Bobba, J. Zhang, P.E. Gaillardon, H.S.P. Wong, S. Mitra, G. de Micheli, System level benchmarking with yield-enhanced standard cell library for carbon nanotube VLSI circuits, ACM Journal on Emerging Technologies in Computing Systems (JETC) 10 (May 2014) 33.

[5] A. Boubekeur, J-L. Patry, G. Saucier, J. Trilhe, Configuring a wafer scale two-dimensional array of single-bit processors, IEEE Computer 25 (April 1992) 29–39.

[6] J.C. Chan, S.K. Gupta, Characterization of granularity and redundancy for SRAMs for optimal yield-per-area, in: IEEE Conference on Computer Design (ICCD), 2008, pp. 219–226.

[7] C. Chiang, J. Kawa, Design for Manufacturability and Yield for Nano-Scale CMOS, Springer, 2007.

[8] V.K.R. Chiluvuri, I. Koren, Layout synthesis techniques for yield enhancement, IEEE Transactions on Semiconductor Manufacturing 8 (Special Issue on Defect, Fault, and Yield Modeling) (May 1995) 178–187.

[9] B. Ciciani (Ed.), Manufacturing Yield Evaluation of VLSI/WSI Systems, IEEE Computer Society Press, 1998.

[10] H. Cho, W. Kang, S. Kang, A very efficient redundancy analysis method using fault grouping, ETRI Journal 35 (3) (June 2013) 439–447.

[11] J.A. Cunningham, The use and evaluation of yield models in integrated circuit manufacturing, IEEE Transactions on Semiconductor Manufacturing 3 (May 1990) 60–71.

[12] N. Dhumane, S. Kundu, Critical area driven dummy fill insertion to improve manufacturing yield, in: 13th Symposium on Quality Electronic Design (ISQED), 2012, pp. 334–341.

[13] S.W. Director, W. Maly, A.J. Strojwas, VLSI Design for Manufacturing: Yield Enhancement, Kluwer Academic Publishers, 1990.

[14] A.V. Ferris-Prabhu, Introduction to Semiconductor Device Yield Modeling, Artech House, 1992.

[15] F. Gong, Y. Shi, H. Yu, L. He, Variability-aware parametric yield estimation for analog/mixed-signal circuits: concepts, algorithms, and challenges, IEEE Design and Test 31 (4) (August 2014) 6–15.

[16] J.P. Gyvez, Integrated Circuit Defect-Sensitivity: Theory and Computational Models, Kluwer Academic Publishers, 1993.

[17] J.P. Gyvez (Ed.), IC Manufacturability: The Art of Process and Design Integration, IEEE Computer Society Press, 1998.

[18] C.W. Hampson, Redundancy and high-volume manufacturing methods, Intel Technology Journal (1997), 4th Quarter, available at http://developer.intel.com/technology/itj/q41997/articles/art_4.htm.

[19] H.L. Kalter, C.H. Stapper, J.E. Barth, J. Dilorenzo, C.E. Drake, J.A. Fifield, G.A. Kelley, S.C. Lewis, W.B. Van Der Hoeven, J.A. Yankosky, A 50-ns 16Mb DRAM with 10-ns data rate and on-chip ECC, IEEE Journal of Solid-State Circuits (October 1990) 1118–1128.

[20] J. Kim, W. Lee, K. Cho, S. Kang, Hardware-efficient built-in redundancy analysis for memory with various spares, IEEE Transactions on Very Large Scale Integration (VLSI) Systems 25 (3) (March 2017) 844–856.

[21] T. Kirihata, Y. Watanabe, H. Wong, J.K. DeBrosse, Fault-tolerant designs for 256 Mb DRAM, IEEE Journal of Solid-State Circuits 31 (April 1996) 558–566.

[22] G. Kitsukawa, M. Horiguchi, Y. Kawajiri, T. Kawahara, 256-Mb DRAM circuit technologies for file applications, IEEE Journal of Solid-State Circuits 28 (November 1993) 1105–1110.

[23] I. Koren, Z. Koren, Yield analysis of a novel scheme for defect-tolerant memories, in: IEEE International Conference on Innovative Systems in Silicon, October 1996, pp. 269–278.

[24] Z. Koren, I. Koren, On the effect of floorplanning on the yield of large area integrated circuits, IEEE Transactions on Very Large Scale Integration (VLSI) Systems 5 (March 1997) 3–14.

[25] I. Koren, Z. Koren, Analysis of a hybrid defect-tolerance scheme for high-density memory ICs, in: IEEE International Symposium on Defect and Fault Tolerance in VLSI Systems, October 1997, pp. 166–174.

[26] I. Koren, Z. Koren, Defect tolerant VLSI circuits: techniques and yield analysis, Proceedings of the IEEE 86 (September 1998) 1817–1836.

[27] I. Koren, Z. Koren, Incorporating yield enhancement into the floorplanning process, IEEE Transactions on Computers 49 (Special Issue on Defect Tolerance in Digital Systems) (June 2000) 532–541.

[28] I. Koren, The effect of scaling on the yield of VLSI circuits, in: W. Moore, W. Maly, A. Strojwas (Eds.), Yield Modelling and Defect Tolerance in VLSI, Adam Hillger Ltd., 1988, pp. 91–99.

[29] I. Koren, D.K. Pradhan, Yield and performance enhancement through redundancy in VLSI and WSI multiprocessor systems, Proceedings of the IEEE 74 (May 1986) 699–711.

[30] I. Koren, D.K. Pradhan, Modeling the effect of redundancy on yield and performance of VLSI systems, IEEE Transactions on Computers 36 (March 1987) 344–355.

[31] I. Koren, C.H. Stapper, Yield models for defect tolerant VLSI circuits: a review, in: I. Koren (Ed.), Defect and Fault Tolerance in VLSI Systems, vol. 1, Plenum, 1989, pp. 1–21.

[32] I. Koren, A.D. Singh, Fault tolerance in VLSI circuits, IEEE Computer 23 (Special Issue on Fault-Tolerant Systems) (July 1990) 73–83.

[33] I. Koren, Z. Koren, D.K. Pradhan, Designing interconnection buses in VLSI and WSI for maximum yield and minimum delay, IEEE Journal of Solid-State Circuits 23 (June 1988) 859–866.

[34] I. Koren, Z. Koren, C.H. Stapper, A unified negative binomial distribution for yield analysis of defect tolerant circuits, IEEE Transactions on Computers 42 (June 1993) 724–734.

[35] D. Kubicek, T. Sullivan, A. Mehra, J. McBride, High-performance processor design guided by system costs, Hewlett-Packard Journal 48 (June 1997) 8, available at http://www.hpl.hp.com/hpjournal/97jun/jun97a8.htm.

[36] N. Kumar, K. Kennedy, K. Gildersleeve, R. Abelson, C.M. Mastrangelo, D.C. Montgomery, A review of yield modelling techniques for semiconductor manufacturing, International Journal of Production Research 44 (2006) 5019–5026.

[37] S.-Y. Kuo, W. Fuchs, Efficient spare allocation for reconfigurable arrays, IEEE Design and Test 4 (February 1987) 24–31.

[38] S.-Y. Kuo, W. Kent Fuchs, Fault diagnosis and spare allocation for yield enhancement in large reconfigurable PLA's, IEEE Transactions on Computers 41 (February 1992) 221–226.

[39] F. Lan, Y. Pan, K-T. Cheng, An efficient network-on-chip yield estimation approach based on Gibbs sampling, IEEE Transactions on Computer-Aided Design of Integrated Circuits and Systems 35 (March 2016) 447–457.

[40] R. Leveugle, Z. Koren, I. Koren, G. Saucier, N. Wehn, The HYETI defect tolerant microprocessor: a practical experiment and a cost-effectiveness analysis, IEEE Transactions on Computers 43 (December 1994) 1398–1406.

[41] X. Li, W. Zhang, F. Wang, S. Sun, C. Gu, Efficient parametric yield estimation of analog/mixed-signal circuits via Bayesian model fusion, in: IEEE/ACM International Conference Computer-Aided Design, 2012, pp. 627–634.

[42] W. Maly, Computer-aided design for VLSI circuit manufacturability, Proceedings of the IEEE 78 (February 1990) 356–392.

[43] W. Maly, W.R. Moore, A. Strojwas, Yield loss mechanisms and defect tolerance, in: W.R. Moore, W. Maly, A. Strojwas (Eds.), Yield Modelling and Defect Tolerance in VLSI, Adam Hillger Ltd., 1988, pp. 3–30.

[44] T.L. Michalka, R.C. Varshney, J.D. Meindl, A discussion of yield modeling with defect clustering, circuit repair, and circuit redundancy, IEEE Transactions on Semiconductor Manufacturing 3 (August 1990) 116–127.

[45] W.R. Moore, A review of fault-tolerant techniques for the enhancement of integrated circuit yield, Proceedings of the IEEE 74 (May 1986) 684–698.

[46] D.P. Munteanu, V. Sune, R. Rodriguez-Montanes, J.A. Carrasco, A combinatorial method for the evaluation of yield of fault-tolerant systems-on-chip, in: International Conference on Dependable Systems and Networks, 2003, pp. 563–572.

[47] B.T. Murphy, Cost-size optima of monolithic integrated circuits, Proceedings of the IEEE 52 (December 1964) 1537–1545.

[48] R. Negrini, M.G. Sami, R. Stefanelli, Fault Tolerance Through Reconfiguration in VLSI and WSI Arrays, MIT Press, 1989.

[49] P. Ohler, S. Hellebrand, H.-J. Wunderlich, An integrated built-in self-test and repair approach for memories with 2D redundancy, in: IEEE European Test Symposium (ETS), May 2007, pp. 91–99.

[50] T. Okabe, M. Nagata, S. Shimada, Analysis of yield of integrated circuits and a new expression for the yield, Electrical Engineering Japan 92 (December 1972) 135–141.

[51] A. Pan, R. Rodrigues, S. Kundu, A hardware framework for yield and reliability enhancement in chip multiprocessors, ACM Transactions on Embedded Computing Systems 14 (January 2015) 12.1–12.26.

[52] E. Papadopoulou, Critical area computation for missing material defects in VLSI circuits, IEEE Transactions on Computer-Aided Design 20 (May 2001) 503–528.

[53] O. Paz, T.R. Lawson Jr., Modification of Poisson statistics: modeling defects induced by diffusion, IEEE Journal of Solid-State Circuits SC-12 (October 1977) 540–546.

[54] J.E. Price, A new look at yield of integrated circuits, Proceedings of the IEEE 58 (August 1970) 1290–1291.

[55] X. Qi, R.J. Rosner, J. Hopkins, T. Joseph, B. Walsh, A. Sinnott, B.K.G. Nair, Incorporating core-to-core correlation to improve partially good yield models, IEEE Transactions on Semiconductor Manufacturing 32 (November 2019) 538–543.

[56] R.B. Seeds, Yield, economic, and logistic models for complex digital arrays, in: IEEE International Convention Record, Part 6, 1967, pp. 61–66.

[57] A. Sehgal, A. Dubey, E.J. Marinissen, C. Wouters, H. Vranken, K. Chakrabarty, Redundancy modelling and array yield analysis for repairable embedded memories, IEE Proceedings. Computers and Digital Techniques 152 (January 2005) 97–106.

[58] R. Spence, R.S. Soin, Tolerance Design of Electronic Circuits, Addison Wesley, 1988.

[59] C.H. Stapper, Defect density distribution for LSI yield calculations, IEEE Transactions Electron Devices ED-20 (July 1973) 655–657.

[60] C.H. Stapper, Modeling of defects in integrated circuit photolithographic patterns, IBM Journal of Research and Development 28 (4) (July 1984) 461–474.

[61] C.H. Stapper, On yield, fault distributions and clustering of particles, IBM Journal of Research and Development 30 (May 1986) 326–338.

[62] C.H. Stapper, A.N. McLaren, M. Dreckmann, Yield model for productivity optimization of VLSI memory chips with redundancy and partially good product, IBM Journal of Research and Development 20 (1980) 398–409.

[63] C.H. Stapper, F.M. Armstrong, K. Saji, Integrated circuit yield statistics, Proceedings of the IEEE 71 (April 1983) 453–470.

[64] T. Sugibayashi, I. Naritake, S. Utsugi, K. Shibahara, R. Oikawa, A 1-Gb DRAM for file applications, IEEE Journal of Solid-State Circuits 30 (November 1995) 1277–1280.

[65] T. Thomas, B. Anthony, Area, performance, and yield implications of redundancy in on-chip caches, in: IEEE Intern. Conference on Computer Design, October 1999, pp. 291–292.

[66] O. Tunali, M. Altun, Yield analysis of nano-crossbar arrays for uniform and clustered defect distributions, in: 24th IEEE International Conference on Electronics, Circuits and Systems (ICECS), 2017, pp. 534–537.

[67] D.M.H. Walker, Yield Simulation for Integrated Circuits, Kluwer Academic Publishers, 1987.

[68] S. Wang, K. Chakrabarty, M.B. Tahoori, Defect clustering-aware spare-TSV allocation in 3-D ICs for yield enhancement, IEEE Transactions on Computer-Aided Design of Integrated Circuits and Systems 38 (October 2019) 1928–1941.

[69] C.L. Wey, On yield considerations for the design of redundant programmable logic arrays, IEEE Transactions on Computer-Aided Design CAD-7 (April 1988) 528–535.

[70] B.P. Wong, A. Mittal, G.W. Starr, F. Zach, V. Moroz, A. Kahng, Nano-CMOS Design for Manufacturability: Robust Circuit and Physical Design for Sub-65 nm Technology Nodes, Wiley-Interscience, NY, 2008.

[71] Q. Xu, S. Chen, X. Xu, B. Yu, Clustered fault tolerance TSV planning for 3-D integrated circuits, IEEE Transactions on Computer-Aided Design of Integrated Circuits and Systems 36 (August 2017) 1287–1300.

[72] T. Yamagata, H. Sato, K. Fujita, Y. Nishmura, K. Anami, A distributed globally replaceable redundancy scheme for sub-half-micron ULSI memories and beyond, IEEE Journal of Solid-State Circuits 31 (February 1996) 195–201.

[73] J-H. Yoo, C-H. Kim, K-C. Lee, K-H. Kyung, A 32-bank 1Gb self-strobing synchronous DRAM with 1GB/s bandwidth, IEEE Journal of Solid-State Circuits 31 (November 1996) 1635–1643.

[74] M.W. Yung, M.J. Little, R.D. Etchells, J.G. Nash, Redundancy for yield enhancement in the 3D computer, in: Wafer Scale Integration Conference, January 1989, pp. 73–82.

FAULT DETECTION IN CRYPTOGRAPHIC SYSTEMS

Cryptographic algorithms are being applied in an increasing number of devices to satisfy their high security requirements. Many of these devices require high-speed operation and include specialized hardware encryption and/or decryption circuits for the selected cryptographic algorithm. A unique characteristic of these circuits is their very high sensitivity to faults. Unlike ordinary arithmetic/logic circuits, such as adders and multipliers, even a single data bit fault in an encryption or decryption circuit will, in most cases, spread quickly and result in a totally scrambled output (an almost random pattern). There is therefore a need to prevent such faults or, at the minimum, be able to detect them.

There is another, even more compelling, reason for paying special attention to fault detection in cryptographic devices. The cryptographic algorithms (also called ciphers) that are being implemented are designed so that they are difficult to break. To obtain the secret key, which allows the decryption of encrypted information, an attacker must perform a prohibitively large number of experiments. However, it has been shown that by deliberately injecting faults into a cryptographic device and observing the corresponding outputs, the number of experiments needed to obtain the secret key can be drastically reduced. Thus incorporating some form of fault detection into cryptographic devices is necessary for security purposes, as well as for data integrity.

We start this chapter with a brief overview of two important classes of ciphers, namely, symmetric key and asymmetric (or public) key, and describe the fault-injection attacks that can be mounted against them. We then present techniques that can be used to detect the injected faults in an attempt to foil the attacks.

11.1 OVERVIEW OF CIPHERS

Cryptographic algorithms use secret keys for encrypting the given data (known as *plaintext*) thus generating a *ciphertext*, and for decrypting the ciphertext to reconstruct the original plaintext. The keys used for the encryption and decryption steps can be either identical (or trivially related), leading to what are known as *symmetric key* ciphers, or different, leading to what are known as *asymmetric key* (or *public key*) ciphers. Symmetric key ciphers have simpler and therefore faster encryption and decryption processes compared with those of asymmetric key ciphers. The main weakness of symmetric key ciphers is the shared secret key, which may be subject to discovery by an adversary, and must therefore be changed periodically. The generation of new keys, commonly carried out using a pseudorandom-number generator (see Section 9.5), must be very carefully executed, because, unless properly initialized, such generators may result in easy to discover keys. The new keys must then be distributed securely, preferably by using a more secure (but also more computationally intensive) asymmetric key cipher.

Fault-Tolerant Systems. https://doi.org/10.1016/B978-0-12-818105-8.00021-8

11.1.1 SYMMETRIC KEY CIPHERS

Symmetric key ciphers can be either *block ciphers*, which encrypt a block of a fixed number of plaintext bits at the same time, or *stream ciphers*, which encrypt one bit at a time. Block ciphers are more commonly used, and are therefore the focus of this chapter.

Some well-known block ciphers include the data encryption standard (DES) and the more recent advanced encryption standard (AES). DES uses 64-bit plaintext blocks and a 56-bit key, whereas AES uses 128-bit blocks and keys of size between 128 and 196 bits. Longer secret keys are obviously more secure, but the size of the data block also plays a role in the security of the cipher. For example, smaller blocks may allow frequency-based attacks, such as relying on the higher frequency of the letter "e" in English language text.

Almost all symmetric key ciphers use the same key for encryption and for decryption. The process used for encryption must be reversible, so that the reverse process followed during decryption can generate the original plaintext. The main objective of the encryption process is to scramble the plaintext as much as possible. This is done by repeating a computationally simple series of steps (called a *round*) several times to achieve the desired scrambling.

The DES cipher follows the approach ascribed to Feistel. The Feistel scheme divides the block of plaintext bits into two parts B_1 and B_2. B_1 is unchanged, whereas the bits in B_2 are added (using modulo-2 addition, which is the logical bit-wise Exclusive-OR (*XOR*) operation) to a one-way hash function $F(B_1, K)$, where K is the key. A hash function is a function that takes a long input string (in general, of any length) and produces a fixed-length output string. A function is called a one-way hash function if it is hard to reverse the process and find an input string that will generate a given output value. The two subblocks B_1 and $B_2 + F(B_1, K)$ are then swapped.

These operations constitute a round, and the round is repeated several times. Following a round, we end up with $B'_1 = B_2 + F(B_1, K)$ and $B'_2 = B_1$. A single round is not secure since the bits of B_1 are unchanged and were only moved, but repeating the round several times will considerably scramble the original plaintext.

The one-way hash function F may seem to prevent decryption. Still, by the end of the round, both B_1 and the key K are available, and it is possible to recalculate $F(B_1, K)$ and thus obtain B_2. Therefore all the rounds can be "undone" in reverse order to retrieve the plaintext.

DES was the first official standard cipher for commercial purposes. It became a standard in 1976, and although there is currently a newer standard (AES established in 2002), the use of DES is still widespread either in its original form, or in its more secure variation called Triple DES. Triple DES applies DES three times with different keys, and offers as a result a higher level of security (one variation uses three different keys for a total of 168 bits instead of 56 bits, whereas another variation uses 112 bits).

The Feistel-function-based structure of DES is shown in Fig. 11.1. It consists of 16 identical rounds similar to the one described above. Each round first uses a Feistel function (the F block in the figure), performs the modulo-2 addition (the $\oplus$ circle in the figure), and then swaps the two halves. In addition, DES includes an initial and final permutations (see Fig. 11.1) that are inverses, and cancel each other. These do not provide any additional scrambling; they were included to simplify loading blocks of data in the original hardware implementation.

The 16 rounds use different 48-bit subkeys generated by a key schedule process shown in Fig. 11.2. The original key has 64 bits, eight of which are parity bits, so the first step in the key schedule (the "*Permuted Choice 1*" in Fig. 11.2) is to select 56 out of the 64 bits. The remaining 16 steps are similar:

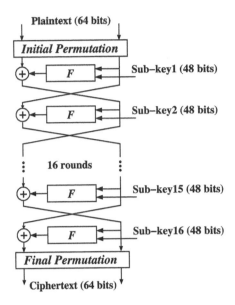

FIGURE 11.1

The overall structure of the Data Encryption Standard (DES).

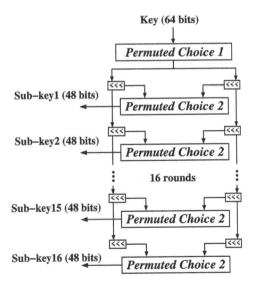

FIGURE 11.2

The key schedule process for DES.

the 56 incoming bits are split into two 28-bit halves, and each half is rotated to the left by either one or two bits (specified for each step). Then, 24 bits from each half are selected by the "*Permuted Choice 2*" block to generate the 48-bit round subkey. As a result of the rotations, performed by the "<<<" block in the figure, a different set of bits is used in each subkey.

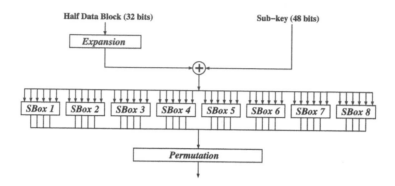

FIGURE 11.3

The Feistel function in DES.

The particular Feistel (hash) function used in DES is shown in Fig. 11.3. It consists of four steps:

1. *Expansion:* The 32 input bits are expanded to 48, using an expansion permutation that duplicates some of the bits.
2. *Adding a key:* The 48-bit result is added (addition modulo-2, which is a bitwise *XOR* operation) to a 48-bit subkey generated by the key schedule process.
3. *Substitution:* The 48-bit result of step 2 is divided into eight groups of 6 bits each, which are then processed by substitution boxes (called *SBoxes*). An SBox generates 4 bits according to a nonlinear transformation implemented as a lookup table.
4. *Permutation:* The 32 bits generated by the eight SBoxes undergo a permutation.

Two crucial properties that every good cipher must have are called *confusion* and *diffusion*. Confusion refers to establishing a complex relationship between the ciphertext and the key, and diffusion implies that any natural redundancy that exists in the plaintext (and can be exploited by an adversary) will dissipate in the ciphertext. In DES, most of the *confusion* is provided by the SBoxes, and the expansion and permutation provide the *diffusion*. If the confusion and diffusion are done correctly, a single bit change in the plaintext will cause every bit of the ciphertext to change with a probability of 0.5, independently of the others.

In 1999 a specially designed circuit was successful in breaking a DES key in less than 24 hours, demonstrating that the security provided by the 56-bit key is weak. Consequently, Triple DES was declared the preferred cipher, and was itself later replaced in 2002 by AES, described next.

AES does not use a Feistel function; instead, it is based on substitutions and permutations, with most of its calculations being finite-field operations. AES uses blocks of 128-bit plaintext and three possible key sizes of 128, 192, or 256 bits. The 128-bit block is represented as a 4×4 array of bytes called the *state*, which is denoted by S with byte elements $s_{i,j}$ ($0 \leq i, j \leq 3$). The state S is modified

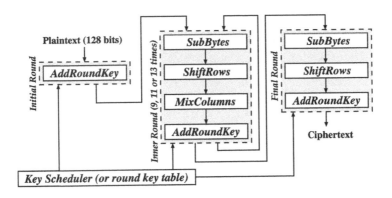

FIGURE 11.4

The overall structure of the Advanced Encryption Standard (AES).

during each encryption round, until the final ciphertext is produced. Each round of the encryption process consists of four steps (see Fig. 11.4):

1. *SubBytes:* Each byte in the state matrix undergoes (independently of all other bytes) a nonlinear substitution of the form $T(s_{i,j}^{-1})$. Due to the complexity of this transformation, its 256 possible outcomes are (in almost all implementations of AES) precomputed and stored in a lookup table called SBox. Unlike in DES, this is an 8- to 8-bit substitution (shown in Table 11.1) rather than a 6- to 4-bit one. The AES SBox has been designed to resist simple attacks.

Table 11.1 The AES SBox: substitution values for the byte xy (in hexadecimal format).

$x \backslash y$	0	1	2	3	4	5	6	7	8	9	a	b	c	d	e	f
0	63	7c	77	7b	f2	6b	6f	c5	30	01	67	2b	fe	d7	ab	76
1	ca	82	c9	7d	fa	59	47	f0	ad	d4	a2	af	9c	a4	72	c0
2	b7	fd	93	26	36	3f	f7	cc	34	a5	e5	f1	71	d8	31	15
3	04	c7	23	c3	18	96	05	9a	07	12	80	e2	eb	27	b2	75
4	09	83	2c	1a	1b	6e	5a	a0	52	3b	d6	b3	29	e3	2f	84
5	53	d1	00	ed	20	fc	b1	5b	6a	cb	be	39	4a	4c	58	cf
6	d0	ef	aa	fb	43	4d	33	85	45	f9	02	7f	50	3c	9f	a8
7	51	a3	40	8f	92	9d	38	f5	bc	b6	da	21	10	ff	f3	d2
8	cd	0c	13	ec	5f	97	44	17	c4	a7	7e	3d	64	5d	19	73
9	60	81	4f	dc	22	2a	90	88	46	ee	b8	14	de	5e	0b	db
a	e0	32	3a	0a	49	06	24	5c	c2	d3	ac	62	91	95	e4	79
b	e7	c8	37	6d	8d	d5	4e	a9	6c	56	f4	ea	65	7a	ae	08
c	ba	78	25	2e	1c	a6	b4	c6	e8	dd	74	1f	4b	bd	8b	8a
d	70	3e	b5	66	48	03	f6	0e	61	35	57	b9	86	c1	1d	9e
e	e1	f8	98	11	69	d9	8e	94	9b	1e	87	e9	ce	55	28	df
f	8c	a1	89	0d	bf	e6	42	68	41	99	2d	0f	b0	54	bb	16

2. *ShiftRows:* The bytes of the first, second, third, and fourth rows of the state matrix are rotated by 0, 1, 2, and 3 bytes, respectively. The state after this step is

$$S = \begin{bmatrix} s_{0,0} & s_{0,1} & s_{0,2} & s_{0,3} \\ s_{1,1} & s_{1,2} & s_{1,3} & s_{1,0} \\ s_{2,2} & s_{2,3} & s_{2,0} & s_{2,1} \\ s_{3,3} & s_{3,0} & s_{3,1} & s_{3,2} \end{bmatrix}, \tag{11.1}$$

so that every column of the matrix is now composed of bytes from all columns of the input matrix.

3. *MixColumns:* The four bytes in each column are used to generate four new bytes through linear transformations, as follows ($j = 0, 1, 2, 3$):

$$\begin{aligned} s_{0,j} &= (\alpha \otimes s_{0,j}) \oplus (\beta \otimes s_{1,j}) \oplus s_{2,j} \oplus s_{3,j}, \\ s_{1,j} &= s_{0,j} \oplus (\alpha \otimes s_{1,j}) \oplus (\beta \otimes s_{2,j}) \oplus s_{3,j}, \\ s_{2,j} &= s_{0,j} \oplus s_{1,j} \oplus (\alpha \otimes s_{2,j}) \oplus (\beta \otimes s_{3,j}), \\ s_{3,j} &= (\beta \otimes s_{0,j}) \oplus s_{1,j} \oplus s_{2,j} \oplus (\alpha \otimes s_{3,j}), \end{aligned} \tag{11.2}$$

where $\alpha = x$ (or 02 in hexadecimal notation), $\beta = x + 1$ (or 03 in hexadecimal notation). $\otimes$ and $\oplus$ are the modulo-2 multiply and add operations, respectively, of the polynomial representations of the state bytes, and the α and β coefficients. These operations are performed modulo the irreducible generator polynomial of AES, which is $g(x) = x^8 + x^4 + x^3 + x + 1$. Polynomial presentations of binary numbers and operations modulo a given generator polynomial have been discussed in Section 3.1. The MixColumns step together with ShiftRows provide the required diffusion in the AES cipher.

4. *AddRoundKey:* The round subkey is added (modulo-2) to the state. As in DES, separate round subkeys are generated using a key schedule process.

All four steps are performed in nine out of the 10 rounds of a 128-bit key implementation, but in the 10th round, the MixColumns step is omitted. In addition, prior to the first round, the first subkey is added to the original plaintext (see Fig. 11.4). The round subkeys are either generated on-the-fly following the key schedule process, shown in Fig. 11.5, or are taken out of a lookup table that is filled up every time a new key is established. The total number of rounds is increased to 12 and 14 for a 192-bit key and a 256-bit key AES, respectively.

Example: A detailed example to illustrate the use of the AES algorithm (or for that matter, any other symmetric key cipher, such as DES) for even the smallest sizes of its parameters (number of bits in the key and plaintext) will be tedious, and not very illuminating. We present therefore only some of the key steps of the example that appears in full detail in the official AES document (see the Further Reading section).
Suppose the 128-bit plaintext is

$$32\,43\,f6\,a8\,88\,5a\,30\,8d\,31\,31\,98\,a2\,e0\,37\,07\,34$$

and the 128-bit key is

$$2b\,7e\,15\,16\,28\,ae\,d2\,a6\,ab\,f7\,15\,88\,09\,cf\,4f\,3c.$$

```
KeyExpansion(byte key[4 * Nk], word w[4 * (Nr + 1)], Nk)
begin
    word temp
    i = 0
    while (i < Nk)
        w[i] = word(key[4 * i], key[4 * i + 1], key[4 * i + 2], key[4 * i + 3])
        i = i + 1
    end while
    i = Nk
    while (i < 4 * (Nr + 1))
        temp = w[i − 1]
        if (i mod Nk = 0)
            temp = SubWord(RotWord(temp)) xor Rcon[i/Nk]
        else if (Nk > 6 and i mod Nk = 4)
            temp = SubWord(temp)
        end if
        w[i] = w[i − Nk] xor temp
        i = i + 1
    end while
end
```

FIGURE 11.5

The key schedule of AES ($Nr = 10, 12, 14$ is the number of rounds, $Nk = 4, 6, 8$ is the number of 32-bit words in the plaintext, and Rcon is an array of round constants, $Rcon[j] = (x^{j-1}, 00, 00, 00)$).

Both have 32 hexadecimal digits and are shown in a matrix format in Figs. 11.6A and B, respectively. The reader can verify that the bytewise *XOR* operation of these two matrices yields the state matrix at the end of round 1, shown in Fig. 11.6C.

The first step in round 2 is SubBytes and its results are shown in Fig. 11.6D. For example, the first byte in the state matrix was $s_{0,0} = 19$, and based on the corresponding entry in Table 11.1, it is replaced by d4. The second step is ShiftRows, and Fig. 11.6E shows the results of rotating the first, second, third, and fourth rows of the matrix by 0, 1, 2, and 3 bytes, respectively. The next step is MixColumns, and its results are shown in Fig. 11.6F. For example, the first byte in the state matrix is calculated based on Eq. (11.2) as follows:

$$s_{0,0} = (\alpha \otimes s_{0,0}) \oplus (\beta \otimes s_{1,0}) \oplus s_{2,0} \oplus s_{3,0} = (02 \otimes d4) \oplus (03 \otimes bf) \oplus 5d \oplus 30$$
$$= 1b8 \oplus 1c1 \oplus 5d \oplus 30 = 04.$$

Note that since the result is smaller than 100 (x^8 in polynomial notation), there is no need to further reduce it modulo-$g(x)$ (recall that $g(x) = x^8 + x^4 + x^3 + x + 1$ is the generator polynomial of AES).

$$
\begin{bmatrix}
32 & 88 & 31 & e0 \\
43 & 5a & 31 & 37 \\
f6 & 30 & 98 & 07 \\
a8 & 8d & a2 & 34
\end{bmatrix}
\quad
\begin{bmatrix}
2b & 28 & ab & 09 \\
7e & ae & f7 & cf \\
15 & d2 & 15 & 4f \\
16 & a6 & 88 & 3c
\end{bmatrix}
\quad
\begin{bmatrix}
19 & a0 & 9a & e9 \\
3d & f4 & c6 & f8 \\
e3 & e2 & 8d & 48 \\
be & 2b & 2a & 08
\end{bmatrix}
\quad
\begin{bmatrix}
d4 & e0 & b8 & 1e \\
27 & bf & b4 & 41 \\
11 & 98 & 5d & 52 \\
ae & f1 & e5 & 30
\end{bmatrix}
$$
(A)   (B)   (C)   (D)

$$
\begin{bmatrix}
d4 & e0 & b8 & 1e \\
bf & b4 & 41 & 27 \\
5d & 52 & 11 & 98 \\
30 & ae & f1 & e5
\end{bmatrix}
\quad
\begin{bmatrix}
04 & e0 & 48 & 28 \\
66 & cb & f8 & 06 \\
81 & 19 & d3 & 26 \\
e5 & 9a & 7a & 4c
\end{bmatrix}
\quad
\begin{bmatrix}
a0 & 88 & 23 & 2a \\
fa & 54 & a3 & 6c \\
fe & 2c & 39 & 76 \\
17 & b1 & 39 & 05
\end{bmatrix}
\quad
\begin{bmatrix}
a4 & 68 & 6b & 02 \\
9c & 9f & 5b & 6a \\
7f & 35 & ea & 50 \\
f2 & 2b & 43 & 49
\end{bmatrix} \cdots
$$
(E)   (F)   (G)   (H)

$$
\begin{bmatrix}
39 & 02 & dc & 19 \\
25 & dc & 11 & 6a \\
84 & 09 & 85 & 0b \\
1d & fb & 97 & 32
\end{bmatrix}
$$
(I)

FIGURE 11.6

Example illustrating the AES algorithm. (A) Initial state matrix. (B) Key added in round 1. (C) State matrix—end of round 1. (D) After SubBytes. (E) After ShiftRows. (F) After MixColumns. (G) The key added in round 2. (H) State matrix—end of round 2. (I) State matrix—end of round 10.

The situation is different when calculating the second byte in the first column. Here,

$$
s_{1,0} = s_{0,0} \oplus (\alpha \otimes s_{1,0}) \oplus (\beta \otimes s_{2,0}) \oplus s_{3,0} = d4 \oplus (02 \otimes bf) \oplus (03 \otimes 5d) \oplus 30
$$
$$
= d4 \oplus 17e \oplus e7 \oplus 30 = 17d.
$$

This value must be reduced modulo-$g(x)$, and since

$$
x^8 \mod g(x) = x^4 + x^3 + x + 1,
$$

we obtain

$$
17d \mod g(x) = 7d \oplus (x^4 + x^3 + x + 1) = 7d \oplus 1b = 66,
$$

which is the final value of the second byte in the first column in Fig. 11.6F.

We now need to calculate a new round key using the procedure in Fig. 11.5. The original key is first rewritten as the following four words:

$$
w[0] = 2b7e1516, \quad w[1] = 28aed2a6, \quad w[2] = abf71588, \quad w[3] = 09cf4f3c.
$$

To calculate $w[4]$ (the first column in the key matrix for round 2), we start with

$$
\texttt{temp} = w[i-1] = w[3] = 09cf4f3c.
$$

Then, we rotate this word by 1 byte obtaining cf4f3c09. Next, we substitute each of the four bytes using the SubBytes transformation in Table 11.1, yielding 8a84eb01. We then perform a bitwise *XOR* operation with

$$Rcon[1] = (x^{1-1}, 00, 00, 00) = 01000000,$$

obtaining 8b84eb01. Finally, we calculate

$$w[i] = w[i-4] \text{ xor temp} = w[0] \text{ xor } 8b84eb01 = 2b7e1516 \text{ xor } 8b84eb01 = a0fafe17.$$

This is the first column in the key matrix in Fig. 11.6G. Adding the resulting key matrix to the state matrix, we obtain the new state matrix shown in Fig. 11.6H. Continuing this process for the remaining rounds (recall that in the last round the MixColumns step is skipped) results in the ciphertext

39 25 84 1d 02 dc 09 fb dc 11 85 97 19 6a 0b 32,

as shown in Fig. 11.6I.
If a single bit is changed in the plaintext, for example, instead of

32 43 f6 a8 88 5a 30 8d 31 31 98 a2 e0 37 07 34,

we use

30 43 f6 a8 88 5a 30 8d 31 31 98 a2 e0 37 07 34,

a very different ciphertext is obtained:

c0 06 27 d1 8b d9 e1 19 d5 17 6d bc ba 73 37 c1.

Similarly, if a single bit is changed in the key, for example, instead of

2b 7e 15 16 28 ae d2 a6 ab f7 15 88 09 cf 4f 3c,

we use

2a 7e 15 16 28 ae d2 a6 ab f7 15 88 09 cf 4f 3c,

the ciphertext produced is

c4 61 97 9e e4 4d e9 7a ba 52 34 8b 39 9d 7f 84.

These two examples illustrate the fact that even a single-bit fault may result in a totally scrambled (almost random) output, demonstrating the significance of detecting such faults.

11.1.2 PUBLIC KEY CIPHERS
Unlike symmetric key ciphers, asymmetric key ciphers (also known as public key ciphers) allow users to communicate securely without having access to a shared secret key. Public key ciphers are, however, considerably more computationally complex than symmetric key ciphers. Instead of a single key

shared by the two entities communicating with each other, the sender and recipient each have two cryptographic keys, called the public key and the private key. The private key is kept secret, and the public key may be widely distributed. In a way, one of the two keys can be used to "lock" a safe, whereas the other key is needed to unlock it. If a sender encrypts a message using the recipient's public key, only the recipient can decrypt it using the corresponding private key.

Another noteworthy application of public key ciphers is sender authentication: the sender encrypts a message with her own private key. By managing to decrypt the message using the sender's public key, the recipient is assured that the sender (and no one else) generated the message.

The best-known public key cipher is the RSA algorithm named after its three inventors Rivest, Shamir, and Adleman, but other public key ciphers have been developed and are in use. Person A wishing to use the RSA cipher must first generate a secret private key and a public key. The latter will be distributed to everyone who may wish to communicate with her. The key generation process consists of the following steps:

1. Select two large prime numbers p and q, and calculate their product $N = pq$.
2. Select a small odd integer e that is relatively prime to

$$\phi(N) = (p-1)(q-1).$$

Two numbers (not necessarily primes) are said to be relatively prime if their only common factor is 1. For example, 6 and 25 are relatively prime, although neither is a prime number.
3. Find the integer d that satisfies

$$de = 1 \mod \phi(N)$$

(d is often called the "inverse" of e).

The pair (e, N) constitutes the public key, and A should broadcast it to everyone who may wish to communicate with her. The pair (d, N) will serve as A's secret private key. The security provided by RSA depends on the difficulty of factoring the large integer N into its prime factors. Small integers can be factored in a reasonable amount of time, allowing the secret private key to be easily derived from the public key. To make the factoring time prohibitively large, each of the prime numbers p and q must have at least hundreds of digits.

Given a message M that person B wishes to send to A, B will encrypt it using A's public key e as

$$S = M^e \mod N.$$

Note that this encryption scheme makes it necessary to restrict the message M to

$$0 \leq M \leq N-1.$$

Upon receiving the encrypted message S, A will decrypt it using her private key d by calculating

$$S^d \mod N = M^{de} \mod N,$$

which can be shown to be equal to the original plaintext message M. The encryption and decryption of RSA messages thus entail exponentiations modulo-N.

Although there are techniques for reducing the complexity of such modular exponentiation (e.g., Montgomery reduction), the complexity of encryption and decryption for the RSA cipher is still considerably higher than that for symmetric key ciphers.

Example: To illustrate the use of the RSA algorithm, consider the following simple example: Suppose we select the prime numbers $p = 7$ and $q = 11$, yielding $N = 77$ and $\phi(N) = 60$. We can then select $e = 7$, which is obviously relatively prime with respect to $\phi(N)$. The pair $(e, n) = (7, 77)$ constitutes our public key. We search now for d that satisfies $7d = 1 \mod 60$, and find $d = 43$ (since $7 \cdot 43 = 301 = 1 \mod 60$). Suppose now that B wishes to send us the message $M = 9$. B encrypts it using the public key $(e, N) = (7, 77)$, which we have given him, obtaining $9^7 \mod 77 = 4782969 \mod 77 = 37$. We receive 37 and decrypt it using our private key by calculating $37^{43} \mod 77$, revealing the plaintext 9.

11.2 **SECURITY ATTACKS THROUGH FAULT INJECTION**

The level of security provided by the different ciphers has not been proved in an absolute sense, and all ciphers rely on the difficulty of finding the secret key directly, and having to resort to exhaustive searches, which may take a prohibitive amount of time. However, attacks on cryptographic systems have been developed, which take advantage of side-channel information. This is information that can be obtained from the physical implementation of a cipher, rather than through exploitation of some weakness of the cipher itself. One example of such side-channel information is the time needed to perform an encryption (or decryption), which in certain implementations may depend on the bits of the key. This allows the attacker to narrow down the range of values, which need to be attempted. Another example is the amount of power consumed in various steps of the encryption process: the power consumption profile of certain implementations may depend on whether the bits of the key are 0 or 1.

Schemes to protect cryptosystems against such attacks have been developed. For example, a random number of instructions that do not perform any useful calculation can be injected into the code, scrambling the relationship between the bits in the key and the total time needed to complete the encryption (or decryption). These randomly-injected instructions can also help protect against attacks based on power measurements. Other countermeasures that have been followed include designs that have a data-independent delay or use dual-rail logic that consumes the same power independently of whether a particular bit is 1 or 0. Most such techniques incur delay and/or power penalties.

An important type of side-channel attacks, which is of particular interest to us in this book, relies on the intentional injection of faults into a hardware implementation of a cipher. Such attacks proved to be both easy to apply and very efficient; an attacker can guess the secret key after a very small number of fault injection experiments. This has been shown to be true for many types of ciphers, both symmetric and asymmetric.

The different techniques for injecting intentional faults into a cryptographic device include varying the supply voltage (for example, by generating a *spike*), varying the clock frequency (generating a *glitch*), overheating the device, or by exposing the device to intense light using either a camera flash, or a more precise laser (or X-ray) beam.

Injecting a fault through a voltage spike or a clock glitch is likely to render a complete byte (or even several bytes) faulty, whereas the more precise laser or X-ray beams may be successful in inducing a single-bit fault. Fault-based attacks have been developed for both cases, and since most of these attacks induce transient faults, they allow the attacker to repeat her attempts multiple times until sufficient information is collected for extracting the secret key, and even use the device after breaking the cipher.

A practical issue that must be considered when mounting a fault-based attack is the need for precise timing of the fault injection. To achieve the desired effect, the fault must be injected during a particular step of the encryption or decryption algorithm. This turns out to be achievable in practice by analyzing the power and/or electromagnetic profile of the cryptographic device.

We next describe briefly possible fault attacks on symmetric and asymmetric key ciphers.

11.2.1 FAULT ATTACKS ON SYMMETRIC KEY CIPHERS

Various fault injection-based attacks on DES have been described, two of which are presented next.

In cryptographic devices that use DES (e.g., smart cards), the secret key is often stored in an EEP-ROM, and then transferred to the memory when a message needs to be encrypted or decrypted. If the attacker can reset an entire byte of the key (set the eight bits of that byte to zero) during its transfer from the EEPROM to the memory, he can figure out the secret key. The attack consists of eight steps as outlined in Table 11.2. In all of these experiments, known (to the attacker), plaintext messages are

Table 11.2 Fault attack on DES.

DES Key	Output
$K_0 = $ xx xx xx xx xx xx xx xx	S_0
$K_1 = $ xx xx xx xx xx xx xx 00	S_1
$K_2 = $ xx xx xx xx xx xx 00 00	S_2
$K_3 = $ xx xx xx xx xx 00 00 00	S_3
$K_4 = $ xx xx xx xx 00 00 00 00	S_4
$K_5 = $ xx xx xx 00 00 00 00 00	S_5
$K_6 = $ xx xx 00 00 00 00 00 00	S_6
$K_7 = $ xx 00 00 00 00 00 00 00	S_7

encrypted with a different number of bytes of the key being forced to 0, as shown in Table 11.2. Based on the ciphertext S_7, the attacker can derive the first byte of the secret key by trying out all possible values of the first byte, until the value that would produce S_7 is found. Since in DES, each byte of the key includes a parity bit, at most 128 values need to be checked rather than 256. In a similar manner, the second byte of the key can be found based on S_6. This procedure is continued until all eight bytes of the secret key are discovered.

Another fault-based attack relies on causing an instruction to fail (most commonly using clock glitches). For example, if the loop variable controlling the number of times the basic round is executed is corrupted and, as a result, only one or two rounds are executed, the task of finding the secret key is greatly simplified.

This type of attack can also be mounted against a device that uses AES and implements the cipher via software. Fault injection attacks on AES that focus, for example, on a byte of either the round subkey or on the state in the last round of the encryption have also been developed. Some of these attacks have been applied in practice to smart cards, yielding the secret key after fewer than 300 experiments. References to the descriptions of these attacks are provided in the Further Reading section.

11.2.2 FAULT ATTACKS ON PUBLIC (ASYMMETRIC) KEY CIPHERS

Unlike symmetric key ciphers, for which both encryption and decryption processes are vulnerable to security attacks, for a public key cipher, only the decryption process may be subject to attacks attempting to extract the secret private key. One easily understood fault attack on the RSA decryption process assumes that the attacker can flip a randomly selected single bit of the private key, d. Given an encrypted message S and its corresponding plaintext M, both of which are known to the attacker, he flips a random bit of d. If the ith bit of d, d_i, is flipped to produce its complement $\bar{d_i}$, the decryption device will generate an erroneous plaintext $\widehat{M}$ instead of M. The ratio between these two is

$$\frac{\widehat{M}}{M} = \frac{S^{2^i \bar{d_i}}}{S^{2^i d_i}} \quad \mod N.$$

If this ratio is equal to $S^{2^i} \mod N$ for some i, the attacker can conclude that $d_i = 0$. A ratio of $\frac{1}{S^{2^i}} \mod N$ for some i implies that $d_i = 1$. Repeating this process will eventually provide all the bits of the secret private key d.

In a similar way, the bits of d can be obtained by flipping a bit in the ciphertext S, and even by flipping two (or more) bits simultaneously. Showing this is left as an exercise for the reader. This type of attack can therefore be successful, even if the attacker is unable to precisely flip a single bit.

> **Example:** Let us use the example discussed in Section 11.1.2 with $(e, N) = (7, 77)$ as the public key and $d = 43$ (or in binary $d_5 d_4 d_3 d_2 d_1 d_0 = 101011$) as the private key. Suppose the decryption device receives the ciphertext 37 and produces the plaintext $M = 9$ if no fault is injected, and the erroneous text $\widehat{M} = 67$ if a single bit fault is injected into d. We now search for i, such that $9 = (67 \cdot 3^{7^{2^i}}) \mod 77$. It is easy to verify that among the possible values of i, $i = 3$ is the one because,
>
> $$(67 \cdot 37^8) \quad \mod 77 = (67 \cdot 53) \quad \mod 77 = 9.$$
>
> Consequently, we deduce that $d_3 = 1$.

11.3 COUNTERMEASURES

We presented above only a small sample out of the large number of possible fault-based attacks that can be mounted against cryptographic devices. Due to the relative ease of applying these attacks, it is obvious that proper countermeasures must be taken to keep the devices secure. Any such countermeasure must first detect the fault, and then prevent the attacker from observing the output of the device after the fault has been injected. Either the output could be blocked (by producing a constant value such as all zeroes), or a random result generated, misleading the attacker. Clearly, the original design of the device must be modified to include any such countermeasure.

Two approaches can be followed when modifying the design of a cryptographic device to protect it against fault injection-based attacks. One relies on duplicating the encryption or decryption process (using either hardware- or time-redundancy) and comparing the two results. This approach assumes that the injected faults are transient and will not manifest themselves in exactly the same time in the two calculations. This approach is easy to apply, but may, in certain situations, impose an overhead too high to be practical. The second approach is based on error-detection codes (see Section 3.1) that usually require a smaller overhead compared with brute-force duplication, although possibly at the cost of a lower fault coverage. Thus a trade-off between the fault coverage and the hardware and/or time overhead should be expected.

11.3.1 SPATIAL AND TEMPORAL DUPLICATION

Applying duplication to the encryption (or decryption) procedure is quite straightforward. Spatial duplication requires redundant hardware to allow independent calculations, so that faults injected into one hardware unit do not affect (in the same way) the other unit(s). Temporal redundancy can be applied by reusing the same hardware unit or reexecuting the same software program, assuming that the manifestation of the injected faults will change from one execution to the other. These schemes are similar to the conventional hardware and time redundancy techniques that are described in Chapter 2. The recalculation with shifted/modified operands techniques described in Section 5.2.4 can be used here to prevent the possibility of both computations being affected by the injected fault in exactly the same way.

A different scheme for applying duplication relies on having a separate hardware unit or software program for executing the reverse procedure. For example, after completing the encryption, the decryption unit or program is applied to the ciphertext, and only if the result of the decryption is equal to the original plaintext is the ciphertext considered fault-free and is output.

The latter approach is costly if applied to an RSA decryption device. The decrypted result $\widehat{M}$ obtained from the received encrypted message S is verified by calculating $\widehat{S} = \widehat{M}^e \mod N$ and comparing $\widehat{S}$ to S. This calculation is time-consuming if the public key e is very large.

11.3.2 ERROR-DETECTING CODES

This section illustrates the use of error-detecting codes (EDCs) for detecting faults in the encryption process of symmetric key ciphers. Similar rules apply to using EDCs during the decryption and key schedule procedures, because these use the same basic mathematical operations as the encryption.

When using an EDC during the encryption process, check bits are first generated for the input plaintext, then for each operation(s) that the data bits undergo, the check bits of the expected result are predicted. Periodically, check bits for the actual result are generated and compared with the predicted check bits, and a fault is detected if the two sets do not match. The general approach is depicted in Fig. 11.7. The validation checks can be scheduled at various granularities of the encryption, be it after every operation applied to the data, after each round, or only once at the end of the encryption process.

The first step, that of generating the check bits for the plaintext, is straightforward. The difficult part is devising the prediction rules for the new values of the check bits after each transformation that the data bits undergo during the encryption process. The complexity of these prediction rules, combined with the frequency at which the comparison is made, determines the overhead of applying the EDC, instead of duplication, as a protection against fault attacks.

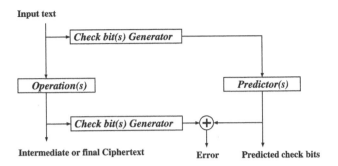

Input text

Check bit(s) Generator

Operation(s)   Predictor(s)

Check bit(s) Generator ⊕

Intermediate or final Ciphertext   Error   Predicted check bits

FIGURE 11.7

The general structure for detecting faults in encryption devices using error-detecting codes.

Various EDCs have been proposed for symmetric and public-key ciphers, most of them being the traditional EDCs described in Chapter 3. In particular, parity-based EDCs were found to be effective for the DES and AES symmetric ciphers. Parity bits can be associated with entire 32-bit words, with individual bytes, or even with nibbles (sets of 4 bits), with each such scheme providing a different fault coverage, and entailing a different overhead in terms of extra hardware and delay.

As an example, we illustrate the procedure for developing parity prediction rules when using a parity-based EDC for the AES cipher. Since most data transformations performed in the AES cipher operate on bytes, the natural choice is assigning a parity bit to each byte of the state. This will simplify the prediction rules and provide a high fault coverage. We discuss next the prediction rules for the four steps included in each round.

The prediction of the output parity bits for the ShiftRows transformation is straightforward: it is a rotated version of the input parity bits, following Eq. (11.1).

Equally simple is the prediction of the output parity bits of the AddRoundKey step: it consists of adding the input parity matrix associated with the state to the parity matrix associated with the current round key.

The SubBytes step uses look-up tables (called SBoxes), in which an SBox is usually implemented as a 256×8 bits memory. The input to the SBox will already have an associated parity bit. To generate the outgoing parity, a parity bit can be stored with each data byte, increasing the number of bits in each location in the SBox to 9. To make sure that input parity errors are not discarded, we will have to check the parity of the input data and, if an error is detected, stop the encryption process. This would add hardware overhead (parity checkers for 16 bytes) and extra delay.

A better choice would be to propagate the input parity errors so that they can be detected later on. This can be achieved by including the incoming parity bit when addressing the SBox, thus further increasing the table size to 512×9. The entries that correspond to input bytes with correct parity will include the appropriate SubBytes transformation result, with a correct parity bit. The other entries will contain a deliberately incorrect result, such as an all-zeroes byte with an incorrect parity bit.

If fault attacks on the SBox address decoder can be expected, the above scheme is insufficient. In this case, we can add a small and separate table of size 256×1, which will include the predicted parity bit for the correct output byte. This separate table will only allow detection of a mismatch between the parity bit of the correct output byte and the parity bit of the incorrect (but with a valid parity) output byte. We can increase the detection capabilities of this scheme by adding one (or more) correct output data bits to each location in the small table, thus increasing its size. Comparing the output of this table to the appropriate output bits of the main SBox table allows the detection of most addressing circuitry faults.

The output parity bits of the MixColumns step are the most complex to predict. As the reader is invited to verify in the Exercises, the equations for predicting these parity bits are as follows:

$$p_{0,j} = p_{0,j} \oplus p_{2,j} \oplus p_{3,j} \oplus s_{0,j}^{(7)} \oplus s_{1,j}^{(7)};$$
$$p_{1,j} = p_{0,j} \oplus p_{1,j} \oplus p_{3,j} \oplus s_{1,j}^{(7)} \oplus s_{2,j}^{(7)};$$
$$p_{2,j} = p_{0,j} \oplus p_{1,j} \oplus p_{2,j} \oplus s_{2,j}^{(7)} \oplus s_{3,j}^{(7)};$$
$$p_{3,j} = p_{1,j} \oplus p_{2,j} \oplus p_{3,j} \oplus s_{3,j}^{(7)} \oplus s_{0,j}^{(7)}, \tag{11.3}$$

where $p_{i,j}$ is the parity bit associated with state byte $s_{i,j}$, and $s_{i,j}^{(7)}$ is the most significant bit of $s_{i,j}$.

The question that remains is the granularity at which the comparisons between the generated and predicted parity bits will be made. Scheduling one validation check at the end of the whole encryption process has the obvious advantage of having the lowest overhead in terms of hardware and extra delay. Theoretically, this could result in the error indication being masked during the encryption procedure, yielding a match between the generated and predicted parity bits despite the ciphertext being erroneous. It can be shown, however, that errors injected at any step of the AES encryption procedure will not be masked and therefore a single validation check of the final ciphertext is sufficient for error detection purposes.

Still, not every combination of errors can be detected by this scheme. Parity-based EDCs are capable of detecting any fault that consists of an odd number of bit errors; an even number of bit errors occurring in a single byte will not be detected. Moreover, if errors are injected in both the state and the round key, some data faults of odd cardinality will not be detected, for example, a single bit error in the round key and a single bit error in the state, occurring in matching bytes, which are added in the AddRoundKeys step. The reason we do not restrict our discussion to single-bit error coverage (as is usually done when benign faults are considered) is that when a malicious fault injection attack takes place, it most likely impacts multiple adjacent bits of the state and/or round key. Still, although we cannot expect a 100% fault coverage when using a parity-based EDC, the fault coverage has been shown to be very high, even when multiple faults are considered.

Parity-based EDCs are suitable for the DES cipher as well, but the situation here is different from that with AES, due to two of the internal operations in the DES encryption process, namely, the expansion (from 32 to 48 bits) and the permutation of the 32 bits. The latter permutation is irregular, and therefore, there is no simple way to predict the individual parity bits of the four bytes. A more practical solution is to verify the correctness of the permutation by duplicating the circuit and comparing the results. In addition, if we wish to detect faults in the remaining steps of the encryption using a parity-based EDC, we must schedule a validation checkpoint within each round prior to the permutation and generate new parity bits afterward. A simple way to overcome the complexity of parity prediction for the 32-bit permutation is to use a single parity bit per 32-bit word. This, however, yields a very low fault coverage and is not recommended.

In a similar way, EDCs can be developed for other symmetric key ciphers. Several such ciphers that rely on modular addition and multiplication will better match residue codes (see Chapter 3). Other symmetric ciphers have been shown to require a very expensive implementation of EDCs, leading to the conclusion that the brute-force duplication is probably a more suitable solution. The cost of providing protection against fault-based attacks should be taken into account when selecting a cipher for a device.

The RSA public key cipher is based on modular arithmetic operations, and as such, it suggests the residue code as a natural choice. First, the check bits for the plaintext are generated, based on the selected modulus C for the residue check ($M \mod C$, where M is the original message). Since all operations performed during the RSA encryption (and decryption) are modular ones, we can apply them to the input check bits and obtain the predicted output check bits. The residue check will fail to detect an error if the faulty ciphertext has the same residue check bits as the correct one. Assuming that the fault injected is random, this match will happen with a probability of $1/C$, and thus a higher value of C will result in a higher fault coverage (but also a higher overhead).

11.3.3 ARE THESE COUNTERMEASURE SUFFICIENT?

The objective of the countermeasures described above is to detect any fault injected during the process of encryption or decryption, and when such faults are detected, prevent the transmission of the erroneous results that may assist the attacker in extracting the secret key. Unfortunately, it has been demonstrated that although the detection of faults is necessary, it is not always sufficient for protecting against fault-based attacks. We illustrate this point through two examples: an RSA decryption, and an AES encryption.

Suppose we use for the RSA decryption a straightforward algorithm that consists of raising the input S to the power d (where d is the private key), as shown in Fig. 11.8. The inputs to this algorithm are the encrypted message S, the modulus N, and the n-bit private key $d = d_{n-1}, d_{n-2}, \cdots, d_0$.

$$\text{Decryption\_Algorithm\_1}(S, N, (d_{n-1}, d_{n-2}, \cdots, d_0))$$

```
begin
    a = S
    for i from n − 2 to 0 do
        a = a² mod N
        if dᵢ = 1 then a = S · a mod N
    end
    M = a
end
```

FIGURE 11.8

A straightforward decryption algorithm for RSA.

Example: Assume a 4-bit private key $(d_3, d_2, d_1, d_0) = (1011)$ (the decimal 11). The algorithm in Fig. 11.8 will calculate $M = ((S^2)^2 \cdot S)^2 \cdot S = S^{11}$.

Fault attacks on this algorithm can be detected either by using a residue code or by calculating M^e mod N, and comparing the result to S. Even with either of these detection techniques, the algorithm is vulnerable to a power analysis-based attack, because a step where $d_i = 0$ will consume less power than a step for which $d_i = 1$. To counter such an attack, the algorithm can be modified so that the power consumed in every step will be independent of d_i. The modified algorithm shown in Fig. 11.9 will, as expected, incur higher delay and power penalties compared to the original algorithm. The check at the end of the algorithm intends to make the algorithm resistant to fault injections.

Decryption_Algorithm_2(S, N, $(d_{n-1}, d_{n-2}, \cdots, d_0)$)
begin
    $a = S$
    for i from $n - 2$ to 0 do
        $a = a^2$ mod N
        $b = S \cdot a$ mod N
        if $d_i = 1$ then $a = b$ else $a = a$
    end
    if (*no error has been detected*) then $M = a$
end

FIGURE 11.9

A modified decryption algorithm for RSA.

However, a careful examination of the algorithm in Fig. 11.9 reveals that it is still vulnerable to fault-based attacks. Since the result b of the multiplication $S \cdot a$ mod N is not used if $d_i = 0$, the attacker can inject a fault during this multiplication, and if the final result of the decryption is correct, he can deduce one bit of the secret private key.

Fortunately, a different algorithm can be devised using what is called a Montgomery ladder, as shown in Fig. 11.10. In this algorithm, the intermediate values of both a and b are used in the next step, and thus, a fault injected in any intermediate step will yield an erroneous result, which will be detected.

Example: Assume, as before, a 4-bit private key $(d_3, d_2, d_1, d_0) = (1011)$. The algorithm in Fig. 11.10 will calculate M as follows: For $i = 3$, $d_3 = 1$, and thus $a = S$ and $b = S^2$. For $i = 2$, $d_2 = 0$, and thus $a = S^2$ and $b = S^3$. For $i = 1$, $d_1 = 1$, and thus $a = S^5$ and $b = S^6$. Finally, for $i = 0$, $d_1 = 1$, resulting in $M = a = S^{11}$ and $b = S^{12}$.

The Montgomery ladder-based decryption algorithm for RSA allows another approach to detect faults injected during the decryption. The computed a and b must be of the form (M, SM), and a fault injected during any intermediate step will destroy this relationship. Thus checking whether a and b satisfy this relationship before providing the final result of the decryption can detect all injected errors, except those that modify either the bits of the secret private key d or the number of times the loop in Fig. 11.10 is performed. By using some EDC for these two, in addition to verifying the relationship between a and b, all injected faults can be detected.

```
Decryption_Algorithm_3(S, N, (dₙ₋₁, dₙ₋₂, ⋯, d₀))
begin
    a = 1
    b = S
    for i from n − 1 to 0 do
        if dᵢ = 0 then
            a = a²  mod N
            b = a · b  mod N
        end
        if dᵢ = 1 then
            a = a · b  mod N
            b = b²  mod N
        end
    end
    if (no error has been detected) then M = a
end
```

FIGURE 11.10

A Montgomery ladder-based decryption algorithm for RSA.

We next describe a fault-based attack on AES encryption that may succeed even if a fault-detection mechanism that prevents erroneous results from being output is incorporated into the design. The attack starts with providing an all-zeroes input to the AES encryption device. In the very first step of the encryption (see Fig. 11.4), the initial round key is added, resulting in the state matrix $s_{i,j} = 0 \oplus k_{i,j} = k_{i,j}$, where $0 \leq i, j \leq 3$. At exactly the same time instant, before the first SubBytes operation, the attacker injects a fault into the ℓth bit ($\ell = 0, 1, \cdots, 7$) of a particular byte $s_{i,j}$ of the state matrix, so that the selected bit is set to 0. If the corresponding bit of the key (bit ℓ of $k_{i,j}$) is 1, the output will be incorrect and the detection mechanism will disallow this output. If, however, the corresponding bit of the key is 0, no error will occur and the encryption device will work properly, providing the attacker with the value of that bit of the secret key.

This attack is very simple to understand theoretically, but may prove to be quite difficult to mount, due to the need for precise timing and location of the injected fault. The secret key can still be extracted, even if the strict timing and location requirements of this attack are relaxed, but this may require a larger number of fault injection experiments. The interested reader can find further details in the original paper referenced in the Further Reading section. The simple attack, described above, shows that implementations of symmetric key ciphers, even those with fault-detection capabilities, are not completely immune to fault-based attacks.

11.3.4 FINAL COMMENT

A final remark is in order: The topic of this chapter is still a very active area of research and a constant stream of new fault-based attacks on cryptographic devices, and of novel countermeasures to protect the devices against these attacks increasingly appear in the literature. The objective of this chapter is to demonstrate the extra difficulties in devising fault-protection techniques to deal with malicious faults injected into cryptographic devices.

11.4 FURTHER READING

The official descriptions of the DES and AES algorithms appear in [30] and [31], respectively. The AES example that is outlined in Section 11.1.1 is detailed in [31]. A more detailed description of AES appears in [15]. The RSA algorithm was first described in [34]. A considerable number of articles on all aspects of cryptography are posted on the website of the International Association for Cryptologic Research [21]. Well-written descriptions of key terms in cryptography appear in the online encyclopedia *Wikipedia* [36].

Fault injection attacks were first discussed in [9]. Many other fault attacks on public and symmetric key ciphers have been later presented in [1,2,11,14,17,20,32,38]. Several surveys of various fault injection techniques have been published [3,4,12,18]. These papers also review some protection schemes against such attacks. Detailed descriptions of ways to protect ciphers from attacks appear in [6–8,10, 13,24–26,28,35]. The derivation of the parity bit prediction rules for AES follows [6]. Simulators for error detection in several ciphers are available online [27]. The insufficiency of fault-detection schemes against fault-based attacks on RSA and AES has been demonstrated in [10,37]. The modified RSA decryption algorithm based on the Montgomery ladder is described in [19,22]. More recent fault injection attacks and countermeasures appear in [5,16,29]. An edited book on several aspects of fault attacks was published in 2012 [23]. The annual Fault Diagnosis and Tolerance in Cryptography Workshop (FDTC) [33] is devoted to papers describing recently developed fault attacks and countermeasures.

11.5 EXERCISES

1. Construct an RSA encryption scheme using $p = 61$ and $q = 53$. Select the public key $e = 17$, which is obviously relatively prime to $\phi(pq)$. Find the corresponding private key d, and for the message $M = 123$, calculate the ciphertext and show that the private key allows the decryption of the ciphertext.

2. Develop a software implementation of DES (or find one on the Internet), and apply the fault-based attack shown in Table 11.2. Modify the program to inject the faults, and write another program to find the secret key.

3. Complete the example (in the chapter) of injecting a fault into the private key d of an RSA decryption device that uses the public key $(e, N) = (7, 77)$ and the private key $(d, N) = (43, 77)$. Assume a ciphertext of 37 as in the example. List all possible single-bit errors and all double-bit errors that can be injected into d. For each error on your list find the erroneous plaintext that the device will produce. Are all the erroneous plaintexts unique?

4. Develop a software implementation of RSA (or find one on the Internet), use the prime numbers $p = 7$ and $q = 11$, as in the example in this chapter, and select $e = 7$. This yields the public key $(e, n) = (7, 77)$ and the private key $(d, n) = (43, 77)$. Inject single-bit failures in your program, and obtain all the bits of the private key.

5. Use the program and parameters from Problem 4, and add a residue check with the modulus 3. Repeat the single bit fault attacks. Will the modified program detect all such faults?

6. Show that $x^8 \bmod g(x) = x^4 + x^3 + x + 1$ for the generator polynomial of AES $g(x) = x^8 + x^4 + x^3 + x + 1$.

7. Verify all 16 results of the MixColumns step that are shown in Fig. 11.6F.

8. Inject a single-bit error in the state matrix shown in Fig. 11.6C, replacing the first byte 19 by 18, and calculate the erroneous state matrix at the end of round 2. Compare your result to the matrix shown in Fig. 11.6H. How many bytes are in error?

9. Suppose you are using AES with data blocks and key of size 128 bits. Your messages, however, are only 50-bit long. What would you put in the unused 78 bit positions?

10. Verify the correctness of the parity prediction equations for the MixColumns step in AES.

11. (a) Why does AES use short keys (e.g., 128 bits) while RSA uses long keys (e.g., 1024 bits)?

    (b) AES has a larger plain text block size than DES (128 vs. 64). Is this an advantage?

12. (a) Will eliminating the MixColumn step in AES make it more vulnerable to attacks? Explain.

    (b) Will a single bit flip in the plaintext always result in 64 flipped bits in the ciphertext after an AES encryption?

REFERENCES

[1] R. Anderson, M. Kuhn, Low cost attacks on tamper resistant devices, in: International Workshop on Security Protocols, in: Lecture Notes in Computer Science, vol. 1361, Springer-Verlag, 1997, pp. 125–136.

[2] C. Aumüller, P. Bier, W. Fischer, P. Hofreiter, J.-P. Seifert, Fault Attacks on RSA with CRT: Concrete Results and Practical Countermeasures, Cryptology ePrint Archive, Report 2002/073, 2002, available at: http://eprint.iacr.org/2002/073.

[3] A. Barenghi, L. Breveglieri, I. Koren, D. Naccache, Fault injection attacks on cryptographic devices: theory, practice and countermeasures, Proceedings of the IEEE 100 (11) (November 2012) 3056–3076.

[4] H. Bar-El, H. Choukri, D. Naccache, M. Tunstall, C. Whelan, The Sorcerer's apprentice guide to fault attacks, Proceedings of the IEEE 94 (2) (February 2006) 370–382, also in the Cryptology ePrint Archive, Report 2004/100, 2004, available at: http://eprint.iacr.org/2004/100.

[5] G. Barthe, F. Dupressoir, P-A. Fouque, B. Gregoire, J-C Zapalowicz, Synthesis of fault attacks on cryptographic implementations, in: ACM SIGSAC Conference on Computer and Communications Security, CCS'14, 2014, pp. 1016–1027.

[6] G. Bertoni, L. Breveglieri, I. Koren, P. Maistri, V. Piuri, Error analysis and detection procedures for a hardware implementation of the advanced encryption standard, IEEE Transactions on Computers 52 (April 2003) 492–505.

[7] G. Bertoni, L. Breveglieri, I. Koren, P. Maistri, V. Piuri, Concurrent fault detection in a hardware implementation of the RC5 encryption algorithm, in: IEEE International Conference on Application-Specific Systems, Architectures and Processors, 2003, pp. 410–419.

[8] G. Bertoni, L. Breveglieri, I. Koren, P. Maistri, An efficient hardware-based fault diagnosis scheme for AES: performances and cost, in: IEEE International Symposium on Defect and Fault Tolerance in VLSI Systems, October 2004, pp. 130–138.

[9] E. Biham, A. Shamir, Differential fault analysis of secret key cryptosystems, in: 17th Cryptology Conference, Crypto 97, in: Lecture Notes in Computer Science, vol. 1294, Springer Verlag, 1997, pp. 513–525.

[10] J. Blöemer, J.-P. Seifert, Fault based cryptanalysis of the advanced encryption standard (AES), in: Financial Cryptography, in: Lecture Notes in Computer Science, vol. 2742, Springer-Verlag, 2003, pp. 162–181, available at: http://eprint.iacr.org/2002/075.

[11] D. Boneh, R. DeMillo, R. Lipton, On the importance of eliminating errors in cryptographic computations, Journal of Cryptology 14 (2001) 101–119.

[12] J. Breier, D. Jap, A survey of the state-of-the-art fault attacks, in: International Symposium on Integrated Circuits (ISIC), 2004, pp. 152–155.

[13] A.S. Butter, C.Y. Kao, J.P. Kuruts, DES Encryption and Decryption Unit with Error Checking, US patent US5432848, July 1995.

[14] M. Ciet, M. Joye, Elliptic Curve Cryptosystems in the Presence of Permanent and Transient Faults, Cryptology ePrint Archive, Report 2003/028, 2003, available at: http://eprint.iacr.org/2003/028.

[15] J. Daemen, V. Rijmen, The Design of Rijndael: AES – The Advanced Encryption Standard, Springer-Verlag, 2002.

[16] H. Eldib, M. Wu, C. Wang, Synthesis of fault-attack countermeasures for cryptographic circuits, in: International Conference on Computer Aided Verification, CAV 2016, 2016, pp. 343–363.

[17] C. Giraud, DFA on AES, Cryptology ePrint Archive, Report 2003/008, 2003, available at: http://eprint.iacr.org/2003/008.

[18] C. Giraud, H. Thiebeauld, A survey on fault attacks, in: Smart Card Research and Advanced Applications VI, CARDIS 2004, in: IFIP International Federation for Information Processing, vol. 153, Springer, 2004, pp. 159–176.

[19] C. Giraud, Fault resistant RSA implementation, in: Fault Diagnosis and Tolerance in Cryptography, FDTC'05, 2005, pp. 143–151.

[20] C. Giraud, H. Thiebeauld, Basics of fault attacks, in: Fault Diagnosis and Tolerance in Cryptography, FDTC'04 – Supplemental Volume of the Dependable Systems and Networks Conference, 2004, pp. 343–347.

[21] International Association for Cryptologic Research, http://www.iacr.org/, ePrint Archive, available at: http://eprint.iacr.org.

[22] M. Joye, S.-M. Yen, The Montgomery powering ladder, in: Cryptographic Hardware and Embedded Systems, CHES 2002, in: Lecture Notes in Computer Science, vol. 2523, Springer-Verlag, 2002, pp. 291–302.

[23] M. Joye, M. Tunstall (Eds.), Fault Analysis in Cryptography, Springer, 2012.

[24] R. Karri, K. Wu, P. Mishra, K. Yongkook, Fault-based side-channel cryptanalysis tolerant Rijndael symmetric block cipher architecture, in: IEEE Symposium on Defect and Fault Tolerance in VLSI Systems, 2001, pp. 427–435.

[25] R. Karri, G. Kuznetsov, M. Goessel, Parity-based concurrent error detection in symmetric block ciphers, in: International Test Conference 2003, ITC 2003 (ISSN 1089-3539) 1 (2003) 919–926.

[26] M.G. Karpovsky, A. Taubin, A new class of nonlinear systematic error detecting codes, IEEE Transactions on Information Theory 50 (8) (2004) 1818–1820.

[27] I. Koren, Fault tolerant computing simulator, available at: http://www.ecs.umass.edu/ece/koren/fault-tolerance/simulator/.

[28] K.J. Kulikowski, M.G. Karpovsky, A. Taubin, Robust codes for fault attack resistant cryptographic hardware, in: Fault Diagnosis and Tolerance in Cryptography, FDTC'05, Sept. 2005, pp. 1–12.

[29] F. Majeric, B. Gonzalvo, L. Bossuet, JTAG fault injection attack, in: IEEE Embedded Systems Letters, 2018, pp. 65–68.

[30] National Institute of Standards and Technology, Data Encryption Standard, FIPS publication No. 46, January 1977.

[31] National Institute of Standards and Technology, Advanced Encryption Standard, FIPS publication No. 197, November 2001, available at: http://csrc.nist.gov/publications/fips/fips197/fips-197.pdf.

[32] G. Piret, J.-J. Quisquater, A differential fault attack technique against SPN structures, with application to the AES and Khazad, in: Cryptographic Hardware and Embedded Systems, CHES 2003, in: Lecture Notes in Computer Science, vol. 2779, Springer-Verlag, 2003, pp. 77–88.

[33] Proceedings of the Annual Fault Diagnosis and Tolerance in Cryptography Workshop (FDTC 2007-FDTC 2019), IEEE Digital Library (IEEE Explore), available at: https://ieeexplore.ieee.org/xpl/conhome.jsp?punumber=1001358.

[34] R.L. Rivest, A. Shamir, L. Adleman, A method for obtaining digital signatures and public-key cryptosystems, Communications of the ACM 21 (1978) 120–126, ACM Press.

[35] A. Shamir, Method and Apparatus for Protecting Public Key Schemes from Timing and Fault Attacks, US Patent 5991415, 1999.

[36] Wikipedia, the free encyclopedia, http://en.wikipedia.org/wiki/Cryptography.

[37] S-M. Yen, M. Joye, Checking before output may not be enough against fault-based cryptanalysis, IEEE Transactions on Computers 49 (September 2000) 967–970.

[38] S-M. Yen, S. Moon, J.-C. Ha, Permanent fault attack on the parameters of RSA with CRT, in: Lecture Notes in Computer Science, vol. 2727, Springer-Verlag, 2003, pp. 285–296.

Index